Worlds of Music

Worlds of Music

An Introduction to the Music of the World's Peoples, Shorter Version

Fourth Edition

Jeff Todd Titon
General Editor

with

Timothy J. Cooley

David Locke

Anne K. Rasmussen

David B. Reck

Christopher A. Scales

John M. Schechter

Jonathan P. J. Stock

R. Anderson Sutton

CENGAGE
Learning·

Australia • Brazil • Mexico • Singapore • United Kingdom • United States

CENGAGE
Learning·

Worlds of Music: An Introduction to the Music of the World's Peoples, Shorter Version
Fourth Edition
Jeff Todd Titon, General Editor with
Timothy J. Cooley, David Locke,
Anne K. Rasmussen, David B. Reck,
Christopher A. Scales, John M. Schechter,
Jonathan P. J. Stock, R. Anderson Sutton

Product Director: Paul Banks

Product Manager: Sharon Poore

Content Developer: Mary Ann Lidrbauch

Product Assistant: Danielle Ewanouski

Marketing Manager: Jillian Borden

Content Project Manager: Rebecca Donahue

Senior Art Director: Sarah Cole

Manufacturing Planner: Julio Esperas

IP Analyst: Christina Ciaramella

IP Project Manager: Betsy Hathaway

Production Service and Compositor:
MPS Limited

Interior and cover design: Dutton &
Sherman Design

Cover Image: David Mbiyu/Demotix/
Demotix/Corbis

For product information and technology assistance, contact us at
Cengage Learning Customer & Sales Support, 1-800-354-9706
For permission to use material from this text or product,
submit all requests online at **www.cengage.com/permissions**.
Further permissions questions can be emailed to
permissionrequest@cengage.com.

Library of Congress Control Number: 2016952182

Student Edition:

ISBN: 978-1-337-10149-3

Loose-leaf Edition:

ISBN: 978-1-337-10157-8

Cengage Learning
20 Channel Center Street
Boston, MA 02210
USA

Cengage Learning is a leading provider of customized learning solutions with employees residing in nearly 40 different countries and sales in more than 125 countries around the world. Find your local representative at **www.cengage.com**.

Cengage Learning products are represented in Canada by Nelson Education, Ltd.

To learn more about Cengage Learning Solutions, visit
www.cengage.com.

Purchase any of our products at your local college store or at our preferred online store **www.cengagebrain.com**.

Printed in United States of America
Print Number: 02   Print Year: 2017

Contents

9   South America/Chile, Bolivia, Ecuador, Peru | 277
John M. Schechter

10   The Arab World | 311
Anne K. Rasmussen

Preface

Why study music? There are many reasons, but perhaps the most important are pleasure and understanding. We have designed this book and digital companion MindTap to introduce undergraduates to the study of music the world over. The only prerequisites are a curious ear and an inquisitive mind.

An Authoritative Case Study Approach

The authors of this textbook agree that the best introduction to the music of the world's peoples is not a survey or musical world tour, which is inevitably superficial. Instead, our approach explores in some depth the music of a smaller number of representative human groups. This approach is not new; we have employed it in every edition of this book since it first appeared thirty-two years ago. It adapts to ethnomusicology the case method in anthropology, the touchstone approach in literature, and the problems approach in history. The object is not to offer students a sampling of a great many musical worlds, but instead to encourage experiencing what it is like to be an ethnomusicologist coming to understand an unfamiliar music on its own terms. We decided on a limited number of case studies rather than a broader survey because that is how we teach the introductory-level world-music course at our colleges and universities. We thought also that by writing about music in societies we know firsthand from our fieldwork, we could produce an authoritative text.

We designed the chapters following six guiding principles.

1. We think a textbook in world music should go beyond merely avoiding elitism and ethnocentrism. Students need to understand an unfamiliar music on its own terms—that is, as the people who make the music understand it.
2. In order to know music as a human activity, not just a sequence of organized sound, we need to ask what the life of a musician is like in different societies and find answers in life histories and autobiographies.
3. We single out the words of songs for special attention because they often convey the meaning and purposes of musical performances as the music makers comprehend them.
4. We have made certain that the musical examples discussed in the book can be heard online.
5. Student music-making projects—singing, and building and playing instruments—should, if properly directed and seriously approached, greatly increase appreciation of a musical style.

6. And most important, an introduction to world music should provide pleasure as well as knowledge. To appreciate and understand the structures and styles of the music under discussion, students are provided with print and digital Active Listening Guides describing musical features as they occur in real time on the accompanying recordings that may be heard via MindTap.

Using *Worlds of Music*

The first chapter of this book introduces the elements of world music. Using as illustrations the popular Ghanaian postal workers' stamp-canceling music and the songs of hermit thrushes, Chapter 1 asks how one draws the line between sound that is music and nonmusical sound. Using everyday ideas of rhythm, meter, melody, and harmony, it sharpens these rudimentary concepts and shows how they can help one understand the various musics presented in this book. In an ethnomusicological context, rudiments include not only those familiar elements of musical organization, but also a basic approach to music's place in human life. For that reason, Chapter 1 introduces a performance model showing how music relates to communities and their history; the chapter also introduces a component model that includes musical sound and structure as well as other elements of a music-culture, including ideas, social behavior, and material culture. We introduce musical worlds as ecological, sustainable, human systems—a theme that is picked up in many of the succeeding chapters.

Chapters 2-10 concentrate on music in a particular geographical and cultural area featuring core recordings, like a demonstration of Javanese *gamelan* in which the orchestral layers are gradually incorporated, thereby showing how the ensemble's parts relate to the whole (Chapter 7). We also include the same kind of demonstration featuring the component parts of the drum ensemble that performs *Agbekor* (Chapter 3). These demonstrations help students to understand the way these complex ensembles function. We encourage instructors to add or substitute a case study based on their own research.

The last chapter guides students through a fieldwork project in which they are encouraged to do original research on nearby music-making. Because any fieldwork project should begin well before the end of the term, we suggest that Chapter 11 be read just after the first case study and that students begin fieldwork immediately afterward, based on a proposal in which they present both a subject and a preliminary topic, describe their projected role and access to the musical culture, and present a tentative work plan. Many students say the field projects are the most valuable experiences they take away from this introductory course, particularly insofar as they must make sense of what they document in the field. The field project encourages original research. Students find it attractive and meaningful to make an original contribution to knowledge.

Worlds of Music comes in two versions: the full one and this shorter one. Based on *Worlds of Music*, 6th Edition (2016), this shorter version offers a textbook aimed squarely at students without prior musical training who want an authoritative and pleasurable entry-level introduction to the music of the world's peoples. It provides readers with curious ears a chance to experience in depth the varying sounds, musi-cal expressions, and aesthetic and cultural principles of varying groups in different parts of the globe.

This edition of the shorter version differs from the previous shorter edition in several ways. Most important, first, a new chapter on Native American music, by Christopher Scales, replaces the former chapter by the late David McAllester. Second, the chapters have been revised and updated with new material. See the following list for details of the revisions.

New to This Edition

Global Changes

- Learning Objectives start every chapter so that students can preview what they will be expected to learn from the chapter.
- Salient Characteristics are featured more consistently throughout the chapters, highlighting musical characteristics and social-cultural characteristics of music cultures.
- The Close Listening feature is now called Active Listening.
- Ten Study Questions appear at the end of every chapter so that students can review and advance their understanding of the chapter's learning objectives.

Chapter 1: The Music-Culture as a World of Music

- New recording of hermit thrushes; updated and revised text.

Chapter 2: North America/Native America

- New to the fourth edition; written by Christopher Scales; replaces the former chapter by the late David McAllester yet retains some of its classic features.

Chapter 3: Africa/Ewe, Dagbamba, Shona, BaAka

- A new section, "Fela and Afrobeat," outlines how Fela Anikulapo Kuti forged the musical style he popularized as "Afrobeat," including an Active Listening feature for his song "Teacher Don't Teach Me Nonsense."

Chapter 4: North America/Black America

- A revised Introduction contrasting an early African-American blues recording, by Ma Rainey (a new musical example), with a typical popular recording from the same period.
- Further discussion of Ma Rainey's "Hustlin' Blues" examines the lyrics.
- A new section, "Blues in the New Millennium," discusses Americana music and the work of James "Super Chikan" Johnson, including a new Active Listening feature for his song "Poor Broke Boy."

Chapter 5: Europe/Central and Southeastern Regions

- Revised Active Listening features.
- Updated interpretations of European musics in the world context.

Chapter 6: Asia/India

- A revised section, "The Aryans," includes a discussion of Vedic chant.
- A new section, "Religion and Music in South India," discusses a major genre of music, the *bhajan*.
- A new section, "A Piece from the Dance Tradition: 'Krishna Nee Begane Baro'," closely examines a song from the dance tradition.
- A revised section, "Pop Music," moves to later in the chapter, and now includes a discussion of the more up-to-date Indian popular song "Urvasi Urvasi."

Chapter 7: Asia/Indonesia

- A revised Introduction compares Javanese musical examples.
- A new section, "Gigi: Indonesian Rock Music," features the popular Indonesian rock group, Gigi, and an Active Listening feature of their song "Dan Sekarang."

Chapter 10: The Arab World

- A revised section, "Wedding Traditions of the Eastern Mediterranean Arab World (The Levant)," discusses how poetry, music, and dance have helped catalyze social protest and resistance in the Arab World.
- A new section, "Musical Biodiversity in the City of Salalah, Sultanate of Oman," discusses the author's recent fieldwork related to how the traditional arts impact the tourism economy as well as the national narrative and her experiences at the Salalah Tourism Festival, including a close examination of and an Active Listening feature for the song "Batal al Bab," including one new transcription.

Chapter 11: Discovering and Documenting a World of Music

- A revised section, "Ethics," includes a discussion of applied ethnomusicology and how the ethnomusicologist's advocacy for and partnership with music cultures has increased in the new millennium.

MindTap MindTap

The Shorter Version can be accompanied by MindTap, a fully online, highly personalized learning experience built upon *Worlds of Music*. MindTap combines student learning tools—readings, multimedia, activities, and assessments—into a singular Learning Path that guides students through their course. Instructors can personalize the experience by customizing authoritative Cengage Learning content and learning tools with their own content in the Learning Path via apps that integrate with the MindTap framework.

The MindTap reader, which contains the full text and all illustrations of the printed chapters introduces concepts and provides context and depth. More than a digital version of a textbook, MindTap is an interactive learning resource that creates a digital reading experience. The robust functionality allows learners to take notes, highlight text, and even find a definition right from the page with the *Merriam-Webster* MindApp. The core musical examples are available online with the chapter reference, either streaming or with suggestions for finding the music online.

All of the core musical examples are accompanied by interactive Active Listening Guides, which provide a real-time visualization of the music playing in perfect synchronization with descriptions of what is happening in the music. Listening activities open every chapter; most chapters provide links to videos related to chapter content; and every chapter includes quizzes with listening questions, content questions, and essay questions. Flashcards of key terms gives students the ability to study while on the go.

The marginal cues in this book signal that music, practice and testing opportunities, and interactive features are available via MindTap. If you'd rather just have access to the music, you can bundle *Worlds of Music* with a pass code to access the streaming music and links to the music not otherwise available.

Ethnomusicology: The Study of People Making Music

The authors of this book are ethnomusicologists; our field, *ethnomusicology*, is the study of music *as* culture, underlining the fact that music is a way of organizing human activity. By *culture*, we do not mean "the elite arts"; rather, we use the term as anthropologists do: Culture is a people's knowledge and their particular way of life, learned and socially transmitted through centuries of adapting to the natural and human world. Ethnomusicologists investigate *all* music: not just music in non-Western societies, but also Western folk, popular, art and ethnic musics.

I like to define ethnomusicology as *the study of people making music*. People "make" music in two ways: They make or construct the *idea* of music—what music is (and is not) and what it does—and they make or produce the *sounds* that they call music. Although we experience music as something "out there" in the world, our response to music depends on the ideas we associate with that music, and those ideas come from the people (ourselves included) who carry our culture. In that way, music also makes (affects) people; the relationship is reciprocal. To use academic language, people make music into a cultural domain, with associated sets of ideas and activities. We could not even pick out musical form and structure, how the parts of a piece of music work with one another, if we did not depend on the idea that music must be organized rather than random, and if we had not learned to make music that way. (Analyzing form and structure is characteristic of some cultures, including Western ones, but in other areas of the world people do not habitually break a thing down into parts to analyze it.)

Furthermore, because ethnomusicologists believe that there is no such reality as "the music itself"—that is, music apart from cultural considerations—we are not satisfied merely to analyze and compare musical forms, structures, melodies, rhythms, compositions, and genres. Instead, we borrow insights and methods from anthropology, sociology, literary criticism, linguistics, science, and history to understand music as human expression. Ethnomusicology is therefore multidisciplinary, combining elements of the arts, humanities, and sciences. Because of its eclectic methods and worldwide scope, ethnomusicology is well suited to students seeking a liberal arts education.

Changing Worlds of Music

When the first edition of this textbook appeared in 1984, formal study of the music of the world's peoples emphasized the musics of indigenous (formerly termed "tribal" or "native") peoples, classical musics of Asia and the Middle East, and the folk, ethnic, and immigrant musics of the Western continents. The integrity of any curriculum in ethnomusicology today requires that a historical, geographic, cultural, and genre-based emphasis continue, and yet in the past twenty years ethnomusicologists have moved toward a more complex and nuanced picture. The older map of a world divided into markedly different human groups, each with its own distinct music, is no longer accurate; perhaps it never was. Transnationalism, which connects individuals and institutions without much regard for national boundaries, has been facilitated by the increasingly globalized world economy and by worldwide information systems such as the internet. This phenomenon has changed many twenty-first-century people into musical cosmopolitans, participating in more than one music-culture.

Musical transnationalism is the result of at least four major changes in the previous century. First, the enormous influence of media on contemporary musical life, not only in the largest cities but also in the remotest villages, has enabled people to hear many new and different kinds of music. Second, increasing migration of people has engendered musical exchange and interchange. In the nineteenth and the first half of the twentieth centuries, these migrations were chiefly one-way trips, forming diasporic settlements linked to a homeland mainly by memory; but today, with globalized information systems and easier travel, migrations are transnational and more fluid, with the migrants moving back and forth among different geographic and cultural spaces. Third, modernization and Westernization throughout the world has brought Western music and musical institutions to non-Western cultures, where they have been variously resisted, adapted, and transformed. Finally, "world music," a new category of popular, mass-mediated music based on a mix or fusion of elements associated with one or more musical cultures, a music with a market niche of its own, has become an intriguing path for musicians and a significant commodity of the media industry. Globalization today characterizes virtually all commerce, and many people regard music primarily as a commodity.

Indeed, some musical consumers equate world music with the music of the world's peoples. Of course, because most music making throughout the world falls outside of that marketing category, no responsible introduction to the music of the world's peoples should focus primarily on world music; yet, the rise of world music and a global economy challenges ethnomusicologists' categories, whether they be categories of genre or geography. It presents new challenges to fundamental concepts such as ethnicity and culture as well.

Worlds of Music has had a long run, going through six major editions, four shorter editions, and translations into Italian, Greek, and Chinese. On its first publication in 1984, it became the bestselling textbook in its field, a position it has never relinquished. As it went through a succession of editions, adding music-cultures (the current edition has nine), we maintained a community of coauthors and our belief that in-depth case studies of particular music-cultures is the best introduction to the music of the world's peoples. The genius of *Worlds of Music*, as one of my colleagues told me, is that it is complete in itself: it not only encourages students to learn the subject but it teaches the professors how to teach it. While no such book could ever be complete, perhaps its combination of depth and user-friendliness has accounted for its success over the years. It has taught generations of students to consider not just the world's musical sounds but also music-cultures; to think not only about musical structures and genres and instruments, but also about the ways in which people within music-cultures experience music; to think about lyrics and their meaning; to learn by doing—by singing and by building and playing instruments; and to accomplish an original fieldwork project and experience what it is like to be an ethnomusicologist. That is, for more than three decades now, this book in all its editions has promoted an in-depth, experiential, hands-on, ears-open, and thoughtful introductory approach to the study of people making music.

Acknowledgments

We have appreciated the assistance, over the years, of several editors at Schirmer Books (now Cengage Learning)—Ken Stuart, Marybeth Anderson Payne, Richard Carlin, Robert Axelrod, Jonathan Wiener, Clark Baxter, Abbie Baxter, Sue Gleason Wade, Sharon Poore, Lianne Ames, Marita Sermolins, and Mary Ann Lidrbauch—in seeing this project through production. We are also indebted to the reviewers who made suggestions for this fourth edition of the Shorter Version: Michael Boyd, Chatham University; Michael Colquhoun, Canisius College; Richard Greene, Georgia College & State University; Tony Jones, Illinois Central College; Sarah Moody, San Diego Christian College; Mary Procopio, Mott Community College; Carol Shansky, Iona College; and Benjamin Smeall, Brandman University.

We are grateful for the contributions of Mark Slobin, who departed for other projects; not only did he write the original chapter on Europe and see it through four editions but, along with David Reck, he also helped me write the first and last chapters for the first edition. We remember the late James T. Koetting, my predecessor at Brown, who authored the chapter on Africa through the first two editions of this book and whose field recording of the Ghanaian postal workers will always remain in it. We are grateful to Henrietta Mckee Carter, who was in Ghana when Jim made that recording and who supplied us with additional information about it. We remember the contributions of the late Linda Fujie, who authored the chapter on Japan that appeared in previous editions. We remember the late David McAllester, one of the original coauthors and one of the cofounders of the Society for Ethnomusicology, whose chapter on Native American music stood from the previous editions as a monument to a great teaching career. It is a testament to its integrity that Christopher Scales, the new author of that chapter, has retained some of McAllester's contributions.

We would be pleased to hear from our readers; you can reach us by contacting the publisher or any of us directly at our respective colleges and universities.

—**Jeff Todd Titon**
Brown University

The Authors

Timothy J. Cooley

is Professor of Ethnomusicology at the University of California, Santa Barbara, Department of Music, where he teaches courses in Polish folk music, American vernacular, folk and popular music, and music and sports, among other subjects. He is also Affiliated Faculty with the university's Global and International Studies Program. He earned a Master's in Music History at Northwestern University and his Ph.D. in Ethnomusicology at Brown University, where he studied with Jeff Todd Titon, Carol Babiracki, Michelle Kisliuk, and Marc Perlman. He enjoys playing Polish mountain fiddle music, American old-time banjo and guitar, and singing in choirs. Cooley's most recent book, *Surfing about Music*, is the first ethnomusicological book about music and sports. In it, he takes a broad view of musical practices associated with surfing, from ancient Hawaiian chants to present-day punk-rock bands. His book, *Making Music in the Polish Tatras: Tourists, Ethnographers, and Mountain Musicians*, won the 2006 Orbis Prize for Polish Studies, awarded by the American Association for the Advancement of Slavic Studies. The collected edition, *Shadows in the Field: New Perspectives for Fieldwork in Ethnomusicology*, edited with Gregory F. Barz (1997; second revised edition, 2008), was instrumental in a discipline-wide rethinking of research methods and objectives. Cooley was the editor of *Ethnomusicology*, the journal of the Society for Ethnomusicology, from 2006 to 2009. His current research continues to ask how people use music to create self- and group-identities, and how this interacts with other cultural practices such as sports, lifestyle decisions, and belief systems.

David Locke

received a Ph.D. in ethnomusicology in 1978 from Wesleyan University, where he studied with David McAllester, Mark Slobin, and Gen'ichi Tsuge. At Wesleyan, his teachers of traditional African music included Abraham Adzinyah and Freeman Donkor. He conducted doctoral dissertation fieldwork in Ghana from 1975 to 1977 under the supervision of Professor J. H. K. Nketia. In Ghana, his teachers and research associates included Godwin Agbeli, Gideon Foli Alorwoyie, and Abubakari Lunna. He has published numerous books and articles on African music and regularly performs the repertories of music and dance about which he writes. He teaches in the Music Department of Tufts University, where he also serves as a faculty advisor to the Tufts-in-Ghana Foreign Study Program and member of the steering committee of the Africana Studies Program. His recent projects include an oral history and musical documentation of dance-drumming from the Dagbamba people, and an in-depth musical documentation of *Agbadza*, an idiom of Ewe music. He is active in the Society for Ethnomusicology and has served as the president of its Northeast Chapter. He founded the Agbekor Drum and Dance Society, a community-based performance group dedicated to the study of traditional Ghanaian music, and the Samanyanga Mbira Club, a community-based performance group dedicated to the study of Shona mbira music. Study of Akan traditional music-culture is Locke's most recent focus.

Anne K. Rasmussen

is Professor of Music and Ethnomusicology and the Bickers Professor of Middle Eastern Studies at the College of William and Mary, where she also directs the Middle Eastern Music Ensemble. Her research interests include music of the Arab and Islamic world; music and multiculturalism in the United States; music patronage and politics; issues of orientalism, nationalism, and gender in music; fieldwork; music performance; and the ethnographic method. Rasmussen received a Ph.D. in ethnomusicology from the University of California, Los Angeles, where she studied with A. J. Racy, Timothy Rice, and Nazir Jairazbhoy. Gerard Béhague and Scott Marcus are also among her influential teachers. Rasmussen is author of *Women, the Recited Qur'an, and Islamic Music in Indonesia* (2010); coeditor with David Harnish of *Divine Inspirations: Music and Islam in Indonesia* (2011), coeditor with Kip Lornell of *The Music of Multicultural America* (1997, 2015); and editor of a special issue of *the world of music* on "The Music of Oman" (2012). She is the author of articles and book chapters in numerous publications and has produced four CD recordings. Winner of the Jaap Kunst Prize for best article in published in 2000, she also received the Merriam Prize honorable mention for her 2010 book from the Society for Ethnomusicology (SEM). Rasmussen has served that society twice as a board member and was elected SEM president in 2014.

David B. Reck

was born in 1935 in Rising Star, Texas. A prodigy, he began musical studies at an early age. He attended the University of Houston (B.Mus.), continuing with graduate studies at the University of Texas (M.Mus.), where he studied with Paul Pisk. His association with Peter Phillips greatly influenced his development as a musician and composer. In the early 1960s, he moved to New York, where he was active in the new music scene with performances of his compositions at venues including Town Hall, Carnegie Hall, the Museum of Modern Art, and at festivals throughout Europe (including London, Paris, Berlin and Rome). In 1968 he received a grant from the Rockefeller Foundation. Enrolling in the College of Carnatic Music (Madras, India), he began a lifetime of study of South Indian classical music in the Karaikudi tradition of *veena*, principally with Ms. Ranganayaki Rajagopalan. While in India, he was awarded a Guggenheim Fellowship in musical composition. Returning to the United States, he enrolled at Wesleyan University (Ph.D.), where he studied with David P. McAllester and Mark Slobin. In 1975 he was appointed to the faculty of Amherst College as a professor of music and of Asian languages and civilizations, where he continued until his retirement. Selected publications include *Music of the Whole Earth*, and "Musical Instruments: Southern Area" in *The Garland Encyclopedia of World Music: South Asia: the Indian Subcontinent*. He has also published numerous articles on South India's classical music and on the influence of India's music on popular and classical music in the United States and Europe. He taught as a visiting professor at Brown University; at Smith, Mt. Holyoke and Hampshire colleges; and at The New School, and he has lectured at numerous colleges and universities in North America, Europe and India. An accomplished *veena* player in the Karaikudi tradition, he has concertized widely on three continents. He has served on numerous committees for, among others, the Guggenheim Foundation, the Broadcast Music, Inc. (BMI) annual composition competition, the Fulbright Scholarship Committee, and the National Endowment for the Arts. While at Amherst College, he initiated numerous courses in Asian music and culture, film, ethnomusicology, classical and popular music and culture, J.S. Bach, the Beatles, world music composition, modernism, and songwriting, along with establishing a pioneering world music concert series which continues to this day.

Christopher A. Scales

is an Associate Professor of Ethnomusicology in the Residential College in the Arts and Humanities at Michigan State University, where he is also affiliated with the American Indian Studies Program. He teaches courses on North American indigenous music, southern Appalachian music, music and technology, intellectual and cultural property, and the North American popular music industry. He received his Ph.D. from the University of Illinois at Urbana–Champaign, where he studied with Bruno Nettl, Thomas Turino, Donna Buchanan, Charles Capwell, and Lawrence Gushee. His book *Recording Culture: Powwow Music and the Aboriginal Recording Industry on the Northern Plains* (Duke University Press, 2012) focuses on contemporary Northern powwow culture and musical creation both on the powwow grounds and in Aboriginal recording studios, specifically engaging the effects of technology and mass mediation on powwow performance aesthetics. His research has also appeared in *Ethnomusicology, the world of music,* the *Canadian University Music Review,* and several edited volumes. Professor Scales has been active collaborating with Native musicians and has produced, recorded, or performed on several powwow and "Contemporary Native music" CD projects for Arbor Records and War Pony Records, independent record labels specializing in North American Aboriginal music. His current research focuses on Native American popular music and, in particular, the influence of Red Power politics on Native musicians during the 1960s and 1970s. An active musician, he regularly performs southern Appalachian music in the East Lansing area on fiddle, guitar, banjo, and mandolin, as well as Shona *mbira* music from Zimbabwe, playing *mbira dzavadzimu*.

John M. Schechter

is Professor Emeritus of Music (Ethnomusicology and Music Theory), at the University of California, Santa Cruz. He received a Ph.D. in ethnomusicology from the University of Texas at Austin, where he studied Latin American ethnomusicology with Gerard Béhague; folklore with Américo Paredes; Andean anthropology with Richard Schaedel; and Quechua with Louisa Stark and Guillermo Delgado-P. Beginning in 1986, he created—and subsequently directed until 2000—the U. C. Santa Cruz Taki ñan and Voces Latin American Ensembles. With Guillermo

Delgado-P., Schechter is coeditor of *Quechua Verbal Artistry: The Inscription of Andean Voices/Arte Expresivo Quechua: La Inscripción de Voces Andinas* (2004), a volume dedicated to Quechua song text, narrative, poetry, dialogue, myth, and riddle. He is general editor of, and a contributing author to, *Music in Latin American Culture: Regional Traditions* (1999), a volume examining music-culture traditions in distinct regions of Latin America. He authored *The Indispensable Harp: Historical Development, Modern Roles, Configurations, and Performance Practices in Ecuador and Latin America* (1992). Schechter's chapter on Víctor Jara appeared in the 2011 volume *Popular Music and Human Rights: Volume II: World Music*, edited by Ian Peddie. His other publications have explored formulaic expression in Ecuadorian Quechua *sanjuán*, and the ethnography, cultural history, and artistic depictions of the Latin American/Iberian child's wake music ritual. Schechter currently serves on the international advisory board of the MUSIKE Project, an ethnomusicological, theme-based journal published under the auspices of the SPANDA Foundation.

Jonathan P. J. Stock

received a Ph.D. in ethnomusicology at the Queen's University of Belfast, where he studied with Rembrandt Wolpert, Martin Stokes, and John Blacking. His field research has been funded by the British Council, the China State Education Commission, the United Kingdom's Arts and Humanities Research Council, the British Academy, and Taiwan's National Endowment for the Arts. It has been carried out in several parts of China, Taiwan, and England, and centered primarily on understanding the transformation of folk traditions in the modern and contemporary worlds. He is the author of two academic books on Chinese music, as well as the multivolume textbook, *World Sound Matters: An Anthology of Music from Around the World*. He is active as an editor, currently coediting the journal *Ethnomusicology Forum*. His current research focus is the music of the Bunun people in Taiwan, but he has also written recently on the history of Chinese music and on the use of world music in science fiction. Formerly the chair of the British Forum for Ethnomusicology and now an executive board member of the International Council for Traditional Music, he founded the ethnomusicology program at the University of Sheffield in 1998 and now serves as Professor and Head of the School of Music and Theatre, University College Cork, Ireland.

R. Anderson Sutton

received a Ph.D. in musicology from the University of Michigan, where he studied with Judith Becker and William Malm. He was introduced to Javanese music while an undergraduate at Wesleyan University, and he made it the focus of his Master's study at the University of Hawai'i at Mānoa, where he studied *gamelan* with Hardja Susilo. On numerous occasions since 1973 he has conducted field research in Indonesia, with grants from the East-West Center, Fulbright-Hays, the Social Science Research Council, the National Endowment for the Humanities, the Wenner-Gren Foundation, and the American Philosophical Society. He is the author of *Traditions of Gamelan Music in Java, Variation in Central Javanese Gamelan Music, Calling Back the Spirit: Music, Dance, and Cultural Politics in Lowland South Sulawesi*, and numerous articles on Javanese music. His current research concerns music and media in Indonesia and South Korea. Active as a *gamelan* musician since 1971, he has performed with several professional groups in Indonesia and directed numerous performances in the United States. He served as the first vice president and book review editor for the Society for Ethnomusicology, and was a member of the Working Committee on Performing Arts for the Festival of Indonesia (1990–1992). From 1982 to 2013, he taught at the University of Wisconsin–Madison, where he was Professor of Music and served three terms as Director of the Center for Southeast Asian Studies. He is now Dean of the School of Pacific and Asian Studies and Assistant Vice Chancellor for International and Exchange Programs at the University of Hawai'i at Mānoa.

Jeff Todd Titon

is Professor of Music, Emeritus, at Brown University, where he directed the Ph.D. program in ethnomusicology from 1986 to 2013. He received a Ph.D. in American Studies from the University of Minnesota, where he studied ethnomusicology with Alan Kagan, cultural anthropology with Pertti Pelto, and musicology with Johannes Riedel. He founded the ethnomusicology program at Tufts University, where he taught from 1971 to 1986. From 1990 to 1995 he served as the editor of *Ethnomusicology*, the journal of the Society for Ethnomusicology. He has done ethnographic fieldwork in North America on religious folk music, blues music, and old-time fiddling, with support from the National Endowment for the Arts and the National Endowment for the Humanities. For two years, he was the guitarist in the Lazy Bill Lucas Blues Band, a group that appeared at the 1970 Ann Arbor Blues Festival. He founded and directed an old-time, Appalachian, string-band ethnomusicology ensemble at Tufts (1981–1986) and then at Brown (1986–2013). He is the author or editor of eight books, including *Early Downhome Blues*, which won the ASCAP–Deems Taylor Award, *Give Me This Mountain*, *Powerhouse for God*, and the *Oxford Handbook of Applied Ethnomusicology*. A documentary photographer and filmmaker as well as author, he is considered a pioneer in applied ethnomusicology, phenomenological ethnography, and ecomusicology. His most recent research may be tracked on his blog (http://sustainablemusic.blogspot.com).

1

The Music-Culture as a World of Music

Jeff Todd Titon

1. SLOVENIA
2. CROATIA
3. BOSNIA AND HERZEGOVINA
4. MONTENEGRO
5. KOSOVO
6. ALBANIA
7. MACEDONIA

Learning Objectives

After you have studied this chapter, you should be able to:

1. Propose a distinction between music and nonmusic, and offer examples of each.

2. Define the term *music-culture*, and offer an example of a music-culture with which you are familiar, discussing its major components (ideas, activities, repertories, and material culture).

3. Define and discuss the elements of form and structure in music, such as melody, meter, rhythm, harmony, texture, and timbre.

4. Discuss a musical performance you have witnessed recently in terms of the four-part model involving affect, community, performance, and history.

5. Decide to what extent mass media shape people's musical preferences and taste, and to what extent mass media reflect these things.

continued

MindTap·

START experiencing this chapter's topics with an online audio activity.

6. Explain what music can tell us about how one group of people over here is different from another group of people over there.

7. Propose various actions to help make a music-culture you admire be sustainable in the long term.

The Soundscape

The world around us is full of sounds. All of them are meaningful in some way. Some are sounds you make. You might sing in the shower, talk to yourself, shout to a friend, whistle a tune, sing along with a song streaming on your phone, practice a piece on your instrument, play in a band or orchestra, or sing in a chorus or an informal group on a street corner. Some are sounds from sources outside yourself. If you live in the city, you hear many sounds made by people and by machines. You might be startled by the sound of a truck beeping as it backs up, or by a car alarm. In the country, you can more easily hear the sounds of nature. In the spring and summer, you may hear birds singing and calling to each other, the snorting of deer in the woods, or the excited barks of a distant dog. Stop for a moment and listen to the sounds around you. What do you hear? The hum of an air conditioner? Your neighbor's dog barking? A car going by? Why didn't you hear those sounds a moment ago? For a moment, stop reading and become alive to the soundscape. What do you hear? Try doing this at different times of the day, in various places: Listen to the soundscape and keep a diary of the sounds you hear.

Just as landscape refers to land, **soundscape** refers to sound: the sounds of a particular place, both human and nonhuman. (The Canadian composer R. Murray Schafer developed this term; see Schafer 1980.) Scientists call the study of sounds within a specific environment **soundscape ecology**. The examples so far offer present-day soundscapes, but what were they like in the past? In medieval Europe, people told time by listening to the bells of the local clock tower. Today we take the sounds of a passing railroad train for granted, but people found them startling when first heard.

The American naturalist Henry David Thoreau was alive to the soundscape when he lived by himself in a cabin in the woods at Walden Pond one hundred and seventy years ago. Writing about his wilderness soundscape, Thoreau first made sure his readers knew what he did *not* hear: the crowing of the rooster, the sounds of animals—dogs, cats, cows, pigs—the butter churn, the spinning wheel, children crying, the "singing of the kettle, the hissing of the urn." This was the soundscape of a farm in 1850, quite familiar to Thoreau's readers. (We might stop to notice which of these sounds have disappeared from the soundscape altogether, for who today hears a butter churn or spinning wheel?) What Thoreau heard instead in his forest soundscape were "squirrels on the roof and under the floor; a whippoorwill on the ridge-pole, a blue jay screaming in the yard, a hare or woodchuck under the house, a screech-owl or a cat owl behind it, a flock of wild geese or a laughing loon in the pond, a fox to bark in the night"; but no rooster "to crow nor hens to cackle in the yard—no yard!" (Thoreau 1971:127-128). In Thoreau's America you could tell, blindfolded, just by hearing, whether you were in the forest, on a farm, or in a town or city. How have those soundscapes changed since 1850?

In Thoreau's soundscape at Walden Pond in 1850, each living species that made a sound had its own acoustic place in what the sound recordist Bernie Krause calls a *biophony*, the combined voices of living things. Krause points out that "non-industrial cultures," particularly those that live in the more-remote regions of the planet, like the BaAka of central Africa we will learn about in Chapter 3, "depend on the integrity of undisturbed natural sound for a sense of place," of where they are as well as who they are (Krause 2002:25). Many soundscape ecologists believe that every nonhuman species communicates in its own **acoustic niche** in the sound-scape, whether it is a bird, whale, or dolphin singing or an insect making noise by rubbing its legs together. But, as we have learned, humans make their own acoustic niches and interact sonically with nonhuman sounds in whatever soundscape they encounter, wherever they happen to be.

Listen to postal workers canceling stamps at the University of Accra post office. The soundscape is a post office, but it is unlike any post office you will likely encounter in North America. You are hearing men canceling stamps at the University of Accra, in Ghana, Africa. Two men whistle a tune, while three others make percussive sounds. A stamp gets canceled several times for the sake of the rhythm. You will learn more about this example shortly. For now, think of it as yet another example of a soundscape: the acoustic environment where sounds, including music, occur.

MindTap·
◀)) **LISTEN TO**
"Postal workers canceling stamps at the University of Ghana post office" online.

The Music-Culture

Every human society has music. Although music is universal, its meaning is not. For example, a famous musician from Asia attended a European symphony concert approximately one hundred and seventy-five years ago. He had never heard Western music before. The story goes that after the concert, his hosts asked him (through an interpreter) how he had liked it. "Very well," he replied. Not satisfied with this answer, his hosts asked what part he liked best. "The first part," he said. "Oh, you enjoyed the first movement?" "No, before that." To the stranger, the best part of the performance was the orchestra tuning. His hosts had a different opinion. Who was right? They both were. Music is not a universal language in the sense that everyone understands what music means. People in different cultures give music different meanings. **Culture** means the way of life of a people, learned and transmitted from one generation to the next. The word *learned* is stressed to differentiate a people's cultural inheritance from what is passed along biologically in their genes: nurture, rather than nature. From birth, people all over the world absorb the cultural inheritance of family, community, schoolmates, and other, larger social institutions such as the mass media—books, video games, television, and the internet. This cultural inheritance tells people how to understand the situations they are in (what the situations mean) and how they might behave in those situations. It works so automatically that we are aware of it only when it breaks down, as it does on occasion when people misunderstand a particular situation. Like the people who carry them, cultures do not function perfectly all the time.

Musical situations and the very concept of music mean different things and involve different activities around the globe. Because music and all the beliefs and activities associated with it are a part of culture, we use the term **music-culture** to mean a group's total involvement with music: ideas, actions, institutions, material objects—everything that has to do with music. A music-culture can be as small as a single human's personal music-culture, or as large as one carried by a transnational group. We can speak of the music-culture of a family, a community, a region, a nation. We can identify music-cultures with musical genres: there is a hip-hop music-culture, a classical music-culture, a jazz music-culture. We can identify subcultures within music-cultures: for example, Atlanta hip-hop within the hip-hop music culture; early music within classical music; or progressive bluegrass within bluegrass. In our example of concert music, the Euro-American or Western music-culture dictates that the sound made by symphony musicians tuning up is not music. But to the listener from Asia, it was music. That we can say so shows our ability to understand (and empathize with) each music-culture context from the inside and then move to an intellectual position outside of them. We can then compare them and arrive at the conclusion that, considered from their points of view, both the stranger and his hosts were correct. Contrasting the music of one culture with the music of another after stepping outside of both is a good way to learn about how music is made and what music is thought to be and do.

People may be perplexed by music outside their own music-culture. They may grant that it is music but find it difficult to enjoy. In Victorian England, for example, people said they had a hard time listening to the strange music of the native peoples within the British Colonial Empire. The expansive and exciting improvisations of India's classical music were ridiculed because the music was not written down "as proper music should be." The subtle tuning of Indian *raga* scales was considered "indicative of a bad ear" because it did not match the tuning of a piano (see Chapter 6). What the British were really saying was that they did not know how to understand Indian music on its own cultural terms. Any music may sound "out of tune" when its tuning system is judged by the standards of another music-culture.

A person who had grown up listening only to Armenian music in his family and community wrote about hearing European classical music for the first time:

> I found that most European music sounds either like "mush" or "foamy," without a solid base. The classical music seemed to make the least sense, with a kind of schizophrenic melody—one moment it's calm, then the next moment it's crazy. Of course there always seemed to be "mush" (harmony) which made all the songs seem kind of similar (posted to SEM-L public list server July 9, 1998).

Because this listener had learned what makes a good melody in the Armenian music-culture, he found European classical melodies lacking because they changed mood too quickly. Unused to harmony in his own music, the listener responded negatively to it in Western classical music. Furthermore, popular music in the United States lacked interesting rhythms and melodies:

> The rock and other pop styles then and now sound like music produced by machinery, and rarely have I heard a melody worth repeating. The same with "country" and "folk" and other more traditional styles. These musics,

while making more sense with their melody (of the most undeveloped type), have killed off any sense of gracefulness with their monotonous droning and machine-like sense of rhythm. (Ibid.)

You might find these remarks offensive or amusing—or you might agree with them. Like the other examples, they illustrate that listeners throughout the world have prejudices based on the music they know and like. Listening to music all over the planet, though, fosters an open ear and an open mind. Learning to hear strange music from the viewpoint of the people who make that music enlarges our understanding and increases our pleasure.

What Is Music?

Music isn't something found in the natural world, like air or sand; rather, music is something that people make, from sounds and silences. They make it in two ways: They make or produce the sounds they call music, and they also make music into a cultural domain, forming the ideas and activities they consider music. As we have seen, not all music-cultures have the same idea of music; some have no word for it, while others have a word that roughly translates into English as "music-dance" because to them music is inconceivable without movement. Writing about Rosa, the Macedonian village she lived in, Nahoma Sachs points out that "traditional Rosans have no general equivalent to

Figure 1.1
Russell Jacobs leading the singing at the Left Beaver Old Regular Baptist Church in eastern Kentucky, 1979. *Jeff Todd Titon.*

the English 'music.' They divide the range of sound which might be termed music into two categories: *pesni,* songs, and *muzika,* instrumental music" (Sachs 1975:27). Of course, this distinction between songs and music is found in many parts of the world. Anne Rasmussen, when chatting with her taxi driver on the way to a conference at the Opera House in Cairo, Egypt, was told by her taxi driver that he liked "*both* kinds of music: singing (*ghina*) *and* music with instruments (*musiqa*)." We can also find this distinction between songs and music in North America. Old-time Baptists in the southern Appalachian Mountains (see Figure 1.1) sometimes say, "We don't have music in our service," meaning they do not have instrumental music accompanying their singing. Nor do they want it.

Some music-cultures have words for song types (lullaby, epic, historical song, and so on) but no overall word for *music.* Nor do they have words or concepts that directly correspond to what Westerners consider the elements of musical structure: melody, rhythm, harmony, and so forth. Many readers of this book (and all of its authors) have grown up within the cultures of Europe and North America. In Chapter 5, the section "The Sounds of European Music" consider specific qualities of European and, by association, North American musical practices that Westerners consider "normal." Consciously and unconsciously, our approaches and viewpoints reflect this background. But no matter what our musical backgrounds are, we must try to "get out of our cultural skins" as much as possible in order to view music through cultural windows other than our own. We may even learn to view our own music-culture from a new perspective. Today, because of the global distribution of music on radio, television, film, digital video, sound recordings, and the internet, people in just about every music-culture are likely to have heard some of the same music. Although the local is emphasized throughout this book, music-cultures should not be understood as isolated, now or even in the past. In particular, thinking about the interaction between the local and the global can help us appreciate music-cultures, including our own.

If we want to understand the different musics of the world, then, we need first to understand them on their own terms—that is, as the various music-cultures themselves do. But beyond understanding each on its own terms, we want to be able to compare and contrast the various musics of the world. To do that we need a way to think about music as a whole.

To begin to discover what all musics might have in common, so that we may think about music as a general human phenomenon, we ask "How do people perceive differences between music and nonmusic?" The answer does not involve simple disagreements over whether something people call "music" is truly music. For example, some people say that rap is not music, but what they mean is that they think rap is not good or meaningful music. Rather, there are difficult cases that test the boundaries of what differentiates sound from music, such as the songs of birds, dolphins, or whales—are these music?

Consider bird songs. Everyone has heard birds sing, but not everyone has paid attention to them. Try it for a moment: Listen to the songs of a hermit thrush at dusk in a spruce forest. At Walden Pond, Thoreau heard hermit thrushes that sounded like these.

Many think that the hermit thrush has the most beautiful song of all the birds native to North America. Most bird songs consist of a single phrase, repeated, but the hermit thrush's melody is more complicated. You hear a vocalization (phrase) and then a pause, then another vocalization and pause, and so on. Each vocalization has a similar rhythm and is composed of five to eight tones. If you listen closely, you also hear that a thrush can produce more than one tone at once, a kind of two-tone harmony. This is the result of the way its syrinx (voice box) is constructed.

Is bird song music? The thrush's song has some characteristics of music—rhythm, melody, repetition, and variation. It also has a function: Scientists believe that birds sing to announce their presence in a particular territory to other birds of the same kind, and also that they sing to attract a mate. Some bird species sing alarm calls to warn other birds of nearby predators, and in wintertime they may sing flight calls to announce their presence and thereby help keep a flock together. Bird song has inspired Western classical music composers. Some composers have transcribed bird songs into musical notation, and some have incorporated, imitated, or transformed bird song phrases in their compositions. Bird song is also found in Chinese classical music. In Chinese compositions such as "The Court of the Phoenix," for *suona* (oboe) and ensemble, extended passages are a virtual catalog of bird calls and songs imitated by instruments.

MindTap
LISTEN TO
"Songs of hermit thrushes" online.

Reflecting today's scientific worldview, most people in the Western music-culture hesitate to call bird songs music. Western culture regards music as a human expression, and bird songs no longer seem so close to the human world. Because each bird in a species sings the same song over and over, bird songs appear to lack human creativity. (Humpback whales, on the other hand, do change their songs over time.) Yet, people in some other music-cultures think bird songs do have human meaning. For the Kaluli people of Papua New Guinea, bird songs are the voices of their human ancestors who have died and changed into birds. These songs cause humans grief, which expresses itself in weeping (Feld 2012). The Kaluli give a different meaning to bird songs than Western-ers do. Does this mean it is impossible to find a single idea of what music is? Not entirely. Euro-Americans may disagree with the Kaluli over whether bird songs have human meaning, but they do agree that music has human meaning. Our thought experiment with bird song and its meanings in different music-cultures suggests that music has something to do with the human world. From an anthropocentric (human-centered) worldview, music is sound that is humanly patterned or organized (Blacking 1973).

For another example of a sound that tests the boundary between music and non-music, we turn back to the postal workers. Throughout the editions of *Worlds of Music*, listeners have found the Ghanaian postal workers' sounds especially intriguing.

These postal workers hand-canceling stamps at the post office of the University of Accra are making drumming sounds, but there are no drums, and two workers are whistling; they are just passing the time. How, exactly? Koetting (Titon 1992:98–99) wrote as follows:

> Twice a day the letters that must be canceled are laid out in two files, one on either side of a divided table. Two men sit across from one another at the table, and each has a hand-canceling machine (like the price markers you may have seen in supermarkets), an ink pad, and a stack of letters. The work part of the process is simple: a letter is slipped from the stack with the left hand, and the right hand inks the marker and stamps the letter. …
>
> This is what you are hearing: the two men seated at the table slap a letter rhythmically several times to bring it from the file to the position on the table where it is to be canceled. (This act makes a light-sounding thud.) The marker is inked one or more times (the lowest, most resonant sound you hear) and then stamped on the letter (the high-pitched mechanized sound you hear). … The rhythm produced is not a simple one-two-three (bring forward the letter—ink the marker—stamp the letter). Rather, musical sensitivities take over. Several slaps on the letter to bring it down, repeated thuds of the marker in the ink pad and multiple cancellations of single letters are done for rhythmic interest. Such repetition slows down the work, but also makes it much more interesting.
>
> The other sounds you hear have nothing to do with the work itself. A third man has a pair of scissors that he clicks—not cutting anything, but adding to the rhythm. The scissors go "click, click, click, rest," a basic rhythm used in [Ghanaian] popular dance music. The fourth worker simply whistles along. He and any of the other three workers who care to join him whistle popular tunes or church music that fits the rhythm.

MindTap·
◀)) LISTEN TO
"Postal workers canceling stamps at the University of Ghana post office," online.

Work song, found in music-cultures all over the world, is a kind of music whose function ranges from coordinating complex tasks to making boring and repetitive work more interesting. In this instance the workers have turned life into art. Writing further about the postal workers' recording, Koetting says,

> It sounds like music and, of course it is; but the men performing it do not quite think of it that way. These men are working, not putting on a musical show; people pass by the workplace paying little attention to the "music." (Titon 1992:98)

Even though the postal workers do not think of this activity as a musical performance, Koetting is willing to say, "It sounds like music and, of course it is." He can say so because he connects it with other music-cultures' work-song activities (see for example, the work songs in Chapter 4). He finds a common pattern in their performance that exists in many music-cultures: people whistling a melody and accompanying it with various percussive rhythms. As a scholar considering people making sounds all over the world, Koetting classifies this activity as music. When he writes "of course it is," he means "of course, within a universal, scientific context it is music." Yet within the postal workers' own cultural context, it is "not quite" music. In other words, the workers are doing this as a part of their work, to pass the time; it is their way of being in the world as workers canceling stamps, not as singers and musicians intent on a musical performance. These cases—bird songs and the Ghanaian postal workers cancelling stamps—bring up questions about the boundaries between music and nonmusic that do not have easy answers. To some, the answer must be one or the other: either bird song is music or it's not; either the postal workers are making music or they are not. To others, the answer may be "Both" or "It depends" or "There is something wrong with the question." What do you think?

Structure in Music

People in music-cultures organize sounds into musical patterns. Although the patterns vary across cultures, all music-cultures pattern sounds into something we call "music." How can we think comparatively about the kinds of musical organization that we find throughout the world? Koetting understood the postal workers' activities to be music when comparing it with other musics he knew. He recognized a familiar pattern of melody and harmony, as you probably did, too. Although this hymn-tune was composed by a Ghanaian, the melody is European, a legacy of Christian missionary music in Ghana. As a student of Ghanaian drumming, he recognized the cross-rhythms of the percussion. He thought about the performance in terms of its melody, harmony, meter, and rhythm.

Indeed, the Western music-culture recognizes these four characteristics of musical performance and talks about them in familiar, ordinary language. These terms describe patterns or structure (form) in sound. It will be interesting to see what happens to these Western (but not exclusively Western) ideas when, for better and worse, they are applied to every music-culture throughout this book. In this section, on musical structure, we briefly review these ideas. Next, we show

how music becomes meaningful in performance. After that, we consider the four components of a music-culture, which in music textbooks are not usually considered rudiments but are no less a part of humanly organized sound: ideas, activities, repertories, and the material culture of music. Last, we return to soundscape and consider the interconnections of music-cultures throughout human history on Planet Earth, as well as the sustainability of music in the future.

Rhythm and Meter

In ordinary language we say *rhythm* when we refer to the patterned recurrence of events, as in "the rhythm of the seasons," or "the rhythm of the raindrops." In music, we hear rhythm when we hear a time-relation between sounds. In a classroom you might hear a pen drop from a desk and a little later a student coughing. You do not hear any rhythm, because you hear no relation between the sounds. But when you hear a person walking in the hall outside, or when you hear a heartbeat, you hear rhythm.

If we measure the time-relations between the sounds and find a pattern of regular recurrence, we have *metrical rhythm.* Think of the soldiers' marching rhythm: HUP-two-three-four, HUP-two-three-four. This is a metered, regularly recurring sound pattern. The recurring accents fall on HUP. Most popular, classical, and folk music heard in North America today has metered rhythm. Of course, most of those rhythms are more complex than the march rhythm. If you are familiar with Gregorian chants of the Roman Catholic Church, you know musical rhythm without meter. Although not music, ordinary speech provides an example of nonmetrical or **free rhythm**, whereas poetic verse is metrical (unless it is free verse). Think of the iambic pentameter in Shakespeare's plays, for example. In a metrical rhythm you feel the beat and move to it. The songs of the hermit thrushes are both metrically rhythmic and not. You can find a beat while the thrush sings a phrase, but after he stops you cannot predict exactly when he will start again.

"Sister, Hold Your Chastity," the Bosnian *ganga* song (Chapter 5), lacks any sense of a beat. You can't tap your foot to it. Although we hear rhythm in the relationship between successive sounds, this rhythm is highly flexible. Yet it is not arbitrary. The singers, who have spent years performing this music together, know how to coordinate the melody and harmony by signals other than a pulse. But the lack of a beat makes it difficult for someone to learn *ganga.* Try singing along with the recording and see for yourself.

Similarly, the rhythm in the Chinese weeding song (Chapter 8) flows in a flexible way as the singer aims to produce a musical effect by lengthening the duration of certain syllables.

On the other hand, the rhythm of *karnataka sangeeta* in "Sarasiruha" (Chapter 6) is intricate in another way. The opening *alapana* section has a flexible, nonmetered rhythm, but the following sections are metrically organized. The *mridangam* drummer's art (see Figure 1.2) is based on fifteen or more distinct types of finger and hand strokes on different parts of the drumheads. Each stroke has its own *sollukattu,* or spoken syllable that imitates the sound of the drum stroke. Spoken one after another, they duplicate the rhythmic patterns and are used in learning and practice.

Although most North Americans and Europeans may not be aware of it, the popular music they listen to usually has more than one rhythm. The singer's

MindTap
LISTEN TO
"Sister, Hold Your Chastity," performed by Azra Bandi'c, Mevla Luckin, and Emsija Tetarvoi'c, online.

MindTap
LISTEN TO
"Yundao ge" ("Weeding Song"), performed by Jin Wenyin, online.

MindTap
LISTEN TO
"Sarasiruha" ("To the Goddess Saraswati") *Kriti* in *raga Natai, Adi tala,* performed by Ranganayaki Rajagopalan, *veena*; Raja Rao, *mridangam,* online.

Figure 1.2
T. Viswanathan, flute; Ramnad
V. Raghavan, *mridangam.*
Courtesy T. Viswanathan.

melody falls into one pattern, the guitarist's into another; the drummer usually plays more than one pattern at once. Even though these rhythms usually relate to the same overall accent pattern, the way they interact with each other sets our bodies in motion as we move to the beat. Rhythm in the postal workers' canceling stamps emphasizes the tugs of different rhythmic patterns. This simultaneous occurrence of several rhythms with what we can perceive as a shifting downbeat is called **polyrhythm**. Polyrhythm is characteristic of the music of Africa and wherever Africans have carried their music. In Arab music, nonmetrical music—that is, singing and instrumental improvisation in free rhythm—is juxtaposed with metered music and sometimes, as we will hear in Chapter 10, metrical and nonmetrical playing are combined in the same moment. In Chapter 3 you will learn to feel yet a further layer of complexity—**polymeter**, or the simultaneous presence of two different metrical systems—as you "construct musical reality in two ways at once" while playing an Ewe (pronounced *eh*-way) bell pattern in *Agbekor*.

Melody

In ordinary language we say *melody* when we want to refer to the tune—the part of a piece of music that goes up and down, the part that most people hear and sing along with. It is hard to argue that melody and rhythm are truly different qualities of music, but it helps our understanding if we consider them separately. When we say that someone has either a shrill or a deep voice, we are calling attention to a musical quality called **pitch**, which refers to how high or low a sound is. When a sound is made, it sets the air in motion, vibrating at so many cycles per second. This vibrating air strikes the eardrum, and we hear how high or low pitched it is depending on the speed of the vibrations. You can experience this yourself if you sing a tone that is comfortable for your voice and then slide the tone down gradually as low as you can go. As your voice goes down to a growl, you can feel the vibrations slow down in your throat. Pitch, then, depends on the frequency of these sound vibrations. The faster the vibrations, the higher the pitch.

Another important aspect of melody is **timbre**, or tone quality. Timbre is caused by the characteristic ways different voices and musical instruments vibrate. Timbre tells us why a violin sounds different from a trumpet when they are playing a tone of the same pitch. Some music-cultures, like the European, favor timbres that we may describe as smooth or liquid; others, like the African, favor timbres that are buzzy; others, like the Asian, favor timbres that we might describe as focused in sound. The construction of instruments in various cultures often reflects the preference for various timbres or a combination of them, as we see with the Moroccan *bendir* in Chapter 10, an instrument that reflects both Arab and African techniques of construction and aesthetic preferences with regard to timbre.

Other important aspects of melody, besides pitch and timbre, include volume—that is, how melodies increase and decrease in loudness.

Another critical aspect of melody in world music is *emphasis:* for example, the way the major tones of the melody are approached: by sliding up or down to them in pitch, as some singers do; by playing them dead on, as a piano does; by "bending" the pitch, as a blues guitarist (Figure 1.3) does when pushing the string to the side and back (Chapter 4).

Yet another way to emphasize a point in a melody is to add decorative tones or what in classical music are called *ornaments*. These, too, occur in many of the musics of the world. See if you can find them as you listen to the audio that accompanies this text online. Concentrate on the way the singers and musicians do not simply sing or play tones, but play *with* tones.

Figure 1.3
Blues guitarists Johnny Winter (left) and Luther Allison, Ann Arbor (Michigan) Blues Festival, August 1970. *Jeff Todd Titon.*

Finding how different music-cultures organize sounds into melodies is one of the most fascinating pursuits for the student of music. If we sing the melody of the Christmas carol "Joy to the World," we hear how Westerners like to organize a melody. Try it:

Joy to the world, the Lord has come! (do ti la so, fa mi re do!)

This is the familiar do-re-mi (solfège) **scale**, in descending order. Try singing "Joy to the World" backwards, going up the do-re-mi scale and using the syllables in this order: "come has Lord the world the to joy." You might find it difficult. But if you first sing the do-re-mi scale using the solfège syllables, and then replace do-re-mi with "come has Lord," and so forth, you will be able to do it more easily.

The white keys of the piano show how most melodies in European and Euro-American music have been organized since the eighteenth century. Do-re-mi (and so forth) represent a *major scale*. Notice that these pitches are not equally spaced. Try singing "Joy to the World" starting on "re" instead of "do." You will see that it throws off the melody. If you are near a keyboard, try playing it by going down the white keys, one at a time. Only one starting key (C) gives the correct melody. This indicates that the **intervals**, or distances between pitches, are not the same.

The Euro-American culture prefers the major scale. As such, Euro-Americans set up many instruments, such as the piano or the flute, so that they can easily produce the pitch intervals of this scale. Timothy Cooley writes more fully about Euro-American scales and melodic organization in Chapter 5, using the same "Joy to the World" tune. But other music-cultures set up their instruments and their scales differently. For example, Javanese musical gongs organize the **octave** (the interval between one "do" and another that usually separates male from female voices when singing the same melody) into five nearly equidistant intervals in their *sléndro* (*slayn*-dro) scale. The Javanese have a second scale, *pélog* (*pay*-log), which divides the octave into seven tones, but the intervals are not the same as those in any Western scales. In the classical music of South India, known as Carnatic music, each melody conforms to a set of organizing principles called a *raga*. Although each *raga* has its own scale (based on one of seventy-two basic scale patterns), it also has its own characteristic melodic phrases, intonation patterns, and ornaments as well as a mood or feeling. A *raga* is an organized melodic matrix inside of which the South Indian singer or musician improvises melodically in performance (see Chapter 6). The modal system of Arab music, *maqam,* is like the Indian *raga* in that characteristic phrases and ornamental patterns are as much a part of the composition of a musical mode as are the notes of its scale, which, in Arab music, can incorporate nontempered "quarter tones" (see Chapter 10).

Harmony

Most readers of this book use the word *harmony* to describe something that can happen to a melody: It can be harmonized. You sing a melody and someone else sings a *harmony,* a part different from the melody, at the same time. You hear the intervals between the tones not only in a sequence, as in a melody, but also simultaneously. These simultaneously sounding tones are called *chords.* Although Western music theory is not always useful in describing music outside the Euro-American traditions, in this case **texture**, a word taken by analogy from the world of textiles to describe the interweaving of fibers, helps describe how melody and harmony interact in various musics throughout the world. Just as threads weave together to make cloth, so melodies can intertwine to make a multimelodic musical whole. *Texture* refers to the nature of these melodic interrelationships.

When the musical texture consists of a single melody only—for example, when you sing by yourself, or when several people sing the same melody in unison—we call the texture **monophonic** ("mono" meaning "single," "phono" meaning "voice"). If you add one or more voices doing different things, the melodic texture changes, and we describe the way the voices relate. The classical music of India commonly includes a *drone,* an unchanging tone or group of tones sounding continuously, against which the melody moves (see Chapter 6). European bagpipes also include drones. When two or more voices elaborate the same melody in different ways at roughly the same time, the texture is **heterophonic**. Heterophony may be heard in the voices of the African-American congregation singing lined-out hymnody "Amazing Grace" (Chapter 4) and among the musicians performing "Ilumán tiyu" (Chapter 9).

Heterophony is the desired texture in much ensemble playing in Arab music, in which each musician performs the same melody, but with their own additions and omissions, nuances, and ornaments, as we hear in several of the musical examples from Chapter 10.

When two or more distinct melodies are combined, the texture is **polyphonic**. Polyphony can also be heard in New Orleans–style jazz from the first few decades of the twentieth century: Louis Armstrong's earliest recordings offer good examples in which several melodic lines interweave. Javanese *gamelan* and other ensemble music of Southeast Asia (Chapter 7) consist of many layers of melodic activity that some scholars have described as polyphony. Polyphony is characteristic of European classical music in the Renaissance period (roughly 1450 to 1600) and the late Baroque (Bach was a master of polyphony).When two or more voices are combined

MindTap·

◀)) LISTEN TO

"Amazing Grace," performed by the deacon and congregation of the New Bethel Baptist Church, Detroit, Michigan, online.

MindTap·

◀)) LISTEN TO

"Ilumán tiyu," performed by "Galo," guitar and vocal, with the Quichua ensemble Conjunto Ilumán, online.

in such a way that one dominates and any others seem to be accompanying the dominant voice— or what most people mean when they say they hear a harmony (accompaniment)—the texture is **homophonic**. Homophony is typical of folk and popular music throughout the world (Figure 1.4).

Piano playing in jazz, rock, and other popular music is homophonic. The pianist usually gives the melody to the right hand and an accompaniment to the left. Sometimes the pianist plays only accompaniment, as when "comping" behind a jazz soloist. Blues guitarists such as Blind Blake and Mississippi John Hurt developed a homophonic style in the 1920s in which the fingers of the right hand played melody on the treble strings while the right-hand thumb simultaneously played an accompaniment on the bass strings.

Figure 1.4
Ladies' String Band, c. 1910. Family photos can be a useful source of musical history, even when identifying information is unknown. *Photographer and place unknown.*

Form

The word *form* has many meanings. From your writing assignments you know what an outline is. You might say that you are putting your ideas in "outline form." You use the word *form* to call attention to the way the structure of your thoughts is arranged. Similarly, in music, painting, architecture, and the other arts, *form* means structural arrangement. To understand form in music, we look for patterns of organization in rhythm, melody, and harmony. Patterns of musical organization involve, among other things, the arrangement of small- to medium-sized musical units of rhythm, melody, and/or harmony that show repetition or variation. Just as a sentence (a complete thought) is made up of smaller units such as phrases, which in turn are made up of individual words, so a musical thought is made up of **phrases** that result from combinations of sounds. *Form* can also refer to the arrangement of the instruments, as in the order of solos in a jazz or bluegrass performance, or the way a symphonic piece is orchestrated. **Form** refers to the structure of a musical performance—the principles by which it is put together and how it works.

Consider the pattern of blues texts (lyrics). The form often consists of three-line stanzas: A line is sung ("Woke up this morning, blues all around my bed"), the line is repeated, and then the stanza closes with a different line ("Went to eat my breakfast and the blues were in my bread"). Blues melodies also have a particular form, as do the chord changes (harmony) in blues (see Chapter 4). In the Jiangnan *sizhu* music of China (Chapter 8), the same music may be played twice as fast in a second section. The form of traditional Native American melodies (Chapter 2) involves the creative use of small units and variation. This form is not apparent to someone listening to the music for the first time, or even the second, which is one of the reasons we pay careful attention to it.

Structural arrangement is an important aspect of the way music is organized. It operates on many levels, and it is key to understanding not only how music-cultures organize music but also how various cultures and subcultures think about time and space in general. For these reasons, musical form is an important consideration in all the chapters that follow.

Our understanding of rhythm, meter, melody, and harmony is greatly enriched when we consider how music-cultures throughout the world practice these organizing principles of human sound. But there is more to music than the structure of sounds. When people make music, they do not merely produce sounds—they also involve themselves in various social activities and express their ideas about music. To ethnomusicologists considering music as a human phenomenon, these activities and ideas are just as important as the music's structure. In fact, the activities and ideas are also part of the human organization of the sound. In other words, ethnomusicologists strive for a way to talk about all the aspects of music, not just its sound. Where, for example, is there room to talk about whether musicians are true to an ideal, or whether they have "sold out" to commercial opportunity? This book presents music in relation to individual experience, to history, to the economy and the music industry, and to each music-culture's view of the world, which includes ideas about how human beings ought to behave. To help think about music in those ways, we next consider music as it exists in performance.

A Music-Culture Performance Model

Even when we are curious about the music of the world's peoples and want to understand more about it, confronting new music can be daunting. When watching a live performance, for example, our first impulse might be simply to listen to it, to absorb it, to see whether we like it or whether it moves us. Our next impulse may be to let our bodies respond by moving to the music. But soon we will ask questions about it: What is that instrument that sounds so lovely? How does one play it? Why are the people dancing? (Or are they dancing?) Why is someone crying? Why are the musicians in costume? What do the words mean? What kind of a life does the head musician lead? To formulate and begin to answer these questions in a comprehensive way, we need some kind of systematic outline, or model, of any music-culture or subculture that tells us how it might work and what its components might be.

In this book we propose a music-culture model that is grounded in music as it is performed (Titon 1988:7–10). To see how this model works, think back to a musical event that has moved you. At the center of the event is your experience of the music, sung and played by performers (perhaps you are one of them). The performers are surrounded by their audience (in some instances, performers and audience are one and the same), and the whole event takes place in its setting in time and space. We can represent this by a diagram of concentric circles (Figure 1.5).

Now we transpose this diagram into four circles representing a music-culture model (Figure 1.6).

At the center of the music (as you experience it) is its radiating power, its emotional impact—whatever makes you give assent, smile, nod your head, sway your shoulders, dance. We call that music's *affect,* its power to move, and place affective experience at the center of the model. Performance brings music's power to move into being, and so we move from performers in Figure 1.5 to performance in Figure 1.6. *Performance* involves many things. First, people mark performances, musical or otherwise, as separate from the flow of ordinary life: "Have you heard the story about ..." or "Now we're going to do a new song that one of the members

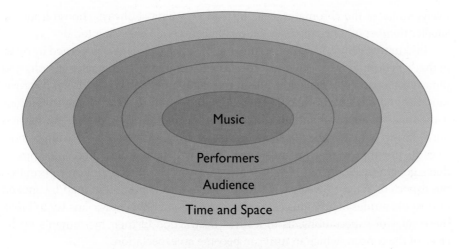

Figure 1.5
Elements of a musical performance.

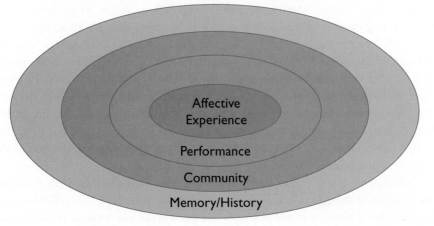

Figure 1.6
A music-culture model (after Titon 1988:11).

of the band wrote while thinking about. ..." When performance takes place, people recognize it as performance. We often mark endings of performances with applause. Second, performance has purpose. The performers intend to move (or not move) the audience, to sing and play well (or not well), to make money, to have fun, to learn, to advance a certain rite or ceremony. The performance is evaluated partly on how well those intentions have been fulfilled. Third, a performance is interpreted, as it goes along, by the audience, who may cry out, applaud, or hiss, and by the performers, who may smile when things are going well or wince when they make a mistake. Even in music that is participatory, without an audience, as in a jam session, the performers interpret and evaluate the music as it moves along.

The most important thing to understand about performance is that it moves along on the basis of agreed-on rules and procedures. These rules enable the musicians to play together and make sense to each other and to the audience. The performers usually do not discuss most of the rules; they have absorbed them and agreed to them. Starting at the same time, playing in the same key, playing in the same rhythmic framework, repeating the melody at the proper point—these are a few of the many rules that govern most of the musical performances that Westerners experience. Even improvisation is governed by rules. In a rock concert, for example, guitarists improvise melodic "breaks," but they usually do not use all twelve tones of the chromatic scale; instead they almost always choose from the smaller number of tones represented by the blues scale (see Chapter 4).

Instrumental improvisation in Arab music, or *taqasim,* is also governed by rules, in that a performer is expected to know how to combine the characteristic riffs and phrases of a particular *maqam,* while at the same time making his or her improvisation sound fresh and original. Audiences, too, often respond to improvisations with shouts of approval and encouragement for the musician, during pauses and after closing phrases called *qafla* (see Chapter 10). In Chapter 5 we will see how rules govern improvisation in music and dance in Poland. Rules or accepted procedures govern the audience, too. In some situations shouting is not only permitted but expected. What to wear, what to say—these, too, are determined by spoken or unspoken rules at any musical performance. Sometimes musicians try to break these rules or expectations, as in a ritual destruction of their instruments at the close of the concert, which in turn can become an expectation.

The music-culture model presented here defines music in performance as meaningfully organized sound that proceeds by rules. (Does bird song conform to this model? How and why?) Finding out those rules or principles becomes the task of analysis. These rules include (but are not limited to) what is usually covered under *musical analysis:* breaking music down into its component parts of mode, motif, melody, rhythm, meter, section, and so forth, and determining how the parts operate together to make the whole. Beyond that, the task in exploring music-cultures is to discover the rules covering ideas about music and behavior in relation to music, as well as the links between these rules or principles and the sound that a group of people calls "music."

You may resist the notion that music, which you think should be free to express emotion, is best thought of as rule-governed behavior. But rules govern all meaningful human cultural behavior in just this way. The point is not that musical performance is predetermined by rules, but that it proceeds according to them. In this view, music is like a game or a conversation: Without rules we could not have a game, and without agreement about what words are, what they mean, and how they are used, we could not hold a meaningful conversation. Nonetheless, just as meaningful conversations can express emotion, so meaningful music can express it as well, though not, of course, in exactly the same way. Further, if a listener does not understand the rules, he or she can understand neither the intention of the composer or musician nor the music's structure.

The circle corresponding to audience in Figure 1.5 becomes community in the music-culture model (Figure 1.6). The *community* is the group (including the performers) that carries on the traditions and norms, the social processes and activities, and the ideas of performance. By community we do not always mean a group of people living close to one another. For our purposes, a community in a music-culture forms when people participate in a performance in some way—as performer, audience, composer, and so forth. We call these communities where people come together over common interests "affinity groups." People in an affinity group may not know each other very well and may not even be in each other's physical presence, as for example in an internet community. Today, some websites allow a person to lay down a bass line, and later someone else from a different part of the world can lay down a guitar track on top of that, while another person can insert a drum track, and another provide a vocal, and yet another add vocal harmony, and so on, until eventually all of it adds up to a song that can be played from the website or downloaded. These "musicians" may never meet in person, yet they form a community.

Performance, then, is situated in community and is part of a people's music-culture. The community pays for and supports the music, whether directly with money or indirectly by allowing the performers to live as musicians. Community support usually influences the future direction of a particular kind of music. In a complex society such as the United States, various communities support different kinds of music—classical, rock, jazz, gospel—and they do so in different ways. When music becomes a mass-media commodity for sale, then packaging, marketing, and advertising become as crucial to the success of musicians as they are to the popularity of a brand of perfume.

How the community relates to the music makers also has a profound effect on the music. Among the folk music-cultures of nonindustrial village societies, the performers are drawn from the community; everyone knows them well, and communication takes place face to face. At the other end of the spectrum is the postindustrial music-culture celebrity who guards his or her private life, performs from a raised platform, offers a disembodied voice coming through electronic devices, and remains enigmatic to the audience. How the community relates to itself is another important aspect of performance. This is the place to consider music in relation to age, gender, identity, region, and class. For example, do men, women, old people, and young people experience music differently? How is poor people's music different from rich people's music? We will consider these issues later in this chapter.

Time and space, the fourth circle in Figure 1.5, become memory and history in our music-culture model (Figure 1.6). The community is situated in history and borne by memory, official and unofficial, whether remembered, recorded, or written down. Musical experiences, performances, and communities change over time and space; they have a history, and that history reflects changes in the rules governing music as well as the effect of music on human relationships. For example, the development of radio, recordings, television, and the internet meant that music did not need to be heard in the performer's presence. This took the performer out of the community's face-to-face relationships and allowed people to listen to music without making or overhearing it in person. Today, music is an almost constant background to many people's lives, with the musicians largely absent.

Music critics and historians also alter the effect of music by influencing the stock of ideas about music. The critic who writes for newspapers, magazines, or the internet helps listeners and music makers understand the impact of performances. When white America became interested in blues music in the 1960s (see Chapter 4), magazine and newspaper writers began asking blues singers questions about their music and its history. Knowing they would be asked these questions, blues singers prepared their answers, sometimes reading and then repeating what writers had already said about blues, sometimes having fun with their questioners and deliberately misleading them, and sometimes answering based on their personal experiences. This pattern repeated itself with hip-hop. Many times the subject of music is history itself. The Homeric poets sang about Odysseus; Serbian *guslars* sang about the deeds of their heroes; European ballads tell stories of nobles and commoners; African *griots* sing tribal genealogies and history, and the Arab *sha'ir*, or poet-singers, recount the travels and definitive battles of their tribal ancestors.

Today, digital recorders, computers, cell phones, tablets, multimedia programs, and the internet are revolutionizing community music history in the West, for they empower musicians and audience alike to record what they want to hear, represent it as they wish, and listen to it again and again; in this way they gain a kind of control over their history never before experienced. In studying the history of a music-culture, or some aspect of it, you need to know not only what that history is but also who tells or writes that history and what stake the historian has in it.

As you read through each of the case studies in the following chapters, bear this underlying music-culture *performance model* in mind. Because each of the case studies focuses on music and performance, you can use this model to understand how each chapter moves among experience, performance, community, memory, and history. Musical analysis is an important part of this procedure. Unlike the analyst who investigates Western classical music by looking at the composer's written score, ethnomusicologists must usually deal with music that exists only in performance, without notation or instructions from a composer. The ethnomusicologist often transcribes the music—that is, writes it down in musical notation—and then analyzes its structure. But it is impossible to understand structure fully without knowing the cultural "why" along with the musical "what."

The Four Components of a Music-Culture

A music-culture ultimately rests in the people themselves—their ideas, their actions, and the sounds they produce (Merriam 1964:32–33). For that reason, we now introduce another way of talking about all these aspects of music—a component model of a music-culture. This model, which complements the performance model we have just discussed, is divided into four parts: ideas about music, activities involving music, repertories of music, and the material culture of music (Table 1.1).

Table 1.1 **The Four Components of a Music Culture**

I. Ideas about music
  A. Music and the belief system
  B. Aesthetics of music
  C. Contexts for music
  D. History of music

II. Activities involving music

III. Repertories of music
  A. Style
  B. Genres
  C. Texts
  D. Composition
  E. Transmission
  F. Movement

IV. Material culture of music

Ideas about Music

Ideas about music are those related to a people's worldview, to their ideas of aesthetics, contexts for music, and histories of music.

Music and the Belief System

What is music, and what is not? Is music human, divine, or both? Is music good and useful for humankind, or is it potentially harmful? Does music belong to individuals, to groups, as if it were private property? Or is music a public resource that should be treated as common property? These questions reach into a music-culture's basic ideas concerning the nature of human society, art, and the universe. Cultures vary enormously in their answers to these questions, and the answers

Figure 1.7

Mr. and Mrs. Walker Calhoun, holding eagle feathers. Big Cove, near Cherokee, North Carolina, 1989. The Calhouns were leaders in preserving traditional ritual songs and dances among the East Coast Cherokee. *Jeff Todd Titon.*

often are subtle, even paradoxical; they are embodied in rituals that try to reconcile love and hate, life and death, the natural and the cultural (Figure 1.7). In Chapter 8 we will see how the Chinese concept of complementarity, yin and yang—often symbolized by 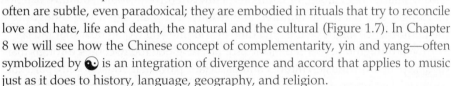 is an integration of divergence and accord that applies to music just as it does to history, language, geography, and religion.

Throughout this book you will see many examples of how belief systems and music-cultures interact. In Chapter 3 you will see that among the Ewe of Ghana, funerals feature singing, dancing, and drumming because the ancestral spirits, as well as their living descendants, love music and dance. Joyous singing and dancing in the presence of death is understood as an affirmation of life. The *ragas* of India, considered in Chapter 6, are thought to have musical personalities, to express particular moods. In Chapter 5 you will learn why music is essential for weddings in Poland and Bulgaria, as well as how major world religions impacted musical practices in many parts of Europe. As you read through the chapters in this book, see how each music-culture relates music to its worldview.

Aesthetics of Music

When is a song beautiful? When is it beautifully sung? What voice quality is pleasing, and what grates on the ear? How should a musician dress? How long should a performance last? Not all cultures agree on the answers to these questions about what is proper and what is beautiful. Harmonic intervals considered "ugly" in some parts of Europe are desirable in others (for example, in "Sister, Hold Your Chastity," in Chapter 5). Some jazz saxophone players (and listeners) favor a "hot," buzzy, honking sound, while others prefer the "cool," smooth, saxophone timbre found in Euro-American classical music. Music-cultures can be characterized by preferences in sound quality and performance practice, all of which are *aesthetic* discriminations; that is, they are concerned with ideas of beauty, pleasure, enjoyment, form, and affect.

Javanese *gamelan* music (Chapter 7) accompanies a family's celebration of a birth, wedding, or other event; people are expected to mingle and talk while the music takes place in the background. The music for the Chinese *guqin* (Chapter 8) was associated many centuries ago with amateur musicians, scholars for whom music was a pastime, not a profession. It was felt that a *qin* musician need not strive for virtuosity in performance nor learn more than a few pieces of music. The story goes that, nearly two thousand years ago, a young scholar went to visit a renowned, older Chinese scholar. On seeing that the elder's *guqin,* hanging on the wall of his study, was in disrepair and missing three of its seven strings, the young scholar inquired as to how it might make music. "Ah," replied the older scholar, "the unplayed melodies are the sweetest to contemplate of all."

Contexts for Music

When should music be performed? How often? On what occasions? Again, every music-culture answers these questions about musical surroundings differently (see Figure 1.8).

In the modern world, where music can be streamed wirelessly from the internet, it is hard to imagine the days when all music was experienced through live performance by its creators. Our great-grandparents had to sing or play music, or hear it from someone nearby; they could not produce it on demand from the radio, television, smartphone, tablet, or computer. How attentively would you have listened to a singer or a band one hundred and twenty-five years ago if you thought that the performance might be the only time in your life you would hear that music?

Even though much of the music around the globe today comes through mass media, people in music-cultures still associate particular musics with particular contexts. The original social context for blues is a bar, juke joint, dance hall, or blues club (Chapter 4). This is a far cry from the concert halls that provide the context for symphony orchestra performances. For many centuries in India, the courts and upper classes supported the classical music that we will consider in Chapter 6. But concerts of classical music in India are more relaxed and informal than those

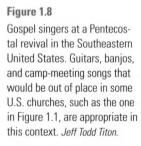

Figure 1.8

Gospel singers at a Pentecostal revival in the Southeastern United States. Guitars, banjos, and camp-meeting songs that would be out of place in some U.S. churches, such as the one in Figure 1.1, are appropriate in this context. *Jeff Todd Titon.*

in Europe, where the patronage of the courts and the aristocracy, as well as the Church, traditionally supported classical music. Today in Europe and North America, the government, the wealthy classes, and the universities supply this patronage. Classical music in various parts of the world, then, is usually associated with patronage from the elite classes, and it is performed in refined contexts that speak of its supporters' wealth and leisure.

Sometimes governments intervene to support other kinds of music. For example, during the twentieth century the Soviet Union and other Communist states encouraged a certain kind of folk music, or workers' music, thought to inspire solidarity. Typically, under government management what had been a loose and informal village musical aesthetic was transformed into a disciplined, almost mechanized, urban expression of the modern industrial nation-state (see Chapter 5). Folk festivals, supported by communist governments, showcased this music. In the United States, government-supported folk festivals have proliferated since the 1960s (Figure 1.9). Here, though, the diversity of ethnic musics is celebrated, and the government encourages the most traditional expressions within the music-cultures that are represented. Folk festivals provide an artificial context for traditional music, but the hope is that in a world where young people are powerfully attracted to new, mass-mediated, transnational popular music, folk festivals will encourage this local music in its home context. When nations modernize and traditional ideas and practices become old-fashioned—as for example in present-day China (Chapter 8)—various individuals and institutions (schools, clubs, societies) get involved in efforts to preserve and revive traditional music for contemporary life; in doing so, they also transform it.

Figure 1.9
Ana Vinagre of New Bedford, Massachusetts, sings Portuguese fado. National Folk Festival, Bangor, Maine, 2002. *Jeff Todd Titon.*

History of Music

Why is music so different among the world's peoples? What happens to music over time and as it spreads from place to place? Does it stay the same or change, and why? What did the music of the past sound like? Should music be preserved? What will be the music of the future? Some cultures institutionalize the past in museums, and the future in world's fairs; they support specialists who earn their living by talking and writing about music. Other cultures transmit knowledge of music history mainly by word of mouth through the generations. Recordings, films, videotapes, CDs, DVDs, and the internet allow us to preserve musical performances much more exactly than our ancestors could—but only when we choose to do so.

Musical history responds to changes in human cultures. The work songs that facilitated human labor gave way to the whine of machines with the industrial revolution (Chapter 4), but today the hum of the computer provides a background to individual musical composition and arranging as well as listening over the internet. European and Asian rural wedding and funeral ceremonies that involved important music making to celebrate these passage rites have become far less elaborate.

Questions about music history may arise both inside and outside a particular music-culture. Most music-cultures have their own community scholars who are historians or music authorities, formally trained or not, whose curiosity about music leads them to think and talk about music in their own culture, ask questions, and remember or document answers.

The four categories of ideas about music overlap. Though we separate them here for convenience, we do not want to suggest that music-cultures present a united front in their ideas about music, or that a music-culture prescribes a single aesthetic. People within a music-culture often differ in their ideas about music. Ragtime, jazz, rock 'n' roll, and hip-hop were revolutionary when they were introduced in the United States. They met (and still meet) opposition from some within the U.S. music-culture. This opposition is based on aesthetics (the music is thought to be loud and obscene, while some question whether it is music at all) and context (the music's associated lifestyles are thought to involve narcotics, violence, free love, radical politics, and so forth).

When organized divisions exist within a music-culture, we recognize music-subcultures, worlds within worlds of music. In fact, as we have seen, most music-cultures in the modern world can be divided into several subcultures, some opposed to each other: classical versus rock, for example, or (from an earlier era) sacred hymns versus dance music and drinking songs. Many Native American music-cultures in the northeastern United States have a subculture of traditionalists interested in older practices that are marked as belonging to their tribe, while other subcultures are involved more with the music of the Catholic Church, and yet others with forms of contemporary popular music (rock, jazz, country) that they have adapted to their needs and desires. Sometimes the subcultures overlap: The performance of a hymn in a Minnesota church may involve region (the upper Midwest), ethnicity (German), and religion (Lutheranism)—all bases for musical subcultures. With which musical subcultures do you identify most strongly? Which do you dislike? Are your preferences based on contexts, aesthetics, the belief system—or a combination of these?

Activities Involving Music

People in a music culture do not just have ideas about music, of course; they put those ideas into practice in a variety of activities—everything from making the sounds to posting music on the internet, from rehearsing in their rooms alone to playing in a band to managing a concert to making and marketing recordings. People have become active rather than passive consumers of music, carefully selecting the music they want to experience from the great variety available.

Human activities involving music also include the way people divide, arrange, or rank themselves in relation to music. Musical ideas and performances are unevenly divided among the people in any music-culture. For example, some perform often, others hardly at all. Some musicians perform for a living, while others play just for the love of it. People sing different songs and experience music differently because of age and gender. Racial, ethnic, and work groups also sing their own songs, and each group may develop or be assigned its own musical role. All of these differences have to do with the social organization of the music-culture, and they are based on the music-culture's ideas about music. We may ask, "What is it like in a given music-culture to experience music as a teenage girl in a West Coast suburb, a young male urban professional, or a rural grandmother of Swedish ethnic heritage who lives on a farm?"

It can be useful to distinguish music which is *presentational* (think of performers presenting music to a separate audience) from music which is *participatory* (everyone in the group makes music, dances, and so on). Alan Lomax thought that the social organization of the musical group was key to how people in various social groups worked together in most activities: in unison, or everyone doing their own thing, sometimes in a coordinated way and sometimes not. In his Cantometrics project, Lomax claimed that musical organization both reflected and reinforced social organization in Europe, Asia, and Africa. For example, traditional Asian music was characteristically solo and presentational, while African music was participatory (Lomax 1968). Thomas Turino (2009) expanded Lomax's categories to include, in addition to presentational and participatory, what he called high fidelity (recordings meant to be faithful copies of live performances) and studio art (computer-synthesized sounds meant to not represent real-time performances). Presentational performances and high-fidelity recordings, he argued, are especially well-suited for capitalist societies, whereas participatory performances and studio art recordings undermine capitalism.

Sometimes the division of musical behavior resembles the social divisions within the group and reinforces the usual activities of the culture. Until 1997, the Vienna Symphony had no women in its orchestra. Throughout most of the nineteenth century men acted the female roles in *jingju* opera (see Chapter 8), as the Chinese government felt it was improper for men and women to appear onstage together. In many traditional ceremonies throughout the world, men and women congregate in separate areas; some ceremonies center exclusively on men, others on women. On the other hand, music sometimes goes against the broad cultural grain, often at carnival time or at important moments in the life cycle (initiations, weddings, funerals, and so forth). People on the cultural fringe become important when they play music for these occasions. In fact, many music-cultures assign a low social status to musicians but also acknowledge their power and sometimes even see magic in their work. The most important features of music's social organization are status and role: the prestige of the music makers and the different roles assigned to people in the music-culture. In the interview with the Iraqi refugee musician Rahim Al Haj in Chapter 10 we read of the familiar reaction of his father, who disapproves of his son's ambitions to be a musician, a sentiment that resonates with the historical accounts of the tenth century written in his native city, Baghdad. When blues arose early in the twentieth century, most middle-class African Americans associated it with the black underclass and tried to keep their children away from it. Blues musicians were assigned a low social status (Chapter 4). Neither the Argentine tango nor the Trinidadian steel band were considered respectable when they arose. Only after they gained popularity abroad and returned to their home countries did they become respectable to the point of becoming national symbols of music in their respective countries.

Ethnomusicologists consider how race, ethnicity, class, gender, region, and identity are embedded in musical activities. When people in a music-culture migrate out of their region, they often use music as a marker of ethnic identity. Throughout North America, ethnic groups perform and sometimes revive music that they consider to be their own, whether Jewish klezmer music, Andean panpipe music, central European polka, Portuguese fado (Figure 1.9), or Beijing (Peking) opera. Musical diasporas and transnationalism have become important themes in twenty-first-century global musical life.

Ever since the twentieth century, the music industry has played an especially important role in various music-cultures. Music is packaged, bought, and sold. How does a song commodity become popular? When is popularity the result of industry hype, and when does it come from a groundswell of consumer interest? How do new kinds of music break into the media? Why do certain kinds of music gain (or fall) in popularity? What makes a hit song? Fortunes are gained and lost based on music producers' abilities to predict what will sell—yet most of the music released commercially does not sell. How should a group of musicians deal with the industry? How can they support themselves while remaining true to their musical vision? What constitutes "selling out"? In the past fifty years, markets have expanded and musicians from all over the globe now take part. Computer-assisted music making and the rise of a market on the internet have empowered consumers to become musicians and have empowered musicians to become teachers, producers, and marketers on YouTube and elsewhere. Music has become an enormously important aspect of the global economy. The current struggles over the future of music delivery on the internet alone involve profits and losses in the billions of dollars. As more people participate in music by making it, not just listening to it, the line between professional and amateur is blurring. For many, the primary experience of listening to music as a commodity is giving way to the experience of making music with the computer and bypassing traditional commercial channels.

As a great deal of money remains at stake in the distribution of music—new as well as old, along with "world music" that is packaged and distributed globally—debates rage over who owns music. When does the composer of a piece of music create something totally new, and when does the composer mainly produce new combinations of old materials? Should music be treated as the composer's intellectual property, for which the composer can charge money, or should it be regarded as free and common property for the public good? Or should it be private property for a limited time, and afterward become common property and pass into the public domain? Here, as elsewhere, ideas about music (and money) generate activities involved with music. People in traditional music-cultures often regard music as common property, but as outsiders and multinational corporations profit from their music, their attempts to protect their musical resources have grown. International agencies such as the World Intellectual Property Organization (WIPO) and United Nations Educational, Scientific and Cultural Organization (UNESCO) have formulated policies to protect what they call cultural rights to "intangible heritage" and traditional arts from commercial exploitation.

Repertories of Music

A **repertory** is a stock of music that is ready to be performed. It consists of six basic parts: style, genres, texts, composition, transmission, and movement. Consider a music with which you are familiar and see if you can understand it using the following terms.

Style

Style includes everything related to the organization of musical sound itself: pitch elements (scale, melody, harmony, tuning systems), time elements (rhythm, meter), timbre elements (voice quality, instrumental tone color), and sound intensity (loudness/softness). All depend on a music-culture's aesthetics.

Together, style and aesthetics create a recognizable sound that a group understands as its own. For example, the fiddle was the most popular dance instrument in Europe and North America from about the eighteenth century until the turn of the twentieth century. In many areas it is still popular; in others, such as Ireland, Sweden, and the United States, it has been undergoing a revival.

Genres

Genres are the named, standard units of the repertory, such as "song" and its various subdivisions (for example, lullaby, Christmas carol, wedding song) or the many types of instrumental music and dances (jig, reel, waltz, schottische, polka, *hambo*, and so forth). Genres come with built-in rules or expectations regarding performance style and setting, with the result that the "same" song, dance, or piece can be classified into different genres depending on how, when, or by whom it is performed or played back. An Irish jig might be played as an instrumental tune in a pub session, used in a film score, or danced professionally as part of an international show.

Most music-cultures have a great many genres, but their terms do not always correspond to terms in other music-cultures. Among the Yoruba in the African nation of Nigeria, for example, powerful kings, chiefs, and nobles retained praise singers to sing to them (Olajubu 1978:685). The praise songs are called *oriki*. Although we can approximate an English name to describe them (praise songs), no equivalent genre exists today in Europe or America. In North America, blues is one genre, country music another. Subdivisions of country music include rockabilly and bluegrass. Country music radio stations may identify themselves as "real country" (along with the latest hits, more of a mix of oldies and southern-oriented country music) or as "hard country" (more of a mix of rock-oriented country music). Consider "electronic" and some of its subdivisions; the website allmusic.com lists more than fifty subgenres, including chiptunes, illbient, trip-hop, left-field house, and goa trance. Subgenres have proliferated and shape-shifted as composition and marketing have grown more sophisticated. How many subgenres can you name in your favorite kind of music?

Texts

The words (or lyrics) to a song are known as its text. Any song with words is an intersection of two very different and profound human communication systems: language and music. A song with words is a temporary weld of these two systems, and for convenience we can look at each by itself.

Every text has its own history; sometimes a single text is associated with several melodies. On the other hand, a single melody can go with various texts. In blues music, for example, texts and melodies lead independent lives, coupling as the singer desires (Chapter 4). *Pop berat* ("heavy pop") compositions fuse Indonesian patriotic texts, traditional Indonesian musical instruments, and electric guitars and synthesizers (see Chapter 7). Navajo ritual song and prayer texts often conclude by proclaiming that beauty and harmony prevail.

Composition

How does music enter the repertory of a music-culture? Is music composed individually or by a group? Is it fixed, varied within certain limits, or improvised spontaneously in performance? Improvisation fascinates most ethnomusicologists: Chapters 3, 4, and 6 consider improvisation in African, African-American, and South Indian music. Perhaps at some deep level we like improvisation not just because of the skills involved but because we think it exemplifies human freedom.

The composition of music, whether planned or spontaneous, is bound up with social organization. Does the music-culture have a special class of composers, or can anyone compose music? Composition is related as well to ideas about music: Some music-cultures divide songs into those composed by people and those "given" to people from deities, animals, and other nonhuman composers.

Transmission

How is music learned and transmitted from one person to the next, from one generation to the next? Does the music-culture rely on formal instruction, as in South India (Chapter 6)? Or is music learned chiefly through imitation (Chapter 4)? Does music theory underlie the process of formal instruction? Does music change over time? How and why? Is there a system of musical notation? Cipher (number) notation in Indonesia did not appear until the twentieth century (Chapter 7). In the ancient musical notation for the *guqin* (Chapter 8), the Chinese writing indicates more than what note is to be played, because many Chinese pictograms (picture writing) suggest something in nature. For example, the notation may suggest a duck landing on water, telling the player to imitate the duck's landing with the finger when touching the string. Such notation can also evoke the feeling intended by the composer.

Some music-cultures transmit music through apprenticeships lasting a lifetime (as in the disciple's relation to a guru, Chapter 6). The instructor becomes like a parent, teaching values and ethics as well as music. Other music-cultures have no formal instruction, and the aspiring musician learns by watching and listening, often over many years. In these circumstances, growing up in a musical family is helpful (Figure 1.10). When a repertory is transmitted chiefly by example and imitation rather than notation, we say the music exists in an *oral tradition* rather than being written. Blues (Chapter 4) is an example of music in oral tradition; so is the *sanjuán* dance genre of highland Ecuadorian Quichua (Chapter 9). Music in oral tradition varies more over time and space than does music tied to a printed score. Sometimes the same music exists both

Figure 1.10

Family photo of a father and son playing music at home, on violin and piccolo, c. 1910. *Photographer and place unknown.*

in oral and written traditions. At gatherings called "singing conventions," people from all over the United States sing hymn tunes from shape-notation in tune books such as *The Sacred Harp.* Variants of these hymn tunes also exist in oral tradition among the Old Regular Baptists (see Figure 1.1) from the upper South, who do not use musical notation but rely instead on learning the tunes from their elders and remembering them.

Movement

A whole range of physical activity accompanies music. Playing a musical instrument, alone or in a group, not only creates sound but also literally moves people— that is, they sway, dance, walk, work in response. Even if we cannot see them move very much, their brains and bodies are responding as they hear and process the music. How odd it would be for a rock band to perform without moving in response to their music, in ways that let the audience know they were feeling it. In one way or another movement and music connect in the repertory of every culture. Sometimes the movement is quite loose, suggesting freedom and abandon, and at other times, as in Balinese dance, it is highly controlled, suggesting that in this culture controlling oneself is beautiful and admirable.

Material Culture of Music

Material culture refers to the material objects that people in a culture produce— objects that can be seen, held, felt, and used. This book is an example of material culture. So are dinner plates, gravestones, airplanes, hamburgers, cell phones, and school buildings. Examining a culture's tools and technology can tell us about the group's history and way of life. Similarly, research into the material culture of music can help us to understand music-cultures. The most important musical objects in a music-culture, of course, are musical instruments (Figure 1.11). We cannot hear the actual sound of any musical performances before the 1870s, when the phonograph was invented, so we rely on instruments for information about music-cultures in the remote past. Here we have two kinds of evidence: instruments preserved more or less intact, such as Sumerian harps over forty-five hundred years old, or the Chinese relics from the tomb of Marquis Yi (see Chapter 8), and instruments pictured in art. Through the study of instruments, as well as paintings, written documents, and other sources, we can explore the movement of music from the Near East to China over a thousand years ago; we can trace the Guatemalan marimba to its African roots; or we can outline the spread of Near Eastern musical influences to Europe. The influence of Near Eastern music on Europe occurred mainly before the Spanish inquisition of 1515, through exchange between a multicultural and multireligious population in Andalusia, the region of southern Europe that we now know as Spain and Portugal; this

Figure 1.11
Young man playing a one-stringed **diddley-bow**. Missouri, 1938. *Russell Lee/Courtesy of the Library of Congress.*

resulted in the development of most of the instruments in the Euro-American symphony orchestra.

We can also ask questions of today's music-cultures: Who makes instruments, and how are they distributed? What is the relation between instrument makers and musicians? How do this generation's musical instruments reflect its musical tastes and styles, compared with those of the previous generation? In the late 1940s and early 1950s, electric instruments transformed the sound of popular music in the United States. In the 1960s, this electronic music revolution spread elsewhere in the world. The computer is the most revolutionary musical instrument today.

Musical scores, instruction books, sheet music, instructional videos, websites devoted to music, YouTube—these too are part of the material culture. Scholars once defined folk music-cultures as those in which people learn to sing music by ear rather than from print, but research shows mutual influence among oral and written sources during the past few centuries in Europe and America. Because they tend to standardize songs, printed versions limit variety, but paradoxically they stimulate people to create original songs. Also, the ability to read music notation has a far-reaching effect on musicians and, when it becomes widespread, on a music-culture as a whole.

One more important part of a music's material culture should be singled out: the impact of electronic media. This technology has facilitated the information revolution, a phenomenon as important as the industrial revolution was in the nineteenth century. Electronic media have affected music-cultures all over the world. People listen to mass-mediated music more than any other kind. Such media are a main reason many now call our planet a global village.

Ecological and Sustainable Worlds of Music

In the eighteenth century, when Europeans began collecting music from the countryside and from faraway places outside their homelands, they thought that "real" traditional music was dying out. From then on, each time a new music-culture was discovered, European and American collectors took the music of its oldest generation to be the most authentic, conferring on it a timeless quality and usually deploring anything new. This neither reflected the way music-cultures actually work nor gave people enough credit for creative choice. At any given moment, three kinds of music circulate within most communities: (1) music so old and accepted as "ours" that no one questions (or sometimes even knows) where it comes from, (2) music of an earlier generation understood to be old-fashioned or perhaps classic, and (3) the most recent or current types of music, marketed and recognized as the latest development. These recent musics may be local, imported, or both. The last is most likely, because today the world is linked electronically; musics travel much more quickly than they did a hundred years ago.

Music-cultures, in other words, are dynamic rather than static. They constantly change in response to inside and outside pressures. It is wrong to think of a music-culture as something isolated, stable, smoothly operating, impenetrable, and uninfluenced by the outside world. Indeed, as we will see in Chapter 4, the people in a music-culture need not share the same language, nationality, or ethnic origin. In the twenty-first century, blues is popular with performers worldwide. People in a music-culture need not even share all of the same ideas about music—as we have seen, they in fact do not. As music-cultures change (and they are always changing) they undergo friction, and the "rules" of musical performance, aesthetics, interpretation, and meaning are negotiated, not fixed. Music history is reconceived by each generation.

In this book we usually describe the older musical layers in a given region first. Then we discuss increasingly more-contemporary musical styles, forms, and attitudes. We wish to leave you with the impression that the world of music is a fluid, interactive, interlocking, overlapping soundscape in which people may listen to music from their ancestors, parents, neighbors, and on computers, tablets, or smartphones all in the same day. We think of people as musical "activists," choosing what they like best, remembering what resonates best, forgetting what seems irrelevant, and keeping their ears open for exciting, new musical opportunities. This happens everywhere, and it unites the farthest settlement and the largest city.

Music is a fluid, dynamic element of culture, and it changes to suit the expressive and emotional desires of humankind. Music is a human adaptation to life on Earth. Whether considered locally or globally, music operates as an ecological system, functioning in the music-culture ecosystem as energy does in an organic ecosystem. Each music-culture is a particular adaptation to particular circumstances. Ideas about music, social organization, repertories, and material culture vary from one music-culture to the next. It would be unwise to call one music-culture's music "primitive," because doing so imposes one's own standards on a group that does not recognize them. Such ethnocentrism has no place in the study of world musics.

Music may be viewed ecologically as a human resource that is produced and consumed. Unlike oil, a finite natural resource that decreases as it is used, music is a renewable human resource that is kept alive in use. Although at times considered an economic resource, as a human resource music has an emotion-based dimension that fosters human relationships outside and apart from the economic realm. But, like natural resources, in most cultures music is experienced as a source of energy, and as something whose qualities can be good or bad, improved or polluted, used wisely or wasted. People are responsible for its wise uses and sustainability, its conservation, management, and continuation as a human resource. Although this stewardship has usually centered on preserving endangered musics, it is helpful also to think of it as encouraging the people who make music, as well as the conditions (ideas and cultural practices, whether traditional or modern) under which human beings remain free to create all music, including new music. In other words, sustainability stewardship is not just about music; it is about the people who make music.

In the chapters that follow, we explore the musical ecosystems of several worlds, and worlds within worlds, of music. Although each world may seem strange to you at first, all are organized and purposeful. Considered as an ecological system, the forces that make up a music-culture maintain a dynamic equilibrium. Some music-cultures are more resilient than others. A change or disturbance in any part of the musical ecosystem, such as the invention of the electric guitar or the latest computer-music technology, may have a far-reaching impact and cause a fundamental change that upsets the old equilibrium state and brings about a new one, as sampling has done. Viewing music this way leads to the conclusion that music represents a great human force that transcends narrow political, social, and temporal boundaries. Music offers an arena where people can talk and sing and play and reach each other in ways not allowed by the barriers of wealth, status, location, and difference. *Worlds of Music* and its accompanying music can present only a tiny sample of the richness of the world's music. We hope you will continue your exploration after you have finished this book.

Study Questions

1. How do anthropologists define the term culture? What is the definition of a music-culture?

2. What is a soundscape? Why should we pay particular attention to it? What sounds do you hear most often in your usual daily round of activities, from waking in the morning to going to sleep at night and everything in between?

3. What are the elements of form and structure in music? Define and discuss rhythm, melody, and harmony.

4. What are the four components of a music-culture? Explain each component and its parts.

5. Think of social organization in a musical ensemble you are familiar with (rock group, symphony orchestra, marching band, church choir, and so on). How are the musical roles divided? Is there a conductor? Are there sections within the group? Are there lead singers or players within the sections? Are there soloists? Do some positions carry more prestige than others? Does this ensemble reflect and embody the divisions within your society at large?

6. Ethnomusicology often is defined as "the study of people making music." What is meant by "making" in this definition?

7. What do various music-cultures within North America think of hip-hop (or some other music that you are familiar with)? In other words, what are some of their ideas about this music? Is it music? Is it good and useful, or potentially harmful? Is it pleasing and beautiful? Is it false, or true? When are the appropriate and inappropriate times for this music? How is it supported? Does it have a history? What is considered "authentic" within this music, and what is considered a sell-out?

8. Consider the role of technology in music, in everything from the construction of musical instruments to the way music is performed and distributed. What was technology's role in a previous century, and how has it changed?

9. Why is it important to keep an open mind when listening to an unfamiliar music?

10. Discuss how ethnicity, class, gender, and region are embodied in country music, hip-hop, classical music, or some other music that you know well.

2

North America/Native America

Christopher A. Scales

Learning Objectives

After you have studied this chapter, you should be able to:

1. Discuss the role and meaning of "tradition" in Native American music.

2. Identify and describe some of the general style features found in many different genres of Native American music.

3. Compare and contrast tribal and intertribal musical styles.

4. Identify similarities and differences between Haudenosaunee, Yuchi, and Navajo musics.

continued

MindTap

START experiencing this chapter's topics with an online video activity.

The author wishes to thank David McAllester for his contributions to this chapter.

5. Give a detailed description of Northern competition powwow music and dance practices.

6. Discuss the historical development of Native American popular music (Contemporary Native American music) in terms of both musical style and how the music relates to larger social and political developments in North America.

Try to recall your first experiences learning about Native Americans. How did you learn about them, and what did you learn? (If you self-identify as Native American, when did you first become aware of your identity *as* a Native American, unique from the dominant Euro-American identity of the majority population?) Perhaps you recall learning about Native peoples in public school through stories of the first American Thanksgiving. Or from Hollywood films like *Pocahontas* or *Dances with Wolves*. Maybe your first encounter involved your favorite sports teams, like the Cleveland Indians or the Chicago Blackhawks. You might recall a family trip through the Southwest during which you encountered Southwestern arts and crafts such as Navajo rugs or Pueblo pottery.

Listen to the song "Straight Up," performed by the Ojibwa powwow drum group The Northern Wind Singers. Does this music conform to your expectations of what "Native American music" is supposed to sound like? If so, why? What musical features in particular do you associate with Native American identity? And if this is not what you expected Native music to sound like, why might this be so? In other words, how do your preconceived ideas about Native Americans, many of which were formed at a very young age, match up with your understanding of their musical practices, which are quite often misunderstood by the larger Euro-American population of North America?

We undertake this brief exercise in order to explore how our collective knowledge of the indigenous peoples of North America—who they are, where they live, how they live, and how and why they make music—is very often partial, fragmented, and typically refracted through the stereotypic and often anachronistic images generated by the mass media and popular culture. Despite centuries of Euro-American intellectual fascination and political entanglements with the Native peoples of North America, they remain largely unknown to most nonindigenous North Americans. This is particularly the case with their music.

The people known as "Native Americans"—also sometimes called American Indians or, in Canada, First Nations peoples—represent hundreds of different tribal groups and communities across North America. There are over five hundred different federally recognized tribes in the United States alone, with over six hundred more in Canada. While these communities are understood by both federal governments and by each other to be distinct cultural and political entities, they may also be usefully understood as a large and very diverse "ethnic" or minority community, although one that is quite unique and particular. Many longstanding treaties between the federal governments of Canada and the United States and numerous Native communities guarantee special rights and privileges and, in certain cases, a degree of political and cultural sovereignty to Native peoples. In Canada, this unique status is further affirmed in the 1982 Canadian Constitution, which recognizes that the indigenous peoples of Canada (which include not only the First Nations but also Inuit and Métis peoples) are guaranteed not only treaty rights but also "Aboriginal rights" (although the nature of these rights continues to be developed and negotiated).

This ongoing concern with political and cultural sovereignty is, in large part, driven by a desire on the part of Native Americans to live their lives *as* Native Americans, which includes the ability to speak not only English but also their own indigenous language; the pleasure of learning about their own unique tribal histories in their schools; and, of particular concern for us in this chapter, the freedom to continue, revive, and elaborate upon the cultural and religious traditions of their ancestors. This, of course, includes a great many music and dance practices that have, throughout the past five hundred years, been subject to myriad forms of government suppression and interference (Ellis 2001).

Tribal Musics

In this chapter we will discuss the great diversity of Native American musical styles and genres by organizing this music into two broad categories: tribal *and* intertribal. *Tribal styles* and genres include all those musical practices that are unique to a particular ethnolinguistic community or group of communities. Tribal styles and genres typically originate from within the tribe and are defined by a unique set of musical style traits. Thus, we can speak in general terms about "Navajo music" or "Ojibwa music" through a discussion of some prominent genres of music and some common musical "style" features that help to define each genre, or that may be more common across a wide range of genres performed by a particular tribal group or community.

Intertribal styles describes the musical genres and practices that are widely dispersed and shared among a number of different Native groups and communities from across North America. In this case, it is perhaps more accurate to talk about intertribal "genres"— named categories of music, such as powwow music— which are so named because of the presence of a cluster of style traits. However, because these genres of music are shared across a wide range of tribal communities, they may also be altered or inflected by local, regional, or tribally defined aesthetic preferences. Thus, for genre categories such as powwow music, there exist several regional or tribally defined substyles. While tribal genres are often identified and understood by tribal community members as "our own music," intertribal genres are more likely to be thought of as "our own *version* of this genre of music."

Tribal styles are also often described, both by Native people and many non-Natives who study this music, as being more "traditional." Tradition has become a troubling and hotly contested term within and across Native communities and also among ethnomusicologists, anthropologists, and folklorists. For many within the academic community, "tradition" is now understood not as a way of describing an object or practice based on a particular set of qualitative traits ("I understand

| **Salient Characteristics of**
Native American Tribal Musics |
|---|
| ■ Predominance of percussion instruments, particularly drums and rattles |
| ■ Predominance of monophonic, solo, or unison singing |
| ■ Frequent use of vocables |
| ■ Larger musical forms derived from the frequent repetition of several shorter, motivically related musical phrases |
| ■ Subtle changes in melody, rhythm, phrase structure, vocal timbre, and many other small musical details are central to many tribal musical aesthetic systems |
| ■ Musical genres are often closely related to specific ceremonial or social activities |

this to be a 'traditional' piece of music based on the age of the composition and a particular set of musical features") but rather as a *social process* whereby social groups selectively preserve elements of their past in order to serve contemporary circumstances (Handler and Linnekin 1984). I believe many Native Americans would agree with this understanding of tradition, and throughout this chapter we will see many instances in which "traditional" forms of music and dance are constantly being renewed, refashioned, or revived in order to suit modern social and cultural needs. Understood in this way, many tribal and intertribal musics that we examine in this chapter can be, and often are, described by Native peoples themselves as "traditional."

Of course, within any one Native community, both tribal and intertribal musics will exist side by side and simultaneously, sometimes even performed by the same individuals. For example, the Navajo hard-rock band Blackfire released a double CD "concept album" in 2007 entitled *Silence Is a Weapon*, which included one CD of punk- and heavy metal–influenced political protest music, and a second CD of traditional Navajo songs. Many of the musicians we will hear and discuss in this chapter live at the intersection of several different social, cultural, and musical worlds. We will examine Native American music through the lens of tribalism and intertribalism in order to highlight this intersection and interpenetration and to explore both the unity and diversity of styles within Native America, a multicultural subsection of the larger North American population.

Haudenosaunee Music

The Haudenosaunee people are members of the Iroquois Confederacy, which historically included the five Iroquoian-speaking tribes: Mohawks, Oneidas, Onandagas, Cayugas, and Senecas. In 1714, the Tuscaroras joined this political alliance, known as the Six Nations Confederacy, which has endured to this day. The confederacy was first enacted through the teachings of the Haudenosaunee culture hero Deganawidah, the Great Peacemaker, who introduced the Great Law of Peace, which is a kind of founding constitution for the Confederacy intended to bring peace and harmony among the five Iroquoian tribes. The central tenets of the Great Law included a politically organized council comprised of fifty sachems (confederacy council members) from the five tribes, who were appointed by clan matrons, and political protocols grounded in the cultural practices of the people, including a consensus-based decision-making process (Starna, Campisi, and Hauptman 1996:279).

> **Salient Characteristics of**
> ## Haudenosaunee Music
>
> - Relaxed, open-throated vocal production, often emphasizing the middle register
>
> - Frequent use of call-and-response forms
>
> - Melodic compass of approximately one octave
>
> - Frequent use of vocables, including the use of stable and "musically meaningful" strings of vocables

In 1777, the council fire was extinguished when tribes could not agree on which side to support during the American Revolution. As a result, a subgroup of the confederacy—those who were sympathetic to the British—left New York and settled on the Six Nations Reserve near Brantford, Ontario, after the war (Olson and Wilson 1986:37). Beginning in 1799, the Seneca sachem and visionary, Handsome Lake, began a revitalization movement within the confederacy nations, preaching a new religion that involved self-sufficiency, sobriety, and adherence to traditional lifeways. This new "code" of living, known as the Code of Handsome Lake, was the basis for what is currently known as the Longhouse Religion, adopted by Iroquois communities in

New York and among the Six Nations during the nine-teenth century (Richter 1992:280). Today, the Haude-nosaunee remain geographically split, most living in a number of reservations in New York state and Six Nations reserves in Ontario and Quebec, although there is also a Cayuga and Seneca reservation in Oklahoma, and an Oneida reservation in Wisconsin. While each community now has a separate political structure, the members of the Six Nations Reserve in Ontario continue to organize themselves according to the tenets of the confederacy (Sutton 2004:324). Haudenosaunee musical and ceremonial life today is centered around the Longhouse Religion and con-tinues to be strongly influenced by both the Code of Handsome Lake and the Great Law of Peace.

Listen to the song "Ho Wey Hey Yo" (Active Lis-tening 2.1), composed by Betsy Buck and performed by the Six Nations Women Singers, a group of tra-ditional singers comprised of musicians from the Seneca, Onondaga, and Cayuga nations from the Six Nations Reserve in Ontario, Canada. The group, whose members have been singing together for decades, was originally organized by Sadie Buck and her sister, Betsy, who are from a well-known, respected family of traditional singers (Figure 2.1). On this recording, the other members include Char-lene Bomberry, Pat Hess, Susan Jacobs, Jayneane Burning, and Janice Martin.

Figure 2.1
Sadie Buck of the Six Nations Women Singers, singing and performing on a water drum.
J. Reid

The group is performing an **Eskanye** or "Women's Shuffle Dance" song, so named because, while the songs can be performed by either men or women, the dance is performed by women only. These songs form a large generic subset within the larger repertoire of "social dance" songs (Diamond 2008:104). Although there are some very old songs in the Eskanye repertoire, many new songs have been com-posed as well. "Ho Wey Hey Yo" is one such newly composed song. Eskanye songs, like many social dance songs, are typically sung to the accompaniment of two instru-ments: the cow horn rattle and the water drum. While water drums are used in sev-eral different traditional tribal musics, the Haudenosaunee version is typically made of a hollowed out log (or sometimes a plastic pipe) sealed at one end and fitted with a tanned hide stretched over the other end. The drum is filled with a small amount of water so that the performer can regularly tip the drum to moisten the hide, which allows the membrane to be tuned and also contributes to the unique clear timbre of the instrument. It is struck with a small wooden drumstick. A cow horn rattle can be hit against the thigh, the palm of the hand, or simply shaken (Figure 2.2).

We can hear several important musical style features in this example. First, note the relaxed, open-throated singing style (which is a preferred vocal timbre for both women and men in traditional Haudenosaunee music). Vocal timbre is often a key feature in distinguishing among different tribal styles. Also instantly noticeable is the use of call-and-response, which structures the larger form of the composition.

MindTap°
◀)) **LISTEN TO**
"Ho Wey Hey Yo," performed by The Six Nations Women Singers, from the album *We Will All Sing* (SOAR) online.

ACTIVE LISTENING 2.1
"Ho Wey Hey Yo" (*Eskanye* ["Women's Shuffle Dance"] Song)

COUNTER NUMBER	COMMENTARY	VOCABLE LYRICS	FORM
0: 00	Drum and rattle introduction starts slowly before increasing in tempo.		
0:07	The solo singer begins by singing and sustaining a lower-octave note before gliding to a note an octave above, which begins the first phrase.	*Eee* *Aaa*	
0:13	Lead singer begins singing the first phrase by herself.	*Ho wey hey yo* *Ho wey hey ya hey yo* *Ho wey hey yo* *Ho wey hey ya he yo ho* *No hey yo "gai na wi ya he ya"*	A
0:27	All performers repeat the first phrase, singing in unison. Note that the instrumental accompaniment changes from a regular pulse articulated by both the drum and the rattle to a "tremolo rhythm" (rapid reiteration of a beat) for the first half of the phrase before returning to the regular pulse for the last part of the phrase. This shift in rhythm is marked by three half-note beats performed by both instruments.	*Ho wey hey yo* *Ho wey hey ya hey yo* *Ho wey hey yo* *Ho wey hey ya he yo ho* *No hey yo "gai na wi ya he ya"*	A
0:43	All singers sing the second phrase of the song in unison, accompanied by the steady quarter-note accompaniment of the drum and rattle.	*Ho wey ya hey yo ho wey* *Ho wey ya hey yo ho wey* *Ho wey hey ya ho wey hey ya* *Ho wey ho wey ya hey yo* *ho wey "gai na wi ya he ya"*	B
1:00	All singers repeat the first phrase, again to the accompaniment of the tremolo rhythm for the first part of the phrase followed by the more regular quarter-note pulse for the second part of the phrase.	*Ho wey hey yo* *Ho wey hey ya hey yo* *Ho wey hey yo* *Ho wey hey ya he yo ho* *No hey yo "gai na wi ya he ya"*	A
1:15	The second phrase is repeated, performed by all singers.	*Ho wey ya hey yo ho wey* *Ho wey ya hey yo ho wey* *Ho wey hey ya ho wey hey ya* *Ho wey ho wey ya hey yo* *ho wey*	B

COUNTER NUMBER	COMMENTARY	VOCABLE LYRICS	FORM
1:29	The cadential vocable phrase "gai na wi ya he ya" is here rendered in a syncopated fashion with cadential rhythmic pattern of three half-notes followed by three quarter-notes, performed by the drum and rattle. Note also that the singers glide up an octave from the low, tonic end note, mirroring how the song began.	*"gai na wi ya he ya"*	
1:39	The entire song form is repeated.		AAB AB

"Ho Wey Hey Yo," by Six Nations Women Singers. Produced by Tom Bee for the SOAR Corporation.

Eskanye songs typically have two melodic phrases (A and B), and the form may be described as a kind of "incomplete repetition." The lead singer performs the A phrase by himself or herself (the call), which is followed directly by a repetition of the melody by the entire group (the response). All of the singers then sing the second phrase, followed by a repetition of both phrases by all singers (omitting the initial solo A phrase heard at the beginning of the song). Thus, the form is spelled AAB AB, and this formal structure is a defining feature of both old and newly composed Eskanye songs. Call-and-response, a widespread form of musical organization, can also be heard in the music studied throughout this textbook, particularly in Chapters 3 and 4 (African and African-American musical styles).

Also instantly noticeable are the predominance of **vocables** (nonlexical or "meaningless" syllables). The lyrics for Eskanye songs can be in Iroquoian or English or use vocables; or they may feature some mixture of the three (Diamond 2008:108). "Ho Wey Hey Yo" uses vocables only and is so named by the vocable pattern that begins the song (a common way that many newly composed Eskanye songs are named). This practice of naming is an indication of the importance of the vocable pattern to the song. While this song does not feature any linguistic text, the vocables are nevertheless recognized as the "lyrics" of the song, and particular

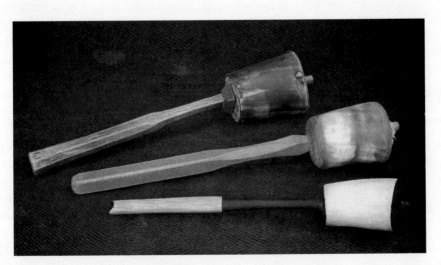

Figure 2.2

Haudenosaunee cow-horn rattles showing a variety of shapes and handles. *Susan W. McAllester*

vocables and vocable patterns are integral parts of a composition. Thus, while vocables have no lexical meaning, they have an essential "musical" meaning. As we will see, this lyrical and musical use of vocables is a widespread phenomenon found in many of the tribal and intertribal musical styles we will encounter in this chapter. The importance of vocable patterns is also evident in the **cadential phrase** "gai na we yo he ya," which is not only used to end both phrases of this song but marks the endings of virtually all Eskanye songs (Diamond 2008:107).

Nowadays, these songs are performed at a gathering called a "Sing," which is a large community event that takes place twice a year in a **longhouse**, a traditional building that once served as living quarters for several families but that now serve as community meetinghouses. They are wood-frame rectangular buildings that feature a stove on each end and wooden benches along the sides. These events feature performances by community "singing societies," which have served many social and ceremonial purposes but today often dedicate themselves to charitable causes and helping to raise money for the needy within the community. Large Sings feature performances from many different singing societies that visit from other Haudenosaunee communities (Diamond, Cronk, and von Rosen 1994:189).

Yuchi Music

The people who identify themselves as Yuchi (numbering approximately twelve hundred) are currently considered a minority group within the larger Creek/Muskogee Nation. Although they differ from the Creek in a number of ways—including the language that they speak, which is unrelated to Muskogean, and a patrilineal rather than matrilineal kinship system—they nonetheless share some cultural, ceremonial, and musical practices with both the Creek and many other tribal communities in Eastern Oklahoma (Moore 1996). For example, tribal groups and communities who live in this area, such as the Caddos, Cherokees, Chickasaws, Creeks/Muskogee, Delawares, Miamis, Nachez, Ottawas, Peorias, Seminoles, Shawnees, Wyandottes (as well as a number of others), all participate in a large social network of ceremonial events known as Stomp Dances. These events are always organized around and hosted at a particular community's "ceremonial grounds." The Yuchi maintain three such ceremonial grounds, known as Polecat (the mother ground), Sand Creek, and Duck Creek. Ethnomusicologist and folklorist Jason Jackson has suggested that these ceremonial grounds, and the communities that surround them, may productively be thought of as similar to Christian "congregations." He writes that, "a ceremonial ground is a group of people sharing a common cultural background that assembles at a fixed location in order to undertake a regular calendar of religious rituals or ceremonies. [They] possess chiefs, orators, and other ritual officers, and they have a corporate identity as a group of people associated with a particular place (their ceremonial grounds)" (Jackson 2005:174).

Salient Characteristics of
Yuchi Music

- Shares a number of characteristics with a more broadly defined Eastern Woodlands ("Eastern Way") musical style

- Moderately relaxed, open vocal production that emphasizes lower and middle register of a singer's vocal range

- Melodic compass of approximately one octave

- Musical scales featuring between four and six pitches

- A preference for melodic shapes that involve either downward melodic lines or undulating lines with an overall descending character

- Frequent use of syncopated rhythms

- A preference for asymmetrical repetition

Stomp dancing is part of a broad repertory of social dances that are known and practiced throughout Eastern Oklahoma, although each community has its own particular sets of dances they like to perform and idiosyncratic ways in which they like to perform them (Levine 2009:6). Thus, the term *Stomp Dance* is used by Eastern Oklahoma Native peoples to refer both to the broader ceremonial practice, which is an all-night song-and-dance event, as well as to the most common genre of song and dance performed at the event. Other song-and-dance genres are also performed at these events, including the Duck Dance and the Alligator Dance (Ibid.).

Stomp Dances take place in the full darkness of night save for the light provided by the ceremonial fire that is maintained at the center of the dance area. Between dances, participants sit on lawn chairs in groups arranged according to the different delegations from other communities and tribes that have come to visit and participate in the Stomp Dance. The dance itself is a line dance with a "leader" at the head of the line who first begins walking and then stomping, leading the line of dancers counterclockwise in an outwardly spiraling circle around the fire. Following directly behind the male leader is the head female "shell shaker," a dancer who is said to "shake for him" (Jackson 2005:177) (Figure 2.3). Behind these two people are a long, alternating line of men and women, who are typically arranged with more knowledgeable singers and dancers toward the front of the line and less experienced performers toward the back.

Stomp Dance songs are structured in antiphonal (call-and-response) style, led by a single male performer who sings short melodies, which are often answered in direct imitation by an all-male chorus. This vocal performance is accompanied by female dancers/instrumentalists who wear "shells," which are leg rattles tied around their calves. As they dance (stomping their feet), they provide the percussive accompaniment to the singing. The more traditional form of this instrument was constructed of five to fifteen tortoise shells that were hollowed out, filled with small stones, and strung together with leather lacing. The more contemporary version uses tin cans linked together with steel wire (Jackson 2003; Levine 2009). Listen to the musical example of a Stomp Dance led by Sonny Bucktrot (Active Listening 2.2), recorded in Bristow, Oklahoma, in 1991.

MindTap*

◄)) **LISTEN TO**

a Stomp Dance, led and performed by Sonny Bucktrot, from the album *Stomp Dance, Vol. 4* (Indian House) online.

Figure 2.3

Stomp Dance shell shakers wearing leg rattles, which can be made from either tortoise shells or tin cans. *Oklahoma Historical Society/PHOTO BY C.R. COWEN., April 16, 1999*

ACTIVE LISTENING 2.2
Stomp Dance led by Sonny Bucktrot

COUNTER NUMBER	COMMENTARY	FORM
0:00	Introductory comments calling people to line up behind the leader and participate. Female dancers wearing shells can be heard walking and taking their places in the line.	
0:41	The lead singer begins the first iterative phrases, focusing on a single low note, which ends in a downward glide. The male chorus responds with the same note but ending in an upward glide. This section is in relatively free rhythm, as the shell shakers have not yet begun to create a steady rhythmic pulse.	Introduction: Section 1
0:51	A series of very short one- or two-note melodic phrases are performed by the leader and imitated immediately by the male chorus. This direct call-and-response pattern quickly becomes rhythmically regular, outlining a steady pulse.	
1:06	The leader begins to stomp in time to the regular pulse of the call-and-response pattern, and the dancers begin creating a steady rhythmic foundation with their leg rattles.	Introduction: Section 2
1:17	The lead singer begins singing a new set of short melodic phrases (all two-beat phrases comprised of two to four notes), now in a middle register, which are imitated by the male chorus.	
1:31	This is the first song in the song set, involving call-and-response patterns in which the leader's melodic call cues a distinctly different repeated response phrase. This section begins with one call-and-response pattern repeated five times, followed by a call-and-response melody that jumps to a higher register, followed again by the first call-and-response melodies.	1st Song
1:58	Leader starts a new song beginning with a new call melody, which triggers a new, different response phrase. Notice that in this song, unlike all of the other songs that follow, there is only a single response melody, here rendered five times.	2nd Song
2:08	The leader twice alternates between an upper-register call and a middle-register call, which are each repeated with slight variation by the chorus. The section ends with one final call-and-response in the middle register.	3rd Song
2:22	The first call-and-response melodic set drops to a lower register and is repeated four times before a second melodic response that jumps up an octave. After the chorus alternates between the upper and lower octaves a few times, the song ends with one final, lower-register repetition.	4th Song
2:50	The alternation between two new lower- and higher-register iterative melodic sets proceeds in a similar way as in the previous section, repeating the lower melody five times before the chorus begins alternating between a lower- and higher-register response melody.	5th Song

COUNTER NUMBER	COMMENTARY	FORM
3:20	This song is performed in a similar way to that of the previous two in terms of repetitions and alternation between lower- and higher-register melodic sets. Note also how the chorus melodies, which are filled with quarter-note rhythmic values, contrast with the leader's melodies, which feature eighth-notes and eighth-note syncopation.	6th Song
3:48	During this song you can clearly hear a "turkey gobble" vocalization, which is a sure sign of appreciation for the song leader and/or the song that he is singing.	7th Song
4:16	This song features a surprising change in phrase structure as we hear, for the first time in the performance, response melodies that are only three quarter-note beats long rather than two or four beats, as in the previous sections. This creates an interesting tension between the now rhythmically asymmetrical call-and-response phrases.	8th Song
5:01	A final call is followed by a falsetto whoop performed by the chorus, which signals the end of the song and dance. Directly after the performance is over, we can clearly hear someone saying "*mado*," which means "thank you" in Muskogee.	

Ethnomusicologist Victoria Lindsay Levine has previously described many of the style features that we hear in this particular example as part of the "Eastern Way" of music making, referring to musical style traits that are broadly found among the many different Woodland tribal groups that live in Eastern Oklahoma (Levine 2009). Some of the musical features that define this style include a moderately relaxed and "open" vocal production that emphasizes a singer's lower and middle vocal range; a melodic compass of approximately one octave with scales that feature between four and six notes; a preference for melodic shapes that involve downward melodic lines or undulating lines that have an overall descending character; and the frequent use of syncopated rhythms and/or the frequent shifting between different beat groupings (Ibid.). Many of these general features can be heard in Sonny Bucktrot's Stomp Dance performance, in which descending, syncopated melodic lines characterize many of the songs.

This Stomp Dance performance is an example of what Levine calls an "iterative form" (a formal structure based on a number of short melodic phrases that are repeated an indefinite number of times) (Levine 2009:4). Here, after some common, introductory call-and-response phrases are exchanged between the leader and chorus, Mr. Bucktrot launches into a set of eight different songs. The introductory material introduces a few different call-and-response techniques. The first section features a long-held single note ending in descending vocal glide followed by the chorus responding by singing the same note ending in an upward glide, which is immediately followed by a series of falsetto cries or yelps. The second introductory section is comprised of a series of short melodic phrases that are performed by the leader and followed in direct imitation by the chorus. These performance practices have become a rather standardized way that many Stomp Dances begin.

After this introductory material, Mr. Bucktrot begins the song set, in which we hear a more unique and complex series of calls and responses, with each song containing one or, more often, two distinct response phrases. When there are two phrases, the first is most often in a lower register than the second (although this is sometimes reversed). Each new song is triggered by the leader and lead singer, who briefly stops dancing and signals the new song with a different "call" melody. The chorus responds with a new melodic response that is thematically related to the leader's melody. Very often, after a variable number of repetitions of this iterative melodic pattern, the leader varies his call melody by singing a phrase in a higher register, which triggers a response melody in a similarly high register. The leader and chorus will then proceed to alternate a few times between the lower-register and higher-register call-and-response melodic sets before the leader again ends that section and begins a new one with yet another new melodic phrase. Also notice that while the leader will often perform subtle changes to his "call" melodic phrases, the response phrases remain relatively consistent and unchanged (which is unsurprising, given that it would be impossible for individual members of the chorus to alter these unison phrases spontaneously during the course of a performance).

While each of the eight songs in this performance adheres to these basic principles of call-and-response, they are also subtly varied. In some instances, the pitch content of the melodic phrases is variable, as the leader and chorus do not confine themselves to any one scale or fixed pitch set but often use pitch sets that are transposed a semitone above or below a previous pitch set (e.g., 4th Song). In other sections, the initial, iterative melodic set begins in a high register and the contrasting set moves to a lower register (e.g., 3rd Song). Other sections contain only one repeated iterative set rather than two (e.g., 2nd Song). In each section, the number of repetitions of each melodic iterative set is also quite variable, as are the number of times the leader shifts from the lower to the higher iterative set. Finally, the sections are varied in how the lower iterative melodic set is related to the higher set. In some instances, it is the same melodic phrase simply transposed (e.g., 6th Song); in other sections, it is varied through an inversion of melodic shape (e.g., 4th Song) or slight rhythmic (e.g., 3rd Song) or melodic (e.g., 1st Song) variation. A larger aesthetic principle at work, governing all of these variations, is a preference for **asymmetrical repetition**, which can be found not only in many Stomp Dance performances, but also in the many other performance genres among Eastern Oklahoma tribes; it is in fact common in a number of tribal styles across North America (Levine and Nettl 2011).

Through this detailed examination we can see that what, upon first hearing, might sound like a relatively "simple" rendering of a series of short melodic phrases in a call-and-response fashion is actually a complex and carefully crafted virtuoso performance by performers who are widely respected experts in this musical style. These performances can last anywhere from two to three minutes to as long as fifteen or twenty minutes and the number of songs (from as few as three to as many as fifteen or more) included in any particular Stomp Dance song set is entirely dependent on the skill, knowledge, and expertise of the song leader (Victoria Lindsay Levine, personal communication).

Because the general forms and style features of this music are widely shared among many Eastern Oklahoma Native groups, Stomp Dance events allow for a broad range of participation by many different tribal communities. Indeed, these events are dependent on a localized network of intertribal participation, and any single event will feature song-and-dance performances by not only the home ceremonial grounds group, but also by visiting delegations of singers and dancers from several other ceremonial grounds. Stomp Dances are an important way to foster and maintain intercommunity bonds among the many Woodlands tribal communities in

Eastern Oklahoma (Jackson and Levine 2002; Jackson 2003). As we will see, in many ways this geographically localized circuit of Stomp Dancing is similar to the much broader intertribal participation and community building that takes place during the intertribal powwow music and dance events that we will study later in this chapter.

Navajo Music

At a population of more than 300,000, the Navajo are the largest Indian tribe in the United States. Descended from Athabascan-speaking nomadic hunters who came into the Southwest as recently as six or seven hundred years ago, they now live in scattered communities ranging from extended family groups to small towns on a reservation of 25,000 square miles (larger than West Virginia) spread over parts of New Mexico, Arizona, and Utah (Figure 2.4). The exact census of the Navajos is uncertain, because thousands live off the reservation in border towns such as Farmington, Gallup, and Flagstaff, and cities such as Chicago, Los Angeles, and San Diego. The reason for these moves is largely economic, as the population has outgrown the support afforded by the reservation.

> ### Salient Characteristics of
> ## Navajo Music
>
> - Traditional music is closely associated with ceremonial life, and is often related to either physical/spiritual health or life-cycle celebrations
>
> - A tense, nasal vocal production
>
> - Use of either strophic forms or complex sectional forms that often interweave several short melodic and/or rhythmic motifs

On the reservation the Navajos' livelihood is based, to a small but culturally significant degree, on farming, raising stock, weaving, and silversmithing. The main part of their $137-million annual income, however, comes from coal, uranium, oil, natural gas, and lumber. Much of their educational and health care funds derive from the Department of the Interior, some of it in fulfillment of the 1868 treaty that

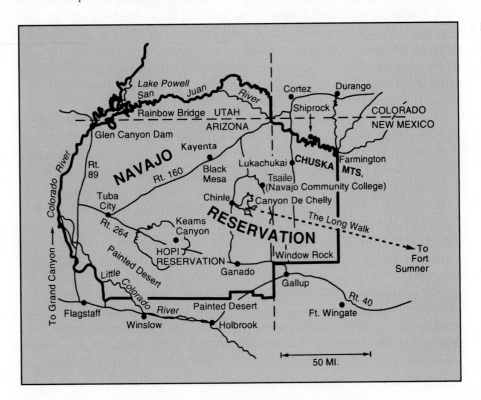

Figure 2.4
Map of the Navajo Reservation and points of interest.

marked the end of hostilities between the Navajos and the U.S. Army. Personal incomes range from the comfortable salaries of tribal administrative and service jobs to the precarious subsistence of marginal farmers.

A Yeibichai Song from the Nightway Ceremony

Most traditional Navajo music is tied in one way or another to Navajo ceremonial life. This repertoire includes music that is more "social" in nature and connected to dancing that occurs either during a ceremony or even sometimes outside of a ceremonial context, like fairs or rodeos, as well as music and chanting that is only performed within the ritual context of a specific ceremony. Navajo ceremonial music is largely tied to physical and spiritual healing and is performed for both curative and prophylactic reasons. The Navajos recognize the disease theory of the Euro-American world, and they take advantage of hospitals, surgery, and antibiotics. In addition, however, they see bad dreams, poor appetite, depression, and injuries from accidents as results of disharmony with the world of nature. Although this view resembles Western psychiatry and psychosomatic medicine in many ways, the Navajos go further. They see animals, birds, insects, and the elements of earth, water, wind, and sky as having a direct and potent effect on human life. Each of these forces may speak directly to human beings and may teach them the songs, prayers, and ritual acts that make up the ceremonials. At the center of this relationship with the natural world is the concept of **hózhó̜ó̜** (beauty, blessedness, harmony), which must be maintained and which, if lost, can be restored by means of ritual and ceremony.

One of the most exciting genres of Navajo music is **Yeibichai** song. *Yé'ii-bi-chái* (gods-their-grandfathers) refers to ancestor deities who come to dance at the major ceremonial known as **Nightway**. The masked dancers who impersonate the gods bring supernatural power and blessing to help cure a sick person. Listen now to the musical example of a Yeibichai song led by Sandoval Begay. The tense energy of the singing is unlike anything that we have encountered so far and is in fact more reminiscent of the powwow singing style that we will encounter later in the chapter. The long introduction (phrases X, Y, and Z), sung almost entirely on the basic note (the **tonic**) of the song, differs strikingly from the other tribal song styles we have heard before. Then the melody leaps *up* an octave. In the first phrase, A, after the introduction, the song comes swooping briskly down to the tonic again to an ending labeled "e^1." This ending appears again later in the song in two variations, "e^2" and "e^3." (Capital letters denote main phrases, and small letters denote motifs within the phrases.) The same descent is repeated (the second A and e^1) and then another acrobatic plunge takes place in B after two "false starts" (labeled ½a) that each closely resemble the first half of A. The song then hovers on the tonic e^2 and e^3 and the phrase *hi ye, hi ye,* which also appears in Y and Z. I call it "Z" because it has the weighty function of ending the introduction and, eventually, the song itself, in the Z phrase. After B, another interesting variation in the use of previous motifs occurs: the *second* half of A is sung twice, a½ and a½, followed by the first half of A, also repeated, ½a and ½a.

The Navajos are noted for their bold experiments in artistic form. This is true in their silversmithing, weaving, sandpainting, and contemporary commercial painting. It is also true of their music, as the play of melodic and rhythmic motifs in the passage just heard suggests. Listen again, following the pattern of this complex and intriguing song (see Active Listening 2.3), and try to sing it yourself along with Sandoval Begay and his group of Yeibichai singers.

ACTIVE LISTENING 2.3
Yeibichai song

COUNTER NUMBER	COMMENTARY	VOCABLES	FORM	RATTLE
0:00	Two high shouts.	*wu-wu-o-o-ho*		Shakes
Introduction				
0:04	Sung almost entirely on the basic pitch (tonic).	*hi ye hi ye hi ye, ho ho ho ho, hi hi hi*		Quick, insistent rhythm
	Ending phrase or bridge.	*hi ye hi ye*		
Song				
0:10	A phrase begins an octave higher then descends.	*hui yi hui-hu'i ho-e*	A	Constant rhythm
0:14	Repeat.	*hui yi hui hu'i ho-e*	A	
	First half of A phrase sung twice.	*yi'au*	½A	
0:19	B phrase opens high and slowly descends.	*hui hui hui hui*	B	
0:23	Melodic phrase from introduction.	*ho ho hi ye, hi ye hi ye hi-i hi ho-e*	C	
	Second half of A phrase sung twice.	*hi-i hi ho-e hi-i hi ho-e*	²⁄₂A	
	First half of A phrase sung twice.	*yi'u*	½A	
0:35	B phrase in melody returns.	*hui hui hui hu-i ho ho*	B	
0:39	C phrase returns.	*hi ye, hi ye hi ye ho ho ho ho hi hi hi hi ye hi ye*	C	
	Bridge ends section.	*ho ho ho ho hi hi hi hi ye hi ye*		
0:50–1:30	Shout begins song's repeat.		A	
1:48–2:00	Shout begins song's repeat. Closes with repeat of introduction.	*hi ye, hi ye hi ye ho ho ho ho hi hi hi hi ye hi ye*	A	Rattle shakes as singing ends

"Yeibichai." Navajo dance song from Nightway. © Archive of Folk Song of the Library of Congress AFS L41. LP. Washington, D.C.

As with the other tribal styles we have heard, this song, sung entirely in vocables, illustrates how far from "meaningless" vocables can be. Almost any Navajo would know from the first calls that this is a Yeibichai song; these and the other vocables identify the type of song. Moreover, this song includes the call of the gods themselves: Although there are hundreds of different Yeibichai songs, they usually contain some variation of this call of the Yei.

Call of the Yei

Hi ye, hi ye, ho - ho ho ho!

Yeibichai singers are organized in teams, often made up of men from one particular region or another. They create new songs or sing old favorites, each team singing several songs before the nightlong singing and dancing end. The teams prepare costumes and masks, and practice a dance of the gods that proceeds in two parallel lines with reel-like figures. A clown follows the dancers and makes everyone laugh with his antics: getting lost, bumbling into the audience, imitating the other dancers. The teams compete, and the best combination of costumes, clowns, singing, and dancing receives a gift from the family sponsoring the ceremony. The representation of the presence of the gods at the Nightway brings divine power to the ceremony and helps the sick person get well.

This dance takes place on the last night of a nine-night ritual that includes such ceremonial practices as purification by sweating and vomiting, making prayer offerings for deities whose presence is thus invoked, and sandpainting rituals in which the "one-sung-over" (the person for whom the ceremony is being performed) sits on elaborate designs in colored sands and other dry pigments. The designs depict the deities; contact with these figures identifies the one-sung-over with the forces of nature they represent and provides their protective power (Figure 2.5). In the course of the ceremony, hundreds of people may attend as spectators, whose presence supports the reenactment of the myth on which the ceremony is based. The one-sung-over takes the role of the mythic hero, and the songs, sandpaintings, prayers, and other ritual acts recount the story of how this protagonist's trials and adventures brought the Nightway ceremony from the supernatural world for the use of humankind (Faris 1990). In addition to the Yeibichai songs, there are hundreds of long, chanted songs with elaborate texts of translatable ritual poetry.

The ritual drama of the Nightway is as complex as "the whole of a Wagnerian opera" (Kluckhohn and Leighton 1974:229). The organization and performance of the entire event is directed by the singer or ceremonial practitioner, who must memorize every detail. Such men and women are among the intellectual leaders of the Navajo communities. Most readers find the Yeibichai song difficult to learn. The shifts in emphasis, the many variations, and the difficult vocal style demand hours of training before one can do it well.

Figure 2.5

Victor M. Begay, a Navajo medicine man, during a sand painting healing ritual. *Arne Hodalic/Terra/Corbis*

At this point in the chapter, after having listened to a few different tribal styles and genres, we can now step back and try to identify some common features that are found across this variety of music. Most obviously, students are no doubt struck by the consistent use of percussion instruments (drums and rattles)—a central element of tribal styles across North America—and the comparative dearth of string and wind instruments. Thus, one important, general style feature of tribal musics includes a musical texture that very often features monophonic singing to the accompaniment of drums and/or rattles. Another common feature is the frequent use of vocables. However, we have seen that while vocables are typically understood to be "nonsense syllables," there is nonetheless a great deal of fixity in how vocables are used. They are, in a very real sense, the lyrics of the song, and I am not aware of any traditional tribal styles in which vocable substitution is tolerated or encouraged. The same vocables and strings of vocables must be used for every performance of a precomposed piece of music.

Another common feature involves how larger musical forms are derived from the repetition of shorter, motif-related musical phrases. This is most evident in the frequent use of call-and-response patterns, which shape larger formal structures. We have also heard how important seemingly small and subtle kinds of melodic and rhythmic variation are a key component of several tribal styles. Hearing beauty in the subtle changes in melody, rhythm, phrase structure, vocal timbre, and many other small musical details is a common feature of many tribal aesthetic systems.

Finally, an important, shared conceptual principle is the idea that the beauty of a musical performance is inextricably tied to its social and/or ceremonial context. The musics that we have examined so far are all closely tied to particular dances and/or ceremonies. Native American listeners (audience members and other performers) will often judge these performances as "beautiful" in response not only to particular compositional or performance practices, but also according to how successful a performance is in fulfilling its contextual or ceremonial role. Is the performance bringing about good dancing or enthusiastic participation, or helping to create a successful ceremony? In other words, the question of aesthetics—"Is this performance beautiful?"—is very closely linked to the question "Is this music doing what it's supposed to be doing, bringing about a successful outcome for this dance or ceremony or social gathering?" Was the musical performance successful in healing the sick? Did it inspire good and energetic dancing? Did it encourage participation on the part of different social constituencies and bring the community, or several different communities, together? These are questions about the cultural *value* of music; about music's ability to do other kinds of social or cultural work. In judging music this way we can see that many Native American aesthetic systems are inextricably tied to wider systems of cultural and social values. Students should continue to keep these common musical features and aesthetic principles in mind as we now turn to an examination of several different *intertribal* musical styles and genres.

Intertribal Music

Native American tribes and communities in North America have a long history of political alliances and social relationships with each other. For example, several regional alliances resulted from cooperative intertribal actions, such as the Pueblo

Revolt of 1680, the ascendancy of the Iroquois Confederacy in the seventeenth and early eighteenth centuries, and the combined efforts of the so-called Five Civilized Tribes (Cherokee, Chickasaw, Choctaw, Creek, and Seminole) to create a self-governing Indian state within Indian Territory (modern-day Oklahoma) in the late nineteenth century. Conceived more broadly, intertribal associations might also include the short-term political alliances established by Pontiac and Tecumseh shortly before and after the American Revolution, respectively. Of course, many intertribal actions were largely based on political expediency (i.e., overt conflicts with Europeans) and were formed for the common political good of tribal groups within a particular region. However, along with these political alliances there has also been a long history of *cultural* sharing and interaction among tribal groups and communities.

Powwow Music

Powwow music is perhaps the most popular and widely dispersed intertribal music and dance practice of the twentieth and twenty-first centuries. Powwows are large, intertribal, social, and generally secular weekend events held year-round (although particularly in the summer months) by both urban and reservation Native American communities across North America. These events are opportunities for community and intertribal celebration involving singing, dancing, travel, camping, feasting, visiting, courtship, "making relatives," honoring elders and veterans, and strengthening and renewing tribal and intertribal social bonds. Powwows are also one of the most vital and active areas of contemporary musical and choreographic creativity and innovation for Native musicians and dancers.

While the general form and structure of these events remain consistent enough across North America that Native dancers and singers from any tribal community are able take part in any particular event, participants recognize significant differences in dance and song styles and in the overall tenor and purpose of different powwows. At present, there are two major powwow "circuits" in North America, each characterized both by geographic region and singing and dancing styles. The "Northern-style" powwow began in the Northern Great Plains and Great Lakes region of the United States; these powwows are now found throughout the Midwest and Northern Plains of the United States (stretching from Michigan and Illinois, through North and South Dakota, to Montana, Idaho, and Wyoming) as well as the central Plains of Canada. "Southern-style" powwows are those typically found in Oklahoma, although these events may be found throughout the Southwest as well. Apart from geography, the distinction between Northern and Southern powwows is also manifest in performance style. Each features a unique style of singing (unsurprisingly known as "Northern-style singing" and "Southern-style singing"), different song genres and categories, and different dance styles. Native American communities on the East and West coasts also host powwows, but often these events are inflected by local song and dance practices, and frequently feature enough stylistic hybridity that they do not easily fall into one or the other of these two paradigmatic types of events.

Salient Characteristics of
Northern Powwow Music

- Unison singing to the accompaniment of the "big drum"

- High, tense, loud vocal production

- Predominance of terraced, descending melodic lines

- Rhythmic displacement between the melody and the drumbeat, glossed by musicians as "off-the-beat" singing

- Call-and-response formal structure, often described as "incomplete repetition" and featuring the phrase structure AA'BCBC or AA' BCDBCD

Within the Northern powwow circuit, another large-scale distinction recognized by powwow participants is the difference between what are known as "competition" powwows (sometimes called "intertribal" powwows) and "traditional" powwows (Scales 2007). As the names suggest, competition powwows feature formal song and dance competitions and (sometimes large) cash prizes for participants, while traditional powwows do not. Several other differences exist as well. Competition powwows are generally much more structured proceedings, with fairly close adherence to a schedule of events. They also place more emphasis on the strict division of dance and song categories and do not regularly emphasize community and tribal concerns or local dance traditions. These events are typically well funded by tribal councils and, increasingly, through money generated by tribal casinos. Drum groups hired to host these events are well paid, and cash prizes can range from $500 to $2,000 or more for dancers and singers.

Conversely, traditional powwows often (although not always) operate on a much smaller budget and emphasize community and intertribal friendship over formal competition. Instead of holding formal contests, each dancer or singer participating receives a modest sum of money from the powwow committee to help offset the expense of travel, food, and lodging for participants. These powwows will, more often than not, offer a feast for all participants and spectators each evening as a way to honor and welcome visitors and community members alike. Dancing and singing activities are undertaken informally, and the proceedings will feature a number of **giveaways**, "honor songs," and other events that highlight or emphasize local community concerns. Friendship and camaraderie are emphasized over contests and competitiveness.

Northern Plains Singing Style

Northern-style powwow singing is so named because of a particular cluster of stylistic features that have historically been associated with a specific geographic region. This style of singing is derived predominantly from the aesthetic practices and preferences of the tribes of the Great Plains, such as the Blackfeet, Crow, Lakota, and Dakota (Powers 1990). Despite regional variation, several musical features typify the Northern style of powwow singing. These general features include the following:

1. A musical texture featuring unison singing to the accompaniment of a steady drumbeat performed on the "big drum" (see Figure 2.6). While the degree to which singers attempt or achieve perfect unison is a matter of both regional and personal choice, most Northern-style singers agree that perfect unison is a performance goal. As one singer succinctly put it to me, a drum group should sound like "One voice, one [drum] beat … One people, one beat!"

2. A high-pitched, tense, loud vocal production is generally preferred, although again this differs by region and singing group. For example, Canadian Cree groups are renowned in the Northern powwow world for their ability to sing with a very high tessitura (vocal range). A tense, pinched, vocal timbre is ideal, and singers go to great length to achieve this, including pinching their larynx while singing. There are generational differences in aesthetic preference in this regard. Older singers generally do not place as great a value on high tessitura or volume, while younger singers often value these characteristics to a much greater degree.

Figure 2.6
The powwow drum group Meskwaki Nation, from Tama, Iowa, performing at the 2011 Saginaw Chippewa Intertribal Competition Powwow in Mount Pleasant, Michigan.
Christopher Scales

3. A terraced, descending melodic line is the typical melodic shape of a Northern song, and there is a startling degree of consistency in this regard. The opening phrase features the highest notes of the song, and each subsequent phrase generally employs collections of pitches lower than the previous phrase. Further, powwow singing in practice does not feature fixed or stable tonal centers; the starting and ending pitches of a song in any given performance are relative, depending on who is singing and how high particular singers are able to begin an opening phrase. Generally, lead singers will start songs at the highest pitch level they can manage. It is not uncommon for subsequent renditions of each verse, if led by other singers in the group, to be microtonally altered either slightly higher or lower according to individual ability and the aesthetic preferences of each singer.

4. One of the most striking and unique features of this musical style is the "rhythmic displacement" of melody and drumbeat, the melody being sung slightly behind or slightly ahead of the beat of the drum. This results in a performance that sounds as if the melody is "floating" above the steady, rhythmic pulse of the drum. Singers and dancers alike recognize singing "off the beat" as an essential stylistic feature. This rhythmic displacement creates a tension that provides much of the energy and dynamism in powwow songs and is a large part of what inspires "good" and energetic dancing.

Listen for these distinct style features in the powwow song "Straight Up," composed by the Ojibwa songmaker Gabriel Desrosiers and performed by his drum group the Northern Wind Singers (Active Listening 2.4). The "off-the-beat" rhythmic tension between the drumbeat and the singing is further intensified by the rendering of the melody in almost a kind of "swing eighth" rhythmic feel that is more closely associated with jazz and blues music. The strong, pulsing vocal vibrato adds a further layer of complexity.

Although powwow musicians possess a high degree of musical expertise and competency, I have found that they rarely speak about their songs or compositions

MindTap
🔊 **LISTEN TO**
"Straight Up," performed by The Northern Wind Singers from the album *21st Century* (Arbor Records), online.

ACTIVE LISTENING 2.4
Straight Up

MindTap·

🎧 **WATCH** an Active Listening Guide of this selection online.

COUNTER NUMBER	COMMENTARY	FORM
0:00	Drum introduction using a driving "straight beat" rhythm.	
First push-up		
0:04	Lead singer begins first phrase.	A
0:10	"Seconds" join in and begin singing.	A'
0:17	Seconds continue to sing the second phrase.	B
0:24	Third phrase begins with a single shout of "ya," followed by the completion of the melody.	C
0:33	"Second side" of the push-up, the beginning of the "incomplete" repetition. Near the end of the phrase we hear "honor beats" (seven in total) that continue into the repetition of the third phrase.	B
0:40	Repetition of final phrase.	C
Second push-up		
0:48	New lead singer begins the lead melodic phrase.	A
0:54	Seconds respond.	A'
1:01		B
1:09		C
1:17	Honor beats performed again, but only 6 this time.	B
1:21	Note that the intensity (speed and volume) of the drumming increases at the end of the phrase leading into the next push-up.	C
Third push-up		
1:32		Form repeats as above
Fourth push-up		
2:15		Form repeats as above
2:20	"Check beating" is performed by all members of the group and begins during the A' part of the push-up as a way of increasing the rhythmic intensity and excitement of final verse.	
2:57	Song ends with 3 "hard beats" followed by a thunderclap sound effect added during studio production.	

in abstract, theoretical terms. However, there are some common terms used to describe the formal and structural elements of songs (Hatton 1974, Powers 1980, Browner 2000). *Push-up* is the Native American term for a verse of a powwow song. Performance practice dictates that the typical rendition of a song should consist of four repetitions of a single verse, or push-up, as is the case with "Straight Up." The number four is imbued with symbolic and spiritual meaning for many Native American groups in North America, particularly among Northern and Southern

Plains tribes. It manifests itself in myriad cultural domains: four directions, four sacred colors in a medicine wheel, and so on.

Each push-up is understood to be divided into two sections: the "lead" section and the "seconds." *Lead* refers both to the opening phrase of the push-up and the singer who performs it (the A phrase). *Seconds* refers both to the remaining phrases of each verse and to all the singers who perform those phrases (the A´ B and C phrases). Non-Native scholars of this music have generally discussed these structural divisions in terms of phrase structure. While there have been some differences in opinion among various scholars as to the exact spelling of the formal structure, the form of a powwow song is usually described as "incomplete repetition" (similar to the form of Haudenosaunee Eskanye songs) and has a phrase structure represented as AA´BCBC, or sometimes AA´BCDBCD (Powers 1990; Browner 2000). There is generally a high degree of motivic relationship between the different phrases; the A´ phrase is a repetition of the A phrase with an extended ending, while the B, C, and possibly D phrases all may share a great degree of melodic material with the A phrase and with each other.

The repetitions of the BC or BCD phrases, sometimes referred to by indigenous musicians as the "second side" of the verse, are structurally marked through the use of "honor beats" (also sometimes called "check beats" or "hard beats") executed on the drum. *Honor beats* refer to a series of louder, harder beats that occur on alternate drum strokes, numbering anywhere from four to nine or ten. These drum strokes are performed by specified members of a drum group, who strike the drum closer to the center and with a marked increase in force while the other members of the group simultaneously reduce the force (and thus volume) of their drumming.

The practice of "check beating" can also refer to other drumming techniques that alter the regular flow of the drumbeat. In practice, drum groups strive to vary the volume, tempo, and intensity of each push-up in order to give dynamic and dramatic shape to their performances. Thus, the leader of the group may use check beats (hard beats) to signal to other members of the group either to pick up the tempo or to increase or decrease the force and volume of their drumming and singing, as we hear in "Straight Up." Each rendition of a push-up is also varied through the use of improvised shouts, cries, or other vocal sound effects rendered by one or more members of a group.

MindTap·

◀») **LISTEN TO**
"Straight Up" performed by The Northern Wind Singers, online.

Listen again to the song "Straight Up," this time paying close attention to the musical features that help to outline the form of the piece. Notice how each of the four push-ups, while seemingly a formal repetition of the same verse, is varied each time through performance details in drumming and through improvised cries and shouts of the singers. However, the larger formal markers—including the hard beats, and honor beats, and the consistently predictable pattern of the different melodic phrases—are all essential features of a powwow song that give cues and clues to the dancers about what is about to happen next in the song. In this way powwow dancers can choreograph their movements to align with the different parts of the song.

Drum groups typically consist of five to fifteen male singers. Many groups are formed according to kinship ties, and encountering groups whose membership is comprised almost entirely of close and distant family relations is common. The men, sitting on folding chairs, form a circle around the drum. Each of them is responsible for both drumming and singing (see Figure 2.6). Women may sometimes join a group, but traditionally their role is limited to singing. In this capacity, women form a secondary circle behind the men and sing an octave higher than them. Although drum groups normally operate in a fairly egalitarian manner, several well-defined social roles exist within a drum group. Each drum group will have at least one lead singer—someone who is responsible for singing the leads to all of the songs (well-established drum groups will have between two and four lead singers who alternate in this capacity). *Seconds* are singers who do not sing leads. Most groups also have at least one songmaker, someone who composes new songs for the group every year. Much like pop music groups, well-known powwow drum groups are expected to have a new collection of songs each new powwow season. Finally, drum groups typically have a "drum carrier" who is responsible for the care and transportation of the drum. Drum carriers may or may not sing in the group but are considered a part of the group because of the importance of their responsibilities. The designation of a drum carrier speaks to the symbolic/spiritual importance associated with the instrument, which is often referred to as "Grandfather." Similar to how one is expected to treat their elders, singers must treat their drum with respect, and many believe that their ability to sing, or sing well, comes directly from the spiritual power of the drum.

The Structure of a Powwow Event

A number of structural components of competition powwows remain consistent across the Northern Plains, including the physical organization of people and the temporal organization of events. Powwow grounds are structured as a series of increasingly larger concentric circles (Browner 2002). At the center of the grounds stands the dance arena, which is surrounded immediately by singing groups who set up their drums on blankets and specially designed drum stands (out of respect, a drum must never be placed directly on the ground), with folding metal or plastic chairs encircling each drum. Behind the drum groups are several rows of lawn chairs where elders, dancers, and relatives of dancers and singers sit and watch the weekend's events unfold. Encircling these rows of chairs, one often finds several stadium-style wooden benches, an informal seating area for the overflow of dancers and singers and for the many spectators. At one end of the dance arena there is typically a permanent, simply designed, wood-framed building, the booth where

Figure 2.7
The dance arbor at the Saginaw Chippewa Intertribal Competition powwow in Mount Pleasant, Michigan, 2013. *Christopher Scales*

members of the powwow committee and the emcees for the event will sit and oversee the proceedings (Figure 2.7).

Myriad vendors' booths and fast-food stands surround the dance arena and seating area on all sides. These businesses travel the northern powwow circuit all summer, setting up makeshift structures from which to conduct business. The craft booths sell a wide assortment of handmade jewelry, clothing, and powwow supplies: beads, feathers, finished hides, belts, fans, roaches (a traditional male headdress, often made from the guard hair of a porcupine), moccasins, and sundry articles needed to make or add to a dancer's **regalia** (dance outfit). The vendors' booths sell commercial items: name-brand clothing and hats, children's toys and games, and sometimes quick-pick lottery tickets. Vendors provide much of the food for singers, dancers, and spectators, selling gallons of coffee, homemade fry bread, soups, hamburgers, hotdogs, "Indian tacos" (fry bread and chili), candy, and soda. Tents, trailers, campers, vans, cars, and lean-tos (the weekend shelter for participants and audience members), fill the rest of the powwow grounds. Portable toilets typically dot the area, and a semipermanent building may serve as a crude shower stall for the dancers. Expecting to find a similar organization at reserve powwows across North America, powwow singers and dancers quickly learn to negotiate the social and geographical space of the powwow grounds. The consistency of this structure makes powwow participants feel "at home" at the powwow no matter where they are in North America.

The order of events has also become somewhat standardized. Typically, powwows begin Friday evening and last until Sunday evening. That time is divided into five different dance sessions, each session beginning with a Grand Entry followed by a series of intertribal dances, then rounds of competition dancing. These sessions generally last between four and six hours. The first Grand Entry begins between 7:00 and 9:00 P.M. Friday night. Saturday's and Sunday's Grand Entries begin at 1:00 P.M. and 7:00 P.M., with a two-hour supper break between afternoon and evening sessions.

Following each Grand Entry procession, a "Flag Song" is rendered, after which a local or visiting elder gives an invocation or prayer. Next is a "Victory Dance" (sometimes called a "Veteran's Dance"), a song that honors all the military veterans in attendance. During this song, all dancers in the arena dance in place. They then post flags, and visiting "royalty" (Powwow Princesses and Braves) and political figures are introduced to the audience. The Grand Entry is then considered officially complete and various rounds of dancing follow. Rounds of "intertribal dancing" directly succeed most Grand Entries. These dances are open to participation by dancers of all ages and styles, and may even include spectators, singers, and others present who wish to join the proceedings. All of the drum groups in attendance provide music for these dances according to a preestablished drum order. The emcees (two or three will often take turns over the course of the weekend) constantly announce the order of events, and the powwow is kept moving by one or sometimes two "arena directors" who work in the dance arena and make sure dancers are ready to dance and drum groups are ready to sing. The arena director, the head judges, and the emcee all work in close contact to make sure events run as smoothly as possible.

Powwow Dancing

The heart of every powwow, whether competition or traditional, is dancing. Singing groups sing in the service of the dancers, and they always perform in the hopes of inspiring energetic and joyful dancing. Most dancing that occurs at powwows may be separated into two broad categories: intertribals and competitions. Intertribal dancing is open to general participation and has no special footwork or regalia requirements (although it is customary for women at least to wear a shawl over their shoulders when entering the arena). During these dances, all who are in attendance are welcome to dance, including singers, spectators, and, upon invitation, even non-Natives. During an intertribal dance it is common to see a wide variety of dance styles and footwork. For many dancers, it is a time simply to circle the dance arena using the basic tap-step dance pattern and visit and talk with fellow dancers or other friends who are in the arena. For other dancers it is a time to warm up and practice dance steps and moves for an upcoming competition. For those who are not in regalia, it may simply be a time to join the dance circle and participate in the event in a more active way.

Dance competitions are organized according to age group (for example, "tiny tots," teens, adults, seniors), gender (male and female), and dance style. Northern competition powwows feature six standard competition dance styles, distinguished by gender, choreography, and regalia; each style constitutes a separate contest category. The three men's styles are Men's Traditional Dance, Men's Grass Dance, and Men's Fancy Dance; the three women's styles are Women's Traditional Dance, Women's Jingle Dress Dance, and Women's Fancy Shawl Dance. A great deal has already been written about powwow dancing and thus only very cursory descriptions of these dance styles will be presented here. For further details, see Browner (2002), McDowell (1997), and Powers (1966), among many others. Online, www.powwows.com features reliable, accurate descriptions and photographs of the different regalia styles. Because so many powwow participants like to share their experiences through social media, there are also literally thousands of videos of powwow dance performances posted to YouTube and other video-sharing sites.

Many of the footwork patterns for these dances derive from a basic form: a four-beat pattern in which the right foot moves forward, taps the ground, and then lands flush to the ground as weight is shifted onto that foot. The left foot then follows exactly as the right foot did: tap-step, tap-step. While a high degree of variation is the norm, both between tribally and regionally specific styles and in accordance with the tastes of individual dancers, some general comments can be made.

Traditional-style dancing in both the male and female form is descended from many pre-reservation, tribally specific dance forms. A circular or U-shaped single feather bustle fastened around the waist of the dancer distinguishes the regalia of the Men's Traditional outfit (Figure 2.8). A Women's Traditional dancer's regalia is either of the buckskin or cloth style. The buckskin outfits are typically decorated with intricate bead designs. Cloth dresses are made entirely of fabric with stitched cloth patterns replacing the decorative beadwork of the buckskin style. The choreography of this dance is one of elegance and grace, featuring subtle, smooth, flowing movements.

The Men's and Women's Fancy styles are similar in name and manner, both emphasizing athleticism, intricate footwork,

Figure 2.8

Men's Traditional dancer Donnie Dowd. Michigan State University American Indian Heritage Powwow, East Lansing, 1995. *Michigan State University Museum.*

and complex, free-form choreography. The men's regalia is distinguished by two brightly colored feather bustles worn around the waist and the shoulders, while the Women's Fancy Shawl Dance regalia is relatively simple, with a decorated cloth dress, leggings, and a shawl worn over the shoulder comprising the basic elements. Both styles feature a great degree of latitude and variation in footwork and choreography, and often feature feats of endurance and athleticism.

The Men's Grass Dance outfit does not feature a feather bustle, but rather consists of shirt and trousers, to which yarn fringe is attached,—a possible simulation of a much older style outfit that featured dried grass tucked into the dancer's belt. A common story associated with the dance maintains that it evolved from the tradition of men tying grass to their outfits and stomping down the long prairie grass so that a dance could begin. The unique choreography and footwork of this dance reflect this activity. The Jingle Dress Dance outfit consists of a dress decorated with a large number of rolled-up snuff can lids attached with ribbon in various patterns. The basic footwork consists of the graceful bouncing on the toes in a right–left alternation to the steady beat of the drum. An alternative dance step, the "side step," involves dancing to a quick, triple-meter song, with the dancer executing rapid slide steps to the left, hands on hips.

Biography of Powwow Singer Gabriel Desrosiers

Gabe Desrosiers (Figure 2.9) is an Anishinaabe (Ojibwa) singer, songmaker, Grass Dancer, and educator who has been participating in powwow culture since child-

Figure 2.9
Powwow singer, dancer, and songmaker Gabriel Desrosiers performs on a hand drum in his Grass Dance regalia, 2010.
Christopher Scales

hood. Born January 25, 1962, in the Lake of the Woods area in Northwestern Ontario, Gabe rose to prominence in the 1980s singing and composing songs for the Whitefish Bay Singers, a powwow group from the Whitefish Bay Indian Reserve. In 1991, he formed his own singing group, the Northern Wind Singers, and since then has been performing regularly with the group, serving as the leader, the lead singer, and the principal songmaker. He is also well known throughout the powwow world as a champion Grass Dancer, winning competitions across North America, and he has toured Europe and the Middle East as a member of two different professional Native American dance troupes. More recently, he has participated in powwows as head singing judge, head dancing judge, arena director, and in several other administrative capacities for celebrations across the United States and Canada. Currently, Mr. Desrosiers works as an Anishinaabe language instructor and the Coordinator of Cultural Programs and Outreach at the University of Minnesota–Morris.

I first met Gabe in 2000, a time when I was carrying out ethnographic research and working as a recording engineer for Arbor Records, an independent music label in Winnipeg, Manitoba, that specialized in the Aboriginal music of North America. Our first collaborative project involved the creation of the Northern

Winds' 2000 CD, *Ikwe Nagamonon: Women's Songs*, a recording project for which I served as recording engineer and producer. Since that time, I have regularly invited Gabe to several of the schools where I have taught to give various lectures, performances, and demonstrations; we also continue to collaborate on academic writing projects (Desrosiers and Scales, 2012; Scales and Desrosiers 2016). Each time we get together, we continue our ongoing conversation about the current state of powwow singing and dancing and the ever-changing nature of Northern powwow culture. The autobiographical sketch that follows was generated from many different formal, recorded interviews that I have conducted with Gabe over the past decade and a half.

> Growing up, my family and I lived in a little town called Sioux Narrows [in the Lake of the Woods region in northwestern Ontario, Canada]. All the other relatives, my uncles and their families and wives, had houses on the North-west Angle reserve through government annuities and treaty rights. And we would have to come into the reserve if we wanted to visit them. But my family wasn't able to live on the reserve, because my father was never considered "status." His name was not on the tribal roll when that community signed their treaty. And then when my mother married him, because of [a rule in] the Indian Act, she lost her status too. So we were—I heard a term back then— the "forgotten people." The Métis people and women who married nonstatus people, Indian or non-Indian, were just totally forgotten and disregarded by the Canadian government. And by their own people, too!
>
> I was about five or six when I went to my first powwow. And my family and I went to this powwow that was way in the bush, in a real secluded area. And that was probably because those people were still hiding; they were still being secretive about their spirituality and religious practices. Anyway, I went there and I vividly remember the people dancing and the elders talking and walking around with their traditional pipes, talking to the people in attendance. But most importantly I remember the songs. I was attracted to the songs at that time for some reason. The powwow didn't go that long because the format wasn't like what you see at a powwow today. There were no emcees, there was no lighting system, there was no PA system. It was just drums in the middle, people dancing around the drum, and occasionally elders taking turns walking around in that arbor [dance area] and talking about old stories and teachings. And typically that's what you see at traditional powwows at roundhouses [among the Anishinaabe people who live in the Lake of the Woods area]. That's what they do. They had a feast. I think they even had a small giveaway.
>
> But I remember going home after that powwow and I could sing those songs that were sung at that powwow. It was just natural. I just remembered them. I remembered the straight songs and the songs with lyrics. And that's when I first figured out that I had this gift of song. And it was kind of strange to me as a kid because I had questions like, "How could I do that?"
>
> It was little while later, when I was about nine, when I was first invited to sing on a drum [in a drum group]. And it was Andy White who approached me. He had heard that I could sing because I was messing around and singing a little in the community at Whitefish Bay. I would sing here and there, I wasn't afraid. So that's probably how he heard. He had already started his drum group, Whitefish Bay, with those Copenace boys and Nazare and

himself. Nazare Henry was the founder of Whitefish Bay. He was Andy's mentor and he taught all the singers of the drum to sing. He got the songs from his grandfather and from singing around the traditional powwow circuit. I joined in a year or so later. So I came in, and the Copenace boys, the two brothers, were around the same age as me. And the younger one was the lead singer. And then we started traveling around to these little powwows.

And I always like to give credit to Andy White for what he did for me. Because for me as a child, singing with Andy and Whitefish Bay was an opportunity for me to get away from all the drinking and many dysfunctional things that were going on in my family life. He saved me from that, because he took me away from that. We would leave weekends and go sing and powwow and have fun. And I have to say he always—it seemed like he always cared. He probably knew what was going on in my life. So I always thank him for doing that because in a lot of ways, I always feel that he saved me from the negative things that were going on. From the abuse, from the alcoholism, you name it. And probably not just within our household because whenever we visited our family on the reserve, it was the same thing: People drinking and fighting. So I also think he did it to get me away from that. Plus he knew that I could sing.

So we would sing at these local community powwows that were being held by the surrounding little reserves. And then a little later, as we kept going, we started traveling a little farther out. Like Manitoba, Red Lake, Ponemah, [Minnesota]. Those were where some of the larger competition powwows were at the time. And Whitefish Bay powwow was a competition powwow at that time as well. And the songs we were singing were just traditional songs from the area. And as time went on, Andy would go out by himself to farther distances, like to Mandaree [North Dakota], or out to Washington or Montana. He'd travel around and he'd go out and take his tape recorder and record music from these different powwows and different drum groups and bring it back to us. And I remember we'd be impressed how different music was in different areas. So we latched on to the idea of learning those songs and singing them. We would experiment with these different kinds of music. I remember we would be amazed by how good some drum groups were sounding back then. Mandaree [Singers], Porcupine [Singers] all these Plains drum groups and western drum groups.

I first started composing music when I was in my early twenties. Maybe I was twenty or twenty-one. And my big influence was a singer named Rob Hunter from [the drum group] Chiniki Lake. They're a group from Morley, Alberta. Nakotas. They were the top drum group at that time. They were winning all over the place, their lead singer was awesome, and their songs were really different. They were a big influence on me. We would see them on the powwow trail and I would just be in awe of them. And they were writing all their own songs; they had their own unique style, and I was inspired by that. I said to myself, "You know, I think I can do that." But I don't really know what made me create the first songs. I was just starting out working in the police force when I was twenty, and I would drive around in my police cruiser by myself and I found one day that I could make a song. And so I recorded it, I put it on tape. And that was the beginning. I started carrying around a cassette player with me and recording whatever songs I would make. I'd put them right onto that tape recorder. And then whenever I had a weekend off I'd go with Whitefish Bay to a powwow and we'd sing those songs.

And at this time we were becoming a popular drum group. I think part of the popularity was because of the song style that I created. I was one of the first in the area to start composing new Ojibwa-style songs, using the Ojibwa language. Before that, before I started composing for Whitefish Bay, all the other drum groups in the area were singing Dakota songs. They were singing word songs and straight songs from different areas. And then there we were. We were traveling around the powwow circuit and I started creating new music and it just really caught on. People liked it. They liked that it was different. Just like Cree-style singing caught on later and all the Cree groups became really popular on the powwow circuit. It was the same for us. I would create this music and we would sing this new stuff at powwows and people just really liked it. So all of a sudden we were getting called to be host drum or an invited drum, and we traveled all over the place. And that's when we went into the studio and recorded our first cassette. And then *that* really caught on and we got *more* invitations to go here and there.

Then, in 1989 I think, I told the guys, "This is it. Let's go to [the Gathering of Nations powwow in] Albuquerque. This is our chance. This is our window of opportunity." I said that if we wanted to make it big in the powwow circuit this was the time. So I convinced them. We all went down to Albuquerque and we won. That was in the spring of 1990. From there we went all the way around the west coast and then went up to Seattle. We were winning contests all over. We won against the big names of the day like Northern Cree and Blacklodge. We were on a great roll. And then in July we finally made it back to our own home powwow at Whitefish Bay. And after that powwow my brother Elliot and I left Whitefish Bay and started Northern Winds. We got together with my other brother, who had never sung before, and a bunch of friends who had also never sung before. They were all guys from Northwest Angle. And we got the Copenace brothers, from Whitefish Bay. We had about fourteen guys altogether. And we went to a few powwows in July and August, but we really didn't have a name for the group yet. We used a new name every powwow. So on the Labor Day weekend we went to Leech Lake powwow and I said, by the time we get there, I'll have a name. And so I thought a lot about it and when we got there I said, "Ok, we're Northern Wind."

But for myself, I believe that all the songs that I make, I don't make them on my own. I have a gift, but that's through the Creator. He gives me that gift. He gives me those songs. They come from somewhere. I absolutely believe that they didn't pop out of the air like that for no reason. They come from the Creator. And so I always take time in my life, when I pray and give tobacco, I always take time to thank Him for all the songs and the ability he gave me to share these songs with the people. I've always believed that's my goal or purpose in life. He's using me to be in the front lines to teach our Indian people. But not only that, I also need to teach non-Indian people about who we are as people. That's what I believe. And these songs are a part of that. They define who I am, because that's been my life. My life is song. I ultimately believe that people will know me, in the end, because of song—because of song and dance. They will know me solely because of that. And in turn I'm going to help them achieve positive things in their life. I really believe that. It just seems like things always happen that lead me in that direction. Maybe I'm doing it on my own, but a lot of times I believe that the Creator is pointing me on that road. Sometimes I go off down a different path but it just seems like I always come back to that road. I have that spiritual guidance that throws me back in the right direction and throws me back into song again. And back into dance. I always think it's my duty to be on that path and to teach. And through singing and dancing these things are happening.

Native American Popular Music

While powwow music has functioned as an important form of popular culture in many Native communities, especially among young people, in the past half century there have also been a number of Native American musicians active in composing and performing in several mainstream, popular music genres, including rap and hip-hop, country, folk, rock, blues, spoken word, a cappella, adult contemporary pop, heavy metal, punk, and many others. However, beyond naming this panoply of musical genres and subgenres, there are few strictly *musical* style features that lend Native American popular music, or "Contemporary Native American" music as it has more recently been labeled within the music industry, a coherent, identifiable "sound." At best, we can identify a few strategies and/or practices undertaken by Native musicians to explicitly mark their music as Native American. Many artists and groups use lyrics that feature overt political statements or deal specifically with either locally or nationally defined Native issues, or at least speak in some way to their own lives as indigenous people; but this is far from a universal feature. Others have attempted to blend traditional, local, or tribally specific musical styles or instruments with mainstream popular styles and genres, or similarly mix English lyrics with their own indigenous language. But there are certainly plenty of musicians, groups, or particular songs that do not fit any of these descriptions that nonetheless are marketed by the recording industry and/or understood by audiences as examples of Native American popular music. In this final section we will briefly examine some of the historical factors that have contributed to the rise of Native popular music, as well listen to a range of musical styles and approaches.

A number of successful and well-known musicians who are known to have varying degrees of Native ancestry have long been celebrated within Native communities, including such luminaries as Hank Williams, Kitty Wells, Jimi Hendrix, and Link Wray. However, it was not until the 1960s that Native performers in contemporary popular musical idioms began to actively self-identify and promote themselves distinctly as "Native American musicians." This new generation of artists arose, in large part, from a series of American federal policies enacted in the 1950s that fundamentally altered the social conditions of countless Native communities and individuals. Fueled by a desire for the rapid assimilation of Indians into mainstream North American society, post-WWII federal Indian policy in the United States featured a strong push toward the urbanization of the Native population. Lured by government programs and the promise of funding and job training and placement, close to 100,000 Native Americans were relocated to certain targeted cities in the United States, resulting in a major demographic shift in the Native population. A similar demographic shift occurred in Canada a decade later. This new, urban Native population began to participate in mainstream North American popular culture and activist politics, which in turn gave rise to the Red Power movement, a politically radical social movement that sought greater public recognition for the political and social issues facing Native Americans.

New urban Natives began to form their own organizations, both social and formal. Relocation funds provided the means for the creation and operation of a number of Indian centers, as well as many intertribal social clubs, athletic leagues, powwow dance groups, Indian newspapers and newsletters, and political organizations. A watershed moment for the movement occurred on November 20, 1969, when a group of eighty-nine Indians calling themselves the Indians of All Tribes landed on Alcatraz Island and laid claim to the land under the terms of the 1868 Treaty of Fort Laramie, which granted the signatories (the Lakota nation, Yanktonai and Santee Sioux, and the Arapaho) the rights to all unused federal property that had previously been Indian land. The occupation grabbed national headlines and sparked nationwide interest on the part of both Indians and non-Indians. Native Americans from all over the country traveled to San Francisco to join the protesters on Alcatraz. Lasting a total of nineteen months, the population of protestors ranged from close to one thousand in June of 1970 to the fifteen that were finally removed by U.S. marshals on June 11, 1971. Alcatraz became a symbolic cornerstone for the political reawakening of American Indians. Over the next several years, Red Power activists engaged in several high-profile occupations and protests in the hopes of drawing more public attention to the social and political injustices experienced by Native peoples across North America. Two of the more (in)famous of these actions were the Trail of Broken Treaties, which involved a caravan of activists who traveled across the country to Washington, D.C., in the fall of 1972 and culminated in the takeover and occupation of the BIA building; and the takeover and occupation of the town of Wounded Knee on the Pine Ridge Reservation in South Dakota by Oglala Lakota and members of the American Indian Movement (AIM)—one of the most militant wings of the Red Power movement. The occupation resulted in a tense, seventy-one-day, armed standoff between the occupiers and U.S. federal marshals and FBI agents (see Matthiessen 1983 for a definitive discussion of the Pine Ridge standoff).

Many Native American musicians who emerged during the late 1960s and early 1970s were explicitly or implicitly connected to the Red Power movement, including folk singers such as Buffy Sainte-Marie and Floyd "Red Crow" Westerman, as well as the mainstream rock groups Redbone and XIT. The group XIT (pronounced "exit"), an acronym for the "Crossing (X) of Indian Tribes," emerged in Albuquerque, New Mexico, in the late 1960s, led by their main songwriter and lyricist, manager, and eventually lead singer, Tom Bee (Dakota; he grew up in Gallup, New Mexico) (see Figure 2.10). The name of the group reflects the intertribal make-up of the band, which at various points in its history featured Dakota, Navajo, Cherokee, and Pueblo musicians. In 1971, Bee secured a recording contract for the group with Rare Earth Records, a subsidiary of Motown Records that was dedicated to the promotion and distribution of non–African-American (mostly rock) acts.

XIT released two albums with Motown: *Plight of the Redman* in 1972 and *Silent Warrior* in 1973. Their first album, *Plight of the Redman*, was almost certainly the first Native American "concept album," as the entire LP was organized as a retelling of

American history from an indigenous perspective, tracing Native American history from precontact through to the arrival of Columbus, the Indian wars, the reservation period, and the eventual rise of the Red Power movement. The LP was a musical analog to Dee Brown's classic text *Bury My Heart at Wounded Knee* (1970), and their commitment and connection to the Red Power movement is explicitly expressed both in their lyrics, which mirror the rhetorical style and strategies found in the speech making and public statements of Red Power leaders, and in their musical style, which very purposefully and self-consciously blended early 1970s rock styles with "traditional" Native instruments (mainly drums and rattles), singing, and chanting. Tom Bee, who wrote all of the lyrics for the *Plight of the Redman* LP and was the driving force behind its political message, took over as lead singer for their second and final LP with Motown, *Silent Warrior*. This LP found great commercial success in Europe and produced the controversial, politically charged "Reservation of Education," which charted in France but was banned or ignored by many radio stations in North America because of its controversial political message (Active Listening 2.5). The song is an excellent example of Tom Bee's songwriting style, with lyrics that feature a sharp, sophisticated critique of the boarding school system and speak directly to some of the larger political concerns of Red Power activists, set to a musical style that sits squarely within the style conventions of early 1970s rock music.

The opening two lines of the song speak directly to Red Power activists and those sympathetic to the movement, the first line articulating an intense dissatisfaction with the social and political marginalization of American Indians, while the second is a call to action. The title of the song, repeated over and over during the chorus, is a clever play on words that critiques both the boarding school system and the reservation system, both of which, at different points in history, were policy instruments used to marginalize and control Native American populations. With this chorus, Bee is suggesting that just as the reservation system of the nineteenth century became a way for the federal government to politically dominate and control

ACTIVE LISTENING 2.5
"Reservation of Education"

COUNTER NUMBER	FORM	LYRICS
0:00	Instrumental introduction	
0:20		You've been born into a world of sorrow
		You've been born to try and change tomorrow
0:41	Verse 1	When I was young I heard of fate
		But not the word segregate
		Oh I was raised in boarding school
		And I was taught to ridicule
	Verse 2	When I was young I heard of hate
		But not the word discriminate
		Oh I was told my way was wrong
		And I must change to get along
1:09	Pre-chorus	When I was very young
		So very, very young
1:23	Chorus	It's a reservation of education [repeated 4 times]
1:50	Verse 3	Big yellow bus took me away
		Where I would talk a different way
		Oh I was told where I would sleep
		Away from stars and my sheep
2:02	Pre-chorus	When I was young
		So very, very young
2:17	Spoken word interlude 1	After all these years
		I have finally come to see the light
		But it's hard for an Indian boy
		To do what's right
		Especially if he's not white
		He's not white [repeated]
2:43	Alternate chorus with Navajo lyrics	*Doo ya'ashooda bilagáana* [repeated 4 times]
3:11	Electric guitar solo	
3:41	Spoken word interlude 2	I wanna tell you
		That all that grit
		You see on them John Wayne movies
		Is painted white
		I said I wanna tell you
		That all that grit
		That you see on them John Wayne movies

COUNTER NUMBER	FORM	LYRICS
		And it's not right
		It's not right [repeated]
4:10	Chorus	It's a reservation of education [repeated 4 times]
4:37	Spoken word interlude 3	I'm sure when you were young
		That you played a game called cowboys and Indians
		I said I'm sure when you were young
		That you played a game called cowboys and Indians
		But we're all grown up now
		But you're still playing a game
		But only now it's called
		Whiteman and Indian [Washington and Indian]
		Whiteman and Indian [Bureaucrats and Indian]
		Whiteman and Indian [BIA and Indian]
		Indian [repeated]
5:23	Chorus	*Doo ya'ashooda bilagáana* [repeated]

"Reservation of Education." Written by Michael Valvano, Tom Bee, and Mac Suazo. Published by Jobete Music Co. Inc. (administered by Sony/ATV Music Publishing LLC.) Produced by Tom Bee for the Soar Corporation.

tribal populations, the boarding school policies of the twentieth century attempted to control how Native peoples felt about their own culture, language, and lifeways. Many of these schools discouraged or forbade Native students from speaking their tribal languages or living according to the cultural practices of their home communities and families. The first and second verses describe this "re-education" experience. Bee sings about being encouraged to "ridicule" one's own tribal beliefs and practices and being taught that one must "change" and assimilate in order to be successful in life. The second verse describes the feelings of dislocation and alienation felt by many boarding school students, many of whom were forced to leave their home communities to attend school. Moving away from the "stars and my sheep" is a specific reference to the experience of Navajo children. While Bee himself is not Navajo, he spent a good deal of time on the reservation, which was close to Gallup.

The first spoken word interlude references the double bind faced by many Native Americans who were educated in the boarding school system: Even if they learned to speak English, converted to Christianity, left the reservation, and tried to assimilate into mainstream Euro-American society, they were often the victims of racism and discrimination. It was indeed hard for an "Indian boy" to do what was "right" (according to what they had learned in boarding school) because he was still understood by the rest of society as a racial "other" ("he's not white"). The second interlude is somewhat of a thematic departure and features a more general critique of the kinds of racist stereotyping of Native American identity found in Hollywood westerns.

In the final spoken word section, the "game" called "Whiteman and Indian" is an explicit reference to the kind of racially based rhetoric that was a common feature of

Red Power statements and speechmaking. In drawing a line between "the White-man" and "Indians," this race-based rhetorical strategy is, intentionally I think, both divisive and essentializing. In referencing the discourse of race—the tacit assumption that "racial" difference (meaning phenotypic traits) equals "cultural" difference (meaning ideology and behavior)—the argument is structured in such a way that bloodline carries with it a certain guarantee of shared cultural history and heritage, a brand of essentialism that was used quite effectively by Red Power activists to build consensus among the many different tribal communities of American Indians across the country. Here, Bee is suggesting that American Indian identity should be understood as a birthright and thus something that is in many ways "beyond culture," which is to say beyond the very real cultural differences that persisted between urban and reservation communities, to say nothing of the social and cultural differences that have existed throughout American history between different tribal communities. It is also worth noting that in the printed lyrics included in the liner notes that accompanied the CD re-release of *Silent Warrior,* Bee chose to replace the repeated lyric "Whiteman and Indian" with the phrases "Washington and Indian," "Bureaucrats and Indian," and "BIA and Indian," listing three of the most common institutional targets of Red Power protests.

Finally, the use of the Navajo language phrase *"doo ya'ashooda bilagáana"* is another important feature of the song. The phrase loosely translates as "The white man is bad" or "the white man is crazy." Using correct Navajo grammar, the word *bilagáana* would be first in the word order, but musically it works better with the order reversed. Bee's use of Navajo language in this song is a particularly interesting choice given that he is a Dakota and not a fluent speaker of Navajo. He commented on this to me in a personal interview, claiming,

> I wrote those [lyrics] in Navajo, having grown up in Gallup, right near the Navajo reservation there. That's a border town. I spent a lot of time on the Navajo Nation, Window Rock, St. Michaels, all those areas. . . . So obviously, because I was living in that region, I wrote them regionally, you know what I'm saying. So I just basically used the language of the area. (Tom Bee, phone interview with author, July 28, 2009)

While the Navajo language lyrics may have been inspired by local concerns, they nonetheless constitute a powerful symbol of cultural difference, marking XIT's music as uniquely "American Indian" and as fundamentally different from the many other kinds of protest music being recorded and performed in the 1970s. Even for American Indians who did not speak or understand Navajo, the presence of a Native language in the music was a powerful reminder of their own cultural difference from the American mainstream and a marker of XIT's cultural authenticity as American Indians, with urban roots, who were still connected to reservation languages and lifeways.

While a great many Native popular musicians are interested in writing lyrics about Native issues and creating music that mixes traditional tribal or intertribal musical styles with mainstream pop idioms, not all musicians fit this mold. For example, the Mohawk (Haudenosaunee) blues–rock guitarist and singer Derek Miller makes little mention of his Native heritage in his songs. Miller was born in 1974 on the Six Nations Reserve in Ontario, Canada. He rose to prominence backing up and touring with well-known Native musicians such as Buffy Sainte-Marie and Keith Secola. In 2002, Miller signed a recording contract with Arbor Records and released his debut CD, *Music Is The Medicine*, which received a Juno Award for Aboriginal Recording of the Year.

Listen to the song "Devil Come Down Sunday" (Active Listening 2.6) from his subsequent release with Arbor Records, *The Dirty Looks* (2006). Based on a riff-based, 12-bar blues form and employing the standard AAB poetic form of many blues songs, this track showcases Miller's considerable talents as a guitarist. His guitar style is reminiscent of some of his self-proclaimed Native American musical

MindTap

🔊 **LISTEN TO**

"Devil Come Down Sunday," performed by Derek Miller from the album *The Dirty Looks* (Arbor Records), online.

MindTap

🎧 **WATCH** an Active Listening Guide of this selection online.

ACTIVE LISTENING 2.6
"Devil Come Down Sunday"

COUNTER NUMBER	COMMENTARY	LYRICS
Introduction		
0:00	Electric guitars, electric bass guitar, and drum set	
1st verse—lyric		
0:21		Devil came down Sunday, offered me a ride
		Devil came down Sunday, offered me a ride
		She's an evil, evil woman, got nowhere to hide
2nd verse—lyric		
0:51		Down at the crossroads, Mohawk road dirt line
		Down at the crossroads, Mohawk road dirt line
		Got to see me a pretty woman, about gettin' me some wine
1:21	Instrumental bridge	
3rd verse—lyric		
1:34		Everybody gamblin', when you're looking for love
		Everybody gamblin', when you're looking for love
		Roll it down with me sugar, show me what you're made of
		Roll it!
2:09	Electric guitar solo	
4th verse—lyric		
2:40		Devil came down Sunday, offered me a ride
		Devil came down Sunday, offered me a ride
		She's an evil, evil woman, I can't wait to ride
Coda—last line of chorus repeats		
3:09	Instrumental ending (same as bridge)	She's an evil, evil woman, I can't wait to ride
		Ride Sally!

"Devil Come Down Sunday," written, published, and performed by Derek Miller.

heroes, including Link Wray and Robbie Robertson. The song is also representative of his musical style more generally, employing dense layers of highly distorted electric guitar and featuring a straight-ahead rock rhythm with drum set and electric bass accompaniment.

Hearing this song, students may well ask (as many students in my classes have when I play this song for them): "In the absence of any obvious musical or lyrical stylistic markers, is this really an example of 'Native music'?" "Could we not also simply classify this as a straightforward blues–rock song that just happens to be performed by a musician of Native American heritage?" These are valid and important questions that begin to hint at the complexity surrounding Native American cultural and social identity in the twenty-first century. Indeed one of the implicit goals of this chapter is that in surveying some of the many diverse and distinctive musical styles developed and performed by Native American individuals and communities across North America, readers will begin to grasp the complexity of Native American identity not only at present, but also throughout the past few centuries of colonial contact.

Figure 2.11

Tom Bee, Dakota musician, music producer, record label owner, and two-time Grammy award winner. *Tom Bee*

Public debate and discussion about the nature and definition of both "traditional" and contemporary Native American music arose in the 1990s and early 2000s when CARAS (the Canadian Academy of Recording Arts and Science) and NARAS (National Academy of Recording Arts and Science) created specific award categories for Native American music (see Figure 2.11). Contemporary Native music posed particular challenges for these award institutions precisely because many prominent Native musicians create and perform music across several genres that, stylistically, are virtually indistinguishable from their non-Native contemporaries. Thus, these organizations faced very pragmatic questions about whether the boundaries for contemporary Native music were defined by bloodline (only Native people perform "Native music") or by musical style and/or lyrical content. While all of these organizations have steered clear of explicitly stating that contemporary Native American music is a category defined by race, to date, no non-Native musician has ever won a Grammy or Juno award for indigenous music. While the stylistic borders that define contemporary Native American music may be blurry, these boundaries are nonetheless vigorously defended, as evidenced by the public controversy and outrage surrounding the nomination of a non-Native musical artist, Sazacha Red Sky, in the inaugural year of the Juno Aboriginal music category (an award eventually won by Cree country musician Lawrence Martin) (Scales 1999).

The Grammy category, which as of 2012 was eliminated and combined with several other "ethnic music" categories into a very broadly defined "Regional Roots" music category, faced similar challenges of definition. The stylistically eclectic Navajo flautist Carlos Nakai, who has been a Grammy finalist four times, suggested that the Native music category "is another example, I guess I would say, of stereotyping us and saying that the only qualifiable music for an award is traditional American Indian music either in chant or in group-chant form with a drum"(Nakai, quoted in Brockman 2002).

Here Nakai is suggesting that NARAS is consciously or unconsciously biased toward more "traditional" or tribally defined musical styles and genres, which are the musical styles that mainstream Euro-American society expects Native musicians to perform. This music more easily fits the widespread stereotype of Native American identity, an identity that is complicated by the stylistically hybrid music of XIT or Derek Miller.

These kinds of public controversies and discussions are part of what anthropologists Levi and Dean (2006) have termed the "risks of being heard." As Native American musicians continue to expand upon, elaborate, or sometimes completely ignore their tribal and intertribal musical traditions—instead embracing and transforming modern technologies, trends in popular culture, and publically lobbying for their aboriginal rights—they may jeopardize their publicly and federally recognized status as Native Americans with a unique cultural history and social position in North America. When Derek Miller composes and performs music that does not overtly engage with his Mohawk identity, is he still performing "Native American music"? I would argue that whether performing Eskanye, Stomp Dance, or powwow songs, whether singing protests songs about political injustices or playing a scorching blues–rock solo, all musicians in this chapter are working through and constructing modern Native American cultural and social identity, an identity that is often "maddeningly complex"(Ibid.:28). Most of the musicians we have heard in this chapter embrace this complexity, as evidenced in the music they perform and the lives they choose to lead. As students of Native American music and culture, all we can do is try to keep up.

MindTap **PRACTICE** your understanding of this chapter's concepts by reviewing flashcards and working once more with the chapter's Active Listening Guides online.

MindTap **DO** an online quiz that your instructor may assign for a grade.

Study Questions

1. What is the difference between tribal and intertribal styles?
2. What is a Sing? What kinds of music occur at this event?
3. In what ways are Stomp Dance songs stylistically similar to the "Eastern Way" of music making that is broadly shared among many tribal groups in the southeastern United States?
4. What is the name of the ceremony that contains the Yeibichai songs? What is the purpose of the ceremony? What are some of its features?
5. What are some general features shared by many different tribal musical styles.
6. What are the differences between "competition" and "traditional" powwows?
7. Discuss the stylistic and formal features that characterize powwow music.
8. Name and describe the six main powwow dance styles in terms of history, regalia, and choreography.
9. What is the "Red Power" social movement, and how did it affect the development of Native American popular music, and the music of XIT in particular?
10. How do we determine what is or is not an example of "Native American music?" How have different institutions dealt with this question?

3

Africa/Ewe, Dagbamba, Shona, BaAka

David Locke

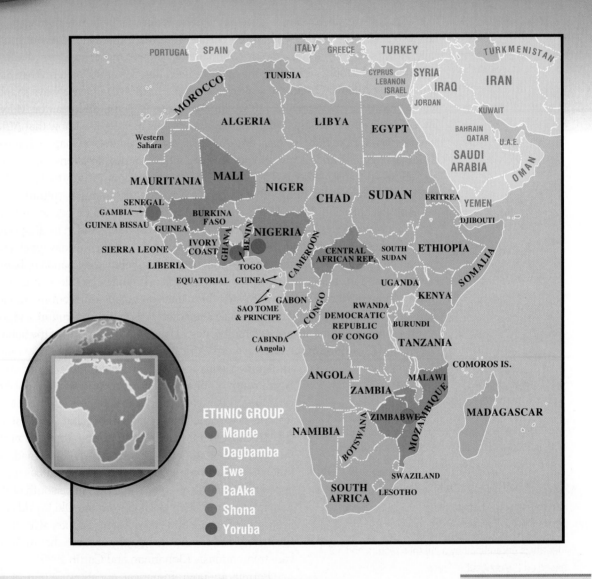

ETHNIC GROUP
- Mande
- Dagbamba
- Ewe
- BaAka
- Shona
- Yoruba

Learning Objectives

After you have studied this chapter, you should be able to:

1. Describe characteristics of musical style that are present in many kinds of African music.

2. Discuss the value and purpose of music-making in several African traditions.

continued

3. Explain the musical uses of **"three-in-the-time-of-two" (3:2)** in examples of African music.

4. Understand the concept of "drum language."

5. Discuss the relationship between African popular music and African traditional music.

Consider a misleadingly simple question: Where is Africa's beginning and end? At first you might say that they lie at the borders that mark the continent. But musi-cally, Africa spills over its geographic boundaries. Calling to mind the narrow Strait of Gibraltar, the historic Suez Canal, the often-crossed Red Sea and Mediterranean Sea, and the vast Atlantic Ocean, we realize that people from Africa have always shaped world history (see Skinner 1973). If we invoke images—Egypt, Ethiopia, the Moors, Swahili civilization, commerce in humans and precious metals—we know that Africa is not separate from Europe, Asia, and America. As pointed out in Chapter 1, music is human-made sound; it moves with humankind on our explorations, conquests, migrations, and enslavements. This chapter, therefore, refers us not only to the African continent but also to the many other places we can find African music-culture.

Another question: What music is African music? We could be poetic and say, "Where its people are, there is Africa's music—on the continent and in its diaspora." The truth, however, is messier. Music is never pure; music-cultures are always chang-ing and being shaped by many outside influences. From Benin and Luanda to Bahia, Havana, London, and Harlem, music-cultures blend along a subtle continuum. African-influenced music now circulates the planet by means of electronic media. After people learn new things about music, their own personal music-cultures adjust.

The African continent has two broad zones: (1) the **Maghrib**, north of the Sahara Desert, and (2) **sub-Saharan Africa**. North Africa and the Horn of Africa have much in common with the Mediterranean and western Asia; Africa south of the Sahara in many ways is a unique cul-tural area. Even so, history records significant contacts up and down the Nile, across the Sahara, and along the African coasts. Just as civilizations from the north (Greece, Rome) and east (Arabia, Turkey) have made an indelible impact on northern Africa, the south has influ-enced the Maghrib as well. Similarly, Africa south of the Sahara has never been isolated from the Old World civi-lizations of Europe and Asia. As this chapter will show, the history and cultural geography of sub-Saharan Africa vary tremendously (Bohannan and Curtin 1995).

Permit an ungrammatical question: When is an African? In everyday circumstances, people in Africa do not usually think of themselves as "African" (Mphahlele 1962). Identity arises from local connections of gender, age, kinship, place, language, religion, and work. Ethnic-ity comes into play only in the presence of people from a different group. One "becomes" a Serer, so to speak, in the presence of a Wolof, an African when among the French, a White in the company of a Black, a Yellow,

Salient Characteristics of
Africa

- Both a geographical place and the people of that place

- African continent has two broad cultural zones separated by the Sahara Desert: Mahgrib to the north and sub-Saharan Africa to the south

- Identity is determined by numerous factors and not based on the concept of "race"

- Can be viewed symbolically, psychologically, spiritu-ally, and geographically

- Many ethnic groups, also called "tribes," "kingdoms," "nations," or "polities" exist

- African music has a profound effect on music throughout the world

a Red (Senghor 1967). These terms suggest relationships among people more than they mark essential characteristics of individuals. Although physical appearance and genetic inheritance do not determine culture, the bogus concept of **race** persists, feeding the ignorance that spawns prejudice and the bigotry that fosters injustice (Appiah 1992). Such labels should therefore be marked: Use With Care.

"Africa" serves as a resonant symbol for many people. People of African descent, wherever they are in the world, may regard Africa as the ancestral homeland, the place of empowerment and belonging (Asante 1987). Industrialized citizens of "information societies" may envision Africa as either a pastoral Eden or the impoverished Third World. Historically regarded as a land of "heathens" by Muslims and Christians, Africa is a fount of ancient wisdom for those who practice religions such as Santería or Vodun. Famine relief and foreign aid, wilderness safari and Tarzan, savage or sage—Africa is a psychic space, not just a physical place.

The sections that follow introduce seven African music-cultures. They show Africa's diversity and some of its widely shared characteristics. Information for two of the sections comes from my own field research; other sections are based on the ethnomusicological scholarship of colleagues—the late James Koetting ("Postal Workers Canceling Stamps"), Paul Berliner ("Nhemamusasa"), Michelle Kisliuk ("Makala"), and Oyebade Dosumnu, Bode Omojola, Marie Agatha Ozah, and Michael Veal ("Teacher Don't Teach Me Nonsense"). The cooperative effort that underlies this chapter seems fitting, because one vital function of African music is to mold separate individuals into a group.

Postal Workers Canceling Stamps

In Chapter 1, you first heard the sounds of African postal workers canceling stamps. As promised, we will revisit this intriguing recording, this time examining how it reflects some of the general characteristics of African music-culture. To start, recall Koetting's description (1992:98–99):

> This is what you are hearing: the two men seated at the table slap a letter rhythmically several times to bring it from the file to the position on the table where it is to be canceled. (This act makes a light-sounding thud.) The marker is inked one or more times (the lowest, most resonant sound you hear) and then stamped on the letter (the high-pitched mechanized sound you hear). . . . The rhythm produced is not a simple one-two-three (bring forward the letter—ink the marker—stamp the letter). Rather, musical sensitivities take over. Several slaps on the letter to bring it down, repeated thuds of the marker in the ink pad, and multiple cancellations are done for rhythmic interest. . . .
>
> The other sounds you hear have nothing to do with the work itself. A third man has a pair of scissors that he clicks—not cutting anything, but adding to the rhythm. . . . The fourth worker simply whistles along. He and any of the other three workers who care to join him whistle popular tunes or church music that fits the rhythm.

How does this musical event exemplify widely shared characteristics of African music-culture?

MindTap·
◀)) LISTEN TO
"Postal workers canceling stamps at the University of Ghana post office," online.

Generalizations about African Music-Culture

Music-Making Events

A compelling feature of this recording is its setting. Canceling stamps can sound like this? How marvelous! Obviously, the event was not a concert, and this most definitely is not **art for art's sake**. Like **work music** everywhere, this performance undoubtedly lifted the workers' spirits and enabled them to coordinate their efforts. The music probably helped the workers maintain a positive attitude toward their job. Music often helps workers control the mood of the workplace (Jackson 1972). (See "Music of Work" in Chapter 4.)

African music often happens in social situations in which people's primary goals are not artistic. Instead, music is for ceremonies (**life-cycle rituals**, festivals), work (subsistence, child care, domestic chores, wage labor), or play (games, parties, lovemaking). Music making contributes to an event's success by focusing attention, communicating information, encouraging social solidarity, and transforming consciousness.

Salient Characteristics of
African Music-Culture

- Usually happens as part of social life and not for its own sake
- One of many kinds of artistic expression in a performance
- Shares features with the style found in Europe and the Middle East
- Exists in a dynamic process of give and take with musics from other world regions
- Usually encourages social participation
- Musicians acquire skill as they grow up in society but also undergo rigorous training
- Is taken seriously as an important part of life
- Often non-Africans make incorrect assumptions about African music

Expression in Many Media

Just as Africans set music in a social context, they associate it with other **expressive media** (drama, dance, poetry, masquerade, sculpture). Indeed, this example is unusual because it is a wordless instrumental. Although music making is usually not the exclusive purpose of an event, people do value its aesthetic qualities. Music closely associated with a life event is also enjoyed at other times for its own sake.

Musical Style

The whistled tune probably seems familiar to many listeners. The melody has European musical qualities such as duple meter, a major **scale**, and harmony. On the other hand, the percussion exhibits widespread African stylistic features such as polyrhythm, repetition, and improvisation.

History

These observations about genre and style lead to an important point about the history of music in Africa: The music-cultures of Europe, Asia, and the Americas have strongly affected those in Africa. Foreigners—Christians and Muslims, sailors and soldiers, traders and travelers—have brought to Africa their instruments, musical repertories, and ideas. Modern media technologies such as radio and audio recording have merely increased the intensity of a very old pattern of border crossing. Like people everywhere, Africans have imitated, rejected, transformed, and adapted external influences in a complex process of culture change.

Many musical traditions have affected African music making. Throughout Africa, Christian hymns and Muslim cantillation (chanting religious texts) have exerted a profound influence on musical style. West Asian civilization has influenced African musical instruments, such as the plucked lutes, double reeds, and goblet-shaped drums of the Sahel area. Euro-American influence shows up in the electric guitar and drum set, although East Asians manufacture many of these instruments. We hear the American influence of Cuban *rumba* on pop music from central Africa, and African-American spirituals on southern African religious music. From praise singers to pop bands, musical professionalism is an idea about music that developed in Africa by means of the intercultural exchange of ideas.

Participation

The postal workers join simple musical parts together to make remarkably sophisticated and satisfying music. This kind of musical design welcomes social engagement. Others could participate by adding a new phrase to the **polyrhythm** or cutting a few dance moves. Undoubtedly, Jim Koetting "got down" while picking up his mail! Much African music shares this generous, open-hearted quality that welcomes participation.

Training

We admire the postal workers because their music seems effortlessly beautiful. The genius we sense in this recording lies in the way the workers are musical together, in their sensitivity to a culturally conditioned musical style. Here, a musical education depends on a society-wide process of **enculturation**—that is, the process of learning one's culture gradually during childhood. Babies move on the backs of their dancing mothers, youngsters play children's games and then join adults in worship and mourning, teenagers groove to pop tunes. Raised in this manner, Africans learn a way-of-being in response to music; intuitively, they know how to participate effectively. Genetic and sacred forces may shape musicality, but culture is the indispensable element in musical training.

Beliefs and Values

Often, Africans conceive of music as a necessary and normal part of life. Neither exalted nor denigrated as "art," music fuses with other life processes. Traditional songs and musical instruments are not commodities separable from the flux of life. In his book *African Music: A People's Art*, Francis Bebey quotes a musician who was asked to sell his instrument:

> He replied rather dryly that he had come to town to play his drum for the dancing and not to deliver a slave into bondage. He looked upon his instrument as a person, a colleague who spoke the same language and helped him create his music. (1975:120)

Intercultural Misunderstanding

These beliefs and attitudes about music make intercultural understanding a challenge, especially for scientifically minded people from what might be called "concert-music-cultures." What a non-African listener assumes is an item of music may be the voice of an ancestor to an African. When he recorded this example, Koetting found himself in this type of cross-cultural conundrum:

ACTIVE LISTENING 3.1
Postal Workers Canceling Stamps

COUNTER NUMBER	COMMENTARY
0:00	Fade in during last phrase of the tune (phrase A^3).
0:07	First complete rendition of tune (phrases A^1, A^2, B, A^3); two-part harmony; restrained percussion.
0:44	Second time through the tune solo whistle; brief interlude without whistling.
2:04	Tune repeats a fourth time with more melodic and harmonic invention in whistling and rhythmic variety in percussive accompaniment.
2:36	Bass part in percussion "takes a solo" as tune finishes.
2:44	Fade-out as next repetition begins.

It sounds like music and, of course it is; but the men performing do not quite think of it that way. These men are working, not putting on a musical show; people pass by the workplace paying little attention to the "music" (I used to go often to watch and listen to them, and they gave the impression that they thought I was somewhat odd for doing so). (1992:98)

This example gives us a feeling for African music in general. The next example affords a more detailed look at a type of music with profound connections to the history of a specific African ethnic group, the Ewe (*eh*-way) people.

Agbekor: Music and Dance of the Ewe People

Drawing on my field research in West Africa during the 1970s, we will now consider a type of singing and drumming, originating as a war dance, called *Agbekor* (ah-*gbeh*-kaw; literally, "clear life"). As we will hear on the recorded example, Agbekor's music features a percussion ensemble and a chorus of singers. A complex lead drumming part rides on a rich polyrhythmic texture established by an ensemble of bells, rattles, and drums of different sizes. Songs are clear examples of call-and-response. Agbekor is a creation of Ewe-speaking people who live on the Atlantic coast of western Africa in the nation-states of Ghana and Togo.

The Ewe People
Ewe History

Triumph over adversity is an important theme in **Ewe** oral history. Until they came to their present territory, the Ewe people had lived precariously as a minority within kingdoms of more populous and powerful peoples such as the **Yoruba** and the Fon. One prominent story in their oral traditions recounts their exodus in the late 1600s from **Agokoli**, the tyrannical king of **Notsie**, a walled city-state located in what is now southern Togo. Intimidating Agokoli's warriors with fierce drumming, the Ewes escaped under cover of darkness. Moving toward the southwest, they founded many settlements along a large lagoon near the mouth of the Volta River. At last, **Wenya**, their elderly leader, declared that he was too tired to continue. Thus, this Ewe group became known as the **Anlo** (*ahng*-law), which means "cramped." Other families of Ewe-speakers settled nearby along the coast and in the upland hills.

In these new lands, the Ewe communities grew and multiplied. Eventually, the small Ewe settlements expanded into territorial divisions whose inhabitants could all trace male ancestors to the original villages. Family heads or distinguished war leaders became chiefs. Despite bonds of common culture and history, each division zealously cherished its independence. The Ewe people have never supported a hierarchical concentration of power within a large state (compare them with the **Dagbamba** kingdom, discussed later in this chapter).

Ever since those early days, the important unit of Ewe social life has been the extended family. Members of a lineage—that is, people who can trace their genealogy to a common ancestor—share rights and obligations. Lineage elders hold positions of secular and sacred authority. The ever-present spirits of lineage ancestors help their offspring, especially if the living perform the necessary customary rituals. The eighteenth and nineteenth centuries saw the Ewes in frequent military conflict with neighboring ethnic groups, with European traders, and even among themselves. The Anlo-Ewe gained a fearsome reputation as warriors.

> ## Salient Characteristics of
> ## the Ewe and Their Music
>
> - Towns and villages east of the mouth of the Volta River along the coast of the Atlantic Ocean
> - Decentralized society based on territorial divisions headed by chiefs, war leaders and priests; extended family is main unit of social life
> - In worldview, religion permeates all aspects of family and community life
> - Ethos emphasizes affirmation of life in challenging circumstances
> - Music with polyphonic instrumental ensembles, dance drumming, and call-and-response singing
> - Musical style features polyrhythm

Ewe Religious Philosophy

An Ewe scholar has commented on the sacred worldview of his people:

> A traveler in Anlo is struck by the predominating, all-pervasive influence of religion in the intimate life of the family and community. . . . The sea, the lagoon, the river, streams, animals, birds and reptiles as well as the earth with its natural and artificial protuberances are worshipped as divine or as the abode of divinities. (Fiawo 1959:35, in Locke 1978:32)

The Ewe supreme being, **Mawu**, is remote from the affairs of humanity. Other divinities, such as **Se** (pronounced seh), interact with things in this world. Se embodies God's attributes of law, order, and harmony; Se is the maker and keeper of human souls; Se is destiny. Many Ewes believe that before a spirit enters the fetus, it tells Se how its life on earth will be and how its body will die. If you ask Ewe musicians the source of their talent, they will most likely identify the ancestor whose spirit they have inherited. Ask why they are so involved in music making, and they will say it is their destiny.

Ancestral spirits are an important force in the lives of Ewe people. The Ewe believe that part of a person's soul lives on in the spirit world after his [or her] death and must be cared for by the living. This care is essential, for the ancestors can either provide for and guard the living or punish them. . . . The doctrine of reincarnation, whereby some ancestors are reborn into their earthly kin-groups, is also given credence. The dead are believed to live somewhere in the world of spirits, *Tsiefe,* from where they watch their living descendants in the earthly world, *Kodzogbe.* They are believed to possess supernatural powers of one sort or another, coupled with a kindly interest in their descendants as well as the ability to do harm if the latter neglect them. (Nukunya 1969:27, in Locke 1978:35)

Funerals are significant social institutions, because without ritual action by the living a soul cannot become an ancestral spirit. A funeral is an affirmation of life, a cause for celebration because another ancestor can now watch over the living. Because spirits of ancestors love music and dance, funeral memorial services feature drumming, singing, and dancing. Full of the passions aroused by death, funerals have replaced war as an appropriate occasion for war drumming such as Agbekor.

Knowledge of Ewe history and culture helps explain the great energy found in performance pieces like Agbekor. Vital energy, life force, strength—these lie at the heart of the Ewe outlook:

In the traditional Anlo society where the natural resources are relatively meager, where the inexplicable natural environment poses a threat to life and where the people are flanked by warlike tribes and neighbors, we find the clue to their philosophy of life: it is aimed at life. (Fiawo 1959:41, in Locke 1978:36)

Agbekor: History and Contemporary Performance
Legends of Origin

During my field research, I interviewed elders about how Agbekor began.* Many people said it was inspired by hunters' observations of monkeys in the forest. According to some elders, the monkeys changed into human form, played drums, and danced; others say that the monkeys kept their animal form as they made percussive sounds and dance-like movements. Significantly, hunters, like warriors, had access to esoteric power.

In the olden days hunters were the repository of knowledge given to men by God. Hunters had special herbs. . . . Having used such herbs, the hunter could meet and talk with leopards and other animals which eat human beings. . . . As for Agbekor, it was in such a way that they saw it and brought it home. But having seen such a thing, they could not reveal it to others just like that. Hunters have certain customs during which they drum, beat the double bell, and perform such activities that are connected with the worship of things we believe. It was during such a traditional hunting custom that they exhibited the monkey's dance. Spectators who went to the performance decided to found it as a proper dance. There were hunters among them because once

_____
*I conducted these interviews with the assistance of a language specialist, Bernard Akpeleasi, who subsequently translated the spoken Ewe into written English.

they had revealed the dance in the hunting customary performance they could later repeat it again publicly. But if a hunter saw something and came home to reveal it, he would surely become insane. That was how Agbekor became known as a dance of the monkeys. (Kwaku Denu, quoted in Locke 1978:38–39)

Although many Ewes consider them legend rather than history, stories like this signify the high respect accorded to Agbekor. Hunters were spiritually forceful leaders, and the forest was the zone of dangerously potent supernatural forces. We feel this power in a performance of Agbekor.

Agbekor as War Drumming

The original occasion for a performance of Agbekor was war. Elders explained that their ancestors performed it before combat, as a means to attain the required frame of mind or, after battle, as a means of communicating what had happened.

> They would play the introductory part before they were about to go to war. When the warriors heard the rhythms, they would be completely filled with bravery. They would not think that they might be going, never to return, for their minds were filled only with thoughts of fighting. (Elders of the Agbogbome Agbekor Society, quoted in Locke 1978:44)
>
> Yes, it is a war dance. It is a dance that was played when they returned from an expedition. They would exhibit the things that happened during the war, especially the death of an elder or a chief. (Alfred Awunyo, quoted in Locke 1978:43)
>
> If they were fighting, brave acts were done. When they were relaxing after the battle, they would play the drums and during the dance a warrior could display what he had done during the battle for the others to see. (Kpogo Ladzekpo, quoted in Locke 1978:43)

The Meaning of the Name Agbekor

I asked whether the name Agbekor has meaning. One elder told me this:

> I can say it signifies enjoying life: we make ourselves happy in life. The suffering that our elders underwent was brought out in the dance, and it could be that when they became settled, they gave the dance this name, which shows that the dance expresses the enjoyment of life. (Kwaku Denu, quoted in Locke 1978:47)

Another elder told me that when people played Agbekor during times of war, they called it **Atamuga** (ah-*tam*-gah), which means "the great oath." Before going to battle, warriors would gather with their war leaders at shrines that housed spiritually powerful objects. They would swear on a sacred sword an oath to their ancestors to obey their leaders' commands and fight bravely for their community. When the Anlo no longer went to war, the name changed to Agbekor (Kpogo Ladzekpo, quoted in Locke 1978:45–46).

The word Agbekor is a compound of two short words: *agbe* ("life") and *kor* ("clear"). The professional performer Gideon Foli Alorwoyie translates Agbekor as "clear life": The battle is over, the danger is past, and our lives are now in the clear (Locke 1978:47). Many people add the prefix **atsia** (plural, *atsiawo*), calling the piece atsiagbekor (ah-chah-*gbeh*-kaw). The word *atsia* has two meanings: (1) stylish self-display, looking good, or bluffing, and (2) a preset figure of music and dance. Perhaps because the word *atsia* means "stylishness," many English-speaking Ewe musicians refer to the preformed drum and dance compositions as "styles." As presented shortly, the form of the lead drumming and the dance consists of a sequence of *atsiawo.*

Learning

In Ewe music-culture, most music and dance is learned through enculturation. Agbekor, on the other hand, requires special training. The eminent African ethnomusicologist J. H. K. Nketia describes learning through slow absorption, without formal teaching:

> The very organization of traditional music in social life enables the individual to acquire his musical knowledge in slow stages, to widen his experience of the music of his culture through the social groups into which he is progressively incorporated and the activities in which he takes part. . . . The young have to rely largely on their imitative ability and on correction by others when this is volunteered. They must rely on their own eyes, ears and memory. They must acquire their own technique of learning. (1964:4)

Gideon Alorwoyie explains how one learns from the performance of an expert:

> All you have to do is know when he is going to play. . . . You have to go and pay attention to what you hear, to how the drums are coordinated and to the drum language, to what the responses are to the calls, and so on. You have to use your common sense right there to make sure that you get the patterns clear. Up to today, if you want to be a drummer, you go to the place where people are playing and then pay attention and listen. That's it. (Davis 1994:27)

Because of its complexity, Agbekor is hard to learn in this informal way. Members of an Agbekor group practice in a secluded area for up to a year before they appear in public. Instruction entails demonstration and emulation. With adept dancers in front, the whole group performs together. No one breaks it down and analyzes it. People learn sequences of movement and music not through exercises but in a simulated performance context. (Compare this with the teaching of *karnataka sangeeta,* described in Chapter 6.)

This style of learning depends on gifted students who can learn long rhythmic compositions merely by listening to them several times. For certain people, drumming comes as easily and naturally as spoken language. Ewes know that drumming talent often comes from one's ancestors. A precocious youngster may be the reincarnation of an ancestor who was a renowned musician. One village drummer told me of a special drummer's ritual:

> My father was a drummer and he taught me. It was when he was old and could no longer play that he gave me the curved sticks. A ceremony has to be performed before the curved sticks are handed over to you. . . . If the custom is not done the drum language will escape your mind. (Dogbevi Abaglo, quoted in Locke 1978:53)

Gideon Alorwoyie explains the effects of this ritual:

> Once the custom has been made, you can't sleep soundly. The rhythms you want to learn will come into your head while you sleep. . . . The ceremony

protects the person in many ways. It protects your hands when you play and protects you from the evil intentions of other people who may envy you. . . . Whenever you see a master drummer in Africa, I'm telling you, he has got to have some sort of backbone. (Locke 1978:54–55)

Performing Organizations

Times have changed since Ewe hunters created Agbekor. Britain, Germany, and France administered Ewe territory during a brief colonial period (1880s to 1950s); now the Ewe people live in the nation-states of Ghana and Togo. Today, relatively few villages have preserved their heritage of Agbekor. But the tradition vigorously continues within drum and dance societies of several types: mutual aid organizations, school and civic youth groups, and theatrical performing companies. Throughout Africa, voluntary mutual aid societies are an important type of performing group (Ladzekpo 1971). Agbekor groups of this kind are formal organizations with a group identity, institutionalized procedures, recognized leaders, and so forth. Many members are poor and cannot afford funeral expenses. People solve this financial problem by pooling resources. When a member dies, individuals contribute a small amount so the group can give money to the family. The society's performance of music and dance makes the funeral grand.

In the mid-1970s, I studied Agbekor with members of this type of cooperative society, the Anya Agbekor Society of Accra (see Figure 3.1). One of their leaders recounted how the group came into existence:

The first Anya Agbekor group in Accra was formed by our elder brothers and uncles. They all scattered in the mid-sixties and that group died away. We, the younger ones, decided to revive it in 1970. Three or four people sat down

Figure 3.1
The Anya Agbekor Society (with the author) in performance. *Godwin Agbeli.*

and said, "How can we let this thing just go away? Agbekor originated in our place, among our family, so it is not good to let it go." We felt that it was something we had to do to remember the old family members. We formed the group to help ourselves. (Evans Amenumey, quoted in Locke 1978:63)

I also studied with school groups trained by my teacher, Godwin Agbeli. In colonial times, missionaries whipped students for attending traditional performance events. These days, most Ewes value their traditional repertory of music and dance as a cultural resource. Since Ghana achieved statehood in 1957, the national government has held competitions for amateur **cultural groups** from the country's many ethnic regions. Young people often join these groups because rehearsals and performances provide social opportunities. Like many African countries, Ghana sponsors professional performing-arts troupes. With its spectacular, crowd-pleasing music and dance, Agbekor is a staple of their repertory.

A Performance

On Sunday, March 6, 1977, in a crowded, working-class section of Accra, the Anya Society performed in honor of the late chief patron of the group. The evening before, the group had held a wake during which they drummed *Kpegisu*, another prestigious war drumming of the Ewe (Locke 1992). Early Sunday morning they played Agbekor briefly to announce the afternoon's performance. Had the event occurred in Anyako, the group would have made a procession through the ward. People went home to rest, then returned to the open lot near the patron's family house by 3:30 in the afternoon for the main event.

The performance area was arranged like a rectangle within a circle. Ten drummers sat at one end, fifteen dancers formed three columns facing the drummers, ten singers stood in a semicircle behind the dancers, and about three hundred onlookers encircled the entire performance area. All drummers and most dancers were male. Most singers were female; several younger women danced with the men. Group elders, bereaved family members, and invited dignitaries sat behind the drummers. With the account book laid out on a table, the group's secretary accepted the members' contributions.

The action began with an introductory section called ***adzo*** (ah-*dzo*), that is, short section. Dancers sang songs in free rhythm. After the *adzo*, the main section, ***vutsotsoe*** (voo-*tsaw*-tso-eh), that is, fast drumming, started. The first sequence of figures honored the ancestors. Following this ritually charged passage, the dancers performed approximately ten more *atsiawo*. The lead drummer spontaneously selected these "styles" from the many drum and dance sequences known to the group. The singers were also busy. Their song leader raised up each song; the chorus received it and answered. One song was repeated five to ten times before another was begun.

After about twenty minutes the ***adzokpi*** (ah-*dzoh*-kpee) or "solos" section of the performance began. Group members came forward in pairs or small groups to dance in front of the lead drummer. The dance movement differed for men and women. As in genres of Ewe social dancing, friends invited each other to move into the center of the dance space. When everyone had their fill of this more individualistic display, the lead drummer returned to the group styles. Soon, he signaled for a break in the action by playing the special ending figure.

Perhaps because the word *atsia* means "stylishness," many English-speaking Ewe musicians refer to the preformed drum and dance compositions as "styles."

During the break, the group's leaders went to the center of the dance area to pour a **libation**. Calling on the ancestors to drink, elders ceremonially poured water and liquor onto the earth. An elder explained later:

> We pour libation to call upon the deceased members of the dance [group] to send us their blessings [so we can] play the dance the same way we did when they were alive. How the Christians call Jesus, call God, though Jesus is dead—they do not see him and yet they call him—it is in the same manner that we call upon the members of the dance [group] who are no more so that their blessings come down upon us during the dancing. (Kpogo Ladzekpo, quoted in Locke 1978:82–83)

The performance resumed with *vulolo* (voo-*law*-law), that is, slow drumming, the processional section of Agbekor. After about fifteen minutes, they went straight to *vutsotsoe*, the up-tempo section, and then *adzokpi*, the "solos" section. After a brief rest they did another sequence of group figures at slow and fast pace, followed by individual display.

At the peak of the final *adzokpi* section, elders, patrons, and invited guests came out onto the dance area. While they danced, singers and dancers knelt on one knee as a mark of respect. After dancing back and forth in front of the drummers, they returned to their position on the benches in back of the drummers.

By 6:00, with the equatorial sun falling quickly, the performance had ended. As the group members contentedly carried the equipment back to the Anya house, the audience dispersed, talking excitedly about the performance.

Although a performance of Agbekor follows a definite pattern, it is not rigidly formalized. A. M. Jones, a pioneering scholar of African music, comments on the elasticity of African musical performance: "Within the prescribed limits of custom, no one quite knows what is going to happen: It depends quite a lot on the inspiration of the leading performers. These men [and women] are not making music which is crystallized on a music score. They are moved by the spirit of the occasion" (Jones 1959:108).

Music of the Percussion Ensemble

We now turn to music of the percussion ensemble for the slow-paced section of Agbekor. Instruments in the Agbekor ensemble include a double bell, a gourd rattle, and four single-headed drums (see Figure 3.2). Listen to Agbekor in Active

MindTap·
◀)) **LISTEN TO**
Agbekor, traditional music of the Ewe people, online.

Figure 3.2
Agkebor ensemble.
© *Emmanuel Agbeli.*

atsimevu   kidi   totodzi   kloboto   kaganu gankogui   axatse

Time Units	01	02	03	04	05	06	07	08	09	10	11	12	01	02	03	04	05	06	07	08	09	10	11	12	01
Four-feel	x			x				x			x				x				x			x			x
Six-feel	x		x		x		x		x		x		x		x		x		x		x		x		x
Gankogui			ko		ko	ko		ko		ko		ko	ko*		ko		ko	ko		ko		ko		ko	ko*
Axatse			pa	ti	pa	pa	ti	pa	ti	pa	ti	pa	pa			pa	ti	pa	pa	ti	pa	ti	pa	ti	pa	pa
Kaganu					ka	ta		ka	ta		ka	ta		ka	ta		ka	ta		ka	ta		ka	ta	
Kidi	gi	de	ge	de	gi	di	gi	de	ge	de	gi	di	gi	de	ge	de	gi	di	gi	de	ge	de	gi	di	gi
Kloboto			de	gi	dege	de	gi		de	gi		de	gi		de	gi	dege	de	gi		de	gi		de	gi
Totodzi			de			de		gi			gi			gi		de		de		gi			gi		gi

Figure 3.3

Parts for the Agbekor drum ensemble.

Listening 3.3, 3.4, and 3.5 for the entire ensemble, then listen to Active Listening 3.2 to hear the bell (*gankogui*) by itself, followed by each instrument with the bell (*axatse, kaganu, kidi, kloboto,* and *totodzi*), and finally the polyrhythm of all the parts. Using a box system to visually represent the temporal structure of the drum ensemble music, we will discuss the parts to help you understand their musical force and to try playing them yourself (see Figure 3.3). (Vocables provide helpful tips for drummers: "d" means strong hand and "g" means weak hand; "e" shows resonant, open tones and "i" means muted, closed tones.)

One by one the phrases are not too difficult, but playing them in an ensemble is surprisingly hard. The challenge is to hear them within a polyphonic texture that seems to change depending on one's point of musical reference. The reward in learning to play these parts is an experience of African musical time.

The Bell

"Listen to the bell"—that is the continual advice of Ewe teachers. Every act of drumming, singing, and dancing is timed in accordance with the recurring musical phrase played on an iron bell or gong called **gankogui** (gahng-*koh*-gu-ee). On first impression, the part may seem simple, but when set in the rhythmic context of Ewe drumming, it becomes a musical force of great potency. Repetition is key.

MindTap·
🔊 **LISTEN TO**
"Demonstration: Agbekor," performed by David Locke, online.

MindTap·
🎧 **WATCH** an Active Listening Guide of this selection online.

ACTIVE LISTENING 3.2
Demonstration: Agbekor

COUNTER NUMBER	COMMENTARY
0:00	*Gankogui* phrase by itself; phrase occurs twelve times; each phrase starts on high-pitched stroke 2 and ends on low-pitched stroke 1.
0:34	*Gankogui* and *axatse* phrases in duet.
1:07	*Gankogui* and *kaganu* phrases in duet.
1:40	*Gankogui* and *kidi* phrases in duet.
2:13	*Gankogui* and *kloboto* phrases in duet.
2:48	*Gankogui* and *totodzi* phrases in duet.
3:20	Full ensemble made up of composite of all phrases.

As the phrase repeats over and over, participants join together in a circling, spiraling world of time.

Seven strokes with a wooden stick on the bell make one pass through the phrase. As you can see in Figure 3.3, the bell part may be thought of as a sequence of short and long notes, that is, notes that are either one or two brief time units in duration. The note marked with the asterisk may be struck on the lower pitched of the *gankogui*'s two bells, a helpful landmark if one becomes rhythmically disoriented. As the part repeats in polyrhythmic context, a listener's musical ear can group the bell tones into a variety of patterns. We experience an aural illusion. Despite the chameleon-like nature of the bell part, enculturated Ewe players hear it as beginning on the third time unit in one cycle and moving towards a temporary feeling of closure on the first time unit of the next cycle.

Tempo, Pulsation, and Time-Feels

Although many contrasting rhythmic phrases occur simultaneously in the percussion ensemble, competent Ewe musicians unerringly maintain a steady tempo. Rather than confusing the players, the musical relations among parts help them maintain a consistent time flow (see Kubik 1962, Locke 1982).

The time-feel (meter) most significant to Ewe performers is the **four-feel**. Together with the explicit bell phrase, these four beats provide a constant, implicit foundation for musical perception. Each is a **ternary beat**, meaning that each has three quicker units within it. When my students first learn a dance step, a drum part, or a song melody, I advise them to lock into the bell phrase and the four-feel beats. Interestingly, this type of groove is widespread in African-American music (see Chapter 4). Practice the bell and four-beat combination by striking your thighs with open palms. When this is flowing easily, bring out the contrast between the parts by changing the weak hand to a fist.

To an Ewe musician, these four-feel beats automatically imply a faster-moving **six-feel**. This is the power of 3:2, or three-in-the-time of-two.

The *axatse* (ah-*ha*-tseh) is a dried gourd, about the size of a cantaloupe, covered with a net strung with seeds. In some Agbekor groups its role is to sound out the four-feel beats. In another frequently heard phrase, downward strokes ("pa") on the player's thigh match the *gankogui*, while upward strokes ("ti") against the palm fill in between bell tones. As the only instrument played by many people at once, the *axatse* "section" provides a loud, indefinite-pitched sound vital to the ensemble's energy.

The high pitch and dry timbre of the slender **kaganu** (kah-gahng) drum cuts through the more mellow, midrange sounds of the other drums. The *kaganu* part articulates offbeats, the moments between the four-feel beats. The late Freeman Donkor, one of my first teachers of Ewe music, said that the rhythm of *kaganu* brings out the flavor of the other parts, like salt in a stew.

In descending order of relative pitch, the three other drums in the ensemble are **kidi**, **kloboto**, and **totodzi** (*kee*-dee, *kloh*-boh-toh, and toh-toh-*dzee*). Each drum adds its own phrase to Agbekor's unique polyphony. There are two ways of striking a drum skin: strokes that bounce off the drum skin produce an open, ringing sound; strokes that press into the drum skin produce a closed, muted sound. Bounces contribute the most to the group's music; presses keep each player in a groove. The parts discussed as follows are widespread, but some Agbekor groups use slightly different versions.

- In the *kidi* part, three bounces and three presses move at the twelve-unit pulsation rate; the phrase occurs twice within the span of one bell phrase.
- The *kloboto* phrase has the same duration as the bell phrase. The part's main idea is a brief bounce-press, offbeat-onbeat figure.
- The *totodzi* part begins and ends with the *kloboto*. Notice the impact of sound quality and body movement on rhythmic shape: The phrase is felt as two strong-hand bounces followed by three weak-hand presses, not according to a three-then-two timing structure.

To get into the drumming, begin by hearing each part "in four" and in duet with the bell. Then, stay "in four" but hear ever-larger combinations with other parts. Next, switch to the six-feel. The point is to explore the potency of these phrases, not to create new ones. Stretch your way of hearing, rather than what you are playing. Strive for a cool focus on ensemble relationships, not a hot individual display (Thompson 1973).

Drum Language

As happens in the instrumental music of many African peoples, Ewe drum phrases often have vernacular texts, called **drum language**. Usually only drummers know the texts. Even Ewe speakers cannot understand drum language just by hearing the music—they must be told. Secrecy makes restricted information valuable and powerful. In many parts of Africa, "speech must be controlled and contained if silence is to exercise its powers of truth, authenticity, seriousness and healing" (Miller 1990:95). During my field research, I asked many experts whether they knew drum language for Agbekor. Saying he learned them from elders in his hometown of Afiadenyigba, Gideon Alorwoyie shared the following with me. Agbekor's themes of courage and service are apparent.

Text, Ewe text, and translation of Agbekor drum language

Totodzi
Dzogbe dzi dzi dzi.
battlefield/ on/ on/ on
We will be on the battlefield.

Kloboto
Gbe dzi ko mado mado mado.
Battlefield/ on/ only/ I will sleep/ I will sleep/ I will sleep
I will die on the battlefield.

Kidi
Kpo afe godzi.
Look/ home/ side-on
Look back at home.

Kaganu
Miava yi afia.
We will come/ go/ will show
We are going to show our bravery.

Songs

Texts

Agbekor songs engage the subject of war. Many songs celebrate the invincibility of Ewe warriors; others urge courage and loyalty; some reflect on death and express grief. Songs memorialize heroes but do not provide detailed historical information. Unlike the freshly composed songs found in contemporary idioms of Ewe traditional music, Agbekor songs come from the past. A song's affective power derives, in part, from its association with the ancestors.

Structural Features

In performance, a song leader and a singing group share the text and melody. As illustrated in the songs that follow, this **call-and-response** idea supports a variety of subtly different musical forms. The tonal system of Agbekor songs has evolved entirely in response to the human singing voice, without being influenced by musical instruments. An ethnomusicologist can identify scales, but in comparison to tuning in South Indian music-culture, for example, an Ewe singers' intonation seems aimed at pitch areas rather than precise pitch points. Melodic motion usually conforms to the rise and fall of speech tones, but Ewe speakers easily understand song lyrics even if the melodic contour contradicts the tonal pattern of the spoken language. Songs add another layer to the rhythm of Agbekor. Not surprisingly, a song's polyrhythmic duet with the bell phrase is all important.

Listen again to Active Listening 3.3, 3.4, and 3.5 for excerpts from my recording of a performance by an Agbekor group from the town of Anlo-Afiadenyigba on August 14, 1976. There are three slow-paced songs, one song in free rhythm, and one fast-paced song.

MindTap•
◀))**LISTEN TO**
Agbekor, traditional music of the Ewe people, online.

Slow-Paced Songs

We begin with the slow-paced songs (see Active Listening 3.3). Song 1 announces that people should prepare for the arrival of the Agbekor procession. It has a rounded form.

In Song 1, the group response sets the leader's lyrics to a new melodic phrase. This section (A) is done twice, followed by a different section (B) that has shorter melodic phrases and a more percussive style of call-and-response. The song ends with leader and group singing together.

ACTIVE LISTENING 3.3
Agbekor *Vulolo* (Slow-Paced Section)

MindTap•
🎧 **WATCH** an Active Listening Guide of this selection online.

COUNTER NUMBER	COMMENTARY
0:00	Fade in on Song 1.
0:05	One time through Song 1.
0:38	Song leader begins Song 1 again, but group raises Song 2 so song leader joins them.
0:42	Song leader continues Song 2 from line B[2] (see Text, Song 2).
0:48	Song 2 repeated seven times, each time taking about 10 seconds.
2:02	Song 3 (see Text, Song 3).
2:21	Song 3 repeated.
2:40	Fade-out during next repetition of Song 3.

Song 2, set at sunrise on the day of battle, urges Manyo, the Ewe commander, and his warriors to "be cunning." Leader and group divide the text: the leader identifies the actors and the action, then the group evokes the scene. Unlike the rounded form of Song 1, this song has a linear, AB musical form: A^1 B^1 A^2 B^2.

Text, Song 2	Leader:	*Agbekoviawo, midze aye*	A^1
	Group:	*Ada do ee,*	B^1
		Kpo nedze ga nu.	
		Ada do!	
	Leader:	*Manyo hawo, midze aye ee*	A^2
	Group:	Repeat lines 2–4.	B^2
	Leader:	Agbekor *group*, be cunning.	
	Group:	The day has come.	
		Beat the double bell.	
		The day has come.	
	Leader:	Manyo's group, be cunning.	
	Group:	Repeat lines 2–4.	

Song 3 expresses an important sentiment in Agbekor songs: celebrating the singers' power and denigrating the opponent—Here, the enemy is a "hornless dog," that is, an impotent person, and "we" are incomparably great. Ewe composers often make this point by means of rhetorical questions: "Who can trace the footprints of an ant?"—that is, Who can defeat us? "Can the pigeon scratch where the fowl scratches?"—that is, Can the enemy fight as strongly as we can? "Can a bird cry like the sea?"—that is, How can the enemy compare to us? In these playful self-assertions and witty put-downs, we see a parallel with the genres of African-American expressive culture called **signifying** (Gates 1988; see Chapter 4 for examples).

Text, Song 3	Leader:	*Avu matodzo,*	A^1
		Dewoe lawuma?	
	Group:	Repeat lines 1 and 2	A^2
	Leader:	*Dewoe?*	B^1
	Group:	*Dewoe lawuma?*	B^2
	All:	*Avu matodzo*	A^2
		Dewoe lawuma?	
	Leader:	A hornless dog.	
		Are there any greater than we?	
	Group:	Repeat lines 1 and 2.	
	Leader:	Any?	
	Group:	Greater than we	
	All:	Repeat lines 1 and 2.	

ACTIVE LISTENING 3.4
Agbekor *Adzo* (Free-Rhythm Interlude)

COUNTER NUMBER	COMMENTARY
2:50	Break in recorded selection.
3:02	Song 4: Leader and group sing first call-and-response.
3:18	Song 4: Leader and group sing second call-and-response.
3:23	Song 4: Together leader and group sing the next section.
3:37	Song 4: Together leader and group repeat the group's first call.
3:39	Exhortation from lead drum and song leader.
3:43	Song 4 repeated: Leader and group first call-and-response; sung twice.
3:56	Song 4: Leader and group second call-and-response.
4:01	Song 4: All sing new section.
4:14	Song 4: All repeat group's first response.

Free-Rhythm Songs

Rhythmically free songs make up the *adzo* section. They have longer texts than do songs from the slow- and fast-paced portions of an Agbekor performance. Like Songs 1 and 3, Song 4 (see Active Listening 3.4) begins with two sections of leader-group alternation but has a noticeably longer third section sung by the whole group. The song lyrics compare the Agbekor group's strength with the power of the ocean and deride the potency of the enemy's weapons.

Fast-Paced Songs

Like many songs from the fast-paced section, Song 5 celebrates heroic passion. For example, another song says simply, "Sweet, to put on the war belt is very sweet." Song 5 (see Active Listening 3.5) opens with the vivid image of a confrontation between two war gods (So). The Fon from Dahomey and the Anlo are about to fight; the beautiful warriors are preparing; will they have the courage to enter the fray?

ACTIVE LISTENING 3.5
Agbekor *Vutsotsoe* (Fast-Paced Section)

COUNTER NUMBER	COMMENTARY
4:19	Break in recorded selection.
4:28	Fade in on Song 5 leader call A and group response B sung twice (see Text, Song 5).
4:39	Song 5 leader-group call and response C and D (see Text, Song 5).
4:44	Song 4 all sing section B (see Text, Song 4).
4:47	Song 5 repeated.
5:05	Song 5 repeated.
5:24	Fade-out as new song is raised.

As we have seen, Agbekor is a group effort. Music and dance help cement social feeling among members of an Agbekor society. Others types of African music depend more on the virtuosity and special knowledge of individuals.

A Drummer of Dagbon

Salient Characteristics of
the Dagbamba and Their Music

- Live in the southern savannah of western Africa in present-day Ghana
- Centralized and hierarchical kingdom (*Dagbon*)
- Drummers (*lunsi*) are members of a hereditary clan
- Drummer may act as a speech artist, a family historian, a royal advisor, a cultural specialist, and an entertainer
- Drumming is based on texts in the local language
- Drumming and singing often are forms of musical praise
- Drummers submit to lengthy and rigorous training under demanding teachers

Musicians have had important functions in the political affairs of many African traditional states. We turn now to the life story of one such person.

In "Nag Biegu" (Active Listening 3.6) we hear the singing and drumming of the Dagbamba people (also known as Dagomba) from the southern savannah of western Africa (Ghana). I recorded the music in 1984. The performers are *lunsi* (*loon*-see; singular **lunga**, *loong*-ah), members of a hereditary clan of "sound artisans" that Westerners sometimes call "griots" (*gree*-oh). A *lunga* fulfills many vital duties in the life of the Dagbamba—verbal artist, genealogist, counselor to royalty, cultural expert, entertainer. The *lunsi* tradition developed in **Dagbon**, the hierarchical, centralized kingdom of the Dagbamba (Chernoff 1979; Djedje 1978; Locke 1990).

The Drums

Lunsi play two kinds of drums—**gung-gong** and *lunga*. For both types, a shoulder strap holds the drum in position to receive strokes from a curved, wooden stick. The gung-gong (goong-*gawng*) is a cylindrical, carved drum with a snare on each of its two heads. The cedarwood of a *lunga* is carved into an hourglass shape. By squeezing and releasing the leather cords strung between its two drumheads, a player can change the tension of the drum skins, which changes the pitch

MindTap•

◀)) **LISTEN TO**

"Nag Biegu" ("Ferocious Wild Bull"), Traditional Praise Name Dance song of Dagbon, performed by *lunsi* drummers of the Dagbamba people, online.

MindTap•

🎧 **WATCH** an Active Listening Guide of this selection online.

ACTIVE LISTENING 3.6
"Nag Biegu" ("Ferocious Wild Bull")

COUNTER NUMBER	COMMENTARY
0:00	Call by leading *lunga* drum.
0:08	Chorus by answer *lunga* and *gung-gong* drums.
0:21	Verse by vocalist and leading *lunga* drum.
0:59	Chorus by answer *lunga* and *gung-gong* drums.
1:09	Verse by vocalist and leading *lunga* drum.
1:45	Chorus by answer *lunga* and *gung-gong* drums.
1:55	Fade-out during verse.

of the drum tones. In the hands of an expert, the drum's sound closely imitates **Dagbanli**, the spoken language of the Dagbamba. *Lunsi* "talk" and "sing" on their instruments. These musicians are storytellers, chroniclers of the history of their people and their nation.

A Praise Name Dance

"Nag Biegu" (*nah*-oh bee-*ah*-oo) is one of the many Praise Name Dances (*salima*) of Dagbon. Its title means "ferocious wild bull," referring to an enemy leader whom Naa Abudu defeated in a dramatic, hand-to-hand

Figure 3.4
Lunsi in performance. *Patsy Marshall.*

duel. This *salima* praises Naa Abudu, a king of Dagbon in the late 1800s who is remembered for his courage and firm leadership. Scoffing at the challenge of a war leader from a neighboring nation, Naa Abudu said, "I am dangerous wild bull. Kill me if you can." As they dance to the drumming, people recall the bravery of the king.

The music has a verse–chorus form (see Active Listening 3.6). In the verse, the vocalist and leading *lunga* drummers praise Naa Abudu and allude to events of his chieftaincy; the answering *lunsi* and two *gung-gong* drummers punctuate the verses with booming, single strokes. The drummed chorus phrase works like a "hook" in a pop song—a catchy, memorable phrase. In this piece, we can hear another case of music built from the temporal duality of 3:2.

Nag Biegu la to to to,	It is *Nag Biegu,*	Drum Language of Chorus Part, "Nag Biegu"
Nag Biegu la to to to,	It is *Nag Biegu,*	
Nag Biegu la to—n nyeo!	It is Nag Biegu—that's him!	
Nag Biegu la to,	It is Nag Biegu,	
Nag Biegu la to,	It is Nag Biegu,	
Nag Biegu la to—kumo!	It is Nag Biegu—kill him!	

Life Story: Abubakari Lunna

I have tape-recorded many interviews with my teacher from Dagbon, Abubakari Lunna (see Figure 3.5). When I met Mr. Lunna in 1975, he was working as a professional with the Ghana Folkloric Company, a government-sponsored performing arts company based in Accra, the capital of Ghana. In 1988, he retired from government service and returned to northern Ghana, where he served his father, Lun-Naa Wombie, until Mr. Wombie's death. Until his death in 2008, Mr. Lunna supported his large family as a drummer, farmer, and teacher. The following excerpt of his life story focuses on his teachers.

Figure 3.5
Studio portrait of Abubakari as a young man. *David Locke/Tufts University Medford.*

There are significant differences of ecology, history, and culture between what Abubakari calls "the North" and "the South."

Whereas his father comes from a long line of drummers, Abubakari's mother comes from a royal family.

"My Education in Drumming"

My father's grandfather's name is Abubakari. It is Abubakari who gave birth to Azima and Alidu; Azima was the father of [my teacher] Ngolba and Alidu was father of Wombie, my father. Their old grandfather's name is the one I am carrying, Abubakari. My father never called me "son" until he died; he always called me "grandfather." I acted like their grandfather; we always played like grandson and grandfather.

When I was a young child, my father was not in Dagbon. My father was working as a security guard in the South at Bibiani, the gold town. I was living with one of my father's teachers, his uncle Lun-Naa Neindoo, the drum chief at Woriboggo, a village near Tolon. When I was six or seven, my mother's father, Tali-Naa Alaasani [a chief of Tolon], took me to his senior brother, a chief of Woriboggo at that time. I was going to be his "shared child." In my drumming tradition, when you give your daughter in marriage and luckily she brings forth children, the husband has to give one to the mother's family. So, I was living in the chief's house.

I was with my mother's uncle for four or five years when he enrolled me in school. They took four of us to Tolon, my mother's home. I lived with my mother's father. We started going to the school. Luckily, in several weeks' time my father came from the South. He called my name, but his uncle told him, "Sorry. The boy's grandfather came and took him to be with the chiefs. Now he is in school." My father said, "What?! Is there any teacher above me? I am also a teacher. How can a teacher give his child to another teacher for training in a different language?" Early in the morning, he walked to Tolon. He held my hand. I was happy because my father had come to take me [see Figure 3.6].

My father spent one month. When he went to the South, he took me with him. Unfortunately, at Bibiani my father didn't have time to teach me. One year when my father came back to Dagbon for the Damba Festival [an annual celebration of the birth of The Holy Prophet Muhammad], he told my grandfather, Lun-Naa Neindoo, "If I keep Abubakari at Bibiani, it will be bad. I want to leave him at home. I don't want him to be a southern boy."

I began learning our drumming talks and the singing. Lun-Naa Neindoo started me with Dakoli Nye Bii Ba, the beginning of drumming [that is, the first repertory learned by young *lunsi*]: "God is the Creator. He can create a tree, He can create grass, He can create a person." Then you say with your drum, "A Creator, God, created our grandfather, Bizung [the first *lunga*]." The elders have given *Dakoli Nye Bii Ba* to the young ones so that they can

practice in the markets. When they know that
you are improving, they start you with drumming stories and singing stories. On every market
day we, the young drummers came together and
drummed by ourselves.

When the Woriboggo chief made my father
Sampahi-Naa, the drum chief second to the *Lun-
Naa* [the highest rank of drum chief], he could
not go back to Bibiani. My father said, "Now, I
am going to work with you on our drumming history talks." He began with the story of Yendi [seat
of the paramount chieftaincy of Dagbon]: how
Dagbon started, how we traveled from Nigeria
and came to Dagbon, how we became drummers,
how it happened that our grandfather **Bizung**
made himself a drummer. If he gave me a story
today, tomorrow I did it correctly.

I was with my father for a long time, more
than five years. My father was hard. I faced difficulty with my father because of his way of teaching. My father would not beat the drum for you.
He would sing and you had to do the same thing
on *lunga.* If you couldn't do it, he would continue
until you got it before adding another.

[Later] my father sent me to my teaching-
father, **Mba Ngolba.** He had a good voice, a good
hand—every part of drumming, he had it. He had
the knowledge, too, and people liked him. When he was drumming, he would
make people laugh. People would hire him: "We are having a funeral on this
day. Come and help us." I traveled with him, carrying his *lunga.* Because of his
drumming, Ngolba never sat at home; every day we went for drumming. That
was how people got to know me. Any time I was walking, people started calling, "Ngolba, small Ngolba." And with my sweet hand and my quick memory,
everyone liked me.

Already I knew something in drumming, so for him to continue with me
was not hard. I only had to listen to his story and follow him. When we went
to a place and he told stories, I tried to keep it in my mind. When we were
resting that night, I asked him, "Oh, my uncle, I heard your talk today. Can
you tell me more about it?" There, he would start telling me something. That
is how I continued my education with Mba Ngolba. I was very young to be
drumming the deep history rhythms with a sweet hand.

My father called Ngolba and advised him, "I am not feeling happy about
all the traveling you and Abubakari are doing. Drummers are bad. Somebody
might try to spoil your lives. Find something to protect yourself. And protect
Abubakari too." Father Ngolba—I can never forget him. Sometimes, when I
was sitting at home, he would call me to get something to drink. I couldn't
ask him, "Father, what is this?" In Dagbon, you can't ask him—you have to
drink it. My Mba Ngolba did it for me several times.

Figure 3.6
Studio portrait of Lun-Naa
Wombie, Abubakari's father.
*David Locke/Tufts University
Medford.*

Just as the royals of
Dagbon have an elaborate
hierarchy of chieftain-
cies, so the *lunsi* have a
pyramid-like system of
titled positions of authority.

Mba means "father"; for
a *lunga* drummer, your
teacher becomes your
teaching-father.

According to Dagbamba
etiquette, children never
question the orders of
their father.

Figure 3.7
Abubakari Lunna with his wife,
Fusena, and son, Wahidu, 2005.
Katherine Stuffelbeam.

Another reason why I liked my teacher, my Father Ngolba, is that despite his quick temper, he didn't get angry with me. He loved me. He didn't take even one of his ideas and hide it from me. Even if I asked him about something common that many drummers know, the thing left—he didn't hide it. He would tell me, "I have reserved something. If you bring all your knowledge out in public, some people with quick learning can just collect it."

I respected Ngolba like my father. During farming time I got up early in the morning and went straight to the farm. When he came, he met me there already. If it was not farming time, I would go to his door, kneel down, and say good morning to him. I would stay there, not saying anything until at last he would ask me, "Do you want to go some place?" Only then could I go. Teachers can give you laws like your own father. That is our Dagbamba respect to teachers.

Father Ngolba died in the South. When an old drummer dies, we put a *lunga* and a drumstick in the grave. The man who was with Ngolba when he died told me, "Your father said, 'Only bury me with this drumstick—don't add my *lunga* to bury me. Give my *lunga* to Abubakari.'" I said thank you for that. We finished the funeral back in Dagbon. The second brother to Ngolba spoke to all their family, "Ngolba told me that if it happens he dies, Abubakari should carry on with his duties. He should take his whole inheritance. And Ngolba had nothing other than his *lunga*." I have his *lunga*; it is in my room now. [See Figure 3.7 for a photo of Abubakari and members of his family.]

Shona Mbira Music

MindTap

🔊 **LISTEN TO**

"Nhemamusasa" ("Cutting Branches for Shelter"), online.

The recording of "Nhemamusasa" features another uniquely African type of musical instrument. It is known outside Africa as "thumb piano"; speakers of the **Shona** language call it (mmm-*bee*-rah). The "kaleidophonic" sound of its music (Tracey 1970:12) provides us with another insight into the musical potential of 3:2 rhythmic structures. Further, the *mbira* tradition shows another way African music can transform a group of separate individuals into a participatory, polyphonic community. Information for this section draws primarily on the research of the ethnomusicologist Paul Berliner (1993).

Cultural Context

History

The Shona, who live in high plateau country between the Zambezi and Limpopo rivers, are among the sixty million **Bantu**-speaking people who predominate in central and southern Africa. Since about 800 C.E., kingdoms of the Shona and neighboring peoples have ruled large territories; stone fortresses such as the Great Zimbabwe number among Africa's most impressive architectural achievements. These kingdoms participated in a lively, Indian Ocean commerce with seafaring powers such as the Arabs, Persians, and Indians (Mallows 1967:97–115). The Portuguese arrived about 1500. Eventually, the large-scale Shona states faded under pressure from other African groups, notably the more militaristic Ndebele in the 1800s. The Shona became a more decentralized, agricultural people.

At the turn of the twentieth century, English-speaking settlers took over the land and imposed their culture and economy on the local Africans. The colonial period in what was then called **Rhodesia** was brief, but it radically affected most local institutions. As in neighboring South Africa, a systematic policy of land grabbing left Africans materially impoverished. Racist settlers scorned African culture; many local people came to doubt the ways of their ancestors. For two decades after the independence of other contemporary African nation-states in the 1950s and 1960s, white Rhodesians maintained their dominance. Finally, a war of liberation (1966–1979) culminated in majority rule and the birth of the nation-state Zimbabwe in 1980.

Music played a part in the struggle. Popular and traditional songs with hidden meanings helped galvanize mass opinion; **spirit mediums** were leaders in the war against white privilege (Frye 1976; Lan 1985). After decades of denigration by some Africans who had lost faith in traditional culture, the *mbira* became a positive symbol of cultural identity.

> ## Salient Characteristics of
> # the Shona and Their Music
>
> - Significant, pre-colonial Shona civilization was supplanted by a long period of European colonialism and invasions by African ethnic groups
>
> - Mbira, a plucked idiophone, is the important traditional instrument; players regard their instrument as a companionable friend
>
> - Mbira music has two interlocking parts and several styles of singing
>
> - Mbira and mbira music are part of the rituals of spirit possession that connect the living with spirits of ancestors
>
> - In the twentieth century, white settlers displaced black Africans from their lands and imposed a racist system that was overthrown in the 1980s by armed resistance
>
> - Music played an important role in the war of liberation
>
> - Music functions as a vehicle for social critique

Shona Spirits

From the perspective inherited from the Shona ancestors, four classes of spirits (literally, *mweya,* or breath) affect the world: spirits of chiefs (*mhondoro*), family members (**mudzimu**), nonrelatives or animals (*mashave*), and witches (*muroyi*) (Lan 1985:31–43). Although invisible, the ancestral spirits nonetheless have sensory experience, feel emotions, and take action to help and advise their beloved descendants. *Mbira* music helps connect the living with their ancestors.

Humans and spirits communicate by means of **possession trances**: a spirit enters the body of a living person, temporarily supplanting his or her spirit. (Note: this spiritual practice is entirely unconnected to the "demonic possession" that may occur in other religious systems.) Once embodied in its medium, an ancestral spirit can advise his or her living relatives, telling them things they have done wrong and how to protect themselves and ensure good fortune. Similarly, a mhondoro spirit may advise a gathering of several family groups regarding matters that affect the entire community, such as the coming of rain. Trances occur at **mapira** (singular, *bira*), all-night, family-based, communal rituals. *Mbira* music and dancing are significant elements in these events (Berliner 1993:186–206; Zantzinger n.d.).

The *Mbira*

Construction

Mbiras of many different styles of construction occur throughout Africa and its diaspora. Most *mbiras* have four features of construction: (1) a set of long, thin keys made of metal or plant material, (2) a soundboard with a bridge that holds the keys, (3) a resonator to shape and amplify the sound of the plucked keys, and (4) jingles that buzz rhythmically when the keys are plucked. The instrument matches the bilateral symmetry of the human body; that is, left-side keys are for the left thumb, right-side keys are for the right thumb and index finger. The longer, bass keys lie toward the center of the soundboard; the shorter, treble keys toward its edges (Berliner 1993:8–18).

On the recording of "**Nhemamusasa**," we will hear an instrument that is frequently used at spirit possession ceremonies: the *mbira dzavadzimu* (mmm-*bee*-rah dzah-vah-*dzee*-moo; literally, "mbira of the ancestors"). Some Shona musicians refer to the tonal qualities of an *mbira*'s sound with the modified English word **chuning** to refer not only to pitches but also to qualities of tone, sound projection, pitch level, and overtones (Berliner 1993:54–72). Musicians debate the affective quality of different *chunings* and symbolically link the *mbira* keys with features of culture such as family relationships, emotional or physical responses to music, and animal imagery. In performance, musicians place the *mbira* within a large gourd resonator (**deze**) that brings out the instrument's full tone; when playing for personal pleasure or during learning–teaching sessions, the resonator may not be needed (see Figure 3.8). Bottle cap rattles or snail shells attached to the soundboard and resonator provide the important buzzing ingredient to the music. Performances usually include hand clapping, singing, and a driving rhythm played on a pair of gourd rattles called **hosho**.

The Player and the Instrument

In performance, the instrument faces toward the player. As noted, the *mbira* has left and right sides, just like the human body. Plucking patterns on the instrument

Figure 3.8

Young *mbira* players Luken Kwari (left) and Cosmas Magaya (right) emulate the demonstration of their elder, John Kunaka (center). *Paul Berliner.*

take full advantage of this **bilateral symmetry**. Repeatedly plucking the keys in prescribed patterns, musicians establish cycles of harmony, melody, rhythm, and counterpoint. Each key on the *mbira* emits a fundamental pitch and a cluster of overtones; the resonator shapes, reinforces, prolongs, and amplifies this complex tone. The buzzing bottle caps not only provide rhythm to the music's texture but also add to the instrument's array of tuned and untuned sounds. Tones overlap. The *mbira*'s sound surrounds the player. In this music, the whole is far more than the sum of the parts (Berliner 1993:127–35).

Creative, participatory listening is an essential aspect of this music-culture. Performer and audience must hear coherent melodies in the *mbira*'s numerous tones. Many pieces exploit the creative potential of 3:2 relationships; often one hand is "in three or six," while the other is "in two or four." Hand-clapping phrases (**makwa**) provide a good way to join in the performance and experience this **polymetric** feeling.

For players immersed in the process, the *mbira* takes on a life of its own. Here is how Dumisani Maraire, one of the first teachers of Shona music to non-Africans, explains it:

> When a mbira player plays his instrument he is conversing with a friend. He teaches his friend what to do, and his friend teaches him what to do. To begin with, the mbira player gives the basic pattern to the mbira; he plays it, and the mbira helps him produce the sound. He goes over and over playing the same pattern, happy now that his fingers and the mbira keys are together. So he stops thinking about what to play, and starts to listen to the mbira very carefully. (Maraire 1971:5–6)

"Nhemamusasa"

According to the Shona, ancestral spirits love to hear their favorite *mbira* pieces. Musical performance is an offering that calls them near, thus making possession more likely. Because of its important social use, this repertory remains stable over many generations. Pieces for *mbira dzavadzimu*, most of which have been played for centuries, are substantial musical works with many fundamental patterns, variations, styles of improvisation, and so forth. These pieces have two interlocking parts: **kushaura**, the main part, and **kutsinhira**, the interwoven second part. Since each part is polyphonic in its own right, the interaction of parts creates a wonderfully multilayered sound. The temporal structure of many mbira pieces consists of a musical cycle of four phrases, each containing twelve fast pulses. The vocal music, which has three distinct styles—**mahonyera** (vocables), **kudeketera** (poetry), and **huro** (yodeling)—adds depth to the musical texture and richness to the meanings expressed in performance. In this discussion we only scratch the surface of the *kushaura* part of a single piece.

In Active Listening 3.7, we hear "Nhemamusasa" (*neh*-mah-moo-*sah*-sah), revered by the Shona as one of their oldest and most important pieces. It was played for *Chaminuka*, a powerful spirit who protects the entire Shona nation. The song title literally means "Cutting Branches for Shelter." One of Berliner's teachers reports that "'Nhemamusasa' is a song for war. "When we [the Shona] were marching to war to stop soldiers coming to kill us, we would cut branches and make a place [tent shelter] called a *musasa*" (John Kunaka, quoted in Berliner 1993:42).

MindTap·
◀)) **LISTEN TO**
"Nhemamusasa" ("Cutting Branches for Shelter"), online.

ACTIVE LISTENING 3.7
"Nhemamusasa" ("Cutting Branches for Shelter")

COUNTER NUMBER	COMMENTARY
0:00–0:46	***Kushaura mbira* part by itself.**
0:00	Fade in during fourth 12-pulse phrase.
0:04–0:13	First full occurrence of 48-pulse cycle.
0:04	First 12-pulse phrase.
0:06	Second 12-pulse phrase.
0:08	Third 12-pulse phrase.
0:10	Fourth 12-pulse phrase.
0:13–0:20	Second occurrence of 48-pulse cycle.
0:13	First 12-pulse phrase.
0:15	Second 12-pulse phrase.
0:17	Third 12-pulse phrase.
0:19	Fourth 12-pulse phrase.
0:20	Third occurrence of 48-pulse cycle; 12-pulse phrases approximately every two seconds.
0:28	Fourth occurrence of 48-pulse cycle.
0:36	Fifth 48-pulse cycle.
0:43	Sixth occurrence of 48-pulse cycle.
0:47	***Kutsinhira* part enters**, which changes the feeling of groove and complicates the composite sound of the instruments.
0:51	Seventh occurrence of 48-pulse cycle.
0:59	Eighth occurrence of 48-pulse cycle.
1:07	Ninth occurrence of 48-pulse cycle.
1:14	Tenth occurrence of 48-pulse cycle.
1:22	Eleventh occurrence of 48-pulse cycle.
1:30	Twelfth occurrence of 48-pulse cycle.
1:38	Thirteenth occurrence of 48-pulse cycle.
1:41	***Hosho* (rattle) enters**, which intensifies the overall sound and reinforces the groove feel of the kutsinhira part.
1:45	Fourteenth occurrence of 48-pulse cycle.
1:54	Fifteenth occurrence of 48-pulse cycle.
2:01	Sixteenth occurrence of 48-pulse cycle.
2:09	Seventeenth occurrence of 48-pulse cycle.
2:17	Eighteenth occurrence of 48-pulse cycle.
2:24	Nineteenth occurrence of 48-pulse cycle.
2:32	Break in temporal flow to announce end of performance.

In 1991, Erica Azim, an experienced American student of *mbira*, heard a contemporary interpretation of the song's meaning from a female Shona friend:

Homeless people sit in their shantytowns
   with nothing to do.
No work.
Trouble is coming.

Text,
"Nhemamusasa"

Evidently, the piece evokes profound feelings. For the Shona, sentiments evoked by pieces such as "Nhemamusasa" make them effective for use in rituals of spirit possession. Even for those of us without inside knowledge of Shona cultural history, the musical sound of "Nhemamusasa" can produce a powerful affect.

Thomas Mapfumo and *Chimurenga* Music

This section on Shona music-culture closes with an example of what might be termed "modern traditional" music: "Nyarai," by Thomas Mapfumo and Blacks Unlimited (Eyre 2015). Mapfumo has named this style ***chimurenga*** music. With its pop band instrumentation and studio production, the music sounds new, but Mapfumo and his audience hear its links to *mbira* music (Bender 1991:163; Eyre 1991:51). Mapfumo and his guitarist, Jonah Sithole, intentionally model their arrangements on traditional music (Eyre 1988:87–88). Like some types of *mbira* music, "Nyarai" is recreational music for dance parties that also comments on topical issues.

Chimurenga music helps us realize that centuries-old traditions need not be obsolete or nostalgic (Waterman 1990). The word *chimurenga* ("struggle") refers both to the war against the white regime in Rhodesia and to a style of music that rallied popular support for the cause (Bender 1991:160–65; Eyre 1991; Manuel 1988:104–6). In the 1970s, the music became popular among Africans despite white censorship of song lyrics and an outright ban on artists and recordings. Just as African slaves in the Americas encoded their own meanings in the texts of African-American spirituals, African freedom-fighting songwriters used allusion to make their points. The baffled censors knew a song was subversive only when it was on everyone's lips, but by then the word was out.

Thomas Mapfumo remembers the development of the *chimurenga* music in the following interview with the music journalist Banning Eyre (square brackets mark Eyre's comments; curly braces mark mine):

> I grew up in the communal lands, which used to be called reserves, for the African people. . . . I grew up with my grandparents, who were very much into traditional music. Each time there was an *mbira* gathering, there were elder people singing, some drumming, some clapping. I used to join them. In the country, there were no radios, no TVs. . . .
>   {Later, Mapfumo lived with his parents in the city and joined bands doing rock 'n' roll covers.}
>   I was into a lot of things, even heavy metal. There were rock band contests held in Salisbury {now Harare}. . . . Some South African bands would cross the Limpopo [River] into Rhodesia to compete. There were a lot of black

bands playing rock 'n' roll music, and we were one of them. But not even one black band ever won a contest. And I asked myself: "What are we supposed to be if this isn't our music? If they [the whites] claim it to be their music, then we have to look for our own music." As a people who had actually lost our culture, it was very difficult to get it back. . . .

{After several years of singing with different bands that toured the beer halls of Rhodesia in the early 1970s, Mapfumo began writing more-serious lyrics.}

One afternoon, we came up with a nice tune opposing Mr. Ian Smith [the final prime minister of white-minority-ruled Rhodesia]. . . . This tune was called "Pa Muromo Chete," which means "It Is Just Mere Talk." Mr. Smith had said he would not want to see a black government in his lifetime, even in a thousand years. So we said it was just talk. We were going to fight for our freedom. This record sold like hotcakes because the people had got the message. Straight away, I composed another instant hit called "Pfumvu Pa Ruzheva," which means "Trouble in the Communal Lands." People were being killed by soldiers. They were running away from their homes, going to Mozambique and coming to live in town like squatters. Some people used to cry when they listened to the lyrics of this record. The message was very strong. . . .

The papers were writing about us. . . . Everyone wanted to talk to us about our music, and the government was very surprised, because they had never heard of a black band being so popular among their own people. They started asking questions. . . .

{In 1979, Mapfumo was detained by the police. After liberation, the popularity of the *chimurenga* style declined, but in the late 1980s he regained local popularity with songs that criticized corruption.}

We were not for any particular party. . . . We were for the people. And we still do that in our music. If you are a president and you mistreat your people, we will still sing bad about you. Never mind if you are black or white or yellow. . . .

{His lyrics still make social comment.}

Today, Zimbabwe is free. . . . So we are focusing our music worldwide. . . . We have been in a lot of world cities. We have seen people sleeping in the streets and governments don't look after these people. That is what our music is there for today. We will never stop singing about the struggle. (Eyre 1991:78)

"Nyarai" ("Be Ashamed") was recorded after the government headed by Robert Mugabe came to power in Zimbabwe. Its traditional stylistic features include musical form based on an 8-beat melodic/harmonic cycle, polyphonic interplay of melodies on two guitars and bass, collective improvisation, occasional climaxes using higher register, and insistent articulation by percussionists of the onbeats and selected offbeats (see Active Listening 3.8). The lyrics celebrate victory by citing the pride of community elders in the achievements of those who struggled for freedom of opportunity, and thanking the ancestors for their unwavering support. Mapfumo chides people ("Be ashamed") who are unreconciled to change, telling them to emigrate if they are unable to live in a democratic nation-state governed

ACTIVE LISTENING 3.8
"Nyarai" ("Be Ashamed")

COUNTER NUMBER	COMMENTARY
0:00	Fade-in.
0:08	8-beat cycles begin.
1:16	Vamp on word *Nyarai*.
1:33	"Shout out" to war heroes.
1:48	Guitar solo break.
2:01	Brass enters; fade-out.

MindTap·

🎧 **WATCH** "Nyarai" ("Be Ashamed"), performed by Thomas Mapfumo and Blacks Unlimited, online.

by majority rule. The song is a praise poem for the warriors, their leaders, their families, and their supporters. Although Mapfumo praises Mugabe for his role in the war of black liberation, subsequent events in Zimbabwe have brought mixed reviews of Mugabe's leadership of that troubled country.

African artists like Thomas Mapfumo adapt traditional music to contemporary realities. They strive to maintain features of their local, culturally grounded musical style while introducing ways of making music that fit more easily into today's global, cosmopolitan music-culture. Bringing noncommercial idioms of African music into the for-profit music industry challenges creative people to modify not only music's sound, but also its social practices and cultural values. Let us consider the case of a performing artist and musical composer who achieved such international attention that he is known by his first name, Fela.

Fela and Afrobeat*

In 1938, Fela Anikulapo Kuti was born into one of West Africa's foremost families of educators, medical specialists, civic activists, and artistic intellectuals (see Dosumnu 2011, Moore 2009, Olaniyan 2004, Omojola 2012 and Veal 2000). His mother characterizes the contribution members of this "elite" extended family have made to their fellow citizens: Funmilayo Thomas Ransome-Kuti was an ardent Pan-Africanist, pioneering feminist, and fearless community organizer. Fela received a colonial-style education in a school owned and operated by his father, which was located in the Yoruba cultural area of what would become the nation-state of Nigeria, and he earned a music degree in 1959 from London's Trinity College of Music. Building upon his familiarity with a wide variety of popular music styles not only from West Africa but also from Europe, the Americas, and the British empire, Fela forged the musical style that he popularized as "**Afrobeat**." Although Fela constructed Afrobeat to function as highly pleasurable dance-party music, he also knew he had created an original art form that responded to the

---

*In addition to the scholarly writing cited in this section, I am indebted to Oyebade Dosunmu, Ian Gendreau, Bode Omojola, Marie Agatha Ozah, and Michael Veal for personal communications.

Salient Characteristics of
Fela Kuti's Music-Culture

- Grounded in traditional Yoruba music-culture but greatly influenced by international black music styles such as jazz, funk, and soul

- Commercial music created for sale and consumption in an urban, cosmopolitan, industrial, and modern African context

- Fully composed works by a self-aware artist who intentionally presents a social critique through his musical works and performances

- Playful use of Nigerian pidgin as well as "the King's English"

disastrous conditions of post-colonial Nigeria. The trenchant analysis of Tejumola Olaniyan says it well:

The oil boom was on, and most of the benefits would be concentrated in the cities. The new breed of Nigerian leaders was brasher and more venal and made no pretense of morality.... [People] were overworked, underpaid, and stressed out by the pressures of the new petrol-fueled economy; and in the overcrowded slums of the metropolises, where primordial loyalties and languages could hold on to only a tenuous existence, they created a unique common symbolic language and mode of social relations.... In that sense, [Afrobeat] is the quintessential music of this new Nigerian social form, the urban masses.... Fela took their daily social life and artistically—musically—monumentalized it in their very own language. (Olaniyan 2004:37–38)

Afrobeat's distinctive combination of musical and lyrical ingredients emerged after Fela unsuccessfully had tried in the mid-1960s to cultivate a Nigerian audience for a style he termed "highlife jazz," an idiosyncratic mixture of mid-twentieth-century West African dance music and small-combo modern jazz. Frustrated both financially and artistically by the tepid response from audiences in Lagos, Fela undertook a ten-month U.S. tour in 1969. The American experience transformed Fela's music, outlook, and behavior. Stranded in Los Angeles, Fela began a lifelong relationship with Sandra Smith Isadore, an African American who introduced him to the political philosophy of black power. By urging him to read *The Autobiography of Malcolm X* (1965), Isadore catalyzed Fela into social activism and an Afrocentric ideology.

Fired with zeal to express African values through a fresh musical style, Fela composed music for a jazz orchestra that featured a steady-state, polyrhythmic groove in minor keys and modal tonalities. The new sound immediately proved successful, first at the Citadel de Haiti nightclub in Los Angeles and then in Lagos after he returned to Africa. Key to Afrobeat's success were Fela's stinging verses in Nigerian Pidgin, a form of English that vividly expressed the widespread dismay at conditions in Nigeria. He himself became the champion of the de-tribalized, impoverished masses, and the anti-imperialist yet sensuous art of Afrobeat was a favorite stimulant of the hip intellectual class. For the rest of his dramatic life as a force for positive change, Fela composed and performed within the style he had created. His prolonged, violent confrontation with oppressive authorities in Nigeria made him one of the world's most famous musicians of political protest. Fela died of AIDS in 1997.

"Teacher Don't Teach Me Nonsense"

Now give close attention to "Teacher Don't Teach Me Nonsense", which Fela composed in 1986 (see Active Listening 3.9). Already his bohemian lifestyle and never-ending battles with authorities in Nigeria had taken a huge physical and mental toll: he had endured several vicious beatings from soldiers and police; his mother had died as a result of an assault on the Kalakuta Republic, Fela's communal

♫ **LISTEN TO**
"Teacher Don't Teach Me Nonsense," performed by Fela Anikulapo Kuti and Egypt 80, online.

home; his performance venue/spiritual temple, the Shrine, had been burned to the ground; and he had earned and spent lots of money. In "Teacher Don't Teach Me Nonsense", we discover many important attributes of the Afrobeat style and also see how Fela used music to challenge abuses of power and educate his listeners to sources of their misery (see the video recording, *Music Is the Weapon*).

The Ensemble and Its Musical Functions

Fela composed for a large orchestra that enabled effects ranging from a full roar to a delicate whisper. Typically, the bass established the music's temporal structure and the pillar tones of its tonality, while electric rhythm guitars played interlocking vamp figures that established the music's modal grooves and fast-paced, interlocking texture.

The horn section consists of two sets of alto, tenor, and baritone saxophones and trumpet; Fela uses them not only for unison riffs but also in interlocking and responsorial relationships. The electric organ is used texturally for interjections between horn riffs, rhythmically as a contributor to the vamps of the guitar section, and as a solo instrument.

The drum set, *sekere* rattle, clips or sticks, and congas parts are centered on an interlocked set of ostinato patterns. The rattle and clips mark the onbeats and their faster subdivisions. The drum set creates the feeling of motion and accentuation.

ACTIVE LISTENING 3.9
"Teacher Don't Teach Me Nonsense"

A	**The band and lyric 1**	**0:00–6:04**
	Intro	0:00–1:56
	Ensemble Theme 1	1:56–2:40
	Lyric 1	2:40–3:40
	Organ solo 1	3:45–5:05
	Lyric 1	5:05–6:04
B	**Instrumental solos**	**6:12–10:47**
	Organ vamps	6:12–6:25
	Tenor sax solo	6:24–8:04
	Baritone sax	8:10–9:03
	Band interlude	9:04–10:47
C	**Musical games**	**10:47–13:10**
	"Spiritual Game"	10:47–12:00
	"Akujugba"	12:12–12:32
	"Kereke"	12:38–13:10
D	**"The message"**	**13:10–19:31**
E	**Reprise**	**19:31–25:45**
	Rhythm Section	25:20–25:45

♫ **LISTEN TO**
"Teacher Don't Teach Me Nonsense," performed by Fela Anikulapo Kuti and Egypt 80, online.

Fela has balanced the accents of each instrument or group of instruments to establish a powerful, rhythmic groove that features an ever-changing kaleidoscope of accents.

Over the first two minutes, we hear the gradual entrance of the rhythm section, the guitar section, and the organ. At 1:56 the entrance of the horn section dramatically changes the mood with its loud volume and forceful tone color. Fela has them state a melodic theme in unison, followed by a texturally dense exchange of interlocking riffs. What broader themes can be read from the music so far? The instrumentation establishes Afrobeat as expensively transnational, and the musicianship shows technical control of a transcultural idiom. The instrumental solos allude to African-American styles such as rhythm and blues, swing, hard bop, and free jazz. The message is that while this particular song is firmly grounded in its local Nigerian context, the musical style of Afrobeat is part of a global black music scene. Fela's role as bandleader/composer places him in league with other masters of black music such as Count Basie, Arensio Rodriguez, and George Clinton in the styles of swing, Latin, and funk, respectively.

Vocal Music and Lyrics

The singers are in three sections: Fela, female chorus, and male chorus. The timbre of the voices is a central feature of the piece: Fela sometimes has a warm sound of seductive intimacy, yet when he is ready to confront his enemies his voice can morph toward the authority of a tenor saxophone. The male chorus seldom becomes the music's focus but instead performs in unison with the females to give the chorus sections strength in the lower register. The cuttingly dry timbre of the female voices, the sound of "the Queens," as they were known, contrasts marvelously with Fela's voice and the rich sound color of the band. The human voices convey feelings of playfulness, ironic humor, incredulity, and indignation. When Fela and a mixed-gendered chorus deliver the first set of lyrics we get not only the fullness of the overall Afrobeat sound, but also its musical-semantic richness.

The words of Nigerian pidgin outline the situation as a rivalry between teacher and student. A listener unfamiliar with Nigerian history or current events might contemplate the relationship in general terms, but audience members "in the know" realize that Fela is hinting at the post-colonial condition between nation-states, with Great Britain as teacher and Nigeria as student. Something has gone wrong. Rather than benefiting from a healthy partnership, teacher and student exist in different conditions—and the students are suffering. Fela's decision to use the word "category" suggests a more profound interpretation: "Fela is here stating that there is an ontological irreconcilable disunity between African and Western systems of knowledge" (Oyebade Dosunmu, personal communication, 2012).

At 10:47, another venerable genre of black music is introduced: interactive musical games. Listeners familiar with Yoruba cultural practices recognize that in these passages Fela references the play of children in the neighborhood and the schoolyard (Bode Omojola, personal communication, 2012). Sounding like a seductive master of ceremonies, Fela invites the audience to "play music together in happiness." Happiness is an important state of being in Fela's ethos because it contrasts with the normal condition of suffering in which most people live. As he told biographer Carlos Moore in a moment of pensive vulnerability:

I'd just like to see happiness in people. That's all. I hate to see brutality. I hate to compromise with wrongdoing. . . . Sadness. Since a child, up till now, I've always been both happy and sad. What makes me sad today is to see people pushed around in life by other human beings. Selfishness by human beings also makes me sad. And the work that has to be done in Africa for Africans to progress. . . . To think of how many Africans are so unaware, how they suffer in oblivion. That makes me sad. (Moore 2009:259–260)

Notice that in his polished diction and vocabulary Fela has adopted the linguistic code of a well-educated person as opposed to the parlance of the street. He takes the role of teacher, but one who can join his students in disarmingly humble and youthful activities.

Thirteen minutes into the piece, we hear what might be referred to as "the message," verses in which Fela delivers a sermon that names obstacles to the people's enjoyment of life: electoral fraud and military coups, corruption by the Nigerian elite, collapse of traditional culture, and dereliction of responsibility by the neo-colonial Western powers. Like a shrewd commander, Fela deploys his musical forces not only to hold the listener's attention but also to dramatize the meaning of the lyrics, sometimes delivering his message alone, sometimes using the rhetoric of litany in rapid-fire call-and-response with female singers, and sometimes adding the horns as a third voice to the responsorial interactions. Sound itself (timbre) is a weapon in Fela's arsenal. For example, the "shrill, businesslike and penetrating" power of the women's unison voices functions like a Greek chorus to confirm the truth that Fela is talking (Olaniyan 2004:117). Fela varies the instrumental backing for the lyrics so that the piece remains musically compelling. He carefully sets the textual rhythm to enhance the natural expressiveness of the pidgin; for example, the word "and" in "culture and tradition" comes on the downbeat (14:04).

In the manner of a courtroom prosecutor, Fela first sets the scene and introduces the characters, then amasses the evidence and finally makes his accusation: African culture and tradition have been broken by European colonialism; immoral greed in the post-colonial nation-state goes unchecked by the former colonialist masters; the neo-colonial economic system punishes the people; and electoral politics are a deceitful illusion. Our consideration of Fela Anikulapo Kuti illustrates how the medium of music enables the expression of cultural criticism in a memorable, socially permissible style. Music, in other words, is a way "to speak truth to power." Let us conclude our inquiry into African music-culture by examining the value of music in a vastly different example: the music-culture of the Forest People of Central Africa.

The BaAka People Singing "Makala"

Our final example of African music-culture differs dramatically from the traditions of the Ewe, Dagbamba, Shona, and Yoruba. It brings us full circle to the communal, inclusive spirit of African music so clearly present in the music of the Ghanaian postal workers. Information for this section relies on the field research of Michelle Kisliuk (1998).

MindTap
◄》 LISTEN TO
"Makala," traditional BaAka song, online.

In "Makala" (Active Listening 3.10) we hear singing, hand clapping, and drumming of the BaAka (bee-*ah*-kah) people. The immense, ancient, thickly canopied tropical forest exerts a powerful influence on life in central Africa. The BaAka are one of several distinct ethnic groups who share certain physical, historical, cultural, and social features as well as adaptations to the natural world (Turnbull 1983). Here I will refer to these groups collectively as **Forest People**. Because of their physical size, non-Africans have called the Forest People "Pygmies." It is an ethnocentric label; their size is a benefit in the forest and plays a minor role in the way they are viewed by their larger African neighbors.

For millennia, the Forest People existed in ecological balance with their environment. Sheltered in dome-shaped huts of saplings and leaves, they lived with kin and friends in small, loose-knit groups. Because these hunting bands needed only portable material possessions, they could easily shift their encampments every few months according to the availability of food. They obtained a healthy diet through cooperative hunting and gathering, allowing them ample time for expressive, emotionally satisfying activities such as all-night sings. The social system was informal and flexible: men and women had roughly equal power and obligations; consensus decisions were negotiated by argument; and children were treated gently. Individuals were not coerced by formal laws, distant leaders, or threatening deities. The forest was God, and people were children of the forest (Turnbull 1961:74).

You may wonder why the preceding paragraph was written in the past tense. During the colonial and post-colonial eras, external forces have confronted the Forest People to a degree unprecedented in their history. They now live within nation-states forged in violent, anticolonial wars; multinational timber and mining companies are at work in the forest; scholars

Salient Characteristics of
the BaAka and Their Music

- Live in forested areas of tropical central Africa
- One of several distinct "Pygmy" ethnic groups who share common characteristics
- Social unit: small, close-knit group of families and friends
- Periodically move from place to place in search of food through cooperative hunting and gathering (semi-nomadic)
- Music-making enacts the egalitarian social structure and communal way of life
- Few musical instruments; emphasis on polyphonic vocal music with a sophisticated, multipart texture

ACTIVE LISTENING 3.10
"Makala"

MindTap
WATCH an Active Listening Guide of this selection online.

COUNTER NUMBER	COMMENTARY
0:00	Music takes shape as male singers, drummers, and women gradually join in.
0:16	Melodic and text theme is sung once.
0:20	Theme is elaborated in rich, multipart chorus.
0:55	Prominent, high-pitched yodeling.
1:16–1:33	Different drumming and prominent countermelody.
1:46	Theme stands out.
1:52	Hand clapping joins in until recording fades out.

and adventurers visit some of them regularly. In short, the Forest People now face great changes.

Earlier I mentioned the Western, ethnocentric view of the Forest People. Throughout history, other peoples have drawn on this culture in various ways. Let us now look at three images that reflect the conflicting roles that the Forest People play in the world's imagination.

Three Images of the Forest People

Primal Eden

For thousands of years, members of the world's imperial civilizations have found renewal in the music of the Forest People. In 2300 B.C.E. an Egyptian pharaoh wrote to a nobleman of Aswan who had journeyed south to the Upper Nile:

> Come northward to the court immediately; thou shalt bring this dwarf with thee, which thou bringest living, prosperous and healthy from the land of the spirits, for the dances of the god, to rejoice and (gladden) the heart of the king of Upper and Lower Egypt, Neferkere, who lives forever. (Breasted 1906, in Davidson 1991:55)

Today, aided by books and recordings, the Forest People continue to exert a pull on the world's imagination. In particular, the beautiful life of the BaMbuti recounted in Colin Turnbull's *The Forest People* (1961) has entranced many. Recordings by Simha Arom have introduced listeners to the intricacy of BaAka vocal polyphony (Arom 1987). For many people, this music-culture evokes cherished values—peace, naturalness, humor, community. In the music of the Forest People we seek to hear an innocence lost to our complex, polluted, violent world.

Primitive Savage

Paired with this image of primal utopia is the notion of **primitive** savagery. According to this view, Pygmies represent an early stage of cultural evolution, a primitive way of life associated with the Stone Age. By definition, primitives do not know the achievements of "high" civilization—science, mathematics, engineering, philosophy; they have no electricity, no industry, no nations, no armies, no books. If this is the stuff of civilization, then, like other native peoples in remote locations on earth, the Forest People must be "primitive."

But calling a human group "primitive" establishes a dangerous inequality. It can justify genocide; enslavement; servitude; colonialism; underdevelopment; land grabbing for lumbering, mining, agriculture, and tourism; and reculturization through evangelism, schooling, wage labor, and military service. From this imperialist perspective, cultures that differ from the "modern" way must change or be eradicated.

Unique Culture in a Global Village

Instead, we can characterize the Forest People with concepts that are less emotionally charged. They are nonliterate and nonindustrial, with a relatively unspecialized division of labor and a cashless, barter/subsistence economy; theirs is a homogeneous society with small-scale, decentralized social institutions, egalitarian interpersonal social relations, and relative gender equality. Their God is everywhere in their world, and they exist within the web of nature. Compared to one's own culture, the Forest People may seem better in some ways, worse in others. Undoubtedly, their culture is unique.

The next section presents a detailed description of a BaAka song. This will set the stage for seeing how the music-culture of the Forest People functions as a resource in their adaptation to change.

"Makala," A *Mabo* Song

Setting

LISTEN TO
"Makala," traditional BaAka song, online.

The performance-studies scholar and ethnomusicologist Michelle Kisliuk recorded "Makala" (*mah*-kah-lah) in December 1988 in the Central African Republic. The setting was a performance event, or *eboka*, of **Mabo** (*mah*-boh), a type of music and dance associated with net hunting (Figure 3.9). Hunting not only provides food but is also a key cultural institution. At this performance, novices (**babemou**) and their entourage from one group had walked to a neighboring camp to receive hunting medicine and related dance instruction from experts (**ginda**) (1998:98ff.).

Form and Texture

An *eboka* of *Mabo* consists of sections of singing, drumming, and dancing. Each song has a theme, that is, a text and tune. By simultaneously improvising melodic variations, singers create a rich polyphony. From time to time, the *eboka* is "spiced up" with an **esime**, a section of rhythmically intensified drumming, dancing, and percussive shouts (Kisliuk 1998:40–41).

Timbre

Men and women of all ages sing "Makala." They obtain a great variety of tone colors that range from tense/raspy to relaxed/breathy. One striking feature, yodeling,

Figure 3.9
BaAka in performance. *Michelle Kisliuk.*

involves quick shifts between head and chest voices. Musical instruments include drums and hand claps. Two different drum parts are played on the drum skins that cover the ends of carved, cone-shaped logs.

Because many different parts occur simultaneously, just listening to the recording does not easily reveal the song's melodic theme. Kisliuk learned the theme when hearing it sung in isolation from other parts by a young woman walking along a path. Singers often do not raise the theme until they have established a richly interwoven polyphony; even then, they are free to improvise on its melodic features.

As in Native American songs, singers mostly use vocables (see Chapter 2). The sparse text of "Makala" is typically cryptic (Kisliuk 1998:99).

		Text, "Makala"
moto monyongo	beautiful person	
Makala	name of an unknown, deceased person from the Congo, where *Mabo* originated	
na lele, oh	I cry [implying a funeral setting in this song]	

Turnbull reports that songs of the BaMbuti often mean "We are children of the Forest" or "The Forest is good." In troubled times they sing a longer text: "There is darkness all around us; but if darkness is, and the darkness is of the forest, then the darkness must be good" (Turnbull 1961:93).

Polyphony

The polyphonic texture of this choral music is complex. Like a well-made, multi-track rock 'n' roll recording, the layered parts in "Makala" sound fresh with each listening. Forest People use many different qualities of multipart song.

Music-Culture as an Adaptive Resource

Restoring Balance

The active force of music-making contributes to the Forest People's enduring yet ever-changing way of life. The BaMbuti encode the practical, moral effect of song in their words for conflict and peace: *akami*, noise or disordered sound, and *ekimi*, silence or ordered sound (Turnbull 1983:50–51). Troubles arise when synergy among people and symbiosis with the forest is disrupted. Communal singing "wakes the forest," whose benevolent presence silences the *akami* forces (Turnbull 1961:92). With yodels echoing off the trees, the forest itself becomes a "musician."

Enacting Values and Creating Self

Improvised, open-ended polyphony embodies egalitarian cultural values such as cooperation, negotiation, argument, and personal autonomy. By making social relations tangible, performance helps individuals develop identity within a group.

Autonomy within Community

Most members of a BaAka community acquire music-making skills as they grow up (enculturation). During times of crisis, the group needs the musical participation of every member. For example, in a memorable scene from *The Forest People*, even when others in the hunting group insult and ostracize a man for setting his hunting net in front of the others', he joins the all-night singing and is forgiven (Turnbull 1961:94–108).

BaAka repertory has a varied history and a dynamic future. Music connects the people to their past, while helping them negotiate their present.

Conclusion

Contrary to the images of chaos and despair conveyed by international mass media, we have encountered African music-cultures of stability, resourcefulness, and self-respect. Abubakari Lunna's life story reveals the rigor of an African musician's education. The erudition, commitment, suffering, and love are profound. Although he says good drumming is "sweet," clearly it is not frivolous or just fun. We could call it "deep," like the music of Frank Mitchell (see Chapter 2). We have seen that many Africans value the achievements of their ancestors. The Ewe rigorously study Agbekor and recreate it with passionate respect in performance. Innovative *chimurenga* music draws its inspiration from classics of Shona repertory. Creative musicians like Fela Anikulapo Kuti set African music within the global flow of black music-culture, using music as an erotic and powerful means of speaking truth to power.

African music-cultures are strongly humanistic. The human body inspires the construction and playing technique of musical instruments such as the *mbira.* The spontaneous performances of postal workers and the Praise Name Dances of the Dagomba point out an important feature of many African music-cultures: Music serves society. As we have experienced, many kinds of African music foster group participation.

Although I encourage African-style **musicking**, musicians who cross cultural borders need to be sensitive to limits and contradictions. To me, nothing approaches the power of time-honored repertory performed in context by the people born into the tradition, the bearers of culture. When non-Africans play African music, especially those of us with white skin, the legacy of slavery and colonialism affects how an audience receives the performance. Thomas Mapfumo, who as a young rock 'n' roller faced discrimination, now competes in the commercial marketplace with international bands that cover African pop songs. How many enthusiasts for African music love its aesthetic surface but regard spirit trance as superstition?

Music is a joyful yet rigorous discipline. The hard work of close listening yields important benefits. By making clear the sophistication of African musical traditions, analysis promotes an attitude of respect. This chapter has musical examples with rhythms based on 3:2. As we have seen, this profound, elemental timing ratio animates many African traditions.

Thinking about musical structure raises big questions that resist simple answers: Can thought be nonverbal? What approach to music yields relevant data and significant explanation? By treating music as an object, does analysis wrongly alienate music from its authentic cultural setting? How can people know each other?

Each chapter in this book benefits from this type of questioning. We seek to know how people understand themselves, but we must acknowledge the impact of our own perspective. Not only does an active involvement in expressive culture provide a wonderful way to learn about other people, but it can change a person's own life as well. From this perspective, ethnomusicology helps create new and original music-cultures.

Inquiry into music-cultures need not be a passive act of cultural tourism. On the contrary, a cross-cultural encounter can be an active process of self-development. When we seek knowledge of African music-cultures, we can also reevaluate our own. As we try our hands at African music, we encounter fresh sonic styles and experience alternative models of social action. Just as African cultures are not static, each student's personal world of music is a work in progress.

MindTap

PRACTICE your understanding of this chapter's concepts by reviewing flashcards and working once more with the chapter's Active Listening Guides online.

MindTap

DO an online quiz that your instructor may assign for a grade.

STUDY QUESTIONS

1. Discuss the education in drumming of Abubakari Lunna, a drummer of Dagbon. How was his education an example of enculturation?

2. Discuss the use of Euro American and traditional African musical features in the postal workers' "work music." How does the question, "Is this music?" relate to this "sound event"?

3. How has Thomas Mapfumo's *chimurenga* music merged Euro American popular music features with traditional African musical features?

4. Discuss Ewe and Agbekor.

5. Discuss some of the problems with trying to answer the questions, "What music is African?" and/or "When is an African?"

6. Discuss ways in which the music-culture of Shona mbira is particularly well-suited to its spiritual purpose.

7. Describe how the BaAka use their music-culture as an adaptive resource.

8. Discuss the Afrobeat music of Fela Kuti in terms of the cultural origin and cultural influences. Which features are African, which are Euro-American, which are African-American, which are universal? What do you think about making differentiations of this kind?

9. Compare and contrast all the examples of music-culture presented in this chapter. What do they have in common? What makes each unique? Given information in the chapter, do you think it is accurate to consider Africa as a distinct geo-cultural region of the world? Justify your argument with evidence from the chapter.

10. Building on the information and ideas developed in answering Study Question #9, undertake a compare-and-contrast study of African music-culture with the music-cultures of other geo-cultural regions of the world presented in *Worlds of Music*. Consider the following topics:
    - Compare elements of musical style such as rhythm, melody, texture, and form.
    - Compare the use of language in music such as the nature of song lyrics or the use of language as a basis for instrumental themes.

- Use the "concentric circles" model to summarize different musical performances and then examine each case for similarities and differences.
- Discuss the issue of generalization. Does a statement that finds similarity among different music-cultures need to be so general that it becomes a stereotype? Or, does the argument become about features of music-culture that are shared among all peoples of the world?
- Discuss the "politics" of global comparisons. On whose terms are comparisons made? What assumptions and preconceptions have impact upon your attitude about comparing African and non-African music cultures? What might be the dangers of this sort of broad generalization? What might be its positive value?

4

North America/Black America

Jeff Todd Titon

Learning Objectives

After you have studied this chapter, you should be able to:

1. Describe the differing functions of work songs, religious songs, and blues songs.

2. Discuss musical and cultural characteristics of African-American music.

3. Discuss the amount of originality and the role of tradition in the composition of blues songs.

4. Assess the advantages and disadvantages of marketing blues today as roots music or Americana.

continued

MindTap·

START experiencing this chapter's topics with an online audio activity.

5. Explain why it is necessary to understand African-American life experiences in order to understand African-American music.

6. Discuss the historical development of blues music in North America and assess its future prospects.

READ, highlight, and take notes on the complete chapter text in a rich, interactive online platform.

🎵 **LISTEN TO**

"My Dream of the Big Parade," by Henry Burr, online.

Salient Characteristics of
African-American Music in the United States

- A unique music, with roots in African music styles, neither African nor European, but fully African American

- Subjects drawn from real life, not fantasy

- Has transformed the style of popular music in North America and throughout the world

MindTap·

🔊 **LISTEN TO**

"Hustlin' Blues," performed by Gertrude "Ma" Rainey, from the album *Mother of the Blues*, online.

Music of work, music of worship, music of play: The traditional music of African American people in the United States has a rich and glorious heritage. Neither African nor European, it is fully a black American music, forged in America by Africans and their descendants, changing through the centuries to give voice to changes in their ideas of themselves. Through all the changes, the music has retained its black American identity, with a core of ecstasy and improvisation that transforms the regularity of everyday life into the freedom of expressive artistry. Spirituals, the blues, jazz—to Europeans, these unusual sounds are considered America's greatest (some would say its only) contribution to the international musical world.

Of course, modern black music does not sound unusual to North Americans because the black style has been so pervasive for many years. Suppose we contrast an early African-American blues recording from the post–World War I era with a typical popular music recording from the same period. Search the internet to find and listen to a performance of the popular song, "My Dream of the Big Parade," recorded in 1926 and sung by Henry Burr; the spoken section is narrated by Billy Murray. Like most other popular music of the early twentieth century, it sounds stilted, square, extravagantly dramatic, unnatural, and jerky—not because of the recording process, but because of the influence of the grand opera singing and marching-band instrumental styles of the period. Burr enunciates the song lyrics very carefully. The tempo speeds up and slows down for dramatic effect. A middle part is narrated. Breaking from song to speech is a signal of sincerity in American popular music. The song is sentimental in style, although the lyrics are detailed, realistic, and anti-war. The musical style is marked by Burr's trilled r's, the onbeat accents throughout, and the blend of the orchestra, in which, apart from the opening bugle, it's hard to hear individual instruments in the mix. Note how the instruments play the same melody while Burr sings it, decorated a bit here and there, as if to underline the sentiments. A chorus also underlines the sentiments.

But in the 1920s, aptly called the Jazz Age, Ma Rainey, Bessie Smith, and other African-American jazz and blues singers revolutionized the craft of singing popular music. Listen to Ma Rainey and Her Tub Jug Washboard Band Orchestra's 1928 recording of "Hustlin' Blues."

Rainey's singing is closer to the sound and rhythms of conversation than Burr's is; Rainey does not trill her r's, and after starting a phrase, she sings through the downbeat rather than on it. The sound of her band couldn't be much more different from the studio orchestra for "Parade." Instead of sweet violins and a brass section, we hear the roughness of a kazoo, backed with the rhythm of a washboard, and the well-defined sounds of a piano. The jug emits a spitting, buzzing sound as it enters in the second stanza (Figure 4.1). This "poor man's trombone" is a stoneware jug, once used to store molasses, that is a couple of gallons in size; to make a sound, the musician blows air across and into the jug's mouth, as you may have done as a youngster with a soda bottle.

The instruments do not blend; each can be heard and identified easily, and the overall sound is meant to be buzzy and raspy. Rainey's voice carries the same buzzy tone quality; Bessie Smith would take that buzz and play with it, turning it on and off for emphasis—a sound that is familiar now, but was not at the time she was performing. Rainey's lyrics, sung as if to a pimp by a prostitute, are equally unusual for their day and of great interest, but we shall return to them later in this chapter. For now, this introductory activity is meant to acquaint your ear with the revolutionary qualities of African-American music as compared with other contemporary sounds one hundred years ago, for black blues and jazz were not recorded until the 1920s. African-American music performances from the stage and on recordings "helped to carve out new space in which black working people could gather and experience themselves as a community" (Davis 1999:137). Almost immediately after hearing these performances, white musicians were playing and recording it as best they could, bringing it to the general North American public, in a pattern that would repeat itself decade after decade. Blues, gospel, jazz, swing, bop, rhythm and blues, rock 'n' roll, Motown, funk, soul music, disco, rap, hip-hop: African-American musical inventions in the twentieth century transformed popular music—first in North America, then in Europe, and eventually throughout the world.

Figure 4.1
Unidentified jug band, Memphis, late 1930s.
Photographer unknown.

Salient Characteristics of
African-American Musical Styles

- Vocals keep close to the rhythms of ordinary talk
- **Improvisation** in performance
- Timbre: The singing tone quality alternates between buttery smooth and raspy coarse
- **Pitch** is variable around the third, fifth, and seventh degrees of the scale, and the tune is playful—ebbing and eddying like the ocean tide
- Movement: Singers sway freely to the music, dancing it with their bodies
- Leader-chorus social organization of the singing group

Music of Worship

The most formative musical experiences for many African Americans occur in church, where youngsters absorb the essentials of their culture's musical style. Listen now to a **hymn** sung by a black Baptist congregation in Detroit (Active Listening 4.1). It is the first verse of the familiar Christian hymn "Amazing Grace," but the rhythm, melody, and performance style are unfamiliar to most people outside the black church. A deacon leads the hymn, opening it by singing the first line by himself: "Amazing grace how sweet it sound." The congregation then joins him, and very slowly they repeat the words, sliding the melody around each syllable of the text.

ACTIVE LISTENING 4.1
"Amazing Grace"

COUNTER NUMBER	COMMENTARY	LYRICS
0:00	Leader gives out the first line.	Amazing grace how sweet it sound
0:09	Congregation joins leader to repeat first line, to a very slow and elaborate melody, with many melismata.	Amazing grace how sweet, ah
0:45	Leader gives out the second line.	That saved a wretch like me!
0:49	Congregation joins leader to sing second line.	That saved a wretch like me!
1:14	Leader gives out the third line.	I once was lost but now am found,
1:20	Congregation joins leader to sing third line.	I once was lost but now am found,
1:56	Leader gives out the fourth line.	Was blind but now I see.
2:01	Congregation joins leader to sing fourth line.	Was blind but now I see.

Salient Characteristics of
African-American Music of Worship

- Shared, participatory musical experiences for many African Americans, early in their lives and influential later on

- Many musical genres and styles, including gospel music, spirituals, and lined out hymnody

- Musical delivery of prayers and sermons

- Performance activates a powerfully affecting presence for many (on affect, see the performance model in Chapter 1)

Next, the deacon sings the second line by himself: "That saved a wretch like me!"; then the congregation joins him to repeat it, slowly and with **melisma** (see Chapter 3). The same procedure finishes the verse (see Active Listening 4.1).

That one verse is all there is to the performance. The singers do not use hymnbooks; they have memorized the basic tune and the words. Notice that the congregation, singing with the deacon, do not all come in at the same time; some lag behind the others a fraction, singing as they feel it. Not everyone sings exactly the same tune, either. Some ornament the basic tones with more in-between or melismatic tones than others do. The singers improvise their ornamentation as they go along. It is a beautiful and quite intricate **heterophonic** performance. Try singing along; you will probably find it difficult to do. This way of organizing the singing in church, in which a leader sings a line and then repeats it with the congregation, is called **lining out**. Lining out psalms–and, later, hymns–was a standard practice in colonial America. Black slaves and freedmen worshipped with whites and picked up the practice from their example. The influence then became mutual. Today you can still hear lining out in a great many black Baptist churches throughout the United States, particularly in the rural South (Figure 4.2).

This version of "Amazing Grace" has many characteristics typical of African-American music in the United States. The words are sung in English, and they fall into **stanzas** (verses or **strophes**), as most English folk songs do. But the style of the performance is black African.

Suppose we enter the black church where I recorded the first song and observed it firsthand (Figure 4.3). It is a Baptist church with a large sanctuary, seating perhaps fifteen hundred on this Sunday morning. When we hear "Amazing Grace," we have come to the **deacons' devotional**, an early part of the worship service consisting of old-time, congregational hymn singing, scripture reading, and a chanted prayer offered by a deacon while the rest of the congregation hum and moan a wordless hymn in the background. The praying deacon improvises his chanted prayer—the words and tune—which begins as speech and then gradually turns to a chant with a definite tonal center, moving at the close in a regular meter; the congregation punctuates the deacon's phrases with shouts of "Yes," "Now," and so forth.

The deacons lead the devotional from the altar area, and after the devotional is through, the activity shifts to the pulpit, where announcements are made, offerings are taken up, and responsive reading is led. Interspersed are modern, lively **gospel songs**, sung by soloists and the high-spirited youth choir, accompanied by piano and organ. The preacher begins his spontaneous sermon in a speaking voice, but after about fifteen minutes he shifts into a musical chant, all the while improvising and carrying on his message. This style of sermon delivery was at least one hundred and fifty years old at the time of my recording, and nearly fifty years later it can still be heard among black Baptist ministers. The change from speech to chant (or **whooping**, as African Americans traditionally call it) is accompanied by a change from a playful timbre that alternates between clear and buzzy to light and coarse to a rather continuously hoarse timbre. As they did for the praying deacon, the congregation responds to the preacher's phrases with shouts of "Well," "Yes," and so forth, on the tonal center.

The Reverend C. L. Franklin of Detroit (Figure 4.4) spoke to me of the rhythm of his whooped preaching: "It's not something I can beat my foot to. But I can feel it.

Figure 4.2
Abandoned rural black church in Manning, South Carolina, June 1939. *Marion Post Wolcott. Courtesy of the Library of Congress/FSA-OWI Collection.*

Figure 4.3
A young deacon chants an improvised prayer. The microphone connects with the church's public address system. Detroit, Michigan, 1978. *Jeff Todd Titon.*

It's in me." It is also in the members of the congregation who sway back and forth with each phrase. Rev. Franklin's sermons were extraordinarily popular—he toured the nation to preach in the 1950s and 1960s, often with his daughter, Aretha. CDs of his sermons can be found even today on the internet and in the gospel bins in record stores in black communities.

Eventually the sermon closes and an invitational song follows, led by a soloist from the choir. Three or four people heed the invitation and come forward to join the church. A final offering is taken up, the preacher gives the benediction, and the choir comes down from the choir stand, locks arms in the altar area facing the pulpit, and joins the congregation in singing "Amen."

Altogether, song and chant have taken up at least half the running time of the worship service: the old-style singing of the deacons' devotional, the traditional chant of the prayer and sermon, and the modern gospel songs. The music is literally moving; it activates the Holy Spirit, which sends some people into shouts of ecstasy, swoons, shakes, holy dance, and trance (Figure 4.5). If they get so carried away that they are in danger of fainting or injuring themselves, they are restrained by their neighbors until members of the nurses' guild can reach them and administer aid. In this setting, music is an extremely powerful activity—and the church is prepared for its effects.

Figure 4.5

Religious music quickens the Holy Spirit and sends a woman into trance. Detroit, Michigan, 1977. *Jeff Todd Titon.*

Much of the music of black Christian worship in the United States is traditional. We have seen that the lining-out tradition dates from colonial America, and many of the hymns sung have the same vintage. The Negro spiritual developed later, born of the camp-meeting revivals in the late eighteenth and early nineteenth centuries, while gospel songs arose in the twentieth.

Music of Work

A **work song**, as the name suggests, is a song workers sing to help them carry on. It takes their minds off the tiring and monotonous bending, swinging, hauling, driving, carrying, chopping, poling, loading, digging, pulling, cutting, breaking, and lifting (Figure 4.6). A work song also paces the work. If the job requires teamwork, work song rhythms coordinate the movements of the workers (Figure 4.7).

Work songs were widely reported among black slaves in the West Indies in the eighteenth century and in the United States in the nineteenth. The widespread, ancient, and continuing African work song tradition is the most probable source.

Work music is hard to find in the United States today. Where people once sang, machines now whine. But in an earlier period, African Americans sang work songs as they farmed and built the canals, railroads, and highways that became the transportation networks of the growing nation.

After Emancipation, the singing continued whenever black people were engaged in heavy work: clearing and grading the land, laying railroad track, loading barges and poling them along the rivers, building levees against river flooding, felling trees, and hauling nets. This included the inevitable farm work: digging ditches, cutting timber, building fences, plowing, planting, chopping out weeds, and reaping and loading the harvest. The words and tunes of these work songs, or **field hollers**, fit the nature of the work. People working by themselves or at their own pace in a group sang slow songs without a pronounced beat; the singer hummed tunes or fit words in as desired, passing the time.

Salient Characteristics of
African-American Work Songs

- Metrical rhythms pace and coordinate group labor
- Field hollers in free rhythm take the mind off the hard labor
- Sung without instrumental accompaniment except for percussion
- Improvisation in lyrics and melodies

MindTap
LISTEN TO
"Field Holler," performed by Leonard "Baby Doo" Caston, online.

Figure 4.6

Chopping cotton on rented land, near White Plains, Greene County/Georgia, June 1941. *Jack Delano/Courtesy of the Library of Congress/FSA-OSI Collection.*

Figure 4.7

Workers lining track. Alabama, 1956. *Frederic Ramsey, Jr.*

MindTap

◀)) **LISTEN TO**

"Field Holler" performed by Leonard "Baby Doo" Caston, online.

As a farm boy, Leonard "Baby Doo" Caston learned to sing these field hollers by copying the practice of older farmhands. In the background of our recording (Active Listening 4.2) you can hear the sound of a stereo playing in the room where the recording was made. Try singing along with Baby Doo Caston.

In group labor that required teamwork and a steady pace, people sang songs with a pronounced beat, which coordinated their movements. A sweet-sounding voice that is always in tune may be desirable in other situations, but it is not important in the group work song tradition. In some Southern prisons, black inmates

MindTap

🎧 **WATCH** an Active Listening Guide of this selection online.

ACTIVE LISTENING 4.2
Field Holler (Work Song)

COUNTER NUMBER	COMMENTARY	LYRICS
0:00	Caston sings first line, drawing out the length of tones as he wishes.	Hey, one of these mornings, mornings, and it won't be long;
0:10	Second line; like the first and all others in a flexible rhythm without a steady beat. Here, "captain" means boss.	You're gonna look for me, captain, and up the road I'll be gone.
0:17	Caston speaks.	"And this other guy named Curtis used to sing a song, says,"
0:21	Caston sings first line of second verse. Notice the melismata in "-try" of "country."	I'm goin' up the country, baby, and I can't take you.
0:33	Caston sings second line of second verse. A "monkey woman" lacks common sense.	There's nothing up the country that a monkey woman can do.

Additional verses

Hey—captain don't you know my name?
I'm the same old fellow who stole your watch and chain.

I'm going away, baby, to wear you off my mind.
You keep me worried and bothered all the time.

sang work songs. For example, the song "Rosie" was used to regulate the axe blows when workers were felling large trees.

Sometimes as many as ten men circled the tree and chopped, five pulling their axes out just before the other five all struck at once. Axes were swinging through the air at all times, back and forth; the work was dangerous and the timing was crucial. Without work songs, the white and Latino inmates chopped two to a tree. With work songs, the black inmates chopped four, six, eight, or ten to a tree. The work went faster and better, and the singing group felt pride and solidarity in its accomplishment. See Active Listening 4.3.

MindTap·
🔊 **LISTEN TO**
"Rosie," performed by prisoners at the Mississippi State Penitentiary, Parchman, Mississippi, online.

ACTIVE LISTENING 4.3
"Rosie"—Excerpt from First Verse with Call-and-Response

MindTap·
🎧 **WATCH** an Active Listening Guide of this selection online.

COUNTER NUMBER	COMMENTARY	LYRICS
0:01	Axes sound, call (leader).	Be my woman, gal I'll
0:04	Axes sound, response (leader and group).	Be your man.
0:07	Axes sound, call (again).	Be my woman, gal, I'll
0:11	Axes sound, response (again).	Be your man.
Text, "Rosie"		
0:00	Verse 1	Be my woman, gal, I'll be your man. Be my woman, gal, I'll be your man. Be my woman, gal, I'll be your man. Every Sunday's dollar in your hand. In your hand, lordy, in your hand. Every Sunday's dollar in your hand.
0:39	Verse 2	Stick to the promise, gal, that you made me. Stick to the promise, gal, that you made me. Stick to the promise, gal, that you made me. Wasn't going to marry till I go free. I go free, lordy, I go free. Wasn't going to marry till I go free.
1:17	Verse 3	Well, Rosie, oh lord, gal. Ah, Rosie, oh lord, gal.
1:29	Verse 4	When she walks she reels and rocks behind. When she walks she reels and rocks behind. Ain't that enough to worry a convict's mind? Ain't that enough to worry a convict's mind?
1:53	Repeat verse 3	Well, Rosie, oh lord, gal. Ah, Rosie, oh lord, gal.
2:05	Verse 5	Be my woman, gal, I'll be your man. Be my woman, gal, I'll be your man. Be my woman, gal, I'll be your man. Every Sunday's dollar in your hand.
2:29	Repeat verse 3	Well, Rosie, oh lord, gal. Ah, Rosie, oh lord, gal.

In African-American music, whether of work or worship, calls answered by responses point up the social nature of this music. This is not a predictable and pre-determined music. Improvisations in lyrics and melodies, created at the moment of performance, as well as changes in timbre, show the high value African Americans place on innovation, creativity, and play.

Music of Play

As we have seen, the performance of religious songs and work songs in the black tradition includes elements of play. For example, churchgoers admire the beautiful performance of a verbally adept preacher as he plays with the resources of language and gesture, and they clap their approval as a solo singer sustains a climactic pitch or goes through intricately improvised melodic variations with great feeling. Work songs introduce a playful, distancing attitude toward the labor at hand. Like call-and-response, this sort of play with pitch, timbre, and rhythm characterizes both African and African-American music.

Although African-American religious songs and work songs contain elements of play, their main purpose is to aid in worship and work. In contrast, music of play serves primarily as entertainment, performed mainly for pleasure even when its effect is also educational, cathartic, or ecstatic.

Blues

Clearly, the music of play in black America offers a dizzying array of genres. The rest of this chapter focuses on just one African-American music of play: blues. The blues is a music familiar to many, but its very familiarity presents problems. Chief among them is the current emphasis on blues as **roots music** or **Americana**. If blues is the root, then rock is the fruit—or so the story goes in the films and radio programs produced in 2003 (see "Additional Listening" and "Additional Viewing" in the References at the end of the book), which the U.S. Congress declared the "year of the blues." (We will learn more about blues, roots, and Americana music near the end of this chapter.) But blues is a music in and of itself. It is wrapped tightly around the history and experiences of African Americans in the United States and deserves to be understood in this light. Blues is tied intimately to African-American experience and cannot be understood without reference to its historical development within African-American culture.

Salient Characteristics of
Blues

- Both a feeling and a musical genre and form

- Lyrics chiefly about love and mistreatment, often ironic and signifying

- Three-line and quatrain refrain stanzas most common

- Improvisation in early blues gave rise to memorized songs after influence of recordings

- Most adhere to common, 12-bar musical form with a standard chord sequence

- Instrumental accompaniment common; guitar most popular accompanying instrument

continued

A second area of confusion about blues arises over the relationship between blues and jazz. Is blues a part of jazz? Did the stream of blues flow into the river of jazz? That common metaphor is not accurate. Historically, blues and jazz are more like parallel highways with crossroads between them. Blues can be understood as a feeling—"the blues"—as well as a specific musical form. Jazz, which engenders complex and varied feelings, is best thought of as a technique, as a way of forming. Jazz musicians applied their technique to the blues form, as to other musical forms.

Muddy Waters (Figure 4.8), Howlin' Wolf, B. B. King, Albert Collins, John Lee Hooker (see Figure 4.16), and Buddy Guy (see Figure 4.15), who rose to national prominence as blues singers, came from a vital tradition. For decades, the blues music-culture—with its singers, country juke joints, barrelhouses, city rent parties, street singing, bar scenes, nightclubs, lounges, recordings, and record industry—was a significant part of the black music-culture in the United States. In the 1960s, the era of desegregation and the Civil Rights Movement, blues faded in popularity among African Americans while it gained a large and appreciative white audience. Nowadays, the blues music-culture incorporates white as well as black musicians and includes a worldwide audience.

- Acoustic instruments before World War II; mostly electronically amplified instruments after

- Different musical substyles associated with different regions ("Mississippi Delta blues," "Chicago Blues," "East Coast Blues," "Urban Blues," "Downhome Blues")

- Invented by African Americans late in the nineteenth century, was most popular entertainment music among African Americans in the first half of the twentieth century

- Became part of the folk music revival in the second half of the twentieth century; has undergone periodic revivals since, with festivals, recordings, celebrity musicians, tours, and so on

- Currently known and played throughout the world; in North America, positioned and marketed today as "roots music"

Blues and the Truth

The best entry into the blues is through the words of the songs. It is hard to talk at length about words in songs, and harder still to talk about music. As Charles Seeger, one of the founders of the Society of Ethnomusicology, reminds us, it would be more logical to "music" about music than to talk about it (Seeger 1977:16). And in the blues music-culture, when the setting is informal, that is just what happens when one singer responds to another by singing verses of his or her own. Another common response to blues is dancing. The most common response to blues music is a feeling in the gut, dancing to the beat, nodding assent, a vocalized "that's right, you got it, that's the truth"—not unlike the black Christian's response to a sermon or a gospel song. A good, "deep" blues song leaves you feeling that you have heard the truth in a way that leaves little more to be said.

We begin by taking an extended look at a single blues performance, "Poor Boy Blues," by the Lazy Bill Lucas Blues Trio. Bill Lucas (Figure 4.9) is the vocalist; he accompanies himself on electric guitar. He is joined by two other musicians, one on acoustic guitar and the other on drums.

Figure 4.8
Muddy Waters (McKinley Morganfield) relaxes between songs at the Ann Arbor Blues Festival, 1969. *Jeff Todd Titon.*

Response to the Lyrics of "Poor Boy Blues"

In Active Listening 4.4, pay particular attention to the lyrics. I did not choose "Poor Boy Blues" because the lyrics are outstanding; they are typical. For me, some of it is good, some not; some of it works, some does not. "I'm just a poor boy; people, I can't even write my name" produces an automatic response of sympathy for the poor boy, but it is not a deep response. I am sorry for the poor boy's illiteracy, but hey, everyone has problems. When the line repeats, I am anxious to hear how the stanza will close. "Every letter in the alphabet to me they look the same" brings to my mind's eye a picture of a strange alphabet in which all letters look alike or, rather, in which the differences in their shape have no meaning. The image is clear—it works, and it involves me. This poor boy may be illiterate, but he is perceptive. And not only does the image itself succeed, but the delay of the most important word in the line, "same," until the end, and the impact of its rhyme with "name" convinces me I am hearing the truth.

Blues singer Eddie "Son" House (Figure 4.10) told me about how he put his blues stanzas together: "I had enough sense to try to make 'em, rhyme 'em so they'd have hits to 'em with a meaning, some sense to 'em, you know" (Titon 1994:47). The inevitable rightness of the rhyme—you expect it and it rewards you—hits harder than an unrhymed close, particularly because the end rhyme always falls, in blues, on an accented syllable.

I do not respond to "Mother died when I was a baby"; I resist a statement that sounds sentimental. This is not because I think of myself as some kind of tough guy, but because I want the sentiment to be earned. I much prefer the statement at the close of the line: "father I never seen." The effect is in the contrast between the mother who died and the father who might as well be dead. In the image of the father who has never been seen is the mystery of not knowing one's parents. It is not just missing love; for all we know the poor boy was raised by loving relatives. But a child takes after parents, inherits the biology, so to speak; without knowing your parents you do not fully know yourself. That is the real terror of the poor boy's life. "When I think how dumb I am, you know it makes me want to scream" is a cliché; okay, scream. The rhyme is forced. Nor do I respond to the third stanza when I hear it; but when I think about it, it seems curious that the poor boy says he began to catch hell from age eleven or twelve. I guess that he was catching it all along but did not fully realize

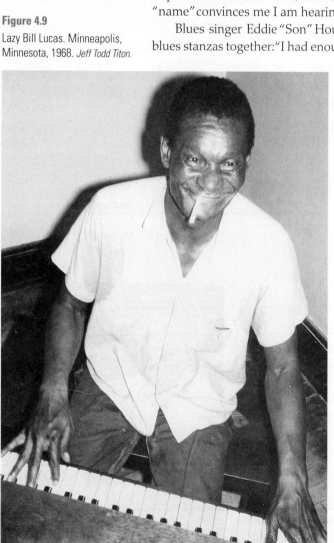

Figure 4.9

Lazy Bill Lucas. Minneapolis, Minnesota, 1968. *Jeff Todd Titon.*

ACTIVE LISTENING 4.4
"Poor Boy Blues"

MindTap°

🎧 **WATCH** an Active Listening Guide of this selection online.

COUNTER NUMBER	COMMENTARY	LYRICS
0:00	Instrumental introduction led by guitar.	
0:13	Lucas sings verse 1. Drums play mostly long-short figures; guitar plays mostly Da-da-da, Da-da-da figures when Lucas is silent between lines.	I'm just a poor boy; people, I can't even write my name. I'm just a poor boy; people, I can't even write my name. Every letter in the alphabet to me they look the same.
0:50	Lucas sings verse 2. Accompaniment as for verse 1.	Mother died when I was a baby; father I never seen. Mother died when I was a baby; father I never seen. When I think how dumb I am, you know it makes me want to scream.
1:26	Lucas sings verse 3. Interplay of the two guitars when Lucas is silent between lines.	Ever since I was the age around eleven or twelve, Ever since I was the age around eleven or twelve, I just been a poor boy; ain't caught nothing but hell.
1:59	Lucas speaks, signaling an instrumental break. "Lay your racket" means "play your instrument."	"Lay your racket, boy, lay your racket."
2:03	Instrumental break the length of one verse. Da-da-da figures mostly throughout on guitar.	"Have mercy."
2:36	Lucas sings verse 4.	When I was a child Santa Claus never left one toy. When I was a child Santa Claus never left one toy. If you have any mercy, please have mercy on poor boy.

Used with permission of William Lucas.

it until then. That is a nice point, but a little too subtle to register during a performance. I would have to sing it several times myself to appreciate that aspect of it.

The final stanza takes great risk with sentimentality, calling up Christmas memories, but it succeeds by a matter-of-fact tone: "When I was a child Santa Claus never left one toy" dispels the scene's stickiness. Santa Claus never left a toy for anyone, but a child who believes in Santa can enjoy an innocent world where presents reward good little boys and girls. If he could not believe in Santa, I wonder if he ever had any part of the innocent happiness people seem to need early, and in large doses, if they are going to live creative lives. Or it could have been the other way around: He believed in Santa, but Santa, never bringing him a toy, simply did not believe in him.

The song now leads up to its final line, a plea for mercy. "You" are addressed directly: If you have any mercy, show it to the poor boy. Will you? If you heard this from a blind street singer, would you put some coins in his cup? Would you be more likely to show mercy to the poor boy than to someone down on his luck who just walks up and asks for spare change? The song will strike some people as sentimental, calling up an easy emotion that is just as quickly forgotten as it is evoked. T. S. Eliot, in an essay still influential nearly one hundred years after he wrote it, argued that in a work of literature any powerful emotion must have an "objective correlative"; that is, the work itself must demonstrate that there is good reason for the emotion (Eliot [1920] 1964). Has "Poor Boy Blues" given you good reason for mercy? Have you been told the truth, or been played for a sucker?

Figure 4.10
Eddie "Son" House.
Minneapolis, Minnesota, 1971.
Jeff Todd Titon.

Autobiography and the Blues

We have been considering the words in a broad cultural context. Considering the effect of "Poor Boy Blues" on a general listener can take us only so far. What do the words mean to someone in the blues music-culture? What did they mean to Lazy Bill Lucas? Does the "I" in the "Poor Boy Blues" represent Lucas? What, in short, is the relationship between the song and the singer?

The blues singer's image as wandering minstrel, blind bard, and untutored genius is idealized, but, according to Samuel Charters, "There is no more romantic figure in popular music than the bluesman, with everything the term involves. And it isn't a false romanticism" (1977:112). The result is that most books on blues are organized biographically. Some writers have gone so far as to derive the facts of an otherwise obscure blues singer's life and personality from the lyrics of his or her recorded songs. On the other hand, published life stories of blues singers completely in their own words are rare (see, for example, Brunoghe 1964; Titon 1974b; Alyn 1993). If we read these first-person life stories properly, we can understand them to be far more reliable expressions of the blues singer's own personality than song lyrics are, because the lyrics are often borrowed from tradition. Nonetheless, most people assume that the lyrics of a blues song do speak for the singer. Paul Oliver wrote, for example, "One of the characteristics of the blues is that it is highly personalized—blues singers nearly always sing about themselves" (Oliver 1998:33).

If that is true, then "Poor Boy Blues" should reflect the life and thoughts of Lazy Bill Lucas.

I was a close friend of Bill Lucas's for six years, playing guitar in his blues band for two of them. During the course of our friendship I recorded his recollections of his life, edited and excerpted for publication first in *Blues Unlimited* (Titon 1969), a British blues research journal, and later in the accompanying notes to his first American LP (Titon 1974a). Let us look, then, at parts of Lucas's life history as he told it to me, and see if "Poor Boy Blues" is autobiographical.

The Life History of Bill Lucas, Blues Singer

I was born in Wynne, Arkansas, on May 29, 1918. I never heard my mother say the exact time I was born: she was so upset at the time I guess she wouldn't remember. I have two sisters and three brothers; I was third from my baby sister, the third youngest.

Ever since I can remember, I had trouble with my eyesight. Doctors tell me it's the nerves. I can see shapes, I can tell colors, and I know light and dark, but it's hard to focus, and no glasses can help me. An operation might cure it, but there's a chance it could leave me completely blind, and I don't want to take that gamble.

My father was a farmer out in the country from Wynne. He was a share-cropper, farming on the halvers. In 1922, we moved to Short Bend, Arkansas, but my father wanted to get where there were better living conditions. A lot of his neighbors and friends had come up to Missouri and told him how good it was up there.

My family moved to Advance, Missouri, in 1924. We moved by night but that doesn't mean we had to slip away. They loaded all our stuff in a wagon and we caught the ten o'clock train. That was my first train ride; I loved the train then. Advance was about twenty-five miles west of the river; it wasn't on the highway, just on the railroad. It was a little town of five hundred. We never did go to town much except on Saturdays. In the summertime we'd go in about every week to carry our vegetables to sell in a wagon: watermelons and cabbage and stuff.

My father wanted to own his own farm, but that was impossible. That was a dream. He didn't have enough money to buy it and there weren't any loans like there are nowadays. We owned cattle, we owned pigs. We had about thirteen milk cows, and we had leghorn chickens that gave us bushels of eggs. We were better off than our neighbors because we would sometimes swap our eggs for something we didn't have.

There weren't many guitars around, but in 1930 my daddy got me a guitar. I remember so well, just like it was yesterday, he traded a pig for it. Our neighbors had some boys that played guitar, but they never did take pains and show me how to do it. I would just watch 'em and listen. I learned from sounds. And after they were gone, then I would try to make the guitar sound like I heard them make it sound. After I got it and come progressing on it, a tune or two here or there, my dad and mama both decided that would be a good way for me to make my living.

My father got me a piano in 1932 for a Christmas present. That was the happiest Christmas I ever had. He didn't trade pigs for that; he paid money for it. Got it at our neighborhood drugstore. Well, at the time I knew how to

Halvers: A sharecropping arrangement in which the landlord supplied the tenant with a shack, tools, seed, work animals, feed, fuel wood, and half the fertilizer in exchange for half the tenant's crop and labor.

play organ, one of those pump organs; so it didn't take me long to learn how to bang out a few tunes on the piano.

I didn't know what chords I was making. We got a little scale book that would go behind the keyboard of the piano and tell you all the chords. It was a beginner's book, in big letters. I could see that. You know, a beginner's book is in big letters. And I wanted to learn music, but after I got that far, well, the rest of the music books were so small that I couldn't see the print. And that's why I didn't learn to read music.

I did learn to read the alphabet at home. My parents taught me, and so did the other kids. I used to go to school, but it was just to be with the other kids, and sometimes the kids would teach me. I was just apt; I could pick things up. I had a lot of mother-wit.

So I bumped around on the piano until 1936, when we left the country and came to Cape Girardeau, Missouri. That was when I started playing the guitar on street corners. My dad had day work; that was the idea of him moving to the city, trying to better his living conditions. But we had to go back to Commerce, Missouri. My dad couldn't make it in Cape Girardeau so we went to Commerce.

At that time I didn't know too much about blues. We had a radio station down there but they all played big band stuff and country and western music. But we didn't call it country and western music back then; we called it hillbilly music. Well, hillbilly music was popular there and so I played hillbilly music on the guitar and sang songs like "She'll Be Coming 'round the Mountain" and "It Ain't Gonna Rain No More" and "Wabash Cannonball." The only time I heard any blues was when we'd go to restaurants where a jukebox was and they'd have blues records. And my daddy had a windup phonograph, and we had a few blues records at home by Peetie Wheatstraw and Scrapper Blackwell and Curtis Jones—the old pieces, you know. So I learned a little bit about blues pieces off the records I'd hear around home.

At that time I didn't have any knowledge of music. I liked any of it. I even liked those hillbilly songs. And when I heard the blues I liked the blues, but I just liked the music, period. And when I played out on street corners, I'd be playing for white folks mostly, and that was the music they seemed to like better, the hillbilly music. So I played it because I'd been listening to it all the time on the radio and so it wasn't very hard for me to play. The blues didn't strike me until I heard Big Bill Broonzy; that's when I wanted to play blues guitar like him.

We lost our mother in 1939. We buried her in Commerce, and we left Commerce after she died. My dad, he went to St. Louis in 1940, still trying to find better living conditions. Later that year he brought me to St. Louis, and that's where I met Big Joe Williams. At that time he wasn't playing in bars or taverns; he was just playing on the street. So he let me join him, and I counted it an honor to be playing with Big Joe Williams because I had heard his blues records while I was still down South. And so we played blues in the street.

But I didn't stay in St. Louis long. My dad and I came to Chicago the day after New Year's in 1941. Sonny Boy Williamson was the first musician I met with up there. I met him over on Maxwell Street, where they had all their merchandise out on the street, and you could buy anything you wanted on a Sunday, just like you could on a Monday. They had groceries, clothes,

Sonny Boy Williamson:
Harmonica player John Lee Williamson (d. 1948).

hardware, appliances, right out on the street, where people could come to look for bargains. That was a good place to play until the cops made us cut it out.

I played a lot with Sonny Boy. We were playing one-nighters in taverns and parties. Sonny Boy would book himself, and I went around with him. There wasn't much money in it; Sonny Boy paid my expenses and a place to stay with his friends. He was known all up around there. I didn't have a name at the time. But I had sense enough to play in time and change chords when he changed; it wasn't but three changes anyhow. We didn't play nothing but the funky blues. He just needed somebody to keep time, back him up on guitar.

Big Bill Broonzy was my idol for guitar, and I'd go sit in on his shows. He'd let me play on the stand between times; I'd play his same songs. Bill knew I couldn't do it as well as he did, so he wasn't mad. In fact he appreciated me for liking his style. I also liked T-Bone Walker (see Figure 4.11), but he made so many chord changes! I was unfortunate to learn changes; I never did know but three changes on the guitar.

I quit playing that hillbilly music when I left St. Louis. In St. Louis I was getting on the blues right smart after I met up with Big Joe Williams. But white folks in Chicago or here in Minneapolis don't like hillbilly music. They tell you right away. "What you think I am? A hillbilly?"

I started in my professional career in 1946, when I joined the union. We all joined the union together, me and Willie Mabon and Earl Dranes, two guitars and a piano. We took our first job in 1946 on December 20, in the Tuxedo Lounge, 3119 Indiana, in Chicago. They paid union scale, but scale wasn't much then. The leader didn't get but twelve dollars a night, the sidemen ten dollars. We worked from 9 P.M. until 4 A.M. It was a real nice club. We had a two-week engagement there, and I thought it was real good money. But then we were kicked back out on the street.

"I didn't have a name": He means that the name Bill Lucas was unknown to the blues audiences.

Figure 4.11
Action at the Ann Arbor Blues Festival, 1969, which took place on the same weekend as the legendary rock festival in Woodstock, New York. Big Mama Thornton sings while T-Bone Walker plays guitar.
Jeff Todd Titon

Little Walter: Walter Jacobs, the most imitated blues harmonica player after World War II.

Little Walter and I used to play along with Johnny Young at a place called the Purple Cat—1947. That's where he gave me the name "Lazy." We'd been there so long Little Walter thought I should go up and turn on the amps, but I never did go up and do that thing, so that's why he started calling me "Lazy Bill," and the name stuck.

In 1948, I started in playing with Homesick James, and sometimes also with Little Hudson. I switched to playing piano in 1950 because they had more guitar players than piano players. But of course I'd been playing piano all along—just not professionally, that's all. Little Hudson needed a piano player for his Red Devils trio. Our first job was at a place called the Plantation, on Thirty-first Street, on the south side of Chicago.

I don't know where he got the idea of the name from, but the drummer had a red devil with pitchforks on the head of his bass drum. And he played in church, too! Would you believe they had to cover up the head of the drum with newspapers? He'd cover the devil up when he'd go to church.

I had a trio, Lazy Bill and the Blue Rhythm, for about three or four months in 1954 [Figure 4.12]. We were supposed to do four records a year for Chance, but Art Sheridan went out of business and we never heard about it again. We did one record ["She Got Me Walkin'," Active Listening 4.5].

Well, I didn't keep my group together long. You know it's kind of hard on a small musician to keep a group together in Chicago very long because they run out of work, and when they don't get work to do, they get with other guys. And there were so many musicians in Chicago that some of 'em were underbidding one another. They'd take a job what I was getting twelve dollars for, they'd take it for eight dollars.

Figure 4.12
Lazy Bill and His Blue Rhythm, studio photo. Chicago, Illinois, 1954. From left to right: Lazy Bill Lucas, James Bannister, "Miss HiFi," and Jo Jo Williams.
Courtesy of Jo Jo Williams.

I was doing anything, working with anybody, just so I could make a dime. On a record session, any engagement at all. For a while I was working with a disc jockey on a radio station. He was broadcasting from a dry cleaners and he wanted live music on his broadcast. I did it for the publicity; I didn't get any money for that. Work got so far apart. Every time I'd run out of an engagement, it would be a long time before another one came through. And so Mojo and Jo Jo, they had come up here to Minneapolis. They had been working at the Key Club, and they decided they needed a piano player. I wasn't doing anything in Chicago; I was glad to come up here. I had no idea I was going to stay up here, but I ended up here with a houseful of furniture.

Mojo and Jo Jo: George "Mojo" Buford, harmonica player, and Joseph "Jo Jo" Williams, bass player.

©1974 by William Lucas and Jeff Todd Titon. (A fuller version accompanies Titon 1974a.)

Lazy Bill Lucas and "Poor Boy Blues"

Bill Lucas's account of his life ends in Minneapolis in 1964. The following year I began my graduate studies at the University of Minnesota and met him at a university concert. By that time he had two audiences: the black people on the North Side of the city who still liked the blues, and the white people in the university community. The 1960s was the period of the first so-called **blues revival** (Groom 1971), during which thousands of blues records from the past four decades were reissued on LPs, dozens of older singers believed dead were "rediscovered" and recorded, and hundreds of younger singers, Bill Lucas among them, found new audiences at university concerts and coffeehouses and festivals. The revival, which attracted a predominantly young, white audience, peaked in the great 1969 and 1970 **Ann Arbor (Michigan) Blues Festivals**, where the best of three generations of blues singers and blues bands performed for the more than ten thousand fans who had trav-

Figure 4.13
Lazy Bill Lucas in his apartment. Minneapolis, Minnesota, 1971. *Jeff Todd Titon.*

eled thousands of miles to pitch their tents and attend these three-day events. Bill Lucas was a featured performer at the 1970 festival. For his appearance he received $400 plus expenses, the most money he ever made for a single job in his musical career.

In the 1960s and 1970s, Bill Lucas could not support himself entirely from his musical earnings. A monthly check (roughly a hundred times the minimum hourly wage) from government welfare for the blind supplemented his income in Minneapolis (Figure 4.13). Most of Minneapolis's black community preferred soul and disco music to blues then, while others liked jazz or classical music. Nor was there sufficient work in front of the university folk music audience for Bill. He sang in clubs, in bars, and at concerts, but the work was not steady. When I was in his band (1969–1971), our most dependable job was a six-month engagement for two nights each week in the "Grotto Room" of a pizza restaurant close to the university. Classified by the musicians' union as a low-level operation, it paid the minimum union scale for an evening's work from 9:00 P.M. to 1:00 A.M.: $23 for Bill, $18 for sidemen. On December 11, 1982, Bill Lucas died. A benefit concert to pay his funeral expenses raised nearly $2,000. Subsequently, he was memorialized by a weekly blues radio show in Minneapolis bearing his name, while in 2003 the Greater Twin Cities Blues Music Society presented a concert and conference entitled "Remembering Lazy Bill Lucas."

Lucas's life history not only gives facts about his life but also expresses an attitude toward it. We can compare both with the words of "Poor Boy Blues" to see whether the song speaks personally for Bill Lucas. Some of the facts of the poor boy's life correspond with Lucas's, but others do not. I asked him whether the line about all the letters in the alphabet looking the same held any special meaning for him, and he said it did. Unless letters or numbers were printed very large and thick, he could not make them out. On the other hand, unlike the poor boy in the song who never saw his father, Lucas and his father were very close. Moreover, his Christmases were happy, and one year he received a piano. What about the attitudes expressed in the song and in the life history? Neither show self-pity. Bill did not have an illustrious career as a blues singer; he scuffled during hard times and took almost any job that was available. Yet he was proud of his accomplishments. "I just sing the funky blues," he said, "and people either like it or they don't."

"Poor Boy Blues" cannot therefore be understood to speak directly for Bill Lucas's personal experience, but it does speak generally for it, as it speaks for tens of thousands of people who have been forced by circumstances into hard times. Thus, in their broad cultural reach, the words of blues songs tell the truth.

Learning the Blues

One question that bears on the relation between Lazy Bill Lucas and "Poor Boy Blues" is the authorship of the song. In fact, Lucas did not compose it; St. Louis Jimmy Oden first put it together and later recorded it in 1942. Lucas learned the song from the record. Learning someone else's song does not, of course, rule out the possibility that the song speaks for the new singer, for he or she may be attracted to it precisely because the lyrics suit his or her experiences and feelings.

In the African-American music-culture, almost all blues singers learn songs by imitation, whether in person or from records. There are no formal lessons. In his life history, Lucas tells how he listened to neighbors play guitar and how he tried to make his guitar sound like theirs did. After he developed a rudimentary playing technique, he could fit accompaniments behind new songs that he learned from others or made up himself.

Listen once again to "Poor Boy Blues" and concentrate now on the instrumental accompaniment. The guitarists and drummer in "Poor Boy Blues" keep a triple rhythm behind Lucas's singing. When Lucas pauses, the guitar responds with a sequence of single-note triplets. This triplet rhythm is a common way of dividing the beat in slow blues songs. Next, listen to the rhythm of Lucas's vocal and try to feel both rhythms, vocal and accompaniment, at the same time. You might find this difficult, because Lucas seldom sings squarely on the beat. Lucas is not having a hard time finding the beat; on the contrary, he deliberately avoids it.

The musical brilliance of "Poor Boy Blues" rests on the difference between vocal and instrumental rhythms. Accents contrast; at times each part has its own meter.

While the accompanying instruments stay in triple meter, Lucas sings in alternating duple and triple. We hear Lucas initiate each vocal phrase in triple meter, then quickly shift to duple, hurrying his phrasing in imitation of speech rhythm.

In Chapter 3, we saw that two-against-three **polymeter** characterizes black African music. Here we see a deep connection between African and African-American music: rhythmic complexity and polymeter. But our example from the blues does not reflect continuous polymeter, as in Africa. Rather, blues music (and jazz and reggae) shifts into and out of polymeter, playfully teasing the boundary. When these shifts occur rapidly, the boundary between single meter and polymeter breaks down. The result is a new sense of time: the graceful forward propulsion we hear as "swing" that makes us feel like moving our whole body in response.

The Blues Scale

Lucas sings "Poor Boy Blues" in a musical scale I have called the **blues scale** (Titon 1971). This scale is found in blues, jazz, spirituals, gospel songs, and other black American music. An original African-American invention, the blues scale also is the most important scale in rock music. It differs significantly from the usual Western diatonic major and minor scales, such as the major scale illustrated in Chapter 1 ("Joy to the World"). The blues scale can be thought of as another example of African-American "playing," this time playing with the pitch on a few of the tones in the major scale. Sing "Joy to the World" again now, pausing on "to" and "Lord":

Joy to the world, the Lord has come.

8 7 6 5 4 3 2 1

For convenience, we will number each of these tones as above. Each number corresponds to what is called a "degree" of the scale. The tones that you paused on, 7 and 3, indicate the regions for the "blue notes," the ones that the blues singer most often plays with: sometimes sounding them right where you sang them, sometimes a little below, sometimes sliding around them about the distance between the tones given off by a white and black key next to each other on the piano. To hear a singer use the blues scale, listen again to Baby Doo Caston's "Field Holler." The first time he sings "morn-ings," notice how he slides down from the initial pitch of "-ings" to a blue note below, while holding the same syllable. The starting pitch of "-ings" is like "Joy" (8) in "Joy to the World," but the ending pitch is a little below "to" (7) yet not quite down to "the" (6). For an even more dramatic example, listen to Baby Doo sing "mornings" the second time (right after the first). Here he slides from the initial pitch on "morn" (4) down through several pitches, going through the blue note around "Lord" (3) in the major scale of "Joy to the World," until he reaches the final pitch (1) on "-ings," comparable to "come" in the Christmas carol. Now listen again to "Poor Boy Blues" and see if you can hear the blue notes.

Composing the Blues

In addition to learning blues songs from other singers and from records, blues singers also make up their own songs. Sometimes they think out a song in advance; sometimes they improvise it during performance. Often a performance embodies both planning and improvisation. The blues song's first composition unit is the line. If you sing the blues most of your life, blues lines may run through your mind like proverbs, which many indeed are: for instance, "You never miss your water till your well runs dry." A male singer might rhyme it with a line like, "Never miss your woman till she say good-bye." (A female singer's rhyme: "Never miss your good man till he say good-bye.") The singer has just composed his stanza:

> You never miss your water till your well runs dry,
> No, you never miss your water till your well runs dry,
> I never missed my baby till she said good-bye.

A traditional blues singer rarely composes a blues song in a single sitting. Instead, lines and stanzas accumulate over a period of time, and whether written down, memorized, or both, they are recalled and configured at the moment of performance. As we have seen, the stanzas may or may not speak directly for the personal experience of the singer. St. Louis Jimmy, the author of "Poor Boy Blues," said this about another of his songs, "Goin' Down Slow":

> My blues came mostly from women....."Goin' Down Slow" started from a girl, in St. Louis—it wasn't me—I've never been sick a day in my life, but I seen her in the condition she was in—pregnant, tryin' to lose a kid, see. And she looked like she was goin' down slow. And I made that remark to my sister and it came in my mind and I started to writin' it.... I looked at other people's troubles and I writes from that, and I writes from my own troubles. (Oliver 1965:101–2)

Songs that blues singers memorize usually stick to one idea or event. A memorized song, Lucas's "Poor Boy Blues" has four stanzas on the circumstances leading to the poor boy's cry for mercy. In contrast, the words in an improvised song seldom show the unity of time, circumstances, or feeling evident in a memorized song. After all, unless you have had lots of practice, it is hard enough to improvise rhymed stanzas, let alone keep to a single subject (compare McLeod and Herndon 1981:59 on improvised Maltese song duels). So an improvising singer usually throws in some memorized, traditional stanzas along with stanzas he or she puts together on the spot.

A Blues Song in the Making

Today, few blues songs are improvised in performance. Most are memorized beforehand. This memorization reflects a later trend in the history of the blues and results from the impact of commercial blues records, which began in the 1920s, on singers born after about 1910. Singers who wanted to make records studied them and got the idea that a song ought to last about three minutes (the length of a 78-rpm record) and stick to one theme—as most recorded blues songs did. So they composed and memorized their songs, and they memorized other singers' songs. Of course, they could not avoid learning traditional stanzas and building a mental storehouse of them, but more and more they sang from memory instead of improvising. The influence of recordings is so overpowering that singers seldom change lyrics when learning other people's songs. Further, like rock bands trying to "cover" hit records, they copy the instruments, too. In short, most blues singers today think a blues song should have a fixed, not a variable, text.

In 1954, Art Sheridan, the owner of Chicago-based Chance Records, asked Lazy Bill Lucas to make a record. During the early 1950s, Lucas had played piano as a sideman on several of Homesick James Williamson's recordings, and he was a member of the Blues Rockers, a group with the minor recording hits "Calling All Cows" and "Johnny Mae." For his own session as leader, Lucas was billed as "Lazy Bill and His Blue Rhythm." He chose an original song, "She Got Me Walkin'." Lucas composed the lyrics in advance and memorized them for the recording session.

The first thing you may notice in "She Got Me Walkin'" is that the stanza form differs from that of "Poor Boy Blues." In that song, Bill Lucas sang a line, then more or less repeated it, and closed the stanza with a rhyming punch line. Most blues stanzas fall into this three-line pattern, particularly traditional stanzas. But some, like stanzas 2 and 3 of "She Got Me Walkin'," fall into a different line pattern consisting of a quatrain (four lines rhymed abcb) and a rhymed, two-line refrain that follows to close out each stanza (Active Listening 4.5). You can easily hear the contrast between the **three-line stanza** and the **quatrain-refrain stanza**. The quatrain fits four short bursts into the first four measures (bars) of the twelve-bar blues,

🎵 **LISTEN TO**

"She Got Me Walkin'," performed by Lazy Bill and His Blue Rhythm, from the album *Street Walking Blues, Vol. 1*, online.

ACTIVE LISTENING 4.5
"She Got Me Walkin'"

COUNTER NUMBER	COMMENTARY	LYRICS
0:00	Instrumental introduction.	
0:14	Lucas sings verse 1. Interplay among all accompanying instruments. Instrumental response to the vocal "calls" (instruments respond when Lucas pauses between phrases and lines).	My baby got me walkin' all up and down the street. My baby got me walkin' all up and down the street. She left me for another man 'cause she wanted to be free.
0:56	Lucas sings quatrain starting verse 2.	My baby told me one day, And I laughed and thought it was a joke; She said I'm going to leave you, You don't move me no more.
1:09	Refrain, verse 2.	She got me walkin' all up and down the street; She left me for another man 'cause she wanted to be free.
1:35	Lucas speaks, signaling an instrumental break.	"Play it for me, boy."
1:37	Instrumental break.	
2:17	Quatrain starting verse 3. "Snook" is James "Snooky" Prior.	I don't want to see Snook, Not even Homesick James; The way my baby left me, I really believe he's to blame.
2:30	Refrain, verse 3.	She got me walkin' all up and down the street; She left me for another man 'cause she wanted to be free.

Words and music by William Lucas. Used by permission.

while the refrain fits into the last eight bars. The quatrain-refrain pattern became popular after World War II. It usually offers vignettes in the quatrain to prove the truth of the repeated refrain. Because any stanza form is by nature preset, it acts as a mold into which the improvising singer pours his or her words. Of course, not just any words will do, because the refrain has to repeat, lines must rhyme, and the whole thing has to make sense.

Lucas told me that he thought getting the names of some of his musician friends into "She Got Me Walkin'" would make the song more popular. The uninitiated listener would find the nicknames a little mysterious and might be intrigued. "Snook" was the harmonica player Snooky Pryor. James Williamson had recorded under the name "Homesick James" and was well known to the people who frequented the Chicago bars and clubs to hear blues. When I asked Lucas whether the lyrics were based on a true story, he replied, "More or less." The "she" of the song turns out to be none other than Johnny Mae, whom Bill had sung about for The Blues Rockers a few months earlier. Johnny Mae was Homesick James's girlfriend.

As Lucas's lyrics show, during the years following World War II blues musicians in Chicago formed a social as well as a musical community. They kept each other company, played on each other's recordings, substituted for one another at various club dates, and both competed with and supported one another in the music business and social world. These relationships persisted for years. For example, Muddy Waters and Howlin' Wolf were rivals. Even as late as 1970, at the Ann Arbor Blues Festival, this rivalry was evident. Waters was scheduled to come onstage after Wolf's set, but Wolf prolonged the set well beyond the agreed-on ending time in a bid to steal time from Waters (Gordon 2002:215–16; Segrest and Hoffman 2004:261–62).

Social Context and the Meaning of the Blues

Blues is best understood as both a musical form and a feeling. The blues songs we have examined—"Poor Boy Blues" and "She Got Me Walkin'"—are typical and can bring us toward a structural definition of blues as a song form. Textually, blues songs consist of a series of rhymed three-line or quatrain-refrain stanzas, each sung to more or less the same tune. Blues tunes usually consist of twelve-measure (bar) strophes, and they employ a special scale, the blues scale. They are rhythmically complex, employing syncopation and, at times, differing rhythms between singing and instruments. Many other attributes of blues songs—melodic shape, for instance, or the typical, raspy timbre—are beyond the scope of this introduction.

Although the emotional aspects of blues are embodied in such musical aspects as the singer's delivery and the way the musicians "play around" with the blues scale and rhythmic syncopation, the most direct expression of blues feeling comes from the lyrics. Most blues lyrics are about lovers, and they fall into a pattern arising from black American life. The blues grew and developed when most African Americans lived as sharecroppers on Southern cotton farms, subject to segregation, disenfranchisement, Jim Crow laws, lynch laws, and violence, from late in the nineteenth century until just before World War II, when farm mechanization began to displace black workers and factory work at high wages in the Northern cities attracted them (Gussow 2002:5–6). Down home, young men and women did not marry early; they were needed on the farm. If a young woman became pregnant, she had her baby and brought the child into the household with her parents. She did not lose status in the community, and later she often married the father of her child. When a woman did marry young, her partner usually was middle-aged and needed a woman to work and care for his children from a prior marriage. It was good to have plenty of children; when they came of age to work, more hands could go into the cotton and corn fields. Adoption was common; when families broke up, children were farmed out among relatives.

Sociologists and anthropologists, some of them black (such as Charles Johnson), studied this sharecropping culture in the 1920s and 1930s. Interested in patterns of love, marriage, and divorce, the fieldworkers found that partners separated because one could not live with the other's laziness, violence, or adultery. These reasons added up to **mistreatment**, the very word they used. A woman was reported as saying her current lover was "nice all right, but I ain't thinking about marrying. Soon as you marry a man he starts mistreating you, and I ain't going to be mistreated no more" (Johnson [1934] 1966:83). Blues songs reflected these attitudes; mistreatment was the most common subject. Once the subject was established, people began to expect mistreatment as the appropriate subject for blues songs, and although many blues songs were composed about other subjects, the majority had (and still have) to do with lovers and mistreatment. After World War II, the sharecropping culture was less important; the action now took place in the cities where most black people had gone: Atlanta, New York, Washington, Detroit, Memphis, St. Louis, Chicago, Dallas, Houston, Los Angeles, Oakland. But black family patterns persisted among the lower classes in the urban ghettos, and so did the blues.

Blues lyrics about mistreatment fall into a pattern. The singer casts himself or herself in the role of mistreated victim, introduces an antagonist (usually a mistreating lover), provides incidents that detail the circumstances of the mistreatment, and draws up a bill of indictment. Then, with the listener's tacit approval, the victim becomes the judge, and the drama turns on the verdict: Will he or she accept the mistreatment, try to reform the mistreater, or leave? Resigned acceptance and attempted reform resolve a minority of blues songs. Most often the victim, declaring independence, steps out of the victim's role with an ironic parting shot and leaves.

Blues music helps lovers understand each other. Because the themes are traditional and shared by the community, blues songs also give listeners community approval for separation in response to mistreatment. The listener who recognizes his or her situation in the lyrics of a blues song receives a good definition of that situation and a possible response to it. At a Saturday night party, or at home alone, a mistreated lover finds consolation in the blues (Figure 4.14).

The Blues Yesterday

It is true that African Americans invented blues, and it is also true that early on people outside the black communities were attracted to it. The white folklorist Howard Odum, for example, collected blues songs in the South prior to 1910. The African-American composer W. C. Handy popularized blues in the 1910s with songs such as "St. Louis Blues," but white singers such as Sophie Tucker recorded blues songs before African-American singers were permitted to do so. African-American blues queens such as Ma Rainey and Bessie Smith made blues the most popular African-American music in the 1920s, attracting a small, white audience as well

Figure 4.14
Dancing at a juke joint.
Alabama, 1957.
Frederic Ramsey, Jr.

as a large, black one. The black poet Sterling Brown told me about an encounter
he had with Rainey when he was a college student. Admirers of her music, Brown
and a friend went to see her stage show; afterward, they went backstage to pay
their respects. Alone with the young men, Rainey was unusually affectionate, which
frightened Brown and his friend into making a hasty exit, he said. Rainey's lyrics
were equally uninhibited: she sang about someone losing her man to another man
("Sissy Blues,"), about a lover's sexual abuse and violence ("Sweet Rough Man"),
and about lesbianism ("Prove It on Me Blues"). Listen again to "Hustlin' Blues," in
which she sings about a pimp who beats her when she doesn't earn any money.

In stanza 1, the singer observes that on account of the rain that night, "tricks"
(men looking for prostitutes) aren't out on the street, so she must go home, where
she knows she will face a fight. In stanza 2, she addresses her pimp, threatening to
take him to court if he strikes her. Stanzas 3 through 5 find her in court, addressing
the judge, from whom she hopes to obtain a restraining order on her pimp, which
she hopes will allow her to leave a life of prostitution. Needless to say, this was not
the typical subject of popular music in the 1920s. The majority of popular songs
were about unrequited love; others commented on current news and events; and
a minority were humorous or "novelty" songs. Most of Rainey's blues lyrics were
about love and mistreatment, yet a few of them rose to this level of gritty realism,
scarcely seen in popular music for another forty years.

Text, "Hustlin' Blues"

1. It's rainin' out here and tricks ain't walkin' tonight, (2x)
   I'm goin' home, I know I've got to fight.
2. If you hit me tonight, let me tell you what I'm going to do, (2x)
   I'm gonna take you to court and tell the judge on you.
3. I ain't made no money, and he dared me to go home, (2x)
   Judge, I told him he better leave me alone.
4. He followed me up and he grabbed me for a fight, (2x)
   He said, "Girl, do you know, you ain't made no money tonight."

5. Oh Judge, tell him I'm through, (2x)
    I'm tired of this life, that's why I bought him to you.

"Hustlin' Blues," sung by Ma Rainey, Chicago, 1928, from the album *Mother of the Blues*.

The 1920s also brought the first recordings of **downhome blues**: Blind Blake, the greatest ragtime guitarist; Charley Patton, a songster regarded as the father of Mississippi **Delta blues** (downhome blues from the Mississippi River delta region); and a host of others brought the music out of the local juke joints and house parties and onto recordings that were circulated back into the black communities (Titon 2002:15). Jimmie Rodgers, the first star of country music, whose brief career lasted from 1927 through 1933, sang many blues songs, particularly his "blue yodels." Rodgers, a white Mississippian, learned many of his songs and much of his relaxed singing style from black railroad men. Blues has remained an important component within country music ever since. African American rhythms, jazz instrumental breaks, and the blues scale were critical in the formation of bluegrass music, which ironically is usually regarded as an Anglo-American musical tradition (see Cantwell 1984). Furthermore, the banjo—the quintessential bluegrass instrument—was derived from an African instrument.

Blues has always been a popular form within jazz and remains so today. In the 1930s and 1940s, blues "shouters" such as Jimmy Rushing (with Count Basie's orchestra) bridged the line between blues and jazz. African American rhythm and blues of the 1940s followed in the tradition of these blues shouters, along with crooners such as Charles Brown. In the meantime an **urban blues** sound arose, featuring singers with small bands led by electric guitar. Aaron "T-Bone" Walker (see Figure 4.11) invented it in the 1940s, and Riley "B. B." (Blues Boy) King made it immensely popular beginning in the 1950s.

Blues played a crucial role in British rock during the 1960s. Groups such as the Rolling Stones (whose name came from a Muddy Waters song and whose early albums featured covers of **Chicago blues**[1]) participated in the British blues revival. Dozens of British blues bands could be found in such cities as London and Liverpool, and talented instrumentalists such as John Mayall and Eric Clapton arose from this ferment in the 1960s. An American blues revival that occurred in the same decade gave white musicians Paul Butterfield and Charlie Musselwhite a start, and a new phenomenon appeared: bands whose personnel included a mixture of black and white musicians. Muddy Waters, for example, featured the white harmonica player Paul Oscher, and in the 1970s had white guitarist Bob Margolin in his band. Lazy Bill Lucas, the leader of the band I played in during the 1960s, led an integrated band. At the 1970 Ann Arbor Blues Festival, Luther Allison and Johnny Winter sang and played a set together (Figure 1.3).

Since the late 1960s, many white American rock bands have covered black blues hits from the 1950s and 1960s. The screaming guitar lines of heavy-metal music are

---

[1]Although Chicago has been an important blues city ever since the 1920s, "Chicago blues" refers to a sound that arose among musicians who had migrated from Mississippi and were living in Chicago just after World War II. Pioneers of this sound included Muddy Waters, Little Walter, and Howlin' Wolf.

Figure 4.15

Buddy Guy performs at the Ann Arbor Blues Festival, 1970. *Jeff Todd Titon.*

Figure 4.16

John Lee Hooker and admirer. Ann Arbor Blues Festival, 1970. *Jeff Todd Titon.*

an interpretation (some would say a misinterpretation) of the blues lead-guitar styles of B. B. King, Albert King, Freddy King, Elmore James, and others. Most rock fans do not realize the debt that rock owes to blues and the African-American community. But in the 1960s, most of black America saw blues as old-fashioned. Outside of strongholds in the Mississippi Delta and Chicago, blues accounted for a small proportion of jukebox records and received little radio airplay. Black intellectuals dismissed blues as a music of resignation, unfit for the contemporary climate of civil rights and black power. **Soul music**—the most popular African-American music in the 1960s, recorded for companies like Stax-Volt and Atlantic by artists such as James Brown, Aretha Franklin, and Otis Redding— proved much more attractive. Yet during this same decade, many blues singers revived their careers, finding a new audience. The blues revival of the 1960s brought commercially recorded blues music and black musicians before a largely white public in North America and Europe. Buddy Guy, popular today, was active but overshadowed in the 1960s revival (Figure 4.15).

The revival of the 1960s was in fact a renewal, a reinvigoration of blues, as older musicians like Howlin' Wolf and Muddy Waters found a new audience. In the film *The Road to Memphis* (2003), B. B. King speaks of his awe at the standing ovation he received at the Fillmore Theatre in San Francisco in 1968 when he sang for a white audience. But in the 1960s, it was still possible to speak of blues as a community-based music among the older African Americans who had grown up with it. I had participated in this blues music-culture when I got to know and to play music with Lazy Bill Lucas and his friends in Minneapolis in the 1960s. In the 1970s and 1980s, that generation passed away while blues fell out of popularity except among a small group of aficionados, largely white, some of whom, like Bonnie Raitt and Stevie Ray Vaughn, became professional blues and rhythm-and-blues musicians themselves. By the end of the 1980s, the movie *The Blues Brothers* had restored blues to the mainstream culture, but in a way that foregrounded white musicians as well as black, with a predominantly white audience, while emphasizing the urban, soul music side of blues. Meanwhile, on the downhome end of the blues spectrum, the reissue of the complete recordings of the Delta blues singer-guitarist Robert Johnson fed, and spread, his legend, while in the 1990s downhome musicians such as Junior Kimbrough and R. L. Burnside were promoted and achieved success with the alternative-rock audience. The continuing careers of some **source musicians**, such as John Lee Hooker (Figure 4.16) and B. B. King, coupled with the arrival of new, young black musicians such as Alvin Youngblood Hart, Corey Harris, and Keb' Mo', continued to invigorate this small corner of American vernacular music.

Modern Blues

Many non–African-American readers of this book already know something about blues, because blues today extends well beyond the boundaries of the African-American music-culture. You can hear blues played in Prague, Dar es Salaam, and Tokyo by citizens of Czechoslovakia, Tanzania, and Japan. Nowadays blues is regarded as a universal phenomenon, accessible to all.

For one example of modern blues style, we turn to a masterpiece by an older singer, Otis Rush. "Ain't Enough Comin' In" was voted the outstanding blues recording of the year 1994 by the readers of *Living Blues* magazine. This song, which Rush wrote and arranged, is as outstanding a performance of urban blues as can be heard even today.

The song (Active Listening 4.6) starts with an authoritative drumbeat, and immediately the electric bass sets a heavy rhythmic riff that repeats until the end of the song, changing pitch when the chords change. In its rhythmic constancy, the bass provides something akin to the bell pattern in Agbekor (see Chapter 3) that anchors the entire performance. The drummer plays simply but forcefully and unerringly, marking the beat 1–2–3–4, with the accent on 3. A rock drummer would be busier than this—and a lot less relentless. The electric bass is louder than the drums, which has been characteristic of black popular music since the 1970s.

> ♫ **LISTEN TO**
> "Ain't Enough Comin' In," performed by Otis Rush, online.

ACTIVE LISTENING 4.6
"Ain't Enough Comin' In"

COUNTER NUMBER	COMMENTARY	LYRICS
0:01	Instrumental introduction.	
0:09	Rush's guitar takes the lead and is accompanied by the band for one verse.	
0:35	Rush sings first verse, with band accompanying.	Oh, I ain't got enough comin' in to take care of what's got to go out. It ain't enough love or money comin' in, baby, to take care of what's got to go out. Like a bird I got my wing clipped, my friends; I've got to start all over again.
1:02	Rush sings second verse.	If the sun ever shine on me again, oh lord if the sun ever shine on me again. Like a bird I got my wing clipped, my friends; I've got to start all over again.
1:28	Bridge section (third verse)–different melodic and harmonic structure.	Now when it's all over and said and done, money talks and the fool gets none. The tough get tough and the tough get goin'; come on baby let me hold you in my arms.
1:46	Rush sings fourth verse while band continues to back him up, as in the second verse.	It ain't got enough comin' in to take care of what's got to go out. Ain't enough love or money comin' in, baby, to take care of what's got to go out. My friends, I got my wings clipped; I've got to start all over again.

continued

COUNTER NUMBER	COMMENTARY	LYRICS
2:12	Rush takes the lead on the electric guitar for an entire verse, accompanied by the band.	
2:38	Rush continues to play an instrumental lead for another verse. Listen to how he "bends" the pitch of some notes by pushing the string to the side.	
3:05	Tenor saxophone lead for a verse; notice the deliberately raspy, buzzy tone.	
3:31	Tenor sax lead for another verse.	
3:57	Rush repeats bridge (third verse).	When it's all over and said and done, money talks and the fool gets none. The tough get tough and the tough get goin'; come on baby let me hold you in my arms.
4:16	Rush sings sixth verse.	Ain't got enough comin' in to take care of what's got to go out. It ain't enough love or money comin' in, baby, to take care of what's got to go out. Like a bird I got my wings clipped, my friends; I've got to start all over again.
4:40	Rush sings seventh verse.	If you don't put nothing' in you can't get nothin' out; You don't put nothin' in, baby, you can't get nothin' out; Like a bird I got my wings clipped, my friends; I've got to start all over again.
5:07	Rush plays instrumental lead guitar to ending fade out. Notice the vibrating guitar (hand tremolo).	

Listeners who can recognize the difference between major and minor chords will realize that this is a minor blues, built on the minor i–iv–v chords instead of the major ones. The first chorus is instrumental. Rush plays the electric guitar lead above a riffing rhythm section that includes a trumpet and saxophone as well as an organ. The direct, spare playing here sets a somber mood for his powerful vocals that follow. The song features a bridge section ("Now when it's all over...") that departs from the usual twelve-bar blues pattern, but you will recognize that otherwise (except for the minor key) the song has a typical blues structure. After the vocals, Rush takes the tune twice through with a guitar solo, and this is followed by two choruses in which a saxophone leads, taking some of Rush's ideas and developing them. The bridge returns, followed by two more verses, and Rush takes it out with one more instrumental chorus. Hear how the sound of the guitar vibrates at the beginning of the last chorus. This is a tremolo, and Rush is known for getting this effect by pushing his fingers from side to side on the strings (a hand tremolo) rather than using the tremolo bar attached to the electric guitar.

Rush's vocal style is striking. Like many blues singers, he hoarsens his voice at times to show great emotion, but he also makes his voice tremble at times, an effect that mirrors his guitar tremolo (and vice versa). Rush's lyrics are clever and subtle. In the beginning of his career he relied on the professional songwriter Willie Dixon, but after his first hit songs he decided that he could "write one better than that" (Forte 1991:159). When I hear the first line, I think "ain't enough comin' in" refers to money; but in the second line, Rush lets me know that I should think of the parallel between love and money: The singer feels that he's giving too much and not getting enough of either in return.

Figure 4.17
Otis Rush performing at the Ann Arbor Blues Festival, 1969. Note that he plays left-handed.
Jeff Todd Titon.

Otis Rush has been a blues legend since the 1950s, well known to musicians and serious blues aficionados if not to the general listening public. Stevie Ray Vaughn named his band Double Trouble in honor of Rush's finest song from that decade. Led Zeppelin covered Rush's "I Can't Quit You Baby," with guitarist Jimmy Page lifting Rush's instrumental break note for note (Forte 1991:156). Rush's guitar playing turned Eric Clapton into a disciple. When Rush met Clapton in England in 1986, he called Clapton a "great guitar player" and modestly went on, "Everybody plays like somebody. It's good to know that somebody's listening . . . I'm not trying to influence nobody, I'm just trying to play, and play well" (Forte 1991:161).

Otis Rush (Figure 4.17) was born in Philadelphia, Mississippi, in 1934 and began playing at age ten. Although B. B. King, T-Bone Walker, and Magic Sam were among the musicians who influenced him most strongly, Rush developed his own version of modern blues guitar. His style is subtle, spare, cool—the instrumental equivalent of caressing a lover. There is nothing egotistical about it, no showing off. His use of silence is brilliant. "Well, I can play fast stuff, but I try to take my time and make you feel what I'm doin'," he told Jas Obrecht. "You can play a bunch of notes so fast, but then you turn around, and somebody out there listening says, 'What did he play?' Sound good, but can't remember nothin'. Take your time and play. Measure it out enough where they got time to hear what you're doing" (2000:243). Like a fine aged wine at its peak, at its best his music has great presence, neither understated nor flashy: it is substantial, direct, powerful, and commands respect.

Blues in the New Millennium

Since the 1960s, blues has undergone periods of revival alternating with periods of decline in popularity. At the turn of the twenty-first century, blues was swept up in the **roots music** phenomenon. The U.S. Public Broadcasting System aired a four-part documentary film, *American Roots Music*, in which blues played a prominent part. Two years later, the U.S. Congress proclaimed 2003 the "Year of the Blues." Yet today, a dozen years later, blues has seemingly turned into one of many small, niche musics, its various "scenes" now chiefly in historical strongholds such as Chicago and the Mississippi Delta. In another ten or twenty years, blues will probably undergo yet another revival.

A dozen years ago, the roots music movement was meant both to recognize early forms of vernacular and ethnic American music and to market them to the general public. "Blues, hillbilly, country, zydeco, Cajun, Tejano, Native American, and rockabilly" were the major early forms of roots music according to Robert Santelli and Holly George-Warren (2002:12). Whereas folk musicians learned their craft primarily from family and neighbors, roots musicians embraced the commercial recording culture that began recording American vernacular music in the 1920s and gradually spread local and regional styles across the nation. Whereas folk musicians were largely illiterate and without much formal education, roots musicians, particularly in the late twentieth century, were literate and educated. In addition, the folk musician traditionally regarded the music she or he played as the music of the community; it did not require labeling according to genre—it was simply "music" or "our music." The roots musician, on the contrary, is well aware of genre and style, usually makes a living from music (or hopes to do so), and "is conscious of being part of the American music tradition. Often he or she feels a personal responsibility to carry on that tradition" (Santelli and George-Warren 2002:13). Whereas the early blues artist Son House (b. 1902) told me he sang about men and women and the troubles they have getting along with each other, the contemporary roots music-culture thinks that blues are about "gender and class relationships" (Ibid.) Yet, marketing blues as roots music had its drawbacks. It branded blues as a music of the past, with its proper place in folk festivals and living history museums where tourists would gaze at it and then move on. The successful film *Ghost World* (2001) featured blues, but it was blues as embodied in the collection of pre–World War II records that belonged to an eccentric loner unable to adjust to contemporary society. After a few years of success, roots backfired as a blues marketing strategy. A world of ghosts seemed more suitable for blues.

Music producers with an interest in roots genres began to use a new name, **Americana**, to describe the evolved roots phenomenon (Americana 2015). Instead of marketing the older roots musics in unvarnished form, they decided to promote the careers of roots music interpreters like Emmylou Harris, Lucinda Williams, Steve Earle, Jimmy Dale Gilmore, and Old Crow Medicine Show. Not traditional roots musicians themselves, these are contemporary performers who have incorporated the roots sound into their new songs. Americana music promoters take pains to distinguish this music from its more commercial counterparts such as country music. As one of the officers of the Americana Music Association puts it, they honor the roots music that influenced Bob Dylan and The Band, but they promote contemporary roots music interpreters, not the roots musicians themselves. The Association defines Americana as a "contemporary music that incorporates various elements of American roots music styles . . . resulting in a roots-oriented sound that *lives in a world apart from the pure forms* of the genres upon which it may draw" (italics mine; Americana 2015).

Overlooked by Americana in the new millennium, the remaining blues music-culture found solace in performers who favored more traditional blues, combining the skillful musicianship of a younger generation with the drive and energy of the old, breathing life into the traditional sounds. One such musician is James "Super Chikan" Johnson. Born in rural Darling, Mississippi, in 1951, Super Chikan got his nickname, "chikan boy," from his habit of talking to chickens on his family's farm. His credentials as a folk blues artist are impeccable: he grew up in the traditional Mississippi blues culture surrounded by family and community musicians (his grandfather played fiddle in string bands, and his uncle is bluesman Big James Johnson). His first instrument was the diddley-bow (see Figure 1.11), and he got his first guitar in a Salvation Army store at the age of thirteen. In his early 20s, he was playing electric bass in his uncle's band and other local groups, but he could not earn a living as a sideman. Driving long-haul trucks for a living, he spent much of his time in the truck cabs thinking of blues song lyrics, and his career as a leader took off during the 1990s, when blues tourism was strengthening in Mississippi. Today, he lives in the center of the blues tourist area, Clarksdale, and sings frequently in blues clubs there when not traveling and performing all over the world. He is a skilled, modern guitarist playing an instrument whose appearance he customized (Figure 4.18). (His custom-made guitars are pictured on his website.) Performing solo at festivals, or in concerts and clubs with small blues combos, his band shows strong Delta roots. Chikan's own guitar style is steeped in traditional Delta and Chicago blues. At the same time, his guitar solos sometimes sound, particularly in their tonal quality, like Jimmy Hendrix, like Muddy Waters' blues album *Electric Mud*, or like San Francisco psychedelic rock music of the late 1960s.

"Poor Broke Boy" (Active Listening 4.7) is a clever twist on a theme as old as the blues—that misfortunes give a person the blues. As in Lazy Bill Lucas's rendition of "Poor Boy Blues" (earlier in this chapter), Super Chikan tells the listener his troubles: no shoes, not enough food, crowded sleeping quarters, no food, no money, dying livestock. Lucas's song was meant to be sincere, but as the poor broke boy's misfortunes pile up, the listener wonders if this singer is being serious or humorous. Meanwhile, the bass and drums lay down the traditional walking bass

♫ **LISTEN TO**
"Poor Broke Boy," performed by James "Super Chikan" Johnson, from the album *Chikan Soup*, online.

Figure 4.18
One of James "Super Chikan" Johnson's custom guitars. American Folk Festival, Bangor, Maine, 2011. *Jeff Todd Titon.*

ACTIVE LISTENING 4.7
"Poor Broke Boy"

COUNTER NUMBER	COMMENTARY	LYRICS
0:00	A full stanza played through without singing, led by guitar, bass, drums, and acoustic piano, in the style of Jimmy Reed.	
0:25	Johnson sings stanza 1 over the same instrumental accompaniment.	I'm just a poor broke boy down in northern Mississippi, (2x) Well when it rains down South, y'all, them old back roads *become so busy*.
0:47	Johnson sings stanza 2 over a similar accompaniment; piano is heard more.	Well I'm walking barefooted on this hot hot Delta land, (2x) I've been working those fields, y'all, and I've got blisters in my hands.
1:07	Johnson sings stanza 3 over a similar accompaniment.	Scorching hot in the summer, we don't even have a fan, (2x) We're sleeping four to a bed, y'all, we're eating whatever we can.
1:30	Johnson plays an instrumental electric guitar break in traditional Delta style and sound, with the now-established accompaniment.	
1:51	Johnson sings stanza 4 over the same accompaniment.	Well my papa went to jail and Mr. Charlie* raised hell, (2x) We had to work all summer just to pay my papa's bail.
2:14	Pianist plays an instrumental break in traditional Delta/Chicago style and sound, with the now-established accompaniment.	
2:34	Johnson repeats stanza 1.	I'm just a poor broke boy down in northern Mississippi, (2x) Well when it rains down South, y'all, them old back roads *become so busy*.
2:55	Johnson sings stanza 5 over the established accompaniment.	We made a bill last summer, down at the general store, (2x) Now *the barter's*† all gone and we can't even charge no more.
3:17	Johnson plays an instrumental electric guitar break, with the now-established accompaniment, but the electric guitar tonal quality has changed to emphasize harmonics in psychedelic style.	

COUNTER NUMBER	COMMENTARY	LYRICS
3:38	Johnson sings stanza 6 over the established accompaniment; guitar timbre reverts to previous tonal quality.	My cow's gone dry, poor hog's about to die, (2x) Well my stomach's got a pain and the poor boy's about to cry.
3:59	Johnson plays another guitar break, using the psychedelic timbre that imitates hens clucking.	
4:21	Instrumental break for the piano; guitar goes back to the traditional timbre.	
4:41	Johnson plays another guitar break, using the psychedelic timbre. This time the choice of notes reflects a more modern practice.	
5:02	Johnson plays another guitar break, more traditional in sound.	
5:23	Johnson signals ending and plays melodic figures on guitar (compare with Fred McDowell's ending of "Kokomo Blues")	

Mr. Charlie is code for "white man."
†Italic type denotes that the accuracy of the lyric is not certain.

"Poor Broke Boy," by James "Super Chikan" Johnson. Performed by James "Super Chikan" Johnson and the Fighting Cocks. © Drop Top Music Cocks.

and backbeat rhythms, while the piano also plays traditional fills. Chikan's guitar style combines the skillful technique that characterizes Americana, yet with a raw edge that reminds knowledgeable listeners of Jimmy Reed and Robert Johnson, all accompanying a traditional blues song form in three-line stanzas.

Chikan's lyrics offer an example of "signifying." **Signifying**, in Afro-American culture, is a way of speaking or writing indirectly about something, using figurative language in a code whose key is hidden from some listeners (Gates 1989). It can be as simple as a euphemism for sex ("How do you want your rollin' done?") or a boast ("I'm gonna build me a mansion out on some old lonesome hill"). In blues, signifying can involve coded language for sex, but it also takes the form of ironic understatement or overstatement directed at lovers, bosses, or both. In Baby Doo Caston's "Field Holler" (Active Listening 4.2), the lyrics refer to the boss as "captain," a word that may sound respectful to the boss, whereas among the working class it is understood to be sarcastic. Language codes are not limited to Africans or African Americans; coded speech characterizes any group that feels oppressed or that wants to hide something from others nearby. But within African-American communities, signifying developed into a fine art. Woven into the thread of black music, whether in spirituals, blues, jazz, or hip-hop, it has been an effective survival mechanism. Super Chikan's song "Poor Boy Blues" is meant to satisfy traditional blues fans while reaching out to a more general Americana audience. Will it do both? That remains to be seen. Super Chikan has been billed on occasion as an Americana performer, but his appeal remains tied primarily to the blues audience, while his credentials as a representative of a "purer" roots form are beyond dispute. Do these historical, economic, and audience changes mean we should abandon our music-culture model (Chapter 1) in the face of real-world complications? No, but we need to keep in mind that it is a model, an ideal. Music-cultures are not isolated entities—they respond to economic, artistic, and interpretive pressures from without as well as within. Their histories reveal that response to these pressures; "catching" or defining a music at any given time comes at the expense of the long view.

MindTap

PRACTICE your understanding of this chapter's concepts by working once more with the chapter's Active Listening Guides online.

MindTap

DO an online quiz that your instructor may assign for a grade.

Study Questions

1. How did African-American music change the sound of popular music in the United States, and then the world, in the twentieth century?
2. What is the difference between the three-line blues stanza and the quatrain-refrain stanza? Illustrate with an example of each.
3. What are the functions of work songs?
4. Do blues singers sing mostly about themselves, or do they represent many people?
5. How do blues singers "compose" their songs?
6. What do field hollers have in common with blues?
7. How and why is traditional African-American worship affecting (moving)?
8. What is a musical revival? Why did blues undergo revivals in the 1960s and again beginning in the 1980s?
9. What are the advantages and disadvantages of marketing blues as a roots music? As Americana music?
10. Why is the history of blues important? Why does it matter that the music was invented and nurtured by African Americans?

5

Europe/Central and Southeastern Regions

Timothy J. Cooley

Learning Objectives

After you have studied this chapter, you should be able to:

1. Describe the most common features of much (but not all) European music.

2. Identify the basic rhythmic and metrical qualities of an example of music.

3. Identify two influential ways that societies are organized in Europe, and explain how they influence musical practices.

4. Interpret a Polish *Góralski* dance suite.

5. Identify the characteristics and significance of world beat fusion projects.

When someone mentions Europe to you, what comes to mind? A particular country, such as France or Germany? Maybe a large city such as Vienna, London, Moscow, or Paris? What sounds play in your mind's ear when you think about European music? Some of you might think of a symphony by Mozart or Beethoven, a Chopin etude you once played in piano lessons, or the popular singer Björk, Eurovision Song Contest winner Conchita Wurst, the bands Lordi, U2, or even the Beatles. But these last two bands are from Ireland and Great Britain, islands off the coast of the continent of Europe. Should they be included in our definition of Europe? If Europe is defined as a landmass, the European continent extends from Portugal in the west to Asia in the east. This certainly extends beyond the concept of Europe most of us have. Perhaps a cultural definition of Europe will clarify our position and help us with the study of European music. But what about North America? Isn't there much that is European about the institutions and cultural practices of Canada, the United States, and Mexico? Defining Europe as a cultural area has its own challenges.

The way we conceive of regions of the world rarely depends solely on physical geography; the human capacity for categorization, naming, and dividing inevitably comes into play. Like music, Europe exists as a concept as well as an entity. For our purposes, the concept of Europe includes several island nations (Iceland, the United Kingdom, and Ireland), and the nation-states on the western end of the European continent, from Portugal in the west to at least the western parts of Russia in the east. In the north are the countries of Norway, Sweden, and Finland; in the south are Spain, Italy, and Greece. At the time of this writing, Turkey is being considered for membership in the European Union; should it be included in our definition of Europe? There are literally hundreds of distinct musics in the nations of Europe. Nonetheless, certain ideas about music and certain ways of creating and organizing sounds can be identified as European. The European settlement of the Americas, not surprisingly, results in many shared musical practices there as well, and for this reason in this chapter we will occasionally reference music from North America and compare it to music from Europe.

Social and Political Organization

We will look at the social and political organization of Europe in two interrelated ways: religion and nationalism. Today, we tend to view Europe as a collection of independent, democratic nation-states, but to the extent that this is true, it is a fairly recent phenomenon. For much of its history, most of Europe's population and land was organized into fiefdoms loyal to particular kingdoms that sometimes expanded into larger empires. The physical borders of these units were rarely exact but rather were contested and changing. Often more stable than the shifting borders of kingdoms and nation-states, religious practices have sweeping, long-term influence on the social, political, and musical practices of Europe.

Religion and Society

The three predominant religions in Europe—though by no means the only religions practiced—are Judaism, Christianity, and Islam. While these three religions are often seen as being in conflict, they have much in common: they are monotheistic, trace their origins to Abraham and the Middle East, and all accept the Torah (Old Testament) as sacred text. Despite these commonalities—or perhaps because of them—the differences between them tend to receive emphasis and shape individuals' and societies' interactions. Tensions between Christian Europe and Muslim Europe in particular did much to define the politics, societies, and cultural practices of the region in the distant and recent past (Davies 1996:253–58). Divisions between different denominations of Christianity are similarly influential in Europe, as illustrated in recent years with *Na Triobloídí* (the Troubles) in Ireland. Here, we will consider how these tensions and ideas of difference influence musicking.

> ## Salient Characteristics of
> ## European Religion and Society
>
> - The predominant religions in Europe are:
>   - Judaism
>   - Christianity
>   - Islam
>
> - Though related historically and doctrinally, these religions create distinct contexts for music

Of the three religions mentioned above, Christianity is the largest and longest established in Europe. Spread throughout Western Europe by the Roman Empire, Christianity became the dominant religion in all of Europe by the fourth century. For most of its history in Europe, Christianity has been divided into several politically and socially significant categories: Roman Catholicism, Orthodoxy (primarily in the east and southeast), and more recently various branches of Protestantism (strongest in northern Europe and the United Kingdom).

Judaism is practiced almost exclusively by ethnic Jews, who over time formed a loosely linked European community. Judaism never obtained a political state within Europe; on the other hand, both Islam and Christianity enjoyed the benefits of becoming state religions. Judaism was introduced to Europe as early as 70 C.E., when Jews, forced into diaspora by the Romans after the destruction of the Second Temple, settled in Mediterranean Europe. Like Christianity, Judaism moved into Central and Western Europe with the Roman Empire. Though several waves of persecution and expulsion diminished Jewish communities over the centuries, significant communities were established by the eighteenth-century Enlightenment era. During World War II, the Nazi regime's genocidal Holocaust and the flight of Jews seeking safety greatly reduced Jewish communities in Europe (Bohlman 2000b:248–49). Today, some communities are rebuilding, and the influence of Jewish music remains strong in many parts of Europe (Rice 2000:11).

Muslim* communities have flourished in Europe since the Moorish Andalusian Empire (eighth to thirteenth centuries) on the Iberian Peninsula and the Turkish Ottoman Empire (fourteenth to twentieth centuries) in Southeastern Europe. Muslim individuals and communities form important components of most European nation-states today, and Islam is a dominant religion in some countries and regions (Albania and Bosnia, for example). Like Jews, however, Muslims have been periodically persecuted and driven from Europe. For example, both Jews and the Muslim Moors were expelled from Andalusian Spain in 1492. Muslim communities are historically strong in many Southeastern European nations (Figure 5.1), and thriving communities of more recent immigrants are found throughout Europe.

Muslim is the term used for one who follows Islam.

Figure 5.1

Mosque in Sarajevo. Bosnia, 2004. *Timothy J. Cooley.*

Religion influences musical practices in ways both subtle and overt. For example, the relationship between Islam and ideas about music is contentious for some Muslims (see Chapter 10). In fact, what may be the most influential sonic production of Islam—the recitation of the Qu'ran (Koran)—is not considered music. Nonetheless, the rules for properly reciting the Qu'ran are reflected in the modal practices of Muslim classical musicians, and these rules also influence vocal ornamentation in some forms of folk music. Likewise, the Call to Prayer—which is traditionally publically broadcast from minarets five times each day in Muslim communities and today may be heard on any number of private audio devices—is a prominent element of the soundscape that structures the practice of Islam. Muslims have also influenced European musical instruments. The guitar (derived from the *'ud* which was introduced to Spain by the Moors) and possibly the violin descended from Middle Eastern instruments.

Likewise, Jewish music and musicians are integrated into the musical practices of many parts of Europe (see Armistead 1979; Bohlman 2000a, 2000b). Jewish music in Europe includes two major traditions: Sephardic and Ashkenazic. Sephardic Jews are from the Iberian Peninsula, but were expelled in the fifteenth century (listen to Judith Cohen and Tamar Ilana, *Sefarad en Diáspora,* for recordings of various Sephardic traditions). Many moved to the Balkans in Southeastern Europe; some settled in the British Isles or the Netherlands; others left Europe. Historically, Ashkenazic Jews were most prominent in Germany, Austria, and Eastern Europe. Identity for many European Jews centered on religion, language, and other cultural practices in addition to association with a particular town, kingdom, or nation. Historically in too many cases, however, Jews and other minority groups were denied nationality or citizenship status through discriminatory laws (Bohlman 2004:214). Yet music expressive of a distinctive Jewish cultural identity developed in response to the inventions of national traditions in the 1800s (Bohlman 2000b:249; for rap and hip-hop among Jews in America, see Cohen 2009). Examples include groups of itinerant musicians called *klezmorim,* who provided music for ritual and secular events both inside and outside Jewish communities. Much later in the twentieth century, **klezmer** became a genre term for a style of music associated with Jews. In many parts of Central Europe, Jewish musicians were essential for non-Jewish weddings, and in some cities and regions across Europe, Jewish musicians were among the most highly sought-after musicians until the Holocaust. Whereas a high degree of integration with other European musics characterized the aesthetic of many Jewish instrumentalists, vocal music served to define a specific Jewish identity through the use of language (Yiddish for many Ashkenazic Jews, Ladino for Sephardic Jews, as well as Hebrew for religious texts, and some secular texts). "Oifn Pripetshik," discussed later (Active Listening 5.1), is an example of a Yiddish language song from an Ashkenazic tradition.

Aligned with the ruling powers that experienced the greatest successes, Christianity has maintained the political advantage in much of Europe. Like mosques and synagogues, Christian churches serve as institutions for spreading sociocultural ideas and practices over wide regions, between kingdoms, and across national borders. For example, the official language of the Roman Catholic Church is Latin. Even though Vatican II reforms, instituted in the 1960s, allowed the worship services to be conducted in the local vernacular, music with Latin texts is still common in churches around the world. Another example is a particular approach toward ideas about **scale** and modality (the organization of pitches typically used in a melody; see Chapter 1) that spread across Europe with the church.

Churches also fostered traditions of literacy, including musical literacy. The five-line system of notating music still used in many parts of the world developed in Europe as early as the eleventh century, and settled into the form used today in the early seventeenth century. The ability to notate accurately many aspects of music (notably pitch, rhythm, and duration) subtly changes one's conception of music itself and forms one of the ideological divisions between classical, popular, and folk music in Europe. Notation also facilitates the conception and composition of large-form abstract music (music without texts such as a concerto or symphony), and to some extent the phenomenon of harmony.

In more region-specific contexts, church traditions encouraged certain types of musical practices. For example, Roman Catholic brotherhoods in Spain have a tradition of snare and bass drum performances reserved for two days of the year during Holy Week, an annual church holiday including Easter (see Plastino 2001, 2003). Beginning in the sixteenth century, the Protestant Reformation resulted in what became a significant division of Christian churches—and often communities as well—in Western Europe into either Protestant denominations (mostly in Northern Europe) or Roman Catholic churches (primarily in the south). The Protestant churches created new musical forms, notably chorales that the entire congregation sang.

All three of the religions considered here influence the music-cultures of Europe and beyond. Their musical practices—approaches toward melody, rhythm, formal structure; the instruments used or prohibited; gendered practice imposed on communities; and so forth—feed the societies' soundscape in inescapable ways. Though religions' influences on musical practices are widespread, it would be a mistake to assume that most music in Europe can be labeled exclusively Christian, Jewish, or Muslim. Musical practices tend to be ecumenical and worldly in the sense that they spread freely from mouth to ear around the world, respecting no religious or political borders.

Salient Characteristics of
Nationalism and Nation-States

- Europe's political organization into democratic nation-states is relatively recent

- The concept of national folk musics is instrumental in creating the sense of national identity

Nationalism and Nation-States

Beginning in the late eighteenth and the nineteenth centuries, kingdoms and empires as the predominant social and political organizational units in Europe gradually gave way to the modern nation-states that today characterize Europe. Key and early events effecting this change include the 1776 American Declaration of Independence (not in Europe, but a declaration of independence from a European monarchy), the 1789 French Revolution, and the short-lived Polish-Lithuanian Commonwealth of 1791. The idea of a nation-state differs fundamentally from the idea of a kingdom or empire (and other forms of dynasties) in that the authority resides in the people of the state, rather than in the dynastic rulers of a kingdom. Another difference is that dynasties, like religions, usually claim to have divine right to rule and govern (White 2000:45–49). Most modern nation-states are officially secular, though politicians in some countries still claim divine authority to support their agendas.

Nationalism as an idea grew out of Enlightenment and Romantic philosophy in Western Europe, including ideas about rational scientific authority, the rights of individuals, and the good of the entire society.* This was a new way of conceiving of the social organization of large groups of people. One way of achieving this was through cultural practices such as language, music, costume, and religion. Today, such social groupings into nations seem both obvious and problematic. After all, we expect Germans to speak German, the French to speak French, Poles to speak Polish, and so forth. But national languages did not grow out of the soil; they are the products of national education as well as forced resettlements and ethnic cleansings. Still, not all nation-states insist on a unique language. For example, Switzerland has four official languages: German, French, Italian, and Romansh; German is the official language in Austria; and so forth.

The challenges to the idea of "nation" (a significantly united people) and "nation-state" (a political unity with a state) become evident upon even a cursory look at any modern nation-state. One common theme in current theories of nationalism is that nations are not natural, inherent, or immutable but must be "invented" (Hobsbawm and Ranger 1983) and "imagined" (Anderson 1991). As Philip Bohlman explains (2004:35–80), music has played an important role in creating national myths ever since the rise of nationalism. As a result, many of our ideas about music in Europe are strongly influenced by a belief that music informs us about the essence of a people (a nation), and that as one moves from nation-state to nation-state, one can expect the change to be reflected in the "national" music. To the extent that this is true, it is the result of nationalism—of proactive national imaginations and inventions. Thus, Ludwig Christian Erk in Germany, Cecil Sharp in England, Béla Bartók in Hungary—and the list

---

*For theories of nations and nationalism, see Anderson 1991; Gellner 1997; Hobsbawm 1990; Hutchinson and Smith 1994; Smith 1998. For statements specifically on music and nationalism, see Austerlitz 2000; Bohlman 2004; Frolova-Walker 1998.

could go on—did not so much discover the folk musics of their respective nations as create the idea of distinct German, English, and Hungarian folk music traditions. In other words, the notion of national musics is itself a human invention.

Though cultural practices are invented and not necessarily natural, they are nonetheless real. We will consider specific examples of music that are Polish, Bosnian, Jewish, and a few that combine ideas and identities from elsewhere within and beyond Europe. Our approach will be to consider the music in its local context, the individuals who created the music, and what we can learn about those people and the places they live from their musical practices.

The Sounds of European Music

European music will be familiar to many readers of this book, and identifying common elements in European music may seem unnecessary. Yet because collectively ethnomusicologists study all musical cultures, including European, it is interesting to see what happens when we ask the same questions about a familiar music that we ask about an unfamiliar one. Sometimes the results are surprising. Taking the four aspects of musical sound introduced in Chapter 1 (rhythm and meter, melody, harmony, and form), we will consider what unique contributions Europeans may have made to the world of music.

Rhythm and Meter

Listen to "Sister, Hold Your Chastity" (Active Listening 5.2, discussed in depth later in this chapter), paying attention to the rhythm. This is an example of a song genre called *ganga* from the Central European nation-state of Bosnia and Herzegovina. Can you tap your foot to the pulse of this music? Not easily. The rhythm in this piece is flexible, and is not metered with an even pulse or repeating pattern of beats. Compare this to the nonmetrical rhythm of a South Indian *alapana* (Chapter 6). Contrast "Sister, Hold Your Chastity" with "ze stary" ("the old one") (Active Listening 5.7), a regional Polish dance piece discussed later in this chapter. We can hear the steady beat or pulse in "ze stary" immediately, especially when a three-stringed cello-sized instrument called *basy* and a violin enter to accompany the voice and the lead violin. This piece is *metered*. Listening to "ze stary," group the pulses into units of four (ONE-two-THREE-four). The *basy* and accompanying violin play a four-beat **ostinato** (a bass and harmony pattern that is repeated again and again). Melodic phrases also take four beats in this piece as does each line of poetry.

The next most common metrical structure in European music consists of **bars** with a number of beats divisible by three, called *triple meter*. Music for a waltz is an example of triple meter (ONE-two-three, ONE-two-three, and so on), though not

Salient Characteristics of
Rhythm and Meter of European Music

- Though some music is unmetered, most tends to be easily counted in even pulses/beats divisible by two (duple-meter) or three (triple-meter)

MindTap
◀) LISTEN TO
"Sister, Hold Your Chastity," performed by Azra Bandić, Mevla Luckin, and Emsija Tetarvoić, online.

MindTap
◀) LISTEN TO
the *alapana* section of "Sarasiruha," performed by Ranganayaki Rajagopalan, online.

all music in triple meter is a waltz. For example, the Yiddish song "Oifn Pripetshik" (Active Listening 5.1) illustrates triple-meter rhythmic organization, though it is not a waltz.

ACTIVE LISTENING 5.1
"Oifn Pripetshik"

COUNTER NUMBER	COMMENTARY/TEXT	TRANSLATION
0:00	Instrumental introduction, guitar and violin. Triple-meter established (four bars of three beats each)	
0:09	Verse 1 (Rhythm: each line takes two bars of three beats in verses and refrain.) *Oifn pripetshik brent a fayerl* *Un in shtub iz hés,* *Un der rebe lerent kléne kinderlach* *Dem aleph béz.* (repeat last two lines)	In the stove a little fire burns And in the house it is warm, And the rebbe is teaching the little children The alphabet.
0:33	Refrain *Zét zhe kinderlach gedenkt zhe tayere* *Vos ir lerent do* *Zogt zhe noch a mol un take noch a mol* *Komets aleph o.* (repeat last two lines)	See now children, remember dear ones, What you are learning here Repeat it again and again *Komets aleph o.* [alphabet chant]
1:05	Verse 2 *Lernt kinder mit grois chéshek* *Azoi zog ich aich on* *Ver s'vet gicher fun aich kenen ivre* *Der bakumt a fon.* (repeat last two lines)	Study, children, with great desire That is what I tell you He who'll know his Hebrew first Will win a banner for a prize.
1:29	Refrain	
2:01	Verse 3 *Az ir vet kinder elter vern* *Vet ir alén farshtén* *Vi fil in di oisyes lign trern* *Un vi fil gevén.* (repeat last two lines)	Children, only when you get older Will you understand How many tears lie in the letters of the alphabet And how much weeping.
2:26	Refrain	
2:58	Verse 4 *Az ir vet kinder dem goles shlepn* *Oisgemutshet zain* *Zolt ir fun di oisyes koach shepn* *Kukt in zé arain.* (repeat last two lines)	Children, when you grow tormented With the struggle of exile Looking to the letters of the alphabet You will draw strength.
3:22	Refrain	

*English translation by Katherine Meizel and Arthur Schwartz.

Pitches, Scales, and Melody

In Chapter 1, you read that Europeans and Euro-Americans prefer a particular way of organizing pitches into scales, the most common scale being a **major scale**. "Joy to the World" was used in Chapter 1 to illustrate the major scale.* If a major scale is the most common scale type in European music systems, the next most common is the **minor scale**. "Oifn Pripetshik" provides a melody in a minor scale or mode. Originally titled "Der alef-beyz" or "The ABC," "Oifn Pripetshik" is a Yiddish-language song by Jewish lawyer and songwriter Mark Warshawsky (ca. 1840–1907) of Kiev (Rubin 1979:270, 272–74). His best-known composition, "Oifn Pripetshik" encapsulates a vernacular or folk style. Warshawsky's evocative tune has been used in several films, including Steven Spielberg's 1993 *Schindler's List.*

Though there are numerous additional scales or pitch sets employed, the vast majority of European music uses either major or minor scales. Readers of this book will know that, in the world of music, there are many varied ways of deriving pitch sets for music, and Europe's contribution to pitch and scale varieties is modest. Europe's unique contributions to the world of music lie elsewhere.

Scales alone do not make for very interesting melodies. Beautiful, memorable, striking melodies are created in the navigation of scales. This includes different ways of emphasizing particular pitches in the scale. Again, the decidedly European-style American composition "Joy to the World" illustrates melodic tendencies for much European music. As explained in Chapter 1, the melody steps down the major scale (do-ti-la-so-fa-me-re-do), yet it does not sound like a simple scale exercise you might hear a singer or piano player practicing. Varying the length of time spent on different pitches, and depending on where they all fall in the metrical cycle, different parts of the melody are emphasized, and the scale becomes a melody. Sing the first line of "Joy to the World" again using the solfége syllables, and pay attention to which syllables are held the longest. The syllables "so" and "do" (corresponding to the words "world" and "come" in the carol text) are held longer than any other syllable/pitch. It is no coincidence that "do" and "so," representing the first and fifth scale degrees, are the most emphasized pitches in many European-style melodies.

Harmony

The examples used to illustrate melody in Europe also illustrate one of this region's most unique contributions: **harmony**. Recall from Chapter 1 that harmony is created by two or more different pitches sounded intentionally at the same time for the purpose of the sound they make together. This can also be called a **chord**, a term familiar to guitar players that is derived from *accord*, implying that the pitches sound pleasant together—in accord with one another. However, exactly which intervals sound "in accord" is a matter of interpretation, and not all music traditions

* The melody for this carol was composed by an American, Lowell Mason (1792–1872), but Mason was a deliberately "European" American composer who used his influence as a music educator to replace the uniquely American fuging-tunes and anthems from the eighteenth century with what he considered to be "correct" European styles (McKim 1993: 47). In fact, "Joy to the World" quotes two melodic ideas from the oratorio *Messiah* by German-born British composer George Frederick Handel (1685–1759). Even if penned in America, "Joy to the World" is a very European-style composition and illustrates a typical European melody and scale type.

Salient Characteristics of
Harmony of European Music

- Pitches artfully performed one after the other produce *melody*

- Two or more pitches played or sung at the same time produce *harmony*

- Changing harmony or chords throughout a performance can be heard as *harmonic rhythm*

- While there is general consensus about which pitch combinations are harmonious or in accord across Europe, there are also significant regional exceptions

in Europe share the same aesthetics of harmony. Europe is not the only part of the world that independently devised ways to combine different pitches simultaneously, but it does seem to have most fully developed the concept of simultaneous pitches that create meaningful sounds independent of melody.

In its most fully realized state, harmonic music has **harmonic rhythm**: the movement of harmonic sounds or chords in time. The chord patterns played by a guitar for a particular song provide an example of harmonic rhythm. Consider "Joy to the World" again. The letters C, F, and G represent a simplified version of the chords—or triadic harmonies—that accompany this melody. "Joy to the World" is given here in the key of C, and these three chords are built on the 1st (C), 4th (F), and 5th (G) scale degrees of that key (solfége syllables *do*, *fa*, and *so*). This is the same basic chord relationship employed in the blues, for example, and the basis of the harmonic system favored in much of Europe since the eighteenth century. Using a guitar or piano, play these chords while you sing the melody. The sounding of the different chords in time is the harmonic rhythm of "Joy to the World," also represented in Figure 5.2.

Some musics of Europe take radically different approaches toward harmony, such as the music heard in "Sister, Hold Your Chastity." This is European music, to be sure, but it employs a different aesthetic from most other European musics with regard to vocal timbre, melody, rhythm, and harmony. This example of *ganga* was performed by three girls from the village of Umoljani in Bosnia and Herzegovina (Figure 5.3). As is the practice for female *ganga* singers, these girls are close friends who have been singing together from a young age. Like the music from the Polish Tatras (introduced next), *ganga* is considered mountain

MindTap·

◀》 **LISTEN TO**

"Sister, Hold Your Chastity," performed by Azra Bandić, Mevla Luckin, and Emsija Tetarvoić, online.

Figure 5.2

Harmonic rhythm of "Joy to the World." Each box represents one quarter-note beat in 2/4 time.

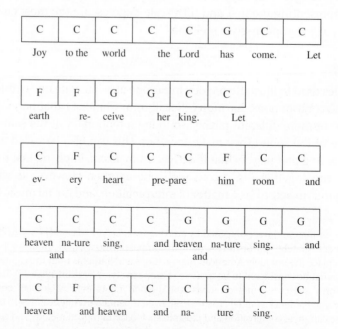

C	C	C	C	C	G	C	C
Joy	to the	world		the	Lord	has	come.	Let

F	F	G	G	C	C
earth	re-	ceive	her	king.	Let

C	F	C	C	C	F	C	C
ev-	ery	heart	pre-pare		him	room	and

C	C	C	C	G	G	G	G
heaven	na-ture	sing,		and heaven	na-ture	sing,	and
and				and			

C	F	C	C	C	G	C	C
heaven		and heaven		and	na-	ture	sing.

Figure 5.3

The singers of the highlander women's *ganga* song "Sister, Hold Your Chastity" (Active Listening 5.2). From left to right, Azra Bandić, Mevla Luckin, and Emsija Tatarović, near the village of Umoljani, 1989. *Mirjana Laušević.*

music, the language is a related Slavic language, and the texture of the singing is **polyphonic**—more than one melodic line performed simultaneously. They are also similar in that the singers take great pleasure in the physical and aesthetic sensation of singing together with loud, powerful voices, preferably outdoors in the mountains. Despite their similarities, what is considered beautiful and consonant harmonically is quite different in Bosnia and Herzegovina than in Poland. In the Polish Tatras, singers sing in unison or at an interval of a third—harmonies generally interpreted as consonant in European music. In the *ganga* example, there are three voices, a leading voice plus two accompanying singers who enter on the second melodic phrase. They begin in unison with the lead singer; all three move together up a step (from G to A); the two accompanying voices remain on the A while the lead singer moves back down to the G, the interval of a major second (Active Listening 5.2). You might hear

ACTIVE LISTENING 5.2
"Sister, Hold Your Chastity"

MindTap·

🎧 **WATCH** an Active Listening Guide of this selection online.

COUNTER NUMBER	COMMENTARY/TEXT	TRANSLATION
0:00	Lead singer sings first line. *Čuvaj seko poštenje ko suze, ko te ljubi,*	Sister, hold your chastity like tears, the one who kisses you,
0:12	Lead singer begins second line and is joined by the other two singers. *(oj) taj te neće uze', čuvaj seko pošte-*	he will not take you, sister, hold your
0:26	Third line. *(oj) -nje ko suze, ko te ljubi.*	chastity like tears, the one who kisses you.

this harmony as harsh or dissonant, but it is considered correct and pleasing to the singers and therefore is consonant in that regional European music tradition. What is consonant and dissonant in music is an aesthetic evaluation, not a law of nature.

European Précis

We can now draw some general conclusions about European musics, though, as we have seen, each conclusion has its exceptions. When compared with music throughout the rest of the world, most music in Europe has relatively simple, symmetrical structures in rhythm and in overall form. European music tends toward rhythmic organization of even pulses in repeating groups of two or three beats. Similarly, melodic structures tend toward pairs of melodic ideas (A and B phrases) and repeating structures (such as the strophic song form). The same can be said about the pitch content of most European music. The major scale is the most prominent scale; the minor scale is the second most common. Much of the beauty of European music comes in the subtle variation and ornamentation of these simple structures.

If European musicians have made any unique contribution to world music, it is the concept of harmony and harmonic rhythm. Polyphony is another hallmark of European music, though it is not unique to Europe. Most colleges and universities offer classes on European polyphony and harmony, and we have only touched on the complexity of these systems here.

Though we have focused on general tendencies in European musics, Europe is host to an amazingly rich variety of regional music styles, genres, and associated cultural practices. While religious and political institutions have contributed to the unification of some musical practices across broad swaths of Europe, much of the music maintained and created anew in any given location provides exceptions to the tendencies described here. Note also that examples used in this chapter span the gamut of the conceptual divisions of European musics into classical, popular, and folk. These categories are not natural but are invented ways of dividing human musical activity. They are more social than sonic, more conceptual than concrete (Cooley 2013; Small 1998). Most often they are deployed within societies to elevate certain musical practices for social and political reasons and to devalue others. For example, distinctions between folk and so-called "art music" (used similarly to "classical music") became particularly significant in Europe in the late eighteenth and early nineteenth century with the rise of nationalism (Gelbart 2007). This was also a moment when the European colonization of other regions of the world was beginning to face new challenges. Some scholars believe that the valuation of European classical music went hand in hand with conceptions of race, class, and power that enabled continued global colonialism. In our society today, how are categories of music used to value or devalue certain groups of people defined by class, ethnicity, and so forth? Understanding this is a very helpful way to begin understanding the meanings of music in any part of the world.

Case Study: Podhale, Polish Tatra Region

"Ze stary," the dance piece used earlier to illustrate rhythmic structures, is from **Podhale**, a region of southern Poland in the Tatra Mountains. The Tatras, the tallest mountains in central Europe (Figure 5.4), form a natural border between the southern tip of Poland and Slovakia (Map 5.1). Though not as tall as the Rocky Mountains or the Alps, the Tatras are steep, rocky, alpine-type mountains that have great influence on those who live on their slopes and in their shadows.

The social and emotional interpretation of mountains has changed over time. Many of us think of mountains as beautiful, dramatic landscapes—desirable locations where we go to ski in the winter and hike in the summer. This, however, is a relatively modern view of mountains created only since the late eighteenth century when traveling to mountainous regions for scientific reasons, leisure, or adventure was a new developmnent in Europe (Hall 1991:41). Before that time, mountains were feared and avoided—obstacles to be crossed at great peril (Cooley 2005:74). Improved roads and the introduction of train service into mountain areas encouraged tourism in the late nineteenth century, further changing the popular image of mountains into destinations of desire. Of course, mountains still do hold real dangers, but in the era of extreme sports, these dangers, too, form part of mountains' attraction. Though mountains often serve as natural borders, they also evoke a sense of freedom and escape rather than containment.

Figure 5.4
View of Giewont, one of the peaks of the Tatra Mountains, viewed from the village of Kościelisko, 1995. *Timothy J. Cooley.*

Map 5.1
Podhale region of Poland.

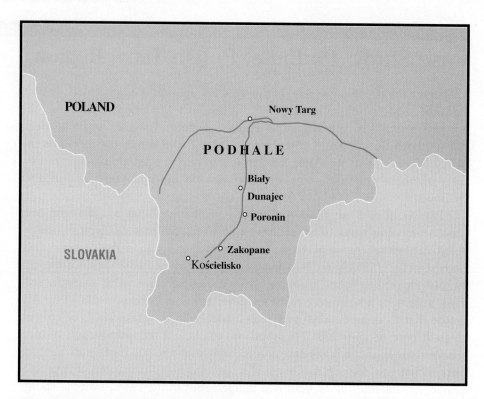

People and Music in Podhale

*Górale** means "mountaineer(s)" (*góra* means "mountain"), and many consider the *Górale* of Podhale to be a particular ethnic group within Poland. Ethnicity is a cultural rather than a biological category. *Górale* express and even create their own and others' understanding of who they are with their cultural practices, including the music that they make. While some of the qualities of the music that *Górale* make are ancient, a clear sense of a music specific to Podhale did not emerge until the end of the nineteenth century and the first few decades of the twentieth. This was the same time that *Górale* as an ethnic group was also being defined (Cooley 2005:67–72). Today, we can identify a music-culture that is indigenous to the Tatra region, that on some level expresses *Górale* as a people, and that we can easily distinguish from music in other regions of Poland, but it would have been more difficult to do this a century ago. *Górale* call this music **muzyka Podhala**. *Górale* musicians also play and sing common, international songs and dances (waltzes, polkas, and *csárdáses*, for example), as well as popular and classical music from Europe and America, but a core repertory of *muzyka Podhala* is still actively performed by and identified with *Górale*.

Muzyka Podhala includes an impressive array of styles and genres, including unmetered singing, topical songs and ballads, and unique instruments such as regional style bagpipes, flutes, and alpine horns. There are also several dance styles, including a dance genre for groups of men associated with legendary Robin Hood-like robbers (see Cooley 2005). Here I will focus on just one genre, a characteristic couples' dance called **góralski** or **po góralsku** (in the *Górale* style).

---

*Following Louise Wrazen (1991:175), I use the plural Polish word *Górale* as both noun and adjective, singular and plural. For an explanation of *Górale* as an ethnic category, see Cooley 2005:67–72.

Music for Dancing

The *góralski* differs from most social dancing that you might be familiar with in that the focus is on a single couple—one man and one woman. Though *Górale* tend to include many group dances such as waltzes and polkas at gatherings, the *góralski* is specifically performed as an expression of *góraleness*. The *góralski* dance and the accompanying music are highly improvised yet fall within elaborate structures. Improvisation is always governed by rules (see the discussion of performance in Chapter 1) and is never completely free of preexisting forms, gestures, and melodic ideas. We will consider three integrated layers of this elaborate *góralski* structure: the social, the musical, and the physical (the dance itself).

The *góralski* may first appear to be social interaction between one man and one woman, but on closer observation we see that it requires the active participation of additional dancers, musicians, and the circle of onlookers. The dance suite begins when a male dancer approaches the band (the traditional string band or **kapela**) and requests a dance, usually by slipping some money into one of the f-holes of the *basy* and singing a song to the tune or **nuta** to which he intends to dance. A *nuta* [plural, *nuty*] literally means "note," but *Górale* musicians use it to refer to a melodic idea or tune family. A *nuta* is not a fixed tune but must be improvised or played a little differently each time. The first *nuta in a góralski* suite is invariably an **ozwodna**, *a* term that refers to a particular type of *nuta* and specific dance steps. While the primary male dancer is telling the band which *nuta* to play, a second male dancer is seeking out and inviting to dance the woman with whom the primary male dancer desires to dance. (The first male dancer arranged this with the second beforehand.) The second man brings the chosen woman to the dance floor and "turns her out"—in a loose embrace they turn first clockwise, then counterclockwise before the man spins the woman. He then leaves the woman to dance with the primary male dancer. The primary male and female dance without touching, and after each *nuta* in the suite, the female dancer leaves the immediate dance area, usually having a seat and chatting with her friends. In other words, she moves back into the community that literally surrounds the dance. For each subsequent dance within the suite, she is reintroduced to the dance floor either by the secondary male dancer or, more typically, by a group of female friends. When the primary male dancer decides he has danced enough, he calls for one of the two closing *nuty* called **"zielona"** (literally "green") while continuing to dance with his partner. When the band hears the call for "green," they shift to the new *nuta* without pausing, and touching for the first time, the couple turns together using the same steps employed when others introduced the female dancer to the dance floor. Thus while most of the dancing is done by one man and one woman, the woman is also introduced to the dance area by other members of the community. For even one couple to dance together, community involvement is required.

Music for the *góralski* consists of a series of distinct *nuty* as called by the primary male dancer and played by the *kapela*. With the exception of the last *nuta*, "zielona,"

Salient Characteristics of
European Music for Dancing

- *Góralski* dance is a performative representation of *Górale* from the Polish Tatra Mountains

- Involves a suite of *nuty* with corresponding dance steps

- Focus is on one male and female couple

- The female is traditionally introduced to the dance area by other community members

- Musicking and dancing require great improvisatory skill

MindTap°

◀)) **LISTEN TO**

Góralski suite part 1: *Ozwodna*; *Góralski* suite part 2: *Ozwodna*; *Góralski* suite part 3: *Krzesana* "trzy a ros"; *Góralski* suite part 4: *Krzesana* "po dwa"; and *Góralski* suite part 5: *Krzesana* "ze stary" and "zielona," online. All performed by Krzysztof Trebunia-Tutka, lead violin; Jan Trebunia-Tutka, second violin and voice; Paweł Trebunia-Tutka, *basy*; with Anna, Marcin, and Aniela Styrczula-Maśniak dancing.

which is performed as a type of coda attached to the penultimate *nuta*, each dance tune is usually clearly separated from the previous dance (Active Listenings 5.3 to 5.7). Dances may have many seconds or even several minutes between each *nuta*, yet the separate *nuty* and dances are considered to be within the same suite or dance sequence. They are distinct events within the larger suite that go together and have a clear beginning and end.

A *Góralski* dance suite always begins with an *ozwodna*. The most common metrical structure of an *ozwodna* is built around five-bar phrases with two pulses in each bar (Active Listenings 5.3 and 5.4). Though unusual for dances in Western Europe, this metrical structure is common in the Tatras and some of the neighboring

ACTIVE LISTENING 5.3
Góralski Suite Part 1: *Ozwodna*

MindTap·

🎧 **WATCH** an Active Listening Guide of this selection online.

COUNTER NUMBER	COMMENTARY/TEXT	TRANSLATION
0:00	Singer Jan Trebunia-Tutka calls for the dance by singing a couplet. The lead violin and *basy* join in on the fifth metrical pulse (third bar) playing the accompanying five-bar ostinato pattern.	
	Ej, dziwcyno kochanie	Girl my love
	Nie lygoj na sianie	Don't lie in the hay
0:06	Jan sings the second couplet, using the same *nuta*.	
	Ej, bo ciy sianko zdradzi	The hay will betray you
	Bedom chłopcy radzi	The boys will be happy.
0:11	Krzysztof Trebunia-Tutka, lead violinist, takes over the melodic lead and plays a variation of the same *nuta*, phrase A. Marcin Styrczula-Maśniak begins to dance with his sister, Aniela. We can hear his shoes stomping on the wooden floor.	
0:16	Lead violin plays a variation of same *nuta* over the same five-bar ostinato, but his variation differs enough that we will call it phrase B.	
0:20	Variation of phrase B, establishing ABB melodic phrase pattern.	
0:24	Phrase A variation.	
0:27	Phrase B variation.	
0:31	Phrase B variation.	
0:35	Phrase A variation.	
0:38	Phrase B variation.	
0:42	Phrase B variation. Dancer Marcin heard clapping while he dances.	
0:45	Phrase A variation.	
0:49	Phrase B variation; dancers heard stomping.	
0:52	Phrase B variation.	

ACTIVE LISTENING 5.4
Góralski Suite Part 2: *Ozwodna*

COUNTER NUMBER	COMMENTARY
0:00	Lead violinist Krzysztof introduces the *nuta*. The accompanying violin and *basy* join on beat five (third bar). *Nuta* is three five-bar phrases long, ABB variation pattern. The ostinato differs slightly in each five-bar phrase, repeating every fifteen bars.
0:05	Phrase B, five bars
0:09	Phrase B, five bars
0:13	Phrase A; *basy* pattern DD EE DD ED EE
0:17	Phrase B; *basy* pattern DE EE AA BC# DD
0:21	Phrase B; *basy* pattern DD EE DE AA DD
0:25	Phrase A (ABB repeats)
0:29	Phrase B
0:33	Phrase B
0:37	Phrase A (ABB repeats)
0:41	Phrase B
0:45	Phrase B
0:49	Phrase A (ABB repeats)
0:52	Phrase B
0:56	Phrase B
0:59	Phrase A
1:03	Phrase B and end

MindTap
WATCH an Active Listening Guide of this selection online.

Carpathian Mountain regions. The opening *ozwodna* is followed by a sequence of *nuty*/dances that may include additional *ozwodne*, and *drobne* ("small") and/or *krzesane* ("striking"). *Drobne* and *krzesane* are closely related tune types combining virtuosic violin playing with elaborate, athletic dancing by the man. They often have four-bar phrases, but many have unusual phrase structures. As we have seen, each dance cycle ends with one of two tunes, or a medley of both, called "zielona" while the dance couple touches for the first time and dances a specific turning step. See Table 5.1 for a summary of the structure of the *góralski* dance suite.

Table 5.1 **Structure of the *Góralski* Dance Suite**

Genre	Description	Key Structural Points
Ozwodna	Opening *nuta*/dance	Second male dancer "turns" the female dancer onto dance area.
Krzesana, drobna, or *ozwodna*	Any number in any order	Usually a group of women reintroduce the primary female dancer to the dance area for each subsequent dance.
"Zielona"	Closing song/*nuta* and dance gesture	No break in the music or dance. Lead male dancer "turns" the female dancer, and the dance suite ends.

Taken together, Active Listenings 5.3 to 5.7 represent a complete *góralski* dance suite as performed in the village of Kościelisko, Poland, by three members of the Trebunia-Tutka family: Krzysztof is on lead violin, his brother Jan on accompanying violin, and their cousin Paweł on *basy*. They were recorded in the home of Ewa and Wojtek Styrczula-Maśniak, where I was staying for a few days in August 2005. I asked Ewa and Wojtek's daughter, Anna, and one of her brothers, Marcin, to dance to inspire the *kapela* while it played and to allow us to hear the sounds of the dancers' shoes on the wooden floor and their occasional claps. Their cousin, Aniela Styrczula-Maśniak, also helped out by turning Anna out onto the dance floor after the first *ozwodna*. Anna, Marcin, and Aniela wore what they had on when I asked them to dance, except they changed into their *kierpce*, tooled-leather shoes with hard leather soles and straps that wrap up the ankles (Figure 5.5). The musicians exclaimed that they played much better with the dancers because the dancing gave them drive and energy. Interaction between musicians and dancers is part of the aesthetic of the music that helps generate pleasure as well as beauty.

Listen carefully to the accompanying ostinato pattern for the first *ozwodna*. The ostinato pattern is a typical, five-bar *ozwodna* type (note the *basy* pattern: DD EE DE AA DD) (see Active Listening 5.3).

The second dance in the suite is an additional *ozwodna*, also in five-bar phrases, but the ostinato differs significantly. The *basy* plays a variation of this pitch pattern—three phrases, each five bars long: DD EE DD ED EE, DE EE AA BC# DD, DD EE DE AA DD. This dance is not introduced by a song (Active Listening 5.4).

The third dance *nuta* is a *krzesana* called "trzy a ros" ("three and one"). As with many of the *krzesana* genre *nuty*, the name refers to the structure of the *nuta* and ostinato. Listen online to *Góralski* suite part 3: *Krzesana* "trzy a ros" and pay careful attention to the accompanying *basy* that changes pitch on the third and fourth beat as follows: DD AD, DD AD, DD AD, and so on. In every four-beat section,

Figure 5.5
Aniela Styrczula-Maśniaka (left) turning out her cousin Anna Styrczula-Maśniaka (center), who will then dance with her brother Marcin (right). This photograph was taken during the session when the *Góralski* Suite examples (Active Listening 5.3 to 5.7) were recorded in the Styrczula-Maśniaka home in Kościelisko, Poland, 2005. *Timothy J. Cooley.*

there are three D pitches and one A pitch, hence the name "three and one." The accompanying violin in this example plays a more elaborate "harmonic" ostinato (Active Listening 5.5). (Harmony is a concept that fits only awkwardly with *muzyka Podhala*. The *basy* and accompanying violin pitch and chord changes function to mark time and musical structure rather than to create the harmonic pull of most European classical music and some Euro-American popular music.)

The fourth dance in the suite is another *krzesana* called "po dwa" ("in two"). The accompanying violin and *basy* change chords every two beats (chords DD AA DD AA, and so on.), hence "in two" (Active Listening 5.6).

The next dance is also a *krzesana*; this one is to a modulating sequence of *nuty* with a changing ostinato pattern called "ze stary" ("the old one") (Active Listening 5.7). Then without stopping, at exactly 1:43 seconds into the audio example, the lead dancer gestures for the end of the dance, and the band immediately shifts into "zielona," the closing coda. Recall that the "zielona" *nuta* marks the end of the dance sequence and the moment when the lead male dancer turns the lead female dancer, ostensibly making physical contact with her for the first time during the dance.

We can make several preliminary interpretations about the social meaning of *góralski* dancing based on the physical structure alone. Before we do this, however, we should remember that *Górale* of Podhale are modern Europeans

ACTIVE LISTENING 5.5
Góralski Suite Part 3: *Krzesana* "Trzy a Ros"

MindTap
🎧 **WATCH** an Active Listening Guide of this selection online.

COUNTER NUMBER	COMMENTARY/TEXT	TRANSLATION
0:00	Jan Trebunia-Tutka introduces the dance by singing. The string band joins in the third bar. *Aśtajrom, aśtajrom,* *Sto śtyrdziyści kacek mom.*	(nonsense vocables) I have one hundred and forty ducks.
0:05	Second sung couplet. *A te kacki mojyj Kaśki,* *Jo siy z Kaśkom dobrze znom.*	Those ducks belong to my Kate, I know my Kate very well.
0:09	Krzysztof plays a variation of the same *nuta* on the violin. Note the unvarying basy/ostinato pattern: DD AD, DD AD, and so on.	
0:33	Note how the string band adjusts tempo to the audible steps of the male dancer.	
0:58	Following the lead violinist, the string band modulates down to the key of G. The *basy* ostinato pattern becomes GG DG, GG DG, and so on.	
1:12	The piece modulates back up to the key of D before ending.	

ACTIVE LISTENING 5.6
Góralski Suite Part 4: *Krzesana* "Po Dwa"

COUNTER NUMBER	COMMENTARY
0:00	Dance called, not by singing, but by calling out *"po dwa!"* The lead violinist begins the *nuta*; the accompanying *basy* and violin join in third bar. *Basy* ostinato pattern: DD AA DD AA, etc.
0:15	Beginning of second variation cycle. Each phrase is four bars long. Variation cycles usually begin with a phrase emphasizing a higher register.
0:28	Beginning the third variation cycle. Note that the number of four-bar phrases varies in each variation cycle.
0:44	Beginning of fourth and final variation cycle.

ACTIVE LISTENING 5.7
Góralski Suite Part 5: *Krzesana* "Ze Stary" and "Zielona"

COUNTER NUMBER	COMMENTARY/TEXT	TRANSLATION
0:00	Jan introduces the fifth dance with two sung couplets. The string band, as usual, joins in the third bar.	
	Ej se ino cina	Hey, only "cina cina" (nonsense vocables)
	Lepso Kaśka niz˙ Maryna	Kathy is better than Mary
	Kaśka uprać, Kaśka usyć	Kathy does laundry, Kathy sews
	Maryniy siy nie kce rusyć.	Mary does not want to move.
0:10	Krzysztof on lead violin picks up the *nuta* with its four-bar phrases and plays for the dance. Note the *basy* ostinato pattern: AA AE, AA AE, and so on.	
0:22	Following a melodic cue played by Krzysztof, the ostinato pattern changes to EE AA, EE AA, and so on.	
0:38	Following the lead violinist again, the ostinato pattern changes back to AA AE, and so on	
1:06	The *nuta* modulates up to D, with a *basy* ostinato pattern: DD DA, DD DA, and so on.	
1:28	The *nuta* modulates to G, with a *basy* ostinato pattern: DD GG, DD GG, and so on.	
1:43	Following a visual cue given by the lead dancer, the *nuta* abruptly changes "zielona" for the ending turn of the dancers.	

who share much culturally with other Europeans and many Americans. Yet traditional cultural practices such as the *góralski* dance contain information concerning core values and ideas about what it means to be *Górale* in the twenty-first century, even if such practices do not describe how any one individual lives his or her life (see also Wrazen 2013). With this in mind, we note that within the overall structure of the dance the primary male dancer exercises considerable freedom and control (Wrazen 1988:197). He determines what dance *nuty* will be used, with whom he will dance, and for how long they will dance together. The primary female dancer must express herself by the way she dances within the context controlled by the man. Her options are limited but her intentions can be read by the community as they observe how she responds to the male dancer with her body language, facial expressions, and general interactions with her partner (Wrazen 1988:200–201). Remember that for most of the dance only one couple dances at a time while all others are free to watch—and they usually do so with great interest. The watching community may also comment on the dance, sometimes singing their commentary and thus creating a fascinating clash of musical sounds as the singing competes with the dance ensemble. As might be expected, dancing *po góralsku* entails a certain amount of showing off within one's own close circle of friends, family, and community. Especially for the man, it is a vigorous, athletic dance that requires skill and stamina in addition to a thorough knowledge of the music.

Life Story: Krzysztof Trebunia-Tutka

A violinist and singer featured on several of the online music examples for this chapter, including the dance suite we just analyzed, Krzysztof Trebunia-Tutka embodies many of the themes of this chapter. He is a traditional musician in that he comes from a long line of family village musicians, he is respected in Podhale as one of the finest musicians and dancers in the *muzyka Podhala* style, and he is an excellent teacher. "Traditional" in this sense means doing things as they were done in the past, the way one's parents, grandparents, and as in Krzysztof's case, even great-grandparents did things. Yet Krzysztof is a modern, cosmopolitan, twenty-first-century global citizen.

Figure 5.6
Norman Twinkle Grant, foreground left, and Krzysztof Trebunia-Tutka, right, performing in a fusion concert at a festival in Zakopane, Poland, 2009. *Timothy J. Cooley.*

He has shared with me in interviews and informal conversations that he believes traditions must change and adapt in order to stay alive in the present day. Therefore, Krzysztof is comfortable and capable playing the violin, shepherd's flute, or dancing *po góralsku* in a local-style costume as his great-grandfather would have done, and later on the same day playing on a festival stage before thousands of fans with a reggae band from Jamaica or a rock-fusion band from Warsaw (Figure 5.6).

I met Krzysztof in Podhale in 1992. He was performing with his father, Władysław, and sister, Anna, at an informal celebration after a small folk festival in Poronin near his home village of Biały Dunajec (Figure 5.7). At the time he was twenty-two years old, a university student in Kraków, and recognized at least locally as an accomplished violinist, dancer, and tradition-bearer. Krzysztof has gone on to became a household name in all of Poland and a popular world-beat music performer and recording artist with several CDs that made the charts in Western Europe. Yet he remains grounded in the Podhale region, where he actively teaches local children how to play *muzyka Podhala,* sing, and dance.

In my interviews and conversations with Krzysztof over the years, two themes consistently emerge: first, deep knowledge of the cultural practices of Krzysztof's ancestors is very important for his self-conception and his understanding of his own musical activities; second, while grounded in this sense of musical heritage, he believes it is his right and responsibility to experiment with his music.

Krzysztof was born in 1970 and raised in the small village of Biały Dunajec, Poland. Whether in conversations with me, in the introductions he makes when performing on stage, or in the liner notes of a published recording, Krzysztof is quick to reference a long line of ancestors who played *muzyka Podhala.* His great-grandfather, Stanslaw Mróz, was a shepherd and a respected bagpipe player.* Mróz is mentioned in the writings of the Polish musicologist Adolf Chybiński, who worked in Podhale before and after World War I (Chybiński [1923] 1961:362), and he was acquainted with the famous Polish composer Karol Szymanowki, who frequently visited Podhale. Krzysztof's grandfather, Jan Trebunia-Tutka (b. 1898), was also a musician, as was Jan's brother, Stanisław (b. 1907). Jan and

Figure 5.7

From right to left: Andrzej Polak, Władysław Trebunia-Tutka, Krzysztof, and Anna (partially blocked by Krzysztof's violin and arm). Poronin, Poland, 1992. *Timothy J. Cooley.*

---

*Bagpipes are often associated with shepherding cultures. The bags themselves are made from the hides of sheep or, as in the case of *Górale* pipes, goats.

his wife had nine children, four boys and five girls. All of the boys were musicians, including the youngest, Władysław (b. 1944), Krzysztof's father. By the 1950s, Władysław was already recognized as a skilled violinist, and the Trebunia-Tutka family band was making a name for itself at the local and national folk music festivals and contests that mushroomed in postwar Poland. When Krzysztof told me about this long line of musicians, he noted with a sense of pride and amusement that in the 1950s there were so many family musicians that the Trebunia-Tutka family could produce three bands to simultaneously play three different weddings or parties.

Here Krzysztof explains how his father reluctantly began teaching him how to play violin:

> When I was about six years old, Mama asked Dad to teach me to play. He gave me a little ***złóbcoki*** [boat-shaped folk violin; Figure 5.8] to play; he did not want me to break a real violin. I did not like it that much, and he did not want to teach me. But little by little I learned, and he would every now and then suggest that we play a tune together. He would tell me how to do something, what I was doing wrong. (interview with author, August 23, 2005)

Even though his father was an excellent music teacher, Krzysztof found it challenging to learn from him at first. However, he did teach Krzysztof how to dance the difficult *ozwodna* steps by the time he was seven. That same year, Krzysztof joined a local school song-and-dance troupe that he enjoyed very much, in part because of the camaraderie with friends. Thanks to his father's teaching, Krzysztof became one of the best dancers in the school.

At that time, in the 1970s, it was quite common for schools, villages, and even businesses to sponsor regional song-and-dance troupes. Poland was then governed by the Communist Party, which encouraged folk music troupes as ideologically appropriate expressions of the people. Whether or not any individual in a troupe accepted that ideology was beside the point. Krzysztof as a young boy was probably not yet that politically aware. He appreciated the song-and-dance troupes for the social and traveling opportunities that they provided. He recalls traveling with his school troupe at age eight or nine to Germany and how inspired he was to meet musicians and dancers from around the world. In the 1980s, Poland was under martial law as the Communist Party attempted to resist the SOLIDARITY* movement that led to the end of communist hegemony in 1989. During martial law, travel outside the

Figure 5.8

Władysław Trebunia-Tutka playing a *złóbcoki*. Poronin, 1992. *Timothy J. Cooley.*

---

*The *Solidarność* movement (SOLIDARITY in English, and typically written in capital letters) achieved free elections and won those elections in 1989. This set off a wave of anticommunist movements throughout Central Europe.

country was severely restricted, but Krzysztof was able to travel around Europe with his troupe.

Krzysztof's father took a greater interest in his son's abilities when he saw him perform with the school group, as Krzysztof relates:

> He showed me how to play on the *fujarka* [wooden flute associated with shepherds]. I liked that very much. I could very quickly learn how to play the tunes. I won first place at a contest on that *fujarka*. That was great motivation, and I would play whenever I had a moment: waiting for my Mama who worked at the hospital, waiting at a bus stop, whenever I had a moment. And all the time I was getting better at the *złóbcoki*. (interview with the author, August 23, 2005)

In 1982, when Krzysztof was about twelve, his father brought him with the family band to a national folk festival in central Poland. Krzysztof recalls the inspiration he received when the family won first prize at the contest. At that time he also started attending a local music school, where he learned how to read music, the basics of European common practice music theory, and the rudiments of playing the piano. Though he did not stick with the music school, he continues to apply these basic skills to his music. For example, he can read the musical notations in books about *góralska muzyka* and uses these books to supplement his understanding of the repertory he learned from his family and community teachers.

When he was thirteen, Krzysztof received an accordion from his father; with his piano keyboard skills, he quickly learned how to play tunes on this new instrument. Though not considered traditional in *Górale* music, and though the equal-tempered tuning of the accordion conflicts with *Górale* tuning practices, the instrument is very useful for pan-European social dance music such as waltzes and polkas. These pan-European dance tunes play an important role at local weddings, and Władysław began taking his son and his accordion with him when he played wedding parties. Wedding celebrations in Podhale typically go on for several days, and the partying lasts until the early morning hours. Though Krzysztof was young for this type of work, he was tall enough to seem a bit older and, besides, he was with his father.

As Krzysztof matured, he shifted his energies back to violin playing and dancing—respected skills for a young man in this region. By the time he was twenty, he was considered one of the best young regional musicians in Podhale. While attending university in Kraków, Krzysztof became the musical director of Skalni, an influential *Górale*-style song-and-dance group that drew its members from university students of the various institutions in Kraków. In 1990, he started a band under his own name (Kapela Krzysztofa Trebunie-Tutki) that recorded a cassette released in 1992, *Żywot Janicka Zbójnika* (*The Life Story of Janicek Zbójnik*).

At about the same time, Krzysztof was involved in another recording project with his immediate family—father Władysław and sister Anna—that opened the doors to many new musical opportunities. In 1991, the Trebunia-Tutka family band made a world-beat fusion recording with a Jamaican reggae band based in London—the Twinkle Brothers. The recording that resulted made the popular music charts in Europe and launched Krzysztof's second career as a professional musician, which included several additional recordings with the Twinkle Brothers (Figure 5.9), as well as rock-fusion, electronic dance, and classical-fusion recordings (for example, the CD *Jubileusz* with Warszawski Chór Międzyuczelnainy [The Warsaw Intercolegiate Choir]). The first recording with the Twinkle Brothers features *muyzka Podhala,* including traditional texts in what we might call a reggae dub sonic context with Jamaican patois glosses on the *Górale* poetry. In my interviews with Krzysztof, he consistently notes that while some may criticize the popularizing of versions of *muzyka Podhala,* he believes that he always treats the music with respect, never performing a parody of his own heritage. In addition, the experience has prompted him to be creative, writing new texts about contemporary life in Podhale, as well as writing new tunes in the *Górale* style. Krzysztof's first new composition was "Kochaj a buduj," a song about building a traditional wooden house; Krzysztof is an architect by profession, specializing in designing modern houses using the traditional log-construction technique.

The Trebunia-Tutka family now tours the world playing a deliberate mix of very traditional-style music using *złóbcokis,* wooden flutes, and bagpipes; modern adaptations of older music; and entirely new compositions that add an electric bass and drum set to the more-traditional ensemble of violins and *basy* (see Figure 5.6).

Krzysztof is a legitimate pop star in Poland, a household name with records in most every CD store. Yet he still takes time to teach groups of children the basics of *muzyka Podhala.* When I asked him about this, he responded that the pay for this teaching is very low and he does not have much time, but that teaching children is a mission. Besides, he says, he has an ability to teach, and many of his students go on to make him very proud.

Krzysztof teaches his students how to read and write music using cipher notation—a system that is a good teaching and memory aid but is not as prescriptive as the music notation system used for European classical music. His introduction of a level of literacy to a musical practice that emphasizes oral transmission is consistent with Krzysztof's interpretation of his own world-beat fusion projects, as well as new compositions that reference traditional style. Deep knowledge of one's own heritage is essential for responsible musical

Figure 5.9

CD cover to *Trebunie-Tutki w Sherwood,* Kamahuk, 1996. From left to right: Della Grant, Krzysztof, Norman "Twinkle" Grant (in *Górale* costume), Anna, and Władysław Trebunia-Tutka. *Photograph by Piotra Gronau; graphic design by Kinga Mazurek-Sforza. CD conception and compilation by Włodzimierz Klesczc and Krzysztof Trebunia-Tutka. Used with permission.*

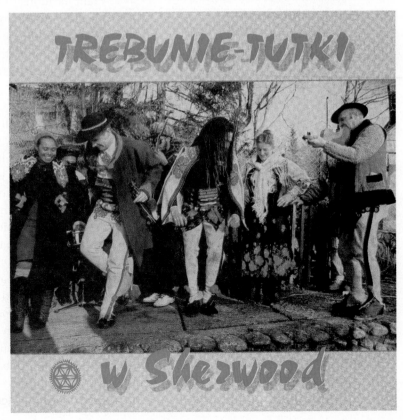

self-representation. This knowledge is also liberating. Grounded in *muzyka Podhala*, Krzysztof is free to go beyond the repertory and style of his ancestors— to play music from Slovakia, lowland Poland, and Hungary, and to collaborate with musicians from Jamaica and elsewhere. As a performer whose popularity extends well beyond his home mountain region and nation, Krzysztof takes seriously the responsibility to educate people about *muzyka Podhala*—what it is as well as what it is not—and he demands the freedom to do this respectfully, on his own terms.

European Regional Musics on the Global Stage: Two Case Studies

Since the 1970s, ethnomusicologists have generally not believed in musical *purity*—music that is created by an isolated group of people reflecting no outside influences. Certainly in Europe it has been a long time since communities have been truly isolated. The Tatra Mountains are still often described as isolated, but even there people (with their musical ideas) have come from distant locations to settle, and since the late nineteenth century the region has been a popular tourist destination. There are qualities of *muzyka Podhala* that are unique and distinct, but not isolated and certainly not pure. Here we examine music that deliberately brings together local and distant musical ideas and sounds.

> ## Salient Characteristics of
> ## European Regional Musics on the Global Stage
>
> - Sounds found in popular European and American music are first heard (reggae in the Polish example, rock guitar and drums in the Bosnian example)
>
> - Less-familiar local sounds are then added, revealing that we are listening to world-beat fusion
>
> - Individuals practicing local traditions are able to access much larger international audiences without compromising the integrity of their traditions

This book offers many examples of the impact of globalization on musical practices. The chapters on South India and Indonesia in particular describe some of the ways that musics from those parts of the world have been combined with Western popular music. This type of synthesis has many names—from fusion, hybrid, and syncretism to creole. I use the term **fusion** because it suggests the combination of different elements through heat, or in the case of cultural practices, through intense contact and interaction. Another useful term is **world beat**, a wide category that combines popular genres of music that have a level of international recognition with a local or indigenous music considered interesting or colorful. Other terms used to refer to the same phenomena are *world music, global music,* and *global pop* (for discussions of these terms, see Erlmann 1996:467; Taylor 1997:1–3; and Feld 2001:191). Perhaps most interesting in the context of this book are the perspectives of indigenous musicians as they embrace globalization. On a closer look and listening, one usually discovers that imitation of Western popular music is not their objective; rather, they intend to stake out a local identity in the context of global media.

Case Study 1: *Muzyka Podhala* and Reggae

Both the discovery of the music of Podhale in Chicago and Krzysztof's life story raise interesting and important questions concerning the relevancy of so-called traditional musical practices in the twenty-first century. One premise of this book—and of ethnomusicology—is that music is conceived of and constructed differently in different regions of the world. Music may change in meaning while maintaining its form when carried by immigrants from the Tatra Mountains to the urban landscapes of Chicago or Toronto. But what happens when a family band of "traditional" *Górale* musicians decides to join forces with another family band, this time of reggae musicians with roots in Jamaica? How does a local musical practice adapt to a globalizing world?

"Krzesany po Dwa" ("Going to the Village") features the Trebunia-Tutka family band together with the Twinkle Brothers band, introduced above. It exemplifies both the process and some of the issues raised by world-beat fusions (see Figure 5.9). Considering the music-sound, we have a piece that is easily recognized as fitting within the popular genre of reggae. But what makes it *sound* like reggae? Is it possible to *hear* it as *muzyka Podhala* instead of reggae, or even simultaneously as reggae?

To answer these questions, we might begin by determining what makes it sound like reggae in the first place. Listen carefully to the first few seconds of "Krzesany po Dwa" and follow Active Listening 5.8. First, we hear a two-second drum introduction, which alone tells us that this is not *muzyka Podhala*—traditionally, there are no drums in Podhale. The drum introduction is followed by what a reggae musician might call the *dub,* a rhythmic/harmonic ostinato played on drum set, electric bass, electric guitar, and piano. What most identifies this dub as reggae is the piano emphasis on the second beat of each measure, supported by the snare drum, which also accents this beat. The second beat of a duple-meter measure (or the 2nd and 4th beats in meter) is usually felt as a weaker beat, and when it is accented, often with a relatively high-pitched instrument, a lilting feeling is created that induces movement in listeners' bodies. This regular marking by a medium- to high-pitched sound of a typically unaccented metrical position also defines a polka. There are differences (a polka is typically much quicker, and the marked position is on an "upbeat" rather than on the beat itself as is the case with reggae, for example), but the principle is the same.

Almost immediately, as the reggae dub is being established, a voice is heard asking, "Hey Johnny, where you goin', man?," to which a second, lower voice responds, "To the village." There is nothing particularly "reggae" about this spoken dialogue, yet the use of the English language again reminds us that this is not *muzyka Podhala.* In fact, there is nothing Polish at all about the music to this point, except for the whistle and vocal call heard in the background starting at five seconds. But most of us would not be able to identify the whistle and call as specifically Polish, and the music remains sonically reggae. Not until fifteen seconds into the piece do our ears receive any real hint that this is not traditional reggae. At this moment, we hear a *Górale* string ensemble playing *Krzesana* "po dwa," one of the *góralski* dance *nuty* introduced earlier. In Active Listening 5.6 you will hear the same ostinato and *nuta* heard in "Krzesany po Dwa" ("Going to the Village"), beginning at 0:15 (see Active Listening 5.8). "Po dwa" means "in two," and careful listening will confirm that the *basy* and accompanying violins, as well as the bass guitar, piano, and electric guitar, change harmony every two beats: two beats on D, two beats on A.

ACTIVE LISTENING 5.8
"Krzesany po Dwa" ("Going to the Village")

COUNTER NUMBER	COMMENTARY/TEXT
0:00	Drum introduction.
0:02	Reggae dub established by drum, bass, electric guitar, and piano. Spoken in English: "Hey Johnny, where you goin', man?" "To the village," and so forth.
0:15	*Krzesany* "po dwa" *nuta* played on violins introduced.
0:25	The Twinkle Brothers begin singing in harmony: "Comin' from the mountains …"
0:41	The Trebunia-Tutka family sings the *Górale* dialect original text (paraphrased in the English texts sung by the Twinkle Brothers).
0:48	The Trebunia-Tutka family band plays a second *nuta* using the same "po dwa" ostinato: DD AA, DD AA, and so on.
0:52	More spoken dialogue in English by the Twinkle Brothers.
1:01	Twinkle Brothers sing a second verse: "The boys are down there drinkin' …"
1:14	Modulation to the key of G, same "po dwa" ostinato: GG DD, GG DD, and so on. Spoken dialogue by the Twinkle Brothers.
1:27	Reggae dub, whistle, and vocal call of a sort used by *Górale* in the Tatras.
1:36	Violin playing a "po dwa" *nuta* over the reggae dub. More vocal calls in *Górale* dialect.
1:56	Reggae band drops out, leaving the *Górale kapela* playing "po dwa" alone.
2:03	Reggae band returns as one of the Trebunia-Tutka family members sings a couplet.
2:37	*Górale kapela* drops out; modulation from key of D to G. Reggae band bass and drum play dub.
2:50	Sung *Górale* text accompanied by reggae drum and bass alone.
3:03	Modulation to C, ostinato: GG CC, GG CC, and so on. Full reggae band and *Górale kapela* return.
3:24	*Górale* dialect texts sung. Accompanied by both the reggae band and *Górale kapela*.
3:32	Modulation back to D, ostinato: DD AA, DD AA, and so on. Both family bands playing.
4:18	Bass and drum dub only.
4:36	*Górale* dialect couplet sung over bass and drum dub.
4:54	*Górale* violin returns for a few phrases before the end.

At twenty-five seconds, two people sing in harmony "Comin' from the mountains, Johnny the outlaw ..." over the reggae dub and *Górale* string ensemble mix. The English dialect verse is a loose translation of the original *Górale* dialect text, *Idzie z góry zbójnici ...*, that we hear at 0:41. *Zbójnici* are legendary mountain robbers, compared by *Górale* to Robin Hood, suggesting that their crimes were justified—robbing the rich to provide for the poor whom the rich had exploited. By now it is clear that this is fusion: music we experience as reggae combined with music from the Polish Tatra Mountains. The music is multivalent; that is, we can hear and interpret it in many ways. The dub establishes the sound as reggae; the violins, the tune that they play, and *Górale* dialect text signal world-beat fusion; a Polish listener and others familiar with *muzyka Podhala* will experience the piece as *Górale* at least on some level. Keep listening, and at 1:56–2:02 the reggae dub drops out completely leaving only the *Górale* ensemble. If someone began auditioning this piece at this moment, it would sound like traditional *muzyka Podhala*—at least for six seconds.

This fusion of *Górale* music with reggae tells us many things about Podhale in the late twentieth and early twenty-first centuries. First, if Podhale ever was a truly isolated corner of Europe, it can hardly make that claim now. People from all around the world travel to the Tatra Mountains, and even family musicians regionally recognized as local culture-bearers are now free to create music with internationally known reggae musicians. Second, ancient stories such as the *zbójnik* legends from Slovakia and Poland can be reinterpreted and given modern meaning. The desire for economic and individual independence, along with the perils of betrayal that are at the center of the *zbójnik* legend, are still relevant in Poland and they resonate with Jamaican Rastafarians as well as an international, world-beat audience. Both *Górale* and Jamaican Rastafarians have traditions of music about independence and heroic efforts to resist exploitation by the wealthy and powerful. Third, though the human desire for independence is probably universal, no single music system is universal. The fusion of reggae and *muzyka Podhala* required outside mediation from Włodzimierz Kleszcz, a Warsaw radio producer who originally conceived of the idea, and a group of studio mixers in Warsaw and London who actually put the reggae and *Górale* musical sounds together.

The Trebunia-Tutka family musicians went on to create many additional fusion recordings with the Twinkle Brothers and with other Polish musicians, ranging from reggae to jazz to modern choral arrangements. A partial listing of their recordings, as well as additional fusion projects, is provided in the Further Listening section at the end of this book.

Case Study 2: Riffing on Music from the "Southern Slavs"

Return for a moment to "Sister, Hold Your Chastity" (see Active Listening 5.2). This example of *ganga* singing was sung by Azra Bandić, Mevla Luckin, and Emsija Tatarović in 1990 on Mount Bjelašnica, south of the city Sarajevo in what was at the time part of The Socialist Federal Republic of Yugoslavia (literally "land of the south Slavs"). Yugoslavia was dissolved in 1992, and Sarajevo is now the capital city of the country called Bosnia and Herzegovina. It is a relatively

MindTap·
◀꜀)) **LISTEN TO**
"Sister, Hold Your Chastity," performed by Azra Bandić, Mevla Luckin, and Emsija Tetarvoić, online.

pluralistic society with three predominant ethnic groups: Bosniaks, Serbs, and Croats. These distinct ethnic identities are tied to histories of religious and other cultural practices rather than to biological differences or origins in different parts of the world. Bosniaks are traditionally Muslims whose ancestors converted to Islam during the four-hundred-twenty-five-year occupation of the area by the Ottoman Empire. Serbs are related historically and culturally to Eastern Orthodox Christianity, and Croats are associated with Roman Catholicism (see also Petrović 2000: 962–65). However, it would be a mistake to assume, for example, that all Serbs are practicing Orthodox Christians or that all Bosniaks are Muslim—just as one would not assume that Roman Catholicism defines the identity of all Italians. Yet, because religious institutions have a profound influence on cultural practices and societies in general, they can play key roles in the development of ethnic concepts as well as interethnic tensions.

Following the 1992 dissolution of Yugoslavia, ethnic tensions were exploited by those in power, and a regional war erupted between 1992 and 1995 that devastated most Bosnian villages, towns, and cities, killing or scattering many of their inhabitants. Thus, the physical and social context in which children would have learned *ganga* was fundamentally altered. For example, Umoljani—the home village of the singers of "Sister, Hold Your Chastity"—was burned down in 1992. Fortunately, the three girls who sang the *ganga* survived and were again singing together as young women in 2000 (see Slobin 2002:233–35 for a recording of these same individuals in 2000). While this story provides hope for the survival of individuals and musical practices, wars, death, and displacement do often result in musical change (see Pettan 1998 for more on the impact of war on music in Croatia).

Here we will consider two examples of change, both resulting from people and music moving from villages to urban centers and around the world. The first has to do with a long practice in Europe of celebrating folk music and adapting it for use in institutions of higher learning—the bastions of classical or art music. In 2005, I visited Sarajevo, where the devastation of the war a decade earlier was still manifest on every building. Even the Academy of Music had a large hole created by a missile that burst through a wall of their performance hall. At this academy, university-aged students are taught to sing *ganga* and other regional music genres, as well as the same European classical repertory found in other elite music schools. Emblematic of a cosmopolitan commitment to religious/ethnic tolerance that defines the spirit of Sarajevo, young Bosniak, Serb, and Croat women sang *ganga* together, socialized together, and laughed together. While cognizant of the real tensions and animosities that drive politics in many parts of the world, musical sounds and practices that travel with people from village to city, and from country to country, may offer counternarratives and cause for renewed hope.

Is *ganga* sung by a few friends in a village the same music as *ganga* sung by a cosmopolitan collection of individuals in a choir at an urban academy? The structure of the music is sonically identical: A lead singer introduces a song and is joined by two or more additional singers who perform "cutting" or "sobbing" accompanying patterns, producing the characteristic, close, harmonic intervals.

However, as cultural practice, the rural and academic *ganga* are quite distinct, reflecting dramatically different ideas about music and activities involving music, especially when we understand *ganga* as gendered practice. Men and women do not sing *ganga* together, and their styles and approaches toward the genre differ. For girls and women in a traditional rural Bosnian context, *ganga* is typically performed by a group of close friends who sing together almost exclusively from the time they are small children until they are married. Men and boys, on the other hand, are socially free to sing *ganga* with different groups and with singers from other villages. So a *ganga* choir at Sarajevo's Academy of Music is all the more extraordinary because the freedom to exchange singing partners is extended to young women who join their voices together with individuals from sometimes contentious ethnic groups to collectively reimagine, at least momentarily, a unified society.

The second example also comes from an elite institution of education, this time in Middletown, Connecticut. It too illustrates a dramatic change in musical structure from traditional Bosnian singing to what we are calling world-beat fusion, and to the aesthetic joining of individuals with diverse backgrounds. "Žuta Baba" was recorded in 1997 by a group of students associated with Wesleyan University who formed a band called Žabe i Babe ("Frogs and Grandmothers" in Serbo-Croatian; roughly equivalent to the American phrase "oranges and apples"). The individuals in Žabe i Babe learned to sing *ganga* at Wesleyan's Music Department from a Bosnian graduate student, Mirjana Laušević, the same woman who made the field recording "Sister, Hold Your Chastity."*

"Žuta Baba" is a version of a genre of traditional Bosnian village singing called *šaljive pjesme* (joking songs). This genre is considered appropriate for elderly women or men, and employing double entendre, the texts are often lascivious. The singing shares some of the musical qualities of *ganga* introduced earlier: loud, open-throated, powerful, and direct; an emphasis on close, harmonic intervals considered dissonant in other European music systems; and phrases ending with a slow, downward glissando or a high yelp (Active Listening 5.9). The musicians in Žabe i Babe also enjoyed playing and singing American rock music and felt these traditional Bosnian music genres shared many of the same sonic qualities, especially the powerful, direct singing and pleasure in harmonic intervals considered dissonant in other contexts. With members from several continents, they did what musicians have been doing for centuries: combining sounds from distant sources to create something new—a musical fusion.

MindTap
◀)) LISTEN TO
"Žuta Baba," performed by Bosnian/American fusion band *Žabe i Babe*, online.

---

*Mirjana Laušević was the source of almost all of the material and information for this interpretation of *ganga* and Bosnia and Herzegovina. I am deeply indebted to her for permission to use her recordings and for her suggestions for improving this chapter. This chapter is dedicated to the memory of Mirjana, who died much too young. Transcriptions and translations of the texts are by Laušević with additional assistance from Marcel Dražila.

ACTIVE LISTENING 5.9
"Žuta Baba"

COUNTER NUMBER	COMMENTARY/TEXT	TRANSLATION
0:00	Instrumental introduction (guitar and drums): Sounds like the intro to a rock song.	
0:25	Vocal introduction: three voices establish close harmony of a major second. Singing style does not sound like rock. Begins to sound like fusion. *Oja, oja, oja* (x4)	Nonsense vocables
0:38	Refrain: Close harmonies (major second then a minor third). First ending in a slow, descending glissando, then ending in a high yelp. *Oja, nina, oja, ne, oja nina, oja* *Oja, nina, oja, ne, oja nina, oja*	Nonsense vocables
0:51	Verse 1: Harmony of a major second on the third "kre" *Žuta baba snutak snuje, kre, kre, kre* *Žuta baba snutak snuje, hm, hm, hm* *U barici na kladici, kre, kre, kre* *U barici na kladici, hm, hm, hm*	Yellow grandma dreams a little dream, ribbit, ribbit, ribbit (frog sounds) In a puddle on a little log, ribbit …
1:03	Refrain	
1:17	Verse 2 *Otud ide rak na konju, kre, kre, kre* *Otud ide rak na konju, hm, hm, hm* *Sta to vic̆e tupa-lupa, kre, kre, kre* *Sta to vic̆e tupa-lupa, hm, hm, hm*	A crawdad on a horse is coming, ribbit … What is it that yells bum-bop, ribbit …
1:30	Instrumental (guitar riff, followed by clackers)	
1:55	Refrain	
2:08	Verse 3 *Sta to vic̆e tamo-vamo, kre, kre, kre* *Sta to vic̆e tamo-vamo, hm, hm, hm* *Sta to lijec̆e gori-doli, kre, kre, kre* *Sta to lijec̆e gori-doli, hm, hm, hm*	What is it that yells here-there, ribbit … What is it that flies up-down, ribbit …
2:20	Refrain	
2:33	Verse 1 repeated	
2:46	Coda *Oja, oja, oja* (x3)	

Reinterpreting Europe

What can we learn from its musics about the place called "Europe" and its peoples? One thing we learn is that there is no single way of being European. We find some general tendencies within European musical practices, but every generalization can be countered with examples from a European musical tradition that does things differently. *Ganga* singing in Bosnia, for example, is every bit as European as Mozart's compositions, even though what constitutes consonant singing differs greatly from Mozart's Salzburg to villages in Bosnia. Whereas some musical characteristics extend to a majority of musical practices in Europe, we can usually associate them with sweeping social and political forces such as the relatively recent institutions of nation-states and the much older influence of religions, especially Judaism, Christianity, and Islam.

Ethnomusicologists find it most satisfying to look at music among particular groups of people in specific locations. Even there they find great diversity of cultural practices, sometimes within individuals. Krzysztof Trebunia-Tutka represents a younger generation of a long line of family musicians in the well-defined region of the Polish Tatras, yet he performs his own identity across regional and national borders in his world beat fusion projects. And though we tend to assume these types of fusions are new, they are not. The nineteenth-century carol "Joy to the World" can be heard as fusion: It was composed in America with a text from Britain by Isaac Watts and melodic ideas from the German/English composer George Frederick Handel. We can conclude that the diversity of cultural practices presented as one of the themes of this chapter extends to even the most local of musical traditions.

Yet even when a performance practice draws on sources from around the world for inspiration, knowledge of the local context (the second theme of this chapter) is essential for understanding musical practice. *Ganga* singing for girls and women in Bosnia is more than an expression of musical aesthetics—it is a way of interacting with one's closest friends. To dance a *góralski* in the Polish Tatras requires knowledge of a series of dance steps and the tune types to which they are danced.

The third theme of this chapter is music and identity. What can we know about the identity of Europeans through the music they produce and enjoy? Merely determining from our listening that music and musicians come from a European music-culture can be challenging, though in some cases we can make a tentative identification. The violin ensembles of the Tatras "sound" European, for example. On closer examination of that music, we learn how *Górale* situate themselves in Poland, culturally and geographically on the edge looking south and east toward the Balkans. Yet no musician simply inherits a musically articulated identity. All musicians make choices and perform their identity musically to reference place, religion, and ideologies as they see fit.

MindTap®

PRACTICE your understanding of this chapter's concepts by reviewing flashcards and working once more with the chapter's Active Listening Guides online.

Study Questions

1. What are the three predominant religions in Europe? What are some of the ways religion influences music?

2. What are the two most common rhythmic meter-types used in much of European music?

3. What is the primary contribution of European music to world music?

4. What is the most characteristic couples' dance of Podhale, and what are the salient characteristics of that dance?

5. Describe a traditional *Górale* instrumental ensemble in Podhale.

6. Compare how *muzyka Podhala* and *ganga* exemplify and contrast with the concept of harmony and harmonic rhythm.

7. What are some typical ways that world-beat fusions are created musically?

8. How might world-beat fusions serve the local needs of traditional musicians?

9. List and compare the ways that *ganga* and *muzyka Podhala* can be seen as representing the social organization and values of their respective communities.

10. How are the invented categories of folk, popular, and classical music used politically in Europe?

6

Asia/India
David B. Reck

TURKMENISTAN
AFGHANISTAN
IRAN
PAKISTAN
HIMALAYA
CHINA
DELHI
NEPAL
BHUTAN
Agra
BANGLADESH
OMAN
INDIA
Calcutta (Kolkata)
MYANMAR
THAILAND
Bombay (Mumbai)
Madras (Chennai)
Andaman Islands
Madurai
SRI LANKA
Nicobar Islands

Learning Objectives

After you have studied this chapter, you should be able to:

1. Gain an overview of the shape and sound of Indian classical music.

2. View Indian music in the context of history and culture.

3. Become familiar with both compositions and the flow of improvisation.

4. Recognize technical aspects of Indian music, particularly the melodic system of *raga*, the rhythmic and intellectual formation of *tala*, and the interplay of musicians in performance.

5. Appreciate the influence of Indian classical music on Western musicians, South Indian pop music, and the Indian diaspora.

Imagine in your mind's eye approaching, from the air, the vibrant city of Chennai in southern India. You first notice in the east the rich blue of the ocean—the Bay of Bengal—spreading out to the horizon. The colonial British had named their provincial capital "Madras," but it had always been called simply "Chennai" by locals. The climate is jokingly described by local citizens as having three seasons: "the hot, the hotter, and the hottest!"

In the old days, Madras was a leisurely and genteel city. Most houses and buildings were one or two stories, with only the ornately sculpted towers (*gopurams*) of Hindu temples projecting up overhead (Figure 6.1). The rich foliage of an array of tropical plants and palm trees enriched the city. Classical Indian music and pop songs echoed from radios, temples, and concert halls. In those days, the day might begin each morning in the cool hours as early as 4:30 A.M., and each evening the town would shut down by 9:30 P.M. At night the air was filled with the perfume of flowering jasmine.

In Chennai today, with its estimated population of close to 5 million, modern buildings—apartments, offices—increasingly give the city an urban look. The chaotic traffic of cars, buses, and trucks, motorcycles, bicycles, and pedestrians clogs the streets as it moves in a cacophony beneath a carbon monoxide haze. Overhead each day, dozens of domestic and international flights approach the busy airport. Shop windows displaying refrigerators, air conditioners, and televisions sit amid Indian restaurants with their pungent array of curries. Computers and electronics are everywhere. Songs from the latest hit movies blare from tea stalls and gatherings.

Down the street from air-conditioned shops with upscale merchandise, one can still find the crowded shops of the bazaar—spices and grains piled high in pyramids, exotic perfumes in dozens of colors and fragrances and silks spread out like a rainbow. Markets offer a veritable paradise of tropical fruits and vegetables. Craft workers follow their traditional trades, such as woodcarving, weaving,

Figure 6.1

The lighted gopuram of Sri Kapaleeswarar temple is reflected in the temple pond, soaring over the neighborhood of Mylapore in Chennai. *Photo © Carol Reck 2014. All rights reserved.*

or making musical instruments. In homes and restaurants, a seemingly infinite variety of traditional deliciously spiced dishes continue to make South India a paradise of fine cooking. Somehow, magically, these ancient traditions persist in a radically changing world, the new and old, the traditional and the innovative, thriving in a unique coexistence. Jawaharlal Nehru, independent India's first prime minister, liked to describe his culture as a palimpsest, a parchment manuscript written on again and again in layers in which everything written before is never fully erased.

History, Culture, and Music

The Indus Valley Civilization (c. 2500–c. 1700 B.C.E.)

India's history begins with the cities of the Indus Valley civilization. Planned, symmetrical streets, water works, a drainage system, and a written language (as yet undecipherable), display links with the high civilizations of the Mesopotamian region. Sophisticated art in clay and metal portrays elephants, tigers, deer, the familiar Indian cows with their shoulder hump, realistic human portraits, and dancing girls. As to music, aside from some clay whistles, no instruments or performances are portrayed in art.

Salient Characteristics of
Indian Music

- Music and spirituality inexorably connected
- Hundreds of different scales underlying melodic system
- Adaptation of European musical instruments to Indian style
- Improvisation important
- Classical music divided into two styles: north and south
- Predominant musical texture of melody + drone + percussion
- Intensive microtonal melodic ornamentation

The Aryans (c. 1700–c. 500 B.C.E.)

From around 1700 B.C.E., a significant immigration (or invasion) was underway by people from Central Asia who moved into India, Iran, and Europe. Now confirmed by DNA testing, these cattle-herding people connect the languages of India, such as Sanskrit and Hindi, with those of Europe. Moreover, the Aryans had a written language in which they notated their sacred chants and collected them into four volumes—the *Vedas*. The manner of chanting the Vedas was preserved by priests who passed the chants down to pupils who memorized their manner of performance by ear. Thus, the Vedas were projected over thousands of years to be used in every major Hindu ceremony (weddings, for example) up to today.

When Indian music in all its intricacies developed, it was preserved and passed on in much the same way, teacher to pupil—by ear, and voluminous memory. Therefore, it perhaps should come as no surprise that the origin of music is seen in Vedic chant. But how? To approach some answers we must delve into some possible clues offered from within India's musical culture. Within the sound world created by great performers is the knowledge that at any given moment, the musician could move into a special "zone." Time seems to stop; specific musical details carry the listener away from mundane analysis. One floats in a mythic ocean of sound: transformed, immersed, infinitely moved.

Ancient Hindu scripture suggests that ultimate reality can be viewed as an ocean of sound, sound that can be heard just as the unmoving background drone instrument, the *tambura*, against which the myriad *raga*-based melodies move and develop. Both music and Vedic chant touch the elusively described but deeply felt "zones" which take us deep within human consciousness.

Vedic chant is one of mankind's deepest links to past millennia. A celebrated song, "Mokshamu," by the South Indian composer Tyagaraja, places music right in the center of some of the most profound concepts of Hindu religious philosophy. The essence of Tyagaraja's song poses these questions: If one has not experienced the inner self ("*atma*"), is enlightenment ("*moksha*" ["release"]) possible? If one has not experienced music in a deep sense, is enlightenment possible? The song then affirms that reality flows into the vital forces of existence and into the holy sound "*om*" (the most powerful sacred sound). From "*om*" the notes of all the *ragas* emerge. Such ideas are encapsulated in Tyagaraja's song.

MindTap·

◀》 **LISTEN TO**

an example of Vedic chant, "Ganesh Vandana," performed by The Brahmins, online.

Kingdoms through the Classic and Medieval Periods (500 B.C.E.–C. 1400 C.E.)

A great many kingdoms, such as that of the great Buddhist emperor Ashoka (268–231 B.C.E.) or of Chandragupta II (c. 340–c. 415 C.E.), appeared in the succeeding centuries. Like Latin in medieval Europe, Sanskrit became the common language of the educated. Remarkable works on religion and philosophy such as the *Upanishads* (the "forest books") explored the nature of reality and, through introspection, the inner self. Sages invented the physical and mental discipline of yoga. Siddhartha Gautama Buddha (fifth century B.C.E.) expounded the new, compassionate faith we know as Buddhism. The various *Puranas* fleshed out the stories of the gods and goddesses, forming the basis of popular Hinduism today.

The greatest of the kingdoms provided royal patronage to the arts. The massive technical book of theater, music, and dance, the *Natya Shastra* (perhaps as early as 200 B.C.E.), describes performance, theory, and professional training in great detail. Many more music theory books—such as *Sarangadeva*'s twelfth-century Sangeeta Ratnakara ("Crest-Jewel of Music")—follow the development of Indian music over the centuries.

Along with the sciences, literature also flourished. Much Sanskrit and vernacular poetry was actually written as lyrics to songs, but without musical notations, the melodies can only be imagined. The two great epics, the *Ramayana* and the *Mahabharata*, were written—remaining important even today—as source material for theater, dance, and lyrics. The great poet and playwright Kalidasa (mid-fourth to early fifth centuries) wrote works which have been translated into dozens of languages.

Painting, sculpture, and architecture also reached pinnacles. The murals in the caves of Ajanta and Ellora, the remarkable *stupa* (hemisphere) at Sanchi, or the breathtakingly beautiful sculptures at temples such as Konarak, Khajuraho, and Mahabalipuram are treasures of world art (Figure 6.2).

The Mughals (1527–c. 1867 C.E.)

Beginning in the twelfth century, Muslim warlords from Central Asia and Afghanistan periodically swept into the plains as far as Delhi, sacking cities and leaving devastation in their wake. However, in 1527, a remarkable general, Babur—a descendent of Genghis Khan and a lover of poetry and books (though he could not read)—decided to stay. The result was the powerful Mughal dynasty, centered in Delhi and Agra, which dominated much of north India until a period of decline beginning in the 1700s. The Mughals were Muslim and, though brutal in war, were lavish patrons of the arts, making their courts centers of learning and culture. Emperors such as Akbar the Great (reigned 1556–1605) and Shah Jahan (reigned 1628–1658) imported scholars, painters, musicians, writers, and architects from as far west as Arabia.

One can stroll around today where the Mughals listened to the great musicians they had assembled. Pavilions and towers held the emperor and courtiers. Down below, between a series of pools to reflect the sound and cool the air, lay the stage under the stars. It was here one night that the greatest singer ever sat and ordered that dozens of unlit oil lamps be placed around the pools. Singing in the *raga Deepak* (literally, "lamp")—associated with fire—he wove ever more intricate improvisations. One by one, the lamps burst into flickering light. Such was the power of his sound and mastery—and the *raga Deepak*! Or so it was said.

The great monuments of Mughal architecture, such as the palace at Fatehpur Sikri or the Taj Mahal, illustrate the Mughals' most impressive artistic accomplishment: the remarkable integration of characteristics indigenous to India with elements derived from the Islamic world of Persia and beyond. This synthesis can be seen in the tradition of "Indian miniature paintings." It can also be heard in music. The melodic concepts of the raga system, soaring improvisations, and the singing of beautiful poetry connect with elements found in Persian, Turkish, and Arabic musical traditions. The connection can also be seen in hybrid musical instruments such as the **sitar** (*sih*-tahr; a plucked, twenty-two-string, classical instrument) and **tabla** (*tahb*-luh; a set of two small drums played with fingers and palms). Again and again over the centuries, foreign cultural ideas have migrated into India, merging in a new and undeniably Indian synthesis.

Finally, the Mughal Era established a division in India's two related but different classical music systems. In the north, musical influences from the Islamic world interacted more strongly with native traditions to form the Hindustani (hindu-*stah*-nee) music tradition. By contrast, in South India, the old Carnatic (car-*nah*-tik) music tradition predominates.

The Period of British Colonization (1600s–1947)

In 1498, only six years after Columbus's epic voyage, Vasco da Gama anchored on Kerala's shores on India's southwestern coast, finding what Columbus had been looking for. The Age of Sail had begun. The British arrived, along with the Dutch, French, and Portuguese, and, through wars and alliances with native maharajas, finally emerged as paramount colonial rulers.

Musically, the contributions of the British regime are less obvious. In the hey-day of the colonial era, the British cut themselves off from meaningful contact with "native" culture. Rather, they imported pianos, violins, and other instruments from Europe for their dance orchestras and military bands.

The establishment of a Pax Britannica, however, provided a peaceful environ-ment in which Indian musical arts could flourish. The golden age of South Indian classical music (c. 1700–c. 1900) was able to develop during this period of relative peace, unnoticed by the foreign missionaries and bureaucrats.

In the 1920s, a recording industry led by the company HMV in Calcutta made it possible to listen to performances of Indian music again and again, a substantial change in an oral tradition. When "talkies" replaced silent films around 1930, the movie indus-try, drawing on traditional theater, was quick to incorporate songs into every film. Movie songs remain the source of most Indian pop music today. In 1936, a national radio, All India Radio (AIR), based on the BBC model, was established. Under enlightened directorship, AIR broadcast hundreds of programs of Indian classical music each year.

A very important development, however, was the discovery by Indian musi-cians that they could adapt European and American instruments to play music in Indian style. The piano was summarily rejected as unsuited, but the violin, harmo-nium (portable, small, reed organ), clarinet, and even the banjo became, in essence, Indian instruments. In recent years, mandolin, guitar, and keyboard have joined the array of "immigrant" Indian instruments.

Independence and the Modern Period (1947–Present)

In 1947, British India achieved independence. The transition from colonies to nation-states has had many ups and downs. Yet modernization has occurred. Culture has been one of modern India's most prestigious exports. Contemporary authors such as Salman Rushdie and Arundhati Roy are among the most famous writers in English today. Since the 1960s, many extraordinary filmmakers have also appeared. Among them is Satyajit Ray (1921–1992), whose works, like "The Apu Trilogy," have gained him recognition as one of the top masters of cinema. Dancers such as T. Balasaraswati and Mrinalini Sarabhai have performed all over the world. Musicians such as Ravi Shankar, Ali Akbar Khan, and Zakir Hussain are megastars. Today, tens of thousands of CDs, DVDs, and videos are available. Musicians now have unlimited access not only to their own traditions but also to music around the globe. With globalization, Indian music, like the culture in general, is absorbing the new as it always has. Yet the old, the traditional, remains.

Many Musics

If you were to spend a day in one of Chennai's flourishing neighborhoods, you might come into contact with many types of musical sound. In the morning the vendors flood the streets. As Barbara Benary pointed out to this author, each vendor has a musical call distinct enough for neighborhood residents to distinguish who is who, and whether to venture out onto the street to make a purchase. As the day wears on, a pilgrim may appear singing a prayer. Once in a great while, the unmistakable whine of the *pungi,* the pair of double-reed pipes (a melody and a drone) with its slithering scale, signals the appearance of a snake charmer. Clearly, we are here in the realm of folk music.

Religion and Music in South India

Religion, primarily Hinduism, looms large in the arts. Lyrics are predominantly religious and may focus on the rich folklore of gods or goddesses and the stories surrounding them.

In the amazingly complex dance forms found in South India—such as *Bharata natyam, Mohiniattam, Kuchipudi,* and *Odissi* or the great dance dramas of *Kathakali, Theru koothu,* and *Yakshagana*—the tales of divinities and mortals are brought to life again and again. Search the internet and explore samples of some of these forms.

A major genre of music is the *bhajan*—a relatively simple song which is sung as an act of devotion. A favorite format is to have a leader singing verses, with a group responding. They are often accompanied by backup melodic instruments such as violin, harmonium, or bamboo flute, and may be joined by percussion. In South Asian culture there is a fascination with symmetry, permutation, or otherwise rational organization, which pervades South India. It can be found, for example, in the patterns and colors of women's saris, or in the geometric designs created by women by sifting fine powder through the fingers onto the ground outside their houses (*kolams*), or by drummers creating rhythmic structures. (See Figure 6.3.)

Figure 6.3

The *kolam*, made by women sifting rice flour or colored powders through their fingers, creating an abstract pattern. Ranging from basic to complex, these auspicious designs—based on a rich, visual vocabulary in this tradition—are freshly drawn each morning on the ground at the entrance to a home. *Photo © Carol S. Reck 2014. All rights reserved.*

Bhajans may be sung formally or informally in many contexts: in a home, a temple, a concert hall, or on the street. In the Tamil winter month of *Margazhi* (usually in December), groups of bhajan singers and instrumentalists walk through the residential streets near a temple in the early hours before daybreak. Finally, in the south, the saxophone-like sound of an ensemble of double-reed pipes combined with drones and *tavil* (cylindrical drums played with stick and hands) is considered an auspicious sound for everything sacred. The *nagaswaram* is played inside temples, in street processions, and at all kinds of celebratory events. The music that the *nagaswaram* plays is the same as South Indian classical music.

Classical Music

The classical music of South India is called **karnataka sangeeta** (car-*nah*-tuh-kuh sahn-*gee*-tuh, with a hard "g") or **Carnatic music**. The roots of this music lie in the courts and palaces of maharajas, in the great southern kingdoms and in the southern temple complexes.

Sculpture in the ancient temples and palaces, as well as murals and miniature paintings, give us vivid visual images of the instruments, orchestras, dance styles, and the where and how of musical performance. They bear a striking resemblance to what is seen in performance today (compare the dancers in Figures 6.2 and 6.4).

Any oral tradition such as that of Indian classical music lives primarily in the hands, voices, memory, and creative imagination of individual human beings. The music, in a sense, lives uniquely in each performance, in the rendition of a song on a particular day, at a particular hour. Today, videos and CDs can preserve a particular

Figure 6.4

The renowned Guru Sudharani Raghupathy (seated in chair) gives a *bharata natyam* dance lesson to Priya Murle. *Photo © Carol Reck 2005. All rights reserved.*

performance, but whether this will change the essentially oral nature of Indian music, and the liquid way musicians approach their tradition remains to be seen.

Music for South India's dance traditions—for example in **bharata natyam** (bha-ruh-tuh *nah*-tyum)—is similar in style to classical concert music. In several genres of dance music, the lyrics are beautiful love poetry. Carnatic music began to take its present shape about one hundred years ago. Three great saint-poet-composers dominate this period: Syama Sastri (1762–1827), Tyagaraja (1767–1847), and Muthuswami Dikshitar (1776–1836). These composers wrote both the melodies and the lyrics to their songs.

The *Kriti*: A Song

Kriti (*krih*-tee) is the principal song form of Carnatic music. "Devi Niye Tunai" is a *kriti*, a classical song with lyrics and melody by Papanasam Sivan (1890–1973). The singer is Shobha Vasudevan, accompanied by drummer David P. Nelson. The Tamil lyrics praise the goddess Meenakshi, chief deity of the ancient temple in the southern city of Madurai.

Notice that each line is repeated, with variations. The opening phrase (beginning *devi niye tunai*) is repeated after sections 2 and 3 as a refrain. The *raga* is *Keervani* (keer-vah-nee) with a basic scale similar to the European harmonic minor scale.

The *tala* (time cycle) is *Adi* (*Ah*-dee *tah*-luh), eight beats, 4 + 2 + 2.

The song floats on the incessant sound of a drone. Against this unchanging background a single melody unfolds. This melody differs greatly from tunes of Western classical or popular music: its lines are sinuous and complex, marked by subtle bends and slides, with intense ornamentation.

A Piece from the Dance Tradition: "Krishna Nee Begane Baro"

We shall now focus on a song from the dance tradition: "Krishna Nee Begane Baro" ("Krishna, Come Soon"), attributed to Vyasatirtha (1460–1539), with lyrics in the Kannada language. It is sung by Jon B. Higgins (1939–1984), who learned his music from T. Viswanathan (1927–2002), a flutist from the dance family of the legendary Ms. T. Balasaraswati (1918–1984).

In the song, the god Krishna, reincarnated in human form, is portrayed and worshipped as an adorable child (Figure 6.5). In the recurring refrain, the child-god is implored, "Come quickly." Since the name of Krishna begins each repetition of the refrain, listen for it! In the song's subsequent verses, the child Krishna is described in detail: wearing silks and jeweled necklaces, holding a bamboo flute. Finally, a well-known story is referred to: His mother catches him eating mud, but when she opens his mouth, she sees the universe.

A drone background of tonal centers and perfect fifths plays behind the vocalist. A violin shadows the melody. A drummer plays a rhythmic accompaniment on the double-headed *mridangam*. The *raga*, or melodic material of the song's melody, is *raga Yamuna Kalyani*. To begin with, Higgins establishes the beauty of the lower notes as they blend with the *tambura* drone in improvised phrases. Listen carefully to how the melody notes blend and interact with the notes of the drone.

After the brief moments of improvisation, the composed song begins and the percussion comes in—and the refrains, each beginning with the word Krishna, are sung. After the singing of the chorus several times, the first verse enters and introduces a raised (sharp) fourth, which contrasts with the earlier natural fourth.

MindTap·
◀)) **LISTEN TO**
"Devi Niye Tunai" ("O Devi! With Fish-Shaped Eyes") online.

♫ **LISTEN TO**
"Krishna Nee Begane Baro—Original," performed by Higgins Bhagavathar (Jon B. Higgins), online.

MindTap·
🎧 **WATCH** a video of "Krishna Nee Begane Baro" as interpreted by the dancer T. Balasaraswati, online.

The raised fourth nudges the *raga* upward toward the fifth, as a resting note or
centering point. There is thus in *raga Yamuna Kalyani* an interplay between F natural
(lower fourth) and F sharp (raised fourth) as they alternate in different phrases
in different contexts in the melody. This expressive contrast between natural and
sharp fourth (F) is a main characteristic of this *raga*.

The beautiful melodies woven from the *raga*, the simple form of repeated
verse and refrain, and the devotional words relating to the well-known concept of
the baby God Krishna, as well as the many stories relating to his incarnation as a god
in human form, fall within a familiar cultural context of Krishna worship in India.
In fact, the song mentions an important Krishna temple in Udupi, a pilgrimage site
in the southern state of Karnataka. The song's expressivity and emotions are
brought out by Higgins in his interpretation of this devotional piece. One may also
view the song as interpreted by the dancer T. Balasaraswati.

The Sound World

If you listen to any performance of India's music, certain characteristics will become apparent. Improvisation plays a key role in performance. All musicians must be able to invent music on the spot. An interesting timbre, or tone color, may strike us. The characteristic sound is *nasal,* whether in the voice or in musical instruments. The performers in Indian music are clearly working by ear in an oral tradition. There is no conductor, but each performer has a comfortable and well-defined role to play. In a performance, when the drum comes in, we are immediately struck by the energy and complexity of the drummer's rhythms, played with the fingers and hands. We can sense a strong beat, but the recurring metrical unit—*tala*— seems to be longer and more complicated than those we are used to (3/4, 4/4, etc.). Finally, lyrics in classical music are touchstones to (primarily) Hindu religion and mythology. For South Indians, these references can be read easily because they are part of the culture in which they have grown up.

Concerts

Concerts in South India usually begin between 5:30 to 6:30 in the evening. Programs are sponsored by **sabhas** (*sah*-bhahs), cultural clubs that bring to their members music, dance, plays, lectures, and movies. The large and prestigious *sabhas* may have their own auditoriums. The audience may sit in rattan chairs or, as in the past, on large rugs or mats spread on the floor. The musicians sit on a rug on a raised platform or stage, with fellow musicians and friends sitting in close proximity. The principal musician always sits in the middle, with the drummer on stage right, and the violinist on stage left. Other musicians, often students of the performers, may also join the group (Figure 6.6).

Compared with classical music concerts in the West, these concerts are relatively relaxed and informal. Members of the audience may count time with their hands, talk with friends, or occasionally get up to buy snacks at the refreshment stand. There are no printed programs. A knowledgeable audience is familiar with the repertoire of songs, *ragas,* and *talas.*

The Ensemble: Musical Texture

In a concert each musician and instrument has a role to play. These roles, creating the musical texture, can be described as *functional layers*: (1) the *melody layer*, (2) the *background* drone, and (3) the *rhythm/percussion*. Within each layer there may be one or more musicians.

Salient Characteristics of
South Indian Music

- Based upon a vast repertoire of songs, each set in a specific *raga* and *tala*

- In performance, is primarily vocal music with violin and (*mridangam*) percussion accompaniment

- Purely instrumental music is not currently popular

- Improvisations are based on the *raga* and *tala* of the song and are an important part of the performance

- A concert today lasts around two hours and may include a variety of types of songs in various South Indian languages

- The song texts are an important part of each song's expressive content

- Almost all songs express devotion to one of the forms of Hindu gods

- Songs in the classical dance repertoire frequently explore the emotions of love

Figure 6.6

An ensemble in concert. The principal artist, the great flutist N. Ramani sits in the middle of the stage in concert. Behind him a student plays the drone *tambura*. The accomplished accompanists are S. D. Sridhar playing violin on stage left and T. K. Murthy, assisted by a student (behind), playing *mridangam* on stage right. Over their heads are prints of great composers. *Photo © Carol Reck 2005. All rights reserved.*

The Melodic Layer

The principal melodic soloist dominates the ensemble. A disciple may support the principal melodic soloist. A singer is principal melodic soloist in perhaps eighty percent of all concerts, but instruments such as violin, bamboo flute, saxophone, *veena,* or mandolin may also be featured.

The next important role within this layer is the *melodic accompanist*. In South India, this is usually a violinist. The melodic accompanist plays three important roles: to (1) play along on the songs; (2) echo and support the soloist's improvised phrases in the *alapana* (*ah-lah*-puh-nuh) (which frequently precedes the song), adding a short *alapana* of his or her own; and (3) alternate with the soloist in later improvisations such as *swara kalpana.*

The *Shruti* Layer

The **shruti** (*shroo*-tee) layer includes one or more specialized instruments. The *tambura* (tahm-*boo*-ruh) is a four-stringed, plucked instrument tuned to the tonal center and fifth. Its buzzing timbre is created by inserting a small length of thread under each playing string on the slightly rounded top of the bridge, creating a rich blend of overtones. The tuned reed *shruti* box may also be used. Played with a bellows, it gives a continuous reed organ sound. Today, most musicians use small synthesizers that can simulate either drone instrument.

The Rhythm/Percussion Layer

Finally, there is the bedrock of the ensemble, the percussion. The double-headed, barrel-shaped *mridangam* (mrih-*dun*-gum) drum is the principal (and often the only) accompanying percussion. The other percussion instruments used in classical music are the **ghatam** (*guh*-tum), a large, clay pot with a ringing, metallic sound; the **kanjira** (kahn-*jih*-ruh), a tambourine with a snakeskin head; and the **morsang** (*mor*-sung), a Jew's harp that is played in the same rhythms as the other percussion instruments.

Now we will explore two concepts that are central to an understanding of India's classical music: *raga* and *tala*.

Raga: The Melodic System

The ancient texts define a **raga** as "that which colors the mind." In Sanskrit the primary meaning of the word is "coloring, dyeing, tingeing." This connection with generating feelings and emotions in human beings—with "coloring" the mind and the heart—is important. A *raga* is an expressive entity with a "musical personality" all its own. Most of all, it includes a portfolio of characteristic musical gestures and phrases that give it a distinct, recognizable identity. One gets to know a *raga* gradually—by hearing one's guru or other master musicians perform it over many years. Traditional texts associate particular **ragas** with human emotions: the nine traditional *rasas* (*rah-suhs*; "flavors")—love, anger, sadness, fear, disgust, wonder, heroism, humor, religious devotion—plus absolute peacefulness. *Ragas* may also be associated with colors, animals, deities, a season, a time of day, or certain magical properties (causing rain, calming the mind, auspiciousness, among others). There is a genre of miniature paintings of *ragas* called **raga-mala** (*rah*-gah *mah*-lah). In the painting of *raga Goda* (Figure 6.7),

Figure 6.7

A *raga-mala,* a painting of the *raga Goda.* Basohli School, late seventeenth century. *Photo © Carol Reck 2005. All rights reserved.*

the mood of the *raga* is created through two colorfully dressed figures in the foreground—a woman playing a frame drum and a dancing nobleman, both frozen in movement—against a dark background. Delicate green leaves connect to a vine wrapping around a tree, a symbol of lovers.

Musicians know these associations and the many folkloric tales about them: for example, *ragas* charming cobras, causing rain, or bringing peace of mind. What is clear in all this is that in India *ragas* are seen as powerful and full of expressive force.

The *Melakarta* System: Classification of *Ragas*

In Carnatic music, all *ragas* relate to a **melakarta** (*may*-luh-*car*-tuh), a basic "parent" or "mother" scale. There are seven notes in each *melakarta* scale: (1) *sa* —(2) *ri* —(3) *ga* —(4) *ma* —(5) *pa* —(6) *da* —(7) *ni* —. In the system the tonal center—(1) *sa*—and the perfect fifth above—(5) *pa*—never change, since they coincide with the drone. The pitches represented by the other five notes are variable and mutate according to a complex system in order to create a wide variety of different scales.

Your teacher will guide you through the simplified chart given in Figure 6.8. Following the lines from left to right, one can discover that there are seventy-two possible tracks, and therefore seventy-two basic seven-note scales in the system, known as the seventy-two *melakarta ragas*.

But the system does not end here. Dozens of other ragas may derive from each of the seventy-two *melakarta* "mothers" by creating other characteristics: (1) omitting notes in ascent and/or descent, (2) zig-zagging the scale in ascent and/or descent, (3) adding "visiting" notes from other scales, and (4) adding other distinguishing elements. *Raga Yamuna Kalyani*, for instance, (in the song "Krishna Nee Begane Baro"), has the characteristic feature of using not just one, but two forms of the fourth, *ma*: F natural and F sharp, as described earlier. There are thus hundreds of *ragas* in common use—and potentially many more.

Tala: The Time Cycle

Tala, the organization of time in music, is part of a conceptual spectrum in Indian thought that moves from a fraction of a second to the great **yugas** (*you*-guhs), or

Figure 6.8

The *melakarta* system (tracks read from left to right).

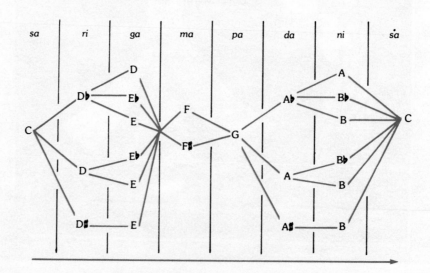

"ages." The musician regards time initially as a beat. On a larger level, beats are grouped into regularly recurring metric cycles, what we call in Western music "measures." In India, these cycles are called *talas*. In Carnatic music today fewer than ten *talas* predominate.

> Counting *talas*:
> *Adi Tala*: 4 + 2 + 2 = 8 beats
> *Rupaka tala*: 1 + 2 = 3 beats
> *Khanda chapu tala*: 2 + 3 = 5 fast beats
> *Misra chapu tala*: 3 + 2 + 2 = 7 fast beats

Except for the **khanda chapu tala** (*kahn*-duh *chah*-pu *tah*-lah) and **misra chapu tala** (*mis*-rah *chah*-pu *tah*-lah), which are generally performed at a brisk tempo, all *talas* may be performed at fast, medium, or slow tempo. In slow tempo, there are two pulses per beat, as in "1 & 2 & 3 & 4 & …" and so forth.

The *tala* cycles differ from the common Western time signatures in that *tala* beats occur in uneven groupings (4 + 2 + 2 = 8 beat *tala*, or 3 + 2 + 2 = 7 beat *tala*, or 1 + 2 = 3 beat *tala*, and so on). These groupings are marked by the accent of hand claps or finger counts.

The Drummer's Art

In performance, the *mridangam* player and other percussionists play in an improvisatory style based on hundreds of rhythmic patterns and drum strokes memorized in their brains and hands. (Until recent decades, percussion has been largely a male endeavor.) In performance, the percussionist may use pre-composed patterns, arranging them in predictable or unpredictable groupings. At the same time, he may spontaneously create different patterns and groupings—or tomorrow, something entirely unexpected might emerge. The drummer's art centers on drum strokes—distinctive tones produced on different parts of the drumhead by different finger combinations. These strokes can be expressed as **sollukattu** (sol-lu-*kuht*-tu), spoken syllables that duplicate drum strokes and rhythmic patterns. The drummer's art is complex. First, he must accompany songs, the *kritis,* and other compositions of the Carnatic music tradition. He must know each song, picking up the flow and feeling, shaping his accompaniment to the internal rhythm of the song.

Second, the drummer emerges from the background during long-held notes in the melody, or at cadences, marking endings of sections of music with a formulaic, threefold repetition called a *mora* (*mo*-ruh) or *korvai* (*kor*-vai).

Third, once in a concert, the *mridangam* player, and other percussionists, if any, emerge and come to the forefront to play a rhythmic solo. This improvised section is called the **tani avartanam**. The scholar and percussionist David P. Nelson's study of the *mridangam* solo, *Mrdangam Mind: The Tani Avartanam in Karnatak Music* (1991), brings out the intricacies of this form.

A Carnatic Music Performance

A concert in South India is marked by a string of songs, each in a specific *raga* and *tala*. While a song may be performed alone for its own intrinsic beauty, the principal musician may choose to perform one or more forms of improvisation before, within, or after the composed song. In a concert, several song forms are used. Among them are the *varnam*, a concert etude, then various *kritis* (compositions) in a variety of *ragas* and *talas*, *bhajans*, and dance pieces. The concert will peak with an extended "main item" (the English phrase is used) in which a major *raga* is expanded with the longest improvisations of the concert, including a drum solo.

A mostly improvised format called ***ragam-tanam-pallavi*** (*rah*–gum, *tah*-num, *puhl*-luh-vee) may also serve as the main item. We will turn our attention to a performance of a *kriti*, "Sarasiruha," as a main item, with improvisations and drum solo played on the plucked *veena* by Ms. Ranganayaki Rajagopalan, accompanied by Srimushnam V. Raja Rao.

Ms. Ranganayaki (Figure 6.9), now in her mid-eighties, in 1936 was a very unruly child. She was sent to live with a childless uncle and his wife in the prosperous southern town of Karaikudi where lived a great *veena* virtuoso, Karaikudi Sambasiva Iyer. (You will notice that South Indian musicians often take their hometown as an identifying "first name" because traditionally there were no surnames in the Western sense.)

Recognizing a rare talent, Sambasiva Iyer took the little girl into his household, into an apprenticeship known as the ***gurukula*** (gu-ru-*koo*-lah) **system**. The discipline was rigorous, with lessons beginning at 4:30 A.M. and continuing throughout the day. Mistakes or laziness were met with slaps from a bamboo rod. Ranganayaki describes her life during that period as "not a normal childhood. I had no playmates or anything. It was *asura sadhakam* ('devil's practice')" (personal communication 2000).

Ranganayaki's musical genius developed. By age twelve she was accompanying her guru in concerts. The close relationship continued after her marriage, and through a move to the big city of Chennai. Her apprenticeship had lasted twenty-two years.

Ms. Ranganayaki has been recognized as one of the great *veena* virtuosi of her time. With her phenomenal memory she is a rare repository of the songs played in the Karaikudi tradition. She has toured Europe and the United States, and been regularly featured in the prestigious AIR radio broadcasts. In 2000, she received one of India's highest artistic awards—the National Award for Music.

MindTap®

🔊 **LISTEN TO**

"Sarasiruha" ("To the Goddess Saraswati") *kriti* in *raga Natai*, *Adi tala*, performed by Ranganayaki Rajagopalan, *veena*; Srimushnam V. Raja Rao, *mridangam*, online.

Figure 6.9

Ranganayaki Rajagopalan with the *veena* she has played since she was a small girl. © *Carol Reck, 2004. All rights reserved.*

Her instrument, the **veena**, has three drone strings and four playing strings. Its carving and ivory trim make it a work of art, and a testimony to the skill of the hereditary craftsmen who made it. The chromatically placed brass frets are set in black wax.

The drummer is Srimushnam (his ancestral village) V. Raja Rao on the *mridangam*. He is one of the great contemporary performers on his instrument. Known as "a musician's musician," he has accompanied most of the leading singers and instrumentalists of Carnatic music. In this performance built upon "Sarasiruha" he illustrates both the art of accompaniment and a brief drum solo.

Raja Rao's instrument, the *mridangam*, has a barrel-shaped body carved from jackwood. Both of its heads are made from multiple layers of leather, the outer layers cut with a circular hole in the middle. The lower (untuned) left-hand head has a blob of damp wheat paste applied to its center to give it a booming sound. The center of the right-hand head (which is tuned to the tonal center) has a specially composed black spot that gives a ringing, metallic sound.

The performance begins with two improvised sections—*alapana* and *tanam*—for *veena* alone. *Alapana* (in free time, with "breath" rhythms and no regular pulse) and *tanam* (marked with strong, energetic, irregular rhythms) precede the chosen composition and introduce the listener to the *raga* in which the song is set. Following the *alapana* is the *tanam*, a more rhythmic melodic improvisation, after which begins the composed song in *kriti* form, "Sarasiruha" in *raga Natai, Adi tala*. This beginning is signaled by the entrance of the drum and the start of *tala* cycles and the song's melody. In this performance, the composed song is performed, followed by a lively, improvised section for *veena* with drum accompaniment called *kalpana swaras* (imagined notes). After this improvised section, a brief drum solo, the *tani avartanam*, ensues. Following the *tani avartanam*, the *veena* player recapitulates the opening phrase of the composed piece, then a brief improvised ending brings the entire piece to a close (see Active Listening 6.1).

ACTIVE LISTENING 6.1
"Sarasiruha" ("To the Goddess Saraswati")

MindTap
🎧 **WATCH** an Active Listening Guide of this selection online.

COUNTER NUMBER	COMMENTARY
Alapana (improvised)	
0:00	*Veena* alone (with drone).
2:05–3:15	Peak of *alapana*. Reaches highest note.
Tanam (improvised)	
3:18	*Veena* alone (with drone). Irregular beat. Rhythmic exposition of *Natai raga*. Listen for the phrases to begin low in the range, then work their way to middle and high range.
7:48–8:18	*Veena* switches back briefly to *alapana* style.
Kriti (composed song) "Sarasiruha"	
8:25	Song begins in *Adi tala* (4 + 2 + 2). Drum enters.
13:31	Repeated variants of musical phrase—invocation of Saraswati, then song continues to the end.

continued

COUNTER NUMBER	COMMENTARY
Kalpana swaras 1 (improvised, short—one cycle or less)	
14:45	Lively, improvised section. Begins with four short *swara* improvisations of less than a half *tala* cycle, each returning to the *idam* "place."
Kalpana swaras 2 (improvised, extended)	
15:10–17:48	Each set of *kalpana swaras* resolves in a return to the *idam* "place."
Tani avartanam (drum solo)	
18:00	Improvised and pre-composed rhythmic solo by the *mridangam*. *Adi tala* continues.
21:30	Listen for the *mora* or *korvai,* a formulaic, rhythmic pattern repeated three times that signals the end of the drum solo.
Kriti return and close	
22:06	*Veena* joins back in with the *kriti's* first bit of melody and an improvised close.

Alapana

The first section of the performance built around the composition "Sarasiruha" is an **alapana** (ah-*lah*-puh-nuh), a free-flowing exposition and exploration of the *raga Natai,* its facets and phrases, its ornamentation, its pushes and pulls of intonation, as well as its mood and character. An *alapana* is nonmetrical, that is, it has no regular beat or recurring *tala* cycles. Instead, its phrases evolve in flowing prose-like "breath rhythms," phrases that eventually come to rest on important pillar tones, or resting notes.

An *alapana* has a general plan set both by the tradition as a whole and by the improvisational habits of the particular musician. In general, the phrases of an *alapana* begin slowly and gradually increase in speed and complexity as they move higher and higher in the range of the voice or instrument. After a peak there is a descent back to the lower register, with an ending on the tonal center *sa* (C). The voice or (as in this case) melodic instrument always performs against the drone background, played on the *tambura* or on the instrument itself.

The *raga* of the *alapana* is determined by that of the *kriti,* the song composition, which it precedes. In our performance the *raga* is *Natai* (*nah*-tai), an ancient and powerful raga associated with the great god Shiva in the form of *Nataraja* (nah-tuh-*rah*-juh)—"the Lord of Dance." The Dance of Shiva, magnificently portrayed in South Indian bronze sculpture, is said to shake the universe with its power and fury. The most noteworthy characteristic of this *raga* is the shake or oscillation on the second note of the scale, *ri* (D# in Western notation) as it descends downward to the tonal center *sa* (C). It is a sound startlingly similar to the major/minor "blues" third found in the African-American tradition (Chapter 4). If you listen carefully or hum along with the performance, eventually you will begin to recognize the series of musical phrases and gestures that give *raga Natai* its character or "musical personality."

Tanam

Tanam (*tah*-nuhm) is a highly rhythmic exposition of the *raga.* It is usually played or sung only once in a concert and is placed after the *alapana* and before the *kriti.*

The musician plucks the playing and drone strings in asymmetrical, improvised patterns on the *veena* while simultaneously working through the various phrases of the *raga*. Although there are no *tala* cycles in *tanam*, there is a strong sense of beat. Just as in *alapana*, the overall shape of a *tanam* follows the range of the instrument from low to high in graduated steps, and then back down again. The Karaikudi tradition is famous for its powerful rendition of *tanam*.

Kriti "Sarasiruha"

All compositions in Carnatic music are songs, melodies with words. Because all these forms are not precisely notated but, rather, are taught and learned orally, songs do not have definitive versions. But in India, within a specific guru's style, students will be expected to follow the guru's version exactly. As a song is passed down from strings of gurus to disciples on its journey over hundreds of years to the present, many variant versions appear. Yet the composition remains recognizably itself—the main turns of phrase and the lyrics remain despite the variations in detail.

A brief *kriti* might be as short as four minutes; a long *kriti* in slow tempo could last for fifteen minutes or more. The structure of the *kriti* form, with its improvisational elements can be amazingly flexible—it may be contracted or expanded in almost infinite ways.

The melody and lyrics of "Sarasiruha" (*sah*-rah-see-*roo*-ha) are by the late-eighteenth to early-nineteenth century composer Puliyur Doraiswamy Ayyar (precise dates are not known). The song is addressed to the goddess of music and learning, Saraswati (Figure 6.10). A free translation of its text follows:

NAVARANA

Figure 6.10
Saraswati, goddess of music and learning. *Drawing © Navarana Reck 2016. All rights reserved.*

Text, "Sarasiruha"

O Mother who loves the lotus seat,
   Ever delighting in the music of *veena*,
   Ever joyful, and ever merciful to me.
Save me who have taken refuge in you!
   O You with feet as tender as sprouts,
   You charm the hearts of poets.
   You dwell in the lotus.
   You of the jeweled bracelets.
   (reprise) 1. O Mother who loves the lotus seat …
Lotus-eyed Mother who is gracious to the lowly who seek your mercy,
   Mother with a face as lovely as the autumn moon,
   Pure Lady! O Saraswati, chaste, ever fond of learning.
   Lady with breasts like ceremonial vessels,
   Complete Being, who holds a book in her hand which bestows all dominion.
   (reprise) 1. O Mother who loves the lotus seat …

Free translation by Indira Viswanathan Peterson, Mount Holyoke College.

Although the words of the song are not audible in an instrumental performance, the musicians and knowledgeable members of the audience know the song text well.

Kalpana Swaras

The term *kalpana swaras* (*kahl*-puh-nuh *swah*-ruhs) means "imagined notes" of the scale of the *raga* being performed. This section of improvised "imagined notes" occurs either in the latter part of the *kriti* (composed song) rendition or after the *kriti* has been completed. Identifying this section in a vocal performance is easy, because the performer sings the names of the notes of the *raga* scale—*sa, ri, ga, ma, pa, da,* or *ni*—instead of lyrics. In performance of *kalpana swaras*, a *veena* player plucks each note, a violinist bows each note, a flutist or *nagaswaram* player tongues each note. The accompanying percussion, once again improvising, can reflect the patterns and lines of the improvised *kalpana swaras*.

In the course of the improvisation, *kalpana swaras* always return to a key phrase from the *kriti*, a familiar island in a sea of improvisation. This phrase, its beginning note, and the place where it begins in the *tala* cycle are important, because ultimately each turn of the *kalpana swaras* will lead back to it. Indeed, it is called the **idam** (ih-*dum*), literally "place." In Ms. Ranganayaki's performance the "place" is the opening phrase of the *kriti*, and it occurs half a beat after the downbeat.

In a performance, at first the improvised phrases of *kalpana swaras* will be short, perhaps only a few counts long, perhaps only filling the last few beats of one *tala* cycle before returning to the phrase of the *idam*. The fertile musical imagination of the performer will gradually spin out reels of imagined notes in ever-widening circles of intricate phrases. The improvisations will develop and grow in length and complexity, extending eventually through more and more cycles of the *tala* as the performer's imagination runs free. Just as in *alapana* improvisation, there is a climb in the tessitura and complexity of the *kalpana swaras*, and an eventual shift to double-time, thereby dramatically increasing the momentum. A final, extended improvisation will bring the *kalpana swara* section to a climax before the final return to the *idam* (the place) and the opening phrase of the composed song.

The Drum Solo: *Tani Avartanam*

As a conclusion of the main item in a concert, the *mridangam* player and other percussionists, if any, come to the foreground with an extended solo. In a full concert, this solo may extend on average for about ten minutes, but the length of the solo is highly variable according to the situation. In our performance, Srimushnam Raja Rao's solo is concise. As noted earlier, the drum solo gives the percussionist the chance to display the full range of his skills and rhythmic imagination. In each section of the solo, the drummer will explore a certain range of patterns and architectural ideas. Finally, the solo will end on an extended *korvai* (kor-vai), a big, rhythmic pattern comprising multiple *tala* cycles, which is repeated three times. This pattern leads back to a brief recap of the *kriti*'s opening phrase by the melodic soloist, followed by a brief, rhythmic closing signaling the conclusion of the piece and its improvisations.

Pop Music

On TV, over the radio, or blasting from the neighborhood snack shops, one can hear Indian popular music, also called "cine songs" because almost all popular music in India originates in movies. The Indian film industry, incidentally, is the largest in the world. The typical film (though there are exceptions) features despicable villains, fearless and clever heroes, gorgeous yet steadfast heroines, romance (always rocky), family problems, utterly surprising plot twists (identical twins separated at birth and the like), broad comedy, heart-stopping fight scenes, and elaborate, sexy, provocative dances. In virtually all movies, songs periodically interrupt the plot with MTV-like visuals in exotic settings or elaborate song-and-dance production numbers. The actors and actresses always lip-sync the words, which are actually sung by "playback singers," who along with the "music director" (composer/arranger) and lyricist are the true stars of India's pop music scene.

Cine music is to some ears a curious and sometimes bizarre blend of East and West. Choppy, hyperactive melodies, often in "Oriental" scales, are belted out by nasal-sounding singers over Latin rhythms and an eclectic accompaniment that may include Western instruments mixed with an array of folk and classical Indian instruments. It is an anything goes, "if it sounds good, use it," approach to music. The "anything" today might include harmony and counterpoint, rap, rock, symphonic music, and jazz, as well as Indian styles and sounds.

The lyrics, like those of pop music everywhere in the world, tend to focus on the eternal emotions and complications of love and romance. A duet/dialogue between female and male singer is thus the norm. But lyrics can also be of a much wider variety than we usually encounter in the West. They may be, for example, comic, religious, ethical, family oriented (such as songs expressing affection for parents), highly poetic, or deeply philosophical.

Read through the lyrics of "Engal Kalyanam" ("Our Wedding") and then listen to the song. This vintage song takes a lighthearted look at the commotion and excitement of an Indian wedding, with the ever-present relatives and the joyful feelings of the happy couple.

MindTap

LISTEN TO
"Engal Kalyanam" ("Our Wedding"), performed by P. Susheela, T. M. Soundararajan, P. B. Sreenivas, and L. R. Eswari, online.

(Chorus) Our wedding is a "confusion wedding"!
Sons-in-law put up the money,
   And the father-in-law puts up the canopy[1] to receive the gifts.
   Morning is the wedding, and evening is the wedding night!
   Enliven! A love marriage![2]
   Tomorrow at the altar we'll exchange garlands, won't we?
   And won't the drums play with the pipes?[3]
The lovers' tale is performed in the eyes.
   It's a great struggle—to perform in the eyes!
   A colorful chariot is running beside me[4]
   Heaven is coming to us!
Mother-in-law puts on eye makeup,
   While the sons-in-law stare at her mirror;
   The [wedding] procession winds along the street with firecrackers,
   While everyone gives their blessings.

Text, "Engal Kalyanam"

Shall we have ten to sixteen children?
　Shall the trimness of our [youthful] bodies be lost?
You claimed you hated men,
　Yet you gave me desire!
　If I am like Kama, the god of love,
　You are the reason!
　Your [blushing] cheeks invite me;
　Your thoughts ask for me, I can tell!
　Your eyes—are like bright lightning …
　What are the pleasures we haven't experienced?
The bride's father had prayed to the god of Tirupati[5]
　That the marriage might be performed there,
　So the bride and groom might have auspicious lives.
　The sons-in-law better come home now
　And give a send-off to the bride's father,
　So that he can take up sanyasin![6]

Free translation from the Tamil by S. B. Rajeswari (1989).

---

[1] The ceremony takes place under a canopy of banana stalks, bamboo, and cloth.
[2] In India, most marriages are arranged by parents. By contrast, a marriage in which the young people choose their own spouse is called a "love marriage" in the Indian context and is unusual, except in the movies.
[3] "Drums … pipes" these are *tavil* and *nagaswaram* with their sacred and auspicious sound.
[4] The groom is like an ancient god-hero riding a chariot.
[5] Tirupati is the hilltop site of the most popular temple in South India.
[6] Now that the bride's father has managed the tension and complications of his daughter's wedding, it is humorously suggested that he can become a recluse (sanyasin) meditating in a hermitage. In sacred texts, this is the last stage of human life.

Although "Our Wedding" is a "golden oldie," one might notice certain strong characteristics that mark this song as unmistakably Indian: the frenetic pace of the clap-hammer rhythms, the alternating male and female voices with backup chorus, an eclectic orchestra, and the culturally specific references in the lyrics. There are three recurring musical sections to the song:

A. The chorus (Engal kalyanam …).
B. Sections marked by a jazz-like "walking" bass, before moving on.
C. Sections marked by an accompaniment exclusively of drums, a very different sound.

Listen to "Engal Kalyanam," Active Listening 6.2, following along with the timeline and noting the recurring sections A, B, and C as shown.

Sections B and C both carry the verses of the song. Instrumental interludes (one of which contains a musical quote from a Woody Woodpecker cartoon) occur between the first four vocal sections.

Older Indian pop music as heard in films from the 1940s, 1950s, and 1960s may approach the semi-classical or even classical in style and instrumentation, as in the classic film *Thillana Mohanambal* (1968) about the romance between a famous dancer and a *nagaswaram* virtuoso.

ACTIVE LISTENING 6.2
"Engal Kalyanam" ("Our Wedding")

COUNTER NUMBER	COMMENTARY	SECTION
0:00	Chorus: *Engal kalyanam* … ("Our wedding …")	A
0:18	Instrumental break	
0:32	Verse 1: Male–female duet in musical dialogue over "walking" bass line	B
0:49	Instrumental break	
0:53	Chorus (repeat): *Engal kalyanam* …	A
1:02	Instrumental break	
1:10	"Woody Woodpecker" call from U.S. cartoon	
1:14	Verse 2: Duet over drum accompaniment; new sound	C
1:42	Verse 3: Duet over "walking" bass line	B
2:12	Verse 4: Duet over drums accompaniment	C
2:35	Verse 5: Duet over "walking" bass line	B
3:14	Chorus: *Engal kalyanam* … and quick fade-out	A

MindTap·
⌂ WATCH an Active Listening Guide of this selection online.

The timbres, forms, and instrumentation of Indian pop music continue to evolve in extremely varied and creative ways, especially when compared with the rigid, industry-controlled formulas for most American pop songs.

For a more up-to-date Indian popular song, listen to "Urvasi Urvasi" by A. R. Rahman from the Tamil film *Kaadhalan* (1994) (also *Kadhalan*). Urvasi is a female name in South India. While most of the lyrics are in Tamil language, the refrain of the song is sung in English and recounts a solution to a variety of frustrations, which are sung in Tamil. The frustrating situations vary from going to a movie to meet girls and finding the theater full of elderly ladies, to settling down to watch your favorite TV show only to have the electricity fail, among others.

The bilingualism of the lyrics illustrates the widespread knowledge of English in post-colonial India today. The musical style will be familiar to anyone who listens to American pop music. The rhythm is set by hand claps and stick clicks, setting up a forceful beat for the entry of rhythm guitar and electric bass. The driving melody of male voices works with fragmented musical phrases, creating an energetic texture supported by sparse orchestration. Ultimately, the refrain punctuating each line presents positive thinking and a philosophic attitude toward life.

The more one listens to Indian popular music, the more one can appreciate its unique qualities, enjoy the beauty of its lyrics and themes, and gain a better understanding of why this is the favorite music of a billion people, old and young, rich and poor, educated and uneducated.

Perhaps someday great, contemporary Indian songwriters such as A. R. Rahman and Ilaiyaraja (who is seen in a large cinema billboard in Figure 6.11) will gain the recognition that they deserve on the world scene.

♫ LISTEN TO
"Urvasi Urvasi," from the Tamil-language film *Kaadhalan*, online.

MindTap·
⌂ WATCH a video of "Urvasi Urvasi" with dances as it appears in the original 1994 Tamil film *Kaadhalan*, online.

Figure 6.11
Composer Ilaiyaraja's head dominates a billboard for the movie *Karagattam-kari* ("Karagattam-girl"). *Karagattam* is a South Indian folk genre in which the female dancer must balance a clay pot on her head as she dances. *Photo © Carol Reck 2005. All rights reserved.*

Indian Music and the West

As a palimpsest, India's culture has long assimilated outside influences and made them its own. The presence of the violin, saxophone, guitar, and mandolin in Carnatic music, and the all-inclusive nature of South India's cinema/pop music industry are obvious examples. As the globalization of music through television, movies, CDs, cassettes, and travel continues, mutual influences between India and the West are bound to increase.

Since the 1970s, South Indian musicians have seen the connections between jazz improvisation and India's classical music traditions. From that awareness the genre known as "fusion" was born, an interface between East and West that continues to excite a younger generation of musicians and listeners. To listen to examples of music of any of the performers mentioned in this section, search the internet for recordings under the performer's name. The Carnatic violinists L. Shankar and L. Subramanian have worked extensively with American and European jazz and rock musicians over the past thirty years, as has the *tabla* wizard Zakir Hussain.

In the early 2000s, the remarkable Australian-British singer of South Indian descent, Susheela Raman, fused a Carnatic *kriti*, "Nagumomo" with an electric, hard-driving Chicago blues style (as in her album *Salt Rain*) played with her Australian compatriots. Her version is based on a *kriti* (classical South Indian song) by Tyagaraja, in the Telugu language. The song's lyrics refer to the charming, benevolent smile of the god-king hero Rama of the epic "Ramayana"; this is, in fact, a devotional love song to the deity in his human incarnation. The *raga* of the song also bears resemblance to the melodic material of American blues. Susheela Raman also has composed her own original songs reflecting her multicultural background.

The brilliant American jazz pianist Vijay Iyer, born in Albany, New York, now of New York City, whose parents are from South India, has worked with

♫ LISTEN TO
Susheela Raman singing "Nagumomo," from her album *Salt Rain* online.

saxophonist/composer Rudresh Mahanthappa and others to bring into jazz a subtle integration of Carnatic music influences and original improvisational procedures, creating a unique, imaginative style that defies definition (search for the album *Reimagining*, 2005, on the internet). He has profoundly influenced the face of jazz in recent years.

Rudresh Mahanthappa, another brilliant musician, has assembled an ensemble of Indian instruments to accompany the Bharata Natyam style choreography of the U.S.-based group Ragamala Dance. In his composition for their dance piece "Song of the Jasmine," Mahanthappa and his ensemble build a powerful, expressive composition combining composed and improvisational elements lasting more than two hours, saturated with *ragas* and *talas* drawn from classical South Indian music. East and West are combined with intelligence, imagination and virtuosity to create an outstanding integration of the two traditions. A sample of their work may be found online at the Ragamala Dance website (with video links).

In the late twentieth and early twenty-first centuries, an increasing number of South Asians have been working, studying, and living abroad. Cohesive communities of transplanted Indians, many trained in music, now appear in almost every major city or university town on Earth. The children of first-generation immigrants often find themselves in a bicultural world where the "Indian-ness" of their home and family must be balanced against the pervasive dominance of the mainstream culture of their adopted country. Cultural clubs and religious institutions support the study and presentation of concerts of classical Indian music and dance. Various Indo-pop styles, such as "bhangra" in Great Britain (note Panjabi MC's album *Panjabi MC Beware*), evolved and moved into the mainstream of their surrounding culture.

"Tassa-beat soca" in Trinidad has also evolved. In the selections mentioned, the drones, scales, and sometimes the instruments and languages of Indian music fuse with the beat and electric sound of mainstream rock and pop styles.

Among a number of musicians who have been strongly influenced by studies of Indian percussion is Dan Reck. With studies in 1991 and the early 2000s on *ghatam* (clay pot drum) and *mridangam* in the United States and in Chennai, he has integrated Indian rhythms into the creation of beats and other rhythmic compositions.

Indian music has infiltrated the West since the late 1950s. The *sitar* virtuoso Ravi Shankar is a seminal figure. Having spent years in Paris as a boy with the dance troupe of Uday Shankar, he has been able to move with ease in the elite worlds of Western classical and pop music. By the late 1960s, his concerts with the *tabla* virtuoso Alla Rakha at venues as varied as the Edinburgh Music Festival and the Monterey Pop Festival eventually gave him superstar status. Over the years, Ravi Shankar has released many collaborative recordings. These include the "West Meets East" dialogues with famous Western musicians—among them the classical violinist Yehudi Menuhin, the flute virtuoso Jean-Pierre Rampal, and the jazz musician Paul Horn. In the album *East Greets East* (1978) he performed with traditional Japanese musicians. His *Shankar Family and Friends*, an early 1970s iconic recording made in San Francisco with several dozen Indian and Western musicians (including one listed enigmatically as "Harris Georgeson"), includes some fascinating music (and some near misses).

♪ **LISTEN TO**
Vijay Iyer playing "The Shape of Things" and "Common Ground" on his album *Raw Materials* online.

MindTap·
🎧 **WATCH** a video of the dancers and musicians in "Song of the Jasmine" online.

♪ **LISTEN TO**
Panjabi MC singing "Jogi" from his album *Beware*, or any of his other songs online.

♪ **LISTEN TO**
"Samsara," by Dan Reck, online.

MindTap°

🎧 **WATCH** . . . a video of "The Inner Light," online.

In the mid-1960s, Ravi Shankar acquired the most illustrious of his students, George Harrison of the Beatles. During the filming of the Beatles' movie, *Help!*, a scene is set with the Beatles eating in an Indian restaurant in London. An ensemble of Indian classical musicians featuring *sitar* and *tabla* is playing in the restaurant. However, the song being played on the *sitar* is not Indian music but rather an instrumental rendition of the Beatles' own song "Hard Day's Night." The Beatles were fascinated by the instruments being played and how unusual and interesting the instruments sounded playing a Beatles tune. As George Harrison recollected, "I remember picking up the *sitar* and trying to hold it and thinking, 'This is a funny sound.'... I went and bought a Ravi record; I put it on and it hit a certain spot in me that I can't explain, but it seemed very familiar to me. The only way I could describe it was: my intellect didn't know what was going on and yet this other part of me identified with it. It just called on me" (http://www.beatlesbible.com/features/india). In the song "Norwegian Wood," George Harrison played the *sitar* in place of the usual solo guitar, the first instance of a musical instrument from India appearing in Western pop music. Harrison's interest in Indian classical music and religious philosophy resulted in a series of finely crafted, India-based songs ranging from "Love You To" and "Within You, Without You" to "The Inner Light" (recorded in Bombay) and the post-Beatles George Harrison song "My Sweet Lord."

🎵 **LISTEN TO**

the song "Love You To," performed by The Beatles, from their album, *Revolver*, online.

In "Love You To," from the Beatles' 1966 album, *Revolver*, the *sitar* begins with a brief introduction of the notes of a *raga*-like scale in unmeasured time—a hint of an *alapana*. A background drone of *tambura* and bass guitar continues throughout.

The *tabla* drumbeat enters, establishing a driving metrical pulse of *tala*-like cycles. Harrison's vocal line is sung in flat tones and ends with a descending melisma of distinct Indian vocal sound. In the second section of the song, the repetitive riffs alternating between *sitar* and voice reflect the "question-and-answer" interplay of Indian musicians in performance. Then there is an instrumental break with the *sitar* and *tabla* improvising first in cycles of seven beats, then in five, and finally in three, all of which leads to a final rendition of chorus and verse. A fast, instrumental postlude corresponds to the ending climactic sections of a North Indian performance. All of this in a three-minute song!

Many of John Lennon's songs of the mid-1960s also had Indian influences, such as "Norwegian Wood" (utilizing the North Indian *sitar*), "Across the Universe," with its Sanskrit phrases, and the beautiful song "Rain." Lennon often used Indian-like sound and textures to indicate the trippiness of drug-induced states (as in "Lucy in the Sky with Diamonds"). In the musical texture of "Tomorrow Never Knows," built over a hair-raising drone and Ringo Starr's hypnotic beat, Lennon (with producer George Martin) used exotic riffs and Indian instruments floating in a hallucinogenic collage of backward tapes and sound effects (described by one critic as "a herd of elephants gone mad!"). All of this backs the otherworldly dream state of the lyrics inspired by the *Tibetan Book of the Dead* as interpreted by the LSD guru Timothy Leary.

It is suggested that you choose a song by one of the artists mentioned in this section that you believe displays an Indian music influence. Write a detailed description of the song, tracking its possible influences and cultural context.

Indo-pop music has continued to flourish in Great Britain, where large immigrant communities from the former colonies continue to generate new genres and sounds. The filmmaker Vivek Bald, in his groundbreaking documentary *Mutiny: Asians Storm British Music,* has brilliantly surveyed the Indo-Brit scene in the late twentieth century.

The singer and composer Sheila Chandra, born in 1965, has treated diverse influences from East and West with intelligence and sensitivity. Trained in both Western and Indian music, in the early 1980s she joined with Steve Coe and Martin Smith to form an innovative, East-West fusion band, Monsoon (see their compilation album, *Silk,* [1991], covering the years 1983-1990). In the exquisite song, "Ever So Lonely/Eyes/Ocean," from her 1992 solo album, *Weaving My Ancestors' Voices,* she sets her English lyrics to *raga*-based melody, drone, and synthesizer. In "Speaking in Tongues" I and II from the same album, Chandra adapts the lightning-fast language of spoken Indian drum patterns with great ingenuity, moving from traditional *sollukattu* to whispers, clicks, and playful gibberish. In her more recent work, Chandra has focused on the unique qualities of her voice set against electronic and acoustic drones, and has explored the synthesis of world vocal traditions from the British Isles, Spain, North Africa, and India. It would be interesting to compare the musical creations of all of these musicians.

As Indian classical and popular musicians continue to absorb the varied musics of the world around them, and as world musical traditions continue to be instantaneously accessible, perhaps the ancient traditions of classical Indian music north and south, Hindustani and Carnatic, will continue to find echoes, reflections, interpretations, and responses in the music of the West.

The author wishes to thank the following for their invaluable contributions: Ms. Lalitha Muthukumar, Drs. M. Muthukumar, Nalini Easwar, Easwar Iyer, and David P. Nelson. Thanks are also due to members of my family, all of whom have contributed greatly to this chapter: my daughter, Navarana, my son, Dan, and my wife, Carol.

MindTap
PRACTICE your understanding of this chapter's concepts by reviewing flashcards and working once more with the chapter's Active Listening Guides online.

MindTap
WATCH videos of Sheila Chandra performing, online.

Study Questions

1. What is the overall role of religion in South India's classical music? South India's classical music and dance is based on Hindu devotional song texts. What genres in Europe and the Americas utilize religious words and/or devotional expression?

2. What are the functioning layers and relationships among musicians in a South Indian classical music ensemble?

3. Why is the relationship between the various notes of a particular raga when juxtaposed with the unchanging notes of the drone important in Carnatic music? In your opinion is there a similar relationship in bagpipe music, Sacred Harp singing, or Appalachian fiddling?

4. In exploring the seventy-two *melakarta* scales, which do you find attractive and interesting? Why?

5. India's civilization is known for absorbing outside influences and "Indianizing" them in a process known as acculturation. Give five examples (in or out of music).

MindTap
DO an online quiz that your instructor may assign for a grade.

6. What are some of the social layers of genres of Indian music? Do American and European music also have musical styles of higher or lower status? How do they reflect various subcultures?

7. Imagine that you are creating a *raga*. What would be its poetic name, time of day, season, and expressive mood (*rasa*)? Could you create a *ragamala* using crayon, chalk, paints, collage, or photographs, abstract or representational, that captures the mood of your imaginary *raga*?

8. South Indian music uses composed songs mixed with improvisational sections. Can you think of a similar approach in Western music-culture? What are the similarities and differences between the two?

9. What are the kinds of improvisation (melodic and rhythmic) used in Carnatic music? Describe their characteristics.

10. Describe the concept of *raga* in Indian music. Do other cultures have something similar?

7

Asia/Indonesia

R. Anderson Sutton

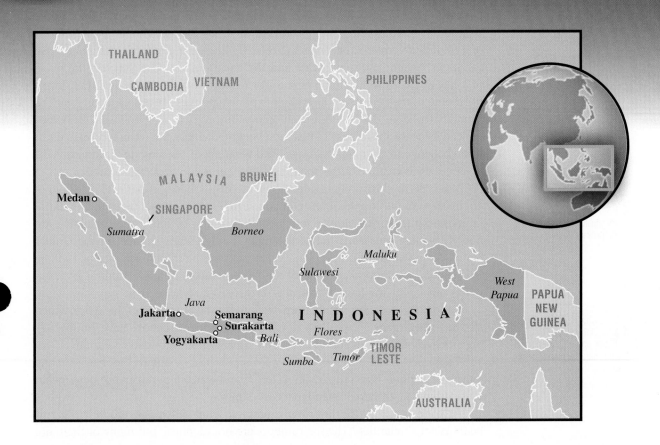

Learning Objectives

After you have studied this chapter, you should be able to:

1. Describe *gamelan* music from Central Java, Indonesia, its instruments, performance styles, and performance contexts.

2. Differentiate the gamelan music of the island of Bali from that of Central Java.

3. Discuss the contrasts between traditional Batak music and the gamelan music of Java and Bali, as well as identify underlying structural similarities.

4. Contrast various styles of Indonesian popular music, and the ways in which they represent different responses to cultural globalization.

MindTap®
READ, highlight, and take notes on the complete chapter text in a rich, interactive, online platform.

MindTap®
🔊 **LISTEN TO**
Ladrang "Wilujeng," performed by musicians of Ngudya Wirama, online.

MindTap®
🎧 **WATCH** a video of "Ladrang Asmaradana Kethoprakan" online.

MindTap®
🎧 **WATCH** videos of Balinese gamelan musicians performing the piece "Sekar Jepun" online.

Indonesia is a country of astounding cultural diversity, nowhere more evident than in the stunning variety of musical and related performing arts found throughout its several thousand populated islands. Before we start to learn more about the country and its music, let's get the sounds of some **gamelan** (*gah*-muh-lahn; percussion ensemble) music in our ears. *Ladrang* "Wilujeng" is our introduction; it is representative of the main musical tradition of the central region of Java. What you hear is a rich blend of mostly percussion instruments, which will be introduced and described later in this chapter. What starts as a single melody played on a fiddle (**rebab**), is joined by the many percussion instruments, mostly playing variations of a central melody that becomes increasingly hidden in the thick texture as these variations become more elaborate and the voices join in. Can you feel the pulse or beat, which slows over the first thirty to thirty-five seconds, and then levels off? Some of the percussion instruments punctuate these beats. Can you hear the sound of the large, deep gong, which occurs only every thirty-two beats? For experienced listeners, this is easy to hear and very predictable, but for newcomers it can be a challenge to get one's bearings. And what about the singing? Javanese vocal quality sounds "natural" to Javanese listeners, but not to most newcomers.

What do the instruments and the musicians look like in performance? There are many examples on the internet if you search for "Javanese gamelan," "Central Javanese gamelan," or similar terms, though many of the videos available are not of Javanese musicians but of the many foreign study groups (in the United States, Australia, and Europe). One video presents a full performance of *Ladrang* "Asmaradana Kethoprakan," one of the best examples of a full, Central Javanese group, albeit with the Javanese vocal texts displayed karaoke-style.

Various styles of performance are exhibited in the unfolding of this piece, which also has a large gong stroke every thirty-two beats. Some sections have group singing and lively drumming; others, solo singing and more subdued drumming.

These first audio and video examples represent but one of Indonesia's many musical traditions. For comparison, listen to and watch a performance of gamelan music from Bali, the small island just east of Java.

In comparison to the Javanese examples, what differences do you see and hear? What similarities? The instruments are not identical, but many of them are similar—percussion instruments with metal keys and knobbed gongs. But notice the sharp contrasts and sudden shifts in musical style in the Balinese example in comparison to the more gradual transitions in the Javanese examples. Indonesians often point to the main contrasts between these two major traditions, identifying the Balinese as more dynamic and exciting and the Javanese as the more steady and predictable. We will come back to these two important varieties of gamelan music shortly, but first some background on Indonesia.

Known formerly as the Dutch East Indies, Indonesia is one of many modern nations whose boundaries were formed during the centuries of European colonial domination, placing peoples with contrasting languages, arts, systems of belief, and conceptions of the world under a single rule. The adoption of a national language in the early twentieth century was a crucial step in building the unity necessary to win a revolution against the Dutch (1945–1949). Today, a pan-Indonesian popular culture has been contributing to an increased sense of national unity, particularly among the younger generation. Nevertheless, strife between ethnic groups and decentralization of political rule after more than three decades of authoritarian rule has challenged this sense of unity. Indeed, though we can identify some general cultural traits, including musical ones, shared by many peoples of Indonesia, to speak of an "Indonesian" culture or style of music is problematic. Regional diversity is still very much in evidence.

Most Indonesians' first language is not the national language (Indonesian) but one of the more than two hundred separate languages found throughout this vast archipelago, comprised of an estimated 6,000 inhabited islands. Further, although many are familiar with the sounds of Indonesian pop music and with such Western stars as Rihanna, Taylor Swift, and One Direction, they also know their own regional musical traditions. In Indonesia, many kinds of music exist side by side in a complex pluralism that reflects both the diversity of the native population and the receptiveness of that population to centuries of outside influences. Indonesia is, then, a country truly home to worlds of music.

What first impression might this country give you? You would probably arrive in the nation's capital, **Jakarta** (jah-*kar*-tah), a teaming metropolis of more than ten million people—some very wealthy, most rather poor. Jakarta is near the western end of the north coast of **Java**, Indonesia's most heavily populated (but not largest) island. (See the map on page 209.) The mix of Indonesia's many cultures among themselves and with Western culture is nowhere more fully realized than in this special city. Many kinds of music are heard here. Western-style nightclubs, karaoke bars, and discos do a lively business until the early hours of the morning. Javanese gamelan music accompanies nightly performances of ***wayang orang*** (*wah*-yang *oh*-rang) theater, an elaborate type of dance-drama from central Java.

You might also run across a troupe from Bali, Sumatra, or any of the many other islands, performing at the national arts center Taman Ismail Marzuki or the Indonesian cultural park Taman Mini. As you begin to find your way around the city by taxi, bus, or three-wheeled *bajaj,* you may develop a taste for highly seasoned food. You will certainly get a sense of Indonesia's many cultures by roaming this complex city. Much of what you encounter, however, has a strong presence in the various regions in which it is rooted.

> MindTap·
>
> 🎧 **WATCH** excerpts of *wayang orang* theater online.

Central Java

Java is an island about the size of New York State (just less than 50,000 square miles). With over 100 million people, Java is one of the most densely populated regions in the world. (Indonesia's total population is about 250 million.) Most of the central and eastern two-thirds of the island is inhabited by Indonesia's largest ethnic group, the Javanese, roughly 85 million people who share a language and other cultural traits, including music, though some local differences persist. In **Sunda** (*soon*-dah), the western third of the island, live the Sundanese, who have a language and arts distinct from those of the Javanese. Despite its dense population, Java remains mostly a farming society, with wet-rice agriculture as the predominant source of livelihood. Most Javanese identify themselves as Muslim, though only a minority follow full orthodox practice such as praying five times a day. Many, however, go to a local mosque on Friday, the Muslim holy day, and fast from dawn until dusk for the month of Ramadhan. And yet many adhere to a blend of Islam with Hinduism and

Buddhism (introduced into Java over one thousand years ago), and with what most scholars believe to be an even earlier layer of belief in benevolent and mischievous spirits and in ancestor veneration. The worldview that embraces these many layers of belief is often referred to as *kejawèn*—literally, "Javanese," or "Javaneseness," a term that indicates the importance of this Javanese self-conception. In the past few decades, however, with increased exposure to global Islam, Javanese have increasingly embraced a less syncretic and more orthodox, though moderate, Islam.

From Jakarta a twelve-hour ride on bus or train through shimmering, wet rice fields, set in the plains between gracefully sloping volcanic mountains, leads to **Yogyakarta** (jog-jah-*kar*-ta; often abbreviated **Yogya** and pronounced *jog*-jah). Yogya is one of two court cities in the cultural heartland of Central Java. The other, about forty miles to the northeast, is **Surakarta** (soo-rah-*kar*-tah or soo-raw-*kar*-taw; usually called **"Solo"**). Most Javanese point to these two cities as the cultural centers where traditional gamelan music and related performing arts have flourished in their most elaborate and refined forms. These courtly developments contrast with the rougher styles associated with the villages and outlying districts.

Yogya is a sprawling city with a population of about 400,000. It has several multistory malls and a growing number of hotels, but few other buildings taller than two stories. Away from the several major streets lined with stores flashing neon signs and blaring popular music, Yogya in many ways resembles a dense collection of villages. Yet at its center stands one of Java's two main royal courts, the official home of the tenth sultan. Unlike any Western palace or court, this is a complex of small buildings and open pavilions appropriate for the tropical climate. It was not designed merely for comfort, however. Endowed with mystical significance as an earthly symbol of the macrocosmos (the ordered universe), the court is oriented to the cardinal directions. The ruler, whose residence is located at the very center of the court, is believed to be imbued with divine powers, as were the Hindu-Javanese kings many centuries ago.

In many of these pavilions are kept the court gamelan ensembles. Some date back many centuries and perform only for rare, ritual occasions, while others have been built or augmented more recently and are used more frequently. Like other treasured heirlooms belonging to the court, most of these sets of instruments are believed to contain special powers and are shown respect and given offerings. Also kept in the palace are numerous sets of finely carved and painted **wayang kulit** (*wah*-yang *koo*-lit; puppets made of water buffalo hide) used in all-night performances of highly sophisticated and entertaining shadow plays. Classical Javanese dance, with gamelan accompaniment, is rehearsed regularly and performed for special palace functions.

Though the court is still regarded as a cultural center, much activity in the traditional Javanese arts takes place outside the court, sponsored by private individuals and by such modern institutions as the national radio station and public schools and colleges. In the rural villages, which long served as a source and inspiration for the more refined courtly arts, a variety of musical and related performing arts continue to play a vital role in Javanese life.

Gamelan

The word gamelan refers to a set of instruments unified by their tuning and often by their decorative carving and painting. Most gamelans consist of several kinds of metal slab instruments (similar in some ways to the Western vibraphone) and tuned, knobbed **gongs**. The word "gong" is one of the few English words derived from Indonesian languages. (Two others are ketchup and amok.) In English, gong may refer to any of a variety of percussion instruments whose sound-producing vibrations are concentrated in the center of the instrument, rather than at the edge—like a bell. In Javanese, it refers specifically to the larger, hanging, knobbed gongs (Figure 7.1) in gamelan ensembles and is part of a family of words relating to largeness, greatness, and grandeur—*agung* ("great," "kingly"), *ageng* ("large"), and *gunung* ("mountain"). In addition to gongs and other metal instruments, a gamelan ensemble normally has several drums and may have other kinds of instruments: winds, strings, and wooden percussion instruments (xylophones).

Some ancient ceremonial gamelans have only a few knobbed gongs and one or two drums. The kind of gamelan most often used in central Java today is a large set, comprising instruments ranging from deep, booming gongs three feet in diameter to high-pitched gong-chimes and slab instruments, with three drums, several bamboo flutes, zithers, xylophones, and a two-stringed fiddle.

Instruments in the present-day gamelan are tuned to one of two scale systems: ***sléndro*** (*slayn*-dro), a five-tone system made up of nearly equidistant intervals, normally notated with the numerals 1, 2, 3, 5, and 6 (no 4); and ***pélog*** (*pay*-log), a seven-tone system made up of large

Salient Characteristics of
Javanese Gamelan Music

- Emphasis on percussion instruments (metal slab and knobbed gongs, drums)

- Bronze preferred for metal percussion instruments

- Use of two scales (five-tone *sléndro* and seven-tone *pélog*) that differ from Western scale

- Gamelan ensemble music is either "loud playing" or "soft playing"

- Stratified texture (main melody, punctuation, elaborations, drum patterns)

- Cyclic repetition of phrases

- Use of different-sized gong instruments to "punctuate" phrases

- Binary orientation in length of phrases and subdivisions

- Ensemble directed aurally by a drummer, not visually by a conductor

- Often accompanies dance, dance-drama, and shadow puppetry

- Flexibility in elaboration of main melody, tempo, dynamics, and number of repetitions

Figure 7.1

The gamelan Kyai Kanyut Mèsem ("Tempted to Smile") in the Mangkunegaran palace, Surakarta, Central Java. In foreground: *gong ageng* (largest gong, on left) and *gong siyem*. *Arthur Durkee, Earth Visions Photographics.*

and small intervals, normally notated 1, 2, 3, 4, 5, 6, and 7. Some gamelans are entirely *sléndro,* others entirely *pélog,* but many are actually double ensembles combining a full set of instruments for each system.

The scale systems are incompatible, and only in a few, rare cases are they played simultaneously. Neither of these scale systems can be played on a Western piano, and neither is entirely standardized, as I shall explain.

The instrumentation of a full *sléndro-pélog* gamelan varies slightly, but it usually includes all or most of the instruments shown in Figure 7.2.

Among these many instruments, it will be useful in listening to the Javanese examples to know the following:

- The **saron** (*sah*-ron) and **slenthem** (*sluhn*-tuhm), instruments with six or seven keys, which play the main melody
- The **gong** (or **gong ageng**) and **siyem** (*see*-yuhm), the two largest, hanging gongs, which mark the end of major phrases of the main melody
- The **kenong** (kuh-*nong*), large kettles resting horizontally, which divide the major phrases evenly (playing simultaneously with the *gong* or *siyem* at the end of major phrases, and subdividing evenly in between: usually two or four times per major phrase)

Figure 7.2

Central Javanese gamelan instruments. *Drawing by Peggy Choy.*

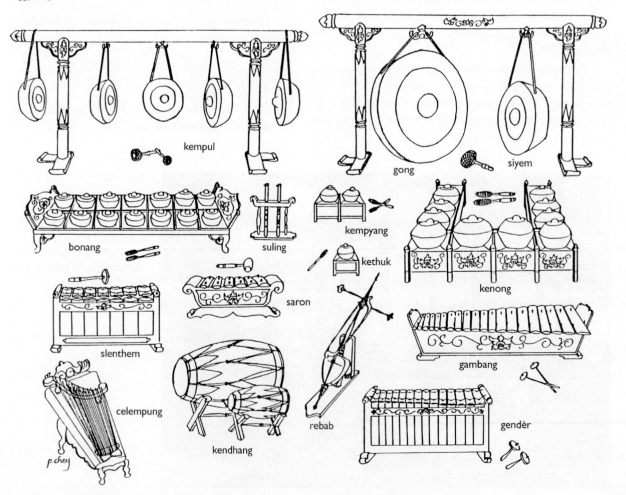

- The **kempul** (kuhm-*pool*), smaller, hanging gongs, suspended vertically, which evenly subdivide phrases (often midway between *kenong* beats)
- The **kethuk** (kuh-*took*), a small kettle, resting horizontally, which subdivides secondary phrases (between *kenong* and *kempul* beats)
- The **bonang** (*bo*-nahng), middle and high-register gong-chimes with ten to fourteen kettles, which embellish the main melody (see Figure 7.3)

Most of the other instruments perform elaborations and variations of the main melody to create a rich and subtle texture.

There is no standard arrangement of these instruments in the performance space except that they are almost always placed at right angles to one another, reflecting the Javanese concern with the cardinal directions (Figure 7.3). Generally, the larger gong instruments are in the back, with the *saron* family immediately in front of them, *bonang* family to the sides, other melodic instruments in front, and drums in the center. The placement of the instruments reflects their relative loudness and their function in the performance of pieces, to be discussed shortly.

The gamelan instruments are normally complemented by singers: a small male chorus (**gérong**, *gay*-rong) and female soloists (**pesindhèn**, puh-*seen*-dehn). Java also supports a highly developed tradition of unaccompanied vocal music, which serves as a major vehicle for Javanese poetry. Although Javanese have recorded their sung poetry in several writing systems for over a thousand years, these are normally sung rather than read silently or aloud. Even important letters between members of the nobility were, until the twentieth century, composed as poetry and delivered as song. Although the postal system has eliminated this practice, vocal music, whether with gamelan or unaccompanied, enjoys great popularity in Java today.

The relation between vocal and instrumental orientations in gamelan music is reflected in the two major groupings of instruments in the present-day Javanese

Figure 7.3

Members of the Pujangga Laras *karawitan* group performing at a wedding in Eromoko, Wonogiri, Central Java, August 2006.
R. Anderson Sutton.

gamelan: "loud-playing" and "soft-playing." Historical evidence suggests that these two groupings were once separate ensembles and were combined as recently as the sixteenth or early seventeenth century. Associated with festivals, processions, and other noisy, outdoor events, loud-playing ensembles were strictly instrumental. Soft-playing ensembles were intended for more-intimate gatherings, often indoors, and involved singing. Even today, performance style distinguishes these two groupings. In loud-playing style, only the drums and louder metal instruments are used (see the left-hand column of Table 7.1). In soft-playing style, these instruments, or most of them, are played softly, and the voices and instruments listed in the right-hand column of Table 7.1 are featured.

Gamelan Construction

Bronze is the preferred metal for gamelan manufacture, owing both to its durability and to its rich, sweet sound quality. Brass and iron are also used, especially in rural areas. They are considerably cheaper than bronze and easier to tune but less sonorous. Bronze gamelan instruments are not cast but instead are forged in a long and difficult process. The metal worker in Java has traditionally been held in high regard. Forging bronze instruments not only requires great skill but also retains a mystical significance. Working with metals, transforming molten copper and tin (the metals that make bronze alloy) into sound-producing instruments, is believed to make one especially vulnerable to dangerous forces in the spirit world. For this reason, the smiths make ritual preparation and may actually assume mythical identities during the forging process (Becker 1988; Kunst 1973:138).

The largest gongs may require a full month of labor and a truckload of coal for the forge that heats the metal. Only after appropriate meditation, prayer, fasting, and preparation of offerings does a smith undertake the making of a large gong. The molten bronze is pounded, reheated, pounded, reheated, and gradually shaped into a large, knobbed gong that may measure three feet or more in diameter. A false hit at any stage can crack the gong, meaning that the process must begin all over.

Gamelan Identity

A gamelan, particularly a bronze set with one or two fine, large gongs, is often held in great respect, given a proper name, such as "Kyai Kanyut Mèsem," (see Figure 7.1),

Table 7.1 **The Two Gamelan Instrument Groups**

Loud-Playing Instruments	Soft-Playing Instruments
gong ageng	gendèr barung
siyem	gendèr panerus
kempul	gambang
kenong	celempung
kethuk	suling
kempyang	rebab
bonang family	
saron family	
slenthem	
kendhang family	

and given offerings on Thursday evenings (the beginning of the Muslim holy day). Though gamelan makers have recently begun to duplicate precise tuning and decorative designs, each gamelan is usually a unique set whose instruments would both look and sound out of place in another ensemble. In the past, it was forbidden even to attempt to copy the tuning and design of palace gamelan instruments, as these were reserved for the ruler and were directly associated with his power.

The variability in tuning from one gamelan to another certainly does not stem from a casual sense of pitch among Javanese musicians and gamelan makers. On the contrary, they take great care in the making and in the occasional retuning of gamelan sets to arrive at a pleasing tuning—one that is seen to fit the particular physical condition of the instruments and the tastes of the individual owner. Bronze has the curious property of changing tuning—rather markedly during the first few years after forging, and more subtly over the next twenty to thirty years, until it has finally "settled." It might seem that the lack of a standard tuning would produce musical chaos, but the actual latitude is rather small.

Gamelan Performance Contexts

Javanese music is more closely interrelated with other performing arts and more intimately bound to other aspects of life than are the arts in the West. Concerts of gamelan music, with an audience sitting quietly and paying close attention to the music, have only recently appeared and serve mostly to present new, experimental works. In contrast, presentations of the more traditional gamelan music are best understood as social events that involve gamelan music. They usually commemorate a day of ritual importance, such as a birth, circumcision, or wedding. Normally, a family sponsors such an event and invites neighbors and relatives, with others welcome to look on and listen. The invited guests are served food and are expected to socialize freely throughout the duration of the event. No one expects the guests to be quiet during the performance of pieces or to pay rapt attention to them the way an audience does at a Western concert. Rather, the music, carefully played though it may be, is seen to contribute to the festiveness of the larger social event, helping to make it *ramé* (lively; busy in a positive way). Connoisseurs among the guests will ask for a favorite piece and may pay close attention to the way the ensemble or a particular singer or instrumentalist performs, but not to the exclusion of friendly interaction with the hosts and other guests. Although the music is intended to entertain those present (without dance or drama), it also serves a ritual function, helping to maintain balance at important transitional points in the life of a person or community.

Though many Javanese listen to popular music for entertainment and relaxation, and some find gamelan music uninteresting or old-fashioned, many also enjoy gamelan music, not only when they hear it live at weddings and other public ceremonies, but also as a pleasant alternative to pop music stations on the radio—for relaxing at home. In these informal contexts, lighter pieces in soft-playing style are usually preferred over the pieces in loud-playing style. Many have learned at least some basic gamelan at some point during their formal education.

More often, gamelan music is performed as accompaniment for dance or theater—a refined, female, ensemble dance (Figure 7.4); a flirtatious female solo dance; a vigorous, martial lance dance; or an evening of drama based on Javanese legendary history, for example. A list of traditional genres currently performed in Central Java with gamelan accompaniment would be long. Some are presented

MindTap·
🎧 **WATCH** an example of a strong, male dance online.

MindTap·
🎧 **WATCH** an example of a refined, female dance online.

MindTap·
🎧 **WATCH** an example of a duet with a refined, male character dancing with a female character online.

Figure 7.4

Dancers at Pujokusuman in Yogyakarta perform a refined, female dance. *Peggy Choy.*

primarily in commercial settings, with an audience buying tickets. Others most often involve a ceremony. You can explore the internet for examples of Javanese dance; there are hundreds, if not thousands, of videos, though quality varies.

The genre held in the highest esteem by most Javanese, and nearly always reserved for ceremony, is the shadow puppet theatre or *wayang kulit* (see Figures 7.5 and 7.6), which dates back no fewer than one thousand years. Beginning with an overture played on the gamelan during the early evening, shadow puppet performances normally last until dawn. With a screen stretched before him (almost all Javanese puppeteers are male), a lamp overhead, and puppets to both sides, one master puppeteer (**dhalang**, *dah*-lang) operates all the puppets, performs all the narration and dialogue, sings mood songs, and directs the musicians for about eight hours with no intermission.

Among the many thousands of hours of high-quality performance of *wayang kulit* on the internet, you can see and hear some truly excellent examples by simply searching for "wayang kulit purba asmara" (leading to many examples by

Figure 7.5
Puppeteer Ki Gondo Darman performing *wayang kulit* at the ASKI Performing Arts Academy in Surakarta. *Arthur Durkee, Earth Visions Photographics.*

the popular, young puppeteer Ki Purba Asmara [kee *pur*-baw as-*maw*-raw]) or "wayang kulit anom suroto" (leading to many examples of the senior puppeteer Ki Anom Suroto [kee *a*-nom su-*raw*-taw]). Both of these puppeteers perform regularly throughout Java and other communities where Javanese currently reside. Both are recognized as top puppeteers for their skills in puppet manipulation, narration, characterization, humor, and singing.

Although the musicians do not play constantly throughout the evening, they must always remain ready to respond to a signal from the puppeteer. He leads the musicians and accents the action of the drama through a variety of percussion patterns he plays by hitting the wooden puppet chest to his left and the clanging metal plates suspended from the rim of the chest. If he is holding puppets in both hands, he uses his foot to sound these signals. He must be highly skilled as a manipulator, director, singer, and storyteller.

The puppeteer delivers not a fixed play written by a known playwright but rather his own rendition of a basic story—usually closely related to versions performed by other puppeteers, but never exactly the same. It might be a well-known episode from the **Ramayana** (rah-mah-*yah*-nah) or **Mahabharata** (ma-hah-bah-*rah*-tah), epics of Indian origin that have been adapted and transformed in many parts of Southeast Asia and have been known in Java for a thousand years.

During a shadow puppet performance, the gamelan plays music drawn from a large repertory of pieces, none specific to a single play and many of which are played in other contexts as well. A good musician knows many hundreds of pieces, but like the shadow plays, the pieces are generally not totally fixed. Many regional and individual variants exist for some pieces. More importantly, the very conception of what constitutes a **gendhing** (guhn-*deeng*)—a "gamelan piece" or "gamelan composition"—differs from the Western notion of musical pieces, particularly within the Western "classical" tradition.

Gamelan Music: A Javanese *Gendhing* in Performance

We can best begin to understand what a Javanese *gendhing* is by considering one in some detail—how it is conceived and how it is realized in performance. Listen to *Bubaran* "Kembang Pacar" (boo-*bah*-rahn kuhm-*bang pa*-char) (Active Listening 7.1). To enable you to hear and understand the individual layers of the music, I had my advanced students of Javanese gamelan at the University of Wisconsin–Madison perform this special version, which begins with only the main melody played by itself (all four major phrases), with successive layers added, one by one.

ACTIVE LISTENING 7.1
Bubaran "Kembang Pacar" (Demo Version)

COUNTER NUMBER	COMMENTARY
Main melody—Phrases A through D	
0:02	*Saron* and *slenthem* play major phrase A, 1st statement, sixteen beats. (metal slab instruments)
0:17	Phrase B, 1st statement, sixteen beats.
0:32	Phrase C, 1st statement, sixteen beats.
0:46	Phrase D, 1st statement, sixteen beats.
1:00	*Gong* enters, marking end of phrase D. (Large, hanging gong; marks the ends of all major phrases)
Phrase A, 2nd statement	
1:04	*Kenong* enters, playing on every fourth beat. (Large kettle, horizontally mounted; subdivides the major phrase)
Phrase B, 2nd statement	
1:20	*Kempul* enters, playing on the sixth, tenth, and fourteenth beats. (Medium, hanging gongs; subdivides the major phrase)
Phrase C, 2nd statement	
1:30	*Kethuk* enters, playing on the first and third beat of every group of four. (Small kettle gong; subdivides the *kenong* phrase)
Phrase D, 2nd statement	
1:43	*Kendhang* (kuhn-*dahng*) enters, playing rhythmic patterns that fill the length of each major phrase (sixteen beats). (Set of large and small barrel drums; directs tempo and dynamics)
Phrase A, 3rd statement	
1:56	*Saron peking* enters, echoing each tone of the main melody. (Smallest, highest-pitched *saron*, metal slab instrument; doubles main melody, except at slower tempos, when it usually varies the melody)
Phrase B, 3rd statement	
2:09	*Bonang barung* enters, playing variations and embellishments. (Larger, lower-pitched gong-chime; elaborates the main melody and subdivides its beats)

COUNTER NUMBER	COMMENTARY

Phrase C, 3rd statement

2:21 — *Bonang panerus* enters, playing variations and embellishments twice as fast as the *bonang barung* earlier.
(Smaller, higher-pitched gong-chime; elaborates the main melody)

Phrase D, 3rd statement

2:34 — Full instrumentation.
2:38 — Drummer speeds up tempo nearing the end of major phrase D.

Phrase A, 4th statement

2:45 — Full instrumentation.

Phrase B, 4th statement

2:56 — Full instrumentation.

Phrase C, 4th statement

3:06 — Full instrumentation.

Phrase D, 4th statement

3:17 — Full instrumentation.
Drummer signals slowing of tempo to end the piece.

Active Listening 7.1 gives the order in which these instrumental layers are added, and the counter number for each. Once all the layers are in place, the ensemble plays the entire piece as it would be heard in Java, including the gradual slowing down to end. This *gendhing* consists of four major phrases of melody (we can refer to them as A, B, C, and D). In this demonstration version, all four are first played alone, with no punctuation, drum, or elaboration. As the *gendhing* repeats, one layer of punctuation, drum pattern, or elaboration is added in each successive major phrase (marked by the gong), as shown in Active Listening 7.1.

You will note that it is an example of loud-playing style throughout. It is in the *pélog* scale system with small and large intervals. Javanese normally refer to *gendhing* by their formal structure, in this case **bubaran** (meaning sixteen beats per major phrase and four *kenong* beats per major phrase); the name of a particular melody, here, **"kembang pacar"** (a kind of red flower); the scale system (*pélog*); and the modal category (*pathet nem* [*pah*-tuht nuhm]).

The structure of this *gendhing*, like most of the Javanese repertory, is based on principles of balance, binary (duple) divisions and subdivisions, and cycles that repeat. The major phrases in a *gendhing* are marked off by the sound of either the large *gong* or the slightly smaller *gong siyem*. For most *gendhing*, these phrases are of regular length as measured in beats of the *main melody*, the part usually played on the *slenthem* and the *saron* family—almost always some factor of two: eight beats, sixteen beats, thirty-two beats, sixty-four beats, one hundred and twenty-eight beats, two hundred and fifty-six beats. (In the genre of pieces that serve as the staple for accompanying dramatic action, as we will see later, the major phrases are of irregular length, and the regular unit is marked instead by the smaller gong, *kempul.*) A major phrase is usually subdivided into two or four shorter phrases by the *kenong*, and these are further subdivided by *kempul* and *kethuk*.

The result is a pattern of interlocking percussion that repeats until an aural signal from the drummer or one of the lead melodic instruments directs the performers to end or to proceed to a different piece. Whereas in Western music composers provide explicit directions for performers to repeat a section, in Javanese gamelan performance repetition is assumed. As we speak of "phrases" in describing music, borrowing the term from the realm of language, Javanese liken the major phrase to a "sentence" and conceive of the subdividing parts as "punctuation." For *Bubaran* "Kembang Pacar," the pattern of punctuation is repeated throughout, the same for each major phrase. Today, many Javanese musicians refer to notation to learn or to recall particular pieces, but they do not generally read from notation in performance. Further, what is notated is usually only the main melody; parts played on the other instruments are recreated in relation to the main melody and are open to some degree of personal interpretation.

The sixteen-beat pattern of punctuation for each major phrase is *kethuk*, rest, *kethuk, kenong, kethuk, kempul, kethuk, kenong, kethuk, kempul, kethuk, kenong, kethuk, kempul, kethuk,* and finally *kenong* and *gong* simultaneously. This is played for each major phrase continuously throughout the piece. The time distribution of the beats is even, but the degree of stress or weight is not (even though no beat is played more loudly than any other on any single instrument). The strongest beat is the one coinciding with the largest and deepest-sounding punctuator, the *gong*, and the *kenong*—at the end of the major phrase. Javanese would count this as one, *two,* three, *four*, etc., with the strongest beat being the sixteenth. This is the only beat where two punctuating instruments (*gong* and *kenong*) coincide. It is this "coincidence" that gives a sense of repose, a release of the rhythmic tension that builds through the course of the major phrase.

Although in the West one may dismiss events as "mere coincidence," in Java the simultaneous occurrence of several events, the alignment of days of the week and dates (like our Friday the 13th), can be profoundly meaningful. It is not uncommon to determine a suitable day for a wedding, or for moving house, based on the coincidence of a certain day in the seven-day week with a certain day in the Javanese five-day market week, and this in turn within a certain Javanese month (in the lunar calendar rather than the solar calendar used in the West). And the simultaneous occurrence of what to Westerners would seem to be unrelated (and therefore meaningless) events—such as the sounding of a certain bird while in the course of carrying out a particular activity—can be interpreted in Java as an important omen.

This deep-seated view of the workings of the natural world is reflected in the structure of gamelan music, where coincidence is central to the coherence of the music. The sounding of the *gong* with the *kenong* marks the musical instant of greatest weight and is the only point at which a *gendhing* may end. Yet, other lesser points of coincidence also carry weight. If we consider the piece from the perspective of the main melody, it is at the coincidence of the main melody with the *kenong* strokes that the next strongest stress is felt.

The ethnomusicologist Judith Becker has argued convincingly that the cyclic structure of Javanese *gendhing* reflects the persistence of Hindu-Buddhist conceptions of time introduced to Java during the first millennium C.E. and not wholly eliminated by the subsequent adoption of Islam. (For an elaboration of this theory, see Becker 1979 and Becker 1981.)

The drummer in the Javanese gamelan acts as a conductor, controlling the tempo and the dynamics (the relative levels of loudness and softness). He or she need not be visible to other musicians, since the "conducting" is accomplished purely through sound signals. He or she does not stand in front of the ensemble but sits unobtrusively in the midst of it. The whole *gendhing* can be repeated as many times as the drummer desires, or as is appropriate to the context in which it is performed. Pieces in *bubaran* form usually are played at the end of performances—*bubar* means "to disperse." The guests or audience are expected to leave during the playing of the piece; thus the number of repetitions may depend on the length of time it takes those in attendance to depart.

Already we have a fairly good understanding of the structure of this piece as performed. Let us focus our attention now on the part played by the drummer, using the smallest and largest drums in combination. Throughout the piece he plays a pattern specific not to this particular piece, but, like the punctuating pattern, generic to the *bubaran* form. That is, the drumming, as well as the punctuation pattern, for any of the forty or so other pieces in this form would be the same: an introductory pattern, several variant patterns for the main phrases, and a special, contrasting pattern reserved only for the playing of the final major phrase and which, together with the slowing of tempo, acts to signal the ending. The patterns are made up of a vocabulary of drum strokes, each with a name that imitates onomatopoetically the actual drum sound (*dung, tak, dang, ket*, and so on) It is the drummer who first begins to play faster, thereby signaling the ensemble to speed up a few phrases before they are to end. To end, other musicians all know they need to slow down during the final major phrase, but the precise rate is determined by the drummer. The playing of a special drum pattern used only for the final major phrase confirms to all the musicians that it is time to end.

We have seen how the punctuating gong parts and the drumming fit with the main melody in *Bubaran* "Kembang Pacar." We can now turn to the elaborating melodic instruments—here the gong-chimes (*bonangs*)—which normally play at a faster rate, providing variations based on the main melody. I mentioned earlier that the only part normally notated is the main melody. The embellishing parts are derived through processes generally understood by practicing musicians. Ideally all musicians can play all the parts. In reality this is true only in the best professional groups, but most musicians have at least a passive knowledge of all the instruments and know how to respond to various signals and subtler nuances.

The two *bonangs* here perform in a style called "walking," usually alternating left and right hands in sounding combinations of tones derived from the main melody. The players have not learned particular *bonang* parts or sets of variations, note for note, for this one piece. Rather, they have thoroughly internalized a vocabulary of traditional patterns known to fit with certain phrases of the main melody. Both *bonangs* embellish or elaborate on the main melody, with the smaller, higher-pitched *bonang* (*bonang* **panerus**) playing at twice the rate of the larger *bonang* (*bonang* **barung**.) Yet it is not simply a matter of mechanical replication throughout, for alternate tones can be substituted (for example, 6 5 3 5 instead of 6 5 6 5) and other choices can be made. The Javanese often refer to the main melody with a word that translates as "outline" or "skeleton," since it can serve as a kind of framework for the elaborating instruments and, in soft-playing style, for the voices as well. The degree to which the main melody actually sounds like an outline depends on its tempo and the resulting levels at which it is subdivided by the elaborating instruments.

Irama Level

In the performances of *Bubaran* "Kembang Pacar" that you have listened to, the *bonang barung* plays at twice the density of the main melody, subdividing it by two. This ratio defines one of five possible levels of subdivision known as **irama** (ee-*raw*-maw) levels. If the tempo had slowed sufficiently, as it does in the first piece you listened to (*Ladrang* "Wilujeng"), the *bonang barung* would have doubled its ratio with the main melody, subdividing each beat by four, instead of two; and the other subdividers (*bonang panerus* and *saron peking*) would also have doubled their ratio. Go back to that first example and listen to the first forty-five seconds or so, during which you'll hear not only these loud-playing subdividers, but the soft-playing ones as well (**gambang**/xylophone, **gendèr**/metallophone, and **celempung**/zither), doubling their subdivision ratio as the tempo slows. Ward Keeler aptly likens the process to a car shifting gears—in this case, downshifting as the car slows to climb a steep grade (Keeler 1987:225). To maintain its relationship with the *bonang barung*, the *bonang panerus* would double as well, resulting in an eight-to-one ratio with the main melody. At the slowest main melody tempo, the *bonang barung* would have a ratio of sixteen beats to one; and the *bonang panerus*, along with the subdividing soft instruments, would play a full thirty-two beats for each beat of the main melody!

Gamelan Music and Shadow Puppetry

Now let's consider some of the music most closely associated with shadow puppet performance (see Figures 7.5 and 7.6). The piece we have studied so far is seldom played for dance or dramatic accompaniment. The musical staples of the shadow puppet repertory are pieces with dense *kenong* and *kempul* playing and phrases of varying length—pieces that generate a level of excitement, partly because of the dense gong punctuation. Each of the three periods of an all-night performance includes at least three of these staple pieces: relatively calm, somewhat excited, and very excited. The gong punctuation is densest in the very excited pieces and least dense in the calmest pieces. The puppeteer determines which piece is to be played,

Figure 7.6
Dhalang (shadow puppeteer) Ki Bawor performing an all-night *wayang kulit* near the town of Purwokerto, western Central Java. *R. Anderson Sutton.*

often signaling the start and stop with knocks against the wooden puppet chest (note the beater held in the puppeteer's left hand in Figure 7.6). He must be just as thoroughly at home with the gamelan music as he is with the many hundreds of characters and stories that comprise this tradition.

We are going to listen to a version of one of these pieces, the Yogyanese ***Playon*** **"Lasem"** (*plah*-yon *lah*-suhm), *sléndro pathet nem,* which exemplifies the "somewhat excited" category (Active Listening 7.2). Depending on the mood the puppeteer

MindTap·

🔊 **LISTEN TO**
Playon "Lasem," performed by Ki Suparman's musicians, online.

ACTIVE LISTENING 7.2
Playon "Lasem"

MindTap·

🎧 **WATCH** an Active Listening Guide of this selection online.

COUNTER NUMBER	COMMENTARY	PHRASE IN MAIN MELODY
Introduction		
0:00	Puppeteer knocks on puppet chest to signal musicians to play.	
0:03	Full gamelan ensemble begins to play in soft-playing style, including female singer.	Phrase A, ten beats of the main melody.
0:11	Puppeteer clangs loudly on metal plaques. Gamelan speeds up and switches to loud-playing style.	Phrase B, twelve beats.
	Female singer and soft instruments drop out.	
0:18	Brief shouts by the puppeteer as rival characters engage in fight.	Phrase C, twelve beats.
0:24	Continued clanging on metal plaques accompanies the fight.	Phrase D, twelve beats.
Central section (repeatable)		
0:31	Drumming and clanging on metal plaques accentuate fight action.	Phrase E, sixteen beats of the main melody.
0:38	Lively accompaniment continues.	Phrase F, eight beats.
0:41	More loud shouts by puppeteer.	Phrase G, sixteen beats.
0:50	Lively action and accompaniment continue.	Phrase H, eight beats.
	Drumming is especially active here.	
0:53	Lively action and accompaniment continue.	Phrase I, twelve beats.
1:00	Lively action and accompaniment continue.	Phrase J, eight beats.
Repeat		
1:04	Section repeat begins; lively action.	Phrase E, sixteen beats of the main melody.
1:10	Puppeteer performs pattern of knocks that signal gamelan musicians to move to ending phrase (K).	Two beats before the end of phrase E.
Coda		
1:12	Puppeteer's signal knocks continue, confirming his intention to end the piece.	Phrase K, six beats of the main melody.
1:15	Performance of *Playon* "Lasem" ends; puppeteer continues knocking on puppet chest to set mood, and he begins to speak.	

wishes to establish, the piece can be played in loud-playing or in soft-playing style, or switched at any point. (The calmest of the three is usually in soft-playing style; the most excited is always performed in loud-playing style.) Also, the length of the piece can be radically tailored to suit the needs of the dramatic moment. Sometimes it may go on, through repetition of a central section, for five or ten minutes. During the course of the all-night performance at which I recorded these examples, the puppeteer (Ki Suparman) signaled this piece to be played eighteen times—all within the first section of the night, which lasted from about 9:00 P.M. to about 1:30 A.M.

This performance begins in soft-playing style but speeds up and gets loud at the end of the first phrase. It then proceeds through the entire *gendhing*, begins to repeat the main section, and ends, on signal, after the first phrase of this repeatable section. Throughout most of the selection, you can hear the puppeteer adding to the excitement by clanging several metal plaques, which hang from the puppet box positioned to his immediate left. While he operates puppets with his hands, he activates the metal plaques with the toes of his right foot! At several points in the selection we hear the puppeteer's shouts as he gives voice to characters who are engaged in a fierce fight.

This *gendhing* and others like it have potential for a great variety of renditions, through changes in tempo, instrumentation, and ending points. This is the essence of shadow puppet music—a very well-known piece, played over and over, but uniquely tailored each time to fit precisely with the dramatic intentions of the puppeteer and kept fresh by the inventiveness of the instrumentalists and singers, who constantly add subtle variations.

Bali

Just east of Java, separated from it by a narrow strait, lies the island of **Bali** (*bah*-lee). The unique culture and spectacular natural beauty of this island have fascinated scholars, artists, and tourists from around the world. In Bali, almost everyone takes part in some artistic activity: music, dance, carving, painting. Although the Balinese demonstrate abilities that often strike the Westerner as spectacular, they maintain that such activities are a normal part of life. The exquisite, masked dancer by night may well be a rice farmer by day, and the player of lightning-fast, interlocking musical passages who accompanies him may manage a small food stall.

Most of the several million people inhabiting this small island adhere to a blend of Hinduism and Buddhism resembling that which flourished in Java prior to the spread of Islam (fifteenth to sixteenth century C.E.). In this, the Balinese and Javanese share elements of a common cultural heritage. As in Java, we find percussion ensembles known as gamelan (or *gambelan*), with metal slab instruments and knobbed gong instruments that look and sound quite similar to those of the Javanese gamelan. Some of the names are the same (*gendèr*, gong, *gambang*, *saron*, *suling*, *rebab*) or similar (*kempur*, *kemong*). Most ensembles employ some version of the *pélog* scale system (some with all seven tones, others with five or six). The accompaniment for Balinese shadow puppetry (as in Java, called *wayang kulit*) employs the *sléndro* scale system, although the instruments used consist only of a quartet of *gendèrs* (augmented by a few other instruments for *Ramayana* stories). Many Balinese pieces employ punctuating gong patterns similar in principle to those of

Java. The Balinese play gamelan for ritual observances, as in Java, though usually at temple festivals, or in procession to or from them, rather than at someone's residence.

While some pieces have strict associations with particular rituals and do not derive their aesthetic appeal from originality of conception, others, such as the one we will listen to next, are appreciated for the beauty and excitement of the particular musical sounds that the composer has created and that the performers execute with skill and sensitivity—something more like appreciation of good jazz or Western classical music.

Nevertheless, certain characteristics clearly distinguish the musics of these neighboring cultures. For example, the Balinese maintain a variety of ensembles, each with its distinct instrumentation and associated with certain occasions and functions. There is no single, large ensemble that one can simply call "the Balinese gamelan." However, the style of music one hears performed in most ensembles in Bali shares several characteristics: (1) strictly instrumental, (2) characterized by changes in tempo and loudness (often abrupt), and (3) requires a dazzling, technical mastery by many of the musicians, who play fast, interlocking rhythms, often comprising asymmetrical groupings of two or three very fast beats. People often comment that Balinese music is exciting and dynamic in comparison with other Indonesian musics, exploiting contrasts in the manner of Western art music.

They may also comment on the "shimmery" quality of the many varieties of bronze ensembles. This quality is obtained by tuning instruments in pairs, with one instrument intentionally tuned slightly higher in pitch than its partner. When sounded together, they produce very fast vibrations. In the West, piano tuners rely on these same vibrations, called "beats," to "temper" the tuning, although on a piano it is intervals that are made intentionally "out of tune" rather than identical strings sounding the same tone. Of course, the intentionally "out-of-tune" pairs of metallophones are perceived to be "in tune" (that is, "culturally correct") in Bali, just as the piano is in Western culture.

The most popular ensemble in Bali today is the gamelan *gong* **kebyar** (kuh-*byar*), which developed during the early twentieth century along with the virtuosic dance it often accompanies (also called *kebyar*—literally, "flash" or "dazzle"). *Kebyar* music is indeed "flashy," requiring not only great virtuosity on behalf of the players, but also a consummate sense of ensemble—the ability of many to play as one.

Listen to "Kosalia Arini" (ko-*sal*-yah a-*ree*-nee), a piece composed by the prolific Balinese composer and skilled drummer Wayan Beratha in 1969 for a gamelan festival. This piece demonstrates features typical of gamelan *gong kebyar* (Figure 7.7), many of which contrast markedly with Javanese gamelan music and with older styles of Balinese music. These include episodic structure—the piece is clearly divided

---

Salient Characteristics of
Balinese Gamelan Music

- Emphasis on percussion instruments, slab, knobbed gongs, and drums (as in Java)

- Use of two scales (*sléndro* and *pélog*) different from Western scales (as in Java)

- Use of different-sized gong instruments to "punctuate" phrases (as in Java)

- Often accompanies dance, dance-drama, and shadow puppetry (as in Java)

- Ensemble directed by melodic instrument player, with drummers (usually two)

- Most gamelan music strictly instrumental, variety of different ensembles

- Shimmery effect from tuning one instrument of a pair slightly higher than the other

- Emphasis on interlocking (often very fast) melodic and rhythmic patterns

- Abrupt shifts in tempo and dynamics (volume level)

- Variety of textures, often stratified

- Cyclic repetition of phrases in some sections; non-repeating phrasing in others

- Flexible in some aspects, but many pieces, melodic patterns, tempo, dynamics, and number of repetitions all determined by composer, before performance

---

MindTap·

◀)) **LISTEN TO**

"Kosalia Arini," performed by STSI musicians, online.

into sections with contrasting instrumentation, rhythm, and texture. Portions of the piece involve cyclic repetition, but the overall design is neither cyclic nor rigidly binary, as is the case in Javanese gamelan pieces.

Michael Tenzer, an American scholar, composer, and performer of Balinese gamelan *gong kebyar,* has provided a detailed analysis of this piece (Tenzer 2000:367, 381–83), from which the following, much briefer commentary derives. Most basic are the contrasts between what Tenzer calls "stable" (cyclic) and "active" (noncyclic) sections.

The overall piece proceeds through four main sections (Active Listening 7.3). As you listen, notice the changes (often abrupt) in tempo, instrumentation, dynamics, and register (high pitch or low pitch). Each section is identified not only by characteristic rhythm and texture but also by tonal center. Though repetitive in

ACTIVE LISTENING 7.3
"Kosalia Arini"

COUNTER NUMBER	COMMENTARY	TONAL CENTER
Noncyclic section		
0:00	*Gendèrs* (metal slab instruments) at different pitch registers play fragments of asymmetrical phrases. Mostly soft dynamic level. Occasional louder, flashy, full-ensemble fragments (*kebyar* interruptions).	C#
0:46	Partial *kebyar* interruption.	
1:43	Full *kebyar* interruption.	
2:16	Flute solo, with low-register *gendèr*. Very soft.	D

COUNTER NUMBER	COMMENTARY	TONAL CENTER
Transition		
2:41	Higher-pitched *gendèrs* enter, marking transition to next section. Mostly soft.	D
Cyclic section		
2:49	*Gendèrs* play four-beat phrases; highly repetitive; alternating between soft and medium dynamic level.	D
***Kebyar* interruption**		
4:39	Full ensemble. Sudden, loud flash.	D
4:41	Short passage featuring the *reyong* (*ray*-yong) (kettle gong-chime played by four musicians).	D
Cyclic section		
4:53	Drum variations (by two drummers) open second cyclic section. Loud and fast, then softer.	D
5:13	*Gendèr* and *reyong* alternate. Mostly soft, fast tempo. Section stops abruptly, with no gong.	E
Transition		
7:22	*Gendèrs* play transition to third cyclic section.	E
Cyclic section		
7:34	*Gendèrs* now play in eight-beat phrases. Mostly loud, full instrumentation, alternating with some soft passages.	C#
Coda		
10:30	Twelve-beat coda, full ensemble.	C#

some sections, the whole piece is much more like a fantasia or an exuberant study in contrasts (especially in dynamics and in rhythm) than even the most dramatic renditions of Javanese pieces.

North Sumatra

Going from Bali or Java to North **Sumatra** (soo-*mah*-trah) involves a considerable distance, both culturally and geographically. Although influenced to some degree by Indian culture during the first millennium C.E., the Batak people, the main inhabitants of the province of North Sumatra, have largely converted to Protestant Christianity or to Islam. The Christian Bataks sing hymns at their Sunday church services with an exuberance and an accuracy of pitch that would put most Western congregations—and even many choirs—to shame. In addition, many indigenous musical genres still thrive among the Batak, and many of these are central to rituals only marginally, if at all, related to Christianity or Islam. Just as the majority of Javanese Muslims partake in rituals involving gamelan music and Hindu-based shadow puppetry, so do the Batak Christians adhere in varying degrees to beliefs and ritual practices that were prevalent prior to the coming of Christianity.

Figure 7.8

Tukang Ginting playing the Karo Batak *kulcapi*. Kabanjahe, North Sumatra. *R. Anderson Sutton.*

Salient Characteristics of
Batak *Gendang Keteng-keteng* Music

- Small, intimate ensemble; no metal percussion

- Plucked-string *kulcapi* plays melody

- Bamboo *keteng-keteng* for low "gong" sound and busy "clickety" filling in

- Stratified texture (melody, punctuation, filling in)

- Cyclic repetition of phrases with variation

Figure 7.9

Members of Tukang Ginting's *gendang keteng-keteng* group, playing the bamboo tube zither (*keteng-keteng*). Kabanjahe, North Sumatra. *R. Anderson Sutton.*

The most celebrated Batak ensembles are the varieties of percussion and wind ensembles known as *gondang* or *gordang,* which usually include a set of tuned drums that are counterparts to the kettle gong-chimes (*bonang* or *trompong*). These can be heard on several fine recordings available commercially (see References). Our brief encounter with music in North Sumatra is from a ritual observance I attended among the Karo Batak, who live in the highlands west of Medan and north of large, beautiful Lake Toba (Figure 7.8). A woman in the town of Kabanjahe was planning to open a beauty parlor in part of her house and wished to have the space ritually purified and to secure blessing for her new business by seeking harmony with the spirit world. This she hoped to accomplish by sponsoring and participating in a ceremony involving music and dance, during which she would contact her immediate ancestors through the help of a spirit medium. Members of her family gathered, along with sympathetic neighbors (but not some of the more orthodox Christians, who were not so sympathetic) and a few foreign visitors, including myself. To my surprise, I was urged to take photographs and record the event.

The ceremony lasted for nearly five hours, with several long sections of continuous music. Family members and some neighbors joined the woman in a traditional line dance. The spirit medium sang incantations, sometimes while dancing. He spoke gently to the woman and, sometimes, loudly to the spirits. With some difficulty the woman eventually went into a trance, and the evening was deemed a success.

The musical group engaged for the evening (Figures 7.8 and 7.9) was a small ensemble performing *gendang keteng-keteng*, a form of traditional Batak

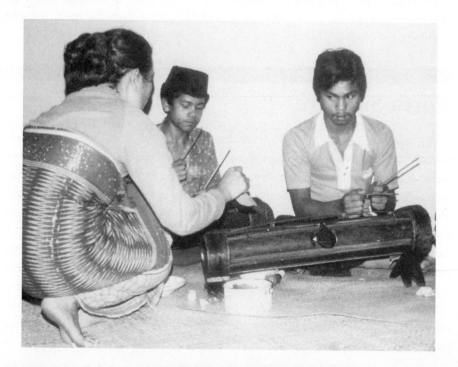

music employing a small, two-stringed, boat-shaped lute (**kulcapi**); two bamboo tube zithers (*keteng-keteng*); and a porcelain bowl. On each of the tube zithers, thin strips had been cut and stretched, forming taut filaments. A small, bamboo disk was attached to one filament on each. These remarkable instruments create a kind of interlocking percussive filigree. In addition, when the filaments with the disks are struck, they vibrate over a hole cut in the bamboo to produce a deep, vibrato sound remarkably like that of a small gong. The ensemble played continually for many hours, with the spirit medium singing part of the time. Melody, filling in, gong punctuation—here were the essential elements, it seemed, for musicmaking not only throughout much of Indonesia but much of Southeast Asia as well.

The few excerpts provided in Active Listening 7.4 cannot give a real sense of the long ritual, but they offer an introduction to musical sounds that contrast

MindTap•

◀)) **LISTEN TO**

the *gendang keteng-keteng* excerpts performed by Tukang Ginting and his group online.

ACTIVE LISTENING 7.4
Gendang Keteng-Keteng, Two Excerpts

MindTap•

🎧 **WATCH** an Active Listening Guide of this selection online.

COUNTER NUMBER	COMMENTARY
0:00	Fade in to performance with *kulcapi*, two *keteng-keteng*, and porcelain bowl.
0:03	First gong sound (from *keteng-keteng*), together with porcelain bowl, which also sounds midway between gong sounds throughout the performance; *kulcapi* plays melody.
0:08	Second gong sound; *kulcapi* continues to play melody.
0:13	Third gong sound; *kulcapi* plays variations of previous melody.
0:18	Fourth gong sound; *kulcapi* continues variations of melody.
0:23	Fifth gong sound; *kulcapi* plays very similar variation of previous melody.
0:28	Sixth gong sound (same).
0:33	Seventh gong sound (same).
0:38	Eighth gong sound (same).
0:43	Ninth gong sound (same).
0:45	Fade out.
0:48	Fade in to later stage of the performance: same instrumentation, faster tempo.
0:49	First gong sound; *kulcapi* plays variation of previous melody, but faster.
0:51	Second gong sound (same).
0:54	Third gong sound (same).
0:56	Fourth gong sound (same).
0:58	Fifth gong sound (same).
1:00	Sixth gong sound (same).
1:03	Seventh gong sound (same).
1:05	Eighth gong sound (same).
1:06	Tempo suddenly doubles; gong sound and porcelain bowl double density (gong sound approximately once every second); *kulcapi* switches to rapid playing, repeating same tone many times.
1:54	Fade out.

with the gamelan ensembles we have heard and yet bear a distant likeness to them. The first excerpt is from the early part of the ceremony. The *kulcapi* player, Tukang Ginting, provides what is basically a repeating, cyclic melody that he varies. The "clickety" sounds are the two *keteng-keteng,* with the two percussionists filling in the texture to give a constant, "busy" sound, which seems to characterize much music throughout Indonesia. What is especially remarkable, in light of the other music we have heard, is how the porcelain bowl and the gong sounds relate. The gong sound occurs at regular intervals, as one so often finds in Java and Bali. It is subdivided by the porcelain bowl sound, which coincides with the gong sound and at the midpoint between them, like a *kenong* subdividing and coinciding with a gong in Java.

The second excerpt is from a climactic moment in the evening when the woman first thought she was going into a trance. (She did not succeed at this point, but did so an hour or so later.) The players increase the musical intensity by compressing the time interval between gong beats; the tempo speeds up and then doubles during this excerpt. The porcelain bowl consistently subdivides the time between gong beats, even in the very fast portion, resembling structurally the *wayang kulit* music of Java (like the *playon* we studied earlier).

With its gong punctuation, coincidence, cyclic melody, binary rhythms, and fast-moving, dense percussion playing, this music seems clearly a relative of the gamelan music we heard earlier. Although this discussion has stressed the similarities, realize that these are only structural similarities, easy to identify from a theoretical perspective. The differences are so profound that the Batak and Javanese care little for each other's music. To the Javanese, clacking bamboo is no substitute for the varied drum strokes of the **kendhang**, the interlocking melodies of the *bonang,* or the elaborate wanderings of the various, soft-playing ensemble instruments in the Javanese gamelan. To the Batak, the thick-textured and often mighty sound of a full Javanese gamelan cannot attain the personal intimacy of the small *gendang keteng-keteng* ensemble or the spontaneity of the *kulcapi* player.

Perhaps these few examples of traditional music from several regions of Indonesia will help you begin to understand the national motto *Bhinneka Tunggal Ika*—an Old Javanese phrase meaning "Unity in Diversity." In the arts we indeed find great variety, but the underlying elements that these arts share attest to the appropriateness of the motto. As we turn to examples of recent popular music, we find another layer of Indonesia's musical diversity—one that many Indonesians experience and is especially meaningful to younger Indonesians from many regions.

Indonesian Popular Music

Most of the music Indonesians would identify as "popular" is, like most popular music anywhere in the world, characterized by the use of at least some Western instruments and Western harmony (Hatch 1989). Essentially a commercial genre, it is disseminated through the mass media and performed by recognized stars. Unfortunately, space does not allow us to explore the interesting history of

Western-influenced music in Indonesia, which has primarily been in the popular vein. We will, however, consider three superstar artists that represent each of three contrasting styles within the pop music world in Indonesia.

Rhoma Irama, *Dangdut*

The first contemporary style is called **dangdut** (*dahng-doot*) in imitation of the sound formerly made on hand drums and more recently on trap set and electric guitar. The musician known from the 1970s through the 1990s as the "king of *dangdut*"—and still an active performer as of 2015—is Rhoma Irama (Figure 7.10). Born in 1947 in West Java, he learned to play electric guitar and showed greater interest in music than in the formal schooling his mother struggled to afford. In his late teens he dropped out

> ### Salient Characteristics of
> ## Indonesian Popular Music
>
> - Use of electrically amplified instruments of Western origin
> - Prominent use of Western harmonies
> - Disseminated through mass media, star system
> - Variety of genres defined by instrumentation, vocal style

Figure 7.10

Rhoma Irama, on stage at the University of Pittsburgh, October 2008. *Courtesy of Andrew Weintraub.*

of school and joined the underground music movement, heavily influenced by Western rock (and banned by then-president Sukarno).

Irama soon became disenchanted with rock. By his own account, he consciously set out to create a sound that would satisfy the craving of Indonesian youth for a "modern" musical style but that would also sound clearly Indonesian (or at least "Eastern") in contrast to Western rock (Frederick 1982:109). He turned to a Western-influenced genre, *orkès melayu* music, which originated in the urban areas of North and West Sumatra. This genre incorporates influences from the soundtracks of the many Indian films that have long enjoyed wide popularity in Indonesia (see Chapter 6). Even with its quasi-Western harmonic basis, this music is clearly Eastern, characterized by highly ornamented singing and flute playing.

Rhoma Irama set out to make a commercial mark, and he succeeded spectacularly. Like most pop stars, he sings about love but also presents forthrightly his own ideas about his country and, perhaps most persistently, about his religion. He was one of the first Indonesian popular artists to make the pilgrimage to Mecca, and he has used both his music and his films to spread his Islamic message. One of his first hits (1977) was a piece about greed, entitled "Rupiah" (the national currency). It was banned by government officials who thought it "debased the national currency" (Frederick 1982:117). Another early song, also banned, was "Hak Azasi" ("Basic Rights"), which described human rights—including freedom of religion and freedom of speech.

Listen to "Begadang II," the most popular song of 1978, which established Irama as a star (Active Listening 7.5). The song bears the same title as the hit film for which it served as the theme song. *Begadang* is a Jakarta term for staying up all or most of the night, usually to socialize with friends. This song provides a typical example of the *dangdut* musical sound as Irama developed it. The text shows Irama's clear orientation toward lower-class youth. Like most of his music, it appeals to the youthful urge to dance and often accompanies popular, social dancing akin to rock or disco dancing in the West.

Almost four decades after this hit, Irama is still producing recordings and performing with his Soneta group, although he no longer dominates the market. Earlier in his career, he starred in several films in which—to the chagrin of more conservative Indonesian Muslims—he proselytizes for Islam through his loud, electric *dangdut* music. Unlikely as it may seem, then, Rhoma Irama gained fame as an Islamic rock star and enjoyed enormous commercial success. His passion for communicating his vision of a more perfect society, holding closely to the teachings of Islam, led him into the realm of politics. In 1982, he endorsed the Islamic opposition party and played at a rally in Jakarta that erupted in violence shortly before the elections took place. Yet, by the early 1990s, he had—most likely with some reluctance—joined the incumbent political party. He even played at functions of the very body that represented the clearest threat to Islamic political power in Indonesia: the army. More recently, Irama has become one of the most outspoken critics of younger, *dangdut* singers who emphasize sexually provocative movements on stage (Weintraub 2010), and he has been a leader in the effort to have the Indonesian government adopt an "antipornography" law that, in its earlier versions, would have banned hundreds of Indonesian performing art forms—traditional as well as modern—in which the costumes of female performers do

MindTap*
LISTEN TO
"Begadang II," performed by Rhoma Irama and his Soneta Group, online.

MindTap*
WATCH the performance of "Perbedaan" ("Difference"), performed by Rhoma Irama and his Soneta Group, online.

ACTIVE LISTENING 7.5
"Begadang II"

COUNTER NUMBER	SECTION/TEXT	TRANSLATION
0:00	Instrumental introduction, featuring Rhoma Irama on electric guitar. Chord progression a variation on standard, American, twelve-bar blues.	
0:22	Verse 1—repeating chord progression; vocal phrases alternate with short guitar phrases.	
	Apa artinya malam minggu *Bagi orang yang tidak mampu?* *Mau ke pesta tak beruang;*	What good is Saturday night For those who are not well-to-do? Want to go to a party, but have no money;
	Akhirnya nongkrong di pinggir jalan.	Wind up squatting by the side of the road.
0:48	Refrain—contrasting chord progression; higher-pitched vocal melody.	
	Begadang, marilah kita begadang, *Begadang sambil berdendang;* *Walaupun kita tidak punya uang* *Kita juga bisa senang.*	Stay up, let's stay up, Stay up and sing; Even though we don't have money We can still have fun.
1:02	Verse 1 (same text and music as previous)	
1:26	Instrumental break, featuring Rhoma Irama on electric guitar.	
1:50	Bridge 1—contrasting chord progression and vocal melody.	
	Bagi mereka yang punya uang *Berdansa-dansi di nite club;* *Bagi kita yang tak punya uang* *Cukup berjoget disini.*	Those who have money Dance at nightclubs; Those of us who have no money Just dance here [by the road].
2:03	Short instrumental break.	
2:10	Bridge 2—same chord progression and vocal melody as previous bridge.	
	Bagi mereka yang punya uang *Makan-makan di restoran;* *Bagi kita yang tak punya uang* *Makannya di warung kopi.*	Those who have money Always eat in nice restaurants; Those of us who have no money Just eat at makeshift roadside stalls.
2:27	Verse 1—same as previous.	
2:57	Refrain—same as previous.	
3:04	Verse 1—same as previous.	
3:29	Sudden stop at the end of verse 1.	

"Begadang II," by Rhoma Irama. Used by permission.

not cover the shoulders or legs. A more moderate version of the law was recently passed, with some flexibility in relation to traditional costuming. Rhoma Irama maintains, with his Soneta musicians, a small group of female musicians whose stage dress is demure but whose movements, while not blatantly erotic, are clearly intended to be alluring.

Responses to Globalization

From Irama's *dangdut*, we now turn to two more recent examples of popular music (one released in 2000, the other in 2009). The forces of globalization have intensified since the 1980s, inundating the Indonesian marketplace with the commercial cultural products of the West, including various forms of American pop, rock, and jazz. Our final two musical examples represent different responses to this process. The first, by a group called Krakatau (named after the famous volcanic island lying just west of Java), involves a careful synthesis of Sundanese (West Javanese) gamelan and fusion jazz. The second is by a rock group known as Gigi, whose music has largely represented a full embrace of Western mainstream and alternative rock styles, with lyrics that often deal with romantic love.

Krakatau, Sundanese Gamelan, and Fusion Jazz

Krakatau (Figure 7.11) was founded in the mid-1980s by Dwiki Dharmawan (*dwee*-kee dar-*ma*-wan), a jazz keyboardist whose skill in imitating the styles of Joe Zawinul (Weather Report) and Chick Corea won him an award as "The Best Keyboard Player" at the Yamaha Light Music Contest in Tokyo in 1985. The early

Figure 7.11
Krakatau in performance. *Courtesy of Krakatau (Dwiki Dharmawan).*

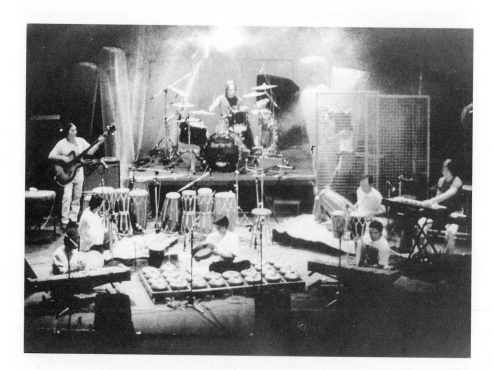

recordings of Krakatau present original, fusion jazz tunes with complex harmonies and rhythms. They include pop and jazz songs, some in English, sung by a female Javanese-Sundanese singer, Trie Utami (tree oo-*ta*-mee) who offers polished, sophisticated imitations of African-American vocal styles. Beginning around 1993-1994, members of the group, particularly Dharmawan and Utami, grew tired of merely imitating the music they admired from the West. Because the core members had all spent much of their youth in West Java (Sunda), they decided to incorporate Sundanese musical elements into their music, adding local experts on *saron, bonang, rebab,* and *kendang.* In short, they set out to create a hybrid variety of music, mixing Western and indigenous Indonesian musical instruments and elements.

Experiments in such combinations have been taking place in Indonesia for centuries. Special challenges are posed by the fact that many Indonesian instruments and songs use tunings and scales, such as *sléndro* and *pélog,* which are not compatible with Western ones. In the nineteenth century, brass band instruments were played with *pélog* gamelan instruments in the courts of Central Java, representing a symbolic fusion of Javanese and Dutch power. In the early twentieth century, Javanese composers began to write pieces combining Javanese singing with Western instruments.

In the 1990s, Indonesia saw a sudden growth in experimental combinations of pop/rock instruments and indigenous Indonesian ones, many inspired by the creative work of Guruh Sukarno Putra (*goo*-rooh soo-*kar*-naw poo-traw, the youngest living son of the founding father of the Republic of Indonesia, President Sukarno). With his group, Gypsy, he released a landmark album in 1976 involving piano, synthesizers, and rock instruments playing along with Balinese *gendèrs* and drums and incorporating Central Javanese vocal styles and West Javanese scales and melodies.

In 1994, Krakatau released *Mystical Mist,* in which some pieces sounded more like jazz fusion and others more Sundanese. In their 2000 release, *Magical Match,* the blend is more even throughout. One ingenious idea they employed is the tuning of their Western instruments to the scales of Sundanese traditional music. Dwiki programmed in a complex alteration of pitches for his keyboard and worked out special fingerings, so that when he strikes certain combinations of black and white keys on his keyboard, he can produce the tones of *sléndro, pélog* or other scales typical of Sundanese traditional music. The bass player, Pra Budidharma, uses an electric bass with no frets (the horizontal, metal strips found on guitars that facilitate production of the Western scale). With skillful placement of his fingers, he can play bass patterns in *sléndro* and other non-Western scales. On this album, Trie Utami sings not like a jazz singer but with the distinctive timbre of a Sundanese female singer. The example we will consider here, however, is purely instrumental, illustrating most clearly the skill of the musicians in creating a piece that tries to be not just Sundanese and not just Western but a "magical match" of the two.

Listen to "Shufflendang-Shufflending" (Active Listening 7.6). The title mixes the English word *shuffle* (a type of African-American ecstatic song/dance combination performed in worship, also known as "ring-shout") and the Sundanese words for drum (*kendang*) and gamelan musical piece (*gendhing*). Krakatau is joined

MindTap·
◀)) **LISTEN TO**
"Shufflendang-Shufflending," performed by Krakatau, online.

ACTIVE LISTENING 7.6
"Shufflendang-Shufflending"

COUNTER NUMBER	COMMENTARY
0:00	Western instruments open piece with a repeating, short phrase.
0:15	Hints of a *pélog* scale (small and large intervals between tones).
0:42	Abruptly, *sarons* (metal slab instruments) play in *sléndro* scale (near equidistant tones).
0:50	*Sarons* play in *pélog* scale.
0:59	*Sarons* return to play in *sléndro* scale.
1:09	Switch to *rebab* (two-string fiddle) playing in *pélog* scale.
1:35	Back to fusion jazz style, as in beginning, although not exact repetition. Similar rotation of scales continues through excerpt.

by Zainal Arifin, Adhe Rudiana (who teaches traditional music at the Indonesian College of Performing Arts in Bandung, West Java), and graduates Yoyon Darsono, Elfik Zulfiqar, and Tudi Rahayu.

While it is possible to enjoy the sounds and the rhythm without knowing their origins, the meaning this music has for Krakatau members and for their fans in Indonesia is its ability to "Sundanize" jazz or pop music and to "jazzify" or "modernize" Sundanese music at the same time. Its ambiguity provides a bridge between the seemingly incompatible worlds of local Indonesian/traditional culture and Western/modern culture. Dharmawan and other members of the group, whom I got to know in August 2000 and hosted for a performance in the United States in 2004, did not have a clear sense of what to call their music. We talked about "new age," "world music," and "ethno-pop." They clearly hope that this music will reach beyond Indonesia and attract listeners from around the world, to appreciate not only their own music but also the rich treasury of Indonesia's traditional music.

In 2005, Krakatau released another album, with Nyak Ina ("Ubiet") Raseuki—a remarkably versatile singer who grew up trained in Western classical and is skilled at singing jazz, mainstream Western pop, and various styles of Indonesian popular and regional music. This album bears the English title *2 Worlds*—again an indication of their intent to blend—and it goes beyond Sundanese styles to incorporate other Indonesian regional traditions in a mix with jazz and pop.

Gigi: Indonesian Rock Music

Let us turn now to an example of Indonesian rock, performed by Gigi, one of the most popular groups. Like many other Indonesian rock groups, Gigi rarely attempts to incorporate indigenous traditional musical influences in their music. Instead their inspirations have come mostly from American and British rock. The name "Gigi" simply means "tooth" (or "teeth"), a humorous moniker for a group that has managed through a steady outpouring of fresh, original, rock music to maintain enormous popularity among Indonesia's teenagers and young adults over the past two decades. In interviews, they acknowledge various international rock musicians as having a profound influence on their style, singling out the Rolling Stones as especially important, as can be seen in the huge poster that graced their studio when I visited in 2009 (see Figure 7.12).

Gigi got their start when guitarist Dewa Budjana joined forces with fellow session musicians Thomas Ramdhan (bass), Ronald Fristianto (drums), and Aria Baron (guitar). They asked singer Armand Maulana to join them as their lead vocalist in late 1993. By mid-1994 they had released their first album (*Angan*) and were performing at major venues. Over the ensuing two decades, they have released numerous albums, toured abroad (to Japan and the United States, among other countries) and maintained consistent popularity in Indonesia. Personnel changes over the years reconfigured the group but did not fundamentally alter their sound. In 2004, they provided the soundtrack for a popular movie (*Brownies*) and released *Raihlah Kemenangan* ("Seize Victory"), the first of what would turn out to be a series (one every two years) of albums with devotional Muslim pop songs. Though still enjoyable as pop music, the songs on these albums address issues of Islamic faith, and are usually released at the time of the Muslim holy fasting month (Ramadhan). "Dan Sekarang" ("And Now") is a love song exhibiting the distinctive voice of lead singer Armand Maulana and the skillful guitar work of Dewa Budjana, together with drummer Gusti Hendy and bass player Thomas Ramdhan, who wrote this song.

"Dan Sekarang" is but one song of nine on Gigi's 2009 album (simply entitled *Gigi*), one of more than a dozen hit albums they have released over the years. The lyrics are in Indonesian. The sound is not uniquely Indonesian, but neither is it foreign to Indonesians, who have had rock music readily available through various media since the mid-1960s. Guitarist Dewa Budjana has developed a separate sphere of musical activity that draws on his Balinese heritage, occasionally employing Balinese gamelan instruments and creating a style that is a soft, fusion music, more meditative than most of the hits by Gigi. (Active Listening 7.7).

Figure 7.12

Poster of Gigi, as displayed in their studio in Jakarta, October 2009. From left to right: Gusti Hendy, Dewa Budjana, Armand Maulana, and Thomas Ramdhan.
R. Anderson Sutton.

ACTIVE LISTENING 7.7
"Dan Sekarang"

COUNTER NUMBER	SECTION/TEXT	TRANSLATION
0:00	Instrumental introduction, featuring Dewa Budjana on electric guitar. Repeating chord progression.	
0:13	Verse 1—same repeating chord progression as in introduction.	
	Kita bertemu,	We meet
	Tanpa rencana di satu kota	Without a plan
	Di satu kota	In a city
	Ku mengenal dirimu	I know you
	Ku ingat wajahmu	I remember your face
0:47	Verse 2—same chord progresssion, drums added.	
	Seminggu sudah	A week after
	Kita saling mengenal	We got to know each other
	Ku merasakan	I feel
	Ada suatu getaran	There is a certain vibration
1:12	Bridge—contrasting chord progression, more intensity in the singing.	
	Ku coba	I try
	Ku ungkapkan	To express (myself)
	Isi hati	What is in my heart
	Kepadamu	To you
1:25	Refrain A—third chord progression, still more intensity in singing.	
	Dan sekarang	And now
	Kau telah menjadi	You have already become
	Bagian hidupku	A part of my life
1:40	Refrain B	
	Dan sekarang	And now
	Kau tempat berbagi	You have a place
	Hati dan hidupku	(in) My heart and my life
1:53	Verse 3—same as previous, but with variation in singing.	
	Kau telah alirkan	You have made to flow
	Cintamu sampai ke jantungku	Your love to my heart
	Tangkanku kau pegang erat	You hold my hand tightly
	Tanpa rencana	Without a plan
2:18	Bridge—same as previous.	
2:31	Refrain A—same as previous.	
2:44	Refrain B—same as previous, with variation in singing.	
2:56	Refrain A—same as previous.	

COUNTER NUMBER	SECTION/TEXT	TRANSLATION
3:10	Refrain B'—slightly varied, new words.	
	Dan sekarang	And now
	Kau telah memberi	You have given
	Permata untukku	A jewel for (to) me
3:23	Instrumental break featuring Dewa Budjana on guitar.	
3:51	Refrain A—same as previous.	
4:04	Refrain B—same as previous, with variation in singing.	
4:17	Refrain A—same as previous.	
4:30	Refrain B'—same three phrases as at 3:10.	
4:42	*Hati dan hidupku*	My heart and my life
4:48	Instrumental postlude	

Used with permission of Thomas Ramdhan.

These three examples of popular music from Indonesia offer some important contrasts in style and message. The contrasts among them can begin to give you an idea of the complexity of Indonesia's popular music—still mostly unexplored by research scholars. Despite his political shift in the early 1990s, Rhoma Irama remains a strong Muslim. His roots are humble, and he speaks to the disenfranchised masses. Krakatau's public image is secular and at once both regional (Sundanese gamelan) and international (jazz fusion). Both Irama and Krakatau perform music that has developed from a blend of disparate musical elements. Gigi, in contrast, strives consciously to create within the stylistic norms of Western rock, producing music that is widely loved by youth throughout the nation, who flock in large numbers to their live concerts and download their music. Where Irama's *dangdut* music and Gigi's rock music have consistently and consciously been molded by mass taste and have found popularity throughout the entire nation, Krakatau's fusion music appeals to a narrower market: sophisticated urbanites (especially Sundanese and Javanese) and the international world music audience.

All three have aspired to use their music to do more than entertain. Through different approaches, Irama and Gigi may offer social and religious messages to their listeners and followers, though Gigi's main hit songs deal with typical pop music issues of love and youth. Krakatau provides a bridge between local tradition and international modernity. Each carves out a social place for its music and maintains a separate artistic style as a result. Despite the upheaval and frequent unrest in parts of Indonesia in recent years, this country still prides itself on its people's ability to tolerate diversity and coexist. These three popular examples offer a glimpse of that diversity, and show us that it applies not only to traditional regional culture but also to popular music disseminated nationally.

Study Questions

1. What is a *gendhing* in Javanese gamelan music?

2. How are loud-playing and soft-playing styles distinguished from one another?

3. What instruments serve what musical functions in a Javanese *gendhing*?

4. What is meant by "*irama* level"? How is it different from "tempo"?

5. Who directs the musicians in a Javanese shadow puppetry performance, and by what means?

6. How do Balinese attain such lightning-fast speed in playing melodic and rhythmic patterns?

7. What features of Balinese gamelan *gong kebyar* music contrast most markedly with Javanese gamelan music?

8. In what ways does the sound of Batak *gendang keteng-keteng* music resemble Javanese gamelan music? In what ways does it differ?

9. What musical influences are combined in *dangdut* music?

10. In what ways is Krakatau's music a response to globalization? How does it differ from *dangdut* and from Gigi's mainstream, popular music?

8 Asia/China, Taiwan, Singapore, Overseas Chinese

Jonathan P. J. Stock

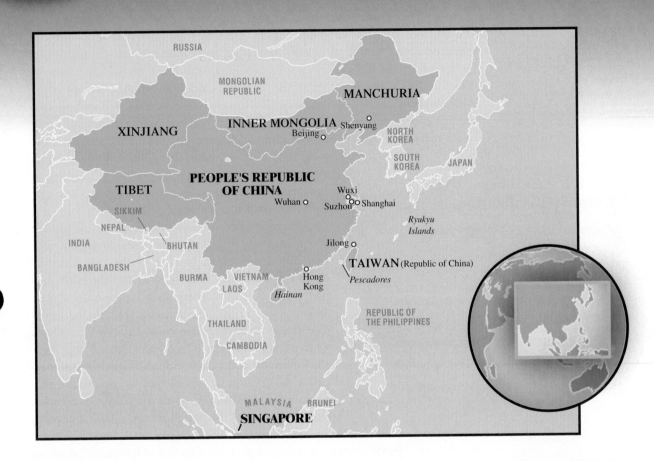

Learning Objectives

After you have studied this chapter, you should be able to:

1. Recognize significant genres of Chinese music, and the instruments and vocal styles they employ.

2. Account for change and continuity in the Chinese musical world.

continued

MindTap°

START experiencing this chapter's topics with an online audio activity.

The author wishes to acknowledge the assistance of the following: Chou Chiener, Pete Fletcher, Gu Chenyuan, Hsu Shuo-Wen, Frank Kouwenhoven, Lee Yachen, Dave Moore, Antoinet Schimmelpenninck, Wang Tingting, and Zhao Yue.

3. Describe the flows of music and musical instruments into China over a lengthy historical period, and identify societies and settings elsewhere in the world that have been impacted by Chinese music in turn.

4. Articulate ways in which the Chinese use music to explore and express their values and priorities.

Salient Characteristics of
Chinese Civilization

■ Huge but diverse, multiethnic population

■ Long-standing idea of a Chinese nation, but highly variable realities over time

■ A single written language; many regional dialects, typically tonal

■ Several key philosophies influential over time, including Confucianism, Daoism, and Buddhism

■ A long tradition of authoritarian government

The Chinese cultural world includes a distinctive cross section of peoples in mainland China, as well as Taiwan, Singapore, and other diasporic groups around the globe. In the People's Republic of China—the heart of this international constituency—we can hear the echoes of long-standing traditions from one of the great, historical centers of civilization. We can also see how these echoes underpin the fast-paced musical multiplicities of a large, contemporary nation and major world market for new, expressive forms. Concentrating on mainland China, but touching on other places along the way, this chapter explores the Chinese musical present by looking at how today's musical styles emerge from and resonate with their particular historical pathways.

The relationship between the past and the present is a fascinating topic for music research anywhere—especially so in China because of the rich historical documentation there. The musical present exists in a permanent state of counterpoint with the musical past, an image we can explore with a concept from the school of Chinese philosophy known as Daoism (sometimes written as Taoism). This is the idea of yin and yang, literally the female and male principles, sometimes symbolized as ☯. The idea is that any entity comprises not only a principal object but also, at the same time, its complementary opposite. The new is not just new, but also is a reaction to the old, which was itself once new. The category "male" seems distinct enough from "female," yet both emerge from the interaction of female and male, so much so that imagining a moment when the categories were truly separate is difficult. The following paragraphs apply this outlook to Chinese society, geography and history, language, formative philosophies and religion, and political organization.

China has the largest population of any country in the world (more than 1.36 billion in early 2015, with one baby born every two seconds). We can find enormous ethnic and cultural diversity within this huge population; the Chinese state officially recognizes fifty-five "nationalities," as well as the majority Han people who form around 92 percent of the total. Most of the Han Chinese inhabit rich agricultural lands in the eastern third of the country—to get a sense of the resulting population density, imagine a billion people living in the United States between the Mississippi River and the Atlantic coast. Meanwhile, Han and many other nationalities (including Zhuang, Uyghur, Hui, Yi, Tibetans, Miao, Manchu, and Mongols) are spread across the extensive deserts and oases of the west, the mountain ranges and grasslands of the north, and the tropical jungle and mountains of the southwest. Ways of life differ in each of these environments. Currently, around 54 percent of the population is urban, but only a generation ago, 75 percent of people worked on the land, inhabiting a social milieu formed primarily around family work and other concerns at the village level. This trend reflects the rapid and significant urbanization and industrialization of the nation. Of course, there were huge cities, elaborate courts, temples, and factories in historical China, and so urban, professional, and elite musics are every bit as well established as the music of the agricultural classes. There have been significant overseas Chinese communities for several centuries, and any account of Chinese music in the present day needs to consider this large and varied diaspora. Most prominent are populations in Taiwan and Singapore. Overseas Chinese are significant markets for Chinese musical trends: Some sustain traditions now infrequently found in the mainland, and many have originated new musical expressions, some of which have become popular in the mainland in turn.

The historical record (Table 8.1) shows that the territory we now know as China has several times been unified by military force into a single nation; at other periods it has fractured into separate, self-governing states. Around 221 B.C.E., for example, the ruler of a state named Qin defeated his rivals across much of present-day China, taking for himself the title of First Emperor (*Qin* is pronounced "chin"—the origin of the term *China;* see the box "Mandarin Chinese Pronunciation"). His important legacy ranged from attempts to standardize the language across the nation to rebuilding and extending the northern defenses—building the Great Wall. Conquest of a different kind occurred in the early thirteenth century, when Genghis Khan led a Mongolian invasion that temporarily unified an enormous portion of Eurasia. A further northern invasion occurred in the mid-seventeenth century, when the Manchus swept southward to found the Qing Dynasty, which endured until 1911. Fragmentation remains part of the contemporary situation. In 1912, the Nationalist Party established a Republic of China and, following Japanese invasion and a bitter civil war, a People's Republic led by the Chinese Communist Party was established in 1949. At this time, the Nationalists retreated to the island of Taiwan, which the Qing had ceded to Japan in 1895 and was reclaimed by the Republic of China in 1945 after Japan's defeat in World War II. Recent years have seen a thawing of the economic and cultural relationship between Taiwan and China, but political reunification remains distant and contested. Meanwhile, a century and a half of British colonial activity in this area encouraged many Chinese to migrate to Southeast Asia; one consequence is that the city-state of Singapore has a majority population of ethnic Chinese.

Table 8.1 **Chinese Dynasties**

Zhou	11th century B.C.E.–221 B.C.E.
Qin	221–207 B.C.E.
Han	206 B.C.E.–220 C.E.
Tang	618–907 C.E.
Song	960–1279
Yuan (Mongols)	1271–1368
Ming	1368–1644
Qing (Manchu)	1644–1911
Republic of China	1912–present (continuing in Taiwan)
People's Republic of China	1949–present

The field of language reflects a similar duality of divergence and accord. Younger Han people in China today mostly speak the national language, Mandarin Chinese, and also a regional variety of Chinese particular to the locality where they were brought up. These regional dialects are often mutually unintelligible, although they all share some words and grammatical structures. Importantly, these are **tone languages**, which means that the pitch (high, low, rising, falling, and so on) at which a syllable is pronounced is as important in determining its meaning as its combination of other components (duration, stress, and the sounds equivalent to consonants and vowels). This characteristic has significant implications for vocal music, as we will see. In contrast to spoken Chinese, writing across the Chinese world has long been unified in a single system of characters. These characters consist of pictorial, phonetic, and other elements; their primary distinction from alphabetic languages is that each written character equals a whole word (with a few exceptions). For centuries, these characters were used across East Asia as the principal form of written language. There are also the native languages of the many minority groups, such as Uyghur or Mongol, learned by those of that ethnicity and often by their neighbors as well.

Many within the Chinese world can disseminate ideas widely in Mandarin Chinese and can read the writings of fellow citizens past and present, but this hardly means that the Chinese have a single outlook on the world. On the contrary, there have long been conflicting schools of thought. Confucianism, which emerged from the writings of Kong Fuzi (literally, Lord Kong, c. 550–479 B.C.E.), argued that good governance required a fixed social hierarchy in which loyalty flowed upward from wife to husband, son to father, common man to ruler, and ruler to heaven. Social responsibility then passed downward, with each individual obliged to care for those on the next stratum below. Confucius saw human nature as basically good but easily corrupted by poor leadership. Meanwhile, Daoists argued for self-cultivation and the importance of severing one's personal ties to an imperfect world. Both systems aimed to explain humanity's place in the universe. However, neither depended on religious belief in the Indo-European sense, although Daoism later cross-fertilized with local folk religions, including spirit and **ancestor worship**. These forms of worship involve rites to pay respect to natural and supernatural forces and to one's forefathers. Buddhism, a third major outlook, came from India to China early in the first millennium C.E. This doctrine held that human beings were inherently imperfect but, through religious practice, could embark on a journey of gradual self-improvement through multiple incarnations toward a purified future.

Each of these doctrines was overlaid by an imperial context that varied widely. At times, a landed aristocracy held the most power; during other periods, the imperial court ruled through a professional elite of scholar-officials selected by public examination and dispatched to oversee districts far from their own homes. Today, the political organization of the Chinese world is no more straightforward. The administrative elite in mainland China is formed principally by members of the Chinese Communist Party. This political system emphasizes social equality, the shared ownership of property, strong central planning, and state control. However, recent decades have seen the encouragement of private enterprise and the rise of business interests, and corruption and the abuse of privilege by those in power has remained a problem. Since 1997, the former British colony of Hong Kong has returned to Chinese rule, with a governor appointed in Beijing but otherwise having a political system somewhat separate from that of the rest of the mainland. The Taiwanese have a multiparty democracy. Chinese in most other countries are typically minority groups with little political say, except in the city-state of Singapore, where the Chinese form the majority population. Singapore is run as a democracy, but the government is notably authoritarian, and the same party (indeed, often the same few families) has held power since independence from Britain half a century ago.

In sum, the Chinese world comprises many highly varied locations even while people within this zone sometimes choose to perceive themselves as a single cultural entity. This same duality applies to Chinese musical culture: On the one hand, there are few musical features that are both uniquely and universally Chinese—characteristics shared in all this music but uncommon in East Asia or more globally; on the other hand, the *idea* of Chinese music is more universal, forming a significant category in Chinese discussions about music, identity, and international cultural contact. Like many around the world, the Chinese believe that their music makes them special and distinct from everyone else. We return to this issue at the end of the chapter.

Mandarin Chinese Pronunciation

Today, Mandarin Chinese is commonly transliterated into an alphabetical system called Pinyin to help those who cannot read Chinese characters. Many Pinyin letters sound similar to their English equivalents. Common sounds requiring special attention are listed here, with approximate English pronunciations.

Pinyin	English Sound	Example	Approximate Pronunciation
A	Ah	Zhang	"jahng"
Ai	Eye	kuai	"kwhy"
Ao	Ow	jiao	"jee-ow" (rhymes with "cow")
E	Uh	ge	"guh"
E	a (long)	Bei	"bay"
I	ee/ir	ni, shi, dizi	"nee," "shir," "dee-zuh"—*i* has an "ee" sound except after c, ch, r, s, sh, z, and zh, when it is "ir," or "uh" if unstressed
Ü	like *ü* in German	Lü	"lue"—shape your lips as if to say "oo" but compress the vocal cavity as in "ee"
C	Ts	can	"tsahn"
Q	Ch	qin	"chin"
R	s (as in "pleasure")	ren	"rjun"
X	Sh	xi	"she"
Y	Ee	Yan	"yen"
Zh	J	zhi	"jir"

Speech tones are normally omitted in Pinyin (but are very important in pronouncing a word correctly). Most syllables are equally stressed (for example, Abing is ah-bing, not AH-bing or ah-BING). A full guide is at https://en.wikipedia.org/wiki/Pinyin. Note that Chinese names are written with family name first, then personal name.

A Cross Section of Chinese Music

How can we begin to grasp this immense subject area? Table 8.2 gives an overview by listing types of music found across the Chinese world today, with a range of imported and newly created genres shown alongside selected age-old, historical styles. Many are discussed in this book, and the sections that follow introduce each in turn.

Listing the items in this way, however, overly separates each. In practice, in China as elsewhere, different kinds of music share many features. Figure 8.1 maps these same examples onto a grid, showing various ways that we might group them according to certain shared characteristics. For example, we might place them by instrumentation into vocal, vocal-instrumental, or instrumental categories. The two folk songs (1 and 2) are performed without instrumental backing and fall into the category of vocal music, as does the ritual song (8). The former were rural forms originally performed during agricultural labor, so it is little surprise that they omit instrumentalists—people needed their hands free to take part in the work—and the latter came from a society of hunter-gatherers who join their hands while singing, as we will see later on. Meanwhile, much music combines vocal and instrumental forces, including all the entertainment genres, from Beijing opera (5) to pop song (9). Some music, though, is designed for instruments alone, such as the solos for the stringed instrument *qin* (6) or the *beiguan* ensemble music (4), although this is a porous boundary in many cases—some *qin* and *beiguan* pieces include singing.

On the same figure, we might instead choose to divide Chinese music into forms intended for the people at large and those aimed at more elite types of listeners. If so, the folk song examples are now joined by several other mass-entertainment forms such as Beijing opera and the pop song as well as religious forms such as the ritual. Meanwhile, the contemporary piano solo (7) is an example of a music mastered only by a specialist minority in China, which places it alongside the *qin* solo, among other examples. None of these categories is static, though. Folk song and Beijing

Table 8.2 Some Examples of Chinese Music

Number	Song Type	Song Title
1	Folk song 1	"Weeding Song"
2	Folk song 2	"Releasing the Horse into Pasture"
3	*Sizhu* ensemble music	"Song of Happiness"
4	*Beiguan* processional music	"Seven-Inch Lotus"
5	Beijing opera	*Third Wife Teaches Her Son;*
6	*Qin* solo	"Three Variations on Yang Pass"
7	Piano solo	"The Joyous Festival of Lunar New Year's Day"
8	Ritual song	*Pasibutbut*
9	Pop song	"Scent"
10	New folk music	"Miracle"

opera are becoming musics of specialist choice in China today, as we will see, and piano learning seems so fashionable in many parts of China that it nearly equals a mass music—there may well be more piano students in China than anywhere else in the world today.

Yet another way to approach these examples is to look at whether each is predominantly rooted in indigenous traditions or was significantly inspired or impacted by Western models. In this case, the two folk songs can now be placed in the indigenous category along with the socially elite solos for the stringed instruments *qin* and *pipa*, among others. The pop song and piano solo, though, arise from imported musical models. We could go beyond these categorizations, dividing up the great mass of Chinese music again and again by musical material, performance context, social function, and the performers' social class to see what patterns emerge. As Figure 8.1 shows, categorization is both a tool for organizing knowledge and an analytic device, which we can deploy to focus in on selected deep musical continuities.

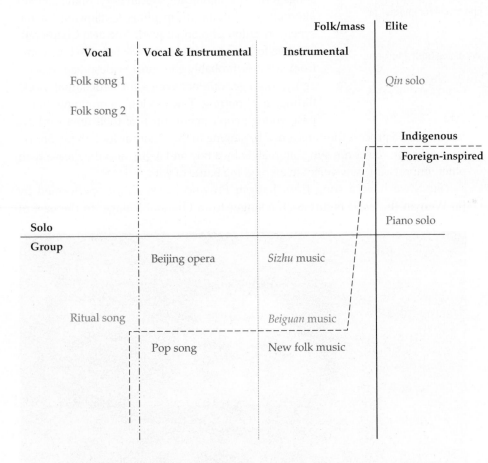

Figure 8.1
Grid of selected genres of Chinese music.

Colors label the primary social function of a performance of each genre:

——— For self-entertainment or use in small-scale, noncommercial settings
——— For religious use (not interpreted as entertainment)
——— For entertainment of the gods (religious entertainment)
——— For paying audiences

Folk Song

Today, the widespread distribution of playback technology has allowed listening to recorded or broadcast music to replace much day-to-day personal music making. Before such technology, singing played an integral role in many events or situations, including courting, funerals, and child care.

Shan'ge (Songs of Agricultural Work, Flirting, and Courting)

There are numerous regional folk song traditions across China, all with distinct musical characteristics. Work songs form one significant subcategory. Some contain alternating solo and group phrases, allowing for the synchronization of manual work (see also Chapter 4). The two folk song examples we will listen to here come from what is probably the most widespread subcategory, ***shan'ge:*** outdoor songs for agricultural work, flirting, and courting. This is a logical grouping. In the past, young people spent much of their time working in the fields, a process they enlivened by singing to the others around them. Sometimes, *shan'ge* verses are sung alternately by a boy and a girl, and they tease each other, improvising new verses in an ongoing battle of wits.

First, we have a song from Jiangsu Province, East China, performed by Jin Wenyin (b. 1927; Figure 8.2), a singer from Qiandai Village, to the east of

Figure 8.2
Folk singer Jin Wenyin.
Courtesy of Antoinet Schimmelpenninck.

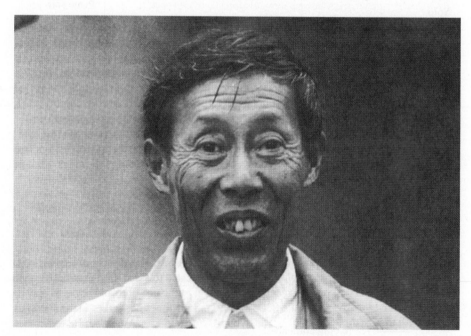

the city of Suzhou (Schimmelpenninck 1997). He worked as a village school teacher and local cultural officer until he became an agricultural laborer during the Cultural Revolution (1966–1976), when many of those associated with cultural activities found themselves fiercely criticized in public meetings, physically maltreated, and thrown out of their former posts. In 1979, he regained cultural employment and actively gathered songs and texts of all kinds from his friends and neighbors.

Jin sings a rice-weeding song (Active Listening 8.1) combining moments during which he cries out using syllables like "e-he-hei," and those where he sings simple lyrics describing the task of weeding a rice paddy.

> Weeding was arduous but essential work during the hot summer months, and all present joined in the calls as they uprooted weeds. The leader improvised lyrics to help the workers forget the heat of the day and their weariness. Jin Wenyin sang alone when he recorded this song in 1987, but had he been singing while weeding, he would likely have developed a short story over several verses or started to challenge other singers within earshot to improvise riddle songs. Jin told Dutch ethnomusicologist Antoinet Schimmelpenninck, who researched folk singing in East China: "Sometimes we sang songs in the fields until we knew no more texts. What to do about it? Well, we could sing 'Shi zhi taizi' ['Ten Tables,' a song counting famous historical and

ACTIVE LISTENING 8.1
"Yundao Ge" ("Weeding Song")

MindTap·
🎧 **WATCH** an Active Listening Guide of this selection online.

COUNTER NUMBER	COMMENTARY	LYRICS	TRANSLATION
0:00	Opening calls	e hehe hehei	
0:09	Line 1 of the lyrics, musical phrase 1a	yingdao ei ...	If you're weeding, sing a weeding song, weeding ...
0:19	Extension of the phrase by repeating a few words from line 1	yingdao ei ...	weeding ...
0:27	Further repetition	aya yingdao ei ...	weeding ...
0:34	Line 2, phrase 1b	liang pang mei ...	With knees bent, squelching in the mud,
0:51	Line 3, phrase 2a	ngei gwa ei ...	I see a six-foot plot, full of weeds,
1:01	Line 4, phrase 2b	(1st time) se zi ...	my ten fingers hold six seedlings.
1:12	Like the opening calls but leads to a repeat of line 4 and phrase 2b	ei hei hei ...	

Yundaoge ("Weeding song"). Copyright © 1997 by Chime Foundation. Used by permission.

Figure 8.3
Singer Zhao Yue. *Courtesy of Jiang Shu.*

legendary figures one by one]. That gave us ten more songs." Or, before marriage, he might have begun to sing about the beauty of one of the girls nearby in the hope of sparking her romantic interest, or at least of initiating some amusing teasing. Jin noted that girls were shy and sang less than men, but if the girl wished, she might sing a verse in reply, and the duet would continue until one singer lost inspiration (and so lost the contest) or a third person chimed in with a verse.

In the same interview, Jin Wenyin noted that the rise of chemical weed killer meant that few people now sang weeding songs. Mechanization also played a part, as did the drift of people to industrial work and the reorganization of land ownership after the 1980s. Before then, much of the land was worked collectively, first by teams of laborers for landlords and later by groups of commune members. From the 1980s on, however, many families were allocated individual plots, with the result that they organized separate work schedules. A better standard of living has resulted, but so has a decline in collective singing. *Shan'ge* are no longer a normal part of work activities, being sustained in some rural areas only by folklore enthusiasts like Jin Wenyin.

But decline is not the full picture, since *shan'ge* have a long history of spreading to new contexts. In ancient China, the emperor sent out officials to gather song texts to help him judge whether or not the people were happy. The seventeenth century saw a literary movement in which certain Chinese authors collected and published songs that they felt had an attractive local character, particularly those with erotic content. The most famous of these writers was Feng Menglong (1574–1646), who published the words of over three hundred *shan'ge*. Feng argued that the songs showed sincere feelings, unlike the contrived, self-conscious love affairs of the social elite. During the 1910s and 1920s, following the example of Christian missionaries and school reformers, social activists of various political outlooks took up mass singing to instill group solidarity or to help their followers disseminate a message. Folk song tunes were often chosen—the activists saw that use of a familiar tune helped people take in the new words. The movie *Yellow Earth* (directed by Chen Kaige, 1984) tells the story of a Communist soldier sent in 1939 to collect village folk songs for just such a purpose. In the 1950s, many of these tunes, with their new lyrics, were published for educational use across the nation. The new social order meant that the lyrics of love songs were largely omitted or rewritten as hymns of admiration for Chairman Mao Zedong (Mao Tse-tung, 1893–1976) and his Chinese Communist Party. Nevertheless, *shan'ge* tunes survived, and songs related to work patterns were sometimes left intact in these collections.

The second recorded example, "Releasing the Horse into Pasture," (Active Listening 8.2) illustrates this more recent situation. Zhao Yue (b. 1977; Figure 8.3) learned this song, which is from Yunnan Province, Southwest China, as a student at the Shenyang Conservatory of Music, in distant Northeast China.

MindTap·

◄)) **LISTEN TO**

"Fang ma shan'ge" ("Releasing the Horse into Pasture"), performed by Zhao Yue, online.

ACTIVE LISTENING 8.2
"Fang Ma Shan'ge" ("Releasing the Horse into Pasture")

COUNTER NUMBER	COMMENTARY	LYRICS	TRANSLATION
0:00	Verse 1 (seven measures long, divided into a three-measure phrase and a four-measure phrase): Phrase 1: a, a', b a is a falling pattern and appears in form a and the more-elaborate a'; b is a sequence pitched a step below	*Zhengyue fang ma wu lu lu de zheng yue zheng yao,*	In the first month I release the horse to pasture,
0:06	Phrase 2: a, b', c, b' b' has one more note than b, to set an extra syllable; c is two rhythmic cries, one to each beat	*Ganqi malai denglu cheng, yao e, denglu cheng.*	I encourage the horse to go into the field.
0:14	Verse 2: same music as verse 1	*Dama ganzai shantou shang, Xiaoma ganlai sui hou gen.*	The big horse climbs the mountain, The little horse follows on behind.
0:26	Verse 3: same music as verse 1	*Eryue fang ma baicao fa, Xiaoma chi cao shenshanli pao.*	In the second month I feed the horse every kind of grass, The little horse eats grass and gallops in the mountain valleys.
0:43	Verse 4; a, a', b, a, b', b', c (the final two elements are reversed to create a distinctive ending)	*Ma wu yecao bu hui pang, Cao wu lushui bu hui fa.*	Without grass the horse won't get fat, Grass without dew won't grow well.

"Fang ma shan'ge" ("Releasing the Horse into Pasture"). Used with permission by Zhao Yue.

"Releasing the Horse into Pasture" shares with the weeding song a two-phrase design and use of vocal cries alongside singing. Yet, the two differ significantly. First, this song has a more straightforward structure than the weeding song does. Second, the greatest contrast is in meter: Jin's *shan'ge* is in free meter, as opposed to Zhao's clear duple meter. Third, Zhao's repertory includes songs from all across China (and overseas), unlike that of Jin, who learned a local set of tunes and songs. Fourth, Jin learned informally in the fields to reshape one main melody to fit a wide range of different song texts, whereas Zhao memorized in the classroom a contrasting series of fixed-format songs. Fifth, while Jin sings in his local Wu dialect, Zhao performs her songs in Mandarin Chinese.

Still, we would be mistaken to describe Zhao's rendition as "inauthentic" as compared with Jin's. After all, neither performance occurred in an agricultural setting, and in the past *shan'ge* were mostly sung by young, single people, much closer in age to Zhao than to Jin. Instead, each performance sustains the tradition in a new setting—Jin's as folkloric hobby, Zhao's in the sphere of music education.

MindTap
WATCH an Active Listening Guide of this selection online.

Instrumental Ensemble Traditions

China is rich in instrumental ensemble traditions. Ancient paintings and court records reveal fascinating details of early ensembles. Other traditions have come down to us through archaeological findings, one of the most remarkable of which is a set of relics from the tomb of Marquis Yi, the ruler of a small Chinese state called Zeng.

Salient Characteristics of
Chinese Ensemble Music

- Heterophonic performance style—multiple instruments share the same melodic line

- Variation during performance—the surface details of the music are not entirely fixed, with room for spontaneous ornamentation and interplay with other musicians

- Notation used when players learn the music, but they perform from memory rather than by reading scores; this increases flexibility but constrains the size of the repertory

- Much music is in suite form: a gradual progression from slow, expanded tunes to fast, compressed versions of the same tune

- Performance is very much part of a wider social event, not a rendition to a paying audience; in the *beiguan* ensemble, performance is part of religious ritual, perhaps the most widespread traditional context for ensemble music in China and Taiwan

In the winter of 1977, a unit of the Chinese People's Liberation Army was called in to level a small, unremarkable hill north of the city of Wuhan in Hubei Province so that a factory could be built. After breaking into a previously unknown burial pit, the soldiers quickly called in the archaeologists. The discovery that followed remains unparalleled among any of the other ancient cultures in Asia, Africa, Europe, or the Americas.

Laid out as a classical Chinese palace, the stone-lined tomb contained everything the Bronze Age despot would need for an upwardly mobile afterlife: an ornately lacquered, wooden double coffin to shield both his bones and his dignity; weapons, armor, and bronze chariot fittings; the skeletons of twenty-one women and a dog; and a full set of ritual musical instruments, including a sixty-five-piece ensemble of studded bronze *zhong* bells and thirty-two tuned *qing* chime stones, as well as drums, strings, and wind instruments. Each woman lay next to an instrument. Beside the bodies were illustrations of the musicians in performance, though sadly no musical notation was found. Inscriptions recorded that the bell set was presented to Marquis Yi in 433 B.C.E. by his powerful neighbor, the King of Chu.

Superbly preserved in the subterranean palace (Figure 8.4), each bell produces two pitches, depending on where it is struck. The set has a range of over five octaves, much of it fully chromatic in semitones. Since the bells are inscribed with the names of the tones they produced, today we know both their actual pitch levels and how they all fit together into a tonal system. The inclusion of five sets of beaters suggests how many musicians might have performed the bells at once. Some of the instruments or other ritual materials found in the tomb show scenes depicting the making of music, providing further clues about performance practice.

A smaller musical ensemble was laid at the foot of the Marquis's coffin in his personal chamber. This comprised a transverse flute, panpipes, two mouth organs, *sheng* (an instrument that would inspire the invention of the accordion), a small drum, three zithers of twenty-five strings with movable bridges, a ten-stringed type of *qin* zither (later in this chapter we discuss its better-known, seven-stringed form), and a five-stringed zither, which appears to have been struck with a handheld stick. All these instruments were very well preserved. The *qin,* for instance, survived with several of its tuning pegs intact, allowing historians to date that technology to at least this period. Coffins of eight young women were close at hand, suggesting that eight of these instruments were played at once to the fortunate Marquis. As if these treasures were not enough, the archaeologists uncovered a second tomb just a few years later. This was thought to be that of the Marquis's consort or close descendant. Here were yet further instruments and more clues to Chinese court music-culture of more than two millennia past.

Figure 8.4
Excavation of the tomb of Marquis Yi (So 2000:15).
Jonathan P. J. Stock

The large, carefully crafted bronze bell set was a hugely expensive gift, and we might wonder what Marquis Yi was doing with such a set—according to Confucian orthodoxy, the largest sets were reserved for kings and emperors. It was also an incredible item to take to the afterlife, not to mention the sacrifice of all those young women (and the dog). This was conspicuous consumption long before Thorstein Veblen coined the term in the last years of the nineteenth century. Veblen linked conspicuous consumption with conspicuous leisure and conspicuous waste. In this view, artistic production is deliberately expensive, time-consuming, splendid, and useless. Useless, that is, in the narrow sense of propelling immediate human survival, but useful indeed in projecting one's elevated wealth, fitness, or status, since only the most superior human being had the surplus time to invest in such cultural display, or, indeed, the authority to take it with him to the grave. If this is so, perhaps the bell ensemble's musical performances were similarly display-oriented, being musically virtuosic and intended primarily to project the Marquis's regal ambitions.

This interpretation of the music played by these ensembles differs from the one put forward in historical writings, which predominantly describe ritual music. Yet we know the ancient Chinese had entertainment-oriented music. The philosopher Mozi (c. 470–c. 390 B.C.E.) made a point of rejecting such music as a wasteful drain on the state and called for the execution of professional musicians. The ancient record of court music, the *Yueji,* described another Marquis, one who had a love for contemporary entertainment music. His sentiments may be familiar to many music students worldwide:

> Marquis Wen of Wei asked Zixia, "When I don my ritual regalia and listen
> to the ancient music, the only thing I fear is that I will keel over [from bore-
> dom]. But when I listen to the tones of Zheng and Wei, I never feel the least
> bit sated with it. May I be so bold as to ask why the ancient music is that way
> when the new is not?" (DeWoskin 1982:94)

The regal bell set may have allowed Marquis Yi to signal royal status when he reached the afterlife, but perhaps its power extended beyond the symbolic. Music is in many senses the least concrete of all the arts. Its sounds—particularly those of the large bells (Figure 8.5)—are readily felt in and around the body while remaining invisible to the eye. Music's special appeal to us as listeners, and its "feelingful invisibility," seem to parallel the agency of the supernatural, which many ancient peoples believed to be present, powerful, and unseen. It is no wonder that music plays a regular role in religious services and funeral ceremonies worldwide, and that people see it as a bridge to the otherworldly.

Because we have no surviving music from 433 B.C.E., but only instruments, tunings, and illustrations, the remainder of this section studies two much more contemporary traditions: Jiangnan *sizhu* from the Shanghai region of East China, and *beiguan* from the city of Jilong in Northern Taiwan. These allow us to focus on contrasting aspects of Chinese ensemble music as found today.

Jiangnan *Sizhu*

Several instrumental traditions are found in and around Shanghai, among them **Jiangnan** *sizhu* (Figure 8.6). Its name means the silk and bamboo music of the Jiangnan region, in East China around the lower reaches of the Changjiang (Yangtze River). The phrase *silk and bamboo* refers to the two major categories of instruments used in this music—silk-stringed instruments and bamboo-tubed wind instruments. The ancient Chinese recognized eight categories of sound-producing materials: silk, bamboo, metal (as in the bells described earlier), stone (as in tuned chimes), gourds (hollowed out to make the body of a mouth organ), earth (baked into clay ocarinas), leather (stretched to make drumheads), and wood (as in clappers). *Sizhu* ensembles are widely distributed across China, their exact instrumentation varying from place to place. In Jiangnan, the ensemble is flexible, but it often includes one or two of each of the following instruments: **erhu**; **sanxian** (three-stringed, long-necked lute), **pipa** (four-stringed, pear-shaped lute),

Figure 8.5
Replica bell modeled on those discovered in the tomb of Marquis Yi. *Jonathan P. J. Stock.*

Figure 8.6
Sizhu performance in a Shanghai tea shop. The back row has an *erhu* player on the left (partially covered), next to him a *pipa* player, and then a *yangqin*. The front musicians are a percussionist (left) and a player of the *sanxian* (we can see the top of its neck only). *Jonathan P. J. Stock*

ruan (four-stringed, round-bodied lute), *yangqin*(hammered dulcimer), and ***dizi*** (transverse bamboo flute); it also includes the *sheng* (mouth organ), and a percussionist plays woodblock and clappers. Sometimes, the ensemble adds a ***zheng*** (also called ***guzheng***; a bridged zither usually with twenty-five strings), and in soft pieces a ***xiao*** (a bamboo, end-blown, vertical flute) replaces the more effervescent *dizi.*

Jiangnan *sizhu* music used to be played by hired instrumentalists at weddings and in local opera, but it is better known as an amateur music today, most typically being performed in tea shops by groups of friends who have formed a music club, rather like Irish music sessions in pubs but with tea as the main drink, not beer. This change reflects a process of gentrification quite widely found in the history of Chinese music. In China, the skills of professional performers have always been appreciated, but music professionals themselves were typically held in low esteem before the twentieth century, which meant that amateur musicians wanted to learn the music but not be taken for professionals. One means of marking their social distance was to transfer the performance to a new context distant from the commercial situations of hired wedding bands or the theater.

In tea shop performances of Jiangnan *sizhu,* musicians seat themselves around a table and play primarily to one another, taking turns as the event proceeds. Other people sit around, possibly listening to the ensemble but more often chatting, smoking, and drinking tea. The brief excerpt recorded in Active Listening 8.3 illustrates how the music actually sounds at a tea shop; compare this track with the concert-style performance cited next.

"Song of Happiness" ("Huanlege") is one of the primary eight pieces that together comprise Jiangnan *sizhu*'s core repertory. It used to be played to accompany a bride on the wedding procession to her new home. The piece makes an effective concert piece, building up gradually to a fast, flamboyant conclusion. A complete performance of "Song of Happiness" is a suite of three renditions of essentially the same melodic material played slowly, moderately, and quickly, in turn. But because there are more decorations at the slower speed, the overall flow of the music actually sounds somewhat similar from one rendition to the next, even though the players perceive the three as having quite different tempos.

ACTIVE LISTENING 8.3
Jiangnan *Sizhu*

COUNTER NUMBER	COMMENTARY
0:00–0:28	Listen first to the duple meter of the percussion part. There are two kinds of sounds, a "tick" from the woodblock and a "tock" from the clapper (played, one to each hand, by the same musician).
	Listen to the melody, which is heterophonic; that is, each musician plays the same tune at once in a version specific to his or her instrument. The *dizi* can be heard clearly, as can some plucked and bowed strings.
	Then consider the background sound—this is not music for a passive audience. Or is the *music* the background sound?

MindTap·
LISTEN TO Jiangnan *sizhu*, performed by musicians at the Huxin Tea Shop, online.

MindTap·
WATCH a video of senior musicians from Shanghai playing "Song of Happiness."

MindTap·
WATCH an Active Listening Guide of this selection online.

Beiguan

The *beiguan* ensemble is a band of wind and percussion players who perform out-door ritual music, predominantly at funerals and temple festivities. Though *beiguan* sounds quite unlike Jiangnan *sizhu*, this contrast is not due to geography or local cultural preference—both Taiwan and Jiangnan have well-blended, introspective, indoor ensembles and strident, outdoor, wind-and-percussion groups. Instead, the two examples allow us to experience the breadth of musics that make up the category of instrumental ensemble traditions.

Beiguan music emanates a muscular self-confidence that perfectly matches its outdoor setting. Here is an extract from my field notes when I began to study *beiguan.* My aim was to capture in words the impression of being surrounded by this remarkably stirring music. (Incidentally, field notes like this normally are not intended for direct publication, and you can see that I was experimenting with a personal, even novelistic style here, one which perhaps jars with the careful writing more normally put forward in textbooks. Still, the idea of using lively prose to directly communicate the sensation of music making has attracted many ethnomusicologists in recent years.)

> Standing near the ensemble, or better taking part as a musician, my ears ring. During and afterward. It could be a rock concert, but it is actually someone's funeral. At the epicenter of the band the air seems to thicken and boil, as streams of molten sound tumble into one another, jostling for supremacy. Each beat of the huge frame gong is felt in the body as much as heard by the ears; the heart thrills to the brilliant clash of the paired cymbals, shot through from moment to moment by the sweet rising tones of the hand gong. Meanwhile, two slim sticks dance balletically on the bald pate of the single-skinned drum. Dance is the word. The movements are visual as well as sonic, signaling the other musicians in a supple staccato punctuated by silent gesticulations and underpinned by the direct rhythmic tattoo of the low-pitched barrel drum or its flat-toned, circular neighbor. But atop all this is the thick, vibrant keening of the massed double-reeds. Blown in near unison, they achieve a visceral resonance I can almost taste. Melodic phrases cascade out of the double-reed instruments, powered by robust circular breathing and a micro-cosm of swirling grace notes. This is indeed music to stir the soul, music to die to (field notes, September 10, 1999).

However imperfectly I could capture it in words, my moment-to-moment enjoyment of musical sound fueled my recognition of the dedication and skills of the *beiguan* musicians whom I had met at the Juleshe ensemble in Baifushequ, Jilong, North Taiwan. They appeared to have memorized vast tracts of technically demanding musical repertory, including numerous suites of up to an hour in length—an achievement about which they were quite nonchalant. Admiring the artistry of these humble experts, I wished to better understand how they had learned so much music.

The musicians showed me how they memorized new tunes by learning to sing them. Their example was the first tune taught to newcomers at Baifushequ. This melody, called "Seven-Inch Lotus" ("Qi Cun Lian"), is often used in celebratory performances.

"Seven-Inch Lotus" is fairly easy to sing, particularly in a group, although there are one or two wide leaps. The lyrics are actually Chinese names of notes (like "do, re, mi" in the West). In learning the tune, musicians keep repeating it over and over, without paying attention to anyone else's mistakes. Vocal quality is not important—formal performances are instrumental, not vocal—nor is exact pitch. I heard one very good musician sing softly a fifth higher than her ensemble colleagues because that pitch level suited her voice better; none of the other musicians gave any sign of complaint. To help keep time, the musicians also beat the tabletop on the main beat of each metrical unit, waving on the off beat (Active Listening 8.4).

Beiguan musicians try hard to be considerate to one another and to be inclusive in their performance activities. They see themselves as members of a community organization, and male members refer to one another as brothers. But they are also serious about their art, and every ensemble recognizes one or two senior players as teachers. It is their responsibility to maintain standards, as shown in this further extract from my field notes.

Mr You, the teacher, stops the ensemble and scolds the young drummer for slipping up. The drummer looks contrite, hanging his head. Two of his friends leap to their feet. "It doesn't matter," one of them cries, "He's trying!" You shakes his head: "He's not memorized it properly. How can other people keep together with him like this?" Discussion ensued, although I suspect You had intended the question to be rhetorical. Everyone agreed they wanted to include the drummer in the forthcoming processional performance. The drummer admitted that he couldn't play the *suona* [double-reed] part either, so he couldn't transfer to that instead. It was decided that a more experienced player should take over, while the beginner sat nearby, imitating his movements closely and drumming onto the back of a nearby wind-player's chair. This would be his final chance to memorize the drum part if he wanted to perform publicly this time (field notes, August 3, 1999).

ACTIVE LISTENING 8.4
"Qi Cun Lian" ("Seven-Inch Lotus"), Vocal Version

COUNTER NUMBER	SECTION	COMMENTARY
0:00	First rendition: *cei gong liu u liu,* *xiang u liu gong liu cei,* *liu gong cei gong liu xiang,* *gong cei xiang u liu xiang,* *gong cei xiang u xiang liu,* *u liu u liu gong,*	Wu Wanyi sings through the notation, beating the start of each measure on the tabletop; another player warms up his reed in the background.
0:20	Start of a second rendition	Recording fades out after a few seconds.

MindTap·
🎧 **WATCH** an Active Listening Guide of this selection online.

MindTap·

◀)) LISTEN TO

"Qi Cun Lian" ("Seven-Inch Lotus"), performed by Baifushequ Juleshe Beiguan Troupe, online.

Once a tune is fully internalized—that is, it can be sung without reference to the notation—the musicians transfer it onto the ensemble's double-reed instrument, or *suona* (Figure 8.7). To do so, they need to convert the vocal melody into a full-scale, instrumental piece. They add notes to fill any gaps in the melody (there is one after the fifth note of "Seven-Inch Lotus") and decorate the surface of the melody with grace notes. The percussionists add their parts, too, which are taught through memorizing patterns of drum syllables. These syllables compress the essential features of the music's percussion patterns into a few **onomatopoeic syllables**: that is, they sound like the sounds they represent ("kuang" represents a strike of the large gong, for example, and "tak" a dry-sounding stoke on the single-skinned drum).

Next, we hear a performance of "Seven-Inch Lotus" by the Baifushequ musicians (Active Listening 8.5).

Often, a *beiguan* group is affiliated with a local temple, which provides rehearsal space in return for the ensemble's participation in rites and processions. This was once common in mainland China and is now returning in many areas, though the political suppression of religious activities there in much of the second half of the twentieth century hit ritual musics particularly hard. In Taiwan, *beiguan* musicians will approach successful businessmen and ask them to act as heads of troupes, providing funding to support the ensemble's activities and regularly inviting all members to dine or socialize together, thereby cementing human relations within the group as a whole.

Earlier, I mentioned the gentrification of the Jiangnan *sizhu* tradition as it turned from the entertainment music of low-class professionals into the repertory of respectable, amateur enthusiasts. *Beiguan* offers similarities and contrasts in this regard. Members of the Baifushequ group are proud of their amateur status, and the music has roots in opera performance. But the opera from which *beiguan* emerged was performed primarily by the sons of the social elite for ritual display.

Figure 8.7

Members of Baifushequ Juleshe *beiguan* ensemble playing *suona*. Jonathan P. J. Stock.

ACTIVE LISTENING 8.5
"Qi Cun Lian" ("Seven-Inch Lotus"), Ensemble Version

COUNTER NUMBER	SECTION	COMMENTARY
0:00	Percussion passage linking this tune to the preceding one	Begins with a slowly accelerating pattern on the barrel drum. The single-skinned drum joins in, with its distinctive, high-pitched click. The cymbals and gongs pick up its cue. The cymbals play regular pulses in time with the single-skinned drum. The higher gong plays a partially syncopated pattern; the large gong reinforces every other beat of the cymbals. The leader slows the speed down to cue the wind instruments.
0:15	"Seven-Inch Lotus"	Gradual entrance of all the *suona*. The percussion continues, and a simple duple meter is established.
0:39	Second rendition	There is a slight increase in speed; small details differ in each rendition—note, for example, that the second drummer switches briefly from barrel drum to bass drum at 0:56.
0:57	Third rendition	
1:16	Fourth rendition	
1:34	End pattern	The *suona* end by drawing out the first note of the tune followed by a note a step below. The percussion then provides a linking passage to the next tune.

In the last generation or two, opera performances have become rare, leaving the instrumental accompaniments as the main musical repertory. Many *beiguan* musicians today have manual trades: construction workers, market stall owners, taxi or truck drivers, and shop workers. These days, the social elite in Taiwan are more likely to send their children for lessons in piano or violin than to apprentice them to a *beiguan* troupe, which they perceive as old-fashioned, working class, and associated primarily with rural funerals.

MindTap*

🎧 **WATCH** an Active Listening Guide of this selection online.

Opera Traditions

In this section we look at *jingju* (Beijing opera). Narrative forms in China range from storytelling with little or no musical setting to fully staged opera with prolific singing and acrobatics. There are now several hundred distinct traditions across the whole of China, so this is just one example of a very broad category.

Jingju (Beijing Opera)

In our look at *jingju*, we will focus on the speech and singing typical of the **qingyi** role. A qingyi is a serious heroine, and good actresses are reputed not only for their vocal powers but also for their evocative use of stance and gesture. Thus, you will gain a deeper appreciation of *jingju* if you see it performed live or on film. (Several internationally distributed Chinese films contain excerpts of *jingju*. For example, *Farewell My Concubine* follows the lives of two singers caught up in the great social changes of the mid-twentieth century, and *Forever Enthralled* presents a biography of the preeminent performer Mei Lanfang.)

The drama *Third Wife Teaches Her Son* is a good example of a story led by a *qingyi*. It concerns the struggles of Wang Chun'e following her husband's death. Men in Confucian society were permitted multiple wives, who were expected not to remarry after their husband's death. In this opera, however, wives one and two have quickly remarried, leaving the dutiful Chun'e to bring up her husband's son by one of the other wives. Wang Chun'e is played by the actress Li Shiji in this performance.

Li is a singer of the Cheng school of performance, which means that she favors a lyrical, graceful style modeled on that of Cheng Yanqiu (1904–1958), a male actor famous for his female impersonations. (In other words, Li is a woman who imitates a man who imitates a woman.)

In the past, melodies were reused from one drama to another—the idea of hiring a composer to write each new opera gained influence in China only during the mid-twentieth century. Reusing music allowed performers to avoid unpaid rehearsal time, and it also encouraged them to develop multiple versions of each tune to better express the needs of the scene in question.

In *jingju,* onstage characters are classified according to role type: *sheng* (male), *dan* (female), *jing* (painted-face), and *chou* (clown). There are subcategories within each type: for example, the *dan* designation includes the *qingyi* (as in our example), *wudan* (military woman), *huadan* (flirtatious maid), *laodan* (elderly woman), and *caidan* (comic woman), among others. Conventions for costumes and makeup vary according to the role type and are often elaborate and expensive, requiring considerable skill in their correct application prior to performance (Figure 8.8). These identify the role type for accustomed viewers.

Though *jingju*'s costuming and makeup are rich, scenery and stage props are often simple, the former consisting perhaps of only a table and two chairs. With the aid of various drapes, these simple objects represent settings from a mountain pass to a courtroom, a palace, a bedchamber, or an inn. Up to the mid-twentieth century, troupes were often migratory, traveling from place to place to perform. As such, it made sense that they took with them only the most basic scenic props.

But explanations for this are not purely logistical. *Jingju* combines four basic expressive means: singing, speech, acting, and fighting (*chang, nian, zuo,* and *da*). Singing and speech embrace a range of modes of voice production, from melismatic arias to the declamation of poems and everyday, conversational speech. Acting and fighting cover a gamut extending from facial expressions to postures, gestures, mime, and choreographed fighting and acrobatics. Each role type draws

Figure 8.8
Cao Man fixes her headdress prior to performing the *wudan* role of Green Snake.
M. Azadehfar.

distinctly on these four expressive means—as a serious heroine, the *qingyi* is normally a specialist in singing and speech, with important acting skills but little scope to fight. Elaborate stage props would limit the chance for performers to display their skills in mime or acrobatics.

The professionals who took part in opera performance in imperial China were much admired for their skill, but they held low status. Some, male and female alike, engaged in prostitution, and officials regularly condemned opera performances as rowdy occasions that encouraged gambling and debauchery. At times, legal restrictions on mixed troupes led performers to form male-only or female-only troupes. In these cases, some actors or actresses specialized in the impersonation of characters of the other gender. In modern times, some of the most famous singers were men who took female roles; for example, Mei Lanfang (1894–1961) and Cheng Yanqiu.

Touring troupes vied for employment at urban theaters and teahouses, aristocratic residences, village fairs, and temples. For this reason, *jingju* isn't well described using the Western term "classical music." While it could be found in elite settings, a wide range of folk occasions also called for opera—from birthday celebrations and funerals to agricultural rites, religious festivals, and clan anniversaries. Some dramas suited each such occasion. In the clan anniversaries, for instance, operas frequently projected a moral message, presenting tales that promoted Confucian virtues such as filial duty and female chastity, as in the example of *Third Wife Teaches Her Son*.

Several significant developments occurred in the twentieth century. The rise of the recording and broadcasting industries, starting in the 1920s, allowed actors to discover something of the musical and dramatic styles of their distant counterparts, and audiences began to select entertainment from a much broader spectrum than before. Some opera ensembles adopted Western musical instruments, and the opening of Western-style theaters led to the greater use of custom-built scenery and props. Specialist directors, scriptwriters, and, by the 1940s, composers were employed to provide new dramatic materials. Developing a tendency already present in certain regional styles, some of the new operas explored contemporary social themes, although historical settings predominated.

After the founding of the People's Republic in 1949, the Chinese Communist Party called for an increase in the number of operas with contemporary themes and working-class characters, as opposed to those peopled with historical heroes and villains, and for some years during the Cultural Revolution only a small number of "model operas" could be performed. The music of these dramas largely resembled that of preceding decades, but the stories described Chinese revolutionary struggles and the war against Japan (1937–1945). In fact, Mao Zedong remained a considerable fan of traditional opera. One official who had worked at the Ministry of Culture told me how he had produced traditional opera tapes for Mao's private listening, sometimes calling performers in to make new recordings. The actors were very frightened, because Mao's government had forbidden performance of those dramas at this time. After the end of the Cultural Revolution, in 1976, the presentation of mythical and historical tales (or newly written stories with a historical setting) resumed, with contemporary settings largely left to other genres.

Opera traditions saw some of their greatest development and sharpest decline in the twentieth century. Many genres that dominated mainstream performance venues and the airwaves two generations ago survive presently only as niche entertainments for enthusiasts. In fact, some of the expressive skills built up in these genres have been transferred to new media, most obviously the acrobatic style of fighting featured in such Chinese films as *Crouching Tiger, Hidden Dragon*, directed by Ang Lee (2000). But the traditional opera performances themselves still repay attentive listening and viewing. Even without understanding the lyrics, we can appreciate the smooth blending of skills—vocal, instrumental, visual, gestural, and so forth—that make a top-level performance successful.

Solo Instrumental Traditions

Salient Characteristics of
Chinese Instrumental Solos

- Many have descriptive titles that set a scene
- Pieces typically comprise several short sections
- Surface-level variation is more important than exact repetition, such that the music repays careful listening

In the Chinese imagination, the *qin* is usually a vehicle for spiritual reflection. A poem by Wang Wei (699–759; cited by DeWoskin 1982:145) captures the historical image of the role of the instrument (Figure 8.9):

Sitting alone in the dense bamboo groves,
I strum my *qin* and accompany with long whistles;
No one to see this deep in the trees,
Only the bright moon appears to shine.

Zither (*Qin*) Solos

The **qin** (also called **guqin**) has an ancient design (a modern *qin* appears in Figure 8.10). Seven-stringed zithers date from over two thousand years ago, and those with different numbers of strings existed even earlier, as we have seen. The *qin* consists of a convex length of wood, narrower at one end than the other. A baseboard, into which two sound holes have been cut, is fixed underneath, leaving a small, hollow cavity between the two boards as a resonating chamber. Makers use old, well-seasoned wood, which produces the best resonance. While selling me a *qin*, the Shanghai-based player Dai Xiaolian told me that the particular instrument she was offering used wood from an old coffin. Catching my surprised look she added, "Don't worry, they clean it first."

Figure 8.9
Detail from Zhao Ji's painting, *Listening to the* qin. *Jonathan P. J. Stock*

Whatever their prior use, the boards are fitted together and coated with a dark lacquer. The seven strings, which differ in thickness, are looped around two feet near the narrower end of the *qin* and drawn across the length of the front board before passing over a low bridge toward the other end. Each string then passes through a hole drilled in the board and is secured by a tuning peg on the underside. Decorative tassels are often attached to the pegs. Traditionally, the strings were made of silk, but recent decades have seen metal strings substituted in China's music conservatories. These are more durable and give a louder tone, but some musicians prefer the timbre of silk strings and still employ them today. Alongside the strings lies a row of thirteen inlaid studs. These function as a guide to the performer, showing where to stop the strings. Nearly every part of the *qin* has a symbolic name. For instance, the two sound holes on the underside of the instrument are known as "dragon pool" and "phoenix pond," respectively, a nomenclature that implies a male–female dualism. The square-shaped and rounded pillars that attach the baseboard to the top board represent earth and heaven, respectively—earth has its bounds, whereas heaven stretches on without end.

Figure 8.10
The hands of a *qin* player. *Jonathan P. J. Stock.*

Although its design is simple, the *qin* is rich in timbres. The strings can be plucked singly, plucked in combination, strummed one after another, and played both open and stopped. Harmonics are sounded by lightly stopping a string while plucking it. The instrument is also rubbed, tapped, and struck by the fingers, and experts claim to be able to produce as many as sixty different kinds of vibrato by moving the finger that stops a string. Different plucking techniques (described later) and slides add further sonic variety.

We can experience much sonic variety in the recorded example, which is the third variation and coda of "Yangguan san die." Like many *qin* pieces, it is performed solo, although there are also songs with *qin* and duos with the vertical, bamboo flute *xiao*. The piece's sectional structure—ending with a coda with a free-meter feel and use of harmonics—also makes it representative of *qin* music more broadly (Active Listening 8.6). Larger pieces typically have more sections and vary musical material from one section to the next but are otherwise similar in many respects.

For much of its extensive history, the *qin* was associated with the elite scholar-officials who governed the Chinese empire. These administrators, often referred to

ACTIVE LISTENING 8.6
"Yangguan San Die" ("Three Variations on Yang Pass")

COUNTER NUMBER	SECTION	COMMENTARY
0:00	Mini-introduction	Uses harmonics—note that the music is very soft. (This is disguised on some recordings by putting the microphone close to the instrument—play this track as softly as you dare.)
0:07	Start of third variation	Switches to normal tones—note also the legato sound (multiple tones coming from one pluck) and the alternation of high and low tones. The music is in free time—it has a regular pace, but there may not be an equal number of beats in each phrase.
0:32		Speed increases. The music is lower pitched overall and gains an insistent quality—this is the most impassioned part of the piece.
0:47		Notes are played here in pairs of the same pitch with a different playing technique the second time. I might be played on an open string first and then on a stopped string, or plucked softly and then plucked strongly with a fingernail, or played cleanly once and then approached with a slide.
1:09		Passage where each tone is plucked simultaneously on two strings at once. Speed then decreases.
1:33	Coda	Harmonics

as the "literati," included many highly cultivated amateur musicians. As an amateur pastime, the *qin* was played either alone for self-cultivation or among a small group of like-minded friends. Even today, some *qin* players call their meetings *yaji,* "elegant gatherings." For this reason, the *qin* was never subject to pressure, until recently, to produce a louder volume in order to entertain a large audience. Instead, and even when the instrument is placed on a specially designed table that acts as an amplifier, the player remains the person to best hear the music.

The literati brought to the *qin* several ideals from their broader societal setting. Poetry and music were combined as *qin* songs, the music of which was designed to bring out the inner spirit of the poetic text. Calligraphy interfaced with *qin* performance. *Qin* techniques were directly stimulated by the hand postures and brush strokes of Chinese calligraphy, and aesthetic dualisms such as movement/stillness or solidity/emptiness were transferred to the musical domain. Because so many performers of the instrument were expert writers who were used to commenting explicitly on the aesthetic qualities of their artworks, it is not surprising that they developed both a sophisticated notational system for the *qin* and a substantial body of accompanying knowledge in the form of paintings, essays, poems, and instructional books.

Like paintings, many *qin* pieces centered on historical or programmatic scenes. Famous examples include "Flowing Waters" and "Geese Landing on a Sandy Beach." Other pieces attempted to capture occurrences from the emotional world of the literati. "Three Variations on Yang Pass" drew on a poem by Wang Wei to portray the feelings of parting friends. One has been assigned to a post in a distant region, and they recognize that they may never meet again. Their emotions become successively less restrained with each of the three final cups of wine they take together.

Today, few people play the *qin*. The scholar-administrators whose emblem it was are long gone, swept away in revolutions and political reorganizations a century ago, and this restrained, sensitive, and flexible solo music seems out of place in today's fast-paced, energetic China. But, as the *qin* expert Liang Mingyue says,

> The small volume of the *qin* stimulates the development of one's subjective auditory sensibility by means of concentration. In fact, there may be a real problem in that today's industrial surroundings, which are full of people and noises, have made us insensitive to a lower sound volume, and that our ancestors of a thousand or more years ago had a more acute sense of hearing than present-day listeners. Therefore, listening with increased concentration and cultivating the "way of the *qin,*" that is, listening with the ear, the heart and the mind, has as much relevance today as it did two thousand years ago. (Liang 1985:211)

Liang is saying that learning to listen to the *qin* is potentially very rewarding indeed, drawing us into a special space of heightened sensitivity. Of course, this is not the only music worldwide that can do this. Other examples of musics that invite close listening include many string quartets, Scots fiddle tunes designed "for listening," contemporary, electroacoustic compositions, and the "songs of contemplation" performed by Gbaya men in the Central African Republic. (The wide geographic distribution of these examples reminds us to remain wary of such stereotypes as the passive, mystical East; the active, rational West; or the energetic, body-driven Africa.) Certainly, learning to listen very carefully is a precondition for many kinds of heightened musical experiences. The soft refinement of the *qin* emphasizes this quality in a particularly outstanding way. Incidentally, it is worth noting that while *qin* music shares some characteristics with certain introspective repertory from Western classical music, it isn't very well described as a classical music per se. While *qin* music can be played in concert-style performances, that isn't its most suitable medium. While musicians do learn from carefully notated scores, the ideal musician is an amateur who gradually forms his or her own version of traditional material, not a professional who cedes creative primacy to the figure of a master composer.

China has become a significant center for the composition and consumption of Western music in the past eighty years. A further instrumental solo illustrates a trend in new music in the twentieth century that accompanied the major social changes mentioned earlier. This is a piano piece by Liao Shengjing (b. 1930)

Piano Solos

Liao Shengjing's piano piece takes the same theme as Liu's composition, now transposed to the village sphere and entitled "The Joyous Festival of Lunar New Year's Day." This is the first of *Twenty-four Preludes for Piano*, subtitled *Chinese Rural Scenes in 24 Solar Terms* (Active Listening 8.7).

Liao's piece exemplifies the socialist realist style that predominated in China from the 1940s until the early 1990s. The socialist realist movement, which Mao Zedong adopted from the Soviet Union, gave artists an important role in society. Their task was to inspire social change by providing positive images of the new society toward which reform aimed, perhaps contrasting these with negative images of the past. Art was not to be created for art's sake—this slogan was criticized as a smokescreen offered by middle-class artists who wished to foist their

ACTIVE LISTENING 8.7
"Li Chun: XinnianJiajie" ("The Joyous Festival of Lunar New Year's Day")

COUNTER NUMBER	SECTION	PART (MEASURES)	COMMENTARY
0:00	A	First part	Opening figure switches from simple to compound duple time in measure five.
			Despite some chromatic notes, the music is in C major. A program note on the score says the music represents a village band merrily playing, and people enjoying the festive atmosphere.
0:11		Second part	Repeats and develops the earlier material.
0:21		Third part	Repeats and develops the earlier material, this time without switching to compound duple meter.
0:28	B		Softer music with a shift to G minor.
0:53	A		Repeats section A. The first two parts are repeated exactly as before; the third part is modified to lead to a loud ending.

own class-based values onto the ordinary people, thereby obstructing real social change. Instead, novels, movies, plays, poems, and music were to be open to the understanding of everyday people. For several decades, students and professionals in the arts were regularly sent to work on the land or in factories and barracks, seeking the comments and suggestions of ordinary people on draft versions of new compositions. The socialist realist style was also applied to new music composed for reformed versions of Chinese traditional instruments.

The happy village scene described in Liao's piece fits the requirement of providing a positive image of life under socialism. The short duration and simple, ABA plan creates music an untrained listener can immediately comprehend and follow. The same can be said of its predominantly tonal orientation.

From another perspective, though, solo piano music like this has close ties to European classical music. There are sets of twenty-four piano preludes by Hummel, Chopin, and Debussy, the number twenty-four allowing the composer to explore each major and minor key in turn. (The equal-tempered piano, of course, is an ideal tool for this kind of exploration.) Liao's set is exploratory, too, but he employs not the twenty-four major and minor keys of Western music but a set of twenty-four pentatonic-based modes that he developed after investigating Chinese pentatonic modal systems in 1985. Liao's preludes reflect his search for a new system of composing music that is both inherently Chinese and also intrinsically modern. And while the title of the music calls to mind the positive imagery important in social realism, the set also points back to presocialist Chinese tradition: Each prelude takes the name of one of the twenty-four phases of the lunar calendar. Much music created in present-day China draws similarly on multiple sources of inspiration.

Religious Traditions

We have already encountered one specifically religious tradition—the music of the *beiguan* ensemble—and several other musics already described have connections with China's religious culture. This short section marks the continued existence—in some cases, the resurgence or transformation—of religious musics in China today.

Communist-led reforms in the middle years of the twentieth century considerably affected the large sphere of Buddhist music. Some reforms were positive, such as the new state supporting researchers who investigated and recorded Buddhist musicians. Many, though, were negative. For example, a large-scale movement against superstition had monks persecuted and forcibly dismissed from their posts. Many temples today struggle to maintain their activities, which traditionally included frequent chanting and, in some cases, instrumental ensemble performance. Some ceremonies were large-scale, elaborate affairs that required numerous participants and lasted over a week. Faced with Communist suppression, some monks moved to Taiwan, a migration that fired a renewal of Buddhist traditions there. A few Buddhists already in pre-Communist Shanghai had begun to disseminate a new kind of Buddhist art music outside the temples. In Taiwan, a Buddhist music industry arose, and its commercial products now range from recordings of chants and rituals to New Age–inflected music and DVDs of large-scale dance extravaganzas.

Instead of delving further into Buddhist religious music, however, we look here at a smaller-scale example that hints at the variety of religious music in the Chinese world. This is an excerpt from *Pasibutbut* singing from the Bunun people who inhabit central Eastern Taiwan. All the examples so far have featured the music of the Han Chinese majority; this excerpt contributes the sounds of one of the many ethnic minority groups across this region. Like many indigenous peoples worldwide who depend on agriculture and hunting (rather than trade) for their food, the Bunun have traditionally prayed for good harvests and good fortune in the hunt. Certain of these prayers have been enhanced by being set to music, and since both agriculture and hunting are group acts, the prayers are sung collectively.

Listen to *Pasibutbut,* or "Prayer for a Rich Millet Harvest." Sung in ritual agricultural or hunting contexts at the start of the New Year, the *Pasibutbut* involves six or more men who don traditional robes and face inward, placing their arms around one another's backs (Figure 8.11). They may also revolve slowly as a group while singing. The overall pitch rises very slowly, and the music forms an offering designed to satisfy the Sky God, Dehanin. One Bunun singer told me (in March 2006) that song should be "stable, like a mountain going up to the sky." The Bunun recognize four different vocal parts in the group, each of which can be taken by multiple singers and plays a distinct role in the musical prayer (Active Listening 8.8).

Like many other of Taiwan's indigenous peoples, the Bunun are now heavily influenced by Christian proselytizing, and according to some sources an estimated 25 percent of Taiwan's indigenous peoples attend church. The Bunun village where I lived for two months has two churches, both well attended. However, it was clear that the church has not served merely as a force for change. The industrialization of Taiwan during the latter half of the twentieth century saw considerable numbers of younger Bunun migrate to the towns and cities. There was little demand for speakers of Bunun language in those locations, and urban schools did not provide mother-language teachers until recently. Language loss among the younger generations has become a serious issue, and some village communities now lack the younger and

Figure 8.11

Bunun men from Haiduan district performing the *Pasibutbut.* Taidong, 2005. *C. Chiener.*

ACTIVE LISTENING 8.8
Excerpt from *Pasibutbut* ("Prayer for a Rich Millet Harvest")

COUNTER NUMBER	COMMENTARY
0:00	First voice enters with an "oh" sound, quickly followed by a second voice a fifth lower singing "eh."
0:06	Third voice enters to "oh," close in pitch to the first; a fourth voice enters singing "eh" a fifth above.
0:13	One voice sings an octave above the starting pitch, quickly falling back to a fifth above—this is a way of marking the climax of a phrase.
0:17	New series of entries; the overall pitch has now slipped up a semitone, one of the special characteristics of this singing style.
0:33	Notice the overlapping entries of voices—the music never falls completely silent.
0:58	A voice farther from the microphone marks the climax of a phrase; again the music slips up a semitone.

MindTap
🎧 **WATCH** a video of a live performance of *Pasibutbut* online.

middle generations so vital for social cohesion and cultural continuity. In this environment, many churches have become community-based cultural centers, using their premises for language education, the promotion of traditional music, and the sustenance of community spirit, as well as for direct Christianization through worship.

Popular Music

Popular music now is strongly established across much of the Chinese world, although the timeline of process differs markedly by location. You can locate much of this music, and a large amount of material relating to it, by searching the internet. Among Chinese commentators, the relationship between national and international ingredients in the music has generated great interest. Meanwhile, many Westerners have looked into the relationship between rock music and politics.

Historians date Chinese popular music to the 1930s. This decade saw the rise of a film industry in China, centered in Shanghai. Popular music was strongly associated with Chinese film almost from its beginning. The roots of film song lay largely in the ballroom and cabaret music of Shanghai's entertainment industry in the 1920s. Many film songs were performed by a small band using idioms influenced by jazz and Tin Pan Alley to accompany a mostly pentatonic vocal melody sung in Mandarin by a female film star, such as Zhou Xuan (1918 or 1920–1957; Figure 8.12).

Salient Characteristics of
Chinese Popular Song

- Reemerged in mainland China in the last thirty-five years after two generations of absence

- Strong music industry roots in Hong Kong and Taiwan

- Now a major force exporting popular music to much of the rest of Asia and worldwide

Figure 8.12
Zhou Xuan in a 1930s publicity photo. *Jonathan P. J. Stock*

Music like this was all but swept away after 1949 in mainland China, to be replaced by the more martial strains of massed song and by further developments of the nationalistic songs already mentioned. The latter were infused with yet more patriotic intensity and increasingly came to be sung by members of state-run entertainment ensembles. Like the earlier film music, these songs were widely broadcast; they still occupied much of the public entertainment sphere in the early 1990s. Unlike the film songs, though, they did not compete in a commercial market for audiences. Instead, they played a prominent role in the sound-world the state produced to teach its citizens roles and feelings appropriate to their lives in socialist China.

The popular music industry shifted to Taiwan and Hong Kong. There, Shanghai-derived film music gradually changed through contact with new trends in Western and Japanese popular music, by the rise of new production techniques, and by the region's changing commercial opportunities. In Hong Kong, for instance, singers initially dropped Mandarin in favor of Cantonese, because this was the native language for most in Hong Kong. Later, with the rise of television, soap operas played a major role in popularizing certain types of songs and their singers. Recently, Korean soaps have become much admired across Chinese-language television networks, leading to a growing Chinese interest in Korean singers and songs. Film remains a significant part of the equation as well, and many of the most prominent singers of Cantopop (Cantonese-language pop song) are prominent movie stars. Examples from the 1980s and 1990s include Jacky Cheung, Andy Lau, Anita Mui, and Faye Wong. Meanwhile, from about 1980, the gradual reintegration of the mainland as a market saw many singers produce Mandarin versions of their songs for sale there as well as Cantonese versions for sale in Hong Kong; sales of the former now far exceed those of the latter.

The return of popular music to the mainland cities coincided with a gradual decline of state-sponsored music and a regrowth of a commercial music industry within China. Among the new, local styles were the *xibeifeng* ("Northwest wind" or "Northwest style"), which featured a deliberately rough, solo, vocal timbre suggestive of northwestern Chinese folk singing, along with lyrics that commented not so much on romance (as in songs from Hong Kong and Taiwan) or on a positive political message (as in state-supported light music), but on the hardships of contemporary life.

Although rock has yet to become part of the musical mainstream in China, many commentators outside of China have written about the rock singer Cui Jian. His brand of Chinese rock, including his rough vocal style, became deeply associated with prodemocracy protests, which sparked military suppression in 1989. Cui denied that his songs criticized government policies, but his co-opting of many of the most potent symbols of the Chinese revolution (red flags, the long march, and so on) clearly raises interpretations that extend beyond the meanings government authorities habitually accorded to those symbols. Moreover, his use of pronouns rather than actual names in certain songs means that a line like "But you always laugh at me," from the song "I Have Nothing," might be taken by different listeners as either a reference to a troubled personal relationship or a complaint about the attitude of the ruling authorities.

The speed with which young people across the country adopted such styles, and the depth of affection they generated, worried government officials. The ideological positions of some songs seemed to them to be potentially damaging to younger listeners' moral outlook, and thus to the socialist state. On the other hand, these same officials wanted China's music industry to become economically self-supporting, and they recognized that this meant that record companies had to be allowed to sell music that people wanted to buy. An outright ban would simply alienate the youth, who would then duplicate and share cassette copies anyway; only the state's music industry would lose out. Their solution has been to allow nearly all music, whether home-produced or imported, to be distributed and sold, but to restrict access to the state-run broadcast media for genres that they view with suspicion (such as rock).

Figure 8.13
Cover of Winnie Hsin's CD featuring the song "Scent."
Jonathan P. J. Stock

Over the longer term, government campaigns against spiritual pollution have faltered. In 1994, for example, the highly sentimental song "Scent" won a major, mainland song prize. Performed by the Taiwanese singer Winnie Hsin (Xin Xiaoqi; Figure 8.13), this song well represents the sentimental mainstream of popular music at that time.

Quite a few websites describe this song using adjectives like "touching" to refer to its emotional world. When the song was released, Hsin emphasized an autobiographical aspect, putting forward an account of her relationship with a man who treated her badly but whom she could not get out of her system. While there is no reason to doubt her, the story allows her to claim an emotional authenticity that establishes this as her own song, not simply one written for her to perform (see Active Listening 8.9). This staking of a personal claim will be familiar to many listeners to Western popular music. Singers there also put themselves forward as "emotional experts" whose primary task is not to recount dramatic action but to explore deeply an emotional state. Contrast this with many kinds of African popular music in which the singer is a "moral expert," a wise man or woman who advises the listener on how best to act in the difficult situations life generates.

The song's music reinforces the compulsive, self-destructive love revealed in the lyrics and described by Hsin in interviews. Instrumentation, blend, and vocal–instrumental balance are carefully deployed to mold a soft, dream-like shell around the singer's perfectly formed voice, embracing it and protecting it by sealing off the outside world. This obsessive reverie—in which a singer lovingly catalogs the traces of her lost love rather than taking action to set matters right—is exactly the kind of emotional state that the Communist Party officials had described as unhealthy. It also, of course, makes the song a suitable vehicle for karaoke performance, one of the main ways in which songs like this are popularized across the Chinese-speaking world. By stepping into Hsin's place in karaoke performance, other women put themselves forward as maltreated but unfaltering lovers.

ACTIVE LISTENING 8.9
"Weidao" ("Scent")

♫ **LISTEN TO**
"Weidao," performed by
Winnie Hsin online.

COUNTER NUMBER	SECTION	LYRICS	TRANSLATION
0:00	Instrumental introduction		
0:33	Verse	*Jintian wanshang de xingxing hen shao, Bu zhi dao tamen pao na qu liao.*	This evening the stars are very few, I don't know where they have run off to.
		Chiluoluo de tiankong, xingxing duo jiliao.	An empty sky, where the stars are so lonesome.
		Wo yiwei shang xin keyi hen shao, Wo yiwei wo neng guode hen hao.	I thought my sorrow would get less, I thought I could get through this.
		Shei zhidao yixiang ni sinian ku wu yao, Wu chu ke tao.	Who could know my every thought is of you, I long for you so bitterly, I can't escape from it.
1:17	Chorus	*Xiangnian nide xiao, Xiangnian nide waitao, Xiangnian ni baise wazi, He ni shenshang de weidao. Wo xiangnian nide wen, He shouzhi dandan yancao weidao. Jiyizhong ceng bei'aide weidao*	I miss your smile, I miss your coat. I miss your white socks, and your body's aroma. I miss your kiss, and the light tobacco smell on your fingers. The once-beloved scent is in my memory.

MindTap·

🎧 **WATCH** a video of the
Twelve Girls Band online.

This example illustrates how the twentieth century saw the rise of many new opportunities for female musicians and performers. Prominent for more than a decade, is an ensemble called the Twelve Girls Band (Figure 8.14). Formed in June 2001, it includes graduates of several of the capital's top conservatories and colleges. It is one of several groups to have established a niche within the popular music market through playing electronically mediated arrangements on Chinese instruments such as *erhu, zheng, pipa,* and *dizi.* Many of the band's works are available on CD and DVD, as well as online. Even here, the long shadow of China's historical past is clear. The Twelve Girls Band uses a classical term (*yuefang*) for the word *band,* which reminds the Chinese speaker of the imperial court entertainers of the ancient past. Despite the rhythm section, electric bass, lightshow, updated costuming, and elements of virtuosic display, the instrumental arrangements lie close indeed to the style of the social realist compositions described earlier. This has not limited the success of similar groups overseas. The case of the Twelve Girls Band illustrates the ongoing internationalization of contemporary musics from China. Clearly, music is actively flowing from China to the outside world.

Figure 8.14
Stage photo of some members of the Twelve Girls Band from the *Beautiful Energy* DVD (JSCP 2003).

Chinese Music/World Music?

At the outset of this chapter, I commented that few musical features are both uniquely and universally Chinese. The examples given bear this out: We cannot set all or most Chinese music apart from other music around the world simply by analyzing sonic elements. The same is true for sectional pieces with pictorial titles, and for Chinese instruments (many of which occur in various forms across East and Southeast Asia). Neither can we define Chinese music tidily on simple geographic terms. As the last examples of popular music emphasize, the roots of much of China's contemporary entertainment arose outside the borders of the People's Republic of China, while performers like the Twelve Girls Band tour worldwide. The same was true in centuries past, which saw widespread musical exchanges, albeit at a slower pace.

We nevertheless encounter in the social world a *concept* of Chinese music, as occurs when Chinese people try to explain what distinguishes their musical lives from those of other peoples. In so doing, they refer not only to sonic and geographic characteristics but also to contexts and usages of performance, and to the emotional and social content generated through acts of music making. Their comments often involve comparison—as in "Chinese music is like this, foreign music is like that,—and they put forward a statement that is as much about the qualities and experiences of life as about music. Here we return to the model of yin and yang, but this time on two levels. On the first, "music" and "life" are opposed but

MindTap*

PRACTICE your understanding of this chapter's concepts by reviewing flashcards and working once more with the chapter's Active Listening Guides online.

inherently interlinked, and any account of the specific sound materials of Chinese music necessarily reflects Chinese life more generally. On the second, "China" is opposed to but conceived in direct acknowledgment of "the foreign." From this perspective, studying Chinese music allows us to gain insight into Chinese life and also to occupy a vantage point from which to comment on trends in global musical culture.

MindTap°

DO an online quiz that your instructor may assign for a grade.

Study Questions

1. Discuss Chinese folk song. Is it dying out today?

2. What four skills are fundamental to the performance art of Beijing opera?

3. Compare two genres to show how political affairs impacted on creativity and performance in the first three decades of Communist rule in mainland China.

4. Using the internet, compare the Chinese rock singer Cui Jian with the Taiwanese singer Zhou Jielun (sometimes called Jay Chou).

5. What are the musical implications of tonal languages?

6. Why can we say that today the piano is a Chinese instrument?

7. Who are the Twelve Girls Band? What do they do, musically speaking?

8. Why did Marquis Wen more than two thousand years ago find ancient music boring, and what has changed in our listening attitudes since then?

9. Why is the *qin* designed to be so soft in sound?

10. How is *beiguan* music sponsored and organized in contemporary Taiwan?

9

South America/Chile, Bolivia, Ecuador, Peru

John M. Schechter

Learning Objectives

After you have studied this chapter, you should be able to:

1. Assess "El aparecido" within the *Nueva Canción* movement in Latin America and within larger traditions of Latin American song.

2. Discuss major traditional aspects of northern Ecuadorian highland Quichua material culture, ecology, and music-culture.

continued

3. Discuss the sound and style of the Andean music ensemble, and propose reasons for its transnational appeal.

4. Define a musical hybrid, and suggest why such hybrids are encountered frequently in Latin American music.

5. Assess the relationship between music and daily life in Latin America. What can music tell us about people's daily experiences and emotions?

Latin America is a kaleidoscope of cultural and ecological patterns, producing myriad distinctive, regional lifeways. It comprises a continent and a half, with more than twenty different countries in which Spanish, Portuguese, French, and dozens of Native American languages in hundreds of dialects are spoken. It is at once the majestic, beautiful Andes mountains, the endless emptiness of the Peruvian-Chilean desert, and the lush rain forests of the huge Amazonian basin. Native American cultures that were not eradicated by European diseases have in many cases retained distinctive languages, belief systems, dress, musical forms, and music rituals. Most Latin American cultures, though, share a common heritage of Spanish or Portuguese colonialism and American and European cultural influences. For instance, several ports in Colombia and Brazil served as major colonial centers for the importation of black slaves; Latin America thus remains a rich repository of African and African American music-culture traditions, including rituals, musical forms and practices, and types of musical instruments.

In Latin American culture, mixture is the norm, not the exception. When you walk through the countryside of Ecuador, for example, you hear a Spanish dialect borrowing many words from Quichua, the regional Native American language. The local Quichua dialect, conversely, uses many Spanish words. South of Ecuador, in the high mountain regions of Peru, the harp is considered an indigenous instrument, although in fact European missionaries and others brought it to Peru. In rural areas of Atlantic coastal Colombia, musicians sing songs in Spanish, using Spanish literary forms, but these are accompanied by African-style drums and rhythms, and by Amerindian flutes and rattles. In northern highland Ecuador, African Ecuadorians perform the *bomba*, a type of song that features African American rhythms, Quichua Indian melodic and harmonic features, and Spanish language—with sometimes one or two Quichua words. Overall, it is hard to maintain strict cultural divisions because the intermingling of Iberian (Spanish and Portuguese), African, and Native American strains is so profound in the Latin American experience.

When you first think of Latin American music, you might hear in your mind's ear the vibrancy of salsa rhythms. There is an enormous variety of beaten and shaken rhythm instruments, such as claves, bongos, congas, and maracas, both in salsa and throughout

Salient Characteristics of
Latin America

- A continent and a half of more than twenty different countries with dozens of different languages, including Naïve American dialects

- A diverse geography that includes the Andes Mountains, the Amazon Basin, and the Peruvian-Chilean deserts

- Merging of Iberian (Spanish and Portuguese), African, and Native American cultures

- A common heritage among Latin American cultures of Spanish/Portuguese colonialism, along with U.S., European, and Native American influences

- Diversity and heritage reflected in enormous variety of regional and local musics

Latin American music. In distinctive sizes and shapes, the guitar figures prominently in Latin American folk music. In Peru and Bolivia, for example, a type of guitar called the **charango** (cha-*ran*-go) may have as its body the shell of an armadillo. There are other types of Latin American music with which you might also be familiar, including bossa nova, calypso, and tango.

Listen to "El aparecido" ("The Apparition"), paying attention to the lyrics, given in Active Listening 9.1 in Spanish with an English translation. The lyrics refer to a "son of rebellion," on the run and pursued. The language is very evocative; in one line this man, never named in the song directly, is compared with Christ ("crucified"). But it turns out that this person is not Jesus; instead, he is a well-known, Latin American revolutionary. Unlike much of the music in this book, "El aparecido" is a song of political protest. Written by Víctor Jara in 1967, "El aparecido" was dedicated "to E.(Ch.)G."—Ernesto Che Guevara, a soldier and activist who joined Fidel Castro's Cuban Revolution, became an official of the Cuban government, and then left to incite political revolution elsewhere. He was killed in Bolivia in 1967. Now famous in this interpretation by Inti-Illimani, the piece speaks of this revolutionary figure's eluding his pursuers; the music reaches a climactic point in its chorus: "*¡Córrele, córrele, correlá; córrele, que te van a matar; córrele, córrele, correlá!*" ("Run, run, run; run, for they are going to kill you; run, run, run!") (Schechter 1999b:428–29). We shall return to consider the music in more detail shortly.

In this chapter, we will take a close look at musics of four Latin American countries: Chile, Bolivia, Ecuador, and Peru. The seven pieces we will address speak eloquently to their own cultures' means for expressing profound grief, to their political concerns, to their "social" forms of music making (Andean panpipe playing), to their histories and ecologies, and, in one case, to the composer's autobiography. A central theme in several instances is that of praise and esteem for one's beloved.

🎵 **LISTEN TO**
"El aparecido," performed by the ensemble Inti-Illimani, from the album *Performs Víctor Jara* online.

Chilean *Nueva Canción*

We began with a contemporary, politically aware music: a powerful folk song composed in 1967 by a great figure in Chilean modern music, Víctor Jara (1938–1973). Jara became a great figure in the modern song movement, **Nueva Canción** (noo-*ay*-va kan-*syon*), or "New Song," of Chile—and, sometimes under a different genre name, of all Latin America. (See Jara 1984 for a full discussion of his life and career, including an accounting of his evolving political consciousness, in a biography written by his wife, Joan.)

Nueva Canción is a song movement through which people stand up for their own culture—for themselves as a people—in the face of oppression by a totalitarian regime, or in the face of cultural imperialism from abroad, notably from the United States and Europe. It developed first in the southern cone of South America—Argentina, Chile, and Uruguay—during the 1950s and 1960s, and it has since spread throughout

Salient Characteristics of
The *Nueva Canción*

- Songs, newly composed by singers and songwriters, employing elements of folksong style
- Lyrics are artful, metaphoric and symbolic, expressing solidarity with traditional values, culture, artisans, and the working classes
- Songs encourage citizens to stand up for their rights in the face of government oppression
- A protest song movement that began in the 1950s spread throughout Latin America

Latin America. As we know from U.S. history, the 1960s in particular witnessed violent upheavals. Latin America echoed the assassinations and urban violence in the United States. Nearly every country in South America, as well as Cuba and the Dominican Republic in the Caribbean, saw revolution, massacre, underground warfare, or other forms of violent social and political confrontation at that time. (For a fuller discussion of the philosophy, political contexts, songs, composers, and ensembles of Chilean *Nueva Canción*, Argentine *nuevo cancionero argentino*, and Cuban *nueva trova*, see Schechter 1999b:425–37, which incorporates study of several Víctor Jara songs, including "Preguntas por Puerto Montt," "Plegaria a un labrador," and "Despedimiento del angelito." You can find a discussion of Jara's song "El lazo" in Schechter 2002:388–91.)

Víctor Jara and Inti-Illimani

♪ LISTEN TO

"El aparecido," performed by the ensemble Inti-Illimani, from the album *Performs Víctor Jara,* online.

Let us listen more closely to one of Víctor Jara's compositions (Active Listening 9.1), "El aparecido" (ell a-pa-reh-*see*-doh), as interpreted here by the noted Chilean *Nueva Canción* ensemble Inti-Illimani (*Inti* = Quechua for "sun"; *Illimani* is the name of a mountain in Bolivia). Active Listening 9.1 provides the full text of "El aparecido" and illustrates the formal structure of this modern-day, composed Chilean *cueca* (*kweh*-ka).

When you listen to Inti-Illimani's version (formulated by that ensemble in 1971) of "El aparecido," you may wonder about the metrical rhythm of the piece (recall the discussion of rhythm and meter in Chapter 1). You may think that you hear the music at one moment in moderate meter, **1**-2-3, **1**-2-3—but at the next moment, in lively meter, **1**-2-3-**4**-5-6, **1**-2-3-**4**-5-6. This version of a traditional Chilean rhythm known as the *cueca* in fact juxtaposes these two types of metrical rhythm at the same time. When this occurs—and it happens in many types of Latin American folk song, from Mexico all the way down to Chile and in many countries in between—it is referred to as **sesquialtera metrical rhythm**: roughly, the simultaneous feeling of 3/4 and 6/8 meter. This metrical–rhythmical ambiguity is the heart and soul of much, though not all, Hispanic-derived Latin American regional folk music. You will hear it in Mexican *son huasteco*, in Colombian *bambuco*, in Ecuadorian *albazo*, in Peruvian *marinera*, in Argentinean *chacarera*, in Chilean/Bolivian *cueca*, and in many other genres as well.

In Active Listening 9.1, you may also wonder about the terms *major* and *minor key* (or *scale*). Chapter 1 explains the concept of the major scale, with the example of the C Major scale built on the consecutive white keys of the piano. Specifically, it noted that the interval between each pitch is not the same. It spoke of this Euro-American major scale, but also of the Javanese *sléndro* and *pélog* scales (see Chapter 7, as well). Different scale types reflect different organizing principles behind the relationships and sequence of their constituent pitches.

"El aparecido" uses variants of the minor scale as well as the major scale. The vocal stanzas and instrumental sections use two forms of the minor scale, while the refrain moves into different major keys, only to conclude on the minor home key. One will often encounter this mix of scales in traditional musics of the Andes region, including Chilean folk music; when Chilean *Nueva Canción* musicians compose contemporary interpretations of traditional musics, they reflect that cultural sensitivity to major and minor keys.

ACTIVE LISTENING 9.1
"El aparecido" ("The Apparition")*

COUNTER NUMBER	COMMENTARY	LYRICS	TRANSLATION
Introduction			
0:00	Ensemble enters in the song's minor home key, 6/8 meter. *Kena* (flute) plays melody and suggests the shape of the vocal stanzas to come.		
1st stanza			
0:10	*Sesquialtera* meter. *Kena* "tail" repeats opening segment of the introduction.	*Abre sendas por los cerros Deja su huella en el viento, El áuila le da el vuelo Y lo cobija el silencio.*	He opens pathways through the mountains, Leaves his mark on the wind, The eagle gives him flight And silence envelops him.
2nd stanza			
0:36		*Nunca se quejó del frío Nunca se quejó del sueño. El pobre siente su paso Y lo sigue como ciego.*	Never has he complained of the cold, Never has he complained of lack of sleep. The poor man senses his step And follows him like a blind man.
Refrain			
0:58	Melody changes to a major key; concludes in minor.	*¡Córrele, córrele, correlá, Por aquí, por aquí, por allá. ¡Córrele, córrele, correlá, Córrele, que te van a matar, Córrele, córrele, correlá, Córrele, que te van a matar, Córrele, córrele, correlá!*	Run, run, run, Here, here, over there. Run, run, run, Run or they'll kill you, Run, run, run, Run or they'll kill you, Run, run, run!
Instrumental interlude			
1:18	*Kena* repeats melody of introduction, with first three pitches an octave higher.		
3rd stanza			
1:29	Minor key. *Kena* "tail."	*Su cabeza es rematada Por cuervos con garra de oro: Como lo ha crucificado La furia del poderoso.*	His head is finished off By ravens with talons of gold: Like the fury of the powerful has crucified him.
4th stanza			
1:57	Minor key.	*Hijo de la rebeldía Lo siguen veinte más veinte. Porque regala su vida Ellos le quieren dar muerte.*	Son of rebellion Twenty, and twenty more pursue him. Because he offers his life They want his death.
Refrain			
2:17	Melody changes to major key; concludes in minor home key.		
Instrumental interlude			
2:37	Minor key. *Kena* repeats melody of Introduction, with first three pitches an octave higher.		

continued

COUNTER NUMBER	COMMENTARY	LYRICS	TRANSLATION
4th stanza repeats			
2:48	Background voices sing stanza in counterpoint with soloist.		
Refrain			
3:09	Major key. Concludes in the minor home key.		

*This Inti-Illimani version—music and text—can be found in Acevedo et al. (ca. 1996:118–23).

Note that in Active Listening 9.1, the word **counterpoint** refers to combining two or more melodic parts. On the repeat of stanza 4 ("Hijo de la rebeldía"), the voices divide, so that one group seems to "follow" the other, with the same text fragments, yet different melodic fragments; thus, we have an example of counterpoint—contrapuntal, or polyphonic, texture.

As noted earlier, the 1950s to 1970s in Latin America was a period of violent upheaval, witnessing the Plaza de Mayo massacre in Buenos Aires and the subsequent fall of Perón in Argentina (1955); the fall of Cuba's Batista government and the victorious Cuban Revolution (1959); the fall of the João Goulart government in Brazil (1964), beginning a fifteen-year, hard-line era; the U.S. intervention in Santo Domingo (1965); an increase in guerrilla activity in Peru, Colombia, and Bolivia; the death of Ernesto Che Guevara in Bolivia (1967); the subsequent spread of guerrilla fighting in Central America and Venezuela, and the Tlatelolco massacre in Mexico (1968); and the victory of the Unidad Popular in Chile (1970), initiating three years of government under Salvador Allende. In 1973, the elected Marxist government of President Allende was overthrown in a bloody coup. Allende and some 2,800 others lost their lives, hundreds disappeared, and thousands were jailed. On September 18, 1973, a young man ushered Joan Jara into the Santiago city morgue, where she found the body of her husband, Víctor Jara, "his chest riddled with holes and a gaping wound in his abdomen. His hands seemed to be hanging from his arms at a strange angle as though his wrists were broken" (Jara 1984:243). The singer who had cried out in word and song on behalf of "him who died without knowing why his chest was riddled, fighting for the right to have a place to live" ("Preguntas por Puerto Montt"), the singer whose songs had so often lauded eloquently the hands of his people (in "El lazo," "Angelita Huenumán," and "Plegaria a un labrador"), had met his fate—in a stroke of terrifying irony—with his own chest riddled with holes, his own hands made lifeless.

After the overthrow of Allende, the music of *Nueva Canción* was prohibited on the airwaves and removed from stores and destroyed. Certain prominent folkloric instruments associated with *Nueva Canción*, such as the *charango*, were also prohibited (Morris 1986:123). But many years later, after changes in political conditions, banished musicians were permitted to return to Chile.

Metaphor plays a major role in *Nueva Canción*. A **metaphor** is an assertion that one thing is also something else, a comparison that typically enhances meaning. So, here, in "El aparecido," Guevara is depicted as a mythological figure ("*Abre sendas ... en el viento*"), one of great power and respect ("*El águila le da el vuelo*");

one of mystery ("*lo cobija el silencio*"); and one pursued by many ("*Lo siguen veinte más veinte*") of the powerful, of the wealthy ("*Su cabeza es rematada/Por cuervos con garra de oro*")."El aparecido" falls within an established Latin American tradition of praising in song individuals—often being pursued—whom some might consider to be outlaws and by others to be heroes. Among the protagonists of the Mexico–Texas border **corrido** (ko-*rree*-do; ballad) tradition, one could point to "Gregorio Cortez" (Paredes 1958, 1976:31) and to two songs about Robin Hood figures, "Joaquín Murieta" and "Heráclio Bernal" (Schechter 1999a:8–10); a Robin Hood figure of twentieth-century Argentina is Juan Bautista Bairoleto (Moreno Chá 1999:267–70).

As to Inti-Illimani, they were victims of the 1973 Chilean coup. One of the original members, Horacio Salinas, recalls, "We were in Italy, on a three-month tour that lasted fifteen years. Against our will, we were very far from our country and alone with our music" (Manz 2005:27). They returned from Italy on Chile's Independence Day, September 18, 1988 (greeted by a crowd of some five thousand at the airport), after fifteen years in exile, during which they toured more than sixty countries (Ibid. 27, 28).

In February 1994, I heard them perform at the University of California at Berkeley. This concert showed how much the ensemble had evolved since a group of Santiago Technical University engineering students had created it in 1967. In addition to the familiar *Nueva Canción* panpipes, *charango*, and **kena** (*ke*-na; Andean vertical, notched flute), the seven-member aggregate now incorporated instruments native neither to Chile nor the Andes: hammered dulcimer and soprano saxophone. The ensemble's multi-instrumentalists now performed sophisticated, tailored arrangements, featuring contemporary, highly coloristic harmonizations of traditional Andean and Caribbean genres. In addition to their renowned version of "El aparecido," the group's repertoire in this highly polished performance was remarkably variegated, showcasing the breadth of Latin American (if elaborately disguised) forms: hocketing panpipes (see the discussion on *k'antu*, next), Peruvian *wayno* (discussed later), Venezuelan *joropo*, Chilean *cueca*, Ecuadorian *sanjuán* (discussed later), Cuban *son*, and Mexican *ranchera*. *Nueva Canción* lives on as an international movement. It has traditional and regional roots combined with a modern, socially conscious musical style and message. It seeks to draw attention to the people—often the forgotten people—and to their struggles for human dignity.

Bolivian *K'antu*

Certain *Nueva Canción* performers such as Inti-Illimani chose the **zampoña** (sam-*pon*-ya), or panpipes, among other traditional instruments, to symbolize their esteem for the native traditions of the Andes and neighboring regions. It is true that panpipes are widely known outside South America. Nevertheless, the depth of the panpipe tradition in South America is remarkable. Today, we can find a huge number of named varieties of panpipes among native peoples from Panama down to Peru, Bolivia, and Chile. In Peru and Bolivia, cultures dating back fifteen centuries knew and played panpipes of bamboo or clay.

Listen to "Kutirimunapaq" (koo-tee-ree-moo-*na*-pakh) as performed by Ruphay, a Bolivian ensemble. They are playing **k'antu** (k-*an*-tu), a type of ceremonial panpipe music from the altiplano, or high plateau, of Peru–Bolivia. The word *k'antu* might be related to a widely known flower of Bolivia, the *kantuta*, or it might be derived from the Spanish word for song, *canto*. Active Listening 9.2 illustrates the formal structure of this Bolivian *k'antu*.

ACTIVE LISTENING 9.2
"Kutirimunapaq" ("So That We Can Return")

COUNTER NUMBER	COMMENTARY
Introduction	
0:00	*Wankaras* (drums) and *ch'inisku* (triangle) only enter. Unmetered, gradually increasing tempo that tapers off.
1st full cycle—A section	
0:10	Full ensemble (multiple *zampoñas, wankaras; ch'inisku*).
0:26	Repeat. Characteristic rhythmic break just before cadence, and start of repeat each time through.
B section	
0:37	Full ensemble. Characteristic rhythmic break just before cadence.
0:53	Repeat.
1:06	Cadence, moves directly into C section.
C section	
1:07	Full ensemble.
1:12	Cadence (no break beforehand).
1:13	Immediate repeat.
1:19	Characteristic break at cadence, leading right back to beginning of A section and second full cycle.
2nd full cycle—A section	
1:20	Full ensemble (multiple *zampoñas, wankaras, ch'inisku*).
1:33	Characteristic rhythmic break just before cadence.
1:34	Repeat.
B section	
1:47	Full ensemble.
2:01	Characteristic rhythmic break just before cadence.
2:02	Repeat.
2:16	Cadence moving directly into C section.
C section	
2:16	Full ensemble.
2:21	Cadence (no rhythmic break beforehand) and immediate repeat.
2:27	Characteristic break at cadence, leading right back to beginning of A section and third full cycle.

COUNTER NUMBER	COMMENTARY
Third full cycle of A—C	
2:29	A section.
2:55	B section.
3:25	C section.
3:31	Repeat.
3:38	Final cadence: *Wankaras* and *ch'inisku* play unmetered/accelerando motif similar to outset.

The entire piece is played three times. Sing some of the melody to get a feel for the rhythm and flow of this *zampoña* music. On a second hearing, the sound may seem richer to you than on the first; you hear a panpipe ensemble playing what seems to be the same melody at various pitch levels, one at an octave below the original pitch level, another a perfect fourth above that lower octave, or a perfect fifth below the original octave.

"Kutirimunapaq" (Quechua for, roughly, "So That We Can Return") is music of the Kallawaya people, who live on the eastern slope of the Bolivian Andes, north of Lake Titicaca, close to the Peruvian border. The Kallawaya **campesinos** (farmers, peasants) live at different altitudes in the Charazani Valley—from 9,000 to 16,000 feet above sea level. Those at the lower elevations speak Quechua and cultivate potatoes, barley, and beans; at the upper elevations, they speak Aymara and keep llamas, alpacas, and sheep. The Incas adopted Quechua as their official language and spread it with them throughout their empire (1200–1533 c.e.). Today, from 5.5 million to 8 million Andeans in Bolivia, Peru, Ecuador, and Argentina speak Quechua (or Quichua), while a minority speak Aymara (Bastien 1978:xxi). "Kutirimunapaq" is a *k'antu* from the community of Niñokorin, at 11,000 feet.

The *k'antu* ensembles for which the Charazani region is famous (Baumann 1985) each comprise twenty to thirty *zampoña*-playing dancers, who move in a circular pattern. Some of them simultaneously beat a large, double-headed drum called a *wankara*. The triangle (in Quechua, *ch'inisku*) which we hear on this track is often present as well.

The Kallawaya play the panpipes in their dry season, which lasts roughly from June to September; they play transverse flutes (played horizontally, like the Western silver flute) or duct flutes (played vertically, and constructed like a recorder) during the rainy season, which lasts from November to at least late February. The preference on the altiplano for duct flutes during the rainy season may be related to the belief that their clear sound attracts rain and prevents frost, both of which are necessary conditions for growing crops.

Our ensemble consists of *zampoñas* of different sizes but with the same basic construction in terms of numbers of tubes. Each musical register is represented by one named pair of panpipes, consisting of an *ira* (*ee*-ra) set of pipes (considered in the Bolivian altiplano to embody the male principle, and serving as the leader) and an **arca** (*ar*-ka) set of pipes (considered to embody the female principle and serving as the follower). In our context, the *ira* set has six pipes and the *arca* set has seven; we may refer to this type as 6/7-tubed. The different instruments play the same melody, which results in the rich musical fabric of parallel octaves, fifths, and fourths.

There are at least two especially interesting aspects of this music. One is the doubling of the melodic line; the other is the way a melody is produced. Doubling the melody at a fixed interval has occurred at other times, in other places. One was in Europe during the Middle Ages. There, by the ninth century, one-line Christian liturgical chant was being accompanied either by one lower part at the octave below or by a lower part at the fourth or fifth below. Another alternative augmented the two-voice complex to three or four voices by doubling one or both lines at the octave. Thus, early medieval Europe had musical textures with parallel octaves, fourths, and fifths very similar in intervallic structure (if not in rhythm) to what we hear in twentieth-century Bolivian *k'antu*. In twentieth-century Africa, songs in parallel fourths and fifths are found among groups that have the tradition of pentatonic, or five-pitch, songs, such as the Gogo people of Tanzania (a good example of a Gogo song in parallel fourths and fifths appears in Nketia 1974:163).

Many peoples have used, and continue to use, the performance practice of **hocketing**: The melody is dispersed among two or more voices or instruments; when one sounds, the others do not. Performing music in hocket is a uniquely communal way of making music: You cannot play the entire melody yourself—you need one or more partners to do it with you. In Africa, the hocketing technique appears among instrumental traditions, in the flute parts of Ghanaian Kasena *jongo* dance music, in the *akadinda* xylophone music of the Baganda of Uganda, and in several flute and gourd-trumpet traditions elsewhere in eastern and southern Africa; for vocal traditions, hocketing can be heard in the singing of the San (Bushmen) of southern Africa (Koetting 1992:94–97). Certain European music of the thirteenth and fourteenth centuries had several parts but used notes and rests in a way that effectively divided the melody line between two voice parts: as one sounded, the other was silent. A hiccupping effect was thus created (*hoquetus* is Latin for "hiccup" and the likely derivation of the term *hocket*). Hocketing with panpipes appears closer in time and space to modern Bolivian music. In Panama, the Kuna Indians play six-tubed *guli* panpipes. Each person holds one tube, with the melody distributed among all six players. The Kuna also play *gammu burui* pan-

Figure 9.1

Left: Seven-tubed *arca* rank.
Right: Six-tubed *ira* rank.

pipes. Each fourteen-tubed set is bound into two groups, or rafts, of seven tubes (two rafts each of four tubes and three tubes, held side by side). The melody is distributed between the two seven-tubed players in hocketing technique (Smith 1984:156–59, 167–72).

As among the Kuna, in Bolivian *k'antu* the hocketing procedure is integral to the overall musical fabric. In fact, hocketing is actually required by the way these panpipes are constructed. Although altiplano panpipes can range from three to seventeen tubes, a widely used type is 6/7-tubed—that is, the "total" instrument has thirteen tubes, consisting of one line, or rank, of six tubes (the *ira*) and one rank of seven tubes (the *arca*), as we have seen.

When the full instrument is combined (six- and seven-tubed ranks joined together or played by two people), we have a thirteen-tubed, e minor scale over the space of an octave and a half (Figure 9.2).

As show in Active Listening 9.2, the formal structure of this performance of "Kutirimunapaq" is ABC, each section being repeated, then the entire piece repeated twice, for a total of three times. This is a characteristic structure for the Bolivian *k'antu*, accommodating the continuous dancing that goes with the music making.

This *k'antu* is primarily five-pitch, or pentatonic. Many traditional dance musics in the Andes region are similarly pentatonic, though certainly not all of them. "Kutirimunapaq" is strongly rhythmic, with the steady pound of the *wankara* supporting the beat. Andean dance music, from Bolivia up to Ecuador, has this powerful, rhythmic cast underscoring its dance function.

Hocketing panpipes, with rhythmic melodies played in parallel fifths and octaves and with a strong, steady rhythm on a large drum, begin to distinguish this Bolivian altiplano stream of Latin American music. The evocation of indigenous cultures such as this high-Andean one, through the use of Andean instruments, begins to demarcate *Nueva Canción*. As we have seen, New Song is not only nostalgic but also politically committed and international. Above all, it speaks of and on behalf of the people—characteristically, the forgotten people.

We now turn our attention north of Chile, Bolivia, and Peru to a nation of many other unsung (or less-sung) individuals and peoples, a country itself frequently overlooked in discussions of Latin America: Ecuador.

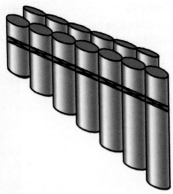

Figure 9.2
Thirteen-tubed *zampoña*.

The Quichua of the Northern Andes of Ecuador

We can best appreciate the traditional nature of northern Ecuadorian Quichua music by knowing something of the traditional setting in which Quichua live. The musicians we will be listening to have traditionally lived in **comunas**, or small clusters of houses, on the slopes of Mount Cotacachi, one of several volcanoes in the Ecuadorian Andes. These *comunas* lie outside the town of Cotacachi, in Imbabura Province.

The Quichua spoken in Cotacachi-area *comunas* was spoken there four hundred years ago. Today in Ecuador, more than one million people speak the language.

The agriculture and material culture of the Andes around Cotacachi are also traditional. In this rich, green countryside dotted with tall eucalyptus, at 8,300 to 9,700 feet above sea level, maize has been the principal cultivated crop for hundreds of years. Quichua homes

Salient Characteristics of
The Quichua and Their Music

- A traditional people who share a common language, agricultural life, and similar material culture

- Live in small clusters of houses (*comunas*) on the slopes of the northern Andes of Ecuador

- The importance of walking is both real and symbolic in the culture, as reflected in the songs and their texts

- *Sanjuanes*, the traditional song of harpists and musical timekeepers, play inside and out of Quichua communities at weddings, private masses, and children's wakes

Figure 9.3

Home of Mama Ramona and Miguel Armando in the *comuna* of Tikulla, outside Cotacachi. May 1980. Today, homes made of concrete block are replacing this older type of dwelling. *John M. Schechter.*

have typically had one room, often with a covered patio, both with dirt floors. Regional Quichua homes have been constructed this way for four hundred years. One such home is shown in Figure 9.3.

Styles of dress have also remained basically the same since the sixteenth century. Everyone covers his or her head to protect it from the intense heat and light of the near-vertical sun at midday. (Cotacachi is almost precisely on the equator.) Women wear cloths, and men wear hats. Quichua women wear embroidered blouses, over which they drape shawls (in Quichua, *fachalina*). They secure their two skirts, one blue and one white, with two woven belts: a wider, inner belt, called the *mama chumbi* (mother belt) and a narrower, outer belt, called the *wawa chumbi* (child belt).

Figure 9.4

Three generations of Quichua men. May 1980. *John M. Schechter.*

Designed in this region, these belts were traditionally woven on home back-strap looms by Quichua families in various *comunas,* and they usually carried the names of Imbabura towns. Men and boys have traditionally worn a white or blue shirt, white pants, and a dark *poncho,* though today in Imbabura you will see Quichua teenagers wearing sweatshirts and jeans emblazoned with English logos. Any large gathering of Quichua—such as for the Saturday market or the Palm Sunday procession—is still largely a sea of blue and white. In Figure 9.4, we see three generations within the same family. The grandfather wears traditional dress; his adult son retains the white sandals, white shirt, pants, and hat; his grandson wears Western-influenced clothes.

Among Cotacachi Quichua, a strong sense of community arises from a common regional dialect, a common dress, and common aspects of material culture. Quichua eat the same diet of beans and potatoes, grown in their own plots. They gather regularly for weekly markets, for periodic community work projects (*mingas*), and for fiestas—such as a child's wake or a wedding. We will discuss harp/vocal music at the Cotacachi-area child's wake later in this chapter. Further, I have examined the ubiquity of the festive child's wake in Latin America in other works (Schechter 1983, 1994a); you can also read of harp performance in the celebration of a Cotacachi-area Quichua wedding, held in October 1990, in Andrade Albuja and Schechter (2004).

In 1980, few Cotacachi Quichua owned vehicles; by 1990, a few community leaders possessed new pickup trucks. In any case, Quichua homes on Cotacachi's slopes are for the most part not located on roads but interspersed along a network of footpaths called **chaki ñanes** (*cha*-ki *nyan*-es). Without telephones, Quichua families have traditionally communicated only by foot, along *chaki ñanes;* these paths bear the weight of Quichua women carrying infants, brush, and food to and from market, and of Quichua men carrying potatoes, milled grain, or perhaps a harp (Figure 9.5). For all Quichua, the way around the slopes on *chaki ñanes* is second nature.

The Musical Tradition: *Sanjuán*

The common language, dress, material culture, and daily labor all find a musical echo in *sanjuán*. The term **sanjuán** (san-*hooan*) arose at least as early as 1860. At that time, it referred to either a type of song played at the festival of St. John (San Juan) the Baptist held in June or a type of dance performed at that festival.

Today, the instrument that Cotacachi Quichua often use to perform *sanjuán* is the harp without pedals, often referred to in English as the diatonic harp because it is usually tuned to one particular scale and cannot be changed quickly to another. Reflecting their other deep-rooted traditions, Quichua have been playing the harp

Figure 9.5
Chaki ñan (Ecuadorian footpath). May 1980. *John M. Schechter.*

Figure 9.6

Harpist Raúl, playing his Imbabura harp. Ecuador, March 1980. *John M. Schechter.*

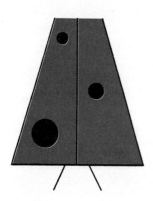

Figure 9.7

Schematic diagram showing the position of sound holes in an Imbabura harp.

in the Ecuadorian highlands for hundreds of years; in the eighteenth century, it was the most common instrument in the region (Recio [1773] 1947:426). The harp's popularity in the Andes is not limited to Ecuador; recall that in the Peruvian highlands, it is so widespread among Quechua that it is considered a "native" instrument. Brought from Europe initially by several different groups of missionaries, especially the Jesuits, and even by the first conquistadors, the harp has been in Latin America for more than four hundred years.

The Imbabura harp, seen and heard here, is common only in Imbabura Province (Figure 9.6). It appears as an oddity among harpists in central highland Ecuador, where musicians play a larger instrument. The harp Raúl plays is made of cedar and uses wooden nails. The sound emanates through three circular holes on the top of the sound box; they are consistently found in the pattern shown in Figure 9.7, on either side of the column, or pole, that connects the neck to the sound box.

You may think Raúl's harp has an unusual shape, compared with Western harps with which you may be familiar. The Imbabura harp's column is straight but short, giving the instrument a low "head," or top. Its sound box is distinctively arched, wide, and deep. On older harps in this region, bull's-hoof glue was used. The tuning pegs are made of iron or wood. The single line of strings is typically a combination of gut, possibly nylon, and steel. The gut strings—used for the bass and middle registers—used to be made by the Quichua themselves from the cut, washed, dried, and twisted intestinal fibers of sheep, dogs, cats, or goats. Sometimes musicians use nylon strings for the middle register, or range, of notes. The steel strings, closest to the performer, play the treble register, in which the melody line is articulated. Once again relying on their environment for necessary materials, Quichua musicians may use the leg bone of the sheep (Quichua: *tullu*, "bone") to turn the tuning pegs on the harp neck.

This Imbabura harp is a descendant of sixteenth- and seventeenth-century Spanish harps, as shown by shared features of tuning, construction, configuration, and stringing. The Imbabura harp has remained essentially unchanged in appearance for one to two hundred years, and possibly longer (Schechter 1992).

Let us now look at the *sanjuán* "Muyu muyari warmigu" ("Please Return, Dear Woman") in Active Listening 9.3, sometimes referred to as "Chayamuyari warmigu" ("Come Here, Indeed, Dear Woman"). This performance is by the highly esteemed Cotacachi-area harpist, Efraín, together with one of his favored singers, Rafael. Having worked with Efraín ten years earlier, in the environs of Cotacachi (see Schechter 2002:405–11), I was pleased to renew our acquaintanceship in 1990. We met to plan the recording session, which would be held in a classroom of the same primary school on Cotacachi's slopes at which my wife and I had resided from October 1979 through April 1980; this stereophonic recording of "Muyu," along with other pieces for harp and voice, took place on October 13, 1990.

Harpists play the higher, or treble strings (treble clef part) with their stronger hand; the lower, or bass, strings (bass clef part) with their weaker hand. Efraín, left-handed, plays treble with the left hand, bass with the right hand (Figure 9.8).

In general, the form of "Muyu muyari warmigu" is typical of Cotacachi Quichua *sanjuanes.* It is fundamentally a repetitive form, in which one or two different phrases, typically contrasting in register, are occasionally inserted into an otherwise similar phrase pattern. In *sanjuán,* the main motive predominates; these are the ones you hear the most, which I refer to as A phrases in "Muyu." These are the melodies one identifies with a particular *sanjuán.* The *sanjuán* phrase often lasts 8 beats, and the rhythm of the first half of the phrase is often identical, or nearly identical, to the rhythm of the second half; we can call this phrase structure, then, **isorhythm**—of "equal rhythm," or the "same rhythm." Here, in "Muyu," the rhythm of the first half of the A phrase is Ta Ta Ta-Ta, Ta Ta Ta Ta; the rhythm of the second half of the phrase is exactly the same: Ta Ta Ta-Ta, Ta Ta Ta Ta. Active Listening 9.3 provides the full text of "Muyu" and illus-

Figure 9.8
Rafael (tapping the *golpe*) and Efraín (playing the Imbabura harp), during the recording of "Muyu muyari warmigu." Mt. Cotacachi, Ecuador, 1990. *John M. Schechter.*

trates its formal structure. *Sanjuanes* are most often in double-couplets: one two-line verse is stated, then immediately repeated; then, another double-couplet or a harp interlude.

As you can hear and can see in Active Listening 9.3, the A phrase predominates in this song. The consecutive A phrases (by harp alone and by harp and voice) are varied by two B phrases, in the harp. Most *sanjuanes* follow this general pattern, although perhaps less regularly, with A phrases predominating and sometimes without any B phrases at all. The A phrases are supported largely by E major, while concluding on its relative minor, c minor; in terms of key relationships, relative major and their own relative minor keys carry identical key signatures (here, three flats for E major and c minor) and the same basic collection of pitches; the relative minor key takes as its home-note the sixth scale degree of its relative major key (C is the sixth degree of the E major scale). The B phrases are in A Major, the subdominant key (IV) of the home-key of Eb major. This scheme of harmony—notably the "bimodality" of a constant alternation between the major and its relative minor key—is characteristic of both northern Ecuadorian highland *sanjuán* and many other Andean traditional musics as well.

The isorhythm discussed earlier is a regular feature of northern highland Ecuadorian Quichua *sanjuanes.* Some combination of sixteenth-eighth-sixteenth and two eighths is characteristic of most *sanjuanes.* Thus, the careful listener can often identify a Quichua *sanjuán* by the presence of these rhythm kernels alone.

It is always interesting to observe how oral tradition works in traditional cultures. Here are three comparable segments of "Muyu" ("Chayamuyari"), all performed by regional Quichua musicians. The first was recorded on December 28,

MindTap•
🎧 **WATCH** an Active Listening Guide of this selection online.

ACTIVE LISTENING 9.3
"Muyu Muyari Warmigu" ("Please Return, Dear Woman")

COUNTER NUMBER	COMMENTARY	LYRICS	TRANSLATION
Introduction			
0:00	Harp plays seven A phrases, then two B phrases.		
1st double-couplet			
0:44	Vocal and harp.	*Muyu muyari warmigu*	Please return, dear woman
		Muyu muyari payagu.	Please return, dear "old lady."
		Muyu muyari warmigu	Please return, dear woman
		Muyu muyari payagu.	Please return, dear "old lady."
2nd double-couplet			
0:52	Vocal and harp. (Couplet repeats.)	*Kambaj shayashka puistuka*	The place in which you've stood
		Sisagullami viñashka.	Just a dear flower has grown.
Instrumental interlude			
1:01	Harp plays six A phrases, then two B phrases.		
1st double-couplet repeats			
1:37	Vocal and harp.		
2nd double-couplet repeats, modified			
1:45	Vocal and harp. (Couplet repeats.)	*Kambaj shayashka puistupi*	The place in which you've stood
		Sisagullami viñashka.	Just a dear flower has grown.
Instrumental interlude			
1:54	Harp plays five A phrases, then two B phrases, then one A phrase.		
3rd double-couplet			
2:30	Vocal and harp. (Couplet repeats.)	*Llakiwanguichu warmigu*	Will you be sad, to me, dear woman?
		Juyawanguichu warmigu?	Or will you be loving, to me, dear woman?
2nd double-couplet repeats, modified			
2:38	Vocal and harp. (Couplet repeats.)	*Kambaj shayashka puistupi*	The place in which you've stood
		Sisagullami viñashka.	Just a dear flower has grown.
Instrumental interlude			
2:47	Harp plays two A phrases, then two B phrases, then six A phrases, then two B phrases.		
1st double-couplet repeats, modified			
3:41	Vocal and harp. (Couplet repeats.)	*Muyu muyari warmigu*	Please return, dear woman
		Muyu muyari urpigu.	Please return, dear turtle dove.
2nd double-couplet, modified			
3:50	Vocal and harp. (Couplet repeats.)	*Kambaj shayashka puistupi*	The place in which you've stood
		Sisagullami viñashka.	Just a dear flower has grown.
Instrumental ending			
3:59	Harp plays three A phrases leading to final chord. Words spoken at end by John Schechter: *"Diusílupagui, maistrugukuna; Alimi llujshirka; disílupa'i."* "Thank you, esteemed maestros; it came out well; thank you."		

1979, by the solo singer César, who was then twelve years old. The second was recorded on September 16, 1990, eleven years later, by the singer-guitarist Segundo "Galo" Maigua Pillajo, the composer of the *sanjuán* "Ilumán tiyu," which we will discuss next in this chapter. The third, our "Muyu," was performed about a month later, on October 13, 1990. All three performances were to roughly the same A phrase with which we are now familiar:

Chayamuyari warmiku	Come here, indeed, dear woman [or wife]	"Muyu": December 28, 1979
Chayamuyari warmiku,	Come here, indeed, dear woman,	
Chayamuyari warmiku	Come here, indeed, dear woman	
Chayamuyari warmiku,	Come here, indeed, dear woman,	
Kampak purishka llaktaka	The community you've walked	
Sumakllamari rikurin,	Appears just beautiful, indeed,	
Kampak purishka llaktaka	The community you've walked	
Sumakllamari rikurin,	Appears just beautiful, indeed	
Kampak shayashka pushtuka	The place in which you've stood	"Muyu": September 16, 1990
Sumbrallamari rikurin,	Appears just shady, indeed,	
Kampak shayashka pushtuka	The place in which you've stood	
Sumbrallamari rikurin,	Appears just shady, indeed,	
Muyu muyari nigragu	Please return, dear dark woman	
Muyu muyari payagu,	Please return, dear "old lady,"	
Muyu muyari nigragu	Please return, dear dark woman	
Muyu muyari payagu,	Please return, dear "old lady,"	
Muyu muyari warmigu	Please return, dear woman	"Muyu": October 13, 1990
Muyu muyari payagu,	Please return, dear "old lady,"	
Muyu muyari warmigu	Please return, dear woman	
Muyu muyari payagu,	Please return, dear "old lady,"	
Kambaj shayashka puistuka	The place in which you've stood	
Sisagullami viñashka,	Just a dear flower has grown,	
Kambaj shayashka puistuka	The place in which you've stood	
Sisagullami viñashka,	Just a dear flower has grown,	

We can hear several things here. First, performers are constrained by an eight-syllable line: every line must be eight syllables long. Quichua performers of *sanjuán* operate under this oral-traditional principle, known as formulaic expression. The pattern is that of Milman Parry's "formula," cited by Lord ([1960] 1978:4): "'a group of words which is regularly employed under the same metrical conditions to express a given essential idea.'" Second, each double-couplet equates to eight quarter-note beats. The melody proceeds sequentially, the first four beats—corresponding to one eight-syllable line—winding down to the fifth scale-degree of the minor key, the last four beats continuing the twisting descent to take the next eight eight-syllable line down to the lower home-note of the key. We also note, as regards the lyrics, a kind of parallel meaning (semantic parallelism): for example, "Please return, dear woman," followed by "Please return, dear 'old lady.'" That is, a couplet like this one often has the two lines nearly identical, with only a small word-shift in the second line; this also facilitates transmission via oral tradition, because the near-repetition of a line means one does not have to remember so much. Young César has identical lines in his first couplet.

This is also a love song; a major theme of all the lyrics is praise for one's beloved. Many traditional songs throughout Latin America speak to the beauty of, and general admiration for, the women of a man's home region (for a fuller discussion, see Schechter 1999a:4–7). Hence, in "Muyu" we read the following: "That place in which you've stood/walked—been, appears beautiful/shady/produces a flower."

Finally, we find that the verbs are interchangeable: Come here—(*Chayamuyari*)/Return—(*Muyu muyari*). In short, we have in "Muyu" a carefully structured, entirely traditional package of oral tradition. It follows rather strict rules having to do with a consistent subject matter, particular syllabic constraints and verb interchangeability, musical isorhythm in an eight-beat phrase, and semantic parallelism in the text.

A Classic *Sanjuán*

At least one Imbabura Quichua *sanjuán* is a classic in its highland region. Popular decades ago and still today, the *sanjuán* "Ilumán tiyu" (ee-loo-*mahn tee*-yoo; "Man of Ilumán") was composed by Segundo "Galo" Maigua Pillajo, a Quichua composer-guitarist-singer of the Imbabura village of Ilumán. Galo Maigua's *sanjuán* compositions are often motivated by autobiographical forces. His fame among Imbabura Quichua is attested to by wide acknowledgment of him as the composer of highly popular *sanjuanes*. His fame is also apparent in the high level of local demand for his ensemble, Conjunto Ilumán, and their having produced a commercial cassette.

My fieldwork in 1990 in Imbabura brought to light the fact that *sanjuán* often takes on the nature of a ballad, even when that fact is not immediately obvious. A *sanjuán* text typically expresses the essence of a large story, making the *sanjuán* a highly distilled ballad form, the synoptic character of the text being in keeping with the elliptical character of Andean poetry dating back to the Inkas (Schechter 1979:193). The ballad nature of "Ilumán tiyu"—the story behind the *sanjuán*—is not at all obvious. We will explore this enigma a bit later, but for now, listen to "Ilumán tiyu" (Active Listening 9.4).

MindTap·

◀)) LISTEN TO
"Ilumán tiyu," performed by "Galo," guitar and vocal, with the Quichua ensemble Conjunto Ilumán, online.

MindTap·

🎧 WATCH an Active Listening Guide of this selection online.

ACTIVE LISTENING 9.4
"Ilumán tiyu" ("Man from Ilumán")

COUNTER NUMBER	COMMENTARY	LYRICS	TRANSLATION	FORM
Introduction				
0:00	Violin outlines home chord four times.			II
0:09	*Kenas* and violin play the principal melody of "Ilumán tiyu"—four A phrases.			AI
0:27	Violin outlines home chord four times.			II

COUNTER NUMBER	COMMENTARY		LYRICS	TRANSLATION	FORM
Quichua-language double-couplets					
0:36	Vocalists sing the two double-couplets to four A phrases. Violin plays in harmony.	A	*Ilumán tiyu cantanmi,* *Ilumán tiyu nijunmi.*	The man [not uncle] from Ilumán sings, The man from Ilumán is saying.	AV
		A	*Ilumán tiyu cantanmi,* *Ilumán tiyu nijunmi.*	The man from Ilumán sings, The man from Ilumán is saying.	
		A	*Sultira kashpa paya kashpa,* *ñuka tunupi bailapai.*	Being a young [unmarried] woman, [or an] old woman, Dance to my song.	
		A	*Sultira kashpa paya kashpa,* *ñuka tunupi bailapai.*	Being a young woman, old woman, Dance to my song.	
Interlude					
0:55	*Kenas* and violin play two B phrases.				B
1:04	Violin plays two A phrases.				AI
1:13	*Kenas* and violin play two A phrases.				(AI)
1:23	Violin outlines tonic chord, four times. Musician shouts, *"Kushi, kushiguta!"* ("Real happy!").				II
The Spanish-language double-couplets					
1:32	Vocalists sing the two Spanish-language double-couplets to four A phrases. Violin plays in harmony.	A	*Este es el indio de Ilumán,* *El que canta (canto)* sanjuanito,*	This is the indígena of Ilumán, He who sings sanjuán,	AV
		A	*Este es el indio de Ilumán,* *El que canta (canto)* sanjuanito,*	This is the indígena of Ilumán, He who sings sanjuán,	
		A	*Para que bailen toditos,* *Para que bailen toditas.*	So that all men might dance, So that all women might dance.	
		A	*Para que bailen toditos,* *Para que bailen toditas.*	So that all men might dance, So that all women might dance.	
Interlude					
1:50	Violin plays two B phrases.				B
2:00	*Kenas* and violin play the principal melody of "Ilumán tiyu"—four A phrases.				AI
2:18	Violin outlines home chord four times. (*"¡Ahora, tshhh!"*)				II
Repeat Quichua-language double-couplets					
2:27	Double-couplets sung to four A phrases, the violin playing in harmony.				AV
Conclusion					
2:46	*Kenas* and violin play two B phrases.				B
2:55	*Kenas* and violin play the principal melody of "Ilumán tiyu," four A phrases.				AI

*Segundo "Galo" Maigua Pillajo sings canto ["I sing"], referring to the fact that he is the composer of the song, about whom its lyrics are centered. Lyrics used with permission of Galo Maigua.

In the village of Ilumán, in the home of a local policeman, I recorded the composer "Galo" Maigua singing "Ilumán tiyu" and playing guitar together with Conjunto Ilumán, on October 27, 1990 (Figure 9.9). Active Listening 9.4 provides the full text of "Ilumán tiyu" and illustrates its formal structure.

If **II** stands for the introduction/interlude, **AI** for the A phrase played by instruments, **AV** for the A phrase vocalized by the ensemble, and **B** for the B phrase, the formal structure of Galo Maigua's composition "Ilumán tiyu" is as follows:

II / AI / II / AV / B / AI / II / AV / B / AI / II / AV / B / AI

The symmetries/balance here are prodigious: three vocal statements and three B statements; four intros/interludes and four instrumental statements; the consecutive pattern, AV-B-AI enunciated three times; the consecutive, overlapping larger pattern, II-AV-B-AI-II occurring twice—itself being framed by the II statements. In sum, a distinctive cohesiveness—strongly reinforced by the Ta-Ta, Ta Ta Ta Ta Ta Ta; Ta-Ta, Ta Ta Ta Ta Ta Ta; eight-beat isorhythm, and by the rising then falling (archlike) melodic shape of the eight-beat A phrase.

Since my 1980 research, when I recorded numerous versions of "Ilumán tiyu" in the environs of Cotacachi, the nature of the lyrics had never been comprehensible. When I was informed that Segundo "Galo" Maigua Pillajo was in fact the composer of this *sanjuán*, I tried, during a visit to his Ilumán home on September 30, 1990, to learn what might lie behind words that seem merely a statement that the man singing and speaking is an *indígena* from Ilumán.

Galo Maigua described the tale behind the text. He told me that before he composed "Ilumán tiyu," he had become extremely ill with tuberculosis; the condition of his lungs had deteriorated, and he believed he was about to die. Although during his 1972–1973 wanderings through the *comunas* around Cotacachi he had sung the melody to a variety of words (Galo says he composes by first hearing a melody and later setting a text), he now determined that he would like everyone— be they young woman or old woman, for example—to dance to this, his song, after his death. In effect, "Ilumán tiyu" was ultimately texted as Galo's final statement

Figure 9.9

Members of the Quichua ensemble Conjunto Ilumán, in the village of Ilumán, Imbabura Province, northern highland Ecuador. October 1990.
John M. Schechter.

of his identity to posterity: "I"—the man singing, speaking—am a man from Ilumán; remember me by remembering my music: "Dance to my song." In sum, what appeared to the uninformed listener to be innocuous words came, on greater understanding, to have profound import for a composer believing himself to be on his deathbed.

Spanish speakers will note that the intermingling of Spanish and Quichua words we spoke of early in this chapter appears prominently in this *sanjuán*. Moreover, the verse *Este es el indio de Ilumán, el que canta sanjuanito* is a rough translation of the first, critically important, verse; Galo Maigua commented to me that a major local radio station had prompted him to produce the parallel text in Spanish. Some of his other *sanjuanes*, such as "Antonio Mocho" and "Rusita Andranga," share the distilled-ballad character of "Ilumán tiyu." Both of these *sanjuanes*, along with "Ilumán tiyu," appear on the commercial cassette *Elenita Conde*, by Conjunto Ilumán; the cassette was mastered in Otavalo and mass-produced in Bogotá, Colombia, somewhat prior to 1990.

Efraín and Rafael, Segundo "Galo" Maigua Pillajo and his Conjunto Ilumán colleagues, and hundreds of other Quichua musicians in the Otavalo Valley, Imbabura Province, are not the only regional stakeholders in the genre that is northern Ecuadorian highland *sanjuán*. *Sanjuán* can also be heard in area mestizo households, and, a few hours up the Pan American highway toward the Colombia border, in African Ecuadorian gatherings. The lesson here is that a prominent regional music can trump racial and cultural barriers and establish itself firmly in a region, with different cultural signatures therein. Let us take a closer look at the musicians up the road, in Chota.

African Ecuadorian Music of the Chota River Valley

When we think of Latin American regions that have large populations of African Americans, Ecuador does not usually come to mind. Yet as much as 25 percent of the country's population are African Ecuadorians. They are heavily concentrated in coastal Esmeraldas Province, which neighbors Imbabura Province. The first Africans arrived in Ecuador in the sixteenth century, after which Jesuit missionaries brought in large numbers of African slaves to work on plantations both on the coast and in the central highlands. Indigenous laborers were hard to find in some areas, and were unwilling to serve as slaves in others. The relatively small pocket of approximately fifteen thousand African Ecuadorians in the Chota Valley, comprising ten to fifteen small villages, has an uncertain origin. The most widely accepted view is that the African Ecuadorians of the Chota Valley are descended from slaves held by the Jesuits on their plantations in the highlands (Lipski 1987:157–58).

During the 1980s and 1990s, the best-known musicians in the Chota Valley were the guitarist-composer-singers Germán, Fabián, and Eleuterio Congo and their colleague, Milton Tadeo. When I first met them in 1980, they played mostly around their home village of Carpuela; when I visited them again in 1990, they had become regional celebrities with regular weekend performances in local villages, on the coast, and in nearby Colombia. As of October 1990 they had recorded six long-playing records within seven years. The Congo brothers are the third generation of composer-performers in their family.

On October 21, 1990, Fabián, Germán, and Eleuterio Congo, with Milton Tadeo and colleague Ermundo Mendes León (on *güiro*), performed "Me gusta la leche" (meh *goo*-sta la *leh*-cheh; "I Like Milk"), heard here. At this time, the full ensemble identified themselves as Grupo Ecuador de los Hermanos Congo y Milton Tadeo ("Ecuador Ensemble of the Congo Brothers and Milton Tadeo"). Germán played lead guitar (*requinto*); Fabián and Milton both played guitar and sang in duet; Eleuterio played the **bomba**, the Chota-area, double-headed drum held between the knees and played with the hands; and Ermundo Mendes León played the *güiro*, a scraper (Figures 9.10 and 9.11).

In this *sanjuán* we find the same eight-beat phrases and double-couplet structure of text that we found in "Muyu muyari warmigu," a Quichua *sanjuán* that would in 1990 have been performed in the Otavalo Valley, a couple of hours down the

Figure 9.10

Grupo Ecuador de los Hermanos Congo y Milton Tadeo. Back row, left to right: Ermundo Mendes León plays the metal *güiro;* Germán Congo, *requinto;* Milton Tadeo, guitar; and Fabián Congo, guitar. In front: Eleuterio Congo plays *bomba*. Imbabura, Ecuador, 1990. *John M. Schechter.*

Figure 9.11

Left to right: Eleuterio Congo, Milton Tadeo, Fabián Congo, John Schechter, Germán Congo, and Ermundo Mendes León. Outside the house of Germán Congo, Imbabura, Ecuador, 1990. *Courtesy of Germán Congo family.*

highway from the Chota River Valley, site of the Congos' home village of Carpuela. However, despite the double-couplet construction and comparable tempo, of the music (one can easily dance Quichua *sanjuán* to "Me gusta la leche"), this is *not* Quichua *sanjuán*, though it is *sanjuán* (Active Listening 9.5).

MindTap
🎧 WATCH an Active
Listening Guide of this
selection online.

ACTIVE LISTENING 9.5
"Me Gusta La Leche" ("I Like Milk")

COUNTER NUMBER	COMMENTARY	LYRICS	TRANSLATION
Introduction			
0:00	*Requinto* guitar plays introductory motive *a* (twice), then		
0:10	introductory motive *b* (twice), then		
0:20	introductory motive *c* (twice).		
	Each motive is eight quarter-note beats long.		
1st stanza (double-couplet)—A phrase			
0:29	Vocals on the A phrase, the principal melody of the *sanjuán*.	*Me gusta la leche, me gusta el café,* *Pero más me gusta lo que tiene Usted.* *Me gusta la leche, me gusta el café,* *Pero más me gusta lo que tiene Usted.*	I like milk, I like coffee, But I like what you have better. I like milk, I like coffee, But I like what you have better.
2nd stanza (double-couplet)—A phrase			
0:38	*Requinto* counterpoint added to vocal melody in A phrase (principal melody).	*Así negra linda de mi corazón,* *Cuando yo te veo, me muero de ilusión.* *Así negra linda de mi corazón,* *Cuando yo te veo, me muero de ilusión.*	So, beautiful black woman of my heart, When I see you, I'm filled with anticipation. So, beautiful black woman of my heart, When I see you, I'm filled with anticipation.
***Requinto* interlude**			
0:48	Lead guitar and ensemble. Lead plays c motive from introduction twice.		
3rd stanza (double-couplet)—A phrase			
0:58	*Requinto* counterpoint added to vocal melody in A phrase (principal melody).	*En esta cuaresma no me confesé* *Porque en viernes santo yo me enamoré.* *En esta cuaresma no me confesé* *Porque en viernes santo yo me enamoré.*	During this Lent I did not go to confession, Because, on Good Friday, I fell in love. During this Lent I did not go to confession, Because, on Good Friday, I fell in love.
2nd stanza repeat			
1:08	Vocals with *requinto* counterpoint.		
Instrumental interlude			
1:18	Ensemble plays two new B phrases.		
1:27	Germán's *requinto* guitar repeats the introduction motives.		
3rd stanza repeat			
1:57	Vocals return with *requinto* counterpoint.		

continued

COUNTER NUMBER	COMMENTARY	LYRICS	TRANSLATION
2nd stanza repeat			
2:06	Vocals with *requinto* counterpoint.		
Requinto interlude repeat			
2:16	Lead guitar and ensemble. Lead guitar plays c motive from introduction twice.		
Final cadence			
2:26	Ensemble with lead guitar playing melodic riff (in the minor home-key). Spoken at end by John Schechter: *Gracias*.		

In the first place, we do not have clear phrase isorhythm: the second four beats are *not* identical here to the first four beats, as in Quichua *sanjuán*. Looking at the stanza 1 (beginning *Me gusta la leche…*):

First 4 beats:	4 sixteenth notes/2 eighths/4 sixteenths/quarter
Second 4 beats:	4 sixteenth notes/sixteenth-eighth-sixteenth/eighth and 2 sixteenths/quarter

This is quite fascinating. In this musical genre "shared" between two neighboring cultures, Quichua and African Ecuadorian, there is a *suggestion* of isorhythm, in that beat 5 is the same as beat 1 (4 sixteenths), and beat 8 is the same as beat 4 (quarter note); the divergence comes with beats 6 and 7. Beat 6 is sixteenth-eighth-sixteenth. The sharp-eyed and sharp-eared among you will recall that this small rhythmic fragment—sixteenth-eighth-sixteenth— was a rhythmic marker for Quichua *sanjuán*. Here it is again, in neighboring African Ecuadorian *sanjuán*. Beat 7 (eighth and 2 sixteenths) is close to beat 3 (4 sixteenths) yet also different. Looking for a moment at stanza 3 (*En esta cuaresma …*), the "noteworthy" beat 6 now gives us a syncopation, accenting the fourth sixteenth-note—a weak beat—thus providing increased rhythmic drive. Quichua *sanjuán* almost never, in my experience, utilizes such weak-beat accent and syncopation.

In the second place, we have the wonderful counterpoint (independent melody and rhythm) of Germán's lead guitar (*requinto*), which provides a remarkable texture, depth, and richness to the music—something Chota musicians often refer to as *dulzura,* or sweetness (Schechter 1994:293). "Me gusta la leche" is a rich, musical expression of a border region: African Ecuadorian, close to a major Quichua cultural zone, within a Spanish-speaking nation. It therefore demonstrates hybrid traits: a genre (*sanjuán*) native to the neighboring Quichua indigenous people, yet here borrowed and—with phrasing twists, rhythmic variance and nuance, and *requinto dulzura*—made unique to Chota.

The Andean Ensemble Phenomenon: Going Abroad

By 1990, the reputation of the Congo brothers and Milton Tadeo had led them to travel throughout Ecuador and into Colombia, playing for substantial fees, and on television (Schechter 1994:288). Segundo "Galo" Maigua and his Quichua colleagues have been to Europe to play. The case of Conjunto Ilumán in particular represents a now-broad phenomenon, both in the Andes and beyond: the itinerant Andean ensemble and the globalization of Andean musics.

In the Otavalo Valley of Imbabura, Quichua ensembles date back at least to the 1940s and 1950s, and began to proliferate in the 1970s (Meisch 1997:200). Groups such as ñanda Mañachi and Conjunto Indígena "Peguche"emphasized in their album liner notes the central role of "music as an expression of indigenous values and its role in [the 1970s indigenous Quichua] cultural resurgence" (Ibid. 201). The Otavalo Quichua musical-ensemble renaissance is evident from Lynn Meisch's listing of numerous, long-playing records produced from 1970 to 1986—nearly all of which were recorded in Ecuador and contained only Ecuadorian music (Ibid. 205–6).

> ### Salient Characteristics of
> # Andean Music
>
> - Traditional music of indigenous, rural peoples who live in the Andean mountain region, including the Quechua and Aymara, descendants of the Inka Empire, in Bolivia, Peru, Ecuador, and Argentina
>
> - Instrumental sound dominated by panpipes with drums
>
> - Often performed in hocketing style, with melodies doubled in octaves
>
> - Underwent a revival and transformation by the *Nueva Canción* movement, spread throughout Latin America, and eventually became part of the world music concert tour and recording mix

In 1990, in this same broad, green valley, teenagers and young men were actively engaged in music making. In Imbabura, one radio station had an annual festival of musical ensembles, in which any and all area village ensembles could participate, each playing perhaps two songs on the radio. In July 1990, this village ensemble marathon featured enough groups to last twelve hours.

Music making provides an important means of socialization among Quichua youths who have long since ceased attending school and who find few community activities available to them, except for volleyball, which is pursued with a vengeance in the village plazas and *comunas* of Imbabura. You will hear Quichua teenagers rehearsing diligently on weekends at an ensemble member's home, performing a few traditional *sanjuanes* and, like their counterparts in the United States, often experimenting with their own compositions.

The 1990s witnessed an explosion of this music as Otavalenian musicians left their homeland to seek larger audiences throughout the world. Meisch (1997, 2002) has documented this phenomenon carefully and in detail. As she notes, "Otavalo music [performed by Quichua indigenous musicians] has now become globalized, part of the world-music beat influencing the music made by others, with Sanjuanitos seen as emblematic of Ecuadorian music" (1997:217). Motivated by potential economic rewards, many Imbabura Quichua ensemble members have, in effect, become **"transnational migrants"** (Ibid.:218) or "immigrants who develop and maintain multiple relationships—familial, economic, social, organizational, religious, and political—that span borders . . . [creating a] multiplicity of involvements . . . in both home and host societies"(Basch, Schiller, and Blanc 1994:7).

Not surprisingly, as the Bolivian ethnomusicologist Gilka Wara Céspedes says, "The Andean Sound is becoming a part of the sonic scene from Europe to Japan" (1993:53). Further, "Otavalo [Quichua] musicians are everywhere, playing in malls, on street corners, at music festivals, and in concert halls and clubs on six continents, and recording and selling their music at locales around the world" (Meisch 1997:243). Where Ecuadorian Andean *indígena* textile manufacturers have for some fifty years traveled the international byways, selling their home-woven ponchos, blankets, and scarves, today the entrepreneurial instinct remains intact but the product has changed: from bulky woolens to featherweight cassettes and CDs, delicate bamboo *zampoñas*, and *kenas.* As one Otavalenian musician, Héctor Lema, told Meisch in 1994, "'We have two ways to earn a living in whatever locale: music and the sales of artesanías [arts and crafts]'" (1997:187). Specifically, Otavalo Quichua ensembles have appeared at First Peoples powwows in Canada and the United States; in folk festivals in Poland and Washington, D.C.; and on street corners, tourist thoroughfares, and subway stations in Quito, New York, San Francisco, Florence, Moscow, Montreal, Paris, Sevilla, Córdoba, and Madrid, among numerous other locales (1997:243).

The United States unquestionably plays a vital role in this international Andean sonic scene. As of about thirteen years ago, Amauta, based in Seattle, comprised of Chilean and Bolivian musicians playing traditional Andean instruments, had appeared at the Seattle Northwest Regional Folklife Festival. Condor, out of Corvallis, Oregon—an ensemble of five professional, college-educated musicians from Argentina, Peru, and Mexico—focused on traditional Andean musics. Andanzas (Spanish: "wanderings") performed music from a variety of Latin American and Caribbean traditions; this widely traveled, four-member ensemble included musicians from Argentina, Bolivia, and Mexico, as well as a classically trained U.S. harpist. Andesmanta (Quichua: "from the Andes"), an ensemble of Ecuadorian musicians playing traditional highland Ecuadorian musics—including *sanjuanes*—as well as other South American folk musics, performed at Carnegie Hall and the Metropolitan Museum of Art. Among the most well-established of U.S.-based Andean groups is Sukay (Quechua: "to work furrows in straight lines" or "to whistle musically"); this group, formed originally in 1974, recorded some eight albums by 1994 and performed at Lincoln Center and major folk music festivals (Ross 1994:19–24). (You can find a list of selected recordings by these and other Andean Ensembles in Ross 1994:27; for recordings of Ecuadorian Andean ensembles, see Meisch 1997:357–65.)

Chaskinakuy

One of the cofounders of Sukay was the Swiss multi-instrumentalist and instrument craftsman Edmond Badoux. With the flautist-percussionist Francy Vidal (self-described as "an eigth-generation 'Californiana' with roots in Mexico and in Europe" (Vidal n.d.), he formed in 1985 the gifted, California-based duo Chaskinakuy (Quechua: "to give and receive, hand to hand, among many"). Chaskinakuy's husband-and-wife members, Edmond and Francy, characterize themselves as "dedicated revivalists" (Figure 9.12). The two musicians sing in Quechua/Quichua and Spanish, and they play more than twenty-five native Andean instruments, some rarely heard outside their highland Andean contexts: Peruvian harp (Edmond plays this instrument, on occasion, upside-down, in accordance with the Peruvian harp's unique procession posture), pelican-bone flute, long, straight trumpet, condor-feathered *zampoña*, and *pututu* (Quechua: "conch trumpet").

Figure 9.12
The duo Chaskinakuy. June
1992. © *Irene Young. Used by
permission.*

Chaskinakuy has appeared in concerts, festivals, university lecture series, and schools in eighteen U.S. states, in Canada, and in Switzerland. They have three times received the Multi-Cultural Grant from the California Arts Council, and for six seasons were picked for the Council's Touring and Presenting Program. Chaskinakuy has three recordings on their own label: *A Flor de Tierra* (2002), *Cosecha* ([1991] 1993), and *Music of the Andes* (1988). They return frequently to the Andes to sustain their performance research into traditional village musics and festivals. Their renditions of Andean musics reflect the musicians' wonderful blend, when singing in duet, and their remarkably close attention to every stylistic detail appropriate to the particular regional music: harmonic underpinnings, melodic lines and inflections, vocal-tone qualities, phrasing, and rhythmic accentuations. Listen to Chaskinakuy's rendition of the Peruvian *wayno*, "Amor imposible."

In this piece, you hear your second Latin American "harp-country genre"; earlier, you heard Ecuadorian *sanjuán*, and now Peruvian **wayno**. As such, we can note four prominent similarities to the "Muyu muyari warmigu" *sanjuán* of Efraín and Rafael. First, note the use of the harp—now as accompaniment to the lively, South Andean *wayno*, then as accompaniment to its lively, North Andean cousin, the *sanjuán*. Second, note the now-familiar Andean bimodality, the use of the minor and its relative major—here, b minor/D major. Moreover, where the B statements of Efraín and Rafael's "Muyu" explored the region of the subdominant of the relative major, similarly, Edmond and Francy's "Amor imposible" employs G major, the subdominant of its relative major, D. Third, those with keen ears will remark that the rhythm is not beaten on a drum, but rather—as in "Muyu"—on the harp sound box; this type of percussive *golpe*, or *cajoneo*, on the harp sound box can be heard in several Latin American countries, including Peru. Fourth and last, we are cognizant of two distinctive, rhythmic motifs. Those of Ecuadorian *sanjuán* revolve around sixteenth-eighth-sixteenth notes. In Peruvian *wayno*, the *golpe* involves something close to an eighth and two sixteenths; this pattern, sometimes close to three triplets, is the near-invariant rhythmic signature of the *wayno*. (You can find a substantial discussion of the history, regional varieties, other musical traits, and poetic substance of the *wayno* in Romero 1999:388–89.)

Again, this performance of "Amor imposible" proves particularly compelling because Edmond captures the distinctive character of Peruvian harp-accompaniment style, and Francy grasps the distinctive, melodic turns of phrase, characteristic portamento, and distinctly focused and clear vocal quality of the female Peruvian singer of *wayno*. Active Listening 9.6 provides the full text of "Amor imposible" and illustrates the formal structure of this Peruvian *wayno*.

As you can tell from its lyrics, "Amor imposible" offers one example of the poetic character of this genre: "Most *waynos* . . . are of an amorous nature. Despite the immense variety of *waynos*, many depict nostalgia for a lost love" (Romero 1999:389). The theme of nostalgia runs powerfully throughout songs that have emerged through the ages in Latin America (Schechter 1999a:2–7).

Each stanza is four lines long. The first three stanzas all have 11-syllable lines, whereas stanzas 4 and 5 have the syllable pattern 6-5-6-5. The formal structure of the music of "Amor imposible," as laid out in Active Listening 9.6, is as follows:

Intro-A-A-A-A-A-B-B-CC'-DD'-EE'-EE'

Raúl Romero (1999:388–90; 414–15) discusses the character and formal structure of the Peruvian *wayno*. One of the possible formal structures, he notes, is roughly AABB (Ibid.:414). In "Amor imposible" we hear an expansion, an extrapolation, of that form: Much of the song is occupied with the A phrase—which correlates with the 11-syllable stanzas, with lesser emphasis being given to the B phrase—which correlates with the 6-5-6-5 stanzas. Then, Edmond's C phrase explores the subdominant key, which lasts into the D phrase; the concluding E phrase dwells on the fifth scale degree, prolonging the final arrival to the home note, the first scale degree.

Other Groups

Finally, the *waynos* and *sanjuanes* of Andean ensembles—as well as *Nueva Canción* musics—have taken root in U.S. universities. For example, the University of Texas at Austin for some years maintained an Andean ensemble, among their other Latin American groups. At the University of California, Santa Cruz, students have, since 1986, performed in intermediate and advanced Andean ensembles called Voces (Spanish: "voices") and Taki Ñan (Quichua: "song path"), respectively.

Taki Ñan, which recorded an in-house cassette in 1992 and an in-house CD in 1998, focuses on traditional Andean musics in Spanish and Quichua/Quechua, as well as on *Nueva Canción* musics. Starting out as a single, ten-student Latin American ensemble in 1986 that focused on Ecuadorian genres, Voces and Taki Ñan became independent of each other in 1991. Over the years, Taki Ñan has tended to follow two approaches: focusing its repertory or presenting a more varied program. When focusing in depth, during one particular quarter of study, the group would emphasize, for example, Colombian musics, Argentinean musics, Afro-South American musics; in Fall 1992, they prepared six different, field-recorded versions of "Ilumán tiyu." Taki Ñan has also presented programs with a variety of traditional and *Nueva Canción* musics. In nearly every one of these programs, from 1989 to the present, both Taki Ñan and Voces have performed South Andean *zampoña* musics—including the *k'antu* "Kutirimunapaq." Over these years, Taki Ñan has benefited enormously from the musical and linguistic assistance of Guillermo Delgado-P., as well as from workshops offered by Chaskinakuy and by the Peruvian musician Héctor Zapana.

ACTIVE LISTENING 9.6
"Amor Imposible" ("Impossible Love")

MindTap·

🎧 **WATCH** an Active Listening Guide of this selection online.

COUNTER NUMBER	COMMENTARY	LYRICS	TRANSLATION
Introduction			
0:00	Harp enters.		
0:05	*Golpe* enters emphasizing long-short-short rhythmic pattern.		
1st stanza—A phrase			
0:13	Harp and *golpe* play main melody. Vocal style with distinctive phrasing and characteristic portamento of the *wayno*.	*Es imposible dejar de quererte,* *Es imposible dejar de amarte,* *Este cariño que yo a tí te tengo* *Es un cariño puro y verdadero.*	It's impossible to stop loving you, It's impossible to stop loving you, This affection that I have for you Is an affection pure and true.
1st stanza repeat—A phrase			
0:28	Harp and *golpe*.		
Harp interlude, "Arpita!"—A phrase			
0:43	Harp.		
2nd stanza—A phrase			
0:58	Harp and *golpe* play main melody.	*¡Cómo quisiera que venga la muerte!* *¡Cómo quisiera morir en tus brazos!* *Quizás así podría olvidarte* *Porque, en mi vida, todo es imposible.*	How so, would I like death to come! How so, would I like to die in your arms! Perhaps that way, I could forget you Because, in my life, everything is impossible.
3rd stanza—A phrase			
1:14	Harp and *golpe* play main melody.	*Ay, cruceñito, amorcito mío* *Este cariño te traigo y te digo* *Aunque mi cuerpo quede sepultado* *Queda mi nombre grabado en tu pecho.*	Ay, dear man from [Santa] Cruz, my dear love This affection I offer you and tell you of Even though my body might be buried My name remains engraved in your breast.
4th stanza—B phrase			
1:29	Harp and *golpe* play contrasting melody.	*Dicen con la muerte* *Se llega a olvidar,* *Quizás en la tumba* *Más nos amamos.*	They say that, with death, One comes to forget, Perhaps in the grave We'll love one another more.
5th stanza—B phrase			
1:37	Harp and *golpe* play contrasting melody.	*Si muero primero* *Yo allá te espero,* *Así para amarnos* *Eternamente.*	Should I die first, I'll wait for you, over there, In that way, to remain loving one another Eternally.
Harp interlude—CC'—DD'—EE'—EE'			
1:46–1:56	Harp plays new C phrase twice.		
1:57–2:06	Harp plays new D phrase twice.		
2:07–2:27	Harp plays new E phrase four times.		
2:28	Final cadence.		

Aconcagua, at Florida State University, performs a variety of Andean musics and has been directed by an alumna of Taki Ñan. Viento, in Berkeley, California, is directed by Chaskinakuy and comprises Berkeley students and community members. Frequently performing at the La Peña Cultural Center in Berkeley, Viento focuses on traditional South Andean musics for *zampoña* and *tarqa* (wooden duct flute). Lydia Mills, another Taki Ñan alumna, directs Los Mapaches, an ensemble of some thirty-five to fifty schoolchildren from the Berkwood Hedge School in Berkeley, who perform Andean musics—on *zampoñas* and other instruments—locally, in concert; on July 24 and 25, 2007, members of Los Mapaches joined forces with a Bolivian young peoples' ensemble, Orquesta de Instrumentos Autóctonos, for two concerts in La Paz, Bolivia.

Afro-Peruvian Music: A Landó

The interpretations and reinterpretations of traditional South American musics continue—both abroad and on the continent itself. One prominent instance of the reconstruction of an imagined music of the past occurs with today's Afro-Peruvian music. In the colonial era, Peru was a major nucleus of African slavery; a substantial segment of eighteenth-century Lima was black (Romero 1994:307). However, the concurrent disappearance of the African marimba and African drum types marked the diminution of African-related musical practice at that time. By the outset of the twentieth century, songs and choreographies of African origins were entering a clouded past (Ibid.:313–14). In 1940, blacks represented only about 0.47 percent of the population of Peru (Feldman 2003:156).

Contravening these demographic and cultural trends, a revival of Afro-Peruvian traditions took place. Raúl Romero, a Peruvian ethnomusicologist, summarizes the mid-twentieth-century revival movement as follows:

> The revival and reconstruction of ancient and almost forgotten "Afro-Peruvian" song-genres began in the late 1950s. Rather than originating in a popular spontaneous movement, this was initiated by local intellectuals interested in the revival and recognition of the contribution of blacks to Peruvian culture. The late historian José Durand (1935–1990), along with Nicomedes Santa Cruz (1925–1992) and his sister Victoria Santa Cruz (1992) were the main collectors, producers, and promoters of black performances during this period. (1994:314)

LISTEN TO
"Azúcar de caña," performed by Eva Ayllón and ensemble, from the album *Afro-Peruvian Classics: The Soul of Black Peru*, online.

Heidi Feldman notes that there was originally a tie between a 1960s black Peruvian political movement (roughly simultaneously with the U.S. Civil Rights Movement) and the Afro-Peruvian musical revival; she claims that, of late, the link to political agendas has been weakened, with Afro-Peruvian music making now serving primarily to divert tourists (2003:156–57). Among the genres and dance-plays considered Afro-Peruvian are the *landó*, the *son de los diablos*, the *festejo*, and the *ingá* (Romero 1994:318).

Let us study, then, an Afro-Peruvian **landó** (lan-*do*)—a reconstructed genre (Romero 1994:318; Feldman 2003:156). It was written by Daniel "Kiri" Escobar and performed in this rendition by the soloist Eva Ayllón. The recording "Azúcar de caña" appears on *The Soul of Black Peru*, "the first recording of Afro-Peruvian music widely available in the United States" (Feldman 2003:157). Active Listening 9.7 provides the full text of "Azúcar de caña" (ah-*soo*-kar deh *kah*-nyah) and illustrates the formal structure of this Afro-Peruvian *landó*.

The rhythmic subtleties of Eva Ayllón's singing impress us. She declaims the text so expressively, with a distinct sensuality: The song incorporates several

ACTIVE LISTENING 9.7
"Azúcar de Caña" ("Sugar Cane")

COUNTER NUMBER	COMMENTARY	LYRICS	TRANSLATION
Introduction			
0:00	Ensemble with vocal solo.	*¡Aha! ¡Vamos temple! ¡Sí!*	Aha! Let's go in [musical] harmony! Yes!
0:02	Distinctive *quijada* sound.		
1st stanza			
0:10	Vocal solo: expressive singing style.	*Salgo de mañana, a tumbar la caña,*	I go out in the morning, to cut sugar cane,
		Salgo de mañana, a tumbar la caña,	I go out in the morning, to cut sugar cane,
		Lucero del alba siempre me acompaña.	The morning star always accompanies me.
		Lucero del alba siempre me acompaña.	The morning star always accompanies me.
2nd stanza			
0:31	Vocal solo.	*Machete en la mano, corazónde vino,*	Machete in hand, heart of wine,
		Machete en la mano, corazónde vino,	Machete in hand, heart of wine,
		El río, mi hermano, zafra mi destino.	The river, my brother, the sugar-cane harvest my destiny.
		El río, mi hermano, zafra mi destino.	The river, my brother, the sugar-cane harvest my destiny.
1st interlude			
0:52	Music reinforces relative minor key.	*Sale el sol tras la montaña,*	The sun rises behind the mountain,
		Sale el sol tras la montaña,	The sun rises behind the mountain,
		Sale el sol tras la montaña,	The sun rises behind the mountain,
1:06		*E, inundando todo el valle con aromas de la caña.*	And, flooding the whole valley with the aroma of the sugar cane.
2nd interlude			
1:14	Relative minor key again reinforced.	*Esta noche en mi cabaña,*	Tonight in my cabin,
		Esta noche en mi cabaña,	Tonight in my cabin,
		Esta noche en mi cabaña,	Tonight in my cabin,
1:27	One-line connector produces tonal instability and introduces text of vocal choral echo.		
		Voy a bailar coba coba con mi mochera,* esta saña.†	I'm going to dance body to body with my mochera,* this dance.†

continued

COUNTER NUMBER	COMMENTARY	LYRICS	TRANSLATION
Choral echo with Ayllón interjections			
1:32		—*con mi mo-chera, esta saña,* —*con mi mo-chera, esta saña,* —*con mi mo-chera, esta saña,* —*con mi mo-chera*— (*"Je-ye, esta saña, señores; ¡pata en el suelo!"*)	—with my *mochera*, this dance, —with my *mochera*, this dance, —with my *mochera*, this dance, —with my *mochera*— ("Yes, yes, this dance, folks; feet to the floor!")
Multipart chorus			
1:42	Chorus with Eva Ayllón and male-voice interjections.	*Azúcar de caña,* *Sombrero de paja,* *Mula resongona,* *Juguito guarapo.* *Azúcar de caña,* *Sombrero de paja,* *Mula resongona,* *Juguito guarapo.* (*"¡Toma! ¡De la negra! ¡Así! ¡Eso es!"*)	Sugar cane, Straw hat, Whining mule, Sugar-cane liquor. Sugar cane, Straw hat, Whining mule, Sugar-cane liquor. ("Drink! My woman's! Like that! That's it!")
Vocal solo			
2:03		*Azúcar, azúcar,* *Azúcar, azúcar,*	Sugar-, sugar-, Sugar-, sugar-,
Instrumental interlude			
2:09	Transition to thirrd stanza.		
3rd stanza			
2:14	Vocal solo.	*Roncan los trapiches, moliendo la caña,* *Roncan los trapiches, moliendo la caña,* *Juguito guarapo, quémame el entraña.* *Juguito guarapo, quéma mis entrañas.* (*"¡Rico!"*)	The sugar mills roar, grinding the sugar cane, The sugar mills roar, grinding the sugar cane, Sugar-cane liquor, burn my innards. Sugar-cane liquor, burn my innards. ("Delicious!")
4th stanza			
2:35	Vocal solo.	*Noche de la zafra, luna de cañero,* *Noche de la zafra, luna de cañero,* *¿Cuándo será´ mío, mi valle, mochero?* *¿Cuándo será´ mío, mi valle, mochero?*	Night of the sugar-cane harvest, moon of the sugar-cane worker, Night of the sugar-cane harvest, moon of the sugar-cane worker, When will my valley be mine, *mochero*? When will my valley be mine, *mochero*?
Repeat from first interlude through multipart chorus and subsequent vocal solo			
2:57–4:13	Vocal solo and call-and-response texture.		
4:13	Reprise of multipart chorus, and fade out.		

* *Mochera/mochero:* woman/man from the Moche region of coastal Peru.
† Saña is also a coastal district, in the Peruvian provinces of Lambayeque and Chiclayo; it has been influenced by older, Afro-Peruvian traditions (Casas Roque 1993:299–300, 331).

terms of flirtation and eroticism. Barely acknowledged in the 1970s, Eva Ayllón by the mid-1980s was among the most esteemed of Afro-Peruvian singing artists (Martínez and Jarque 1995). We hear the distinctive buzz of the **quijada** (kee-*ha-da*)—a donkey, horse, or cow jawbone that is a traditional instrument dating back in Peru to the eighteenth century (for an eighteenth-century drawing, see Casas Roque 1993:308; see also Romero 1994:312–13). Also known as *carraca llanera* in the Plains of Colombia, this instrument is a struck idiophone; the animal's molars, when loosened by exposure to the elements, produce a clear, dry crack when struck with the fist. In some Colombian ensembles, the molars may be scraped with a stick. We also hear a sense of exchange between the solo vocalist Ayllón and a chorus; this resounds with the call-and-response texture that we typically associate with an African or African-derived music.

Then there are the lyrics. The entire piece resounds with the culture and ecology of its home region. First, the Moche culture (*mochera, mochero*) existed prior to the time of the Incas, in northern coastal Peru; the *Muchik* (Moche) irrigation systems were taken up by the Inkas. One can still observe remnants of the Moche culture, both in the physical features of the inhabitants of this coastal zone and in their surnames and place names (Casas Roque 1993:299). Today, in fact, in political and lexicographic efforts in the region, aided by the distinguished anthropologist Richard P. Schaedel (d. 2005), one sees a remarkable revival of Moche culture underway (Delgado-P. and Schechter 2004:x). Second, "Azúcar de caña" oozes with the harvest, milling, aroma, and drink of the *caña*—sugar cane, grown in lowland areas. *Guarapo* is an alcoholic beverage made from the cane—a *licor* that can burn one's insides. *Trapiches*, or sugar mills, process the *caña.*

Trapiche and *caña* emerge in music not only along the Peruvian coast, but also to the north in Ecuador and Colombia. In an October 31, 1990, interview with Milton Tadeo and Ermundo Mendes León, these Chota Valley musicians told me that the *bomba*—a traditional, emblematic genre of Chota—had actually emanated from the *trapiche* (sugar-mill) culture of the older generations of Chota: Jesuit missionaries derived a degree of wealth, up to the eighteenth century in Ecuador, through several sugar plantations located near today's Carpuela, the Congo brothers' home village. Milton recounted to me this traditional *bomba* text: "'A la culebra verde, negrita, no hagas caso, mete *caña* al trapiche, chupa y bota gabazo.' (Don't pay attention to the green snake, dear woman; put cane to the sugar mill, suck on it, and throw away the waste pulp.)" (Schechter 1994:288–89; for a discussion of this version and a slightly different one, see Coba Andrade 1980:42. Coba Andrade provides a deeper discussion of this entire phenomenon.). Farther north, in Colombia, we find a lively, raucous festive *bambuco* called "El guaro." As William Gradante notes, "The terms *guaro* and *guarapo* refer to the sugary juice squeezed from sugar cane—in this case in its fermented, highly intoxicating, homemade form" (1999:341). This upbeat, *sesquialtera* folk song, made famous in an interpretation by the renowned Colombian duo of Garzón y Collazos, speaks to the same joy of the *caña* that we have seen in Peru and Ecuador: "De la *caña* sale el *guaro*—¡Qué caramba!—Sí la *caña* es buena fruta. Si la *caña* se machaca—¡Qué caramba!—El *guaro* también se chupa…." ["*Guaro* comes from sugar cane—Whew!—Sugar cane sure is great. If the cane is squeezed—Whew!—Then you can even drink it…."] (Ibid.:347).

Despedida, or Farewell

In this chapter, we began with the comment that Latin America was a kaleidoscope of cultural patterns, and we explored the musical manifestation of several of these. In our *despedida,* or farewell, to Latin American music-culture, we can begin to appreciate the richness of ensemble and solo music making in Latin America. These *Nueva Canción* songs, *k'antus, sanjuanes, waynos, albazos,* and *landós* speak to strongly felt political concerns; deep-rooted musical forms of expression; detailed and attentive attempts, from afar, to capture the overall character of an Andean song-dance type; and dedicated efforts to recreate local musical style. From "El aparecido" and "Muyu," to "Amor imposible" and "Azúcar de caña," we have feasted on a substantial buffet, one that I hope will entice you to savor the many other pungent and satisfying flavors of Latin American music.

Study Questions

1. What are two musical instruments—both of which were mentioned and heard in this chapter—whose "ancestors" go back at least two hundred years, in the Andes of South America?

2. How can one demonstrate that the phenomenon of the Andean music ensemble is now truly an international one?

3. What are two particularly interesting aspects of the Bolivian *k'antu,* "*Kutirimunapaq*"?

4. Describe two examples, discussed in this chapter, of the revival/reinterpretation/ transplantation of traditional Latin American musics.

5. How is it that the African-Ecuadorian *sanjuán,* "*Me gusta la leche,*" is actually an example of a hybrid music?

6. How do the lyrics of the Afro-Peruvian *landó,* "*Azúcar de caña,*" reflect the ecology and culture of its home region?

7. What are some traditional aspects of northern Ecuadorian highland Quichua material culture and music culture?

8. What is the Quichua *sanjuán,* "*Ilumán tiyu,*" really about?

9. What are some features of the Peruvian *wayno*? How is it that the husband-and-wife ensemble, Chaskinakuy, captures its character so well, in their rendition of "*Amor imposible*"?

10. What is the song "*El aparecido*" about? How does it fit both within the *Nueva Canción* movement, in Latin America, and within larger traditions of Latin American song?

10

The Arab World

Anne K. Rasmussen

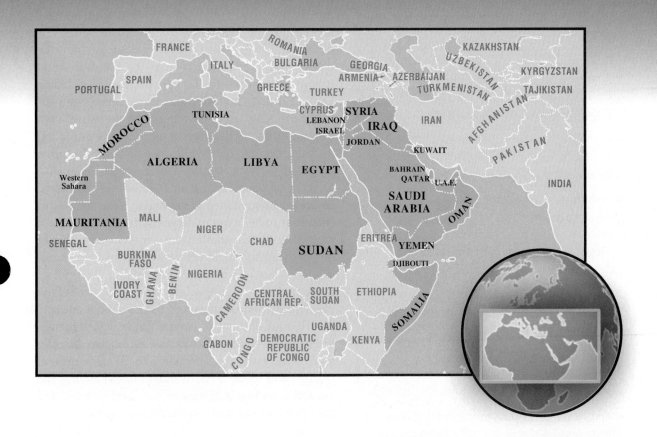

Learning Objectives

After you have studied this chapter, you should be able to:

1. Appreciate the great variety of traditional, folk, and popular music from various regions in the Arab world and its diaspora.

2. Understand the complexities involved in the geographic distinctions between the *Middle East*, the *Arab world*, and the *Muslim world*, and how these terms are important for an understanding of the region's music.

3. Know the specific vocabulary of terms related to: the material culture of music (musical instruments, etc.); the building blocks of music (modes and rhythms, etc.); aesthetic

continued

MindTap·

START experiencing this chapter's topics with an online audio activity.

concepts about music; historical events related to music; the influence of religious ideologies and practices on music; and the names of important musicians, historical figures, groups, and communities relevant to this chapter's overview of music in the Arab world.

4. Discuss the effects of human migration on the transmission, preservation, and intensification of musical practice in the Arab world and its diaspora.

5. Pursue your own investigation of Arab music and musicians.

Salient Characteristics of
Arab Music

- Arab music has a written history that dates back to the eighth century and plays a very important role in the intellectual life of the early Arabs

- Due to the prominence of the Ottoman Empire, Arab countries never really developed their own court or national music

- Arab scales include quarter tones or microtones, which are notes that fall between the black and white keys of the piano (some find that this quality makes the music sound out of tune, while aficionados often say quarter tones contribute to the sweetness of Arab music)

- Arab music features both metric and nonmetric rhythm, and both can be combined in performance as in "Shaghal"

- The Arabic language, including Quranic recitation and sung poetry, are key to Arab musical aesthetics

- Arab instruments include a wide variety of drums, frame drums, flutes, double reed instruments, and plucked and bowed lutes, and are relatively transportable (in comparison to, say, the instruments of the Javanese *gamelan* or a grand piano)

- Heterophony is one of the most compelling aspects of Arab musical texture and performance practice

- Arab music thrives today both as a modern, popular phenomenon, as well as a living, traditional practice despite social, cultural, and political turmoil and constant migration

- The slow violence of economic destitution and sociopolitical constraints can have irreversible effects on the sustainability of musical ecosystems

This chapter introduces music of the Arab world. A vast collection of twenty-two countries, where Arabic is the official spoken and written language, the Arab world is home to a surprising diversity of peoples, including Jews, Christians, and Muslims. Furthermore, the people of the Arab world have been "on the move" both historically and in the present time. So, the music and the culture of the Arab world spread out in a **diaspora**: Rather than being confined to a single geographic location, its people and their traditions are dispersed beyond the boundaries of the region. One aim of this chapter is to help you understand the routes of these musical traditions. Another aim is to share an appreciation of the historical and literary legacy of Arab music-culture. While it is modern and dynamic, Arab music today also offers a glimpse into the roots of some of the oldest ideas, philosophies, and theories about music.

Through looking at several kinds of Arab music making, we explore the influence of religion, the history of the region, relationships to Western musical practice and ideas, some wonderful celebrations, the musical roles and activities of men and women, and the importance of music in the Arab diaspora.

"Arabia"

For centuries, the Western world has consumed fanciful images of a timeless "Arabia" though art, literature, film, and popular culture. Some of these images originate in the stories of *The Arabian Nights,* which are set in Persia and Mesopotamia (present-day Iran and Iraq) as early as the seventh century C.E. The stories relate a variety of adventures on the **Silk Road**, an ancient network of trade that ran from China to Morocco (Map 10.1). A corresponding Maritime Silk Road connects the regions around the **Indian Ocean** and further east

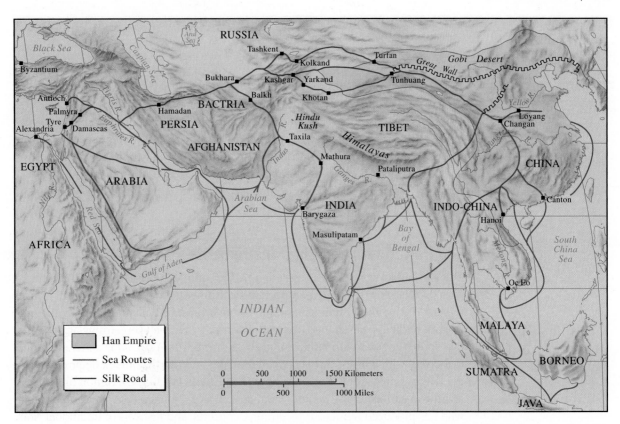

Map 10.1
The Silk Road

to the South China Sea. Versions of the *Arabian Nights* were written in Arabic on papyrus (a fibrous paper made from a plant of the same name; used by ancient Egyptians, Greeks, and Romans) and date to the ninth century. However, familiar tales such as "Aladdin and the Magic Lamp," "Ali Baba and the Forty Thieves," and "Sinbad the Sailor" have been rewritten and retold by a wide range of authors— from those living in different parts of Asia to the literati of nineteenth-century England (such as Robert Louis Stevenson) to teams of screenwriters at Disney and Dreamworks studios.

The reimagining of Arabia through art, literature, and music has produced wonderful images as well as misleading stereotypes. Every period of Western art music includes masterpieces inspired by the so-called Orient. During the Tin Pan Alley era of American popular music in the 1920s and 1930s, songs such as "Leena from Palesteena" or the "Sheik of Araby" were standard fare. In the 1950s and 1960s, the soundtracks of motion pictures such as *Casablanca* (with a score by Max Steiner) and *Lawrence of Arabia* (with a score composed by Maurice Jarre) created the evocative soundscape of the unpredictable desert and the animated bazaar. This music became a springboard for later musical explorations heard in the soundtracks of James Bond and Indiana Jones films, and of animated productions such as *Aladdin* or *The Prince of Egypt,* marketed to children and their parents. The popular imagination is also fueled by political history and current events, particularly today, with the news media's constant focus on the turbulent instability of many Arab countries. But let us leave the imaginary world of Arabia behind and turn instead to the reality of Arab music and culture.

The *Takht* Ensemble

Listen to the excerpt of the performance of "Al-Shaghal" (ash-sha-*ghal;* the gh is similar to the French "r," and the "a" of *ghal* is pronounced like that of "apple;" the article *al,* meaning "the," is elided with the initial sh sound of the subject, *shaghal* and is, thus pronounced *ash-shaghal* and not *al-shaghal*). It was recorded live at a concert at Mount Holyoke College in Massachusetts, at the end of a weeklong summer workshop called the Arabic Music Retreat. The title means "Obsession," referring to an obsession or preoccupation with the beloved, a common theme in Arabic-language poetry and literature.

The Performers and Their Instruments

The ensemble you hear is called a **takht** and comprises seven instrumentalists who play the most important instruments in Arab traditional music (Figure 10.1). Simon Shaheen and his younger brother William both play the *'ud*, a short-necked, pear-shaped, fretless lute, usually with eleven strings arranged in five double courses with a fifth, single bass string. The Arab *'ud* is generally tuned in fourths (with a major third between the third and fourth course). Beginning with the lowest single string, the *'ud* is tuned C2, F2, A2, D3, G3, C4. Simon Shaheen is a virtuoso performer on *'ud* and violin as well as a composer and ensemble leader who has produced numerous recordings, concerts, and festivals of traditional Arab and Middle Eastern music. He is also known for his more fusion-oriented projects with musicians specializing in jazz and other world music traditions; in 1996, he founded the Arabic Music Retreat, an intensive, summer music workshop.

Figure 10.1

The *takht* ensemble. Pictured from left to right, Nasim Dakwar (violin), William Shaheen (*'ud*), Simon Shaheen (*'ud*), A. J. Racy (*buzuq*), George Sawa (*qanun*), Bassam Saba (*nay*), and Michel Mirhige (*riqq*). *Anne Rasmussen.*

Dr. A. J. Racy (Figure 10.2), an ethnomusicologist, composer, and performer and professor at the University of California, Los Angeles, plays the *buzuq*, a long-necked lute with twenty-four movable frets, two sets of strings in triple courses C and G, and a single bass string tuned to C. Racy's name is cited frequently in this chapter because he is one of the most important scholars of Arab music. He is also the codirector of the Arabic Music Retreat.

Nasim Dakwar of Haifa, Israel, plays the violin, which is identical in construction to the Western violin or fiddle except that most Arab musicians tune the highest two strings down a whole step. Thus, rather than the Western tuning G3, D4, A4, E5, the Arab violin is tuned G3, D4, G4, D5.

Bassam Saba of New York plays the *nay*, a reed flute that is blown obliquely at an angle. Jamal Sinno of Boston plays the *qanun*, a zither with seventy-five strings in triple courses with a series of small tuning levers that allow the strings to be retuned in the course of performance. Michel Mirhige, formerly one of the most important percussionists in Lebanon, now living in New York, plays the *riqq*, the Arab tambourine, also known as the *daff*.

Musical Texture

All of the musicians play virtually the same melody, a piece by the Egyptian composer, singer, instrumentalist, and actor Muhammad'Abd al-Wahhab (d. 1991). Even though they play the same melody, the musicians are not playing precisely in **unison** (together on the same pitches); rather, they are free to add their own ornaments and nuances. Some instruments leave notes out, while others double them. The plucked stringed instruments, *'ud, buzuq,* and *qanun,* create a thicker, more sustained texture by employing evenly paced double or quadruple picking, or **tremolo** (fast strumming or picking up and down on a string). They also decorate their melodies with **grace note pickups** (playing the note above or below very quickly before landing on the main note) and **octave leaps** (jumping up or down an octave). The reed flute, or *nay,* and the violin can sustain longer tones. Although the *nay* is an aerophone and the violin is a chordophone, the instruments are similar in that they can both vary their sustained tones by altering the **timbre**, or tone color, of those tones with bow pressure in the case of the violin, air pressure in the case of the *nay,* or vibrato; both instruments can slide between notes—an important aesthetic technique of Arab music. Each instrument of the *takht* decorates the melody with **trills** (oscillations between two adjacent notes), **turns** (ornaments including a note above or below the main note), slides, and variations in the tone color characteristic of that instrument. The *qanun,* for example, can easily do a run of an octave or more. The *nay* can sustain pitches, bend them, and shift the tone color from the breathy tone that is characteristic of the instrument to a purer, more focused sound similar to that of the Western silver flute. The *'ud* can reinforce important tones by quickly playing the same note an octave lower. The musicological term for the texture produced by the *takht* is **heterophony** (see Chapter 1), something that occurs rarely in Western art and pop music but that is easy

Figure 10.2
A. J. Racy playing the *buzuq. Dan Neuman.*

to find in many musical styles around the world. Heterophony is one of the most compelling aspects of playing and listening to Arab music, even though many Arab musicians rarely comment on this remarkable aspect of Arab performance practice, perhaps considering it one of the more unteachable aspects of performance. (See Chapter 8 for examples and a discussion of heterophony in Chinese music.)

Rhythm

The *riqq,* a tambourine with an extremely sensitive skin head (traditionally made of fish skin) and heavy cymbals, is an instrument that alone can sound like an entire percussion section. The rhythmic pattern or *iqa'* played by Michel Mirhige is made up of eight beats and is called *wahda.* First, listen for the difference between the low-sounding *dumm* (D) and the higher, drier-sounding *takk* (T). The name *wahda* comes from the Arabic word *wahad,* or "one," because there is only one *dumm* to each eight-beat cycle. Second, notice that Mirhige can fill or sometimes simplify this repeating pattern with an almost infinite number of rhythms and variations. Third, when the ensemble is playing all together (during the refrains, for example), Mirhige plays on the head of the instrument but lets the jingles ring through slightly (listen, for example, at 0:05 and 2:10). Fourth, when the ensemble features a soloist within the group, he may choose to play only on the head of the instrument, still producing several variations but silencing the potentially clamorous jingles.

Form, Melody, and Improvisation

Now we will focus on the melody and form of "Al-Shaghal" (Active Listening 10.1). After an eight-measure melody, the ensemble plays a kind of melodic, rhythmic **ostinato** (repetitive pattern), during which each individual plays a solo **taqasim**, or improvisation. Prior to the excerpt you'll hear, the violinist has already performed a solo. As we join the performance, it is Racy's turn to solo on the *buzuq.* The solid rhythmic and melodic ostinato provides the canvas upon which Racy paints his improvisation, or *taqasim.* Notice the way the rhythm of the *buzuq taqasim* has a regular pulse in some places but is nonmetrical or in free rhythm in others (see Chapter 1). At times it seems as if Racy is in synchrony with the other musicians but for the most part he seems to be doing his own thing. The juxtaposition of nonmetered rhythm and metrical rhythm, and the possibility of combining them, as we hear when Racy plays his relatively unmetered solo against the regular ostinato of the other musicians, is a distinctive feature of the music of the Arab world, and the of Middle East in general.

A **maqam** is a musical mode or scale, and there are several kinds of *maqams* described by name, as we will discuss later in the chapter. "Al-Shaghal" is in *maqam Bayyati* (ba-*yeah*-tee), beginning on the note G. One might also hear *maqam Bayyati* beginning on the note D or A, for example.

The second degree of the scale is a half-flat (indicated in this text with the sign ♭), also sometimes called a neutral interval or a quarter tone. The A♭ falls between the notes A♭ and A natural on the piano. Try humming along with the recording and then singing the scale of *maqam Bayyati.* If you have grown up in Europe or North America, you have heard these kinds of intervals in popular and folk music, but if you have been trained as a pianist or in the tradition of Western classical music you may find this difficult to do. One way for someone new to this music to approach the quarter tone might be to first sing the A as an A natural: G A B♭ (just like the do-re-mi

ACTIVE LISTENING 10.1
"Al-Shaghal" ("Obsession")

MindTap·

🎧 **WATCH** an Active Listening Guide of this selection online.

COUNTER NUMBER	COMMENTARY: MUSICAL ACTION	COMMENTARY: PERFORMER–AUDIENCE INTERACTION
0:00	End of violin solo (*taqasim*)	Exclamation: "Allah" by either a musician or someone in the audience
0:05	Eight-measure refrain played by the whole ensemble or *takht*	Audience applause
0:14	Second phrase of 8-measure refrain (measures five through eight)	
0:23	Two measures of rhythmic/melodic ostinato played by the *'ud*	
0:28	Beginning of *buzuq taqasim* after the "*dumm*" or downbeat by the ensemble	
0:33	Silence: pause between phrases	Audience murmers: "Ahh"
0:37	Tiny idea or fragment	
0:39	Silence	
0:41	Longer phrase with repeated notes, emphasized notes, and **sequences** (musical ideas that are repeated a step higher or lower)	
0:58	**Qafla**, or ending idea of the first "paragraph" of the improvisation	Complete silence
1:08	Paragraph 2 of the *taqasim*	
1:14	Melodic development, sequence, and another cadential phrase, or *qafla*	Vocal response by the audience members and other musicians
1:15–1:48	The *buzuq* continues the solo and concludes it with a *qafla* at 1:41 that is met with another vocal response by audience members and musicians. The *taqasim* ends as the main melody of the refrain is reintroduced at 1:48; some ensemble members join him subtly, with "fillers" and bits of the main melody.	Vocal response by the audience members and other musicians at 1:41
2:05	Descending run of notes by the *'ud* to lead the ensemble back into the repeat of the refrain melody	
2:10	Eight-measure refrain repeated by ensemble	Huge audience applause
2:28	Beginning of *nay taqasim*	Exclamation of "Allah!" at the end of the first phrase of the *nay taqasim*

of a minor scale). Then return to the A and slide down ever so slightly to a note that creates some tension with that A natural but is not as low as the full A ♭. The best way to get a sense of the intervals in *maqam Bayyati* is to sing along with this and other music in that *maqam,* and match your voice to the pitches of the performers.

Listen again to the *buzuq taqasim* by Racy. Let us call the first section of the solo (0:28–1:05 on the recording) a "paragraph." We hear several phrases or sentences, separated by pauses, that emphasize the four notes of the bottom of the scale (G A♭ B♭ C), with particular emphasis on the 4th degree C, the 5th degree D, and the **tonic** (first or bottom) note, G. The second paragraph of the improvisation, beginning at 1:08, showcases the lower range of the instrument. This paragraph extends to about 1:41 on the recording. The final phrase features a purposeful ascent up the scale of *maqam Bayyati,* and then a descent down the steps of the scale with a few twists and turns at the bottom. This concluding musical statement or **cadential phrase** is called a *qafla* (plural, *qaflat*). See if you can notice the raised 6th degree (E♭) that Racy employs on the way down the scale. While this is an occasional note, it is very much a part of the character of this *maqam,* especially when it occurs as effectively as it does in this *qafla.*

After a couple of seconds during which we hear only the ostinato pattern, the *buzuq* comes quietly back into the main melody of the composition (1:43). The rest of the musicians hang back, allowing the soloist's moment to continue, and do not join in until Racy reaches the repeat of the melody, which has become a kind of recurring refrain. The dramatic, descending run by the *'ud,* played by the virtuoso Simon Shaheen, brings the group back into the refrain definitively, and all join in at this repeat of the melody (2:05). At this moment we might describe Shaheen's deviation from the ensemble a **vamp** (rhythmic or melodic ostinato)—more as polyphony (see Chapter 1) than heterophony because he is really creating a countermelody that becomes a "pickup" to the group's return. The descending *'ud* line underscores the end of Racy's solo and receives resounding approval from the audience.

Tarab

To many, this music sounds beautiful in and of itself, but the fact that you can hear the live audience in the background tells even the novice that this is an exciting event. Even after the first phrase of Racy's *taqasim* on the *buzuq,* we can hear the audience murmur acknowledgment. In fact, rather than remaining respectfully silent, this audience participates actively in the music making. Listen again to the juncture between Racy's solo and the group refrain (2:05 to the end of the excerpt). Following this refrain, we hear just the beginning of Basam Saba's *nay taqasim.*

This concert follows the parameters of performance, or the principles of a musical event, which are at first learned and later expected or even desired by the participants (see the performance model in Chapter 1). Active listeners, including members of the ensemble, might respond to the music with exclamations of "Oooh" and "Ahhh," and words like *Allah* (God), *Ya Salam* ("Oh, peace"), or *Ya 'Ayni* ("Oh, my eye"). With these exclamations, the audience encourages the musicians by making a statement that the music is moving and exciting. The musicians in turn respond to the audience's acclamations with more good music.

In this context, interaction between musicians and audience is at the same time a catalyst for and the result of **tarab**, which translates roughly as "ecstasy" or "enchantment." The concept of *tarab* gets to the very heart of Arab musical aesthetics. The term refers to a repertory of traditional compositions as well as to a style of performance that both embodies and invokes *tarab* (Racy 2002). (You will notice later in this chapter that the female and male singers Sana and Amer Khadaj are called *mutriba* and *mutrib,* literally "enchantress" and "enchanter"; both the terms derive from *tarab*.) In "*tarab* culture," musicians and audiences expect performances to be inspired and inspiring (like, for example, the performance of "Amazing Grace" at the New Bethel Baptist Church, in Chapter 4). Listeners are expected to contribute to the overall atmosphere of an evening's music by offering complementary exclamations of encouragement to singers and instrumentalists alike. A performance without such participation would be considered lifeless, uninspired, and more like a concert of Western classical music, where the audience is expected to be silent while the music is playing and to applaud only after it is over.

During the performance of "Al-Shaghal," the conditions were ripe for *tarab*. And although the concert was in Massachusetts, rather than somewhere like Cairo, Egypt, what made it an evening of Arab music (as opposed to an evening of New England music) was—along with the musicians, their repertory, and the instruments on which it was performed—the experiences and expectations the participants shared.

Religion and Music in the Arab World

Newcomers to this music and culture sometimes assume that all Arabs are Muslims (people of the Islamic religion), and that Arab music is therefore Muslim music. On the contrary: with the exception of music used in religious rituals, Arab music is part of a tradition shared by Jews, Christians, and Muslims. In fact, in spite of the emigration of significant communities of both Jews and Christians away from Arab lands, many historically prominent musicians were Jews and Christians, and the three religious communities share a long history of musical and cultural exchange that continues today in spite of mass exodus and political rupture. So, although the performance of much music can be correctly categorized as Arab music *and* Middle Eastern music, it is not necessarily Islamic or Muslim music.

The religion of Islam is prominent throughout the Arab world and the Middle East; however, only about 20 percent of the world's Muslims live in the Arab world. The majority of Muslims live in South and Southeast Asia. In fact, Indonesia, Pakistan, India, and Bangladesh are the countries that have the largest Muslim populations, and none of these countries are part of the Arab world. The Arab world is actually the birthplace of three monotheistic religions—Judaism, Christianity, and Islam—which share many cultural attributes, from liturgical texts and stories, to traditions of religious chant, to philosophical ideas regarding mysticism. We turn now to the Islamic "Call to Prayer" and the recitation of the Qur'an.

The "Call to Prayer": *Azan*

The entire text of the "Call to Prayer" is printed here. Listen to several versions of the call to familiarize yourself with this ubiquitous aspect of the soundscape. Numerous recordings of the "Call to Prayer" may be found on YouTube from many places in the Middle East and Muslim World (search "call to prayer," "azan," or "adhan" on YouTube). Note that each phrase is repeated except for the final phrase. Pay attention to the often beautiful, virtuosic melodies created by a **muezzin** (the person who does the call). Sabri Mudallal (1918–2006), who I recorded in Aleppo, Syria, in 1993, is an exemplar of this art and of virtuosic, traditional singing. I was fortunate

MindTap•
◀)) **LISTEN TO**
"Call to Prayer" (*Azan*), performed by Sabri Mudallal, online.

MindTap•
🎧 **WATCH** video of Sabri Mudallal online.

to have met this "first muezzin" of the Great Zakariyya Mosque of Aleppo because I admired the recordings I had heard of his singing. When I inquired about this great master, our self-appointed guide, Hamid, took us straight to Sabri Mudallal just as he was about to recite the noon "Call to Prayer." Over the next few days, Sabri Mudallal invited us to make a series of recordings.

Text, The "Call to Prayer"

Allahu Akbar, Allahu Akbar	God is Great, God is Great
Ashshadu an la ilaha illa Allah (x2)	I testify that there is no God but God (x2)
Ashshadu anna Muhammad rasul Allah (x2)	I testify that Muhammad is the prophet of God (x2)
Hayya 'ala salah (x2)	Come to prayer (x2)
Hayya 'ala falah (x2)	Come to salvation (x2)
Il salah ghairu min al-noum	Prayer is better than sleep [for the morning call]

In Muslim communities throughout the world, the "Call to Prayer" emanates from every mosque five times a day. While most contemporary muezzins, like Sabri Mudallal at the Great Mosque in Aleppo, use a sound amplification system, the minarets of mosques were originally built so that those with beautiful, powerful voices could broadcast their call throughout the community. The call to prayer is not considered music, but it *is* musical. Notice the way the phrases are separated by long pauses during which you can hear the sounds of the city. At the appointed times for the call (predawn, noon, midafternoon, dusk, and about an hour and a half after sunset), the soundscape of Aleppo, like that of many cities in the Muslim world, is a loose tapestry of *azans,* all of them starting just a few seconds or minutes apart, with each proceeding at its own pace. Listen for the way the *azan* progresses. Each phrase, when repeated, becomes longer and more ornamented. Listen also to the declamatory nature of Sheikh Mudallal's voice. Finally, though the timbre or color of the voice might to a Western ear seem nasal or harsh, it is a model of beauty in this cultural context, a sound to which reciters throughout the Islamic world—even in Indonesia, South Africa, or Bosnia—might aspire.

Two other aspects of this singing that make it so distinctive are: (1) a nasal vocal timbre, called **ghunna** in Arabic, and (2) the way the muezzin holds or sustains vowelless consonants. Listen, for example, to the held "nnnnnnn" at 1:30 on the track. While these vocal techniques are undesirable to trained singers of Western classical music, nasalization and sustaining or "sitting on" consonants are a part of the sound of American country and western music, as well as many other American popular music styles (see Chapter 4).

These vocal techniques, which are cultivated in the performance of the *azan,* the recitation of the Islamic **Qur'an,** and the singing of religious songs, are considered the hallmarks of excellent singing in other Arab contexts as well. Reciters are acknowledged for their talent by their fans and connoisseurs alike; those like Sabri Mudallal, who was also known for his performance of traditional vocal repertory, may live a life similar to that of a professional singer, with a busy schedule of performance engagements and lively concerts packed with admiring fans and students. We were treated to his singing one evening when he invited us to a gathering of muezzins (Figure 10.3).

Figure 10.3
Muezzins of Aleppo.
Anne Rasmussen.

Once the singing started, the music continued for two hours. There was no break, no pause for applause, no conversation, and no introductions—all behaviors that one might associate with either a performance or a rehearsal. Social activity occurred through the sharing of songs.

Music and Islam

The widespread notion that "Muslims do not approve of music" is problematic. Certainly, in the past and particularly today, some Muslim individuals and communities have condemned music and musicians in the name of religion. Sometimes thought of as "fanatic," "fundamentalist," "extremist," or just conservative, these groups—the most well-known of which is the Afghani-based Taliban—use arguments they say are based on religious dogma to close theatres, destroy musical artifacts, and persecute musicians (Shiloah 1997). In truth, however, a wealth of musical genres and styles exists in Islamic communities throughout the world. At the most basic level, ritual speech, like the "Call to Prayer," the verses of the Qur'an, and even group prayer is almost always intoned or chanted. Some performances of religious language can be remarkably musical. Furthermore, in certain social contexts such as public celebrations or family-based rites of passage, religious language often occurs alongside singing, sometimes with instrumental accompaniment. As such, the performance of religious language—from prayer to many different kinds of song—constitutes a dense constellation of Islamic vocal arts and music (Figure 10.4).

The Arabic language is used in ritual performance throughout the Muslim world—from Indonesia to Pakistan, and from South Africa to Bosnia to California. But while the language of the Qur'an, Arabic, along with various daily rituals and key holidays are shared across the Muslim world, every country, region, culture, and community has developed its own local religious practices. In Indonesia, for example, there are a multitude of unique, Islamic musics. We can also find a prevalence of

MindTap•
◀)) **LISTEN TO**
various reciters online.

Figure 10.4
Contestants Abdul Hamid and Isa Siswatika, both age twenty, in preparation for upcoming competition in Quranic recitation, Jakarta, Indonesia.
Anne Rasmussen.

women in public religious life, which might seem remarkable when compared with practice in other Muslim regions (see Nelson 1985, Rasmussen 2010, and Harnish and Rasmussen 2011).

Music in History/Music as History

The Qur'an is not only essential for Muslim ritual, but it also provides an important source of guidance in matters of everyday life, including those that involve music. Alongside the Qur'an, people look to the **Hadith** (ha-*deeth*), the traditions of the prophet Muhammed that were preserved in the statements of his closest companions and eventually recorded in writing. Together, the Qur'an and the Hadith contain much information related to the attitudes toward and the practice of music during the dawn and development of Islam (the seventh and eighth centuries). These are the first in a rich library of early, written sources on music history in the Arab world.

Musical Life in Medieval Mesopotamia

Formerly called Mesopotamia (literally "the land between two rivers": the Tigris and the Euphrates), Iraq has long been recognized as the site of phenomenal human invention: the wheel, written **cuneiform** script, and ingenious architectural and agricultural techniques. Baghdad was for centuries a cosmopolitan city humming with intellectual activity and music. Cities such as Baghdad, as well as Aleppo and Damascus (both in Syria), served as cultural crossroads and mercantile centers along the overland Silk Road that were characterized by a multicultural mix of peoples from Mesopotamia, Syria, Byzantium (Turkey), and Persia (Iran) (Racy 1984).

The medieval Arab world witnessed rich intellectual and scientific investigation. During the ninth century, the translation into Arabic of the treatises of Plato, Pythagoras, Plotinus, and Aristotle took place at the **Bayt al-Hikma** (House of Learning) under the patronage of the Abassid Caliph al Ma'mun. Works written between the ninth and thirteenth centuries in this environment considered the scientific nature of music—from its importance in the universe, to the measurement of pitch intervals, to the construction of musical instruments such as the 'ud. Authors were preoccupied with the cosmological and metaphysical meanings of music (Racy 1984:9; Turner 1995), as well as with its applications for healing and therapy (Shiloah 1991). Arabic translations of Greek treatises became available in medieval Europe and greatly influenced the development of music there, where the ancient world's ideas about music and its relationship to both the mundane and the sublime caught on. The Latin concept of the *quadrivium,* which allied music with the study of mathematics, geometry, and astronomy, was directly influenced by Greek philosophies that were made known, in part, through the Arabic translations originating in Mesopotamia. Let's meet a musician from contemporary Mesopotamia, Rahim Alhaj.

Interview with Rahim Alhaj, Musician from Baghdad

Given Iraq's contemporary history, you may find it difficult to imagine Baghdad as a city bustling with cosmopolitanism, intellectual activity, and music. During the Second Gulf War (begun in 2003), an Iraqi 'ud player and composer, Rahim Alhaj (also known as Al Haj) visited my campus in January 2004. His concert was standing room only; in fact, more than one hundred people were turned away. Our curiosity to know and share something with "a real musician from Baghdad" was apparent. During Rahim's visit I kept an audio recorder running: in the car, at restaurants, and during his formal presentations. What follows is an edited version of his story. I have polished his English, which he humorously refers to as "a disaster"; Rahim reviewed the transcript to make sure I had not misinterpreted anything that he said. Because this was a very personal exchange, I refer to Mr. Alhaj as Rahim.

Owing to fortuitous circumstances and new friendships, Rahim began to build a life in the United States. He began to perform live, tour, and record. In 2015, Rahim was the recipient of a National Heritage Fellowship Award, the most distinguished honor bestowed upon folk and traditional musicians in the United States. Rahim's story exemplifies the dynamic nature of musicians and a music-culture that can survive the harshest of circumstances. Furthermore, the story of any individual musician shows us again that, even though we can generalize about the music-culture of a nation, an ethnic group, a religious community, a town, a community, a band, or even a family, the trajectory of each and every person making music—and "people making music" includes musicians, patrons, audiences, dancers, and producers—is unique. Here is Rahim's story.

Salient Characteristics of Rahim Alhaj's Music

- Attributes his discovery of the 'ud to a teacher who took the time to mentor him
- His father was not in favor of music as a profession
- Describes his relationship with his instrument and with music as a love affair (see Figure 10.5)
- Even though he was "only a musician," he was persecuted for his politics (as is the case with many political refugees and emigrants, a family member went to extraordinary lengths and great expense so that Rahim could leave his homeland for a better life)
- One of the side effects of war and religious extremism can be cultural genocide; musicians can be disempowered, and entire traditions can be wiped out
- As a newcomer to the United States, he was an unknown whose life's work no longer had a context

Rahim was able to leave Iraq in 1991 with a false identity: his mother purchased a real passport for him.

Rahim provided some details about the process of resettlement in the United States. After being granted refugee status and placement in Albuquerque, New Mexico, his case was taken up by a local charity. Given a month's rent and some money for food, Rahim was on his own, with no friends and just a few phrases of English.

I was born in Baghdad to a middle-class family. I was the only musician. I started playing the *'ud* when I was nine. I was a little boy compared to the big *'ud*. I was trying to find my way [just to hold the instrument]. But I watched my teacher and how he played with the instrument. So fortunately, or unfortunately, I could make some noise. Anyway, so he said, "You are a musician," and he gave me his instrument and he gave me some lessons, and I was … by myself … practicing all day. Then I found myself totally in love with the instrument. In fact, I couldn't sleep without it … sometimes I had to hold it and just sleep, until my father said, "He is insane!" My father was fighting with my mom a lot, because he didn't want me actually to be a musician. He wanted me to be a doctor. It is like this in America, [too]: parents don't like their children to be musicians. You know: "Go be a doctor!" "Money! A lot of money!"

Anyway, the great thing was, my mom, she supported me a lot … she made me a musician. My first concert was when I was in elementary school. And actually, because my father refused to let me study music unless I studied something else, I also studied Arabic literature to be a teacher. During that time, I entered my career as a professional musician. I graduated from the Conservatory of Baghdad under one of the greatest *'ud* players in the world, Munir Bashir. And up until 1991, I was politically active against the regime [of Saddam Hussein]. I was against the Iran–Iraq War, and I was imprisoned [twice because of that].

In 1991, I had the chance to leave Iraq under false travel documents. My mom bribed a man. She bought me this Iraqi passport under another name, so I got the chance to leave from Iraq to Jordan, which cost one million *dinari*, which is like twenty thousand dollars. When I left Iraq, I had a bad experience— and this was the saddest moment in my whole life. At the border between

Jordan and Syria they took my instrument from me because the Iraqi constitution does not allow a musician to take an instrument out of Iraq to another country unless you have permission from the minister of culture. This instrument was … it wasn't just an instrument, it was my life: my love, my wife, my mom, my life. And I let go of it.

Anyway, I stayed a while in Jordan, two or three years as a teacher, and then left for Syria where I stayed quite a while, five years or so until I came here with my wife, who I met in Syria, in March 2000. The United Nations granted me political asylum and arranged for me to come to the United States, and they chose New Mexico for me. Now I am here playing a lot of music, and composing, and doing some lectures.

It's a funny story. After a month this guy came to me, and he said, "We found you a job." And I said, "Okay!" And he said, "McDonald's." And I said, "So which kind of institute is that? Is that teaching history, musicians, music… ?" Yeah, so I swear to God I asked him, "Is this Western music they teach or Eastern music?" And he said, "No. This is McDonald's." "I don't know what McDonald's is!" I said. And he said, "It's McDonald's. It's a restaurant." I told him, "What?! A restaurant? I'm not playing in a restaurant! I'm a concert musician!" And he said, "Well, you're not *going* to play there. Your job is dishwasher." I was astonished. I had no English, but I told him, "Do you know me? Have you read my résumé?"

Well, the Iraqi people are proud of two things in Iraq, basically. Not just because the first civilization started in Iraq; we are proud of music and art. But the time under Saddam was a long disaster for a lot of reasons. The music scene and environment in the Iran–Iraq War [was like this]: All of the songwriters and poets wrote songs about Saddam: how great he is, and how the [Iran–Iraq] War was justified. As a musician, if you are not against the government, you will continue as a musician. In Iraq, when you are a musician, you have a salary. You take money from the government that allows you to live. And then you don't need to go to bars and play. That's nice. So that's what happened with the music.

But it was *after* what happened during the Iran–Iraq War in Iraq under Saddam [that was really bad]. Unfortunately, as you know, after the First Gulf War, we had sanctions for fifteen years, and it had an undeniable impact on the Iraqi people. We lost two million kids as a consequence of sanctions [because there was a shortage of medicine and supplies]. And all the musicians, you know, composers and so forth, left Iraq. Music became more of a secondary thing, not a way to live. So all the musicians could not make a living in Iraq, so they left Iraq.

The 'ud in Iraq is different from other Arab world traditions. It's not just associated with other instruments [as in the example of the *takht* ensemble heard in Active Listening 10.1]. No! The 'ud becomes a solo instrument. The new music for the 'ud as a solo instrument has a meaning: There are stories behind the music, not just something like a *taqasim* or improvisation [which is more abstract]. This is a different concept. You express *feelings*: compassion, love, and peace. We in Iraq have moved beyond the traditional forms. We are just a few, really, who are doing this kind of thing. My composition called "Helum" ("Dream") is about the desire we have to touch our dreams. The piece is actually based on a phone conversation with my nieces and nephews. Before my recent trip to Iraq, I asked them, "What are you, you know, *dreaming*

Fortunately Rahim met someone who spoke Arabic and understood his predicament. She and some others supported his first concert, and then another and another. As his career as an Arab musician in the United States became more established, he began to see his role as a cultural ambassador, something he speaks about passionately. Rahim told me about music during the regime of Saddam Hussein, who was ousted from power and captured in 2003, during the Second Gulf War, and subsequently executed in 2006.

The notes accompanying his CD, *When the Soul Is Settled*, (2006) report that the conservatory he attended was "empty, burned, and silent" when he visited Iraq in 2004. When Rahim studied there, the curriculum included two years of Western art music, two years of Iraqi/ Arab music, and two years during which a student focused on a more specific area, such as composition or solo performance. He also described the importance of the 'ud in Iraq and of various musicians such as the teacher Sharif Muhi ud-Din Haydar (1892–1967) and his students, Munir Bashir and Jamil Bashir, who advanced a new style of virtuosic, Western-influenced 'ud playing that has been very popular among younger Iraqi musicians such as Rahim.

right now?" They were in college, and they said, "Well, just to have a regular life." That's the dream: to have a regular life, to go to school, get an education, and start lives. And to have a safe, basic life, which includes clean water and electricity. Their dream is to have a life.

For example, when I came to the United States, I composed this piece: [Rahim plays the beginning of "Horses" for a group of students (Active Listening 10.2)]. And so this is called "Horses." I composed this piece the third day I was in the United States. I was in the Albuquerque desert, and I found myself like a horse, able to run anywhere, you know, to touch my freedom. So I thought, how can I make horses? So I took [the idea of] galloping, and I composed this. That's totally, totally new in the music of the *'ud*.

As Rahim introduced his compositions, he juxtaposed the despair of his nieces and nephews—who hope for the basic privileges of clean water, electricity, and safety—and the destruction of a cultural practices—like playing music in a public venue or at a community wedding, or the freedom to walk down the street carrying an instrument—with the sensations of hope and freedom he felt when he began to

ACTIVE LISTENING 10.2
"Horses"

COUNTER NUMBER	SECTION	COMMENTARY
0:00	Introduction (two measures/eight beats)	Three-note idea (or motive) repeated.
0:03	Introduction (two measures/eight beats)	Three-note idea repeated one octave lower.
0:06	More of the introduction; transition	Three-note idea repeated in various ways, with a transitional passage at the end.
0:17	Section A	Interplay between a bass line and repeated notes in the upper register of the instrument.
0:30	Section A repeated	
0:43	Section B Here the melody moves to the upper range of the scale, and a descending pattern is heard twice: C to B C B, A B A, G A G— repeated at m. 24: C D C, B C B, A B A, G A G. At m. 29, a descending sequence leads into a dramatic, octave-and-a-half-run at m. 31, down to the tonic note C—which then leads back into the melody. (The run begins on A and concludes on C in m. 31.)	Last measure of this melody features a descending line into the lower register of the 'ud, which leads in to the return of the A section.
1:04	1st melody (A) repeated	
1:18	2nd melody (B) repeated	

establish his home in Albuquerque, New Mexico. Rahim summed up his philosophy, evident in his performances, his frequent interviews with the press, and his public presentations, as follows:

> I believe, profoundly believe, that there is nothing called Western music and Eastern music. This is an illusion. There is one something that's called music. You listen to this or that kind of music because you were born here or there. That's the way I see it. Just music.

Based on his first feelings in Albuquerque, of being free like a wild horse, Rahim Alhaj's composition "Horses" is what we call *programmatic.* He told us: "I composed this piece the third day I was in the United States. I was in the Albuquerque desert, and I found myself like a horse, able to run anywhere, you know, to touch my freedom."

All of Rahim's music is *about* something: galloping horses, lovers on the beach, destruction in Baghdad, or the dreams of his nieces and nephews; in concert, Rahim prefaces all of his performances with a story. The programmatic aspect of his style contrasts with the traditional music of Egypt and the Levant, which includes as its core a canon of pieces inherited from Ottoman Turkey. This Turko-Arabic music is often *abstract* and identified only by the name of the piece's form and its mode (*maqam*) or, in some cases, an impressionistic title, as in "Al-Shaghal" ("Obsession"). Although the newcomer to Arab music might find "Horses" quite similar to "Al-Shaghal," this performance differs from the Arab tradition exemplified by the latter, in the many ways.

By jumping from medieval Baghdad to the Baghdad of Rahim Alhaj, which he left in the year 2000, we skipped about ten centuries of Arab music history, so we now return to our thumbnail sketch of the rich history of Arab music.

Salient Characteristics of "Horses"

- Is programmatic: There is a story behind the piece
- Favors major and minor diatonic scales rather than Arab modes, which feature characteristic phrases and progressions and, in many cases, quarter tones
- An emphasis on virtuosity over emotionality (*tarab*), which can be heard in fast passages, Western-style scalar runs, harmonics, and arpeggios
- Use of harmonics and arpeggios requires the player to exploit the upper range of the instrument, something not heard in traditional 'ud playing
- Repetitive, sequential phrases combined with the use of arpeggios and sometimes chords suggests the application of Western harmonic progressions in ways that are uncommon in traditional Arab music

The Ottoman Empire and the Colonial Era

Up until the late nineteenth century, Arab world countries were subject to the cultural and colonial powers of the Ottoman Empire, which lasted from about 1326 to 1918. The Ottoman Turks created a musical legacy that still provides the basis for the "classical" tradition, particularly in the nearby Arab countries of Syria, Lebanon, Jordan, Palestine, and Egypt. Their political power combined with their cultural achievements allowed the widespread distribution of many developments in musical form and style—in the theory and practice of musical modes and rhythms, in the art of improvisation (*taqasim*), in the adaptation of Western musical notation, and in the development of modern instruments. Thus, Turkish Ottoman music-culture greatly influenced music throughout the Maghrib and the Mashriq.

Following and overlapping the Ottoman rule, European colonialism extended well into the twentieth century—with certain North African countries not gaining independence from the French until 1956 (Morocco and Tunisia) and 1962 (Algeria). Colonialism influenced music in the Arab world as much as the Ottoman rule had. In fact, because foreign occupying powers (both Turkish and European) dominated large-scale government in so many Arab-world countries, an official music of the court or government-sponsored musics never developed in most Arab countries. Rather, tradition remained unrestrained, to wax and wane according to circumstances.

The twentieth century saw new attempts to collect Arab music and to codify repertory, musical forms, scales, and rhythms. Baron Rodolphe d'Erlanger, a French musicologist who settled in Tunisia, published several books that include not only the French translation of historical writings but also transcriptions of the music that he collected from throughout the region. D'Erlanger was a driving force behind the **Congress of Arab Music**, an event sponsored by the Egyptian government in 1932 that assembled Arab theorists and performers along with European music scholars such as Erich von Hornbostel, Béla Bartók, Curt Sachs, Paul Hindemith, and Robert Lachmann. A particularly exciting aspect of the congress was that it produced more than one hundred and seventy-five 78-rpm audio recordings that captured the sounds of Arab music at the time. These recordings were archived, and some of them have been reissued on CD. The seven committees of the congress recorded and codified various Arab music traditions. They also discussed and documented musical elements such as rhythm, modes, and musical instruments, and they described and debated such subjects as music history, manuscripts, education, recording, and general issues (Racy 1991:71). The 1932 conference illustrates the points of convergence and divergence between Arab and Western approaches to the study and performance of music, many of which remain relevant today. The records of the conference, and the historical works of authors like d'Erlanger, also highlight the differences between the musical practices of the Mashriq and those of the Maghrib.

The Maghrib

North Africa is the area above the Sahara Desert, as opposed to sub-Saharan Africa, described in Chapter 3, and comprises the part of the Arab world called the **Maghrib** (also Maghreb)—literally "the place where the sun sets." In addition to Morocco, the Maghrib includes the countries of Mauritania, Algeria, Tunisia, and Libya. Egypt and the Sudan, although technically in North Africa, are not considered part of the Maghrib but are in the **Mashriq** ("where the sun rises"), the eastern Arab world. The Maghrib became part of the Arab empire through the trade fostered by the trans-Saharan caravan routes, beginning in the eighth century. Along with the silks and spices of the Arabian Peninsula and Mesopotamia came the religion of Islam. Islamic ideas and practices took hold more firmly in the lowland and coastal cities and where urban trade centers flourished, as opposed to the Atlas Mountains where the people preserved their Berber language and culture and continue to do so today. This Arab Islamic Empire extended North into Europe into an area then referred to as Andalusia. Beginning in 711 and for about the next seven hundred years until the Spanish Inquisition in 1515, a diverse civilization developed in Andalusia, anchored by court centers in Granada, Córdoba,

Figure 10.6
The *Association Ahbab Cheikh Salah* of Oujda, Morocco, in concert in May 2014.
Anne Rasmussen.

and Seville, which boasted a rich artistic life. With a series of expulsions after the Christian conquest of Granada in 1492 (the **Reconquista**), the art musics of the Andalusian cultural centers Córdoba, Granada, and Seville were transplanted to the new urban coastal centers of Algeria, Tunisia, Morocco, and Libya (Figure 10.6). The classical Andalusian musical traditions of the Maghrib, while related to those of Egypt and the Levant, have a distinct **repertory** and instrumentation and thus deserve their own musical study (see, for example, Davis 2004, Ciantar 2012, Davila 2013, and Glasser 2016).

Independent Morocco

The sites and sounds of old Arab Andalusia—for example, the splendid architecture of the Alhambra in Granada, or the sounds of the urban song genres **fado** in Portugal and **flamenco** in Spain, both thought to resonate with Arab-Andalusian influence—are now tourist attractions of the Iberian Peninsula. A ninety-minute boat ride across the Straits of Gilbraltar transports you from Europe and old Andalusia into the contemporary Arab world. Morocco gained independence from the French in 1956, so it is impossible *not* to notice the French presence in Morocco. Excellent baguettes and espresso can be procured along the grand boulevards of the cities and even in the small coffee shops of the Atlas Mountain roads, where buses stop to collect passengers. French is learned in schools, and everyone in the cities speaks it, along with Arabic and Berber. Just as Moroccans exhibit the cultural influences of past colonial domination, France also benefits from its inextricable involvement with Arab North Africa: *Maghrebi* culture is one of France's most notable cultural features, from the wonderful couscous restaurants of Paris, to first-class literature and film, to the *rai* North African pop music that has become a staple sound of commercially marketed World Music. Rai is well worth exploring. Sometimes referred to as the "blues" of North Africa, the music is rooted in the coastal Algerian city, Oran, and in the protest and wedding music of women, the most famous of whom is Cheikha Remitti (1923–2006). The superstars of rai music include Cheb Mami, Cheb Khalid, and Rashid Taha. The international hit songs "Didi," "Aicha," and Taha's cover of "Rock the Casbah" propel rai music into the category of classic Arab rock (see their recommended recordings in the discography, or search for rai music on YouTube).

Owing in part to the proximity of Morocco to Europe, this North African country has been much more accessible to Westerners than, say, Syria in the eastern Arab world or Saudi Arabia in the Gulf. Following independence, the country became a magnet for counterculture musicians such as the jazz saxophonist Ornette Coleman and the English rock group the Rolling Stones, as well as for writers who, like Brion Gyson and Timothy Leary, visited and in some cases stayed (Schuyler 1993). Fifty years later, the accessibility and allure of North Africa still draws artists from the United States and Europe who want to collaborate with musicians in North Africa. Examples include Peter Gabriel, producer of the WOMAD festival and the soundtrack for *The Last Temptation of Christ;* Sting, who collaborated with Cheb Mami for the song, "Desert Rose," from his album *Brand New Day;* and Jimmy Page and Robert Plant from the group Led Zeppelin, who recorded the album *No Quarter* and launched their "UnLedded" tour featuring a cast of Middle Eastern musicians. Such collaborations have helped introduce North African music and musicians to an international fan base, and numerous annual festivals such as the Fes Festival of World Sacred Music, held annually in Fes, Morocco, create an international meeting ground for musicians and audiences from all over the world. As World Music projects like this explode in all directions, it invites us to think about the implications of this kind of global exchange for musicians and audiences as well as for students of ethnomusicology and their professors. The case studies in Chapter 2 and elsewhere in this volume present other examples of global musical exchange that increasingly influence popular and traditional music throughout the world.

The Music of Celebration: Communal Music Making at a Wedding in Morocco

To provide a contrast to our focus up to this point on concert and ritual music and aesthetics, music in and as history, and the performances of male musicians, we next explore women's communal music making in the Maghrib. A few years ago, I traveled to Casablanca, Morocco, to attend my friend's wedding. My experience of that city and the multiday wedding festivities began with a visit to the public baths.

The Public Baths

The evening I arrived I learned that some of the groom's sisters were planning to go the next morning to the **hamam** for the traditional prenuptial communal bath. The sisters woke me around 6:00 A.M., all prepared with kits of soaps, towels, lotions, brushes, and natural, rough loofa sponges from the sea. We piled into a little car and drove down the wide boulevards in the modern part of the city, which is modeled after the French *Nouvelle Ville* (New City). We arrived at a building in a modest neighborhood of Casablanca and entered a gallery made of stones lit only by the natural light seeping in through the cracks. The walls and floors glistened with moisture. The experience of the communal bath was unquestionably physical, but it was not at all like the erotic depictions of the *hamam* by French Orientalist painters or colonial-era photographers; rather, it was intensely social. In Morocco, as elsewhere in the world, women socialize together when they can. They cook together, have their children together, and care for them and their extended families together. During Barbara's wedding, they sang together and played the frame drum called the **bendir**. My companions from Casablanca worked regular jobs, too, as teachers, flight attendants, and retail salespeople. That morning I participated in a kind of gender-specific socializing that also generates music, poetry, and performance specifically by and for women. The experience helped prepare me for the particular role that the women, including me, would play in the wedding that would take place over the next few days.

The Wedding Celebration

Two days after my trip to the *hamam*, I awoke to the sounds of women serenading the bride with boisterous, cheering songs accompanied by their own playing of the *bendir*. My friend, the bride, sat immobile, her arms resting on towers of pillows, her legs propped up by an ottoman. Her skin had become a canvas for delicate curlicues of henna, a natural, red dye used for staining the skin and hair in a widespread ritual of beautification practiced most prominently by women of the Middle East and South Asia (Figure 10.7). Many of the other women also had their hands dyed by the wedding attendant (she also turned out to be the ritual specialist who would accompany us for the next two days). For most of the day and on into the evening, the gathering of women drank mint tea, visited, and sang songs of congratulations to the bride, accompanied by vigorous, polyrhythmic playing of the *bendir*.

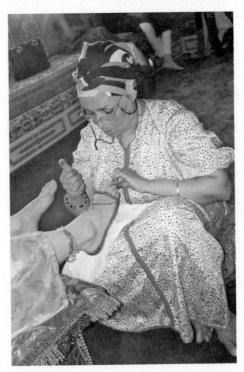

Figure 10.7
The henna party.
Anne Rasmussen.

The **bendir** is a variation of the frame drum, an instrument found throughout the entire Middle East and virtually everywhere in the Islamic world. The instrument is held in one hand and supported with the other in a way that frees some of the fingers of each hand to strike the skin on various places, producing *dumms* and *takks* in a remarkable variety of timbres. Although a staple of the Middle East and Arab world, the construction of the Moroccan *bendir* also reflects the preferred aesthetics of Africa. Two or three semi-taut strings across the inside of the *bendir* actually touch the skin's surface and vibrate, acting as snares when the instrument is struck. To my ear, the snares (added also to other Moroccan drums) reflect the African aesthetic delight for "buzz" (also discussed in Chapters 3 and 4). Just like the metal plate with its rattling rings on the bridge of a Gambian *kora* (Knight 1984), or the bottle caps or shells sewn onto the perimeter of the large gourd resonator of the *mbira* of Zimbabwe (Turino 2001), the snares on a *bendir* add another timbral component to the *dumm* and *takk* of this Arab frame drum.

Playing frame drums is the provenance of women in Morocco and throughout much of the Middle East, and even in much of central and southern Europe. Similar to the way the piano was once considered an acceptable "ladies' instrument" in the West, the frame drum is the one instrument that women of the Arab world have historically been allowed to play. Associated with healing, spirituality, and celebration, learning to play percussion may be as natural as learning to sing the songs that propel these social contexts. Another aspect of Arab weddings that adds to the excitement and the ritual is the *zaffa*, a procession in which the new couple is literally danced or paraded into the public space.

> ### Salient Characteristics of
> # *Zaffa* Wedding Procession
>
> - Weddings are important contexts for gendered music making
>
> - Several groups of musicians at the Moroccan wedding signified the multiple identities of the family
>
> - A ritual specialist helped with the henna night and also with the various sub-rituals within the wedding
>
> - The construction of the *bendir* and the polyrhythms evident in the playing and singing reflect African aesthetics

The *Zaffa* Wedding Procession

The *zaffa* procession for my friend's wedding was splendid. The couple arrived by car at a rented hall already filled with guests. They were whisked out of the car and escorted up the steps to the blaring of trumpets and the beating of *bendirs*. We all fell into line and walked with the couple and the musicians around the room in a regal procession, which resumed several times that evening and through the night until sunrise. For each procession, the bride and sometimes the groom wore different clothes, and each time they were announced musically by the various bands of musicians, who, along with the wedding attendant, pictured above, and the emcee, are all ritual specialists, hired for the occasion.

Three hired groups of musicians entertained us until about 8:00 in the morning. The first was a band of men who sat on a stage and performed Egyptian and North African urban pop—the music you might hear on the radio. The second group included four Berber women who sang and danced in a style unique to the Atlas Mountains, to the accompaniment of *bendir* and *rabab* (Figure 10.8). The men who played *bendir* and *rabab* at the beginning of the evening were also part of the third musical configuration, which animated the *zaffa* procession by playing huge tambourines called *mazhars* and long, straight, valveless trumpets called *nafirs* (Figure 10.9), which are rather unusual in the Arab world, where brass instruments of any kind are rare. As you hear in Active Listening 10.3, both the *nafir* trumpets and the *mazhars* play a repeating, ostinato pattern. In the context of performance, the focus of the overlapping patterns—which are organized into 6-beat units—can shift from two groups of three (**123456 123456 123456**—ONE two three FOUR five six) to three groups of two (**123456 123456 123456**—ONE two THREE four FIVE six). And during the night, as these various musics played on, the guests also clapped in patterns that alternately accented groups of two and three beats: a two-beat rhythm (two groups of three) and a three-beat rhythm

Figure 10.8

Performers at a Casablanca wedding. *Anne Rasmussen.*

Figure 10.9
Zaffa procession at Casablanca wedding, with *nafir* trumpets in the rear and *mazhars* in the front. *Anne Rasmussen.*

ACTIVE LISTENING 10.3
Zaffa **Procession at a Casablanca Wedding**

COUNTER NUMBER	COMMENTARY
0:07	*Zagareet* (high-pitched, excited, trilling calls) by the women.
0:12	Loud percussion pattern played by *bendirs*.
0:15	*Nafirs*, long trumpets, enter playing an ostinato pattern on a single tone; percussion continues.
0:55	Voices of the trumpeters heard in the background (here the music has a three-beat feel).
1:19	Trumpet ostinato resumes with percussion.
	Try to hear the polyrhythm, the alternation of or simultaneous accents within the groupings of six beats:
	1 2 3 **4** 5 6 — ONE two three FOUR five six
	1 2 3 4 5 6 — ONE two THREE four FIVE six

MindTap·
🎧 **WATCH** an Active Listening Guide of this selection online.

(three groups of two). This aspect of polyrhythm, discussed at length in Chapter 3, is, like the snares on the *bendir*, an aspect of Arab *Maghrebi* music that is distinctly African.

The ways in which music is used to articulate, explore, or even teach identities serve as a fascinating aspect of ethnomusicological inquiry. (See the music-culture model from Chapter 1.) By featuring both the pop band, who played tunes from the Arabic-language hit parade on amplified instruments including electric keyboard, electric viola, electric guitar, trumpet, and drum set, and the Berber groups, who played traditional music on acoustic folk instruments, the groom's family seemed to

MindTap·
🎧 **WATCH** a video of this *zaffa* procession of the wedding of Barbara and Najib, online.

be making a statement about both the richness of Moroccan culture and their multiple identities: urban and rural, Arab and Berber. Sometimes music and dance can encapsulate feelings about identity, about "who we are," with unmatched power.

Wedding Traditions of the Eastern Mediterranean Arab World (The Levant)

Dancing is certainly an important aspect of celebrations worldwide, but among Arab families, singing and poetry recitation are also communal and obligatory expressions of joy. In Dearborn, Michigan, where we find the largest community of Arab people outside of the Arab World, Palestinian and Lebanese women call out, in a high-pitched declamatory voice, improvised verses to the bride and groom, or to their own family and friends, on any occasion when hospitality is celebrated (Rasmussen 1997). These little poems, half-sung, half-shouted, are generally punctuated with **zagareet**, the high-pitched, trilling cries that proclaim excitement. The tradition that is preserved in Arab American communities today is consistent with practices in "the homeland"; in fact, wedding traditions such as these may be even more robust in the Arab diaspora then they are in their land of origin. Khadija Fayoumi, a member of my extended family, an elderly woman from Raffa, a city on the far eastern tip of the Gaza Strip in Palestine, told me about her role at Palestinian weddings. She explained that, before the first **intifada** (Palestinian uprising against Israeli occupation, 1987–1991)—before curfews, before security concerns, and before the rampant unemployment that renders marriage less frequent and much less extravagant today—when celebrations were still abundant, the neighborhood women always called on her for weddings. Not because she was a great singer, she clarified modestly, but because she knew all the songs! One evening she sang song after song for our family, drumming along on the bottom of a plastic bucket, giving us a taste of a special brand of Palestinian women's music making that, in better times, used to be commonplace (personal communication, 1993, 2000). Khadija's story reminds us that the slow violence of economic destitution and sociopolitical constraints can have irreversible effects on the sustainability of musical ecosystems. (See Chapter 1 for a discussion of music and sustainability).

Listen to the Palestinian Popular Arts Troupe (*Firkat El-Funoun Al-Sha'biyyah Al-Filastiniyyah*), also known as *El-Funoun* (The Arts), from the Palestinian territories. In this modern recasting of folk performance, we first hear the high-pitched, poetic cries of a woman who calls for blessings on the groom, who is, possibly, referred to as "the moon" (see Active Listening 10.4). Women respond with *zagareet*. A drum enters, and then we hear a male voice singing vocables (meaningless syllables) in free rhythm: "Ooof, ooof, ya bay"; another overlapping voice is heard toward the end of this sung melody. This is followed by a solo introduction by the **mijwiz**, a single-reed, double-piped folk clarinet, typical of the Levant (Syria, Lebanon, Jordan, and the Palestinian territories). The **mijwiz** drops out, and the *nay, buzuq,* and *qanun* play in call-and-response. The song proper begins with a man singing the beginning of each line of poetry and a group of women completing each line. The musical material, poetic form, and singing style draw on folk models, and the poetry contains metaphoric language that is as rich as any classical verse. A

ACTIVE LISTENING 10.4
"Initiation of Ecstasy"

MindTap·

🎧 **WATCH** an Active Listening Guide of this selection online.

COUNTER NUMBER	COMMENTARY	ARABIC TRANSLITERATION*	TRANSLATION
0:00	Female solo voice	*Aay yay yay* *Ya Rabb khalli bayya* *Aay yay yay* *Wa'tî wa'tî il-ghâli* *Aay yay yay* *Wa shufi-it-'amar fi darû* *Aay yay yay* *Ya rub kattir malû*	Aay, God keep his Father Aay, God give him the big gift Aay, I saw the moon in his house Aay, God increase his wealth
0:21	Zagareet by women		
0:25	Male solo(s)	Vocables	Oooh oooof ooof oooof ooof ya bay
0:36	Solo *mijwiz* with percussion		
0:56	*Nay, buzuq,* and *qanun* enter.		
1:18	Male solo with female chorus singing the second half of each line as a response; the response is underlined.	*Ya-bû-l-shhûr mrakhiyyîn* <u>*foug-l-hdûm*</u> *Min yowm frâqaq 'anni* <u>*ma shuft-l-hdûm*</u> *Min yowm-l-hajartûni tibki 'ayouni* *'ala-l-firqa jan-antuni w-il khad-i- 'ahh.*	You whose hair flows gracefully over your garments From the day you left me, sleep has evaded me From the day you deserted me, my eyes have wept incessantly The day you left me, you made me crazy, and, your beautiful cheeks are like buoys (bobbing about)
1:38	Instrumental interlude		
1:49	Singing in a non-metrical improvisatory style	Vocables	We yeh ho ho yeh willa ya bye

person, man or woman, who has been abandoned by his beloved, or a community whose friends have deserted them, in both cases usually without saying good-bye, are common themes of Arabic poetry and song. The images of hair flowing over the garments, weeping eyes, sleepless nights, and the distraught lover who is left with images of his beloved's cheeks are well known. Later, the singer continues by touching on scenes of village life and the wedding celebration. For the troupe *El-Funoun,* the staged performance of traditional expressive culture, including poetry, music, ritual, and dance, is part of their mission to "revive regional folklore as a form of Palestinian identity" (El-Funoun 1999; see also http://www.el-funoun.org). Poetry, music, and dance have also helped to catalyze social protest and resistance in the West Bank and Gaza, the occupied Palestinian territories of Israel, among Israeli Arabs and among Palestinians in diaspora communities in other Arab world countries, as well as in Europe and North and South America. Taking their cue from the rich traditions of folk poetry and the artistic use of language, resistance poets and political activists use English- and Arabic-language poetry in performance, as well as comedy and hip-hop, to extend and endorse their heritage with messages of resistance and affirmation. The work of poet Suheir Hammad and the hip-hop group, DAM, and comedy tours like "The Muslims Are Coming," or the biting humor of Amer Zahr, who writes a blog called "The Civil Arab," are all well represented on the internet and merit exploration by anyone interested in Arab music, culture, and contemporary issues (see MacDonald 2013).

Musical Biodiversity in the City of Salalah, Sultanate of Oman

The Arabian Peninsula is the region in the Arab world where the customs and values of the desert tribes are publicized and performed as part of a contemporary, national identity. The Arab countries of the Persian Gulf (also commonly referred to as the Arabian Gulf)—Kuwait, Bahrain, Qatar, the United Arab Emirates, Saudi Arabia, Yemen, and Oman—commonly advertise the **Bedouin** lifeways of the powerful tribes of Arabia as among their most precious cultural attributes. With the exception of Yemen, which has not enjoyed the prosperity of the oil-rich countries of the Gulf Cooperation Council (GCC), the cities of these modern nations, established within the past half century, are renowned for the splendor of their modern skyscrapers, world-class museums, and developing knowledge industries—attributes that have been enabled by the region's oil wealth. Alongside the ultra-modern features of the Gulf, visitors to the region will learn of desert encampments, medieval forts, falconry, dune bashing, and the possibility of extreme, adventure sports offered by the splendid natural environment. The traditional arts are important both for the tourism economy and for the story that people tell about themselves and their country, the national narrative. (See Chapter 5 for a discussion of music and nationalism.) My fieldwork in Oman over the past five years has opened my eyes and ears not only to an extraordinarily spectacular natural environment comprised of 1,000 miles of coast along the Gulf of Oman and the Indian Ocean, vast deserts, and rugged mountains, but also to a people whose history and culture has percolated within the contexts of the Maritime Silk Road around the Indian Ocean region: from Africa to the east, Iran and the Indian Subcontinent to the west, and Island Southeast Asia to the south.

The Salalah Tourism Festival, also known as the *Mahrajan al-Khareef* (Festival of the Monsoon), takes place every summer in Oman's coastal city, Salalah, in the southwestern-most Dhofar province, which shares borders with Yemen to the west and Saudi Arabia to the north. Although far from the capital city, Muscat, with its many attractions, Salalah brings in thousands of international tourists during the summer **monsoon** season because of the cool, moist, breezy climate that enshrouds the city and the green mountains at a time when the rest of the Arabian peninsula and most of the Middle East is scorching hot. We will use the song "*Batal al-Bab*" as an entrée into the special region of Salalah and the musical biodiversity of the Dhofar province.

Summer 2011: I have just two days left to experience the Salalah Festival. I concentrate my time at the "Traditional House" and open-air stage, where several local bands are scheduled to play each evening (Figure 10.11 and Figure 10.12). I sit behind the soundboard with various important men. Said, whose watch always matches his colorful *dishdasha*, is the manager of the traditional house and stage; he has welcomed and made a place for me behind the soundboard every evening. Although the audience is segregated, with women on one side of the open-air performance space, and men on the other, as a Westerner, and a researcher, I am a sort of "de-gendered" other, able to transcend social norms and sit with the men behind the soundboard. Even though we are positioned *behind* the band, this is the place to be: I can watch the sound engineer as he manipulates the channels to balance a band's sound, usually a loud mix of multiple drums, keyboard synthesizer(s), bagpipes, conch shells, male solo vocalists, and backup chorus made up of anywhere from three to ten women. The "manager" of the performing band also sits behind the soundboard, and artists and other festival personnel mill around in the Traditional House, which also serves as a green room for the musicians and dancers at the Salalah Festival (Figure 10.10).

On this very misty evening, I sit in the cold, clammy night air, wondering if I have had about enough. Shamis, the manager of the band *Al-Atar* (The Perfume), and I introduce ourselves to one another. I have gotten pretty good

Figure 10.10
Shamis Nasib Awab (right), manager of the band *Al-Atar*, and singer Askree Hajeeran seated behind the soundboard. *Anne Rasmussen.*

Figure 10.11
Rajab Khamis, Director of the Folklore Troupe Al-Majd (in black, smiling at the camera) and stage manager, Said (in Green turban) in front of the Traditional House looking out onto the open-air stage. Others pictured are members of the various bands performing that evening. *Anne Rasmussen.*

Figure 10.12
The Traditional House (Bayt Turathy) and open-air stage. Note the audience, with the women (many of whom are in black), on the right and the men (in white) on the left. Al Majd troupe, directed by Rajab Khamis, performs. *Anne Rasmussen.*

about explaining who I am and what I am doing. When Shamis (Figure 10.10) asks me if there is anything he can do to help me, I take a gamble and say:

> "I have heard so much about the singer and poet, Jam'an Diwan, and I keep hearing one of his songs, '*Batal al-Bab*'; I would like to know more about this and other important Salalah singers of the past, and to get some recordings at a proper shop."
>
> "Jam'an Diwan," Shamis exclaims, "I am the grandson of Jam'an Diwan."

At that moment a door opened to the lineage of the most important poets of Salalah, in the Dhofar region, this very special and musically rich region of the Arabian Peninsula and the Sultanate of Oman. The next day, Shamis took me to meet his uncle, Mana Diwan, the son of Jam'an Diwan, and we all met again in the summer of 2012 and again in January 2015, when they told me about the legacy of this poet laureate of Salalah.

Jam'an bin Ramadhan Diwan Al-Nubi was born in Salalah sometime during the first decade of the twentieth century. He died in 1995, and his life and works reflect the complex trajectory and birth of the modern, ancient nation of Oman. His family was from Africa and, in the early part of the twentieth century, they were likely slaves or servants. He inherited his talent from his mother, herself a distinguished poet known for the genre *tabl nisa'*, or women's drumming and singing. Although Diwan was illiterate, his life experience was rich. As Rajab Khamis (Figure 10.11) exclaimed to me: "If you follow the songs of Jam'an Diwan you will know the history and culture of Salalah: the sea life, the mountains, dances, love, work and life on the boat, traveling to other ports of call in Oman and in Africa, everything!" (Rajab Khamis, personal communication, 2015). He is said to have worked as a ship captain sailing out of the historic port town of Mirbat, and later as a security officer for large companies stationed in the desert. He composed hundreds of songs, and he and his family were patronized, first by Sultan bin Taimur and his wife, Mazoon al-Mashani, and then by their son, His Majesty Sultan Qaboos bin Said, who assumed power from his father in a bloodless coup in 1970, the year that the modern nation was born, accompanied by a self-declared renaissance or *nahda*. The coastal city of Salalah, home of Jam'an Diwan and the site of the annual summer festival, was continuously identified to me as among one of two important regions for music and dance (the other being the port city of Sur). In addition to the music and dance of Afro Omani communities, whose lifeways are associated with Oman's seafaring past and present, are the unique arts of the Jabali people, the mountain Arabs whose Jabali language and dialect has yet to be fully recorded. Combined with the desert culture of the noble tribes of Oman, Salalah's history as chronicled in the poetry of Diwan is rich.

Unlike many songs heard on the radio in Oman, Diwan's lyrics for *"Batal al Bab"* are lacking in any nationalist content; rather, the protagonist pleads, "Open the door, oh door keeper" and reminisces about the good times with loved ones, who seem to be oblivious to his requests. The song is composed in rhyming quatrains, with each verse of two lines, each with two hemistiches, following, for the most part a rhyme scheme of aaax, bbbx, ccccx etc., except for the chorus (*matla'*), which is rhymed aaba (Active Listening 10.5). The singers you hear are Khula Al-Siyabia (female) and Salah Ba'bad (male). Note the gender complementarity in the arrangement of male and female soloists and choruses: the male soloist sings a verse; the female soloist sings another verse; the women's chorus repeats the first verse; and the male chorus repeats the second verse. The song was recorded by the Omani Ministry of Information, where most of Oman's traditional music has been collected, studied, and reproduced, due to extraordinary initiatives of Sultan Qaboos, early in his reign, to establish the Oman Center for Traditional Music. The song was arranged, I am told, by Ali Al Hashele, who is ensemble (*takht*) director in the private Arabic orchestra of the

MindTap
◄)) LISTEN TO
"Batal al Bab," performed by vocal soloists Salah Ba'bad and Khula al Siyabia and with *'ud* soloist Salim Maqrashi, online.

ACTIVE LISTENING 10.5
"Batal Al-Bab"

MindTap·
🎧 **WATCH** an Active Listening Guide of this selection online.

COUNTER NUMBER	DESCRIPTION OF RECORDING	TRANSLITERATION OF ARABIC LYRICS	TRANSLATION
0:00–0:49	Dramatic introduction by strings followed by the establishment of the *bar'a* rhythm (at 0:10), a quick, four-beat pattern, comprised of interlocking patterns on double-headed kasir and rahmani drums. Also note the hand claps on beats two and three of the four-beat pattern.		
0:49	Salah Ba'bad, male vocal solo	1. *Batal il-bab ya bowab/ khalini kalam il-ahbab*	1. Open the door O Bowab!/ Let me talk to the loved ones.
		Alathi safaru 'ani/b'ada hum khatari ma tab	Those who traveled away from me./After they left, my heart/ mood (*khater*) has not been sweetened/healed
1:01	Khula Al Siyabia, female vocal solo	2. *Batal al-bab wa arhimni/ wa an khataitha tasamahni*	2. Open the door and have mercy on me/If I've done you wrong, forgive me.
		Ma baghaitk t'atibni/yasdini min shaqa wa- 'athab	I didn't mean for you to reproach me/it blocks me from longing and torture
1:12	Female chorus repeats verse 1		
1:24	Male chorus repeats verse 2		
1:35	Instrumental interlude: same as the introduction. The violins lead with the melodic phrase of four measures. The phrase is repeated, this time with *qanun* taking the lead on the first two measures, complemented by violin response. The full phrase is repeated twice, with the *qanun* finishing out the instrumental interlude by putting its own twist on the melody we've heard before. 8 m. (violins, tutti)		
1:44	2 m. (violin, tutti response) 2 m. (*qanun* call)		
1:49	2 m. (violin, tutti response) 12 m. (*qanun* solo)		
1:53	2 m. bridge/vamp		
2:09	Salah Ba'bad, male vocal solo	3. *Fuka li-l bab ya insan/tawal layla w-ana sahran*	3. Unlock the gates for me, O human/I have spent the whole night awake [staying up]
		Bisima tathkar al-ikhsan/la sadaqa wa la ashab	Don't you remember a good deed?/Neither friendship nor friends

COUNTER NUMBER	DESCRIPTION OF RECORDING	TRANSLITERATION OF ARABIC LYRICS	TRANSLATION
2:20	Khula Al Siyabia, female vocal solo	4. Qala li ruh wa tawakal/min hina ma m'ak madkhul	4. He told me to go and rely upon God (get out of here)/you don't have an entry
		Wa lub ay maghluq tatswasul/qultulu khatri ma tab	And if you try to go through any creature, I told him my heart/mind has not been sweetened/healed
2:32	Female chorus repeats verse 3		
2:43	Male chorus repeats verse 4		
2:54	Instrumental interlude, this time with the 'ud taking the solo lead.		
3:29	Khula Al Siyabia, female vocal solo	5. Qala li wa aish turid mini/yom kul yom tata 'ani	5. He said what do you want from me?/Day upon day, you are weary
		Qultihu qul watamani/Li turidha bi ghair hasab	I told him, tell me and wish for what you want without account
3:41	Salah Ba'bad, male vocal solo	6. Batal al-bab ya insan/If'al al-zaini w-alahsan	6. Open the door O you (human)!/Do what is right and beneficent
		Shuf nakhatari wa lahan/kayf saru bighair asbab	See that my heart/mind is longing/how they left (walked about) without reason
3:52	Female chorus repeats 5		
4:03	Male chorus repeats 6		
4:15	Instrumental Interlude, this time with the keyboard synthesizer taking the solo lead.		
4:48	Salah Ba'bad, male vocal solo	7. Safaru laylat il-jum'a /ma darai la mini al-raj'a	7. They traveled on the eve of Friday; not knowing when the return would be
		Shuf qalbi kamma al-sham'a/li sabarat daqiqa thab	Look, my heart is like a candle; If you were patient with me for one minute, it would melt.
5:01		1. Batal al-bab ya bowab/khalini kalam il-ahbab	1. Open the door O Bowab!/Let me talk to the loved ones.
		Alathi safaru 'ani/b'ad hum khatari ma tab	Those who traveled away from me. After they left heart/mind has not been sweetened/healed.
5:11	Female chorus repeats verse 7		
5:23	Male chorus repeats verse 1		
5:34	Male and female chorus both sing verse 1		
5:46	Instrumental coda		

Sultan. Listen to the incredible rhythmic picking technique of Oman's premier 'ud player, Salim Maqrashi. It is this rhythmic picking style that also identifies the tune as being from the Gulf region and, more specifically, as the Salalah-based **bar'a** style.

Since the rhythmic pattern is chugging along in two beats (**1**+2+**1**+2+), but the lines of poetry are sung in groups of ten beats, the beginning of each line falls alternately on a different beat of the *bar'a* rhythmic pattern.

The text is full of local referents but also resonates with some of the classic themes of Arabic poetry. The singer pleads for the doorkeeper to let him/her in. He refers to the people who have traveled away, who have hardened their heart, perhaps forgetting about him/her. He/she asks for forgiveness, pleads to the *bowab* and the community to do the right thing. He/she describes the loved ones (*ahbab* from the noun *hub*, or love) as departing on Thursday evening, the eve of Friday or Yom al-Jum'a, Friday being the day of prayer. He/she implores that if the loved ones would be patient one minute they would see that his/her heart would melt like a candle. Whether or not the protagonist has done wrong is unclear; however, songs of separation from one's community are legion in Arab poetry. In the context of the desert Bedouin, nomadic peoples are always on the move, returning to find that the loved ones (*ahbab*) have departed. In the Indian Ocean context of Oman, sailors departed for months, sometimes years, at a time, traveling West and South around the Indian Ocean basin along the coast of East Africa when the monsoon winds went in one direction and then when the annual winds shifted to the other direction to the East and South along the coast of India. In the music of the sea, called *fann al-bahr,* many songs celebrate departure and arrival and tell tales of travel and the hardship of separation.

The production values of this recording of "*Batal al-Bab*" hardly sound "traditional." The use of synthesizer, chimes, and a big, syrupy-sounding violin section along with plenty of reverb, cloak this old poem in a modern veneer. (See works by Rasmussen 2012 and Al-Harthy and Rasmussen 2012 for more on the development of Omani national music aesthetics.) The song is in the dance style, *bar'a,* a distinctly Afro-Omani groove.

While the music for this dance style, *bar'a,* is performed by a community of male and female musical specialists (Figure 10.13), the dance, which is a male dance, may be seen all over Oman. It is enjoyed by men, particularly at weddings and other social events, who hold their ceremonial dagger (the *khanjar*) above their head while dancing forward and back in front of the band. The dance was inscribed into the United Nations Educational, Scientific and Cultural Organization (**UNESCO**) registry of items of "**intangible cultural heritage**" after a long process of application and documentation by Oman's ministry of heritage and culture. Similar styles of dancing may be seen elsewhere in the Gulf, in Yemen, and even in the circum-Indian ocean region of Southeast Asia, where music and dance from the Gulf have been assimilated as performative expressions of Islam. However, the recognition of *bar'a* by UNESCO as an item of "intangible culture heritage" signals the importance of the dance for the region, and signals the dance as uniquely Omani—an important feat as Oman establishes and promotes a national culture that is distinct from neighboring nations in the Gulf.

Figure 10.13
The female chorus, *radida,* is an essential component of a band in Salalah.
Anne Rasmussen.

Homeland and Diaspora: An Unexpected Reaction

In the summer of 2000, I made a trip to Israel and the Palestinian territories (the West Bank and Gaza) to explore the possibility of bringing a group of college students to the area in order to study with Arab musicians there. I was introduced to the al-Asadi family, who welcomed me warmly, served delicious food, and, after I described the chapter I was preparing for this book, agreed to let me record our conversations about music and poetry along with their performances of sung poetry and instrumental improvisations. The father, Saud al-Asadi, was an accomplished poet who specialized in various forms of vernacular sung Arabic poetry. He presented me with two published books of his poetry and also sang some traditional genres of Palestinian poetry called *'ataba* and *mijana.* I gave the family a copy of the CD I produced in 1997, *The Music of Arab Americans: A Retrospective Collection* (Rounder 1122). The recording is a kind of "greatest hits" of the Arab American community from about 1915 to 1955; all of the original performances were recorded on 78-rpm records, so the production values and techniques are obviously out of date.

Saud al-Asadi's reaction to my CD was completely unexpected. He insisted we put it on and listen to it—all fourteen tracks—right away. He showed a deep interest in these archival performances and seemed to be particularly captivated by the music of people who had emigrated from Palestine. Mr. al-Asadi went on to tell me that during the first half of the twentieth century, when people left Palestine for the United States, everyone assumed it was "just for money." He was completely astonished that two musicians on my CD, originally singers for *Radyu*

Figure 10.14

Photograph of the original Alamphon paper sleeve for the 78-rpm recordings made by Sana Khadaj. The Arabic between the photographs translates as "The new records of the singing stars, the enchanting singer Sana and her husband, the enchanting singer Amer Khadaj." *Courtesy of Lila Kadaj.*

al-Sharq al-Adna, a radio station established by the British in Palestine, were never able to return to home to Palestine after what they thought, in 1947, would be just a six-month tour to the United States, because of the Arab–Israeli war and the establishment of the state of Israel in 1948. Their home and the radio station in Jerusalem were destroyed as a consequence of the war, so the musicians made a life in the United States. What struck Mr. al-Asadi even more profoundly was not their unsuspected exile but rather that his Palestinian countrymen had been perpetuating their culture, particularly their poetry and music, in places like Brooklyn, New York, and Dearborn, Michigan. He couldn't believe that this music had been living on in Arab American communities for more than half a century. This was all a complete revelation for him. As he listened to the music of these Arab immigrant musicians, Mr. al-Asadi was moved to tears.

Listen to the first few phrases of "Lamma Ya Albi" ("When, O Heart of Mine"). It features the singer Sana Khadaj accompanied by her husband Amer Khadaj, with Jalil Azzouz, and Naim Karakand on violin and Muhammad al-Aqqad on *qanun.* This New York session was recorded by Farid Alam for his label, Alamphon, and the 78-rpm record circulated widely within the Arab American community during the 1940s and 1950s (Figure 10.14).

In Chapter 1, you considered recordings as a part of the material culture of music (Table 1.1), and in Chapter 11, you will learn about commercial music as domain of music-culture. This recording, like thousands of non-English-language-based musics recorded by immigrant musicians on 78-rpm records, exemplifies the ways in which commercial, "disembodied" records can reflect the initiatives and needs of very localized communities. In a way similar to the independent labels of today, as well as music that is only shared on the Web, these records were made by and for the Arab community in the U.S. diaspora, a phenomenon that Saud al-Asadi, living in the homeland, could hardly believe. The song is preceded with the announcement *Istiwanat Alamphon, al mutriba Sana* ("Alamphon Records, the singer [literally, "enchantress"] Sana; Active Listening 10.6). Sana Khadaj alternates between metrical, strophic verses and solo vocal lines in free rhythm, in which she demonstrates her range of vocal color and ornamentation. Although this "commercial" record may not be up to par in terms of today's production values, the quality of the recording is remarkably good considering the technology available in the 1940s. The lyrics exhibit typical themes of Arabic literature and poetry: love, longing, and nature.

ACTIVE LISTENING 10.6
"Lamma Ya Albi" ("When, O Heart Of Mine"), Excerpt

MindTap·
🎧 **WATCH** an Active Listening Guide of this selection online.

COUNTER NUMBER	COMMENTARY	ARABIC TRANSLITERATION	TRANSLATION
0:00	Spoken introduction	*Istiwanat Alamphon, al mutribah Sana*	Alamphon Records, the singer, Sana
0:02	Instrumental introduction		
0:47	First vocal line, repeated; each half-line complemented by deliberate "fillers" or *lawazim* by the *qanun*	*Lamma ya albi habı̄bak 'a⁻d Tili' il-'amar min ghayr mi'a⁻d (x2)*	When, O heart of mine, your beloved returned The moon came out early (without an appointment)
1:19	Refrain	*Lamma ya albi, ya albi, ya albi, ya albi*	When, O heart of mine
1:28	Improvisatory vocal line by the singer in free meter with instrumentalists following along	*Ya...* *Ya... albi*	My heart...
1:46	Instrumental beginning of the next metrical section of the song		

When, O heart of mine, your beloved returned
The moon came out early (without an appointment)
Our nights returned again, all of them joys
I forgot my pains and sorrows as my mind relaxed
How much, my spirit, have I stayed up with you, with passion like torture
And remained alone until the farewell appeared
Refrain
Why don't you tell me where you have been? You make me confused!
You whose beauty is in the antimony of the eye, come back and make me happy.

Text, "Lamma Ya Albi" (translation)

From Diaspora to Globalization: Ofra Haza and World Beat

We have just considered a very specific example of Arab music in diaspora—immigrant musicians who recorded their own music on their own labels for their own community, and the way in which their recordings deeply touched someone from their original homeland fifty years afterward. We end our exploration of Arab music with an example of a local musician whose music went global. Israel and the Palestinian territories are one of the most dynamic areas of the Middle East. This small area, about the size of the state of Connecticut, is home to Jews, Muslims, and Christians who differ in terms of ethnicity, socioeconomic class, and political orientation. Everyone there is affected by political histories that have dictated family trajectories for hundreds of years and that, today, keep decision-making and daily mobility beyond the control of ordinary people. If we look at the performer Ofra Haza and her music as one window into the music and culture of the Middle East and Arab world, we quickly discover that our window is more like a dynamic prism that refracts various histories, trajectories, and interactions than a static tableau that presents a panoramic view. Jews lived in ancient Palestine well before the birth of Jesus Christ or the revelations of the Prophet Muhammad. A significant number of them immigrated to Yemen in the southern part of the Arabian Peninsula about two thousand years ago after the destruction of the first temple (586 B.C.E.). They lived in isolation for hundreds of years, perpetuating a supposedly pure style of Jewish music and liturgy that was thought immune to foreign influence—a phenomenon I have called **marginal preservation** (Rasmussen 1997).

In 1948, the same year that Jalil Azouz and Sana and Amer Khadaj found themselves exiles on the streets of New York, Israel organized an exodus for Yemeni Jews known as "The Magic Carpet." Israelis sent planes to evacuate virtually the entire Jewish community (about fifty thousand) from Yemen to Israel. There are perhaps a couple of thousand Jews who remain in Yemen today, but for the most part the Yemeni Jewish community now resides in Israel. Ofra Haza (1957–2000) grew up in Israel performing community theater. She was eventually awarded the Israeli equivalent of the Grammy award in 1980, 1981, and 1986 owing to the sales of her immensely popular records. After being picked up on the nascent mediascapes of international pop music, by the 1990s she was a strong player in a relatively new music/marketing category called World Beat or EthnoPop, something we now more often find under the ambiguous term World Music.

"Im Nin'alu" is from the traditional collection of religious songs of the Yemenite Jews called the Divan and was written by a seventeenth-century poet, Rabbi Shalom Shabbezi. "The basic idea, expressed in the first two lines is that heaven is attentive even when men are not. The poem, which is filled with images from Jewish mysticism, alternates between Hebrew and Arabic" (Zahavi-Ely, personal communication, 2006). (The verse following the two you hear is in Arabic.) In addition to a quasi–Western-sounding chamber ensemble that includes oboe and violin, you can hear a brass tray and tin can, household items that acquired the function of percussion instruments during a time of musical repression in Yemen (Active Listening 10.7). Ofra Haza's recording of "Im Nin'alu" was sampled and remixed several times, notably for the title track to the film *Colors,* a movie directed by Dennis Hopper, about African American gangs in Los Angeles (listen at about 18 minutes: https://www.youtube.com /watch?v=3nLISecTkUw).

Ofra Haza's voice was later heard in households across North America when she became the voice of Yocheved, the mother of Moses, for the Dreamworks film *Prince of Egypt.*

MindTap®

🔊 **LISTEN TO**

"Im Nin'alu," performed by Ofra Haza, vocal, with instrumentalists Iki Levy, Chaim Gispan, Eli Magen, Yigal Tuneh, Rima Kaminkowski, Yuval Kaminkowski, Israel Berkowitch, Yitchak Markowetzki, Israela Wisser, Abraham Rosenblatt, Elchanan Bregman, Abigail Erenheim, Meril Grinberg, Lesli Lishinski, and Ilan School Shlomo Shochat, online.

MindTap·

🎧 **WATCH** an Active Listening Guide of this selection online.

ACTIVE LISTENING 10.7
"Im Nin'alu"

COUNTER NUMBER	COMMENTARY	HEBREW TEXT*	TRANSLATION*
0:00	Exposition of the Hebrew text in six phrases free meter	Im nin'alu daltei n'divim Daltei marom lo nin'alu El Chai, marei-mawam al kawruvim Kulawm b'rucho ya'alu	Even when the doors of the generous ones (the wealthy) are locked, the doors of heaven will never be barred.
			Oh! Living God, up high above the cherubim
			They all go up through His spirit.
		El Chai	Oh! Living God!
0:48	Verse 1 begins, first line of text	Im nin'alu daltei n'divim	Even when the doors of the generous ones (the wealthy) are locked,
		Daltei marom lo nin'alu	The doors of heaven will never be barred.
0:55	Listen for percussion		
0:58	2nd line of text, same melody as first line	El Chai, mareimawam al kawruvim	Oh! Living God, up high above the cherubim
		Kulawm b'rucho ya'alu	They all go up through His spirit.
1:04	Listen for percussion		
1:07	"B" part of melody (refrain)	El Chai	Oh! Living God!
1:16	Verse 2, similar in arrangement to verse 1	Ki hem elai kis'o kawruvim Yodu sh'mei weihal'lu	They are near to His throne They thank His name and praise (Him).
		Chayet shelhem rotzeh washawvim	Beasts who have been running back and forth
		Miyom b'ri'aw nichlawlu	Since the day the world was created, they have been crowned.
		El Chai	Oh! Living God!
1:44	Instrumental rendition of the melody		
2:02	Return of the "B" section at verse 3	El Chai	Oh! Living God!

*The Hebrew text is a transliteration of Yemenite Hebrew as Ofra Haza sings it; the English translation was provided by Na'ama Zahavi-Ely.

Concluding Remarks

At the turn of the twenty-first century, the Middle East was known for its complex politics and rich natural resources. In the aftermath of the unparalleled events of September 11, 2001, the Second Gulf War, which began in the spring of 2003, the so-called Arab Spring (2011), which many in the United States took as a harbinger of new freedoms but which instead has led in some cases to less stability, many U.S. citizens are being forced to take a hard look at their ideas, attitudes, and knowledge about the Middle East and Arab world. In many parts of the Arab world

MindTap·

PRACTICE your understanding of this chapter's concepts by working once more with the chapter's Active Listening Guides online.

today, particularly in Iraq, Syria, and the Palestinian territories, grave security risks, rampant unemployment and economic strife, the loss of music patronage, and the dearth of the material culture of music from concert halls to blank tape to violin strings have taken their toll. Such everyday conditions make things like planning a wedding—or even walking down the street carrying an instrument to play music with a friend or take a music lesson—unthinkable. At the same time music thrives in diaspora and in new globalized contexts in the cosmopolitan countries of the Arabian Peninsula. Music lives on as one of the most tenacious elements of culture. For centuries, Middle Eastern and Arab music have proven to be of great interest to musicians and audiences worldwide. Explorations of Middle Eastern history, culture, religion, and politics in the news media and cultural industries have never been more vigorous. The introduction to Arab music in this chapter comes with an invitation to learn more. Listen, read, and explore the internet resources that make performers and performances throughout the Arab world available to you. Investigate the recordings and works listed in the References and discover the arts and culture of the Arab world by engaging with the people who create it throughout the world and in our own midst.

MindTap•

DO an online quiz that your instructor may assign for a grade.

Study Questions

1. How is the performance of "Shaghal" an example of Arab music in diaspora?

2. What are some examples of women's music making? How does the wedding provide a context for expressions of gender and of group identity?

3. What are some common themes in Arab poetry? Give specific examples.

4. What are some of the ideas and misconceptions surrounding "music and Islam"? What are some representations of Arab and Middle Eastern cultures and peoples in the mass media and popular imagination?

5. Discuss rhythm in Arab music. What is the difference between metric and non-metric performance? Give examples of each from this chapter, and find other examples on the internet, from the *Worlds of Music* musical examples, or from your own collection.

6. What is special about Arab scales (*maqamat*) and Arab intonation? Name a few other musical features that contribute to Arab musical aesthetics.

7. What important role did Arab civilization and culture play in Europe during the seventh to the fourteenth centuries? How did the Ottoman era and the colonial regime influence music in the Arab world?

8. How are Sana and Amer Khadaj's story and performance illustrative of the immigrant experience in general and of Arab immigration to the United States specifically? How is their story similar to or different from that of Rahim Alhaj? Explore the stories of other immigrant musicians in the United States.

9. What is the UNESCO Commission on Intangible Cultural Heritage, and how might it contribute to the sustainability of various kinds of music cultures throughout the world?

10. How is the Arab world and/or the Middle East multiethnic, multilinguistic, and multireligious? Give specific examples. How does the music presented in this chapter reflect this diversity?

11 Discovering and Documenting a World of Music

Jeff Todd Titon and David B. Reck

Learning Objectives

After you have studied this chapter, you should be able to:

1. Examine the music in your "backyard" and choose a music-culture that you will document and interpret, making sure it is one that you like and one to which you will have access.

2. Considering the music-culture you have selected, determine a subject for your study.

3. Describe the difference between a subject for a study and a topic.

4. Considering the subject you have selected, determine a topic for your study.

5. Consider the ethical aspects of what you intend to do, and discuss these with your instructor.

continued

6. Locate the gear you will need for your documentation, and obtain consent from the people whose music you intend to document and interpret.

7. Write a proposal indicating what you intend to do in your field project—the who, what, where, and when of your documentation, and some thoughts about the why (your interpretation)—and submit this proposal to your instructor for approval.

8. Complete your field project and deliver it to your instructor.

Music in Our Own Backyards

In our explorations of the world's musics, we—as students and scholars alike—are fascinated by cultures and peoples greatly separated from us by place or time, in sound and style, or in ways of making and playing music. But there is also a music-culture surrounding us, one that we see and hear only partially because it is too close to us—because we take it for granted, as fish do water. Our musical environment is held both within us, in our thoughts; and outside us—by other members of our community. It expands outwardly from us (and contracts into us) in a series of circles that may include family, ethnic groups, regional styles, geographic location, and cultural roots (Western Europe, Africa, Asia, and so on).

This chapter is all about gathering reliable information on today's music. We encourage you to seek out a nearby musical world, observe it in person, talk with the people involved in it, document it with recordings and photographs, and interpret the information in a project that will contribute to knowledge about today's musical activities. If this research project is part of a course, check with your instructor for specific directions. What follows is a general guide, based on the experience that we and our students have had with similar projects at our colleges and universities.

Selecting a subject for your research is the first step in the project. Songs and instrumental music serve a great many purposes and occur in a wide variety of contexts, from singing in the shower to opera, from the high-school marching band to the rock festival, from the lullaby to the television commercial, from music videos to computer music input via midi keyboards, and from smartphones and tablets to the internet. Whether trivial or profound, it is all meaningful. To help you select a subject, consider a few organizing principles: family, generation and gender, avocation/leisure, religion, ethnicity, regionalism, nationalism, and commercialization. Here we focus on North American examples, but if you are using this book elsewhere you should apply these (and perhaps other) organizing principles to examples from your own music-culture. Later we will give you some specific suggestions on how to move from a subject to a topic, and how best to proceed from there to gather information.

Family

As is true of all cultures, most North Americans first hear music in family life (Figure 11.1). Much of that music comes from the radio, television, computer, smartphone, or tablet. People often say that the kind of music they heard before they were old enough to have their own recordings and playlists strongly influenced

Figure 11.1
A sharecropper family sings hymns in front of their home. Hale County, Alabama, 1936. *Walker Evans. Courtesy of the Library of Congress.*

them. Families also usually provide some live music. Many mothers and grand-mothers sing lullabies, for example. Sometimes lullabies are the only songs in a foreign language that North American children with strong ethnic backgrounds hear, because people (particularly grandparents) often fall back on old, familiar languages for intimate songs.

In short, most North Americans have an early layer of songs learned in childhood in a family setting. Children then work in harmony with (or work against) this basic musical background as a part of growing up and finding their identity. As they grow up, if they are attracted to making music, they will be able to listen to a great many different kinds of music, inside and outside of their families and communities. By the time they are adult musicians they may have multiple musical identities as a result of choices they made along the way. While growing up in Maine, Erica Brown (see Figure 11.12) learned Franco-American music from her family and community; later, she took classical violin lessons and was a member of the Bates College "Fighting Bobcats" Orchestra and of the Maine All-State Orchestra. Now she performs Franco-American music of New England at ethnic festivals; she also serves as the leader of a bluegrass band playing music associated with the southern Appalachian Mountains.

Generation and Gender

Much North American music making is organized along age-group or generational lines. Schools, church classes, scouting groups, children's sidewalk games, college singing groups, and many other musical situations include people of about the same age. Songs learned by these groups may stay with them as they grow older.

Fewer gender differences exist with regard to music today than in the past. Just as women now take up sports like race-car driving and become professional jockeys, so do more women play instruments, such as the drums and saxophone, which used to be largely limited to men (Figure 11.2). A whole genre that used to

Figure 11.2
"The boys in the band." Grove
Lake Concert Band, a brass
band from Oregon, 1911.
Photographer unknown.

be exclusively male—barbershop quartet singing—now has a parallel female style, exhibited by such groups as the Sweet Adelines. One women's bluegrass group called themselves the All Girl Boys, while today's bluegrass stars include Alison Krauss, Rhonda Vincent, Claire Lynch, Alison Brown, and Laurie Lewis. But gender differences remain important, as many of today's musical groups, like other North American social groups, are organized along gender lines.

Leisure

Music as a recreational, leisure activity is an important part of North American life. Many North Americans feel the need for a strong group pastime, and of course some of this impulse is channeled into musical organizations. A local American Legion Post or an ethnic group such as the Polish Falcons may have a band; here the music making affirms group solidarity. Fielding a band for the local parade or festival brings the group visibility and pride. Black youngsters in high school and college form extracurricular, informal, hip-hop or gospel groups; sometimes these groups become semiprofessional or even fully professional. Most high schools and colleges can boast a few rock bands, some rappers and possibly even a jazz group, as well as cocktail pianists, folk-singing guitarists, and chamber music ensembles.

The computer has facilitated music making as a hobby. Using their instruments with sampling and software, composers can create and arrange songs and instrumental compositions, then record a final version with the computer supplying the instrumental accompaniment. Amateur and professional composers and musicians can access websites at which they collaborate to produce layered arrangements of musical compositions (see Chapter 1).

Religion

Religion is one of the better-documented areas of North American musical life. Scholars know about music's role in many religious movements, ranging from the eighteenth-century Moravians through the revival movements of the nineteenth century and the founding of sects such as the Mormons or Pentecostals. Scholarly study focuses on the Negro spiritual, while the tent-revival preacher, the snake handler, and the old-time churches also receive attention (Figure 11.3). But the musical activities of contemporary, mainline, middle-class churches, synagogues, and mosques offer equal interest, though few people study them. The songs of new religious movements, such as small meditation groups based on Christian or Eastern religious thinking, also deserve attention. These groups need to encourage solidarity and teach their message, but they have no traditional music. Often they change the words of well-known songs as a way of starting, just as Martin Luther changed the words of German drinking songs 450 years ago to create a body of sacred songs we know as Protestant chorales. The new groups may also work hard on developing an "inner music" for their members, through which the believer reaches the desired state of tranquility.

Ethnicity

Ethnicity is the oldest consideration in the study of the North American music-culture in the sense that the United States is usually regarded as a nation of immigrants. It is also one of the newest considerations because of the interest in ethnic identity, diversity, and multiculturalism, a trend that has gathered force since the late 1960s (Figure 11.4).

Throughout North America, ethnicity has played a major role in musical history. Whether in the dialect and songs of the French Acadians in New Brunswick, the heroic *corrido* ballads sung along the Rio Grande by Mexican Americans, the retelling of the story of hard-hearted Barbara Allen by British-American ballad

Figure 11.3
Music almost always accompanies formal rites of passage such as this old-time baptism. Eastern Kentucky, 1990. *Jeff Todd Titon.*

Figure 11.4

Alan Shavarsh Bardezbanian plays *'ud* with his Middle Eastern ensemble. National Folk Festival, Bangor, Maine, 2003. *Jeff Todd Titon.*

singers, or the singing of a Yiddish lullaby in a Brooklyn tenement, North Americans have built and maintained ethnic boundaries through music. Students in the United States whose grandparents stopped publicly singing Old World songs on their way to becoming "one-hundred-percent American" have become enthusiastic about joining ethnic music groups or studying their group's heritage. Other parents and grandparents, of course, never stopped singing their native songs.

North American ethnic music has always involved transnational exchange. On the one hand, Greek Americans are influenced by new developments in popular music in Athens, while on the other, Polish American records find great favor among farmers in far-off mountain villages in Poland. American jazz, hip-hop, and country music have spread around the world, from Holland to Russia and Japan. A complicated interplay goes on between black music in the United States and the Caribbean (Figure 11.5). A single song may embody layer upon layer of musical travel. Reggae developed in Jamaica, where it represented a blend of Afro-Caribbean and black, U.S. soul music. This already complicated style came to America from England, where pop groups repackaged it and exported it, and the cycle continues: Reggae is now popular in most parts of Africa; and in the Tatra Mountains in Poland, where we might not expect reggae (see Chapter 5), it has fused with traditional village music.

In today's world, family- and community-based musics have become markers of ethnic identity and an older way of life. At the same time, they are packaged, bought, and sold in the marketplace; this encourages originality and virtuosity, qualities that may not have been important in the musics' traditional contexts.

Regionalism

Just as ethnic groups never really dissolved into the so-called melting pot, so ways of life still differ according to region, by speech, food, music, and so forth.

Figure 11.5
One of Boston's Caribbean steel-drum bands performs at a women's prison, 1979. *Jeff Todd Titon.*

Regionalism crops up in the names of styles, such as the Chicago blues sound and the Detroit "Motown" soul sound, or even within ethnic styles, as in the distinction between a Chicago and an East Coast polka. The crisp bowing, downbeat accents, and up-tempo performance of a fiddle tune in the Northeast (Figure 11.6)

Figure 11.6
Fiddler Ed Larkin, Tunbridge, Vermont, 1941. *Jack Delano. Courtesy of the Library of Congress.*

bears little resemblance to the same tune's performance in the Southwest, with its smooth bowing and more-relaxed beat. The same hymn tune shows considerable variation even within the same denomination in different parts of the country. One Indiana Primitive Baptist was overheard to comment on the slow, highly decorated tunes of her Primitive Baptist neighbors to the Southeast: "They take ten minutes just to get through 'Amazing Grace'!"

Like ethnicity, regionalism is coming back into fashion. Farmer's markets and local food economies breathe new life into regional agriculture. There are now many local festivals, and event listings can be found on the internet. Even if it sometimes seems the result of shrewd marketing to promote local cultures, regional musical diversity has not yet given way to a one-size-fits-all music. North America is still too large and diverse to turn all music into brand names, or to have the entire population respond equally to all music, and the search for revival or for novelty continues.

Commodified Music

While amateurs still make most of the music in North American culture, paid professionals supply much of it as well. It is remarkable that this complex culture carries musical events that are also typical of nonindustrial or preindustrial societies. Though some genres, such as the funeral lament, have largely disappeared in the United States, rituals that mark a change of life, such as weddings and initiations (bar mitzvahs, debutante parties, senior proms, graduations), still demand solemnization by music. A wedding may take place in a park with an ice-cream truck, balloons, and jeans instead of in a formal church setting, yet music remains indispensable, even if it consists of pop tunes instead of an official wedding march.

A great deal of the commoditized music with which North Americans come into daily contact may be described as "disembodied"—that is, the listener does not feel the physical presence of the performer and many times cannot even see the original musical situation (as in Figure 11.7). Some of this music can be partially controlled by the listener, who selects recordings from his or her playlist to suit a mood. Although the listener can imagine an original musical situation—a concert or recording studio—there is no possibility of interaction with the performers, and the music is the same each time it is heard. Indeed, much of this music is never performed "live" in concert or in a recording studio at all; rather, it is generated partly in live performance and partly by engineers and musicians who add tracks in a recording studio or by means of a computer.

One of the most significant recent developments in commoditized music is the rise of mp3 technology and the distribution of music over the internet. Musicians who think that the music industry takes too much profit from album sales are able to market their recordings directly to consumers via the internet. Consumers now flock to websites and download apps that enable them to stream music.

Ethnomusicologists pay close attention to how people use music in their daily lives. Many young people today have become active consumers who not only select music but engineer and package it for themselves and their friends. Mix tapes—tracks selected from CDs and recorded to cassettes (nowadays to devices or via the internet) and given to friends—were popular in the last decades of the twentieth century. One model for this kind of musical activity was the "Deadhead," who recorded and traded recordings of live Grateful Dead concerts. The practice

Figure 11.7
Dancing to records on a juke-box. West Virginia, 1942. *John Collier. Courtesy of the Library of Congress.*

continues with today's jam bands. Long before the Deadheads, jazz buffs were recording after-hours jam sessions and trading the results. Today, the person who downloads music from the internet, edits it, and arranges the music on a playlist plays quite an active role in choosing music to suit a lifestyle. Music making on the computer does not require singing or playing a traditional instrument; instead, the computer becomes both the instrument and the recording studio.

Public background music is another kind of commoditized music heard in daily life. There is no logical connection between buying groceries and hearing piped music in an elevator, supermarket, boutique, or shopping mall. In offices and factories, the employer may choose to have background music that is manufactured and programmed to increase worker productivity. This, of course, represents a particularly powerful type of unrequested music, and some do not even notice it.

This brief survey of music making organized around family, generation and gender, leisure, religion, ethnicity, regionalism, and commoditized music should help you select a subject for your project: a nearby musical world that you're interested in, have access to, and can gather information about.

Doing Musical Ethnography

Your aim in discovering and documenting a world of music is a **musical ethnography** —a written representation, description, and interpretation of some aspect of a music-culture. The *subject* of your musical ethnography is the aspect of the music-culture that is being represented; the *topic* of your musical ethnography enables your analysis and interpretation of your subject. Approaching a music-culture for the first time, you may feel overwhelmed, but if you use Table 1.1 from Chapter 1 to organize your thinking about what you see and hear, you will see how you might go about gathering information on specific aspects of it so that you may write on a particular topic within the music-culture. Your writing could be accompanied by photographs, recordings, or even video that you make while documenting the music-culture.

The music in the repertory can be recorded for later study and analysis. Much of social organization and material culture can be observed. By listening to musicians talk with each other, and by talking to them, you can begin to understand their ideas about music; through interviews you can learn more about those ideas, the repertory, musical activities, and material culture, as the conversations and interviews formed the basis for the musicians' life histories in this book. But discovering and documenting a world of music is not like examining an amoeba under a microscope. People differ in how they behave, what they believe, and what they say to you. Different people will sing "the same tune" differently. Under these conditions, accurately representing and interpreting a music-culture, even a single aspect of it, in a musical ethnography is a complex and subtle undertaking. It is probably not something you have done before.

Selecting a Subject: Some Practical Suggestions

It is obvious that your project requires you to collect, understand, and organize information about music in order to present it. It differs from the usual school research paper in that it focuses on a musical situation that you seek out directly from people rather than chiefly from publications. In ethnomusicology, as in anthropology and folklore, this in-person witnessing, observing, questioning, recording, photographing, and in some cases performing is called **fieldwork**. Fieldwork is research "in the field" rather than in the laboratory or library. Of course, library research is often quite helpful as part of this endeavor. You might find background information on your topic in the library and by searching the internet, and you should not overlook the opportunity to do so. But most of your project will take you into the field, where you will obtain your most valuable and original information.

Collecting, understanding, and organizing information about music are, of course, interrelated. You will begin with certain insights about the information you collect. As you organize it, you will gain new insights. After you organize it, you will be able to describe it and move toward an interpretation of it.

You can approach your subject in different ways. First, you might try to chart the music you hear daily:

1. Keep a log or journal of all the music you hear over three or four days or a week. Note the context, style, and purpose of the music. Calculate how much of your day is spent with music of some sort.
2. Record, video, or simply describe in words several television or internet advertisements that employ music. Note the style of the music and the image it attempts to project. How is the music integrated into the message of the advertisement? Is it successful? Offensive? Both?
3. Map the uses of music in various movies or television shows as you watch them. For contrast, select a daytime serial and a crime-fighting show, or a situation comedy and a popular dramatic series, for example.

4. Survey the uses of background music in local stores. Interview salespeople, managers, owners, and customers (always obtaining their permission) about music and sales.

5. Survey the music that you listen to on the internet. On what occasions do you seek out music there? What is your relationship to this music, and how does it compare with your relationship to other music in your daily life? Is there a group of people interested in the same music you are? If so, does this group chat over the internet about this music? What kind of a community does this constitute?

A second approach is to examine the music in your personal background. Explore your memory of songs and music. Note how your religious and ethnic heritage may have influenced the music you heard and your current musical interests. How has your musical taste changed as you have grown older? Survey the contents of your music collection or your preferences in listening to music on the radio, television, or the internet. You can ask your friends and family the same questions.

A third approach is to explore music in your community—your school community or your hometown—where you can interview people, listen to musical performances, possibly take part in them yourself, and gather substantial information. Here are several possible subject headings:

Ethnic groups
Piano teachers
Private instrumental instruction (music stores, private lessons in the home)
Choir directors
Church organists, pianists, and so on
School music (elementary, junior high, high school)
Music stores
Musical instrument makers
Background music in public places
The club scene (bars, coffeehouses, restaurants, clubs)
Musical organizations (community choral groups, bands, barbershop quartets, and so forth)
Part-time (weekend) musicians
Professional or semiprofessional bands (rock, pop, jazz, rhythm and blues, country, gospel, and so forth)
Chamber music groups
Parades and music
Disc jockeys
Symphony orchestras

A fourth approach narrows the subject and concentrates on an individual musician's life, opinions, and music. Often we focus our attention on the musical superstars, but in the process we forget many fine and sensitive musicians, many of them amateurs, who live in our communities. Senior citizens, teachers, owners of music shops, or tradespeople have sometimes had rich musical experiences as professional or part-time musicians. To search out such people is not always easy. Try the musicians' union, ethnic organizations, word of mouth, school or college music teachers, radio station disc jockeys, the clergy, club owners, newspaper columnists and feature-story writers, or even local police stations and fire departments. Musicians can be approached directly at fairs, contests, festivals, concerts, and dances (Figure 11.8). Many colleges and universities have foreign-student associations that include amateur musicians, and they can tell you about others in the area. Ethnic specialty restaurants and grocery stores provide another resource.

The musical world that surrounds you is so diverse that you may feel swamped, unable to focus your energy. But when it finally comes down to deciding on a subject for your project, two guiding principles will help you: *Choose something you are interested in* and *choose something you have access to*. Succeeding will be hard if you are not curious about the music you examine, and you must be close to it in order to look at it carefully. Most students find it helpful to discuss their proposed subjects with the instructor, and with classmates as well.

Collecting Information

Once you have chosen a subject, your next move is to immerse yourself in the musical situation, consider what aspects of it interest you, and select a topic. Then you need to plan how to collect information—what you'll observe and hear, what questions to ask when you talk to the musicians or others involved, what rehearsals or performances to record, and so forth. Almost always you will need time and flexibility to revise your plans as you collect the information you need. For that reason you should get started as early in the term as possible. Most people will be happy to tell you about their involvement with music as long as you show them you really are interested.

Gaining Entry

Musical activities usually have a public (performance) side and a private (rehearsal) side. The performance is the tip of the iceberg; you will want to understand what lies beneath, and that is best learned by observing and listening to the people

Figure 11.8
Nathan, Chris, and Robin Sockalexis, Penobscot Nation, Old Town, Maine, singing and drumming. Bangor, Maine, 2003. *Jeff Todd Titon.*

involved. If you must approach a stranger, you may want to arrange an introduction, either by a mutual friend or by a person in authority. If, for example, you want to talk with musicians in an ethnic organization, it is wise to approach the president of the organization and seek his or her advice first. This not only allows you to get good information but also to share your plans with the president, who needs to know what is going on in the group. In other situations, it is best to let the people in authority know what you intend to do, and why, but to avoid having them introduce you, particularly if their authority is legal only and they do not belong to the same ethnic group as the people whose music you will be studying.

The first contact is especially important, because the way you present yourself establishes your identity and role. That is one reason why you must take the time to be honest with yourself and others about your interest in their music and the purpose of your project. If you are a college student, you may find yourself being assigned the role of the expert. But this is a role to avoid. Tell the people who give you information that they are the experts and that you are the student who wants to learn from them—that otherwise you would not seek their help. Let them know that you hope they will be willing to let you talk with them, observe them, and, if appropriate, participate in the music.

Participation and Observation

Doing research in the field requires a basic plan of action. Which people should you talk with? Which performances should you witness? Should you go to rehearsals? How might you just hang out and overhear people's normal conversations about their music, interfering as little as possible? What about a visit to a recording studio? If you are studying a music teacher, should you watch a private lesson? Should the teacher teach you? Will you take photographs? Videos? What kind of recording equipment can you get? Who will pay for it? You have probably been thinking about these and many similar questions. One more that you should pay attention to at this time regards your personal relationship to the people whose music you will study. Should you act as an observer—as a detached, objective reporter? Or should you, in addition to observing, also participate in the musical activity if you can?

Participating as well as observing can be useful (and quite enjoyable). You hope to learn the music from the inside. Rather than staying around the edges of the action, depending on others to explain all the rules, you will come to know some of the musical belief system intuitively.

But participating has its drawbacks. The problem with being a **participant-observer** is that you sometimes come to know too much. It is like not knowing the forest for the trees: The more of an insider you are, the less you are aware of those unspoken assumptions that "everyone knows"; and so in order to address your project to an outside reader, you will need to imagine yourself as an outsider, too. If you are participating as well as observing, you must make a special effort to document some of the basic things about the music culture an outsider would need to know, and take nothing for granted. This dual perspective—the view of the participant-observer—is not difficult to maintain while you are learning how to participate in the musical situation. In fact, when you are learning, the dual perspective is forced on you. The trouble is that after you have learned, you can forget what it was like to be an outside observer. Therefore, it is very important to keep a record of your changing perspective as you move from outsider to participant. This record should be written in your field notes or spoken into your tape recorder as your perspective changes.

In fact, you may already be a full participant in the music-culture you intend to study. Writing a musical ethnography about a music-culture in which you have been involved for some time may seem quite appealing. Although this kind of research appears easy, it is not. Your knowledge usually is too specialized for general readers. Furthermore, the issues that matter to you as a member of the music-culture may not interest anyone outside the music-culture very much; and if that is the case, your musical ethnography will find a limited audience. You may feel that because of the depth of your knowledge, you do not need to interview any other members of the music-culture, but this is not so. Other participants' perspectives will differ from yours, and although you may favor your own, in a musical ethnography all perspectives are important. You may also, without even realizing it, express a particular point of view as if it is a generally accepted truth rather than a bias coming from inside the music-culture.

What if you work as an observer only and forego participation? There are some advantages to doing so. It saves time. You can put all your energy into watching and trying to understand how what people tell you is going on matches what you can actually see and hear going on. You can follow both sides of "what I say" and "what I do" more easily when you are merely observing as opposed to participating. On the other hand, you do not achieve objectivity by keeping yourself out of the action. Your very presence as an observer alters the musical situation, particularly if you are photographing, or making videos or audio recordings. In many situations, you will actually cause less interference if you participate rather than intrude as a neutral and unresponsive observer. If you are studying dance music, it is a good idea to dance (Figure 11.9).

Figure 11.9
Fiddler and guitarist playing for a dance at a fiesta. Taos, New Mexico, 1940. *Russell Lee. Courtesy of the Library of Congress.*

Selecting a Topic

After you have narrowed your subject, your next step is one of the most difficult: selecting a good *topic* to write about. In most undergraduate writing projects, students work on assigned topics. But for this project you are being asked to generate your own topic. A topic is not the same as a subject. A subject may be a music-culture, a musical scene, a musician, or a group of musicians. A topic is your subject viewed from a particular perspective, and with a thematic question in mind. By themselves, subjects cover too much ground; topics focus your attention on specific questions that will: (1) help you organize the information you collect and (2) lead you from documentation to interpretation. For example, "the Jewish cantor" is a subject, something to investigate. "Musical education of Jewish cantors in New York City" is a topic. The cantor is viewed from a thematic perspective: education. You want to understand what the education of a cantor consists of and what the results are. Putting this into a thematic question, you ask "What is the musical education of cantors in New York City?" Another example of a subject is "The Outlaws, a local country music band." A topic turned into a thematic question that involves the band might be "How is gender a factor in the music of the Outlaws, a local country music band?" Here, the focus is on the band members' attitudes, interactions, lyrics, social scene, and so forth, as they relate to gender. This topic is in itself too large and would have to be refined further, narrowed down perhaps to "What roles does gender play in the social scene that surrounds the Outlaws, a local country music band?" The social scene would include the members of the band, their activities, and their interactions with the music industry and their audience.

The process of refining a topic is gradual and involves much thought. To begin, go back to Chapter 1 and use the music-culture model to select aspects of your subject that interest you. Do you want to focus on conceptions of music, activities involving music, repertories, or material culture? Of course, these aspects are interrelated, and ignoring any of them completely will be difficult; nevertheless, concentrating most of your attention on one of them will help you select a topic you can manage. It will also give you some initial ideas to think about as you gather your information. While doing field research, you will find that some areas of your topic yield better information than do others. As you assess the results of your research-in-progress you should be able to refine and refocus your topic to take advantage of the good information you have gathered. As you do so, you may have to deemphasize, or possibly even discard, other aspects of your topic that you have found difficult to research.

Your instructor can help you move from a subject to a topic. Many teachers ask students to begin their field research early in the term and to make a short written proposal in which they describe their subject and, if they have done enough fieldwork up until now, their topic. Instructor feedback at this point can save you a lot of time later. As we have suggested, students at first often choose topics that are too broad, given the limitations on their time and the instructor's guidelines for the paper's length. Another common problem is a topic that is too vague. Interpretation—figuring out what your documentation means—always goes in the direction of answering increasingly specific questions about your topic. If you have decided to focus on one band's repertory, a thematic question like "What is the repertory of the Accidental Tourists, a campus rock band?" should be made more precise with theme-related questions that you now ask yourself, like "How does the band choose, learn, arrange, and maintain songs for their repertory?" A series of questions like this can help you focus your observations and interviews. In this case, you would want to ask the band members these questions and to attend some rehearsals and see how the band chooses, learns, and arranges their songs. After starting field research, working with your thematic question to generate a series of more precise, related questions will help you, in that you can organize your project around those questions. When you write your project up, the answers to those questions, and how the answers relate to each other, will lead you to an overall interpretation of the topic and the main point you want to make.

For example, you may be interested in bluegrass music and find a local group of bluegrass musicians who allow you to observe a rehearsal. Or possibly you go to a bluegrass festival and observe the jam sessions in and around the RVs and tents on the site. You may become interested in how bluegrass harmony works. "What are the principles of bluegrass harmony?" is your thematic question. As you do your fieldwork observation and interviewing, you will find that you can ask more-specific questions. You would hear the musicians use terms for the different harmony parts, like "lead" and "tenor" and "baritone," and you could observe, hear, and ask about the role of each part and how the parts relate to the whole. Alternatively, you may become interested in the etiquette of the jam sessions. What is the purpose of these elaborate social arrangements, and how does jam session etiquette promote social and musical harmony as well as minimize conflict? What are the rules of jam session etiquette? In both cases, you have proceeded from a subject (bluegrass) to a topic (bluegrass harmony or bluegrass jam sessions), and you have narrowed down and further sharpened those topics through questions that will lead you from documentation to interpretation of those aspects of the music-culture.

In other words, gathering information is not simply a matter of recording it all, as a sponge soaks up water. You will want to be selective in what you document, because after documentation you will need to interpret your material. In the bluegrass rehearsal you will pay particular attention to the way the musicians work out the harmonies, and when you interview them you will ask them about that. If your topic involves jam session etiquette, you will focus on that rather than on other aspects of bluegrass.

To take another extended example, suppose that your subject is music on the campus radio station, and your topic has to do with the radio station's attitude toward women's hip-hop groups. Your topic will be phrased as a thematic question: "What is the station's attitude toward women's hip-hop groups?" To find out, you listen carefully to the station over a period of time. You decide to interview some of the people who work at the station, and you try to figure out a way to approach your topic during these interviews. One deejay might play a lot of women's music on a particular show, and you might find out something about this deejay's attitude by asking. As you gather information, you try to estimate how well theory is put into practice—the station people say they are in favor of women's music, but you find that overall they do not play very much of it. You wonder why. Do the station people think the audience does not want to hear it? How do the station people know what does the audience want to hear, and should they play what the audience wants to hear, anyway?

Questions that arise during the course of your research can help you to select the kind of documentation that you will do—whether, for example, to survey the recordings in the radio station's library or to interview members of the listening audience—and help you to focus your interpretation so that by the end of your project you will have some answers to your questions. You will not merely be gathering material but also focusing that material on a topic; the heart of your project is your own interpretation of the material in light of the topic you have chosen. In our example about women's hip-hop on campus radio, perhaps the station does not express a coherent attitude toward this music at all. Perhaps you find that female deejays have a different attitude than male deejays do. The answers to your questions should lead you to your main point, or the thesis of your interpretation.

One thesis might be "On the campus radio station, male deejays ignore women's hip-hop, while many female deejays are very much aware of it, play it, and expect their listeners to enjoy it." If your fieldwork led you to a different conclusion, your thesis might be something like, "On the campus radio station, male deejays feel obligated to play women's hip-hop, and they do, but without much knowledge or understanding of it. Female deejays play women's hip-hop because it represents a point of view they understand and sympathize with, but they also realize they can't overdo it because they don't want women as their main audience." Or maybe they do; maybe there is one show that does. Such a narrow topic might be the best of all, as you discover after learning about this particular deejay and show. This very narrow focus would have the advantage of specificity—you would not feel like you were generalizing about the station all the time and then making exceptions for different points of view. But this narrow topic would fall into place only after you had done a good deal of fieldwork.

Library and Internet Research

Depending on the topic you have selected, you may want to search the internet to see whether anyone has published information on your topic. Wikipedia is often helpful on music topics. Do not neglect your library's physical collection either. It might be useful to spend a couple of hours in the library stacks, opening books on your subject to see if they contain relevant information, because finding everything you need in the electronic card catalog can be challenging.

The American Folklife Center, at the Library of Congress, and the Smithsonian Institution's Center for Folklife and Heritage, both of which have extensive collections of recorded sound, can be accessed on the internet via the following addresses:

http://www.loc.gov/folklife
http://www.folklife.si.edu

You may find some of the following periodicals helpful:

American Music
Asian Music
Black Music Research Journal
The Black Perspective in Music
Bluegrass Unlimited
Ethnomusicology
Ethnomusicology Forum
Ethnomusicology Review
Journal of American Folklore
Journal of Country Music
Journal of Folklore Research
Journal of Jazz Studies
Journal of Popular Culture
Journal of Popular Music and Society
Latin American Music Review
Living Blues

Music Educators' Journal
MUSICultures
Popular Music
Southern Spaces
the world of music
Yearbook of the International Council for Traditional Music (ICTM)

If your library subscribes to JSTOR or other electronic databases with articles from scholarly journals, you should search for your subject and topic there. Look also in the reference section of your library or on the internet for such bibliographies as *The Music Index* and RILM, as well as specialized bibliographies and reference works. There may even be discographies (a list of musicians, titles, record numbers, places, and dates) of recordings in music in the area you are researching. For example, Richard Spottswood's *Ethnic Music on Records: A Discography of Ethnic Recordings Produced in the United States, 1893 to 1942* is a five-volume work that lists 78-rpm recordings made during that period (Spottswood 1990). If your research topic involves a U.S. ethnic music, then this could be a valuable resource for you. Music and photographs on the internet can also be helpful in your research (Figure 11.10). The bibliographies will point you toward books and articles on your subject. The reference librarian can help you find these. Many of these music-related bibliographies and discographies are now available electronically on the internet through your school library portal.

The internet has become a vast resource for information about music. Try searching on keywords that surround your topic. You will probably have to refine your search greatly in order to make it efficient. Also, realize that some of the information you find on people's websites, such as their opinions about music, does not carry the authority of a scholarly book published by a university press. Nevertheless, some of these specialized sites offer a good deal of useful information that you might not be able to find in books; amateur research has contributed significantly to certain areas of music, such as discographic information.

Figure 11.10

Corozal, Puerto Rico. Orchestra furnishing music for dancing at a tenant purchase celebration, 1941. Two men, one with guitar and one with *cuatro*, and a boy with maracas. *Jack Delano. Courtesy of the Library of Congress.*

The internet is particularly good for gathering groups of people together to discuss a subject of common interest and share insights. For example, numerous bluegrass websites reflect how bluegrass fans think and talk about their music. Music clubs devoted to single genres such as *qin* or polka often have a presence on the internet. Social media offers several music interest groups. Various music "hangout" sites can be valuable as well. Of course, the internet also offers a great deal of music and video; no doubt you are familiar with various streaming sites.

Remember that you will gather most of your information directly by observing a music-culture in action and by speaking with people who participate in the music-culture. Library and internet research provides background information, and sometimes it cannot even do that—your subject may not have received attention yet, or the little that has been written may not be useful. But if research on your topic has been published, learning about it will help you undertake a better project. Further, the people whose music you are studying often can suggest good books and articles for you to read, saving you time in your search.

Ethics

Doing fieldwork involves important ethical considerations. The people you photograph, record, and interview have ethical rights to their musical performances and their images. Most colleges and universities have a policy designed to prevent people from being harmed by research. Be sure to find out from your instructor whether your project is bound by your institution's human subjects research policy and whether you need to get it reviewed and approved by your institution. Also be sure to discuss the ethics of the project with your teacher before you begin and, if things change, as you proceed.

Whether your project is part of a course or not, think carefully about the impact of what you propose to do. *Always* ask permission of the people involved. Besides ethical rights, people have legal rights to privacy and to how they look, what they say, and what they sing, even after you have recorded it. Be honest with yourself and with the people you study about your interest in their music and the purposes of your project. Tell them right from the start that you are interested in researching and documenting their music. If you like their music, say so. If the project is something for you to learn from, say so. Explain what will happen to the project after you finish it. Is it all right with them if you keep the photographs and videos you make? Would they like a copy of the project? (If so, make one at your own expense.) Is it all right if the project is deposited in the college or university archive? Most archives have a form that the people (yourself included) will sign, indicating that you are donating the project to the archive and that it will be used only for research purposes. If this project is not merely a contribution to knowledge but also to your career (as a student or otherwise), admit it and realize that you have a stake in its outcome. Ask the people whose music you are studying why they are cooperating with you and what they hope to achieve from the project, and bear that in mind throughout. *Never* observe, interview, make recordings, or take photographs or videos without your subjects' knowledge and permission.

Today, many ethnomusicologists believe that simply going into a musical situation and documenting it is not enough. The fieldworker must give something back to the people who have been generous with their thoughts, music, and time. In some cultures, people expect money and should be paid. Fieldworkers sometimes act not simply as reporters or analysts, but also as cultural and musical advocates, doing whatever they can to help the music they are studying to flourish. Not all ethnomusicologists work in colleges and universities. Some in the United States work for arts councils, humanities councils, and other public agencies, where they are expected to identify, document, and present family- and community-based arts to the public. Some work for government or nongovernment agencies that formu-late cultural policy. Many ethnomusicologists believe that diversity is as important in the musical world as it is in the biological world. For that reason, many think advocacy and support for music cultures are necessary in the face of all the forces that endanger them.

Giving back, advocacy, and partnership are part of what ethnomusicologists call **applied ethnomusicology**, a field that has grown enormously in the new millennium. Many ethnomusicologists today believe that research that adds to the storehouse of knowledge is not enough. Whether employed inside or out-side of the academic world, we feel that ethics requires that we go beyond docu-menting and interpreting a music-culture and thanking the people afterward. Applied ethnomusicology puts this knowledge and understanding to practical use with, and for, the musical community, whether the intention is a musical benefit, a social improvement, an economic advantage, a cultural good, or some combination of these.

Field Gear: Notebook, Recorder, Camera

The perfect fieldworker has all-seeing eyes, all-hearing ears, and total recall. Because none of us is so well equipped, you must rely on written notes, recordings, and photographs that you make in the field. To do this, you may be able to rely on a smartphone or tablet; or you may have access to better-quality equipment such as a DSLR or micro 4/3 still camera, a video camcorder, or a portable digital recorder meant for music, not just speech. These original documents you make serve two purposes: (1) they enable you to reexamine your field experiences when you write up your project, and (2) they may be included in your final project because they are accurate records of performances, interviews, and observations. On the other hand, field equipment presents certain difficulties: It costs money, you need to know how to work it properly, and you may have to resist the temptation to spend much of your time fiddling with your gear when you should be watching, thinking, and listening instead.

Fifty years ago, fieldworkers relied primarily on note taking, and it is still necessary today. No matter how sophisticated your gear is, you should carry a small, pocket notebook. It will be useful for writing down names and addresses, directions, observations, and thoughts while in the field. Today, some people make notes on their smartphones. In the days before sound recording, musical tran-scription was accomplished by notating the performance on the spot. While this is still possible, it is not advisable except when performances are very brief and you have the required music dictation skills. Performing a song slowly for a transcrip-tion, and sometimes trying to repeat parts of it, puts the musician in an unnatural context and changes the performance. Still, notebooks are especially useful for preserving information learned in interviews, particularly if a recording device is unavailable or awkward in the interview situation. In addition, you should write down your detailed impressions of the overall field situation: (1) your plans, ques-tions, any difficulties you meet with; (2) as complete a description as possible of the musical situation itself, including the setting, the performers, the audience, and the musical event from start to finish; and (3) your reactions and responses to the field experience. Your field notebook becomes a journal (and in some instances also a diary) that you address to yourself for use when you write up your project. As such, writing in it daily is useful.

Many colleges and universities have media centers that loan inexpensive, portable recorders to students for use in fieldwork projects. Whether you use a recorder—and if so what type it is (smartphone, tablet, digital with a microphone)—largely depends on the nature of your project and your instructor's expectations. Although they may be adequate for some interview situations, voice recorders do not record music well enough for documentation purposes. Sound quality can be improved dramatically if you use an external microphone plugged into the recorder's microphone input jack. Some external mics are available for smartphones. Of course, you need to be thoroughly familiar with the recorder's operation *before* you go into the field in order to make accurate recordings.

The best way for beginners to improve the sound of a recording is to place the microphone in a good spot. If the sound is soft or moderate and comes from a small area (a solo singer, a lesson on a musical instrument, or an interview, for example), place the microphone close to the sounds and in the middle of them. If the sounds are loud and spread out (a rock band or a symphony orchestra, for example), search out "the best seat in the house" and place or hold the microphone there. For an interview, a lavalier microphone attached to your subject's shirt will give a good sound, but don't forget to speak loudly when you ask a question, or the microphone won't "hear" you very well. Make a practice recording for a few seconds and play it back immediately to check microphone placement and to make certain the equipment is working properly (Figure 11.11). If you are not interviewing, it can be helpful to wear headphones to monitor the sound. Take along spare batteries or an external charger.

If properly used, even the simplest cameras take adequate pictures of musical performances. A picture may not be worth a thousand words, but it goes a long way toward capturing the human impact of a musical event. A smartphone or separate digital camera is useful because it allows you to see the photograph and correct mistakes (such as standing too far from the action) immediately.

Using video to document a musical event offers the advantage of sound combined with a moving picture. It may allow you to focus selectively on certain aspects of the musical event, such as dancers or particular musicians, so that they can be seen as well as heard in action. Video accompanying your project should be edited down to a manageable size, and it should reveal those aspects of the music-culture that are related directly to your topic. The latest smartphones shoot video, as do some DSLR cameras, but dedicated video camcorders offer the best quality.

Figure 11.11
A chief checks the quality of a recording of his musicians. Kasena-Nankani Traditional Area, Ghana. *James T. Koetting.*

Interviewing

Interviews with people whose music you are studying can help you get basic information and feedback on your own ideas. Ethnomusicologists used to call such people *informants,* but today they are often called *consultants.* Be careful not to put words in your consultants' mouths and impose your ideas. The first step in understanding a world of music is to understand it as much as possible in your consultants' own terms. Later, you can bring your own perspective to bear on the musical situation. Remember that much of their knowledge is intuitive; you will have to draw it out by asking questions. Observe the relationships among the musicians in the music-culture you are documenting and interpreting (Figure 11.12). This will help you formulate questions for interviews.

Come into an interview with a list of questions, but be prepared to let the talk flow in the direction your consultant takes it. In his 1957 preface to *Primitive Man as Philosopher,* Paul Radin distinguished between two procedures for obtaining information: question-and-answer and "letting the native philosopher expound his ideas with as few interruptions as possible" ([1927] 1957). Your consultants may not be philosophers, but they should be given the chance to say what they mean. Some people are talkative by nature, but others need to be put at ease. Let the person know in advance what sorts of questions you will be asking, what kind of information you need, and why. Often you will get important information in casual conversations rather than formal interviews; be ready to write down the information in your field notebook. For example, you may be able to gather information informally by listening to conversations that musicians have in the normal course of their music-making activities. Some people are by nature silent and guarded; despite your best intentions, they will not really open up to you. If you encounter that sort of person, respect his or her wishes and keep the interview brief.

Beginning fieldworkers commonly make two mistakes when doing interviews. First, they worry too much about the recorder, and their nervousness can carry over to the person they interview. But if you have already gotten the person's consent to be interviewed, then getting permission to record the interview should not be hard. One fieldworker always carries her digital recorder and camera so they are visible from the moment she enters the door. Then she nonchalantly sets the recorder down in a prominent spot and ignores it, letting the person being interviewed understand that the recorder is a natural, normal part of the interview. Still ignoring the recorder, she starts off with the small

Figure 11.12
Erica Brown performs the traditional Franco-American music of her family and community with her teacher, Don Roy. She is also the leader of a bluegrass band. American Folk Festival, Bangor, Maine, 2005. *Jeff Todd Titon.*

talk that usually begins such a visit. Eventually the other person says something like, "Oh, I see you're going to record this." "Sure," she says steadily. "I brought along this recorder and mic just to make sure I get down everything you say. I can always edit out any mistakes, and you can always change your mind. This is just to help me understand you better the first time." She says that once they have agreed to be interviewed, nobody has ever refused her recorder. But she adds that if anyone asked her to keep the recorder shut off, she would certainly do so.

A second problem is that beginning fieldworkers often ask leading questions. A *leading question* is one that suggests or implies (that is, it leads or points to) one particular answer. Leading questions make the information obtained unreliable. In other words, it is not clear whether the person being interviewed is expressing his or her own thoughts or just being agreeable and giving the answer the consultant thinks the interviewer wants. In addition, leading questions usually result in short, uninteresting answers. Study this first dialogue to see how *not* to interview:

FIELDWORKER 1: Did you get your first flute when you were a girl?

CONSULTANT: Yeah.

FIELDWORKER 1: What was the name of your teacher?

CONSULTANT: Ah, I studied with Janice Sullivan.

FIELDWORKER 1: When was that?

CONSULTANT: In college.

FIELDWORKER 1: I'll bet you hated the flute when you first started. I can remember hating my first piano lessons.

CONSULTANT: Yeah.

The trouble here is that the consultant gives the kinds of answers she thinks are expected of her. She is just agreeing and not necessarily telling the fieldworker what she thinks. She is not even giving the conversation much thought. The fieldworker has asked the wrong kind of questions. Now look what happens when another fieldworker questions the same person.

FIELDWORKER 2: Can you remember when you got your first flute?

CONSULTANT: Yeah.

FIELDWORKER 2: Could you tell me about it?

CONSULTANT: Sure. My first flute—well, I don't know if this counts, but I fell in love with the flute when I was in grade school, and I remember going down to a music store and trying one out while my father looked on, but I couldn't make a sound, you know!

FIELDWORKER 2: Sure.

CONSULTANT: So I was really disappointed, but then I remember learning to play the recorder in, I think it was third grade, and I really loved that, but I didn't stick with it. Then in college I said to myself, I'm going to take music lessons and I'm going to learn the flute.

FIELDWORKER 2:   Tell me about that.

CONSULTANT: Well, I had this great teacher, Janice Sullivan, and first she taught me how to get a sound out of it. I was really frustrated at first, but after a while I got the hang of it, and she would always tell me to think of the beautiful sounds I knew a flute could make. I used to think a flute could make a sound like water, like the wind. Well, not exactly, but sort of. And then Mrs. Sullivan suggested I borrow a tape of *shakuhachi* music—you know, the Japanese flute?— and I heard different kinds of water, different kinds of wind! I knew then that I would play the flute for the rest of my life.

Compare the two fieldworkers' questions: "Did you get your first flute when you were a girl?" is a leading question because it leads to the answer, "Yes, I got my first flute when I was a girl." What is more, fieldworker 1 implies that most people get their first flutes when they are young, so the consultant probably thinks she should answer yes. By contrast, the question of fieldworker 2—"Can you remember when you got your first flute?"—is open-ended and invites reflection, perhaps a story. When the consultant says "Yeah," fieldworker 2 asks for a story and gets a much better—and different—answer than fieldworker 1. Go over the rest of the first interview and notice how fieldworker 1 injects her opinions into the dialogue ("I'll bet you hated the flute when you first started") and fails to draw out the consultant's real feelings about her lessons, whereas fieldworker 2 establishes better rapport, is a better listener, asks nondirective questions, and gets much fuller and truer answers.

If your project concentrates on a single consultant, you may want to obtain his or her life story (Titon 1980). For this purpose you truly need a recorder to capture the story accurately. Because the way your consultants view their lives can be as important as the factual information they give, you should try to get the life story in their own words as much as possible. This means not asking questions that direct the story as you think it should go. What matters is how your consultant wants it to go. "Tell me about your life in music; start at the beginning" is a good opener for a life story. Come back later, in another interview, to draw out specific facts and fill in gaps by direct questioning. In the initial interview, begin by explaining that you would like your consultant to tell you about his or her life as a musician (or whatever is appropriate—composer, disc jockey, and so forth) from the beginning until now. Once begun, allow plenty of time for silences to let your consultant gather thoughts. If he or she looks up at you expectantly, nod your head in agreement and repeat what has just been said to show that you understand it. Resist any impulse to ask direct questions. Write them down instead, and say you will come back to ask questions later—for now you want the story to continue.

Not everyone will be able to tell you their autobiography in relation to music, but if you are fortunate enough to find someone who can, it may turn out to be the most important part of your project. On the other hand, if your consultant's life story is a necessary part of your project, but you cannot obtain it except by direct and frequent questioning, you should certainly ask the questions. If you get good answers, the result will be your consultant's life history, a collaborative biography rather than an autobiography.

Interviews, then, with the people whose music you are studying (and perhaps with their audience) help you obtain factual information and test your ideas. They also help you begin to comprehend the musical situation from your consultants' point of view: their beliefs, their intentions, their training, their feelings, their evaluations of musical performance, and their understanding of what they are doing—what it is all about. Ultimately, because this is your project, you will combine their ideas with your own interpretations when you write the project up using the information you have collected.

Other Means of Collecting Information

Some people, especially as they get older, become curators of their own or their families' lives. You might find information already gathered: autobiographical manuscripts, diaries, photos, scrapbooks and recordings made by people for themselves, family and friends. Clubs, fraternities, schools, churches, and various organizations often store away old materials that shed light on musical activities. At concerts, the programs handed out may be rich in information, ranging from descriptions of the music to the type of advertisers that support the concerts. Membership lists and patrons' lists may be included as well.

Finishing the Project

As you do all the hard work of organizing and collecting information, always think ahead to what you will do with it. As you go along, return to the list of questions you formulated in relation to your topic—the questions you wanted to ask about the musical situation. You also will have formulated more questions during your fieldwork and other research. These questions and the information you have gathered are related, and they offer a natural organization for your project around your main idea, the answer to the question posed by your topic. Remember that the point of your project is to document some aspect of a nearby music-culture and to interpret it based on the topic you have chosen. Your instructor may ask you to write a preliminary proposal describing your subject and a topic phrased as a thematic question; then, after you have been immersed in your fieldwork for a week or two, you may need to write a final proposal describing both your subject and your refined topic. Feedback on these proposals, from your instructor and possibly from other students, will be helpful; they may know some things that will help your field research go better, or they may have some good suggestions for questions to ask of the music-culture you are documenting and interpreting.

As you're writing, you may want to clarify certain things; check back with your consultants. As you interview, collect information, and think about the musical situation you study, new questions will always occur to you. It is no different when you write up your project. Unlike some term papers, a fieldwork project is built up and accomplished gradually over at least several weeks' time, not quickly near the end of the term. Start early.

You are not the only one affected by your finished project. Your work reflects other people's feelings and, on occasion, their social position. Be clear in what you state about your consultants. Confidentiality may be important; if people asked you not to use their names or repeat what they said to you, respect their wishes.

As is customary in many anthropological works, you may decide to change names of people or places to make certain no one is identified who does not want to be. Imagine the problems created for the member of a band who criticizes the leader if word gets back to the group, or for a school music teacher if he criticizes the school board to you in private and you then quote him.

The authors of this book intend that our readers experience "what it is like to be an ethnomusicologist puzzling out his or her way toward understanding an unfamiliar music." A good field project inevitably provides just that experience and makes an original contribution to knowledge. Valuable and enjoyable in and of itself, discovery, documentation, and interpretation of a world of music takes on added significance, because even the smallest project illuminates our understanding of music as human expression.

Study Questions

1. What gear will you need when you do your fieldwork project? How will you obtain it?

2. What organizing principles can help you study "music in your own backyard?"

3. What four approaches can you take to select a subject for your musical ethnography?

4. What is documentation, description, and interpretation, and how are they related in a musical ethnography?

5. Why are interviews useful in fieldwork? What makes an interview good or bad?

6. What is the difference between the subject of a musical ethnography and its topic? How are the two related?

7. How do thematic questions help you move from a subject to a topic?

8. How do questions that arise in your mind during your research help you arrive at the thesis, or main point, of your interpretation?

9. In your fieldwork study, what are the pros and cons of participating versus observing?

10. What ethical problems arise in fieldwork? Discuss some problems and possible solutions.

Glossary

absolute pitch and **relative pitch** The pitch of a musical tone can be referred to both by the number of vibrations per second (absolute pitch) and by the tone's position in a scale or mode (relative pitch).

acoustic niche Scientific hypothesis that each species that communicates by sound has evolved its signals, over time and according to habitat, in terms of frequency, duration, timbre, and so on, so as to avoid interference from other sounds.

adzo Introductory section of the fast-paced section of an *Agbekor* performance.

adzokpi Section of the fast-paced part of *Agbekor* in which people dance in pairs or small groups.

Afrobeat Musical style created by Fela Kuti that presents politically charged Afrocentric lyrics within attractive, dance-party grooves.

Agbekor War dance of the Ewe people; the name means "clear life."

Agokoli The tyrannical king from whom the Ewe fled.

akami Noise; disordered sound; an out-of-balance social condition.

alapana (*ah-lah*-pah-nah) Improvised introduction to a *raga* in free rhythm.

Americana Traditional styles and sounds within modern musical genres that have evolved from **roots music**.

ancestor worship Rites to pay respect to natural and supernatural forces and to one's forefathers.

Anlo Segment of the Ewe ethnic group that lives along the Atlantic coast.

Ann Arbor Blues Festival The first major U.S. festival devoted entirely to blues; it began in 1969 and attracted more than ten thousand fans annually for the first few years.

applied ethnomusicology Ethnomusicology (the study of people making music) put to practical use for the benefit of musicians and music-cultures; usually based on principles of reciprocity and social responsibility.

arca Name of the "female" or follower set of panpipes in *k'antu* ensemble. The "male" or leader set is called *ira*.

art for art's sake Art that is produced for no reason other than its value as aesthetic experience.

asymmetrical repetition A term ethnomusicologists Bruno Nettl and Victoria Lindsay Levine employ to refer to an aesthetic principle of structural form found in many different Native American tribal and intertribal musical styles.

Atamuga "Great oath"; another name for *Agbekor*.

atsia (plural, *atsiawo*) 1. Stylish self-display, looking good, or bluffing. 2. Preset figure of music and dance.

axatse Dried gourd rattle; its musical phrase fills out the bell part.

azan (also *Adhan*) Islamic "Call to Prayer," heard five times a day from mosques and over mass media among Muslim communities throughout the world.

BaAka One of several ethnic groups known to Europeans as Pygmies.

babemou Novices.

Bali (*bah*-lee) Island just east of Java.

Bantu General classification of people with similar language who live in Central and Southern Africa.

bar Unit of measure in the European system for writing music. Sometimes also called a "measure," each bar has a set number of beats or pulses in metered music.

bar'a Omani music and dance genre of which "Batal al-Bab" is an example. *Bar'a* was inscribed into the UNESCO registry of intangible cultural heritage in 2010.

barang (*bah*-rang) Name of a tone in each of the two Javanese scales (tone 7 in *pélog*, tone 1 in *sléndro*), and name of mode/*pathet* in *pélog*.

barung (*ba*-roong) Indicates middle or lower register *bonang, gendèr,* or *saron*.

basy Three-stringed, cello-sized instrument used in Central Europe.

Bayt al-Hikma During the Abbasid Kalifite, "the house of learning/knowledge" where the translation of Greek treatises were written.

Bedouin Nomadic groups that inhabit the desert regions throughout the Arab world.

bendir See *daff*.

bharata natyam (*bhah*-ruh-tuh *nah*-tyum) A South Indian classical dance style.

bilateral symmetry Symmetry between right and left sides of the human body.

binary beat Unit of musical time with two shorter time units (pulses) within it; see **quaternary** and **ternary beats**.

birimintingo Virtuosic instrumental passages in a performance on **kora.**

Bizung First Dagbamba *lunga* player and founder of the *lunsi* occupational clan.

blues revival The period between 1959 and 1971 when blues gained a large audience among young white people in Europe and North America. A second blues revival took place from the late 1980s through the mid-1990s, and yet another was centered on the "Year of the Blues," 2004.

blues scale Musical scale characterized by intervals of the flatted seventh, both the perfect and flatted fifths, and both the major and flatted thirds.

bomba (*bom*-ba) In the context of African Ecuadorians living in the Chota river valley of northern highland Ecuador, a double-headed drum held between the knees and played with the hands. Also used to describe a traditional musical genre, of this same cultural region, in *sesquialtera* meter. (Also a name for a genre of African-derived traditional dance music in Puerto Rico, and for drum types used in those ensembles.)

bonang (*bo*-nahng) Gong-chime, with ten, twelve, or fourteen kettles arranged in two rows.

bottleneck Neck of a Bordeaux type of wine bottle, used in playing the blues by moving along the top of guitar strings above the fingerboard to produce various tones; by extension, the name of any slide device for this purpose.

bubaran (boo-*bah*-ran) A type of formal structure in Javanese *gamelan* pieces/*gendhing*, sixteen16 beats per gong, four beats per *kenong;* usually used for dispersal of the audience after a performance.

buzuq A long-necked lute with twenty four movable frets and two sets of strings in triple courses C and G and a single bass string tuned to C.

cadential phrase A musical idea (series of notes) that concludes a musical phrase or section.

call-and-response One singer or group or instrumentalist sings or plays a musical phrase (the "call"), and another singer or group or instrumentalist answers (the "response") with another musical phrase. Although found in the music of many cultural groups, it is especially strong in African and African American music.

campesinos (kam-pe-*see*-nos) Peasants, farmers. In the south-Andean context (Peru, Bolivia), specifically, one who speaks either the Quechua or Aymara language.

Carnatic music (car-*nah*-tik) South India's classical music style.

celempung (chuh-*luhm*-poong) Zither, usually with twenty-four to twenty-six strings in double courses.

chaki ñane (*cha*-ki *nyan*) In Northern Andean Ecuador, a mountain footpath alongside agricultural plots.

charango (cha-*ran*-go) A small, fretted guitarlike instrument of Andean Bolivia, Peru, and northern Argentina, often with ten strings in five pairs, and used in peasant (Quechua-speaking First Peoples) and mestizo music in courting, festival, and/or ensemble (stage) contexts. May have a flat or a round back made of either wood or armadillo shell.

Chicago blues Electrically amplified blues that arose among African-American musicians who had migrated from the South to Chicago just after World War II. Pioneers of this sound were Muddy Waters, Little Walter, and Howlin' Wolf.

chimurenga War of liberation against white rule; a style of popular music.

chord Two or more pitches played simultaneously for the sound they make together.

chuning Slang term among Shona *mbira* players that refers not only to the tuning of the *mbira* keys but also the instrument's overall sound quality.

comunas (ko-*mu*-nas) Small clusters of houses in which the Quichua of the northern Ecuadorian highlands (the Otavalo valley) have traditionally lived.

Congress of Arab Music A conference in 1932 held in Cairo, Egypt that assembled Arab theorists and performers along with European music scholars such as Eric von Hornbostel, Bela Bartok, Curt Sachs, Paul Hindemith, Robert Lachman, and Baron Rudolphe D'Erlanger.

corrido (ko-*rree*-do) A ballad genre from the Mexico–Texas border region, characteristically performed by a male duo self-accompanied on guitars and often containing formulaic elements and a characteristic opening and closing; often addresses the exploits of heroic figures, migration experiences, romance, or tragedy.

counterpoint Combining two or more melodic parts.

cultural group Ghanaian-English term for a formally organized, amateur performance group that performs folkloric arrangements of traditional music and dance.

culture Ideas and behavior, learned and transmitted from one generation to the next, which make up the way of life of a people; usually distinguished from a people's biological (genetic) inheritance.

cuneiform A writing system of the ancient Near East in which wedge-shaped impressions were made in soft clay.

daff (also *duff*) All frame drums in which skin is stretched over one side of a cylindrical frame that is anywhere from about 12 inches to about 36 inches in diameter, sometimes including snares or jingles, found primarily throughout the Arab and Muslim worlds.

Dagbamba Ethnic group of Abubakari Lunna.

Dagbanli Language of the Dagbamba people.

Dagbon Kingdom of the Dagbamba people.

dangdut (dahng-doot) Hybrid genre of Indonesian popular music, combining influences from Indian film music, Western rock, and Indonesian regional styles from eastern Sumatra.

deacons' devotional A period before the service proper, in which the early congergants gather for traditional worship activities in song and prayer. Church deacons lead "Dr. Watts" hymns, lining them out, and chant ("whoop") prayers.

Delta blues Downhome blues from the Mississippi River Delta; regarded by some as the deepest or most profound downhome blues. Pioneers included Charley Patton, Son House, and Robert Johnson.

deze Large gourd resonator for *mbira*.

dhalang (*dah*-lahng) Puppeteer in Javanese and Balinese shadow puppet theater/*wayang kulit*; also, narrator in Javanese dance drama/*wayang orang*.

diaspora A dispersion of a people that was formerly concentrated in one place.

diddley-bow A one-stringed instrument, usually strung with thick wire, attached to a barn wall; often the earliest stringed instrument downhome blues guitarists played (as children). The rock'n'roll singer Bo Diddley took his stage name from this instrument.

dishdasha The loose, flowing garment worn by men in Oman.

dizi Transverse bamboo flute.

donkilo In *kora* music, a tune with several phrases of text.

downhome blues Early blues, chiefly sung by men accompanying themselves on acoustic guitar. Sometimes called "country blues" even though the music was sung and played in cities by people who grew up there.

drum language Vernacular meaning of a drummed phrase.

eboka Performance event.

ekimi Silence; ordered sound; a harmonious social condition.

enculturation Process of gradually acquiring cultural competency by living in a community, especially during childhood.

erhu Two-stringed fiddle.

esime Section of rhythmically intensified drumming, dancing, and percussive shouts.

Eskanye Women's Shuffle dance songs, a genre of traditional Haudenosaunee music.

Ewe Ethnic group that performs *Agbekor*.

expressive media Mode of aesthetically enhanced or intensified communication of affect and emotion.

fado An urban song genre of Portugal.

field holler African-American work song in free or flexible rhythm, sung solo, without instrumental accompaniment, in a work environment such as a cotton field. One of the ancestors of the blues.

fieldwork In-person observing, questioning, recording, photographing, and in some cases participating, which leads to information about a culture. Work "in the field" rather than at the library, on the internet, or in a laboratory.

flamenco An urban song genre of Spain.

Fon West African ethnic group with powerful historic polity in what is now Benin (see **Yoruba**).

Forest People Name used in *Worlds of Music* to collectively refer to many distinct groups of Pygmies, each having their own ethnicity.

form Structure of a musical performance; how a musical performance is put together, and how it works.

four-, six-feel Quality of musical pacing expressed in terms of number of beats within the time span of the bell phrase.

free rhythm Rhythm without recurring accents; unmetered rhythm.

fujarka Wooden flute associated with shepherds in Poland and Slovakia.

fusion Bringing together musical sounds from different traditions through intense contact and interaction.

gambang (*gahm*-bahng) Xylophone, with seventeen to twenty-two wooden keys.

gamelan (*gah*-muh-lahn) Ensemble of instruments, predominantly percussion (central, eastern, and western Java; Bali; and southern Kalimantan and Malaysia).

ganga Small-group singing genre from Bosnia emphasizing the harmonic interval of a major second.

gankogui Double bell; molds time into distinctive shape.

gendang keteng-keteng (guhn-*dahng kuhtuhng kuhtuhng*) A Batak musical genre employing two-stringed, boat-shaped lute, bamboo tube zithers, and porcelain bowl.

gendèr (guhn-*dehr*) Instrument with ten to fourteen metal slabs, suspended over tube resonators.

gendhing (guhn-*deeng*) Musical piece for *gamelan*, with regular beat and punctuation.

genre Named, standard units of a musical repertory.

gérong (*gay*rong) Small male chorus.

ghatam (*guh*-tum) A large, clay pot played with fingers and hands.

ghunna Nasality, a technique of vocal production recognized in the Call to Prayer, the recitation of the Qur'an, and traditional singing in the Arab world.

ginda Experts.

giveaway A special event that takes place at a powwow; involves formalized distribution of gifts to powwow singers, dancers, and audience members.

gong (*gong*, = *gong ageng*) Largest variety of hanging, knobbed gong.

gongche Form of notation found in China using simple symbols to represent the pitches of a musical scale.

Górale Polish word for people from the mountains; sometimes used as an ethnic category.

góralski Polish adjectival form of "gora" (mountain) but used here to refer to a genre of dance for one couple in Podhale, Poland. Also called *po góralsku* (in the Górale manner or style).

gospel song A song with lyrics focused on the Christian life. Usually more lively than a **hymn**.

grace note pickup Approaching a note by singing or playing the note above or below it very quickly before landing on the main note.

griot Term used by Europeans for the hereditary sound artisans of West African polities such as the Mande (**jalolu**) or Dagbamba (**lunsi**).

gung-gong Cylindrical, carved drum with a snare on each of its two heads.

guoyue "National music" a style of Chinese music that arose in the twentieth century and drew on aspects of Western means while attempting to preserve and develop national musical content as an alternative to Western music.

guqin See *qin*.

guru A teacher who passes on knowledge to his or her disciples.

gurukula system (gu-ru-*koo*-lah) A tradition in which young students live in the house of their teacher for many years to learn music, a craft, or ritual.

guzheng See *zheng*.

Hadith The traditions of the Prophet Muhammad often used by Muslims as a source of guidance in legal, social, and cultural matters.

halvers A sharecropping arrangement in which the landlord supplied the tenant with a shack, tools, seed, work animals, feed, fuel wood, and half the fertilizer in exchange for half the tenant's crop and labor.

hamam Traditional public baths found throughout the Middle East.

harmonic rhythm The movement of harmony or chords in time.

harmony Two or more different pitches sounded at the same time for the purpose of the sound they make together.

heterophonic/heterophony Musical organization that occurs when two or more voices or instruments elaborate the same melody in different ways at approximately the same time.

hocketing Dispersing the tones of the melody among several voices and/or instruments, which play it in alternation or sequence rather than simultaneously. Traditional performance practice for south Andean panpipe music, such as "Kutirimunapaq," but also found elsewhere in the world.

homophonic Musical organization characterized by a single, dominant melody and its musical accompaniment.

hosho Pair of gourd rattles played in Shona *mbira* music.

hózhó͟ó͟ A Navajo concept meaning beauty, blessedness, or harmony. Navajo seek to restore *hózhó͟ó͟* through rituals such as the Nightway ceremony.

huro Style of Shona singing that uses yodeling.

hymn A song of praise to God.

idam (ih-*dum*) Literally the "place" in a melodic line in a song having a pitch and a particular point in the *tala* cycle to which improvisations periodically return.

improvisation The art of composing music at the moment of performance rather than in advance of performance.

Indian Ocean Area of water and surrounding landmasses, countries, and continents that have been in contact with one another through maritime trade and travel for centuries.

intangible cultural heritage Traditional cultural practices deemed worthy of recognition and safeguarding according to UNESCO.

interval Distance between two pitches in a musical scale.

intifada Palestinian uprising against Israeli occupation.

ira (*ee*-ra) One rank, or line, of south Andean panpipes; represents, on the Bolivian high plateau (altiplano), the male principle; serves as the "leader." Shares the full melody, with the *arca* rank of pipes, playing in hocket.

irama (ee-*raw*-maw) Level of subdivision of main melody beat by elaborating instruments.

isorhythm Equal rhythm, the same rhythm. In the setting of northern Ecuadorian highland Quichua *sanjuán*, this concept denotes an established tradition, in which the rhythm of the first half of the phrase is characteristically identical, or nearly so, to the rhythm of the second half.

Jakarta (jah-*kar*-tah) Indonesia's national capital city.

jaliya What **jalolu** do.

jalolu (singular, **jali**) Hereditary sound artisans and musical specialists within Mande music-culture.

Java (*jah*-vah) Indonesia's most densely populated island, home to Javanese, Sundanese, and Madurese.

Jiangnan *sizhu* A genre from the Jiangnan region, in East China, around the lower reaches of the Changjiang (Yangtze River). Historically, two major categories of instruments were used in this music, silk-stringed instruments and bamboo-tubed wind instruments.

jianzipu Tablature score for the Chinese *qin* that shows string stopping and plucking techniques.

jingju Beijing opera.

kaganu Highest-pitched *Agbekor* drum; "salt in the musical stew."

kanjira (kahn-*jih*-ruh) A tambourine made of wood and lizard skin, with jangles.

k'antu (k-*an*-tu) A type of ceremonial panpipe music from the altiplano, or high plateau, of Peru and Bolivia.

kapela Traditional string band in Podhale, Poland. Elsewhere in Poland the term usually refers to a choir.

karnataka sangeeta (car-*nah*-tuh-kah sahn*gee*-tah with a hard "g") Carnatic music, South India's classical music style.

kebyar (kuh-*byar*) Literally, "flash," "burst forth." Type of *gamelan* (and dance) created in twentieth-century Bali.

kembang pacar (kuhm-*bahng pah*-char) A type of red flower; title of a *gamelan* piece.

kempul (kuhm-*pool*) Smaller, hanging, knobbed gong.

kena (*ke*-na) An Andean vertical notched flute.

kendhang (kuhn-*dahng*) Double-headed, barrel-shaped drum (Java); similar term used in West Java and Bali (*kendang*).

kenong (kuh-*nong*) Large kettle gong, horizontally mounted.

kethuk (kuh-*took* [as in English "took"]) Small kettle gong, horizontally mounted.

khanda chapu tala (kahn-da *chah*-pu *tah*lah) A five-beat *tala* cycle subdivided 2 + 3.

kidi Second-highest-pitched *Agbekor* drum; three bounces and three presses.

klezmer Ashkenazic Jewish music for secular and sacred occasions such as weddings; instrumental and vocal; texts often in Yiddish. Musicians who play this music are called *klezmorim*.

kloboto Higher-pitched of paired set of *Agbekor* drums; creates displacement.

konkong Ostinato part in *kora* music made by knocking on the resonator.

kora Bridge-harp played by **jalolu** of **Mande** music-culture.

kriti (*krih*-tee) The principal song form of South Indian classical music.

kudeketera Style of Shona singing that uses poetry.

kulcapi (kool-*cha*-pee) Two-stringed, boat-shaped lute of the Karo Batak, North Sumatra.

kumbengo Instrumental ostinato played on *kora* that establishes the tonal and metric framework of a piece.

kushaura Main part in a two-part arrangement of *mbira* music.

kutsinhira Interwoven second part in a two-part arrangement of *mbira* music.

landó (lan-*do*) Reconstructed genre of Afro-Peruvian music. An example is "Azúcar de caña."

libation Ritual communication to the spirit world involving drinks and speech.

life-cycle ritual Ceremony marking an important juncture in life such as birth, death, coming-of-age, or marriage.

lining out A form of call-and-response in psalm or hymn singing. A leader speaks or chants each line of the verse, and the congregation repeats the line to a different tune.

longhouse Among the Haudenosaunee, a meetinghouse with a stove at each end of the hall and benches along the sides and used for social and ceremonial events.

lunga (plural, *lunsi*) 1. A Dagbamba verbal artist, genealogist, counselor to royalty, cultural expert, and entertainer. 2. Hourglass-shaped tension drum.

Mabo Type of music and dance associated with net hunting.

Maghrib The part of the Arab world that is in the western part of North Africa (Morocco, Tunisia, Algeria).

Mahabharata (ma-hah-bah-*rah*-tah) One of two major Indian epics widely known in Java and Bali; centers on conflict between rival sets of cousins, culminating in major war.

mahonyera Style of Shona singing that uses vocables.

major scale Most common arrangement of pitches used in European and North American melodies "Do-re-mi-fa-sol-la-ti-do."

makwa Hand-clapping phrases that accompany mbira music.

Mande General term for West African ethno-linguistic groups whose music-culture features specialist "sound artisans" and stringed instruments such as *kora*.

mapira All-night, family-based, communal rituals at which spirit possessions occur; singular, *bira*.

maqam Musical mode in the Arab tradition; *maqam bayyati* is the name of a mode; this conceptualization of scale is found in variation throughout the Arab world and Middle East region, including parts of Central Asia.

marginal preservation Aspects of culture that are preserved in migrant communities long after they have died out or developed into something new in the place where they originated (see Rasmussen 1991).

Mashriq The part of the Arab world that is the Eastern part of North Africa as well as the Mediterranean (Egypt, Lebanon, Jordan, Syria, Iraq).

material culture Tangible objects produced by humans, such as tools, furniture, and so on, resulting from knowledge transmitted from one generation to the next.

Mawu Ewe Supreme Being.

Mba Father (teaching-father).

Mba Ngolba Abubakari Lunna's second teaching-father.

mbira Plucked, tuned idiophone.

melakarta (*may*-luh-*car*-tuh) A system of seventy-two basic seven-note "parent" or "mother" scales for classifying *ragas*.

melisma Elaboration of the melody with three or more tones per syllable of text.

metaphor A figure of speech comparing one thing to another, usually involving similarities not immediately obvious.

mijwiz A single-reed, double-piped folk clarinet that is typical of the Levant (Lebanon, Syria, Jordan, and the Palestinian territories).

minor scale After major scale, the second most common arrangement of pitches in European and North American melodies. Distinguished by a lowered third scale degree.

misra chapu tala (*mis*-rah *chah*-pu *tah*-lah) A *tala* cycle of seven beats divided 3 + 2 + 2, usually played at fast speed.

mistreatment Chief theme of blues lyrics, when one person (usually a lover) treats another badly or unjustly.

monophonic Single-part music.

monsoon The rainy seasonal winds that dictate yearly migration patterns and the direction of boat and ship travel around the Indian Ocean region.

morsang (*mor*-sung) An Indian type of Jew's (or jaw) harp.

mridangam (mrih-*dun*-gum) Principal South Indian drum, barrel-shaped, two-headed, and played with fingers and palms.

mudzimu Shona ancestral spirits.

muezzin The man who performs the Call to Prayer.

music-culture A group's total involvement with music: ideas, actions, institutions, material objects—everything that has to do with music.

musical ethnography A written representation in the form of documentation, description, and interpretation of a subject within a music-culture, organized from the standpoint of a particular topic.

musicking An invented word that turns the static noun "music" into an action "to make music."

muzyka Podhala Music considered indigenous and unique to the Podhale region of southern Poland.

Natai raga A *raga* with two ascending scales: (a) a seven-note, ascending scale C D# E F G A# B C, and (b) a five-note, ascending scale C E F G B C. They are used interchangeably. *Natai* has one form of the descending scale: C B-flat G F E-flat C.

nay A reed flute that is blown obliquely, at an angle.

ngara A superior female singer who excels at public performances.

"Nhemamusasa" One of the oldest and most important Shona *mbira* pieces.

Nightway Nine-day, Navajo curing ceremony performed for the purpose of restoring *hózhóó* in the one-sung-over.

Notsie Historic city-state from which Ewe people escaped.

Nueva Canción (nu-*e*-va kan-*syon*) or "New Song." A political song movement through which people stand up for themselves in the face of oppression by a totalitarian government or in the face of cultural imperialism from abroad. Developed first in Argentina, Chile, and Uruguay during the 1950s and 1960s, it spread throughout Latin America.

nuta Literally "note," but is used by *Górale* of Poland to refer to a melodic idea or tune family.

octave The interval between one musical pitch and another that is twice (or half) its frequency.

octave leaps Jumping up or down the interval of an octave, for example from the note G below middle C to the note g above middle C.

onomatopoeic syllables Syllables that sound like the sounds they represent.

ostinato Repeating rhythmic or melodic pattern that is usually played "underneath," "against," or as a backdrop for the main melody.

ozwodna Dance tune-type for *góralski* dance in Podhale, Poland. An *ozwodna* may be introduced by singing, but it is primarily instrumental and is metered, usually with five-bar phrases.

panerus (pa-nuh-roos) Indicates highest register *saron, bonang,* or *gendèr*.

participant-observer A person who studies a culture by joining in its activities as well as by observing it from an outside perspective.

pathet (*pah*-tuht) Musical mode; also major section of shadow play.

peking (puh-*keeng*) Smallest and highest pitched *saron* in Javanese *gamelan*, also called *saron panerus*.

pélog (*pay*-log) Seven-tone scale, of small and large intervals.

pesindhèn (puh-*seen*-den) Female singer (Java).

phrases (musical) Like a phrase within a sentence; a group of tones that makes up a unit.

pipa Pear-shaped, Chinese lute with four strings.

pitch The perceived highness or lowness of a sound, related to the frequency of its vibrations.

Playon "Lasem" (*plah*-yon *lah*-suhm) Title of *gamelan* piece played in first major section of shadow play, Yogyakarta style (Java).

po góralsku See *góralski*.

Podhale The Tatra Mountain region of southern Poland.

polymeter Simultaneous presence of different structures of music's temporal organization, such as time span and/or beats.

polyphonic Multipart music.

polyrhythm Simultaneous occurrence of more than one rhythm, with a shifting downbeat.

possession trance Ritual process in which the body of a living person becomes the "medium" for a spirit being.

powwow A Native American social, ceremonial, and spiritual gathering featuring food, singing, and dancing.

primitive Derogatory English term placing an ethnic group at an early stage of cultural or technological evolution.

qafla The Arabic term for a cadential melodic phrase. A phrase at the end of a "sentence" or "paragraph" of improvised music.

qanun A zither with seventy-five strings in triple courses with a series of small tuning levers that allow the strings to be retuned in the course of performance.

qin (also *guqin*) Chinese seven-stringed zither with an ancient history and delicate tone.

qingyi A serious heroine in Beijing opera, one of several significant role-types used in theatrical tradition.

quaternary beats Unit of musical time with four shorter time units (pulses) within it; compare to **ternary** and **binary beats**.

quatrain-refrain stanza Form of a blues verse (stanza) in which a four-line quatrain is followed by a two-line refrain, usually spread over twelve bars (measures) of music. Compare **three-line stanza**.

Quichua (or Quechua) (*kee*-chooa) (*keh*-chooa) Dating back to the Inca civilization, a language spoken by up to eight million First Peoples (Native Americans) in the Andes region of South America, including Ecuador, Peru, Bolivia, Argentina, and Colombia. Heard in both "Muyu muyari warmigu" and "Ilumán tiyu."

quijada (*kee*-*ha*-da) A percussive instrument made from the jawbone of a donkey, horse, or cow; the animal's molars, when loosened by exposure to the elements, produce a clear dry crack when struck with the fist. Used today in Afro-Peruvian musics.

Qur'an (also Koran) The holy scriptures of Islam, comprised of 114 chapters and believed by Muslims to be the word of God as transmitted through the angel Gabriel to the Prophet Muhammad.

race Concept that categorizes groups of people on the basis of their physical appearance.

raga (*rah*-guh) A musical entity characterized by distinctive elements (scale, ornaments, and so on) that provides the raw material for melodic composition and improvisation.

raga-mala (*rah*-guh *mah*-luh) A genre of miniature painting depicting a *raga*.

ragam-tanam-pallavi (*rah*-gum, *tah*-num, *puhl*-luh-vee) Extensive, improvisational form based on a single phrase of melody and text; often performed as the main piece in a concert.

rai A genre of North African pop music; also popular in France.

Ramayana One of two major Indian epics widely known in Java and Bali; centers on story of Prince Rama.

rasa (*rah*-sah) An emotion generated by a work of art.

rebab (ruh-*bab*) Two-string fiddle (Java; also found in Bali and elsewhere).

Reconquista The progressive "re-conquest" in the early 1500s of southern Europe (also known as "the Spanish Inquisition") by European Christians that resulted in the gradual exile and migration of Muslims and Jews.

regalia A term used by Native Americans to refer to all of the elements of a powwow dancer's outfit, including both articles of clothing (e.g., headdress, moccasins, ribbon shirt, etc.) and other decorative and/or ceremonial accessories (e.g., wing fan, blanket, etc.).

repertory A stock or supply of ready musical performances, consisting chiefly of style, genres, texts, composition, transmission, and movement.

Rhodesia Former name of a white-ruled state; renamed Zimbabwe.

riqq The Arab tambourine.

roots music Musical genres such as blues, gospel, Cajun, zydeco, hillbilly, bluegrass, polka, or klezmer that are either identified as source musics that contributed to mainstream popular musics such as rock, or as the musics of ethnic groups in the United States. As a marketing term, it replaced "folk music" and competes with **Americana.**

sabha (sah-*bhah*) Cultural organization that sponsors concerts, dance recitals, and plays.

Sahel Ecological zone in West Africa south of the desert and north of the tropical forest.

salima Praise Name dances of Dagbon (for instance, "Nag Biegu").

sanjuánes (san-*hooan*) Originally (c. 1860) either a type of song played at the festival of St. John (San Juan) the Baptist held in June or a type of dance performed at that festival. Today, it is a northern Ecuadorian highland Quichua genre.

sanxian Three-stringed, long-necked lute.

saron (*sah*-ron) Instrument with six or seven metal slabs, resting on a trough resonator.

scale An ordered arrangement of the pitches used in a musical performance.

Se Divinity that personifies fate or destiny.

sequence Musical ideas that are repeated a step higher or lower.

sesquialtera metrical rhythm Music that can be felt in both 3/4 and 6/8 metrical rhythm—either simultaneously or alternatively. This metrical-rhythmic ambiguity is the heart and soul of much Hispanic-derived Latin American regional folk music.

shan'ge Outdoor songs from China used for agricultural work, flirting, and courting.

Shona Ethnic group in Zimbabwe noted for its *mbira* music.

shruti (*shroo*-tee) The tonal center chosen by a performer.

signifying African-American expressions that express things indirectly, couched in metaphoric, coded, and often witty language.

Silk Road An ancient network of trade routes running from Japan to Morocco in North Africa and Southern Europe.

sitar (sih-*tahr*) Plucked, twenty-two–string classical instrument of North India.

siyem (*see*-yuhm) Middle-sized, hanging, knobbed gong.

sléndro (*slayn*-dro) F-tone scale, with nearly equidistant intervals (Java and Bali).

slenthem (*sluhn*-tuhm) Instrument with six or seven metal slabs, suspended over tube resonators.

sollukattu (sol-lu-*kuht*-tu) Spoken drumming patterns.

Solo (*soh*-loh) Short name for Surakarta.

soul music The most popular African-American music in the 1960s, recorded for companies like Stax-Volt and Atlantic, featuring singers such as James Brown, Aretha Franklin, and Otis Redding.

soundscape All the sounds that can be heard in a particular place.

soundscape ecology Scientific study of the relationship among sounds and how they interact with beings and objects in a particular environment.

source musician An elder musician thought to be authentic by virtue of birthright and participation in the music-culture during an earlier age, rather than its present-day revival.

spirit medium Person whose body is temporarily occupied by a spirit so that it can communicate in the material world.

stanza A song form in which successive verses are set to the same melody. Sometimes the words "stanza" and "verse" are used interchangeably. A more technical term is *strophe*.

strophe Structural division of a poem or song, such as a stanza or a verse.

strophic Song form in which each new verse reuses the same musical outline.

style Includes everything related to the sound of a music characteristic of a particular culture in a particular period.

sub-Saharan Africa Africa south of the Sahara Desert.

Sudan Region of Africa just south of the Sahara Desert; called "land of the Blacks" in Arabic.

suling (*soo*-leeng) End-blown bamboo flute.

Sumatra (soo-*mah*-trah) Large Indonesian island, west of Java.

Sunda (*soon*-dah) West Java (western third of the island of Java).

Surakarta (soo-rah-*kar*-tah; also pronounced soo-raw-*kar*-taw) One of two famous court cities in central Java.

Suzhou tanci Classical genre of narrative singing from the city of Suzhou in East China.

swara (or *svara*) (swah-ruh) A note or pitch in a scale of Indian music. The seven notes (*swaras*) of a scale are named *sa, ri, ga, ma, pa, da, ni*. The scale has a movable tonic.

The actual pitch of each note is defined by the *raga* in which it occurs.

tabla (*tah*-bluh) Principal north Indian drum comprising a set of two small drums one of metal and pot-shaped, the other of wood and cylindrical, played with fingers and palms.

takht Arabic, an ensemble of three to eight instrumentalists, sometimes including a singer, who perform traditional Arab music on Arab stringed, wind, and percussion instruments.

tala (*tah*-luh) A recurring time cycle. Can be counted with fingers and hands.

tanam (*tah*-nuhm) A melodic improvisation, strongly rhythmic but without *tala*.

tani avartanam (*tah*-nee ah-*vahr*-tuhnuhm) Percussion solo in a concert.

taqasim An instrumental improvisation in Arab and Middle Eastern music.

tarab A term used for a repertoire of Arab music as well as the social dynamics enacted in the course of performance. Translated as ecstasy, rapture, enchantment.

ternary beat Unit of musical time with three shorter time units (pulses) within it; compare to **quaternary** and **binary beats**.

text Words or lyrics of a song or poem.

texture Melodic interrelationships within a musical performance.

three-in-the-time-of-two (3:2) A span of time that is simultaneously divided in two parts and three parts.

three-line stanza One form of a blues verse (stanza) in which the first line is repeated, and then the third line closes out the thought with a rhyme, usually spread over twelve bars (measures) of music. Compare to **quatrain-refrain stanza**.

timbre Color and quality of a tone produced by an instrument or the voice; reason why the same note played on two different instruments sounds different.

tone language The pitch (high, low, rising, falling, etc.) at which a symbol is pronounced is as important in determining its meaning as its combination of other components (duration, stress, and the sounds equivalent to consonants and vowels).

tonic In Western music theory, the basic tone, or note, of a melody or a section of a piece; the most important pitch; usually the pitch that occurs most often; often the last tone of a melody, the pitch that the melody seems to be gravitating toward. The tonic note of C major is C. Also called "do," as in "do-re-mi-fa-so…"

Torah The most important book of the Jewish tradition, transmitted by God to Moses, chanted orally according to specific rules and guidelines, in a public practice that is central to Jewish life.

totodzi Lower-pitched of paired set of drums; three-then-two timing.

transnational migrant Members of a particular ethnic group residing—at different moments in time—both in their home territory and in different nations. In Chapter 9, it applies specifically to Quichua musicians of the Otavalo valley, northern highland Ecuador, and their social networks both in that valley and abroad.

tremolo On a stringed instrument, strumming or picking up and down on one or more strings rapidly to create a sustained tone.

trills Oscillating between two notes that are right next to each other.

turns An ornament that includes a note above and below the main note.

'ud A short-necked, pear-shaped, fretless lute, usually with eleven strings in double courses.

UNESCO United Nations Educational, Scientific and Cultural Organization.

unison Singing or playing the same melodic line.

urban blues Later blues, closest to rhythm and blues than any other form of blues, which arose after World War II. Electric instruments, a saxophone or horn section, and lead guitar work characterize this music. T-Bone Walker and B. B. King were its early stars.

vamp Rhythmic and melodic ostinato.

veena (*vee*-nuh) A plucked, seven-stringed, South Indian lute.

vocable A nonlexical syllable used in many different kinds of vocal music from around the world.

vulolo Slow-paced, processional section of *Agbekor*.

vutsotsoe Fast-paced part of an *Agbekor* performance.

wayang kulit (*wah*-yang *koo*-lit) Shadow puppetry, using flat, leather puppets made of water-buffalo hide.

wayang orang (*wah*-yang o-rang) Javanese dance drama; dancer-actors presenting episodes derived from the *Ramayana* and *Mahabharata*, accompanied by *gamelan*.

wayno (*wahy*-no) Known by various regional names, a deeply rooted, lively musical genre native to the south-Andean region of Peru and Bolivia. Texts may speak to a lost love; musically characterized by

duple—or a combination of duple and triple—meter, and bimodality (minor, together with relative major). An example is "Amor imposible."

Wenya Historic leader of the Anlo-Ewes during their exodus.

whooping African American name for the preacher's traditional, musical part chanted, part-sung sermon delivery.

world beat Deliberate combinations (fusions) of popular genres of music that have a level of international recognition with a local or indigenous music; usually considered "exotic."

work song/work music Songs or instrumental music in oral tradition, used to accompany work and make the time pass more pleasantly and/or to pace and coordinate the work itself.

xiao Bamboo end-blown vertical flute.

Yeibichai Traditional music genre of the Navajo found in the Nightway ceremony.

Yogya (*jog*-jah) Short name for Yogyakarta (sometimes spelled "Jogja" or "Jogya").

Yogyakarta (jog-jah-*kar*-tah; also pronounced yog-yaw-*kar*-taw) One of two famous court cities in central Java (sometimes spelled "Jogjakarta").

Yoruba West African ethnic group with powerful, historic polity in what is now Nigeria (see **Fon**).

yuga (*yoo*-guh) One of the four ages of Indian mythological time.

zaffa A procession of the bride and groom that includes musicians, dancers, instrumentalists, and all of the invited guests.

zagareet A high-pitched trilling cry that proclaims excitement, usually performed by women.

zampoña (sam-*pon*-ya) In Andean South America, refers to panpipes, a set of endblown bamboo rubes lashed together, each tube producing a particular pitch. In the southern Andes (Peru and Bolivia), *zampoñas* are in two ranks, or lines, of pipes and, in traditional performance format, are played in hocket, with the two ranks being divided between two different performers. The south Andean *zampoñas* are traditionally played in large ensembles, accompanied by drums.

zheng (also *guzheng*) A bridged zither with usually twenty-five strings.

zielona Literally "green,"; in Polish *muzyka Podhala* the term refers to a tune-family used as the final part of a *góralski* dance suite.

złóbcoki Small, boat-shaped folk violin used in the Polish Tatra Mountains.

References

CHAPTER 1—THE MUSIC-CULTURE AS A WORLD OF MUSIC

References

Blacking, John. 1973. *How Musical Is Man?* Seattle: Univ. of Washington Press.

Feld, Steven. 2012. *Sound and Sentiment: Birds, Weeping, Poetics and Song in Kaluli Expression*. 3rd ed. Durham, NC: Duke Univ. Press.

Krause, Bernie. 2002. *Wild Soundscapes*. Berkeley, CA: Wilderness Press.

Lomax, Alan. 1968. *Folksong Style and Culture*. New York: Transaction Publishers.

Merriam, Alan P. 1964. *The Anthropology of Music*. Evanston, IL: Northwestern Univ. Press.

Olajubu, Chief Oludare. 1978. "Yoruba Verbal Artists and Their Work." *Journal of American Folklore* 91:675–90.

Sachs, Nahoma. 1975. "Music and Meaning: Musical Symbolism in a Macedonian Village." Ph.D. diss., Princeton Univ.

Schafer, R. Murray. 1980. *The Tuning of the World: Toward a Theory of Soundscape Design*. Philadelphia: Univ. of Pennsylvania Press.

SEM-L Archives. 1998 (July 21, 17:03:53). No subject. Posted by A. K. May be accessed via http://www.ethnomusicology.org/?Resources_ELists

Thoreau, Henry David. 1971. *Walden*. Princeton, NJ: Princeton Univ. Press.

Titon, Jeff Todd. 1988. *Powerhouse for God: Speech, Chant, and Song in an Appalachian Baptist Church*. Austin: Univ. of Texas Press.

———, ed. 1992. *Worlds of Music*. 2nd ed. New York: Schirmer Books.

Turino, Thomas. 2009. "Four Fields of Music Making and Sustainable Living." *The World of Music* 51(1):95–118.

Additional Reading

Barz, Gregory, and Timothy J. Cooley. 2008. *Shadows in the Field: New Perspectives for Fieldwork in Ethnomusicology*. 2nd ed. New York: Oxford Univ. Press.

Crafts, Susan D., Daniel Cavicchi, Charles Keil, and the Music in Daily Life Project, 1993. *My Music*. Hanover, NH: Univ. Press of New England.

Mundy, Rachel. 2009. "Birdsong and the Image of Evolution." *Society and Animals* 17:206–223.

Nettl, Bruno. 1995. *Heartland Excursions: Ethnomusicological Reflections on Schools of Music*. Urbana: Univ. of Illinois Press.

Pantaleoni, Hewitt. 1985. *On the Nature of Music*. Oneonta, NY: Wellkin Books.

Pettan, Svanibor, and Jeff Todd Titon, eds. 2015. *The Oxford Guide to Applied Ethnomusicology*. New York: Oxford Univ. Press.

Reck, David. 1997. *Music of the Whole Earth*. New York: Da Capo.

Rice, Timothy. 2014. *Ethnomusicology: A Very Short Introduction*. New York: Oxford Univ. Press.

CHAPTER 2—NORTH AMERICA/NATIVE AMERICA

References

Blackfire. 2007. *Silence Is a Weapon*. Flagstaff, AZ: Tacoho Records 881131000844. CD.

Brockman, Joshua. 2002. "Beyond Drumbeats: New Sounds from Indian Country." *New York Times*, January 16, 2002. Retrieved from http://www.nytimes.com/2002/01/16/arts/arts-in-america-beyond-drumbeats-new-sounds-from-indian-country.html.

Brown, Dee. 1970. *Bury My Heart at Wounded Knee: An Indian History of the American West*. New York: Holt, Rinehart & Winston.

Browner, Tara. 2000. "Making and Singing Pow-Wow Songs: Text, Form, and the Significance of Culture-Based Analysis." *Ethnomusicology* 44(2):214–233.

———. 2002. *Heartbeat of the People: Music and Dance of the Northern Pow-wow*. Urbana: Univ. of Illinois Press.

Desrosiers, Gabriel, and Christopher Scales. 2012. "Contemporary Northern Plains Powwow Music: The Twin Influences of Recording and Competition." In *Aboriginal Music in Contemporary Canada: Echoes and Exchanges*, edited by Anna Hoefnagels and Beverley Diamond. Montreal: McGill-Queen's Univ. Press.

Diamond, Beverley. 2008. *Native American Music in Eastern North America*. New York: Oxford Univ. Press.

Diamond, Beverley, M. Sam Cronk, and Franziska von Rosen. 1994. *Visions of Sound: Musical Instruments of First Nations Communities in Northeastern America*. Chicago: Univ. of Chicago Press.

Ellis, Clyde. 2001. "'We Don't Want Your Rations, We Want This Dance': The Changing Use of Song and Dance on the Southern Plains." In *American Nations: Encounters in Indian Country, 1850 to the Present*, edited by Frederick Hoxie, Peter Mancall, and James Merrell. New York: Routledge.

Eyabay. *Ain't Nuthin' But a "E" Thang*. Winnipeg, MB: Sunshine Records SSCD4397. CD

Faris, James C. 1990. *The Nightway: A History and a History of Documentation of a Navajo Ceremonial*. Albuquerque: Univ. of New Mexico Press.

Handler, Richard, and Jocelyn Linnekin. 1984. "Tradition, Genuine or Spurious." *Journal of American Folklore* 97:273–290.

Hatton, O. Thomas. 1974. "Performance Practices of Northern Plains Pow-Wow Singing Groups." Department of Music, Institute of Latin American Studies, Univ. of Texas at Austin, *Yearbook*, 123–137.

Jackson, Jason Baird. 2003. *Yuchi Ceremonial Life: Performance, Meaning, Tradition in a Contemporary American Indian Community*. Lincoln: Univ. of Nebraska Press.

———. 2005. "East Meets West: On Stomp Dance and Powwow Worlds in Oklahoma." In *Powwow*, edited by Clyde Ellis, Luke Eric Lassiter, and Gary H. Dunham. Lincoln: Univ. of Nebraska Press.

Jackson, Jason Baird, and Victoria Lindsay Levine. 2002. "Singing for Garfish: Music and Woodland Communities in Eastern Oklahoma." *Ethnomusicology* 46(2):284–306.

Kluckhohn, Clyde, and Dorothea Leighton. 1974. *The Navajo.* Cambridge, MA: Harvard Univ.

Levi, Jerome, and Bartholomew Dean. 2006. "Introduction." In *At the Risk of Being Heard: Identity, Indigenous Rights, and Postcolonial States,* edited by Jerome Levi and Bartholomew Dean. Ann Arbor: Univ. of Michigan Press.

Levine, Victoria Lindsay. 2009. "Music and Dance the Eastern Way in Oklahoma." Paper presented at the Native American Arts Festival, Idyllwild Arts Foundation.

Levine, Victoria Lindsay, and Bruno Nettl. 2011. "Strophic Form and Asymmetrical Repetition in Four American Indian Songs." In *Analytic and Cross-Cultural Studies in World Music,* edited by Michael Tenzer and John Roeder. New York: Oxford Univ. Press.

McDowell, Marsha (ed.). 1997. *Contemporary Great Lakes Pow Wow Regalia: "Nda Maamawigaami (We Dance Together)."* East Lansing: Michigan State Univ. Museum.

Matthiessen, Peter. 1983. *In the Spirit of Crazy Horse.* New York: Viking Press.

Moore, John H. 1996. "Yuchi." In *Native America in the Twentieth Century: An Encyclopedia,* edited by Mary B. Davis. New York: Garland Publishing.

Northern Wind Singers. 2002. *Ikwe Nagamonan: Women's Songs.* Arbor Records AR-11282. CD.

Olson, James S., and Raymond Wilson. 1986, *Native Americans in the Twentieth Century.* Urbana: Univ. of Illinois Press.

Powers, William K. 1966. *Here Is Your Hobby: Indian Dancing and Costumes.* New York: Putnam.

———. 1980. "Oglala Song Terminology." In *Selected Reports in Ethnomusicology* 3(2), edited by Charlotte Heth. Los Angeles: Program in Ethnomusicology, Univ. of California, Los Angeles; 23–41.

———. 1990. *War Dance: Plains Indian Musical Performance.* Tucson: Univ. of Arizona Press.

Richter, Daniel K. 1992. *The Ordeal of the Longhouse: The Peoples of the Iroquois League in the Era of European Colonization.* Chapel Hill: Univ. of North Carolina Press.

Scales, Christopher. 1999. "First Nations Popular Music in Canada: Musical Meaning and the Politics of Identity." *Canadian University Music Review* 19(2):94–101.

———. 2007. "Powwows, Intertribalism, and the Value of Competition." *Ethnomusicology* 51(1):1–29.

Scales, Christopher, and Gabriel Desrosiers. 2016 "Nimiidaa!" ['Let's all dance']: Music and Dance on the Northern Plains Powwow Trail." In *Musics of Multicultural America, Revised,* 2nd ed., edited by Kip Lornell and Anne Rasmussen. Jackson: Univ. Press of Mississippi.

Starna, William A., Jack Campisi, and Laurence M. Hauptman 1996. "Iroquois Confederacy." In *Native America in the Twentieth Century: An Encyclopedia,* edited by Mary B. Davis. New York: Garland Publishing.

Sutton, Mark Q. 2004. *An Introduction to Native North America,* 2nd ed. Boston: Pearson Education.

XIT. 1999. *Plight of the Redman.* SOAR 101. CD

Additional Reading

Bailey, Garrick, and Roberta Glenn Bailey. 1986. *A History of the Navajos: The Reservation Years.* Santa Fe, NM: School of American Research Press.

Browner, Tara (ed.). 2009. *Music of the First Nations.* Urbana: Univ. of Illinois Press.

Deloria, Vine, Jr. 1969. *Custer Died for Your Sins: An Indian Manifesto.* London: Collier-Macmillan.

Gill, Sam D. 1981. *Sacred Words: A Study of Navajo Religion and Prayer.* Westport, CT: Greenwood Press.

Howard, James H., and Victoria Lindsay Levine. 1990. *Choctaw Music and Dance.* Norman: Univ. of Oklahoma Press.

Lassiter, Luke E. 1998. *The Power of Kiowa Song.* Tucson: Univ. of Arizona Press.

McAllester, David and Susan. 1980. *Hogans: Navajo Houses and House Songs.* Wesleyan, CT: Wesleyan Univ. Press.

McCullough-Brabson, Ellen, and Marilyn Help. 2001. *We'll Be in Your Mountains, We'll Be in Your Songs: A Navajo Woman Sings.* Albuquerque: Univ. of New Mexico Press.

Nakai, R. Carlos, James Demars, David P. McAllester, and Ken Light. 1997. *The Art of the Native American Flute.* Pacific, MO: Mel Bay Publications.

Nettl, Bruno. 1989. *Blackfoot Musical Thought: Comparative Perspectives.* Kent, OH: Kent State Univ. Press.

Samuels, David W. 2004. *Putting a Song on Top of It: Expression and Identity on the San Carlos Apache Reservation.* Tucson: Univ. of Arizona Press.

Scales, Christopher A. 2012. *Recording Culture: Powwow Music and the Aboriginal Recording Industry on the Northern Plains.* Durham, NC: Duke Univ. Press.

Additional Listening

Traditional Tribal and Intertribal Music

Akipa, Bryan. 2001. *Eagle Dreams.* Makoché 0186.

Bear, Keith. 2000. *Earth Lodge.* Makoché 0153.

Bear Creek and Sizzortail. 2004. *When Worlds Collide.* Drum Hop.

Black Lodge Singers. 1996. *Kid's Pow-Wow Songs.* Canyon 6274.

Locke, Kevin. 1999. *The First Flute.* Makoché 0147.

Nakai, R. Carlos. 1987. *Earth Spirit.* Canyon 612.

Nakai, R. Carlos, and William Eaton. 1993. *Ancestral Voices.* Canyon 7010.

Nakai, R. Carlos, with James Demars, Blacklodge, and the Canyon Orchestra. 1997. *Two World Concerto.* Canyon 7016.

Natay, Ed Lee. *Natay: Navajo Singer.* 1951. Canyon 6160.

Primeaux and Mike. 2001. *Bless the People.* Canyon 6317.

Primeaux and Mike with Joe Jakob. 1997. *Sacred Path.* Canyon 6306.

Red Bull. 2000. *Millennium.* Sweet Grass Records 11200.

Red Bull. 1998. *World Hand Drum Champs '98.* Sweet Grass Records 90498.

The Boyz. 2004. *For a Lifetime.* Drum Hop 0300.

Various Artists. 1997. *Wood that Sings: Indian Fiddle Music of the Americas.* Smithsonian Folkways 40472.

Various Artists. 2004. *Beautiful Beyond: Christian Songs in Native Languages.* Smithsonian Folkways 40480.

Whitefish Jrs. 2003. *In Honor of Percy Dreaver: Round Dance Songs.* Sweet Grass Records 010803.

Native American Popular Music

Aglukark, Susan. 1992. *Arctic Rose.* EMI Canada 72438 28605.

Blackfire. 2001. *One Nation Under.* Canyon 7049

Burch, Sharon. 1989. *Yazzie Girl.* Canyon 534.

Donavan, Mishi. 2007. *Storm Beauty.* Arbor 12572.

Eagle and Hawk. 2003. *Mother Earth.* Arbor 12162.

Harjo, Joy. 1997. *Letter from the End of the 20th Century.* Silver Wave 914.

Humphrey, Annie. 2004. *Edge of America.* Makoche 0182.

Indigenous. 2003. *Indigenous.* Jive 53480

Kashtin. 1994. *Akua Tuta.* Tristar 67203.

Litefoot. 1996. *Good Day to Die.* Red Vinyl 9607.

Miller, Derek. 2002. *Music Is the Medicine.* Arbor 11842.

Pura Fe. 1995. *Caution to the Wind.* Shanachie 5013.

Redbone. 2003. *The Essential Redbone.* Epic/Legacy 86072.

Robertson, Robbie. 1994. *Music for the Native Americans.* Capitol 28295.

Robertson, Robbie. 1998. *Contact from the Underworld of Redboy.* Capitol 54243.

Sainte-Marie, Buffy. 1992. *Coincidence and Likely Stories.* Chrysalis 21920.

Sainte-Marie, Buffy. 1996. *Up Where We Belong.* EMI Premier 3745.

Salas, Stevie. 2007. *Sun and the Earth, Vol. 1.* Arbor 12572.

Secola, Keith. 1998. Wild Band of Indians. Oarfin 70002.
Shenandoah, Joanne. 2003. *Covenant*. Silver Wave 983.
Trudell, John. 1992. *AKA Grafitti Man*. Rykodisc 10223.
Ulali. *Mahk Jchi*. 1997. Thush 7582.
Westerman, Floyd. 1993. *The Land Is Your Mother/Custer Died for Your Sins*. Trikont 0170.

Major Sources for Recordings

Sound of America Records (SOAR). 5200 Constitution NE, Albuquerque, NM 87110; (505) 268-6110. www.soundofamerica.com. SOAR offers a wide range of both contemporary genres, including rock, country, rap/hip-hop, spoken word, and Christian/gospel recordings, along with a large number of traditional products, including powwow, tribe-specific genres, and flute music. SOAR is comprised of five main sublabels, with each label specializing in a particular genre or set of genres: SOAR (which features a wide range of contemporary and traditional recordings), Natural Visions (Native American flute and New Age music), Warrior (various contemporary genres), Dakotah (children's stories/ spoken word), and Red Sea (Christian).

Sunshine Records. 275 Selkirk Ave., Winnipeg, MB, Canada. R2W-2L5; (800) 307-8057 Sunshine Records is one of the longest-running and most successful independent music labels in Canada. Started by Ness and Linda Michaels in 1975, this label has produced a wide variety of local musics, including a large catalog of Métis fiddle music (in particular local Manitoban fiddle legend Reg Bouvette), Ukrainian wedding music, Native and non-Native rock, folk, and country artists, and is responsible for one of the largest collections of powwow music available in Canada. A large part of their marketing strategy involves creating recordings targeted to Winnipeg's large Aboriginal (First Nations and Métis) population, as well as the surrounding indigenous communities in Manitoba.

Arbor Records. www.arborrecords.com Although no longer recording and releasing new music, Arbor Records products are still available for online purchase. The label has a large catalog of both traditional (mostly powwow music) and contemporary music. Arbor has pursue a two-pronged marketing strategy, targeting a good deal of their powwow recordings to indigenous customers while using more mainstream distribution networks to bring their contemporary Native music products, as well as select traditional recordings to the mainstream (i.e., nonindigenous) market.

Drumhop Productions. 325 East Capitol Ave., Bismarck, ND 58501. www.drumhop.net Drumhop Productions was started in 2004 by graphic artist and champion powwow Grass dancer Rusty Gillette, along with Everett Moore, a longtime member of a very popular powwow drum group. While their products can typically be found only on the Web or at a vendor's booth at a powwow, they have managed to record some of the top Northern- and Southern-style powwow groups, including Bear Creek (Ojibwa), Midnite Express (intertribal), The Boyz (intertribal), as well as Southern groups like The Southern Boys (Comanche) and Sizzortail (Pawnee), among others.

Canyon Records Productions, 3131 W. Clarendon Ave., Phoenix, AZ 85017-4513; (800) 268–1141. http://www.canyonrecords.com This is an important distributor of Native American recordings. It not only stocks a large inventory under its own label but it also keeps in print many of the recordings of smaller distributors, some of which might otherwise have gone out of business. It carries recordings of mostly traditional music as well as some rock, gospel, and country and western.

Indian House, Box 472, Taos, NM 87571; (505) 776–2953. http://www.indianhouse.com This company specializes in traditional Indian music and typically devotes an entire recording to one genre, such as Taos Round Dance songs or Navajo Yeibichai songs. The abundant examples and the excellent notes make these recordings valuable for scholars as well as other interested listeners.

Library of Congress. Archive of Folk Culture, Motion Picture, Broadcast, and Recorded Sound Division, Library of Congress, Washington, DC 20540; (202) 707-7833. http://www.loc.gov/folklife/rec.html. This collection includes the Willard Rhodes recordings of Native American music: excellent recordings and notes from all across the country.

Smithsonian/Folkways. The Folkways Collection, Smithsonian Institution, Washington, DC 20560; (202) 287–3262. http://www.folkways.si.edu/index.html. The inventory of the Ethnic Folkways Records and Service Corp., formerly of New York City, has been preserved at the Smithsonian Institution, and new recordings on a joint label are being produced. Their holdings include many early recordings of Native American music.

Internet Resources

Omaha Indian Music, a website maintained by the Library of Congress, featuring music from the 1890s to 1980s. http://lcweb2.loc.gov/ammem/omhhtml/omhhome.html

Index of Native American Musical Resources on the internet http://www.hanksville.org/NAresources/indices/NAmusic.html

Directory of sites on Native American music, languages, powwows, and Native Languages. http://www.georgiejessup.com/links3.htm

Native American music and arts: organizations and individuals. http://www.nativeculturelinks.com/music.html

Native American Radio has five streams playing Native American music twenty-four hours a day. They have one of the largest online archives of digitized Native American music in the world. Search for music by artist, album, label, or song title. http://www.nativeradio.com

CHAPTER 3—AFRICA/EWE, DAGBAMBA, SHONA, BaAKA

References

Appiah, Anthony. 1992. *In My Father's House*. Cambridge, MA: Harvard Univ. Press.
Arom, Simha. 1987. *Centrafrique: Anthologie de la Musique des Pygmees Aka*. Ocora CD559012 13.
———. 1991. *African Polyphony and Polyrhythm*. Cambridge, England: Cambridge Univ. Press.
Asante, Molefi. 1987. *The Afrocentric Idea*. Philadelphia: Temple Univ. Press.
Bebey, Francis. 1975. *African Music: A People's Art*. Translated by Josephine Bennet. New York: Lawrence Hill.
Bender, Wolfgang. 1991. *Sweet Mother: Modern African Music*. Chicago: Univ. of Chicago Press.
Berliner, Paul. 1993. *The Soul of Mbira*. Rev. ed. Berkeley: Univ. of California Press.
Bohannan, Paul, and Phillip Curtin. 1995. *Africa and Africans*. 4th ed. Prospect Heights, IL: Waveland Press.
Breasted, J. H. 1906. *Ancient Records of Egypt*. Chicago: Univ. of Chicago Press.
Chernoff, John. 1979. *African Rhythm and African Sensibility*. Chicago: Univ. of Chicago Press.
Davidson, Basil. 1991. *African Civilization Revisited: From Antiquity to Modern Times*. Trenton, NJ: Africa Word Press.
Davis, Art. 1994. "Midawo Gideon Foli Alorwoyie: The Life and Music of a West African Drummer." M.A. thesis, Univ. of Illinois, Urbana-Champaign.
Djedje, Jacqueline. 1978. "The One-String Fiddle in West Africa." Ph.D. diss., Univ. of California–Los Angeles.
Dosunmu, Oyebade Ajibola. 2011 *Afrobeat, Fela and Beyond: Scenes, Style and Ideology*. Doctoral Dissertation, University of Pittsburgh.
Eyre, Banning. 1988. "New Sounds from Africa." *Guitar Player* (October): 80–88.
———. 1991. "On the Road with Thomas Mapfumo." *The Beat* 10(6): 48–53, 78.

———. 2015. "Lion Songs: Thomas Mapfumo and the Music That Made Zimbabwe." Durham and London: Duke University Press.

Fiawo, D. K. 1959. "The Influence of the Contemporary Social Changes on the Magico-Religious Concepts and Organization of the Southern Ewe-Speaking People of Ghana." Ph.D. diss., Univ. of Edinburgh.

Frye, Peter. 1976. *Spirits of Protest.* Cambridge, England: Cambridge Univ. Press.

Gates, Henry Louis. 1988. *The Signifying Monkey: A Theory of Afro-American Literary Criticism.* New York: Oxford Univ. Press.

Jackson, Bruce. 1972. *Wake Up Dead Man: Afro-American Worksongs from Texas Prisons.* Cambridge, MA: Harvard Univ. Press.

Jones, A. M. 1959. *Studies in African Music.* London: Oxford Univ. Press.

Kisliuk, Michelle. 1998. *"Seize the Dance!": BaAka Music Life and the Ethnography of Performance.* New York: Oxford Univ. Press.

Koetting, James. 1992. "Africa/Ghana." In *Worlds of Music.* 2nd ed. New York: Schirmer.

Kubik, Gerhard. 1962. "The Phenomenon of Inherent Rhythms in East and Central African Instrumental Music." *African Music* 3(1): 33–42.

Ladzekpo, Kobla. 1971. "The Social Mechanics of Good Music: A Description of Dance Clubs among the Anlo Ewe-Speaking People of Ghana." *African Music* 5(1):6–22.

Lan, David. 1985. *Guns and Rain.* Berkeley: Univ. of California Press.

Locke, David. 1978. "The Music of *Atsiagbekor.*" Ph.D. diss., Wesleyan Univ.

———. 1982. "Principles of Offbeat Timing and Cross-Rhythm in Southern Eve Dance Drumming." *Ethnomusicology* 26(2): 217–46.

———. 1990. *Drum Damba.* Tempe, AZ: White Cliffs Media.

———. 1992. *Kpegisu: A War Drum of the Ewe.* Tempe, AZ: White Cliffs Media.

Mallows, A. J. 1967. *An Introduction to the History of Central Africa.* London: Oxford Univ. Press.

Manuel, Peter. 1988. *Popular Musics of the Non-Western World.* New York: Oxford Univ. Press.

Maraire, Dumisani. 1971. *The Mbira Music of Rhodesia.* Booklet and record. Seattle: Univ. of Washington Press.

Miller, Christopher. 1990. *Theories of Africans.* Chicago: Univ. of Chicago Press.

Moore, Carlos. 2009. *Fela: This Bitch of a Life.* Chicago: Lawrence Hill Books.

Mphahlele, Ezekiel. 1962. *The African Image.* London: Faber and Faber.

Nketia, J. H. Kwabena. 1964. *Continuity of Traditional Instruction.* Legon, Ghana: Institute of African Studies.

Nukunya, G. K. 1969. *Kinship and Marriage among the Anlo Ewe.* London: Athlone Press.

Olaniyan, Tejumola. 2004. *Arrest the Music! Fela and His Rebel Art and Politics.* Bloomington, IN: Indiana Univ. Press.

Omojola, Bode. 2012. *Yoruba Music in the Twentieth Century: Identity, Agency and Performance Practice.* Rochester, NY: Univ. of Rochester Press.

Senghor, Leopold Sedar. 1967. *The Foundations of "Africanite" or "Negritude" and "Arabite."* Translated by Mercer Cook. Paris: Presence Africaine.

Skinner, Eliot, ed. 1973. *Peoples and Cultures of Africa.* Garden City, NY: Doubleday.

Thompson, Robert F. 1973. "An Aesthetic of the Cool." *African Arts* 7(1): 40–43, 64–67, 89.

Tracey, Andrew. 1970. *How to Play the Mbira (Dza Vadzimu).* Roodepoort, Transvaal: International Library of African Music.

Turnbull, Colin. 1961. *The Forest People.* New York: Simon & Schuster.

———. 1983. *The Mbuti Pygmies: Change and Adaptation.* New York: Holt, Rinehart, & Winston.

Veal, Michael. 2000. *Fela: The Life and Times of an African Music Icon.* Philadelphia: Temple Univ. Press.

Waterman, Christopher. 1990. "Our Tradition Is a Modern Tradition." *Ethnomusicology* 34(3): 367–80.

X, Malcom. 1965. *The Autobiography of Malcolm X; With the Assistance of Alex Haley.* New York: Grove Press.

Zantzinger, Gei. n.d. "Mbira: Mbira dza Vadzimu: Religion at the Family Level." Film. Available from University Museum, Univ. of Pennsylvania.

Additional Reading

Agawu, Kofi. 1995. *African Music: A Northern Ewe Perspective.* Cambridge, England: Cambridge Univ. Press.

Berliner, Paul. 2006. "Grasping Shona Musical Works: A Case Study of Mbira Music." In *Art from Start to Finish,* edited by Howard S. Becker, Robert R. Faulkner, and Barbara Kirshenblatt-Gimblett, 126–34. Chicago: Univ. of Chicago Press.

Brincard, Marie-Therese, ed. 1989. *Sounding Forms: African Musical Instruments.* New York: American Federation of Arts.

Collins, John. 1992. *West African Pop Roots.* Philadelphia: Temple Univ. Press.

Jackson, Irene, ed. 1985. *More Than Drumming.* Westport, CT: Greenwood Press.

Nketia, J. H. Kwabena. 1974. *The Music of Africa.* New York: Norton.

Nzewi, Meki. 1991. *Musical Practice and Creativity.* Bayreuth, Germany: Iwalewahaus, Univ. of Bayreuth.

Stone, Ruth. 2000. *Garland Handbook of African Music.* New York: Garland.

Additional Listening

Berliner, Paul. 1995. *Zimbabwe: The Soul of Mbira.* Nonesuch Explorer Series 9 72054-2.

Chernoff, John. 1990. *Master Drummers of Dagbon.* Vol. 2. Rounder CD 5406.

Locke, David. n.d. *Drum Gahu: Good-Time Drumming from the Ewe People of Ghana and Togo.* White Cliffs Media WCM 9494.

Lunna, Abubakari. 1996. *Drum Damba featuring Abubakari Lunna, a Master Drummer of Dagbon.* White Cliffs Media WCM 9508.

Additional Viewing

Konkombe: Nigerian Music. n.d. Produced and directed by Jeremy Marre. Harcourt Films.

The Language You Cry In. 1998. Directed and produced by Alvaro Toepke and Angel Serrano. Inko Producciones. San Francisco: California Newsreel.

Mbira Dza Vadzimu Urban and Rural Ceremonies with Hakurotwi Mude. 1978. Devault, PA: Constant Spring Productions.

Music and Culture of West Africa: The Straus Expedition. 2002. Gloria J. Gibson and Daniel B. Reed. Indianapolis: Indiana Univ. Press. CD-ROM.

A Performance of Kpegisu by the Wodome-Akatsi Kpegisu Habobo. 1990. Produced by David Locke. Boston: Educational Media Center, Tufts Univ.

Rhythm of Resistance: The Black Music of South Africa. 1988. Directed by Chris Austin and Jeremy Marre. Produced by Jeremy Marre. Harcourt Films/Shanachie Records.

Internet Resources

African Music Encyclopedia http://www.africanmusic.org

African Music on RootsWorld http://www.rootsworld.com/rw/africa .html

Afropop Worldwide http://www.afropop.org

AllAfrica.com: Music: Newsfeed source for news and reports on music in Africa http://allafrica. com/music

The International Library of African Music http://www.ilam.ru.ac.za

Stern's Music http://www.sternsmusic.com

CHAPTER 4—NORTH AMERICA/BLACK AMERICA
References

Americana. 2015. "Who We Are," Americana Music Association. http://americanamusic.org/who-we-are. Accessed January 3, 2015.

Brunoghe, Yannick, ed. 1964. *Big Bill Blues*. New York: Oak.

Cantwell, Robert. 1984. *Bluegrass Breakdown*. Urbana: Univ. of Illinois Press.

Charters, Samuel. 1977. *The Legacy of the Blues*. New York: Da Capo.

Davis, Angela Y. 1999. *Blues Legacies and Black Feminism*. New York: Vintage Books.

Eliot, T. S. [1920] 1964. "Hamlet and His Problems." In *The Sacred Wood*. Reprint, New York: Barnes & Noble.

Forte, Dan. 1991. "Otis Rush." In *Blues Guitar*, edited by Jas Obrecht, pp. 156–62. San Francisco: GPI Books.

Gates, Henry Louis, Jr. 1989. *The Signifying Monkey: A Theory of African American Literary Criticism*. New York: Oxford Univ. Press.

Gordon, Robert. 2002. *Can't Be Satisfied: The Life and Times of Muddy Waters*. Boston: Little, Brown.

Groom, Bob. 1971. *The Blues Revival*. London: Studio Vista.

Gussow, Adam. 2002. *Seems Like Murder Here: Southern Violence and the Blues Tradition*. Chicago: Univ. of Chicago Press.

Johnson, Charles S. [1934] 1966. *Shadow of the Plantation*. Reprint, Chicago: Univ. of Chicago Press.

Lucas, William ("Lazy Bill"). 1974. *Lazy Bill Lucas*. Philo LP 1007.

McLeod, Norma, and Marcia Herndon. 1981. *Music as Culture*. 2nd ed. Darby, PA: Norwood Editions.

Obrecht, Jas. 2000. "Otis Rush." In *Rollin' and Tumblin': The Postwar Blues Guitarists*, edited by Jas Obrecht. San Francisco: Miller Freeman.

Oliver, Paul. 1965. *Conversation with the Blues*. London: Cassell.

———. 1998. *The Story of the Blues*. Boston: Northeastern Univ. Press.

Santelli, Robert, and Holly George-Warren. 2002. *American Roots Music*. New York: Abrams.

Seeger, Charles. 1977. *Studies in Musicology, 1935–1975*. Berkeley: Univ. of California Press.

Segrest, James, and Mark Hoffman. 2004. *Moanin' at Midnight: The Life and Times of Howlin' Wolf*. New York: Pantheon.

Titon, Jeff Todd. 1969. "Calling All Cows: Lazy Bill Lucas" *Blues Unlimited* 60:10–11; 61:9–10; 62:11–12; 63:9–10.

———. 1971. "Ethnomusicology of Downhome Blues Phonograph Records, 1926–1930." Ph.D. diss., Univ. of Minnesota.

———. 1974a. Brochure notes to *Lazy Bill Lucas*. North Ferrisburg, VT: Philo Records 1007.

———, ed. 1974b. *From Blues to Pop: The Autobiography of Leonard "Baby Doo" Caston*. Los Angeles: John Edwards Memorial Foundation.

———. 1994. *Early Downhome Blues: A Musical and Cultural Analysis*. 2nd ed. Chapel Hill: Univ. of North Carolina Press.

———. 2002. "Labels: Identifying Categories of Blues and Gospel." In Allan Moore, ed., *The Cambridge Companion to Blues and Gospel Music*. Cambridge: Cambridge Univ. Press.

Additional Reading

Baker, Houston. 1987. *Blues, Ideology, and Afro-American Literature: A Vernacular Theory*. Chicago: Univ. of Chicago Press.

Finn, Julio. 1992. *The Bluesman*. New York: Interlink.

Grissom, Mary Alle. [1930] 1969. *The Negro Sings a New Heaven*. Reprint, New York: Dover Books.

Jackson, Bruce. 1972. *Wake up Dead Man: Afro-American Worksongs from Texas State Prisons*. Cambridge, MA: Harvard Univ. Press.

King, B. B., with Dave Ritz. 1996. *Blues All Around Me: The Autobiography of B. B. King*. New York: Avon.

King, Steven. 2013. *I'm Feeling the Blues Right Now: Blues Tourism and the Mississippi Delta*. Jackson, Mississippi: Univ. Press of Mississippi.

Palmer, Robert. 1981. *Deep Blues*. New York: Viking Press.

Salvatore, Nick. 2006. *Singing in a Strange Land*. Urbana: Univ. of Illinois Press. Biography of Rev. C. L. Franklin.

Titon, Jeff Todd. 1990. *Downhome Blues Lyrics*. 2nd ed. Urbana: Univ. of Illinois Press. Anthology of post–World War II lyrics.

Tracy, Steven, ed. 1999. *Write Me a Few of Your Lines: A Blues Reader*. Amherst: Univ. of Massachusetts Press.

Additional Listening

The following albums may be purchased on the internet.

Alan Lomax Collection. Prison Songs, Vol. 1: Murderous Home. Rounder.

B. B. King Live at the Regal. Geffen.

Bessie Smith: *The Complete Recordings, Vols. 1-4*. Columbia Legacy.

Blind Blake: All the Published Sides. JSP Records.

Charley Patton: Complete Recordings, Vols. 1 and 2. Acrobat.

Chicago Blues: The Chance Era. Charly. (Lazy Bill Lucas.)

The Essential Gospel Sampler. Columbia Legacy.

James "Super Chikan Johnson: *Chikan Supe*. Gzbc/kcr.

Muddy Waters: His Best. Geffen.

Negro Blues and Hollers. Rounder 1501. Out-of-print Library of Congress recording.

Otis Rush: *Ain't Enough Comin' In*. Mercury.

Rev. C. L. Franklin: *Legendary Sermons*. MCA Universal Special Products.

Robert Johnson: The Complete Recordings (2011). Sony.

Roots 'n' Blues: The Retrospective. Columbia Legacy.

T-Bone Walker: *The Ultimate Collection (1929-1957)*. Acrobat.

Menhaden fishermen's work songs preserved by the Northern Neck Chantey Singers may be heard online at http://www.npr.org/templates/story/story.php?storyId=6605894&ft=1&f=1021

Additional Viewing

Check YouTube for footage of performances by many of the blues singers mentioned in this chapter. Search under the singer's name, such as Otis Rush, Johnny Shines, Ma Rainey, Fred McDowell, T-Bone Walker, Big Mama Thornton, Bessie Smith, Howlin' Wolf, Magic Sam, Super Chikan, and so forth.

For performances of religious music and work songs search YouTube and other video websites under Rev. C. L. Franklin, Soul Stirrers, Swan Silvertones, Northern Neck Chantey Singers, etc.

Blues Like Showers of Rain. 1970. Directed by John Jeremy. Documentary based on Paul Oliver's 1960 field trip to the South. May be streamed for free at http://www.folkstreams.net/film,283

Bukka White and Son House. 2000. Yazoo DVD, black and white, 60 minutes. Riveting performances of Mississippi Delta blues.

Delta Rising: A Blues Documentary. 2008. Directed by Michael Afendakis and Laura Bernieri. Color, 79 minutes. Centered on blues in Clarksdale, Mississippi. James "Super Chikan" Johnson is one of the performers.

Gandy Dancers. 1994. Directed by Maggie Holtzberg and Barry Dornfeld. Color, 30 minutes. Documentary film about traditional work songs of railroad men as they lined up railroad tracks on the roadbed. May be streamed free at http://www.folkstreams.net/film,101

Ghost World. 2001. Directed by Terry Zwigoff. Color, 111 minutes. Distributed by United Artists. Based on the comic by Daniel Clowes. Bittersweet, perceptive story of a high school senior's infatuation with pre–World War II blues and an eccentric, middle-aged man who collects old blues recordings.

The Land Where the Blues Began. 1993. Directed by John Bishop, Alan Lomax, and Worth Long. Color, 58 minutes. Based on Alan Lomax's field trips to Mississippi in 1978 and 1985.

Otis Rush: Mastering Chicago Blues Guitar. (c. 1993). VHS videotape, color, 90 minutes. Pound Ridge, NY: Hot Licks Productions. Instruction and some footage of Rush's fine playing. No longer in print.

The Road to Memphis. 2003. Directed by Richard Pearce, written by Robert Gordon. One of seven films in the series *Martin Scorsese Presents the Blues*. PBS Videos. http://www.pbs.org/theblues. Features B. B. King and Bobby Rush.

St. Louis Blues. 1929. 15 min., black and white. Directed by Dudley Murphy. Music Direction by W. C. Handy. Starring Bessie Smith, who sings the title song. Often on YouTube.

A Singing Stream. 1987. Online video, color, 57 minutes. Directed by Tom Davenport. Delaplane, VA: Davenport Films. http://www .folkstreams.net. African American gospel music.

Wild Women Don't Have the Blues. 1989. VHS videotape, color, 58 minutes. Directed by Christine Dall. San Francisco: California Newsreel. A documentary on women blues singers. Out of print, but used copies are available.

Internet Resources

Among many, these are worth attention:

Blues World: Essays, with links to organizations, magazines, discographies, auctions: http://www.bluesworld.com/Blueslinks.html

Blues Hangout forum. http://blindman.fr.yuku.com/forums/2# .VJ7oOCwALA

The Folkstreams website contains many documentary films about African American music, including blues. http://www.folkstreams.net

Yahoo Groups: Pre-War Blues.

CHAPTER 5—EUROPE/CENTRAL AND SOUTHEASTERN REGIONS

References

Anderson, Benedict. 1991. *Imagined Communities: Reflections on the Origin and Spread of Nationalism.* Rev. ed. London: Verso.

Armistead, Samuel G. 1979. "Judeo-Spanish and Pan-European Balladry." *Jahrbuch fuur Volksliedforschung* 24: 127–38.

Austerlitz, Paul. 2000. "Birch-Bark Horns and Jazz in the National Imagination: The Finnish Folk Music Vogue in Historical Perspective." *Ethnomusicology* 44(2): 183–213.

Bohlman, Philip V. 2000a. "East-West: The Ancient Modernity of Jewish Music." *East European Meetings in Ethnomusicology* 7: 67–90.

———. 2000b. "Jewish Music in Europe." In *Europe: The Garland Encyclopedia of World Music.* Vol. 8, 248–69. New York: Garland.

———. 2004. *The Music of European Nationalism: Cultural Identity and Modern History.* Santa Barbara, CA: ABC-CLIO.

Chybiński, Adolf. [1923] 1961. *O polskiej muzyce ludowej: Wybór prac etnograficznych.* Edited by Ludwik Bielawski. Kraków, Poland: Polskie Wydawnictwo Muzyczne.

Cohen, Judah. 2009. "Hip-Hop Judaica: The Politics of Representatin' Heebster Heritage." *Popular Music* 28(1): 1-18.

Cooley, Timothy J. 2005. *Making Music in the Polish Tatras: Tourists, Ethnographers, and Mountain Musicians.* Bloomington: Indiana Univ. Press.

———. 2013. "Folk Music in Eastern Europe." In *Cambridge History of World Music.* Edited by Philip Bohlman, 352–70. Cambridge, England: Cambridge Univ. Press.

Davies, Norman. 1996. *Europe: A History.* Oxford, England: Oxford Univ. Press

Erlmann, Veit. 1996. "The Aesthetics of the Global Imagination: Reflections on World Music in the 1990s." *Public Culture* 8(3): 467–87.

Feld, Steven. 2001. "A Sweet Lullaby for World Music." In *Globalization,* edited by Arjun Appadurai, 189–216. Durham, NC: Duke Univ. Press.

Frolova-Walker, Marina. 1998. "'National in Form, Socialist in Content': Musical Nation-Building in the Soviet Republics." *Journal of the American Musicological Society* 51(2): 331–71.

Gelbart, Matthew. 2007. *The Invention of "Folk Music" and "Art Music": Emerging Categories from Ossian to Wagner.* Cambridge, England: Cambridge Univ. Press.

Gellner, Ernest. 1997. *Nationalism.* New York: New York Univ. Press.

Hall, Derek R., ed. 1991. *Tourism and Economic Development in Eastern Europe and the Soviet Union.* London: Belhaven Press.

Hobsbawm, Eric J. 1990. *Nations and Nationalism Since 1780: Programme, Myth, Reality.* Cambridge, England: Cambridge Univ. Press.

Hobsbawm, Eric J., and Terence Ranger, eds. 1983. *The Invention of Tradition.* Cambridge, England: Cambridge Univ. Press.

Hutchinson, John, and Anthony D. Smith, eds. 1994. *Nationalism.* Oxford, England: Oxford Univ. Press.

McKim, LindaJo H. 1993. *The Presbyterian Hymnal Companion.* Louisville, KY: Westminster/John Knox Press.

Pasternak, Velvel, ed. 1994. *The International Jewish Songbook.* Cedarhurst, NY: Tara.

Petrović, Ankica. 2000. "Bosnia-Hercegovina." In *Europe: The Garland Encyclopedia of World Music.* Vol. 8, 962–71. New York: Garland.

Pettan, Svanibor. 1998. *Music, Politics, and War: Views from Croatia.* Zagreb: Institute of Ethnology and Folklore Research.

Plastino, Goffredo. 2001. *Tambores del Bajo Aragón.* PRAMES Aragón LCD D.L.Z 635-2001.

———. 2003. "Fifteen Fragments on My (Field)work." *British Journal of Ethnomusicology* 12(1): 97–112.

Rice, Timothy. 2000. "The Music of Europe: Unity and Diversity." In *Europe: The Garland Encyclopedia of World Music.* Vol. 8, 2–15. New York: Garland.

Rubin, Ruth. 1979. *Voices of a People: The Story of Yiddish Folksong.* Philadelphia: Jewish Publication Society of America.

Slobin, Mark. 2002. "Bosnia and Central/Southeastern Europe: Music and Musicians in Transition." In *Worlds of Music: An Introduction to the Music of the World's Peoples,* 4th ed., edited by Jeff Todd Titon, 211–41. New York: Schirmer.

Small, Christopher. 1998. *Musicking: The Meanings of Performing and Listening.* Middletown, CT: Wesleyan Univ. Press.

Smith, Anthony D. 1998. *Nationalism and Modernism.* London: Routledge.

Taylor, Timothy D. 1997. *Global Pop: World Musics, World Markets.* New York: Routledge.

White, George W. 2000. *Nationalism and Territory: Constructing Group Identity in Southeastern Europe.* Lanham, MD: Rowman & Littlefield.

Wrazen, Louise. 1988. "The Góralski of the Polish Highlanders: Old World Musical Tradition from a New World Perspective." Ph.D. dissertation, Univ. of Toronto.

———. 1991. "Traditional Music Performance among Górale in Canada." *Ethnomusicology* 35(2): 173–93.

———. 2013. "Marysia's Voice: Defining Home through Song in Poland and Canada." In Women Singers in Global Contexts: Music, Biography, Identity, edited by Ruth Hellier, 146–60. Urbana: Univ. of Illinois Press.

Additional Reading

Bartók, Béla. 1981. *The Hungarian Folk Song,* edited by Benjamin Suchoff. Translated by M. D. Calvocoressi. Annotated by Zoltán Kodály. Albany: State Univ. of New York Press.

Buchanan, Donna. 2005. *Performing Democracy.* Chicago: Univ. of Chicago Press.

Cartner, Holly. 1991. *Destroying Ethnic Identity: The Gypsies in Romania.* New York: Helsinki Watch.

Cooley, Timothy J. 1999. "Folk Festival as Modern Ritual in the Polish Tatra Mountains." *The world of music* 41(3): 31–55.

———. 2001. "Repulsion to Ritual: Interpreting Folk Festivals in the Polish Tatras." *Ethnologies* 23(1): 233–53.

Czekanowska, Anna. 1990. *Polish Folk Music: Slavonic Heritage, Polish Tradition, Contemporary Trends.* Cambridge, England: Cambridge Univ. Press.

Kligman, Gail. 1988. *The Wedding of the Dead.* Chicago: Univ. of Chicago Press.

Laušević, Mirjana. 2007. *Balkan Fascination: Creating an Alternative Music Culture in America.* New York: Oxford Univ. Press.

Ling, Jan. 1997. *A History of European Folk Music.* Rochester, NY: Univ. of Rochester Press. [First published in Swedish by Akademiförlaget, 1988.]

Nettl, Bruno. 1973. *Folk and Traditional Music of the Western Continents.* 2nd ed. Englewood Cliffs, NJ: Prentice Hall.

Rasmussen, Ljerka V. 2002. *Newly Composed Folk Music of Yugoslavia.* New York: Routledge.

Rice, Timothy. 2004. *Music in Bulgaria: Experiencing Music, Expressing Culture.* New York: Oxford Univ. Press.

Rice, Timothy, James Porter, and Chris Goertzen, eds. 2000. *Europe: The Garland Encyclopedia of World Music.* Vol. 8, 962–71. New York: Garland.

Silverman, Carol. 2013. "Global Balkan Gypsy Music: Issues of Migration, Appropriation, and Representation." In *The Globalization of Musics in Transit: Musical Migration and Tourism,* edited by Simone Krüger and Ruxandra Trandafoiu, 185–208. New York: Routledge Univ. Press.

Slobin, Mark, ed. 1996. *Retuning Culture: Music and Change in Eastern Europe.* Durham, NC: Duke Univ. Press.

Sugarman, Jane C. 1997. *Engendering Song: Singing and Subjectivity at Prespa Albanian Weddings.* Chicago: Univ. of Chicago Press.

Titon, Jeff Todd, and Bob Carlin, eds. 2002. *American Musical Traditions.* Vol. 4: *European American Music.* New York: Schirmer.

Wrazen, Loise. 2007. "Relocating the Tatras: Place and Music in *Górale* Identity and Imagination." *Ethnomusicology* 51(2): 185–204.

Additional Listening

Judith Cohen and Tamar Ilana. 2005. *Sefarad en Diáspora.* Pneuma PN780.

Kapela Staszka Ma´sniaka. 1997. *Muzyka Ko´scielisk.* Folk CD 009.

Márta Sebastyén and Ókrös Ensemble. 1993. *Transylvanian Portraits: Hungarian Village Music from Transylvania.* Koch 3-4004-2H1.

Márta Sebastyén, Alexander Balanescu, and Muzsikás. 1999. *The Bartók Album.* Rykodisc/Hannibal HNCD 1439.

Plastino, Goffredo. 2001. *Tambores del Bajo Aragón.* PRAMES Aragón LCD D.L.Z 635-2001.

Trebunie-Tutki. 2000. *Folk Karnawał.* Folk CD-029.

Twinkle Brothers & Tutki. 1992. *Twinkle Inna Polish Stylee: Higher Heights.* Twinkle Music. http://www.twinklemusic.com

Various Artists. 1990. *Polish Folk Music: Songs and Music from Various Regions.* Polskie Nagrania Muza PNCD 048.

Various Artists. 1993. *Bosnia: Echoes from an Endangered World.* Smithsonian Folkways Recordings SFW40407.

Various Artists. n.d. *Bring It All Home.* Kamahuk kcd-1. http://www.kamahuk.net

Warszawski Chór Międzyuczelniany (Warsaw Intercolegiate Choir). 1999. *Jubileusz.* With guests, Trebunia-Tutki. Cantica CTCD 002.

Additional Viewing

Ashkenaz: The Music of the Jews from Eastern Europe. 1993. Created and directed by Tzipora H. Jochsberger. Written and directed by Asher Tlalim. Teaneck, NJ: Ergo Media; Jerusalem: Israel Music Heritage Project. A compilation of Jewish music from Eastern Europe, including Yiddish folksongs, the liturgical music of the synagogue, and Klezmer and Yiddish theater tunes. The film also features rare archival footage of Jewish life in Eastern Europe as it existed prior to World War II, providing an understanding of the environment from which the music grew.

The JVC Smithsonian Folkways Video Anthology of Music and Dance of Europe. c. 1996. Directed by Kunihiko Nakagawa. Japan: JVC, Victor Company of Japan. Barre, VT: Distributed by Multicultural Media. These videos are mixed in quality and in their supporting documentation, but at least the section on Bulgaria is useful. They were filmed during the communist period but do not feature professional folklore groups. The booklet notes are helpful.

The Popovich Brothers of South Chicago. 1977. Directed by Jill Godmilow. Distributed by Balkan Arts Center. This video is a dated but moving portrayal of a family of musicians who for decades provided music for the Serbian American community in and around Chicago.

The Romany Trail. c. 1992. Directed and produced by Jeremy Marre. Harcourt Films. Newton, NJ: Distributed by Shanachie Records. 2 videos. Part of the *Beats of the Heart* series. Part 1 is a search for the "lost" gypsy tribes of Egypt and traces their route into Spain. Part 2 first goes to India to find what are believed to be the original gypsy families whose descendants migrated across the Middle East to Africa and Europe, then it goes to Eastern Europe, among the oppressed gypsy communities of then-communist Europe. See the essay on these films in the *Beats of the Heart* booklet.

CHAPTER 6—ASIA/INDIA
References

The Beatles. 1966. *Revolver.* Parlophone CDP 7 464412. CD.

Chandra, Sheila. 1991. *Silk.* Shanachie 64035. CD.

———. 1993. *Weaving My Ancestors' Voices.* Caroline CAROL 2322-2. CD.

Iyer, Vijay. 2005. *Reimagining.* Savoy Jazz SVY 17475. CD.

Panjabi MC (Rajinder Rai). 2003. *Panjabi MC Beware.* Sequence SEQ 8015-2.

Raman, Susheela. 2001. *Salt Rain.* Narada B00005BJIG. CD.

Shankar, Ravi. 1978. *East Greets East.* Deutsche Grammophon 2531-381.

Films

Bald, Vivek, 2003, *Mutiny: Asians Storm British Music.* Groundbreaking documentary film surveying the Indo-Brit music scene in the late twentieth century. For further information and contact, see info at http://bengaliharlem.com. Profile: http://cmsw.mit.edu/profile/vivek-bald.

Additional Reading and Viewing

Mohan, Anuradha. 1994. "Ilaiyaraja: Composer as Phenomenon in Tamil Film Culture." M.A. thesis, Wesleyan University.

Nelson, David Paul, 2008. Solkattu Manual: An Introduction to the Rhythmic Language of South Indian Music. Middletown, CT: Wesleyan Univ. Press.

———, 1991. Mrdangam Mind: The Tani Avartanam in Karnatak Music. 3 vols. Ph.D. dissertation, Wesleyan University.

Reck, David. 2008. "The Beatles and Indian Music." In *Sgt. Pepper and the Beatles: It Was Forty Years Ago Today,* edited by Julien Olivier. Burlington, VT: Ashgate.

Shankar, Ravi. 1968. *My Music, My Life.* New York: Simon & Schuster.

Viswanathan, T. and Allen, Matthew H. 2003. *Music in South India: The Karnatak Concert Tradition and Beyond.* Oxford, England: Oxford Univ. Press.

Additional Listening: Carnatic Music

Annotated Website: The website http://www.medieval.org/music/world/carnatic/cblsup.html has an annotated list of CDs, plus relevant information on South Indian (Carnatic) music, composers, performers, and music styles. In particular, you might want to look for the CDs listed below.

An Anthology of South Indian Classical Music. Ocora 5900001/2/3/4. Four CDs.

Chandramouli, Sreevidhya, *Maruta* [veena and voice; no number, date]. SonicSoul Acoustics. 15183 Dane Lane, Portland, OR 97229; (503) 531-0270; http://kartha1.tripod.com

Jayaraman, Lalgudi J. *Violin Virtuoso: Lalgudi J. Jayaraman.* Oriental AAMS-125.

Moulana, Sheik Chinna. *Nadhaswaram.* Wergo SM-1507. [nagaswaram]

Narayanaswamy, K.V. *Guru Padam.* Koel 063. [vocal]

Padmanabhan, Rajeswari. *Surabi.* SonicSoul Acoustics. [veena; no number; released in 1998]. http://kartha1.tripod.com

Ramani, N. *Lotus Signatures.* MOW CDT-141. [flute]

Ranganayaki Rajagopalan. *Makar* 029. [veena]

Sankaran, Trichy. *The Language of Rhythm.* MOW 150. [mridangam]

Subbulakshmi, M. S. *M. S. Subbulakshmi: Live at Carnegie Hall.* EMI India 147808/809. Two CDs. [vocal]

———. *M. S. Subbulakshmi: Radio Recitals.* EMI India CDNF 147764/65. Two CDs. [vocal]

Viswanathan, T. *Classical Flute of South India.* JVC VIGG-5453.

Other Recordings

Ilaiyaraja. n.d. *How to Name It.* Oriental Records ORI/AAMS CD-115. CD.

Shankar, Ravi. 1971. *Concerto for Sitar and Orchestra*. Angel SPD 36806.

———. n.d. *Ragamala: Concerto for Sitar and Orchestra No. 2*. Angel DS 37935.

Dance DVDs

Bharatanatyam Legends—Prof. Sudharani Raghupathy. 2008. Geethanjali. DVD (also available on Netflix)

Bharatanatyam Legends—Prof. C.V. Chandrasekhar. n.d. Geethanjali. DVD

Priyadarshini Govind. *Abhinaya—Recital: The Beauty and Breadth*, n.d. Kalakriya

(Kalakriya has an extensive list of DVDs by this artist and others. http://kalakriya.com)

———, *Abhinaya / Rama Krishna Leela*. n.d. Kalakriya

———, *Thillana / Mohana Thillana—The Details & Delineation*. n.d. Kalakriya

———, *Varnam / Varnam—The Sum & Substance*. n.d. Kalakriya

Films

Ray, Satyajit. *The Apu Trilogy*. 1956–1959. Written, directed, and produced by Satyajit Ray, music by Ravi Shankar.

———. 1958. *The Music Room (Jalsaghar)*. Written, directed, and produced by Satyajit Ray. (Available online.) With music and dance by Begum Akhtar, Roshan Kumari, Waheed Khan, Bismillah Khan (on screen); Dakhshinamohan Thakur, Ashish See Ray's information http://www.satyajitray.org/and discography: http://www.satyajitray.org/films/filmo_directed.htm

Additional Listening: Hindustani Music

Compiled by Peter Row, New England Conservatory of Music

Buddhadev Das Gupta—Nayak ki Kanra. Buddhadev Das Gupta (sarod) with Anand Gopal Bandopadhyay (tabla): *raga* Nayak ki Kanra. Raga Records: RAGA 210.

Gathering Rain Clouds. Vishwa Mohan Bhatt (mohan vina) with Sikhvinder Singh Namdhari (tabla): *ragas* Miya ki Malhar and Gavati. Water Lily Acoustics: WLA-ES-22-CD.

Kanhra. Hariprasad Chaurasia (flute) with Sabir Khan (tabla): *raga* Kaunsi Kanhra. Nimbus Records: NI 5182.

Lakshmi Shankar: The Hours and the Seasons. Lakshmi Shankar (khyal and bhajan) with Sadanand Naimpalli (tabla): *ragas* Ahir Bhairav, Dhani, Khafi and Bhajans in *ragas* Megh and Bhairavi. Ocora: C 581615.

Padmabhushan Nikhil Banerjee—Sitar Recital. Nikhil Banerjee (sitar) with Kanai Dutt (tabla) and Swapan Choudhury (tabla): *ragas* Komal Rishabh Asavari, Jaunpuri, Mand and Dhun (Baul folk song). EMI: CDNF 150043.

Ravi Shankar in Celebration—Classical Sitar. Ravi Shankar (sitar) with Chatur Lal (tabla), Kumar Bose (tabla), Anoushka Shankar (sitar), Zakir Hussain (tabla), Alla Rakha (tabla), and Kanai Dutt (tabla): *ragas* Charu Keshi, Bhatiyar, Adarini, Marwa, and Dhun Kafi. Angel: 7243 5 55578-2.

Ustad Ali Akbar Khan, Signature Series: Vol. 1: Three Ragas. Ali Akbar Khan (sarod) with Mahapurush Misra (tabla): *ragas* Chandranandan, Gauri Manjari, and Jogiya Kalingra. Alam Madina Music Productions: AMMP CD 9001.

Ustad Amjad Ali Khan (Compilation). Amjad Ali Khan (sarod) with Samta Prasad, Chandra Mohan, and Shafaat Ahmed Khan (tabla): *ragas* Sughrai Kanada, Bihag, and Tilak Kamod. Gramophone Company of India: CDNF 150209.

Ustad Vilayat Khan—Sitar. Vilayat Khan (sitar) with Akram Khan (tabla): *raga* Jaijaivanti. India Archive Music: CD 1010.

Major Sources For Recordings

Music of the World (MOW label). P.O. Box 3620, Chapel Hill, NC 27515; (888) 264-6689; http://www.musicoftheworld.com

Oriental Records. P.O. Box 387, Williston Park, NY 11596; http://www.orientalrecords.com

Raag Music. Los Angeles, CA; (310) 479-5225; http://www.raaga.com

Supplementary Internet Resources

"Yengal Kalyanam" song from the film "Galaatta Kalyanam" (1968) https://www.youtube.com/watch?v=ZpDSEwPYu6w

Classical Music and the Dance Tradition

Malavika Sarukkai demonstrating Bharatanatyam https://www.youtube.com/watch?v=jobattuH_v0 and https://www.youtube.com/watch?v=iIfmI27Nh_Q

Devotional, Bhajan

"Thillana Mohanambal—Superhit Classic Cult Tamil Movie—Sivaji Ganesan, Padmini." https://www.youtube.com/watch?v=FjyeYV _pr2c The nagaswaram ensemble scene of the film, beginning at about 5:20, shows the performance of the piece as well as the cultural context of sacred music played in a temple concert. Indian Music and the West

Vijay Iyer, Rudresh Mahanthappa

Vijay Iyer & Rudresh Mahanthappa—Aftermath—Bridgestone Music Festival 2008 https://www.youtube.com/watch?v=lKSwmgFGoVE

The Beatles

"Across the Universe" https://www.youtube.com /watch?v=zC4poOpZG9w

Beatles promo video. https://www.youtube.com /watch?v=vrL-bYpY9Cc

"India," the Beatles ("super rare John Lennon demo") A visual collage of photos from the Beatles visit to India, with a John Lennon song composed for a later stage play about his life. https://www.youtube.com/watch?v=zzltijILEfA

"Norwegian Wood," https://www.youtube.com /watch?v=HcikqVOD8is

"Tomorrow Never Knows," https://www.youtube.com /watch?v=tisjsgsgtZU

CHAPTER 7—ASIA/INDONESIA

References

Becker, Judith. 1979. "Time and Tune in Java." In *The Imagination of Reality: Essays in Southeast Asian Coherence Systems*, edited by A. L. Becker and Aram A. Yengoyan, 197–210. Norwood, NJ: Ablex.

———. 1981. "Hindu-Buddhist Time in Javanese Gamelan Music." In *The Study of Time*, 4, edited by J. F. Fraser. New York: Springer-Verlag.

———. 1988. "Earth, Fire, Sakti, and the Javanese Gamelan." *Ethnomusicology* 32(3): 385–91.

Frederick, William. 1982. "Rhoma Irama and the Dangdut Style: Aspects of Contemporary Indonesian Popular Culture." *Indonesia* 34:103–30.

Hatch, Martin. 1989. "Popular Music in Indonesia (1983)." In *World Music, Politics and Social Change*, edited by Simon Frith. Manchester, England: Manchester Univ. Press.

Keeler, Ward. 1987. *Javanese Shadows, Javanese Selves*. Princeton, NJ: Princeton Univ. Press.

Kunst, Jaap. 1973. *Music in Java: Its History, Its Theory, and Its Technique*, edited by Ernst Heins. 3rd ed. 2 vols. The Hague: Martinus Nijhoff.

Tenzer, Michael. 2000. *Gamelan Gong Kebyar: The Art of Twentieth-Century Balinese Music*. Chicago: Univ. of Chicago Press.

Weintraub, Andrew. 2010. *Dangdut Stories: A Social and Musical History of Indonesia's Most Popular Music*. New York: Oxford Univ. Press.

Additional Reading

On Music

Bakan, Michael B. 1999. *Music of Death and New Creation: Experiences in the World of Balinese Gamelan Beleganjur.* Chicago: Univ. of Chicago Press.

Becker, Judith. 1980. *Traditional Music in Modern Java: Gamelan in a Changing Society.* Honolulu: Univ. of Hawaii Press.

Becker, Judith, and Alan Feinstein, eds. 1984, 1987, 1988. *Karawitan: Source Readings in Javanese Gamelan and Vocal Music.* 3 vols. Ann Arbor: Univ. of Michigan Center for South and Southeast Asian Studies.

Benamou, Marc. 2010. *Rasa: Affect and Intuition in Javanese Musical Aesthetics.* New York: Oxford Univ. Press.

Brinner, Benjamin. 2008. *Music of Central Java: Experiencing Music, Expressing Culture.* New York: Oxford Univ. Press.

Gold, Lisa. 2004. *Music of Bali: Experiencing Music, Expressing Culture.* New York: Oxford Univ. Press.

Harnish, David D., and Rassmussen, Anne K., eds. 2011. *Divine Inspirations: Music and Islam in Indonesia.* New York: Oxford Univ. Press.

Herbst, Edward. 1997. *Voices in Bali: Energies and Perceptions in Vocal Music and Dance Theater.* Hanover, NH: Univ. Press of New England, Wesleyan Univ. Press.

Kartomi, Margaret. 1980. "Musical Strata in Java, Bali, and Sumatra." In *Musics of Many Cultures,* edited by Elizabeth May, 111–33. Berkeley: Univ. of California Press.

Lindsay, Jennifer. 1992. *Javanese Gamelan: Traditional Orchestra of Indonesia.* 2nd ed. New York: Oxford Univ. Press.

Manuel, Peter. 1988. *Popular Musics of the Non-Western World: An Introductory Survey.* New York: Oxford Univ. Press. (See especially pp. 205–20.)

McPhee, Colin. 1966. *Music in Bali.* New Haven, CT: Yale Univ. Press.

Perlman, Marc. 2004. *Unplayed Melodies: Javanese Gamelan and the Genesis of Music Theory.* Berkeley: Univ. of California Press.

Rappoport, Dana. 2009. *Songs from the Thrice-Blooded Land: Ritual Music of the Toraja (Sulawesi, Indonesia),* translated from the French by Timothy Seller. 2 vols. and DVD. Paris: Éditions Épistèmes, Éditions de la Maison des sciences de l'homme.

Simon, Artur. 1984. "Functional Changes in Batak Traditional Music and Its Role in Modern Indonesian Society." *Asian Music* 15(2): 58–66.

Sumarsam. 1995. *Gamelan: Cultural Interaction and Musical Develop- ment in Central Java.* Chicago: Univ. of Chicago Press.

Sutton, R. Anderson. 1987. "Identity and Individuality in an Ensemble Tradition: The Female Vocalist in Java." In *Women and Music in Cross–Cultural Perspective,* edited by Ellen Koskoff, 113–30. Westport, CT: Greenwood Press. Reprint, Urbana: Univ. of Illinois Press, 1989.

———. 1993. *Variation in Central Javanese Gamelan Music.* DeKalb, IL: Center for Southeast Asian Studies, Northern Illinois Univ.

Tenzer, Michael. 1991. *Balinese Music.* Berkeley, CA: Periplus.

Vetter, Roger. 1981. "Flexibility in the Performance Practice of Central Javanese Music." *Ethnomusicology* 25(2): 199–214.

Yampolsky, Philip. 2013. "Three Genres of Indonesian Popular Music: Their Trajectories in the Colonial Era and After." *Asian Music* 44(2): 24-80.

On Indonesia

Anderson, Benedict R. O'G. 1965. *Mythology and the Tolerance of the Javanese.* Ithaca, NY: Cornell Modern Indonesia Project.

Becker, A. L. 1979. "Text Building, Epistemology, and Aesthetics in Javanese Shadow Theater." In *The Imagination of Reality: Essays in Southeast Asian Coherence Systems,* edited by A. L. Becker and Aram A. Yengoyan, 211–43. Norwood, NJ: Ablex.

Cohen, Matthew Isaac. 2006. *The Komedie Stamboel: Popular Theater in Colonial Indonesia, 1891-1903.* Athens: Ohio Univ. Press.

Geertz, Clifford. 1960. *The Religion of Java.* New York: Free Press.

Holt, Claire. 1967. *Art in Indonesia: Continuities and Change.* Ithaca, NY: Cornell Univ. Press.

Ricklefs, Merle C. 2001. *A History of Modern Indonesia since c. 1200.* 3rd ed. Stanford, CA: Stanford Univ. Press.

Taylor, Jean Gilman. 2003. *Indonesia: Peoples and Histories.* New Haven, CT: Yale Univ. Press.

Additional Listening

Java (including West Java and Jakarta)

Bedhaya Duradasih, Court Music of Kraton Surakarta II. King Record, World Music Library, KICC 5193.

Betawi and Sundanese Music of the North Coast of Java: Topeng Betawi, Tanjidor, Ajeng. Music of Indonesia, 5. Smithsonian Folkways SFW CD 40421.

Chamber Music of Central Java. King Record, World Music Library, KICC 5152.

Court Music of Kraton Surakarta. King Record, World Music Library, KICC 5151.

The Gamelan of Cirebon. King Record, World Music Library KICC 5130.

Indonesian Popular Music: Kroncong, Dangdut, & Langgam Jawa. Music of Indonesia, 2. Smithsonian Folkways SF 40056.

Java: Langen Mandra Wanara, Opéra de Danuredjo VII. Ocora CD C559014/15.

Java: Palais Royal de Yogyakarta. Volume 4: La musique de concert. Ocora (Radio France) C 560087.

Javanese Court Gamelan. Elektra/Nonesuch Explorer Series 972044-2.

Klenengan Session of Solonese Gamelan I. King Record, World Music Library, KICC 5185.

Langendriyan, Music of Mangkunegaran Solo II. King Record, World Music Library, KICC 5194.

Music from the Outskirts of Jakarta: Gambang Kromong. Music of Indonesia, 3. Smithsonian Folkways SF 40057.

The Music of K. R. T. Wasitodiningrat. CMP Records CD 3007.

Music of Mangkunegaran Solo I. King Record, World Music Library, KICC 5184.

Shadow Music of Java. Rounder CD 5060.

Songs Before Dawn: Gandrung Banyuwangi. Music of Indonesia, 1. Smithsonian Folkways SF 40055.

The Sultan's Pleasure, Javanese Gamelan and Vocal Music from the Palace of Yogyakarta. Music of the World CDT-116.

Bali

Bali: Court Music and Banjar Music (Musique de cour et musique de banjar). Réédition Auvidis, Unesco collection, Musiques et musicians D 8059.

Bali: Gamelan and Kecak. Elektra Nonesuch Explorer Series CD 979204-4.

Bali: Les Grands Gong Kebyar des Anneés Soixante. Ocora, Harmonia Mundi, C 560057–C 560058. 2 CDs.

Gamelan Gong Gede of Batur Temple. World Music Library, King Records KICC 5153.

Gamelan Gong Kebyar, Bali. Elektra Nonesuch CD 79280-2.

The Gamelan Music of Bali. World Music Library, King Records KICC 5126.

Gamelan Semar Pegulingan "Gunung Jati," Br. Teges Kanginan. World Music Library, King Records KICC 5180.

Gender Wayang of Sukawati Village. World Music Library, King Records KICC 5156.

Golden Rain: Gong Kebyar of Gunung Sari, Bali. Elektra Nonesuch CD 79219-2.

Kecak Ganda Sari. Kecak from Bali. Bridge BCD 9019.

Music in Bali. World Music Library, King Records KICC 5127.

Music of the Gamelan Gong Kebyar, Bali. Vital Records 401-2. 2 discs.

Other Indonesian Islands

Batak of North Sumatra. New Albion Records NA 046 CD.

Gongs and Vocal Music from Sumatra. Music of Indonesia, 12. Smithsonian Folkways SFW C 40428.

Indonesian Guitars. Music of Indonesia, 20. Smithsonian Folkways SFW CD 40447.

Kalimantan: Dayak Ritual and Festival Music. Music of Indonesia, 17. Smithsonian Folkways SFW C 40444.

Kalimantan Strings. Music of Indonesia, 13. Smithsonian Folkways SFW CD 40429.

Lombok, Kalimantan, Banyumas: Little-known Forms of Gamelan and Wayang. Music of Indonesia, 14. Smithsonian Folkways SFW CD 40441.

Melayu Music of Sumatra and the Riau Islands. Music of Indonesia, 11. Smithsonian Folkways SFW CD 40427.

Music from the Forests of Riau and Mentawai. Music of Indonesia, 7. Smithsonian Folkways SFW CD 40423.

Music from the Southeast: Sumbawa, Sumba, Timor. Music of Indonesia, 16. Smithsonian Folkways SFW CD 40443.

Music of Biak, Irian Jaya. Music of Indonesia, 10. Smithsonian Folkways SFW CD 40426. *Music of Madura.* Ode Record Company CD ODE 1381.

Music of Maluku: Halmahera, Buru, Kei. Music of Indonesia, 19. Smithsonian Folkways SFW CD 40446.

Music of Nias and North Sumatra: Hoho, Gendang Karo, Gondang Toba. Music of Indonesia, 4. Smithsonian Folkways SF CD 40429.

Night Music of West Sumatra. Music of Indonesia, 6. Smithsonian Folkways SFW CD 40422.

Sulawesi: Festivals, Funerals, and Work. Music of Indonesia, 18. Smithsonian Folkways SF CD 40445.

Sulawesi Strings. Music of Indonesia, 15. Smithsonian Folkways SFW CD 40442.

Vocal and Instrumental Music from East and Central Flores. Music of Indonesia, 8. Smithsonian Folkways SFW CD 40424.

Vocal Music from Central and West Flores. Music of Indonesia, 9. Smithsonian Folkways SFW CD 40425.

Additional Viewing

Karya: Video Portraits of Four Indonesian Composers. 1992. Videocassette. Produced and Directed by Jody Diamond. Distributed by American Gamelan Institute, Box 5036, Hanover, NH 03755. Balinese, Javanese, and Batak composers talk about their recent work.

The JVC Video Anthology of World Music and Dance. 1990. Thirty video cassettes plus guide. Edited by Fujii Tomoaki, with assistant editors Omori Yasuhiro and Sakurai Tetsuo, in collaboration with the National Museum of Ethnology (Osaka). Produced by Ichikawa Katsumori. Directed by Nakagawa Kunihiko and Ichihashi Yuji. Victor Company of Japan, Ltd., in collaboration with Smithsonian Folkways Recordings. Distributed by Rounder Records, Cambridge, MA 02140.

- Volume 9 contains footage of Javanese shadow puppetry (poor quality), along with studio footage of Balinese *kecak* ("monkey chant") and Sundanese music (recorded in Japan).
- Volume 10 contains a variety of Balinese examples, recorded in Bali, mostly employing a *gamelan semar pegulingan* (even for contexts in which this ensemble is not appropriate).

Bali

Bali Beyond the Postcard. 1991. Videorecording and 16 mm. Produced and directed by Nancy Dine, Peggy Stern, and David Dawkins. Distributed by Filmakers Library, 124 East 40th St., New York, NY 10016; and by "Outside in July," 59 Barrow St., New York, NY 10014. *Gamelan* and dance in four generations of a Balinese family.

Compressed Version of a "Gambuh" (Dance Drama) in Batuan. 1981. 16 mm. Produced by T. Seebass and G. van der Weijden. Distributed by Institut für den Wissenschaftlichen Film, Göttingen, Germany. Performance of *gambuh,* "classical" Balinese dance drama.

Releasing the Spirits: A Village Cremation in Bali. [1981] 1991. Videocassette. Directed by Patsy Asch, Linda Connor, et al. Distributed by Documentary Educational Resources, Watertown, MA. Cremation rituals in a central Balinese village.

Shadowmaster. 1980. Videocassette and 16 mm. Directed by Larry Reed. Distributed by Larry Reed Productions, 18 Chattanooga St., San Francisco, CA 94114. Fictional film about the social and artistic life of a shadow puppeteer in Bali.

Java

Bird of Passage. 1986. 16 mm. Directed by Fons Grasveld. Distributed by Netherlands Film Institute, Postbus 515, 1200 AM Hilversum, The Netherlands. Javanese traditions in Java, Suriname, and the Netherlands.

The Dancer and the Dance. (1990?). Videocassette and 16 mm. Produced by Felicia Hughes-Freeland. Distributed by Film Officer, Royal Anthropological Institute, 50 Fitzroy St., London, England W1P 5HS. Javanese court dance in its current social context.

Traditional Dances of Indonesia, Dances of Jogjakarta, Central Java: Langen Mandra Wanara. 1990. Videocassette from 16-mm film made in 1975. Directed and produced by William Heick. Distributed by University of California Extension Media Center, 2176 Shattuck Ave., Berkeley, CA 94704. Dance-opera presenting episode from the Ramayana.

Traditional Dances of Indonesia, Dances of Surakarta, Central Java: Srimpi Anglir Mendung. 1990. Videocassette from 16-mm film made in 19 75. Directed and produced by William Heick. Distributed by University of California Extension Media Center, 2176 Shattuck Ave., Berkeley, CA 94704. Refined female court dance. (Ten additional videorecordings from the same distributor present additional dances from Java, Bali, and West Sumatra.)

North Sumatra

Karo-Batak (Indonesien, Nordsumatra)—Gendang-Musik "mari-mari" und "patam-patam." 1994. 16 mm. Directed by Artur Simon. Distributed by Institut für den Wissenschaftlichen Film, Göttingen, Germany. Ceremonial music performed by *gendang keteng-keteng* ensemble.

Karo-Batak (Indonesien, Nordsumatra)—Tänze anlässlich einer Haarwas chzeremonie in Kuta Mbelin. 1994. 16 mm. Directed by Franz Simon and Artur Simon. Distributed by Institut für den Wissenschaftli chen Film, Göttingen, Germany. Dances associated with the hair–washing ceremony of Kuta Mbelin, North Sumatra. (Fourteen additional films from the same distributor cover performing arts of Karo and other Batak groups in North Sumatra and of Kayan- Dayak groups in West Kalimantan [Borneo].)

Internet Resources

American Gamelan Institute. Home page with links to archived materials, musical examples, and other information pertaining to traditional and contemporary *gamelan* music—Javanese, Balinese, Sundanese, and experimental/international. http://www.gamelan.org

Central Javanese Gamelan. Introductory essay, followed by descriptions of some Central Javanese *gamelan* CDs. http://www.medieval.org/music/world/java.html

Dewa 19. In Indonesian; official website of the popular Indonesian rock group Dewa 19, with links to various Indonesian music sites, mostly pop. http://dewa19.com

Gamelan Hawaii. University of Hawaii *gamelan* website; includes link to useful introductory article "Towards an Appreciation of Javanese Gamelan," by Hardja Susilo. http://remus.shidler.hawaii.edu /gamelan/home.htm

Gamelan Kyahi Telaga Madu, University of Michigan. Background information on central Javanese *gamelan,* with focus on the *gamelan* set at the University of Michigan. http://www.ii.umich .edu/cseas/resources/gamelan

The Gamelans of the Kraton Yogyakarta. Exquisite photos, sound excerpts, and thorough commentary, covering the many palace *gamelan* ensembles and their cultural contexts, by Roger Vetter. web.grinnell.edu/courses/mus/gamelans/open.html

Gendhing Jawa. Thorough set of Javanese *gamelan* pieces in cipher notation, organized by tuning system and *pathet,* neatly and clearly presented. www.gamelanbvg.com/gendhing/gendhing.html

Gigi music site. http://www.last.fm/music/Gigi Photos of the popular Indonesian rock group Gigi and streaming of selected songs.

Grading the Top Ten Songs in … Indonesia! A dynamic site with videos of current hit Indonesian pop songs http://grantland.com/hollywood-prospectus/grading-the-top-10-songs-in-indonesia

Indonesian Music. General introductory material on Javanese and Balinese *gamelan* music. http://trumpet.sdsu.edu/M151/Indonesian_Music1a.html

Indonesian Music's Stream on SoundCloud. Direct access to streaming of current and recent Indonesian pop music. https://soundcloud.com/groups/indonesian-music

Krakatau. In English; official website of Indonesian fusion group Krakatau, led by Dwiki Dharmawan. http://www.krakatau.net

Musik Pop Indo. Download site for contemporary Indonesian pop music audio files (mp3). http://ariftea.heck.in/category/musik-pop-indo-1/1.xhtml

Northern Illinois University SEASite, Arts and Culture. Basic back ground on arts and culture from across Indonesia. http://www.seasite.niu.edu/Indonesian/Budaya_Bangsa

UK Gamelan Information. Comprehensive site with information on *gamelan* for students and for people traveling in Indonesia, description of instruments, annotated discography, links to vario us *gamelan* sites, including *gamelan* groups in Europe and the United States, as well as the United Kingdom. http://www.gamelan.org.uk/links.htm

CHAPTER 8—ASIA/CHINA, TAIWAN, SINGAPORE, OVERSEAS CHINESE

DeWoskin, Kenneth. 1982. *A Song for One or Two: Music and the Concept of Art in Early China*. Ann Arbor: Univ. of Michigan.

JSCP. 2003. *Beautiful Energy*. Guangzhou: JSCP. [DVD]

Liang Mingyue. 1985. *Music of the Billion: An Introduction to Chinese Musical Culture*. Berlin: Heinrichshofen.

Schimmelpenninck, Antoinet. 1997. *Chinese Folk Songs and Folk Singers: Shan'ge Traditions in Southern Jiangsu*. Leiden: CHIME Foundation.

So, Jenny, ed. 2000. *Music in the Age of Confucius*. Washington, DC: Freer Gallery of Art and Arthur M. Sackler Gallery.

Additional Reading

Always check standard reference sources, like the *New Grove Dictionary of Music and Musicians*, and the *Garland Encyclopedia of World Music*, both available online.

Adshead, S. A. M. 2000. *China in World History*. 3rd ed. London: Palgrave.

Baranovitch, Nimrod. 2003. *China's New Voices: Popular Music, Ethnicity, Gender, and Politics, 1978–1997*. Berkeley: Univ. of California Press.

Farrer, James, and Andrew Field. 2015. *Shanghai Nightscapes: A Nocturnal Biography of a Global City*. Chicago: University of Chicago Press.

Han Kuo-Huang. 1978. "The Chinese Concept of Program Music." *Asian Music* 10(1): 17–38.

———. 1979. "The Modern Chinese Orchestra." *Asian Music* 11(1): 1–43.

Harris, Rachel, Rowan Pease, and Shzr Ee Tan, eds. 2013. *Gender in Chinese Music*. Rochester: Univ. of Rochester Press.

Jones, Andrew. 2001. *Yellow Music: Media Culture and Colonial Modernity in the Jazz Age*. Durham, NC: Duke Univ. Press.

Jones, Stephen. 1995. *Folk Music of China: Living Instrumental Traditions*. Oxford, England: Clarendon Press.

Lau, Frederick. 2007. *Music in China: Experiencing Music, Expressing Culture*. New York: Oxford Univ. Press.

Lum, Casey Man Kong. 1996. *In Search of a Voice: Karaoke and the Construction of Identity in Chinese America*. Mahwah, NJ: Erlbaum.

Mackerras, Colin P. 1972. *The Rise of the Peking Opera 1770–1870: Social Aspects of the Theatre in Manchu China*. Oxford, England: Oxford Univ. Press.

Mittler, Barbara. 2003. "Cultural Revolution Model Works and the Politics of Modernization in China: An Analysis of *Taking Tiger Mountain by Strategy*." *the world of music* 45 (2): 53–81.

Moskowitz, Mark L. 2010. *Cries of Joy, Songs of Sorrow: Chinese Pop Music and Its Cultural Connotations*. Honolulu: Univ. of Hawai'i Press.

Rees, Helen. 2000. *Echoes of History: Naxi Music in Modern China*. New York: Oxford Univ. Press.

———, ed. 2009. *Lives in Chinese Music*. Urbana: Univ. of Illinois Press.

Riddle, Ronald. 1983. *Flying Dragons, Flowing Streams: Music in the Life of San Francisco's Chinese*. Westport, CT: Greenwood Press.

Stock, Jonathan P. J. 1995. "Reconsidering the Past: Zhou Xuan and the Rehabilitation of Early Twentieth-Century Popular Music." *Asian Music* 26(2): 119–35.

———. 2003. *Huju: Traditional Opera in Modern Shanghai*. Oxford, England: Oxford Univ. Press.

Thrasher, Alan R. 1985. "The Melodic Structure of Jiangnan Sizhu." *Ethnomusicology* 29:237–63.

———. 2000. *Chinese Musical Instruments*. Oxford, England: Oxford Univ. Press.

van Gulik, Robert. 1940. *The Lore of the Lute: An Essay in Ch'in Ideology*. Tokyo: Sophia Univ.

Wichmann, Elizabeth. 1991. *Listening to Theatre: The Aural Dimension of Beijing Opera*. Honolulu: Univ. of Hawai'i Press.

Witzleben, J. Lawrence. 1995. *"Silk and Bamboo" Music in Shanghai: The Jiangnan Sizhu Instrumental Ensemble Tradition*. Kent, OH: Kent State Univ. Press.

———. 1999. "Cantopop and Mandapop in Pre-Postcolonial Hong Kong: Identity Negotiation in the Performances of Anita Mui Yim-Fong." *Popular Music* 18(2): 241–58.

Wong, Isabel K. F. 1984. "*Geming gequ*: Songs for the Education of the Masses." In *Popular Chinese Literature and Performing Arts in the People's Republic of China 1949–1979*, edited by Bonnie S. McDougall, 112–43. Berkeley: Univ. of California Press.

Yung, Bell. 1989. *Cantonese Opera: Performance as Creative Process*. Cambridge, England: Cambridge Univ. Press, 1989.

———, ed. 1997. *Celestial Airs of Antiquity: Music of the Seven-String Zither of China*. Madison, WI: A-R Editions.

Additional Listening

Anthology of World Music: China. 1998. Cambridge, MA: Rounder Records CD 5150.

Chine: Fanbai. Chant liturgique bouddhique. Hymnes aux Trois Joyaux. 1997. Ocora Radio France C560109.

Chine: Le pêcheur et le bûcheron: Le qin, cithara des lettrés. 2007. VDE- Gallo CD-1214.

The Music of the Aborigines on Taiwan Island Vol. 1: The Songs of the Bunun Tribe. 1992. Taipei: Wind Records.

Songs of the Land in China: Labor Songs and Love Songs. 1996. Taipei: Wind Records.

Yangguan san die: Parting at Yangguan. 2002. Berlin: Wergo.

Internet Resources

Rock singer Cui Jian http://www.cuijian.com/ENGLISH/Pages/main_interface.html

Tomb of Marquis Yi of Zeng http://depts.washington.edu/chinaciv/archae/2marmain.htm

John Thompson's site on the *qin* http://www.silkqin.com/

Twelve Girls Band http://www.12girls.org

CHAPTER 9—SOUTH AMERICA/CHILE, BOLIVIA, ECUADOR, PERU

References

Acevedo, Claudio, Rodolfo Norambuena, José Seves, Rodrigo Torres, and Mauricio Valdebenito. [1996?]. *Víctor Jara: obra musical completa: Textos partes I y II, Rodrigo Torres.* Santiago, Chile: Fundació n Víctor Jara.

Andrade Albuja, Enrique, and John M. Schechter. 2004. "'*Kunan punlla rimagrinchi…*': Wit and Didactics in the Quichua Rhetorical Style of Señor Enrique Andrade Albuja, Husbandman-Ethnographer of Cotacachi, Imbabura [Ecuador]." In *Quechua Verbal Artistry: The Inscription of Andean Voices/Arte Expresivo Quechua: La Inscripción de Voces Andinas,* edited by Guillermo Delgado-P. and John M. Schechter, 311–36. Bonn, Germany: Bonner Amerikanis tische Studien (BAS, Volume 38); Aachen, Germany: Shaker.

Basch, Linda, Nina Glick Schiller, and Christina Szanton Blanc. 1994. *Nations Unbound: Transnational Projects, Postcolonial Predicaments and Deterritorialized Nation-States.* Langhome, PA: Gordon and Breach Science Publishers.

Bastien, Joseph W. 1978. *Mountain of the Condor: Metaphor and Ritual in an Andean Ayllu.* St. Paul, MN: West. American Ethnological Society Monograph 64.

Baumann, Max Peter. 1985. "The Kantu Ensemble of the Kallawaya at Charazani (Bolivia)." *Yearbook for Traditional Music* 17:146–66.

Casas Roque, Leonidas. 1993. "Fiestas, danzas y música de la costa de Lambayeque." In *Música, danzas y máscaras en los Andes,* edited by Raúl R. Romero, 299–337. Lima: Pontificia Universidad Católica del Perú, Instituto Riva-Agüero.

Cespedes, Gilka Wara. 1993. "Huayño, Saya, and Chuntuqui." *Revista de Música Latinoamericana/Latin American Music Review* 14 (1): 52-101.

Chaskinakuy. 1993. *Music of the Andes: Cosecha.* Produced by Edmond Badoux and Francy Vidal. Occidental, CA, 1993: CD. All arrangements are by Chaskinakuy. http://www.chaskinakuy.com/recording.htm

Coba Andrade, Carlos Alberto G. 1980. *Literatura popular Afroecuatoriana.* Series: Cultura Popular. Otavalo, Ecuador: Instituto Otavaleño de Antropología.

Conjunto Ilumán. n.d. (pre-1990). *Elenita Conde.* Ecuador. Cassette.

Delagado-P., Guillermo, and John M. Schechter, eds. 2004. *Quechua Verbal Artistry.* Bonn: Bonner Amerikanistische Studien (BAS, Vol. 38). Aachen, Germany: Shaker.

Feldman, Heidi. 2003. "The International Soul of Black Peru." In *Musical Cultures of Latin America: Global Effects, Past and Present: UCLA Selected Reports XI,* edited by Steven Loza, 155–61. Los Angeles: Univ. of California, Los Angeles Department of Ethnomusicology and Systematic Musicology.

Gradante, William J. 1999. "Andean Colombia." In *Music in Latin American Culture: Regional Traditions,* edited by John M. Schechter, 302–82. New York: Schirmer.

Jara, Joan. 1984. *An Unfinished Song: The Life of Víctor Jara.* New York: Ticknor and Fields.

Koetting, James T. 1992. "Africa/Ghana." In *Worlds of Music: An Introduction to the Music of the World's Peoples,* 2nd ed., edited by Jeff Todd Titon, 67–105. New York: Schirmer.

Lipski, John M. 1987. "The Chota Valley: Afro-Hispanic Language in Highland Ecuador." *Latin American Research Review* 22(1): 155–70.

Lord, Albert. [1960] 1978. *The Singer of Tales.* New York: Atheneum; reprinted by arrangement with Harvard Univ. Press. First edition 1960.

Manz, Beatriz. 2005. "A Journey Toward Simplicity." In *Berkeley Review of Latin American Studies.* Berkeley: Center for Latin American Studies, Univ. of California, Winter, 25–28.

Martínez, Gregorio, and Fietta Jarque. 1995. Liner notes to *The Soul of Black Peru.* Warner Bros. Records Inc. 9 45878-4. Cassette.

Meisch, Lynn A. 1997. "Traditional Communities, Transnational Lives: Coping with Globalization in Otavalo, Ecuador." Ph.D. dissertation, Stanford Univ.

Moreno Chá, Ercilia. 1999. "Music in the Southern Cone: Chile, Argentina, and Uruguay." In *Music in Latin American Culture: Regional Traditions,* edited by John M. Schechter, 236–301. New York: Schirmer.

Morris, Nancy. 1986. "*Canto porque es necesario cantar:* The New Song Movement in Chile, 1973–1983." *Latin American Research Review* 21(2): 117–36.

Nketia, J. H. Kwabena. 1974. *The Music of Africa.* New York: Norton.

Paredes, Américo. 1958. *"With His Pistol in His Hand": A Border Ballad and Its Hero.* Austin: Univ. of Texas Press.

———. 1976. *A Texas-Mexican Cancionero: Folksongs of the Lower Border.* Urbana: Univ. of Illinois Press.

Recio, P. Bernardo. [1773] 1947. *Compendiosa relación de la cristi andad (en el reino) de Quito.* Madrid: Consejo Superior de Investigaciones Científicas, Instituto Santo Toribio de Mogrovejo.

Romero, Raúl R. 1994. "Black Music and Identity in Peru: Reconstruction and Revival of Afro-Peruvian Musical Traditions." In *Music and Black Ethnicity: The Caribbean and South America,* edited by Gerard H. Béhague, 307–30. Coral Gables, FL: Univ. of Miami North-South Center.

———. 1999. "Andean Peru." In *Music in Latin American Culture: Regional Traditions,* edited by John M. Schechter, 383–423. New York: Schirmer.

Ross, Joe. 1994. "Music of the Andes." *Acoustic Musician Magazine* (June): 18–27.

Schechter, John M. 1979. "The Inca—*Cantar Histórico*: A Lexico-Historical Elaboration on Two Cultural Themes." *Ethnomusicology* 23(2): 191–204.

———. 1983. "*Corona y Baile*: Music in the Child's Wake of Ecuador and Hispanic South America, Past and Present." *Revista de Música Latinoamericana/Latin American Music Review* 4(1): 1–80.

———. 1992. *The Indispensable Harp: Historical Development, Modern Roles, Configurations, and Performance Practices in Ecuador and Latin America.* Kent, OH: Kent State Univ. Press.

———. 1994. "Los Hermanos Congo y Milton Tadeo Ten Years Later: Evolution of an African-Ecuadorian Tradition of the Valle del Chota, Highland Ecuador." In *Music and Black Ethnicity: The Carib bean and South America,* edited by Gerard H. Béhague, 285–305. Coral Gables, FL: Univ. of Miami North-South Center/Transaction.

———. 1999a. "Themes in Latin American Music Culture." In *Music in Latin American Culture: Regional Traditions,* edited by John M. Schechter, 1–33. New York: Schirmer.

———. 1999b. "Beyond Region: Transnational and Transcultural Traditions." In *Music in Latin American Culture: Regional Traditions,* edited by John M. Schechter, 424–57. New York: Schirmer.

———. 2002. "Latin America/Ecuador." In *Worlds of Music: An Introduction to the Music of the World's Peoples,* 4th ed., edited by Jeff Todd Titon, 385–446. Belmont, CA: Schirmer.

Smith, Sandra. 1984. "Panpipes for Power, Panpipes for Play: The Social Management of Cultural Expression in Kuna Society." Ph.D. dissertation, Univ. of California–Berkeley.

Vidal, Francy. n.d. "Biography." http://www.chaskinakuy.com/biography.htm

Additional Reading

Béhague, Gérard. 1990. "Latin American Folk Music." In *Folk and Traditional Music of the Western Continents,* 3rd ed., edited by Bruno Nettl; revised and edited by Valerie Woodring Goertzen, 185–228. Englewood Cliffs, NJ: Prentice Hall.

———, ed. 1994. *Music and Black Ethnicity: The Caribbean and South America.* Coral Gables, FL: Univ. of Miami North-South Center/Transaction.

Den Otter, Elisabeth. 1985. *Music and Dance of Indians and Mestizos in an Andean Valley of Peru.* Delft, The Netherlands: Eburon.

Fairley, Jan. 1985. "Annotated Bibliography of Latin-American Popular Music with Particular Reference to Chile and to Nueva Canción." In *Popular Music, vol. 5, Continuity and Change,* 305–56. Cambridge, England: Cambridge Univ. Press.

Harrison, Regina. 1989. *Signs, Songs, and Memory in the Andes: Translating Quechua Language and Culture.* Austin: Univ. of Texas Press.

Mendoza, Zoila S. 2000. *Shaping Society through Dance: Mestizo Ritual Performance in the Peruvian Andes*. Chicago Studies in Ethnomusicology. Chicago: Univ. of Chicago Press.

Olsen, Dale A. 1980. "Folk Music of South America: A Musical Mosaic." In *Musics of Many Cultures: An Introduction*, edited by E. May, 386–425. Berkeley: Univ. of California Press.

Olsen, Dale A., and Daniel E. Sheehy, eds. 1998. *South America, Mexico, Central America, and the Caribbean*. Vol. 2 of *The Garland Encyclopedia of World Music*. New York: Garland Reference Library of the Humanities, vol. 1193.

Romero, Raúl, ed. 1993. *Música, danzas y máscaras en los Andes*. Lima, Peru: Pontificia Universidad Católica del Perú: Instituto Riva-Agüero.

Schechter, John M., ed. 1999. *Music in Latin American Culture: Regional Traditions*. New York: Schirmer.

Tompkins, William David. 1998. "Afro-Peruvian Traditions." In *The Garland Encyclopedia of World Music, Volume 2: South America, Mexico, Central America, and the Caribbean*, edited by Dale A. Olsen and Daniel E. Sheehy, 491–502. New York: Garland.

Turino, Thomas. 1993. *Moving Away from Silence: Music of the Peruvian Altiplano and the Experience of Urban Migration*. Chicago: Univ. of Chicago Press.

Additional Listening

Afro-Hispanic Music from Western Colombia and Ecuador. 1967. Recorded and edited by Norman E. Whitten, Jr. Folkways FE 4376.

The Inca Harp: Laments and Dances of the Tawantinsuyu, the Inca Empire [Peru]. 1982. Recorded by Ronald Wright. Lyrichord LLST 7359.

Música folklórica de Venezuela. n.d. (post-1968). Recorded by Isabel Aretz, Luis Felipe Ramón y Rivera, and Álvaro Fernaud. International Folk Music Council, Anthologie de la Musique Populaire. Ocora OCR 78.

Pre-Columbian Instruments: Aerophone [Mexico]. 1972. Produced by Lilian Mendelssohn, with Pablo Castellanos. Played by Jorge Daher. Ethnic Folkways Library FE 4177.

Traditional Music of Peru 1: Festivals of Cusco. 1995. Annotated by Gisela Cánepa-Koch. Series compiled and edited by Raúl R. Romero, director of the Archives of Traditional Andean Music, Lima, Peru. Smithsonian Folkways SF 40466. 25-page booklet.

Traditional Music of Peru 2: The Mantaro Valley. 1995. Produced in collaboration with the Archives of Traditional Andean Music. Series compiled and edited by Raúl R. Romero, director of the Archives of Traditional Andean Music, Lima, Peru. Smithsonian Folkways SF 40467. 21-page booklet.

Traditional Music of Peru 3: Cajamarca and the Colca Valley. 1996. Series compiled and edited by Raúl R. Romero, Archives of Traditional Andean Music of the Riva-Agüero Institute of the Catholic University of Peru, Lima, Peru. Smithsonian Folkways SF 40468. 25-page booklet.

Traditional Music of Peru 4: Lambayeque. 1996. Series compiled and edited by Raúl R. Romero, Archives of Traditional Andean Music of the Riva-Agüero Institute of the Catholic University of Peru, Lima, Peru. Smithsonian Folkways SF 40469. 25-page booklet.

Additional Viewing

Benson-Gyles, Anna, producer. 1980. *The Incas*. Odyssey Series. Coproduction of British Broadcasting Corporation (BBC) and Public Broadcasting Associates, Inc., Boston, MA. Incas/Odyssey Series/Box 1000, Boston, MA 02118. PBS Video, 1320 Braddock Pl., Alexandria, VA 22314.

Cohen, John, director. 1979. *Q'eros: The Shape of Survival*. 53 minutes. 16 mm film/video. Color. Berkeley: Univ. of California, Extension Center for Media and Independent Learning, 2000 Center St., 4th Floor, Berkeley, CA 94704.

———. 1984. *Mountain Music of Peru*. 16mm film/video, 60 min. Color. Berkeley: Univ. of California, Extension Center for Media and Independent Learning, 2000 Center St., 4th Floor, Berkeley, CA 94704.

Cross, Stephen, director. 1977. *Disappearing World: Umbanda: The Problem Solver*. In English and in Portuguese with English subtitles. Peter Fry, narrator. Brian Moser, series editor. Public Media Video, 5547 N. Ravenswood Ave., Chicago, IL 60640-1199. Granada Colour Production, Granada, United Kingdom.

Rivera, Pedro A., and Susan Zeig, directors. 1989. *Plena Is Work, Plena Is Song*. 16 mm film/video. Cinema Guild, Inc., 1697 Broadway, Suite 506, New York, NY 10019-5904.

Internet Resources

Chaskinakuy: http://www.chaskinakuy.com http://www.chaskinakuy.com/recording.htm http://www.chaskinakuy.com/biography.htm

Florida State University School of Music Center for Music of the Americas. http://www.music.fsu.edu/ctr-americas.htm

Latin American Music Center, Indiana University School of Music. http://www.music.indiana.edu/som/lamc

LAMC-L: Academic Discussion of Latin American Music. At the Latin American Music Center, Indiana University School of Music. LAMC-L is an e-mail discussion list and file server for the Latin American Music Center at the School of Music, Indiana University, Bloomington. http://www.music.indiana.edu/som/lamc/edusearch/lamc-l

Latin American Music Review/Revista de Música Latinoamericana. http://www.utexas.edu/utpress/journals/jlamr.html

Revista Musical Chilena. Published by the Universidad de Chile, Facultad de Artes. One of the major musicology/ethnomusicology journals published in Latin America. http://www.scielo.cl/scielo.php?script¼sci_serial&pid¼0716-2790&lng¼en&nrm=iso

CHAPTER 10—THE ARAB WORLD

References

Alhaj, Rahim. 2006. *When the Soul Is Settled: Music of Iraq*. Smithsonian Folkways SFW 40533.

Al-Harthy, Majid and Anne K. Rasmussen. 2012. "Music in Oman: An Overture." *the world of music* New Series 1/2: 9–43

Ciantar, Philip. 2012. *The Ma'Tuf in Contemporary Libya: An Arab Andalusian Musical Tradition*. London: Ashgate.

Davila, Carl. 2013. *The Andalusian Music of Morocco: Al-ˉAla: History, Society and Text*. Wiesbaden, Germany: Reichert.

Davis, Ruth. 2004. *Ma'luf: Reflections on the Arab Andalusian Music of Tunesia*. Scarecrow Press.

El-Funoun. 1999. *Zaghareed: Music from the Palestinian Holy Land*. Sounds True STA M109D.

Glasser, Jonathan. 2016. *The Lost Paradise: Andalusi Music in Urban North Africa*. Chicago: Univ. of Chicago Press.

Harnish, David, and Anne K. Rasmussen, eds. 2011. *Divine Inspirations: Music and Islam in Indonesia*. New York: Oxford Univ. Press.

Knight, Roderic. 1984. "Music in Africa: The Manding Contexts." In *Performance Practice*, edited by Gerard Béhague, 53–90. Westport, CT: Greenwood Press.

MacDonald, David A. 2013. *My Voice Is My Weapon*. Durham, NC: Duke Univ. Press.

Nelson, Kristina. 1985. *The Art of Reciting the Qur'an*. Austin: Univ. of Texas Press.

Racy, A. J. 1984. "Arab Music—An Overview." In *Maqam: Music of the Islamic World and its Influences*, edited by Robert Browning, 9–13. New York: Alternative Museum.

———. 1991. "Historical Worldviews of Early Ethnomusicologists: An East-West Encounter in Cairo, 1932." In *Ethnomusicology and Modern Music History*, edited by Stephen Blum, Philip V. Bohlman, and Daniel M. Neuman, 68–94. Urbana: Univ. of Illinois Press.

———. 2002. *Making Music in the Arab World: The Culture and Artistry of Tarab*. Oxford: Oxford Univ. Press.

Rasmussen, Anne. K. 1997. "Theory and Practice at the 'Arabic Org': Digital Technology in Contemporary Arab Music Performance." *Popular Music* 15(3): 345–65.

Rasmussen, Anne K. 2010. *Women's Voices, the Recited Qur'an, and Islamic Music in Indonesia.* Berkeley and Los Angeles: Univ. of California Press.

———. 2012. "The Musical Design of National Space and Time in Oman." *the world of music New Series* 1/2: 63–97.

Schuyler, Philip. 1993. "A Folk Revival in Morocco." In *Everyday Life in the Muslim Middle East,* edited by Donnal Lee Bowen and Evelyn A. Early, 287–93. Bloomington: Indiana Univ. Press.

Shiloah, Amnon. 1991. "Musical Modes and the Medical Dimension: The Arabic Sources (c.900–c.1600)." In *Metaphor: A Musical Dimension,* edited by Jamie C. Kassler. Sydney: Currency Press.

———. 1997. "Music and Religion in Islam." *Acta Musicologica* 69 (July–December): 143–55.

Turino, Thomas. 2001. "The Music of Sub-Saharan Africa." In *Excursions in World Music,* 3rd ed., edited by Bruno Nettl, Charles Capwell, Philip V. Bohlman, Isabel K. K. Wong, and Thomas Turino, 227–54. Upper Saddle River, NJ: Prentice Hall.

Turner, Howard R. 1995. *Science in Medieval Islam: An Illustrated Introduction.* Austin: Univ. of Texas Press.

Additional Reading

The Garland Encyclopedia of World Music. Volume 6: The Middle East. 2002. Edited by Virginia Danielson, Scott Marcus, and Dwight Reynolds, with Alexander J. Fisher. New York: Routledge. The first source to turn to for further information on the Middle East, this encyclopedia is a collection of the best and most concise work of most of the major scholars in the area of Middle Eastern music. The volume also includes extensive bibliographic references and the comprehensive "A Guide to Recordings of Middle Eastern Music."

Abu-Lughod, Lila. 1986. *Veiled Sentiments: Honor and Poetry in a Bedouin Society.* Berkeley: Univ. of California Press

Ahmed, Leila. 1992. *Women and Gender in Islam.* New Haven, CT: Yale Univ. Press.

Bowen, Donna Lee, and Evelyn A. Early. 1993. *Everyday Life in the Muslim Middle East.* Bloomington: Indiana Univ. Press.

Danielson, Virginia. 1997. *The Voice of Egypt: Umm Kulthûm, Arabic Song, and Egyptian Society in the Twentieth Century.* Chicago: Univ. of Chicago Press.

Danielson, Virginia. 1992. "Artists and Entrepreneurs: Female Singers in Cairo During the 1920s." In *Women in Middle Eastern History: Shifting Boundaries in Sex and Gender,* edited by Nikki R. Keddie and Beth Baron. New Haven, CT: Yale Univ. Press.

Doubleday, Veronica. 1999. "The Frame Drum in the Middle East: Women, Musical Instruments and Power." *Ethnomusicology* 43(1): 101–34.

Eickelman, Dale F. 1989. *The Middle East: An Anthropological Approach.* Upper Saddle River, NJ: Prentice Hall.

Farmer, Henry George. 1929. *A History of Arabian Music to the XIIIth Century.* London: Lyzac and Co.

Kulthum, Umm. 1967. "Umm Kulthum: Famed Egyptian Singer (1910–1975)." In *Middle Eastern Muslim Women Speak,* edited by Elizabeth Fernea and B.Q. Bezirgan. Austin: Univ. of Texas Press.

Marcus, Scott L. 2006. *Music in Egypt: Experiencing Music, Expressing Culture.* Global Music Series. Bonnie C. Wade and Patricia Shehan Campbell, general editors. Oxford, England: Oxford Univ. Press.

Lane, Edward W. [1908] 1963. *The Manners and Customs of the Modern Egyptians.* London: Everyman's Library.

Marcus, Scott L. 1992. "Modulation in Arab Music: Documenting Oral Concepts, Performance Rules and Strategies." *Ethnomusicology* 36(2): 171–95.

———. 1993. "The Interface Between Theory and Practice: Intonation in Arab Music." *Asian Music* 24 (2): 39–58.

Racy, A. J. 1983. "Music in Nineteenth-Century Egypt: An Historical Sketch." *Selected Reports in Ethnomusicology* 4:157–79.

———. 1988. "Sound and Society: The *Takht* Music of Early-Twentieth Century Cairo." *Selected Reports in Ethnomusicology* 7:157–79.

———. 1991. "Creativity and Ambience: An Ecstatic Feedback Model from Arab Music." *the world of music* 33(3): 7–28.

Rasmussen, Anne. K. 1991a. "'An Evening in the Orient': The Middle Eastern Nightclub in America." *Asian Music* 23(2): 63–88.

———. 1991b. "Individuality and Social Change in the Music of Arab Americans." Ph.D. dissertation, Univ. of California–Los Angeles.

Regev, Motti, and Edwin Seroussi. 2004. *Popular Music and National Culture in Israel.* Berkeley: Univ. of California Press.

Reynolds, Dwight F. 1995. *Heroic Poets, Poetic Heroes: The Ethnography of Performance in an Arabic Oral Epic Tradition.* Ithaca, NY: Cornell Univ. Press.

Said, Edward W. 1979. *Orientalism.* New Work: Vintage Books.

Sawa, George D. 1985. "The Status and Roles of the Secular Musicians in the *Kitab al-Aghani* (Book of Songs), of Abu al-Faraj al-Isbahani (d. 356 A.H./967 A.D.)" *Asian Music* 17 (1): 69–82.

———. 1989. *Music Performance in the Early 'Abbasid Era 132–320 A.H./ 750–932 A.D.* Toronto: Pontifical Institute of Mediaeval Studies.

Schade-Poulsen, Marc. 1999. *Men and Popular Music in Algeria: The Social Significance of Rai.* Austin: Univ. of Texas Press.

———. 1984. "Moroccan Andalusian Music." In *Maqam: Music of the Islamic World and Its Influences,* edited by Robert Browning, 14–17. New York: Alternative Museum.

Shaheen, Jack G. 1984. *The TV Arab.* Bowling Green, OH: Bowling Green State Univ. Popular Press.

Sells, Michael A. 1999. *Approaching the Qur'an: The Early Revelations.* Ashland, OR: White Cloud Press.

Touma, Habib Hassan. 1996. *The Music of the Arabs.* Expanded ed., translated by Laurie Schwartz. Portland, OR: Amadeus Press.

Van Nieuwkerk, Karen. 1995. *A Trade Like Any Other: Female Singers and Dancers in Egypt.* Austin: Univ. of Texas Press.

Villoteau, M. 1823. *Description de L'égypt: De l'état Actuel de L'Art Musicale en égypt.* Vol. 14, 2nd ed. Paris: Imprimerie de C.L.F. Panckoucke.

Additional Listening

Alhaj, Rahim. 2003. *Rahim Alhaj: Iraqi Music in a Time of War.* (Live in concert, New York City April 5, 2003). Voxlox. Original compositions.

———. 2006. *When the Soul Is Settled: Music of Iraq.* With notes by D.A. Sonneborn. Smithsonian Folkways SFW 40533.

Bashir, Munir. n.d. *The Stockholm Recordings.* VDL 688. Original music by the Iraqi master of the 'ud.

———. n.d. *Masters of Oud: Munir Bashir and Omar Bashir.* BR 001. Original music by the Iraqi master of the 'ud with his son.

Congrès du Caire. 1988. *Muhammad al Qubbanji, Dawud Hosni, Muhammad Ghanim, … * 2 CDs made from historical recordings in the occasion of Cairo Congress in 1932. Including a special book let. Edition Bibliogeque Nationale-L'institute du Monde Arabe. Paris. APN 88-9, 10.

Jones, Brian. 1971. *Brian Jones Presents the Pipes of Pan at Joujouka.* LP. New York, NY: Rolling Stones Records. COC 49100. Rereleased by Phillips. 1995. CD. Recording from 1968, of musicians from the Moroccan village of Jahjoukah, produced by Brian Jones, former member of The Rolling Stones.

El-Funoun. n.d. *Zaghareed: Music from the Palestinian Holy Land.* Sounds True STA M109D. Folkloric troupe presents creative renditions of musical folk traditions.

Ensemble Morkos. 2000. *Cedre: Arabo-Andalusian Muwashshah.* L'empreinte Digitale. ED 13067. Traditional music from Arab–Andalusian tradition. Instrumental compositions and improvisations and *vocal muwshshahat* performed by Lebanese ensemble.

Fakhri, Sabah, and Wadi al Safi. 2000. *Two Tenors and Qantara: Historical Live Recording of Arabic Masters.* Ark 21. Live concert recording of two fine singers from Syria and Lebanon accompanied by excellent ensemble led by Simon Shaheen.

Gabriel, Peter. 1989. *Passion: Music for the Last Temptation of Christ.* Geffen Records. Soundtrack for film of the same title. Music chosen and arranged based on creative imagination of music during the time of Jesus Christ.

The Musicians of the Nile (*Les Musiciens du Nil*). 2001. *Mizmar Baladi.* Ocora C582006. Music in the style of epic traditions described in this chapter, as well as other Egyptian folk music.

Page, Jimmy and Robert Plant. 1994. *No Quarter: Unledded.* Atlantic.

Racy, A. J. 1997. *Mystical Legacies.* Lyrichord Discs LLCT 7437. Original compositions and improvisations and traditional music interpreted by Racy performing on *'ud, buzuq,* and *nay* with Soheil Kaspar, percussion.

Racy, A. J., and Simon Shaheen. 1993. *Taqasim: The Art of Improvisation in Arabic Music.* Lyrichord Discs LLCT 7374. Racy and Shaheen perform in traditional Arab style of improvisation on *'ud, buzuq,* and violin.

Rimitti, Cheikha, 1994. *Les Racines Du Rai / Rai Roots.* CMM Productions 82874-2, Buda Musique 82874-2.

Shaheen, Simon. 2002. *Turath: Master Works of the Middle East.* CMP Recordings 3006. Shaheen and traditional ensemble perform canon of Turkish/Arab repertory.

Sting. 1999. *Brand New Day.* Interscope Records. This CD features the Algerian singer Cheb Mami for the song "Desert Rose," which was hailed as an unprecedented collaboration.

Taha, Rashid et. al., 1998. 1, 2, 3, Soleils: Taha, Khaled, Faudel. Ark 21.

Tasat, Ramon. n.d. *Como la Rosa en la Güerta.* CD produced by Ramon Tasat. Collection of Sephardic ballads and paraliturgical songs primarily in Ladino language with texts and translations; accompanied by Tina Chauncy and Scott Reiss.

Various Artists. 1997. *The Music of Arab Americans: A Retrospective Collection.* Rounder 1122. Collection of the most important artists from within the Arab American community between 1915 and 1955. Informative notes and photographs in booklet.

Additional Viewing

100% Arabica. 1997. Feature film, 85 min. Directed by Mahmoud Zemmouri. Coproduced by Fennec Productions, Les Films de la Toison d'Or, and Incoprom. Screenplay by Mahmoud Zemmouri. Music by Mohamed Maghni. New York: ArtMattan Productions.

A Little for My Heart a Little for My God. 1993. Documentary film, 60 min. Directed by Brita Landoff. Produced by Lindberg and Landorg Film HB. New York: Filmmaker's Library.

The Master Musicians of Jahjouka. 1983. Videocassette. A. J. Racy, Narrator. Long Beach, CA: Mendizza and Associates Mendiza Films.

Sallamah. 1943. Feature film. Starring Umm Kulthum and Anway Wajd. Lyrics by Bayram al-Tunsi. Music by Zakariya Ahmad. Ave 44 Arabian Video Entertainment.

Silences of the Palace (Samt al-Qusur). 1994. Feature film, 127 min. Written and directed by Moufida Tlatil. Produced by Ahmed Baha Eddine Attia and Richard Magnien. Music by Anouar Brahem. Produced by Mat Films and Cinétéléfims. Magfilms coproduction. Bethesda, MD: Capitol Home Video.

Wedding in Galilee (Hatunah B'Galil). 1987. Feature film, 113 min. Directed by Michel Khleifi. Original screenplay by Michel Khleifi. New York: Kino on Video.

A Wife for My Son. 1990s. Feature film, 93 min. Directed by Ali Ghanem. Produced by Mohammed Tahar Harhoura. Script by Françoise Penzer. Seattle WA: Arab Film Distribution.

Internet Resources

Here are just a few websites of the performers and related traditions mentioned in the chapter. All of these sites have been reliable for several years; however, I encourage you to explore Internet and YouTube sites frequently; new sites and resources emerge as others disappear.

Association Ahbab Cheikh Salah. https://www.facebook.com/Jmyt.Ahbab.Alshykh.Salh

DAM: http://www.damrap.com

Electronic Intifada. http://electronicintifada.net

Fex Festival of World Sacred Music. http://fesfestival.com/en/

El-Funoun http://www.el-funoun.org

In Their Own Voices. Henrietta Yurchenco's website leads to the table of contents of her book *In Their Own Voices: Women in Judeo-Hispanic Song and Story* and to the lyrics of the songs described and to audio files of performances. http://henriettayurchenco.com/ITOV/ITOV1.html

Jewish Devotional and Liturgical Poetry http://www.piyut.org.il/English

Kakish, Wael. Video explaining frets on the long-necked lute, *buzuk* https://www.youtube.com/watch?v=S2B3_RUWJKM

Maqam http://www.maqam.com

Maqam World. Extensive, multitiered website featuring information and demonstration of musical modes, rhythms, and forms. http://www.maqamworld.com/index.html

Mijwiz solo by A.J. Racy. http://www.youtube.com/watch?v=i2zx1KUZP6c and http://www.youtube.com/watch?v=OdDwGTZ0zLQ

NPR: "In Baghdad, a Rare Musical Performance." Report by Jamie Tarabay, *Morning Edition,* National Public Radio, June 20, 2007. http://www.npr.org/templates/story/story.php?storyId=11202774

Simon Shaheen and Arabic Music Retreat http://www.simonshaheen.com

A. J. Racy http://www.ethnomusic.ucla.edu/people/racy.htm

Rahim Alhaj http://www.rahimalhaj.com

Naseer Shamma http://www.naseershamma.com

Silk Road http://www.silkroadproject.org/silkroad/map.html

Slingshot Hip Hop: http://www.slingshothiphop.com/about

Al Jadid: A Review and Record of Arab Culture and Arts http://www.aljadid.com/music

The Store: Rap and Hip-Hop. Compilation of Palestinian and other rap/hip-hop in the Arab diaspora. http://www.freethep.com/tunage.htm

CHAPTER 11—DISCOVERING AND DOCUMENTING A WORLD OF MUSIC

References

Radin, Paul. [1927] 1957. Preface to *Primitive Man as Philosopher.* New York: Dover.

Spottswood, Richard. 1990. *Ethnic Music on Records: A Discography of Ethnic Recordings Produced in the United States, 1893 to 1942.* 5 vols. Urbana: Univ. of Illinois Press.

Titon, Jeff Todd. 1980. "The Life Story." *Journal of American Folklore* 93: 276–92.

Additional Reading

Barz, Gregory F., and Timothy J. Cooley. 2008. *Shadows in the Field: New Perspectives for Fieldwork in Ethnomusicology.* 2nd ed. New York: Oxford Univ. Press.

Emerson, Robert M., Rachel I. Fretz, and Linda L. Shaw. 2011. *Writing Ethnographic Fieldnotes. 2nd ed.* Chicago: Univ. of Chicago Press.

Ethnomusicology 36(2). 1992. [Special issue on fieldwork in the public interest]

Fife, Wayne. 2005. *Doing Fieldwork.* London: Palgrave Macmillan.

Golde, Peggy, ed. 1986. *Women in the Field: Anthropological Experiences.* 2nd ed. Berkeley: Univ. of California Press.

Lassiter, Luke. 2005. *The Chicago Guide to Collaborative Ethnography.* Chicago: Univ. of Chicago Press.

Lornell, Kip, and Anne K. Rasmussen. 1997. *Musics of Multicultural America.* New York: Schirmer Books.

Pettan, Svanibor, and Jeff Todd Titon, eds. 2015. *The Oxford Guide to Applied Ethnomusicology.* New York: Oxford Univ. Press.

Van Maanen, John. 1988. *Tales of the Field: On Writing Ethnography.* Chicago: Univ. of Chicago Press.

Wolcott, Harry F. 2005. *The Art of Fieldwork.* 2nd ed. Walnut Creek, CA: Alta Mira Press.

Internet Resources

American Folklife Center, Library of Congress. Excellent advice for beginning documentarians; many examples of documentary projects from the 1920s on. http://www.loc.gov/folklife

Transom: A Showcase and Workshop for New Public Radio. Advice on documentation with sound recording, aimed at producing and editing radio documentaries. Useful reviews of recording and editing equipment; some instructions on using editing software. http://transom.org

Vermont Folklife Center. Advice and examples of documentary projects, some music-related; also good advice on gear, including some older formats likely still in use in school AV departments. http://www.vermontfolklifecenter.org

Credits

Photo Credits

Chapter 1. Chapter banner: © RODINA OLENA/ShutterStock.com; **Page 5**: Jeff Todd Titon; **Page 10**: Courtesy T. Vishwanathan; **Page 11**: Jeff Todd Titon; **Page 13**: Photographer and place unknown; **Pages 19–21**: Jeff Todd Titon; **Page 26**: Photographer and place unknown; **Page 27**: Russell Lee/Courtesy of the Library of Congress;

Chapter 2. Chapter banner: © pzAxe/ShutterStock.com; **Page 35**: J. Reid; **Page 37**: Susan W. McAllester; **Page 39**: Oklahoma Historical Society/Photo BY C.R. Cowen., April 16, 1999; **Page 46**: Arne Hodalic/Terra/Corbis; **Pages 50, 53**: Christopher Scales; **Page 55**: Michigan State University Museum; **Page 56**: Christopher Scales; **Page 62**: Sound of America Records (SOAR); **Page 67**: Tom Bee.

Chapter 3. Chapter banner: © pzAxe/ShutterStock.com; **Page 79**: Godwin Agbeli; **Page 81**: © Emmanuel Agbeli; **Page 89**: Patsy Marshall; **Pages 90, 91**: David Locke/Tufts University Medford; **Page 92**: Katherine Stuffelbeam; **Page 94**: Paul Berliner; **Page 106**: Michelle Kisliuk.

Chapter 4. Chapter banner: © gudimm/ShutterStock.com; **Page 113**: Photographer unknown; **Page 115**: Marion Post Wolcott/Courtesy of the Library of Congress/FSA-OWI Collection; **Pages 115, 116**: Jeff Todd Titon; **Page 117**: Jack Delano/Courtesy of the Library of Congress/FSA-OSI Collection; **Page 118**: Frederic Ramsey Jr.; **Pages 121, 122, 124, 127**: Jeff Todd Titon; **Page 128**: Courtesy of Jo Jo Williams; **Page 129**: Jeff Todd Titon; **Page 136**: Frederic Ramsey Jr.; **Pages 138, 141, 143**: Jeff Todd Titon.

Chapter 5. Chapter banner: © RODINA OLENA/ShutterStock.com; **Page 150**: Timothy J. Cooley; **Page 157**: Mirjana Lausevic; **Page 159**: Timothy J. Cooley; **Pages 164, 167–169**: Timothy J. Cooley; **Page 171**: Photograph by Piotra Gronau; graphic design by Kinga Mazurek-Sforza. CD conception and compilation by W.Çodzimierz Klesczc and Krzysztof Trebunia-Tutka. Used with permission.

Chapter 6. Chapter banner: © De-V/ShutterStock.com; **Page 182**: © Carol Reck 2014. All rights reserved; **Page 185**: Photo © Carol S. Reck 2005. All rights reserved; **Page 187**: Photo © Carol S. Reck 2014. All rights reserved; **Page 188**: Photo © Carol Reck 2005. All rights reserved; **Page 190**: Photo © Carol Reck 2015. All rights reserved; **Pages 192,** **193**: Photo © Carol Reck 2005. All rights reserved; **Page 196**: © Carol Reck, 2004. All rights reserved; **Page 199**: Drawing © Navarana Reck 2016. All rights reserved; **Page 204**: Photo © Carol Reck 2005. All rights reserved.

Chapter 7. Chapter banner: © RODINA OLENA/ShutterStock.com; **Page 213**: Arthur Durkee, Earth Visions Photographics; **Page 214**: Drawing by Peggy Choy; **Page 215**: R. Anderson Sutton; **Page 218**: Peggy Choy; **Page 219**: Arthur Durkee, Earth Visions Photographics; **Page 224**: R. Anderson Sutton; **Page 228**: Wayne Vitale; **Page 230**: R. Anderson Sutton; **Page 233**: Courtesy of Andrew Weintraub; **Page 236**: Courtesy of Krakatau (Dwiki Dharmawan); **Page 239**: R. Anderson Sutton.

Chapter 8. Chapter banner: © pzAxe/ShutterStock.com; **Page 250**: Courtesy of Antoinet Schimmelpenninck; **Page 252**: Courtesy of Jiang Shu; **Pages 255, 256, 260**: Jonathan P. J. Stock; **Page 263**: M. Azadehfar; **Page 265**: Jonathan P. J. Stock; **Page 270**: C. Chiener; **Pages 272, 273**: Jonathan P. J. Stock; **Page 275**: Beautiful Energy DVD (JSCP 2003).

Chapter 9. Chapter banner: © pzAxe/ShutterStock.com; **Pages 288–291, 296, 298**: John M. Schechter; **Page 298**: Courtesy of German Congo family; **Page 303**: Irene Young. Used by permission.

Chapter 10. Chapter banner: © gudimm/ShutterStock.com; **Pages 314, 315**: Anne Rasmussen and Dan Neuman UCLA; **Pages 321, 322, 324, 329, 331–333, 337, 338, 343**: Anne Rasmussen; **Page 344**: Courtesy of Lila Kadaj.

Chapter 11. Chapter banner: © RODINA OLENA/ShutterStock.com; **Page 351**: Library of Congress Prints and Photographs Division [LC-USZ62-13830]; **Page 352**: Photographer unknown; **Pages 353–355**: Jeff Todd Titon; **Page 355**: Jack Delano/Courtesy of the Library of Congress; **Page 357**: John Collier/Courtesy of the Library of Congress.; **Page 360**: Jeff Todd Titon; **Page 362**: Library of Congress Prints and Photographs Division/[LC-USF33- 012865-M1]; **Page 366**: Jack Delano/Library of Congress Prints and Photographs Division; **Page 369**: James T. Koetting; **Page 370**: Jeff Todd Titon.

Frontmatter, Endmatter. Design banners: © De-V/ShutterStock.com

Text Credits

Chapter 2. 36–37: "Ho Wey Hey Yo" by Six Nations Women Singers. Produced by Tom Bee for the Soar Corporation. **45:** "Yeibichai". Navajo dance song from Nightway. © Archive of Folk Song of the Library of Congress AFS L41. LP. Washington, DC. **63–64:** "Reservation of Education" Written by Michael Valvano, Tom Bee, Mac-Xit Suazo Published by Jobete Music Co. Inc. (administered by Sony/ATV Music Publishing LLC.). Produced by Tom Bee for the Soar Corporation. **66:** "Devil Come Down Sunday" Written, Published and Performed by Derek Miller.

Index

Note: Glossary terms appear in boldface type.